The History of Italian Marxism

Historical Materialism Book Series

The Historical Materialism Book Series is a major publishing initiative of the radical left. The capitalist crisis of the twenty-first century has been met by a resurgence of interest in critical Marxist theory. At the same time, the publishing institutions committed to Marxism have contracted markedly since the high point of the 1970s. The Historical Materialism Book Series is dedicated to addressing this situation by making available important works of Marxist theory. The aim of the series is to publish important theoretical contributions as the basis for vigorous intellectual debate and exchange on the left.

The peer-reviewed series publishes original monographs, translated texts, and reprints of classics across the bounds of academic disciplinary agendas and across the divisions of the left. The series is particularly concerned to encourage the internationalization of Marxist debate and aims to translate significant studies from beyond the English-speaking world.

For a full list of titles in the Historical Materialism Book Series available in paperback from Haymarket Books, visit:
https://www.haymarketbooks.org/series_collections/1-historical-materialism

The History of Italian Marxism

From its Origins to the Great War

Paolo Favilli

Translated by David Broder

Haymarket Books
Chicago, IL

First published in 2016 by Brill Academic Publishers, The Netherlands

Published in paperback in 2017 by
Haymarket Books
P.O. Box 180165
Chicago, IL 60618
773-583-7884
www.haymarketbooks.org

ISBN: 978-1-60846-803-4

Trade distribution:
In the US, Consortium Book Sales, www.cbsd.com
In Canada, Publishers Group Canada, www.pgcbooks.ca
In the UK, Turnaround Publisher Services, www.turnaround-uk.com
All other countries, Ingram Publisher Services International, ips_intlsales@ingramcontent.com

Cover design by Jamie Kerry of Belle Étoile Studios and Ragina Johnson.

This book was published with the generous support of Lannan Foundation and the Wallace Action Fund.

Printed in Canada by union labor.

10 9 8 7 6 5 4 3 2 1

Library of Congress Cataloging-in-Publication data is available.

Contents

Preface to the English Edition

What is the History of Marxism?

'Marx was Russian'. So I was told by a student taking a Contemporary History exam, in response to a question of mine seeking to establish a connection between Marx's place of birth/early formation and a wholly 'Western' geographical/cultural context. I did not find such a paradoxical answer shocking – and for two reasons. Firstly, on account of my long teaching experience; anyone with a similar working career will have heard many things worthy of those collections that they sometimes produce of students' 'beastliest' errors. Secondly – and of some significance to the logic of this book – because this paradoxical answer in a way mirrors the paradox of 'Marxism' transitioning from West to East. Anyone wholly ignorant of biographical facts and the paths of 'Marxian' and/or Marxist texts could easily associate Marxism with what was a fundamental element of its twentieth-century periodisation: the birth, development and end of the 'profane experiment'.[1] Naturally, a student preparing for a Contemporary History exam cannot do without knowing the basic characteristics of these events, and the student in question thus failed. But even so, the paradox in question sparks reflections of some importance to better bringing 'Marxism' into focus as an object of history. What we call 'Marxism' is a highly unstable, non-homogeneous composite; and it was precisely in the Soviet experience that the tensions in its components' system of relations reached their maximum extent.

Let us try to reflect on the way in which Marxism was presented in two works of a very high standard that both appeared in the context of Soviet literature: *Dr. Zhivago* and *Life and Fate*. These were the works of two Soviet authors, Boris Pasternak and Vassily Grossman, who were also critics of fundamental aspects of the 'profane experiment'. These were works in which Marxism could not but appear as the *necessary* reference for thought and action.

> The *sun* set
> and at once
> *electricity* fired *Potemkin*[2]

---

1 Di Leo 2012.

2 From Pasternak's *1905*.

This was the metaphorical Marxism of 1905; the lightning-enlightening Marxism that we will go on to look at more closely. It was the Marxism of the poetic and cultural atmosphere of Alexander Blok in which Pasternak and his friends spent part of their youth.[3]

In *Dr. Zhivago* this 'fire, penetration, [and] personal vision of the world' found its translation into prose through the memory of Pavel Antipov, a very young man during the 1905 Revolution, who then became Strelnikov, the Red military commander in the Civil War that began in the 'great and terrible ... year of Our Lord 1918'.[4]

Here were

> Revolutions, young men dying on the barricades, writers racking their brains in an effort to curb the brute insolence of money, to save the human dignity of the poor. Marxism arose, it uncovered the root of the evil and it offered the remedy, it became the great force of the century.

While

> the whole of the workers' movement of the world, the whole of Marxism in the parliaments and universities of Europe, the whole of this new system of ideas with its newness, the swiftness of its conclusion, its irony, and its pitiless remedies elaborated in the name of pity – all of this was absorbed and expressed in Lenin, who fell upon the old world as the personified retribution for its misdeeds.[5]

Yet the conjugation between revolution and this way of understanding Marxism, of which Pasternak considered 1905[6] to be paradigmatic, would soon be transformed:

> It has often happened in history that a lofty ideal has degenerated into crude materialism ... Blok says somewhere: 'We, the children of Russia's terrible years'. Blok meant this in a metaphorical, figurative sense ... the terrors were not terrible but sent from above, apocalyptic; that's quite different. Now the metaphorical has become literal, ... and the terrors are terrible, there you have the difference.[7]

---

3 Pasternak 1958, pp. 27–8.

4 Bulgakov 1971, p. 4.

5 Pasternak 1958b, Chapter Fourteen, p. 17.

6 See his poems *1905* and *Lieutenant Schmidt*.

7 Pasternak 1958b, Chapter Sixteen, p. 5.

Forty years on from 1905, and almost thirty years after October, such was the thinking of Misha Gordon and Nika Dudorov, friends of the now-departed Yuri Zhivago who had been very young participants – like Antipov/Strelnikov – in the great days of 1905.

Marxism had become an arid textbook catechism, an ideology ever-changed in conformity with even the most contradictory political turns, the ultimate justification of 'constant, systematic duplicity'.[8]

Now, Marxism had picked up its rifle as the Red soldier Taraska, who had seen during the 'imperialist' war how powerful arms really were.

> 'He wanted to be a power himself. An armed man isn't just a man like any other ... You just try to take Taraska's rifle away from him now! Well, then came the slogan "Turn your bayonets against your masters", so Taraska turned. That's the whole story. There's Marxism for you'. 'That's the most genuine kind – straight from life'[9]

Using power for victory – this was the 'crude materialism' of 'authentic' Marxism. Here, power was the key to judging the correctness of thoughts and actions.

In his *Life and Fate*, Vassily Grossman particularly brought these two elements into relief, portraying the following dialogue between Getmanov (an army corps political commissar), Novikov (a commander of the tank corps), and Nyeudobnov (Novikov's chief in the high command). The great pincer movement that would soon encircle Paulus in Stalingrad was about to begin, and discussion turned to the choice of a new commander for an armoured brigade:

> 'We could appoint Major Basangov temporarily', said Novikov. 'He knows what's what. And he was taking part in tank-battles right at the beginning of the war, near Novograd-Volynsk. Does the commissar have any objections?'
>
> 'Of course not,' said Getmanov. 'It's not for me to object ... There is one thing, though. The second-in-command of the second brigade is an Armenian; you want the chief of staff to be a Kalmyk – and we've already got some Lifshits as chief of staff of the third brigade. Couldn't we do without the Kalmyk?' He looked at Novikov, then at Nyeudobnov. 'That's how we all feel', said Nyeudobnov. 'And on the face of it you're right. But

8 Pasternak 1958b, Chapter Fifteen, p. 7.

9 Pasternak 1958b, Chapter Six, p. 5.

> then Marxism's taught us to look at things differently'. 'What matters is how well the comrade in question can fight the Germans', said Novikov. 'That's what Marxism tells me'.[10]

Faced with the invocation of Marxism as the highest judge of this matter, the political commissar's Russian nationalism – a nationalism that would struggle to find a way to understand such a judge – was forced to take a backward step.

But if we think the problems of Marxism's history through the analysis of 'Marxism, according to the texts',[11] then how could the Marxisms of Novikov and Nyeudobnov gain mastery over such a judge? And what about all the other forms outlined by a great writer like Pasternak?

None of these *forms* of Marxism has a place in a history conducted within the terms of 'Marxism, according to the texts'. Yet these Marxisms coming 'straight from life' itself – and thus, for Pasternak, 'authentic' ones – have been very significant in 'collective life': that is, in history. As for their 'authenticity', it is entirely clear that this is a literary term that has nothing to do with the practices of textual philology. The great writers' literary expressions do, however, have the ability to help us grasp elements of truth that stand beyond the narration of facts. If this was 'authenticity' because it was 'straight from life' itself, then the 'authenticity' in question represents an amalgam revealing an ideal world – no matter how simplified or falsified – through behaviours and ways of being that are profoundly interconnected. That is to say, through its necessary contextualisations.

Above, I used the expression '*forms* of Marxism'; and I think that the history of Marxism cannot be anything other than the history of the *system of relations among its forms*. And each of these forms in turn appear as crossroads at the end of multiple paths; 'the overlapping of references whose meaning is plural', as one French reviewer of this book put it.[12]

This is, therefore, a type of multiplicity different to that of the long-practiced history of *Marxisms*. While this latter has produced knowledge-results of some significance, it is a multiplicity that almost exclusively pertains to theoretical Marxism – that is, to one *form* of Marxism.

A history conducted through an analysis of the 'forms of Marxism' could suggest elements of analogy with what was a typically Marxian methodology. Indeed, Marx systematically used the term 'form/s' from the *Grundrisse*

10 Grossmann 2011, p. 205.

11 An expression from Macchioro 1999.

12 *Mil neuf cent*, 1997, pp. 221–3.

onward, in particular in *Capital* Volume I, and it is a concept of decisive importance in his elaborations: the nodal point of a true and proper theoretical language.

It is wholly evident that the explanatory language used to give account of the metamorphoses of 'value', through the multiplication of its phenomenal forms, cannot be applied to the system of relations running between the various forms of historical Marxism. Even so, it does suggest mechanisms for analysing the relation between the 'concrete' and the 'abstract' that can hardly be foreign to a history in which the 'abstract' reference (theory) was always evoked as the explanation of 'concrete' phenomena (structures, mentalities, behaviours).

Certainly, the historian's mechanism for understanding the 'forms of Marxism' cannot enjoy the same analytical compactness as that which is used to explain the changes in the 'forms of value'. Rather, it is often necessary to use different analytical categories in accordance with the contexts in which the different forms are located. Indeed, some categories can be used to understand 'long-term' forms, while others can only be used by way of specific periodisations. We will try to give two examples of this. In the first case, we will see that the form of Marxism in question must be analysed using a plurality of categories, some of which transcend the period in which this form is most manifest. In the second case, conversely, we will see that the category (singular) used is exclusively capable of giving account of one particular form, linked to a specific and limited periodisation.

a) The form of Marxism that emerges from Pasternak and Grossman's literary representations owes its genesis to a particular historical period: it is a 'war-Marxism'. They baptise it in two terrible events, namely the Great War and the Russian Civil War. The former signalled a sharp break with the way in which this culture had developed the system of mediations between theory (be it philosophical, economic or social) and political practice. The latter solidly attached the new phase beginning with the 'catastrophe' to a particular history – Russia's history – with the 'glue' of rivers of blood that were spilt amidst extreme cruelty. This was a history little-favourable to the development of the universalistic elements of Enlightenment ancestry typical of the great majority of the Marxist cultures preceding the 'catastrophe'. In general, when we think of the tension between Russian and Western European history we tend to counterpose a long and unbroken experience of autocracy with a tradition of liberal modernity, with its implicit lines of descent to democracy. What ultimately bore greater influence on what I have called 'war-Marxism' was the deeper aspect of Russian society: the peasant question.

'The Russian Enlightenment has become the Russian Revolution',[13] Pasternak wrote, within the already-mentioned logic of the transformation of a noble thought into 'crude materialism' that, nonetheless, came 'straight from life' – or more precisely, from the historical context in which that life is immersed. And the pages of Pasternak devoted to the revolutionary upheavals, together with those written by other great Soviet writers, with their 'capacity to penetrate the real, which could truly ground their sense of history and respond to the questions that it poses',[14] allow us to 'see more' in the folds of the 'life' that also shaped the forms of Marxism.

> And then I stomped my master Nikitinsky. I stomped him for an hour or more than an hour, and in that time I got to know life to its fullest. With shooting – I'll put it this way – with shooting all you do is get rid of a man. Shooting's a pardon for him, and too damn easy for you. Shooting, it won't get you to the soul, to where it is in a man, how it shows itself. But, when the time comes, I don't spare myself – when the time comes, I stomp the enemy for an hour or more than an hour. I want to get to know life, what life's all about.[15]

It was thus that the little Jewish Red soldier in Budionny's army – the great writer Isaac Babel – laconically dealt with an abyss as vast as it was deep: a historical abyss. In the 'year of '18' the Red general Pavlichenko, a former serf of the 'landowner' Nikitinsky, kills his old master such as to get to his 'soul' and take it away from him. And the illiterate Pavlichenko thrashes his master after having read him a letter of Lenin's from a white piece of paper. He thrashes him in the name of Lenin, in the name of 'the most genuine kind' of Marxism – the Marxism coming 'straight from life'. Perhaps when Babel was shot on Stalin's orders in 1940 it was following the same reading of Lenin's letter as Pavlichenko's.

The same motivations as Pavlichenko's – the 'spasm of hatred'[16] that had built up over such a long time – were at the basis of other massacres of landowners, at the hands of the anti-Bolshevik, anti-Marxist nationalism of a Symon Petliura:

> the peasants hated that same Lord Hetman as though he were a mad dog ... in the peasants' minds the Hetman's so-called 'reform' was a swindle on

13 Pasternak 1958b, Chapter Sixteen, p. 5.

14 Esposito 2013, p. 46.

15 Babel 2014.

16 Bulgakov 1971, p. 107.

> behalf of the landlords and ... what was needed once and for all was the true reform for which the peasants themselves had longed for centuries: All land to the peasants.[17]

And the landowners, officers, had their badges of rank carved directly on their skin.[18] These were anti-Bolsheviks and anti-Marxists whose actions were based on the same watchwords, the same programme, that allowed the 'Reds' to win the civil war.

> I accept the *comrades* being rigid and even tyrannical with regard to the party's political conduct. But as for comrades having the authority to pronounce as arbiters of questions of science ... no, science will never be put to the vote, even in the so-called society of the future![19]

Without the context we have described, this observation of Labriola's would have remained entirely obvious, just as it was at the moment in which he wrote it. Yet this context also developed elements that had been present within the very manner in which the genesis of socialism, the social sciences and the overall cultural dimension had been interlinked. The consequences of this would have been unthinkable before the emergence of 'war-Marxism'. Here was the conviction – and it was a fundamental conviction – that the strategic terms of politics (and sometimes even the tactical ones) necessarily depended on 'scientific' guidance. Naturally, in the context of Marxism's foundation, this could only be a matter of 'positive science'; but in different contexts this same relation would again be proposed using the different epistemological moments of the status of 'science' and/or 'the sciences'.

Arthur Koestler described one of these moments in literary terms, when he referred to the discussions of the Bolshevik Central Committee before Lenin's death, as remembered by the now 'Old Bolshevik' Rubashov, about to be crushed under the wheel of the Moscow Trials of the 1930s:

> during the lifetime of the old leader, no distinction between 'theorists' and 'politicians' had existed. The tactics to be followed at any given moment were deduced straight from the revolutionary doctrine in open discussion ... Each one of the men with the numbered heads on the

17 Ibid.

18 Bulgakov 1971, p. 135.

19 Antonio Labriola, 'Marxismo, Darwinismo, eccetera', *Critica Sociale*, 1897, p. 189.

> old photograph which had once decorated Ivanov's walls, knew more about the philosophy of law, political economy and statesmanship than all the high-lights in the professorial chairs of the universities of Europe. The discussions at the congresses during the Civil War had been on a level never before in history attained by a political body; they resembled reports in scientific periodicals – with the difference that on the outcome of the discussion depended the life and well-being of millions, and the future of the Revolution.[20]

This attitude was a deep undercurrent throughout the whole development of Marxism and socialism, if with rather differentiated, controversial and even contradictory results. It produced a constant attention to structural phenomena, an attentive study of the general conditions within which political action must play out, a consideration of politics itself as a moment in a more complex web of interdependencies, and a consideration of culture as a primary and indispensable moment of this politics.

At the same time, however, the 'scientific' justification of 'tactics' has even in the best of cases powerfully impoverished the depth of the epistemological problems that are necessarily connected to this, reducing the necessary flexibility of contingent political choices to rigid and doctrinaire schemas. In the worst cases, 'science' became a merely instrumental appendage of tactics, reduced to an ideology of immediacy. The reduction of 'science' to ideology – even with regard to the 'tactical' dimension – was almost taken for given, once these premises were assumed. All things considered, even an ideology can play a noble function, and not necessarily be transformed into an ignoble tool. In the reality of the historical process involving socialism and Marxism there has, certainly, been a place for science, and also for a noble use of ideology; but so, too, for its ignoble use. The bayonet of the Red soldier Taraska has often been misguided, in the search for 'the other side'.

We thus have a long-term *form of Marxism* whose origins can be analysed only by way of a very general interpretative framework. But over this long period, a variety of rather more specific codes would each make reference to an original archetype that was little more than their canvas. Each of these codes can only be explained by way of specific categories. Recourse to the original archetype is not only insufficient, but can also prove misleading. There is no *necessary* relation between the archetype and these codes. These codes' *forms of Marxism* must be contextualised individually, with analytical categories that

20 Koestler 1968, p. 142.

do not coincide temporally with that of the archetype; that is, using analytical categories that must be set in a problematic relation with the archetype.

b) In the first part of this book, we will often encounter the expression 'Marxism outside of Marxism'. We have conceived and used this category *only* in order to explain the formation process of cultures *preceding* the moment in which Marxism took on its structuring elements.

In our twentieth-century experience we encountered 'Marxism' above all in its form as a school and system of doctrines, as a political movement, or even as a set of state institutions. This was, then, a rather structured Marxism. The fact that there was also a plural Marxism (a plurality of Marxisms) does not stand in contradiction with the 'organised' character of a large part of its history.

The historical literature on Marxism must necessarily be considerably influenced by an experience in which this structured dimension was of such significance. As such, in general the *starting point* of this history has been fixed in Marx and Engels's *oeuvre*, as concerns its theoretical coordinates, and the early formation of the 'Marxist parties', as concerns the coordinates of the political movement.

Nonetheless, the paths of Marxism's development when Marxism *as such* did not exist also *fully belong* to this history. They indicate possibilities of another relation between theoretical elaboration and real movement, one operating outside of the political organisations entrusted with this relation precisely because of their claimed possession of the 'right' theory.

Even at the end of the nineteenth century, what we are accustomed to calling Marxism already had a rather substantial and relatively structured presence among the realities of Italian culture. Moreover – and this is a consideration of no little significance – in the 1890s a party formed that avowedly assumed 'Marxism' as the foundational element of its own identity. Even back then, there were in truth multiform ways of identifying the 'object' Marxism, which was a set of rather different 'things'; but it is difficult to deny its overall, organised character.

The discourse regarding the previous period is a rather different one. *Beyond* any 'Marxist party', in these years Italy – and not only Italy – saw the development of the 'Marxist' logics with which the workers' unions related to the tasks of resistance and to the possible political role that the organised 'class' could play. 'Marxist' logics here meant only a coincidence – whether it was a conscious one or otherwise; and often it was, indeed, unknowing – with Marx's indications regarding the workers' movement. These latter had principally matured through the experience of the First International, though he had elaborated them starting with the English experiences of the 1850s.

Throughout the development of the First International – at least until the very severe clash with Bakuninism brought the distinction between doctrinal choices to the centre of discussion, as well as the tendency for them to be defined negatively, as labels – 'Marxism' did not particularly stand out as a 'doctrine', a 'party' or a 'sect'. The development of this type of Marxism was a hypothesis wholly extraneous to Marx's intentions, and, indeed, would have been entirely unrealistic given the actual tendencies of the European workers' movement. In his 'Instructions for the Delegates of the Provisional General Council' to the 1866 Geneva Congress, Marx clearly stated that the International Association's task was 'to combine and generalise the *spontaneous movements* of the working classes, but not to dictate or impose any doctrinary system whatever'. Moreover, such an 'imposition' would have been impossible.

The relation between Marx, a very influential member of the General Council, and the most important workers' organisations in Europe, in particular the trade unions, was not an easy or one-dimensional one. It became an essential aspect of the far from linear establishment of a Marxian framework regarding the role of workers' organisation, even despite the absolute lack of any current in the International that could itself be defined as 'Marxist'.

Even where there was a 'battle for Marxism' as in France and Germany, this 'outside' component would prove essential.

For example, the members of the *chambres syndicales* were also members of International sections, and often their meeting places and headquarters were the same. Their socialistic frame of reference was very much defined, but it was a Proudhonian and certainly not a 'Marxist' one (even Marx's name was almost unknown in working-class circles in France until after the Commune). They defended their positions using Proudhonian arguments, thus maintaining their traditional frame of ideological reference. But as concerned the International's general line on the role and function of workers' organisation, and the conjugation of resistance and political initiative, they were always entirely convinced in siding with the General Council. Ideological choices would remain an element 'external' to the 'internal' logic of the International Working Men's Association. Meanwhile in Germany, was it not, as Marx himself recognised, the 'Lassallean' Schweitzer who was more 'internal' to the International's logics than was the 'Marxist' Liebknecht?

This was all the more the case in the Italy of the 1870s and 1880s, where a cultural amalgam formed that was structurally incompatible with being divided into an 'internal' and 'external' consciousness standing in a hierarchy of ideological priorities. It was precisely in the Italy of those years that the loadbearing structure of what would become 'Marxism' principally developed through the experience of the *Partito Operaio Italiano* and the elaborations of the 'non-Marxist' Gnocchi Viani. This was, indeed, a 'Marxism outside of Marxism'.

This category thus arises for use in a specific, limited context. Yet the analytical whole in which it is inserted, and which provides its justification, is the same one that defines (indeed, does not 'define') our object, Marxism, as it takes shape in this volume: namely, as a set of *historically determinate forms*.

The Times through Which This Book Has Lived

I began working on this volume at the peak of the 'crisis of Marxism' of the 1980s, and I finished it after the 'death of Marxism' and the 'end of history'. The present English edition is being published in the time of the 'Marx renaissance'.

The path from 'crisis' to 'death' of Marxism was a decisive element of the *zeitgeist* that surrounded the elaboration and in particular the reception of this book. So powerful was the effect of the spirit of the times – and in many senses, we continue to feel its impact – that even the so-called Marx renaissance does not seem, at least for now, to have the power to shift its direction in any decisive sense. The Marx renaissance is, without doubt, an extremely important phenomenon that has today gone beyond the academic context and become a central element of one of the world's most important artistic events: the Venice *Biennale*. The 'cornerstone' of its 2015 programme was 'the imposing live reading of the three volumes of Karl Marx's *Das Kapital. Das Kapital* [would] become a kind of Oratory: throughout the seven months of the Exhibition, the live reading would be an uninterrupted appointment'.[21] As the curator of the Venice show explained, 'I am bringing Marx to the *Biennale* because he speaks to us today'.[22] Yet the spheres of studies, of art, of high culture in general, seem rather separate from processes of change in the present state of things.

The 'Marx renaissance' phenomenon began to take shape very soon after the proclaimed 'death' of the Trier thinker; and not by chance, this occurred in concomitance with the first ominous creaking of the financial-recessionary crises of the 1990s. This phenomenon then grew exponentially with the beginning of the 'great crisis' in which we are still today immersed. The reasons for this are entirely obvious ones: the inability of mainstream economic thought – which today almost wholly coincides with 'vulgar economics', given its emi-

21 *La Repubblica*, 6 March 2015.

22 *La Stampa*, 3 March 2015.

nently ideological function – to explain the deeper logics of the manner in which the imbalances of 'the world economy', namely world capitalism, are now appearing. Posing the right questions about the current phase of capitalist accumulation, and attempting to give some answers, demands *thinking capitalism itself as a problem*. Is it possible to do that without Marx?

Evidently not. Hence the resumption of a very rich amount of writing – much of it scholarly – on Marx and Marxism. This almost amounts to a new library, adding to the true and proper library of Alexandria (and fortunately, it is one that is still with us) collected over time with the infinite contributions dedicated to Marxian and Marxist problematics.

The Italian contribution to the construction of this new library has been anything but marginal, with scholars of economics, philosophy and sociology producing a high-level literature. Marx's fundamental texts have been scrutinised by new and attentive philological studies. More particularly, *Capital* has been the object of an important recent critical edition, indeed one including all the texts that Marx explicitly composed with a view to the realisation of Volume I.[23] This volume also includes all the main variants of the editions preceding the Fourth German Edition, and thus allows us directly to enter into Marx's laboratory. This is what Gramsci called 'preliminary detailed philological work ... carried out with the most scrupulous accuracy [and] scientific honesty'.[24] It is philology placed in service of the critical interpretation of theory.[25] Of theory, in short.

Up till this point, history scholars have remained on the margins of the Marx renaissance's central threads: in the best of cases, they have gone along with its dominant logic. Historians' reception of the very wide panorama of studies produced by this Marx renaissance has been apparent above all in works relating to new interpretations of the history of thought, the history of analysis and the history of ideas in general.

In Italy, the history of theory has a long and very interesting tradition. The fact that the Italian contribution to the theoretical debate on Marxism was very important both at the end of the nineteenth century (with Antonio Labriola) and in the twentieth century (with Antonio Gramsci) could not fail to influence a whole tradition of studies. Moreover, Marxism's Italian interlocutors/adversaries in 'pure economics' (Vilfredo Pareto) and 'pure concepts' (Benedetto

---

23 *Il capitale. Critica dell'economia politica*, published by La città del sole in 2011 as Volume XXI of the *Marx Engels Opere Complete*.

24 Gramsci 1975, p. 420.

25 Fineschi 2008.

Croce) represented the international high points of both economic theory and idealist philosophy.

This tradition has had – and still has – important results for our knowledge. In the *Trente Glorieuses* following the Second World War, the paths of Marxist culture's social history were explored with varying fortunes. This historiographical framework did not replace the preceding one, but rather combined with it. Notwithstanding certain frictions, the set of relations between these two historiographical dimensions doubtless itself represented an enrichment of Marxist culture. After the 'end of Marxism' and the 'end of history' made the connection with 'the real movement' a rather problematic one, the history of theory was reinvigorated. But now its references were wholly external to the *forms of Marxism* such as they related to the *forms* of the subalterns' 'antithesis', both in their history and in terms of their future prospects. It is possible that the current excavation of Marx's theoretical materials will also lend itself to a renewed history and a new synthesis: but for now the model of the general works published during the period of the 'Marx renaissance' has again been that of the history of theories. We could note, for example, a recent *Storia dei marxismi in Italia*:[26] a book of considerable and scrupulous analytical intelligence, but one that explicitly presents itself as a 'history of theoretical Marxism'.[27] The same is also true of a still-ongoing publishing initiative – a monumental work planned to appear in six volumes, three of which have come out already[28] – to which numerous Italian scholars have contributed. This is a very useful work of comparative analyses, but again one that remains internal to the logic that we have mentioned.

In short, it does not seem that we are about to see a history of twentieth-century Italian Marxism inspired by the same criteria as the book now being presented to the Anglophone reader.

The *spirit of the times* to which I referred above had no telling influence on the toolbox that I employed in putting together this book. This was, rather, a toolbox that had taken shape very much *internally* to the epistemological and methodological problems of an intense cycle of historiographical innovation. This was a cycle in which the project of historiography *qua* social science – albeit one with its own peculiarities – was going through a process of gradual disciplinary theorisation. Here, it was passing through the search for – and proposal of – a specific theory for a specific model. In short, the history-theory

26 Corradi 2005.

27 Corradi 2005, p. 7.

28 Jaca Book's *L'altro Novecento. Comunismo eretico e pensiero critico*, edited by Pier Paolo Poggio.

relationship was becoming the central element of what has been called the logical-historical method, the keystone of a materialist approach to history. All this was part of the attempt to make a contribution to the 'Marxist history in the making' to which a whole generation of young scholars devoted themselves.[29]

'We can move between narrower or wider models of theorisation, but we cannot do without a history that is closely shaped by the demands of theory. And the relation with the economic sphere – the social science that developed the most rigorous theoretical framework, the science of reference for a generally diffuse historical materialism – ended up also becoming the measure of the degree of Marxism in historical culture'.[30] Again in the case of the history of Marxism, a first approach by way of economics (economic history, the history of economic thought, the history of economic analysis) seemed compulsory. This approach was both the result of the aforementioned Italian tradition of the history of theory, and the obligatory reference point for whoever thought of writing history in a materialist vein. My first monograph on the history of Italian Marxism, published in 1980, was a fruit of this same climate.[31] It was a work moving substantially in harmony with the Italian tradition of the history of theory, even if it did also seek to grasp all the possible articulations of theory with the political sphere. It was an attempt to translate theory into ethical-political – and thus historical – terms, as well as an intellectual history and history of high politics.

The other aspect of the Italian tradition that fed into this monograph concerned the philological dimension. This dimension occupied an absolutely central position in my formation at university in Florence. For all 'serious studies', Delio Cantimori continually repeated, he and Eugenio Garin were compulsory reference points in history and the history of philosophy, and Gianfranco Contini and Giacomo Devoto in Romance and classical literature. Obviously in this history of theories, the philological approach was reserved only for texts of recognised importance, meaning texts of high culture.

Absent from that book, then, was the whole sphere of the workers' movement's use/fulfilment of the theoretical complex in question. I was aware – as I wrote at the time – that the path toward such a widening of my theme would require addressing 'a set of problems implying different investigations and different methodologies'; a set of problems 'awaiting a synthesis that the current

29 Vilar 1973.

30 Favilli 2006, pp. 232–3.

31 Favilli 1980.

state of studies [did] not seem to promise any time soon'.[32] It was a synthesis that I myself would attempt, and which would appear sixteen years later.

Moreover, as the 'crisis of Marxism', latent in the first half of the 1980s, transformed into the 'end of Marxism' at the conclusion of that decade, the 'toolbox' used with regard to both Marxism and the history of Marxism was further enriched. There was no need for an ideological 'culturalism' with a postmodern substrate in order for cultural history – also by way of social history – to become a catalyst for research, including research related to the history of Marxism.

We can see significant traces of this in Turin publisher Einaudi's monumental *Storia del marxismo*, a work published in four volumes (five books) between 1978 and 1982, and whose architects not by chance included Eric Hobsbawm and Georges Haupt. The differences with another imposing (1,499 page) work conceived at the beginning of the 1970s[33] could not have been more stark. This latter work's novelty related to its attempt to 'give account of Marxism in its theoretical dimension', not only in its 'essential principles', but also 'in its concreteness and diversities'.[34] In substance, it was a question of articulating the 'Marxism' within the 'Marxisms'. Conversely, in the Einaudi *Storia del marxismo* this aspect was wholly obvious, and the articulation that it sought was a rather different one, notwithstanding the continued prevalence of theoretical aspects and political thinking. It also paid attention to the history of the concepts used, to their semantic contextualisation, and to questions regarding the spread of theory and thought in terms of vertical stratification. As Hobsbawm suggested, the 'irradiation'[35] of Marxism acted in all directions: horizontally in the 'movements inspired by, or which declared themselves inspired by Marx's ideas',[36] and vertically in the processes of the use 'from below' of aspects of theory considered useful in a determinate context.

Hobsbawm's role in Einaudi's *Storia del marxismo* was evidently a central one. He was entrusted not only with specific essays but also with the introductions to the individual volumes, and particular the important prefaces to Volumes I (1978) and IV (1982), at a time when the crisis of Marxism – or as he preferred to call it, the 'crisis in Marxism'[37] – had become an expression commonly used in public discourse. This, indeed, was the direct consequence of the

32 Favilli 1980, p. 11.
33 The *Storia del marxismo contemporaneo* published by Feltrinelli in 1974.
34 Zanardo 1974, p. xi.
35 Hobsbawm 1979, p. 61.
36 Hobsbawm 1978a, p. xii.
37 Hobsbawm 1982, p. 49.

continuous dialogue that had now been established between the British tradition of the likes of Thompson and Hobsbawm and the Italian historiography of Marxism and the workers' movement.

Thompson's studies delving into the ways in which the subalterns' oppositional consciousness manifests itself within a wide range of organised forms, as well as Hobsbawm's studies delving into the consciousness of 'uncommon people' and the forms in which the subaltern conceive their emancipation, would also bear considerable influence on scholars rethinking the history of Italian Marxism.

As concerns the construction of this book, it was precisely at the beginning of the second half of the 1980s that the effects of the dialogue to which I earlier referred became decisively important. I now felt that the intensive studies of theory, and in particular of economic theory, on which I had concentrated in previous years had now yielded all that they could do *in terms of the history of Marxism*. High-culture texts remained the parameters that I was familiar moving within, though I was clearly aware of their one-dimensional character. In 1986 the Fondazione Feltrinelli and the Friedrich Ebert Stiftung entrusted me with preparing an exhibition on the Italian editions of Marx and Engels's works as well as a seminar on the paths that these works took in Italy, to be held at the Studienzentrum at Trier's Karl-Marx-Haus.[38] The philological work that I conducted into the trajectories of these Italian editions set me in contact with texts that had remained wholly extraneous to my previous studies of economic theory.

Hobsbawm's *Labouring Men*, published by Einaudi in Turin in 1972, had already become a classic among the studies of labour movement history, and in 1986 another work of Hobsbawm's was released in Italy, dedicated to the cultures of labour.[39] In one of the finest essays in this volume, on 'political shoemakers', the role that common people with an ideological function play among other common people came sharply into definition. These were the key figures of the 'subaltern who speak to the subaltern'; exactly the same figures that I would find, for example, as I studied papers like *Il Fascio Operaio*.

I entered into contact with lowly publications, some of which were newspapers exclusively produced by workers: and yet these were publications that sometimes featured passages of Marx and Engels's works. The modalities and the factors behind these choices became a new chapter in the history of Marxism, and, indeed, a very interesting one. This was not a dimension substituting

38 Favilli 1988.

39 Hobsbawm 1986.

for the history of theoretical Marxisms; rather it was a fundamental component of the system of relations between different *forms* – a system of relations necessary to any history of Marxism. This was a study entailing epistemological and methodological reflections different from those of my past experiences. This meant, then, being totally immersed in my toolbox. Given that these analytical demands were essential to the work in question, matters concerning the *spirit of the times* – however powerful – ultimately remained external.

Once my work was finished, however, the political-cultural context became a factor of anything but secondary importance in how the resultant work was received. This was a context in which it seemed difficult to understand how someone could have dedicated almost ten years to studying and researching a history of Marxism, given that Marxism was now finally dead.

'You're still spending your time on Marxism?', a friend asked me with an air of commiseration – this being a friend who was a top leader of the *Partito democratico della sinistra* (the first of the names that the PCI assumed after it dropped the communist 'C') and a future minister in a centre-Left government. He was not a culturally unaware person inclined to *trasformismo*, like the greater part of those journeying from the PCI to the *Partito democratico* via a series of staging posts. Indeed, he would then prove as much with choices that wholly contrasted with the dominant conception of politics as a career. With excellent studies behind him and a passion for books, he preserved the Communist tradition of a constant search for the connections between cultural elaboration and political praxis. It was for these reasons that his reaction faced with the 'spectre of Marx' in 1995 was such an interesting one: it provided the surest indication of how far the conviction had spread that after the fall of the Berlin Wall there was no place either for the complex of theories critical of capitalism, or for a politics in some way informed by these theories.

Naturally, this was not only an Italian phenomenon; but it was here that it took on a dimension unequalled anywhere else in all Western European history. In Italy, indeed, a party defining itself as 'Marxist' enjoyed a prestige and 'intellectual heritage' incomparable with that of other countries. 'At its peak the PCI could make recourse to an extraordinary array of social and moral energies, which combined popular roots deeper and an intellectual influence more widespread than that of any other force'.[40] It was a political and cultural reference point for the Left, and not only in Europe.

40 Anderson 2014, p. 79.

> For the PCI the crisis ... arrived from the outside and it consequently had a solely 'imported', superstructural and wholly ideological character: the crisis of a name and a memory that had with one fell swoop become unsustainable. A still strong and united party marked by only marginal disagreements was almost suddenly forced, with the precipitation of a defeat that it had almost certainly not foreseen, and for which it was not directly responsible, to shed its own skin – literally to renounce its own soul – and to adopt a new path in order to be able to survive. And so it was, after a brief discussion – and everything was resolved rather quickly, though it also meant the trauma of a split. Positions and slogans that had until recently been considered heretical now became its daily bread. Authors and doctrines that had up till that moment constituted the core of a cohesive and shared education were suddenly forgotten ... Men and women with decades of impassioned commitment behind them, were suddenly and without notice detached from their own history – the long march that had produced the construction of their 'themselves' – and reattached to a new identity, with respect to which the first was nothing but a useless (and embarrassing) accumulation of detritus.[41]

The Italian historian who described this reversal in such dramatic and pathos-filled terms nonetheless considered it *necessary* after the implosion of the USSR: an event that 'changed the meaning of the whole narrative' that had gone before.[42] This meant reducing to nothing all the existing laboratories and sites of elaboration. As has rightly been noted, 'the calm with which this suicide was carried out' was truly impressive.[43]

In history there are no events that reduce everything to nothing. Critical discussion on other 'events' that supposedly reduced everything to nothing today fill up entire libraries. The fact that a historian could advance such an argument is one further indication of a phenomenon that needs to be studied and explained.

Another history scholar and protagonist of microhistory – an Italian historiographical theory that was both innovative and of great international importance – would declare: 'All of us have in some way been influenced by Marxism ... and I am gobsmacked when I see that *all of a sudden* no one is a Marxist any more: it is something atrocious, appalling'.[44]

41 Schiavone 1999, pp. 5–7.

42 Schiavone 1999, p. 21.

43 Asor Rosa 1996, p. 40.

44 Levi 1990, p. 225. My italics.

Practically right up till 1989, Italian Communist intellectuals were nourished on reflections that dated back across a long period. A considerable proportion of them now very rapidly moved almost entirely to cancel out the whole theoretical tradition within which they had formed their whole scholarly persona (some of them across several decades) and their coordinates of reference (which they had also used in the formation of others). This opens up multiple questions concerning the very fine line where the great epochal turning points encounter the individual ways of experiencing them, as well as individual responsibilities.

Here, there truly was an epochal turning point. A long period so heavily charged with the future instead concluded with the negation of that future; and this was a deep and genuine historic caesura, light years away from the countless turning points and/or revolutions as portrayed by the media. Events of this kind overwhelm everything else. Nonetheless, professional scholars have the duty to distinguish between different levels, logics and paths, even as the darkness that always accompanies the great cataclysms makes everything look indistinct. This means distinguishing between ideology and analysis, utopia and dystopia, and the immediately political use of a theory and its hard kernel, as well as distinguishing among the different times of a long-term experience not all of whose periods conform to the same logic. This is an operation that involves long studies and much research, as well as the writing of many books, but it is one intimately connected with (*necessary to*) the life choice that is 'science as a vocation', to use an expression from someone else who is 'no longer current'.[45] It is not easy to make distinctions when the spirit of the times is so powerful, but the alternative is the ever wider spread of the 'Ciccotti paradox'. Ettore Ciccotti, to whom I have referred repeatedly over the course of this book, was from the late nineteenth century to the beginning of the twentieth century one of the most important and innovative Marxist historians in Italy. During the Fascist *ventennio* Ciccotti ended up agreeing to become a senator, and when he died in 1939 he was thus to be considered wholly compromised by the regime. Yet this last phase of his existence does not appear – or appears only episodically, purely as a biographical curiosity – in any study devoted to Ciccotti. The role that he occupies in Italian and European culture – and it is not an unimportant one – is attached to Ciccotti the *Marxist historian*, and not his subsequent fate as a 'Fascist'.

45 The expression is Max Weber's, the title of a 1917 lecture of his.

Our time, so rich in political rethinking – which is, of course, indispensable, but also entails genuine biographical traumas if it means seeing the past as a univocal and indistinct bloc – must be preparing us many 'paradoxical' cases *à la* Ciccotti. If in that past historians or philosophers or scholars of social sciences calling themselves Marxists produced significant works, that does not lose its meaning on account of the radical changes that have taken place since then.

Some of these people were truly important to postwar Italian – and not only Italian – culture. They produced works that, even if they are read today outside of the mood of their times (but doesn't every work conserve that mood?), display a still-intact theoretical solidity and critical awareness. And yet some of them are particularly dogged in their commitment to *damnatio memoriae*, in which cause they combine with scholars who were of no significance yesterday, but make a great deal of noise today.

We might ask ourselves what overall meaning people who now have almost all of their works behind them manage to ascribe to their lives as scholars (and perhaps not only as scholars) when, considering that the 'great task' they had assigned themselves has now been dragged into the abyss by the fall of their 'great hope', they also drag in their whole past scholarly activity, effectively also putting in doubt (at least their past) probity and intellectual capacity.

Paradoxically, when the history of the Italian culture of the second half of the twentieth century is written, some of them will be there – and with no little honour – precisely as *Marxists*. The last part of such figures' lives will appear to scholars as an insignificant biographical detail, exactly as in the case of Ettore Ciccotti. The only difference is that Ciccotti would not have been displeased to be remembered as such by historians. Notwithstanding his changed political coordinates, he never repudiated his past scientific work, and did not regret having been a *Marxist historian*, conscious that this dimension was the foundation of his life as a man and a scholar.

Such a prospect must, however, terrify some of these ex-Marxists, judging by the tone of their incursions into the media (and many of them now appear only in the media).

In a delightful film that came out twelve years ago, *The Barbarian Invasions*, a group of French-Canadian friends, history professors at Quebec University, melancholically discuss their cultural experience, so intensely interlinked with the rest of their life experience. They recall their allegiance to each of the 'isms' of the times: structuralism, Maoism, situationism, and so on. The only ism they kept away from – they conclude – is cretinism. When professionals of the study of history, philosophy, economics and so on restrict themselves to bobbing along with the waves of history, we might doubt that they could even console themselves with that much.

These forms of the end of Italian Marxism are still awaiting 'serious studies'. Certainly, though, they are a chapter of the history of Marxism, and of the history of the Italian Marxism of the twentieth century.

Lugano, March 2015

CHAPTER 1

The 1860s and 1870s: Marxism Rejected, and the Humus of Marxism

1 The Democratic Antithesis

'Over more than a century the term "worker" has become an element of all cultural discourse, whether explicitly or implicitly, as a denomination of a social or professional condition'.[1] These words appeared in an early 1960s text by Italo Calvino, in one of those discourses of which he was the unsurpassed master, constructed in a careful and calibrated balance between the specifically literary and social theory. Getting to grips with the question of the centrality of the term 'worker', Calvino underlined the genesis of a profound phenomenon of very great significance: 'the worker has entered into history of ideas as the personification of the antithesis'.[2]

The cultures of Marxism have been essential in determining the immanently universalistic value through which the term 'worker' has expressed both the subjectivity and objectivity of an historical process concluding in the horizon of total liberation, negating what currently exists. These cultures have given theoretical explanations of the worker's antithetical nature, within a genesis that was largely common to the formation of both the 'worker' and these cultures: an antithesis that a symbiotic construction of theory and historical objectivity almost seemed to have made apparent.

Workers and the cultures of Marxism represented the *antithesis* in a dialectical process that saw the negation long maturing within the *thesis*; within the given reality. This would, then, arrive at a separation in which it was still possible to see elements that would be recomposed in the perspective of a far-off but hoped-for *synthesis*. Over the course of a long-term process, 'democracy' and 'democrats' were now the thesis, now the antithesis, now the synthesis. Moreover 'the forms of a prior stage always emerge among the ideas of a more recent one ... and the vital kernel of an era, a nebulous mass in expansion, is channelled into forms that are the historical precipitate of rather older eras'.[3]

---

1 See Calvino 1980, pp. 100, 101.

2 Ibid.

3 R. Musil, 'Geist und Erfahrung', *Der Neue Merkur*, March 1921.

If Marx and Engels first appeared in Italy in the guise of authoritative exponents of European democracy, we can explain this not only in terms of chronological coincidence – with the great democratic uprisings of the late 1840s – but also with regard to a dimension of European democracy that was both extremely widespread and radical. There is an obvious – even if problematic – continuity tying the Marx and Engels presented as 'German democrats' in 1847 as they commemorated the anniversary of the 1830 Polish revolution[4] to the Marx who referred to 'democratic principles' in his famous 1848 letter to *L'Alba*, and the positions of Tucci and Cafiero at the November 1871 Rome Congress of the *Società Operaie*, when they sought to demonstrate that Mazzini's position stood in contradiction to 'being democratic' and the International itself.[5] This is a web whose threads make visible both the developments of a line of thinking and the milieus that served as the mediation for its development.

In the 1860s and immediately after the Paris Commune, essential elements of what would later become 'Marxism' were being spread by the democratic press across Italy.

From 1864 onward there was an early and widespread divulgation of both the *Inaugural Address* and the *Provisional Rules* of the International Workingmen's Association. In July 1865 the first full translation (notwithstanding a few small omissions) of these two documents appeared in Genoa's *Il Dovere*.[6] The *Rules* had already appeared alone in the February 1865 issue of Milan's *L'Unità Italiana*. Previous to the *Il Dovere* translation there had only been three English editions and two German ones. Yet by the end of the decade there were a total of five Italian editions of the *Provisional Rules*, six of the *General Rules* agreed at the Geneva Congress, one complete edition of *The Inaugural Address*, and two of its concluding section; and moreover, in 1871 the *General Rules* would be published a further fourteen times. However, not until the historian Ettore Ciccotti's new translation published by Mongini in 1901 would the *Inaugural Address* again be published in Italy.

The circle of newspapers involved in producing these editions was relatively broad: as well as the ones that we have already mentioned, they included *Libertà e Lavoro* and *Il Popolo d'Italia* in Naples; *Il Gazzettino Rosa* in Milan; *Il Proletario Italiano* in Turin; *L'Eguaglianza* in Girgenti; *Il Romagnolo* in Ravenna; *La Favilla* in Mantua; and *La Plebe* in Lodi. This latter would then distribute the *General Rules* separately from its normal run, selling them at 10 *centes-*

4 See *La Rivista di Firenze*, 24 December 1847.

5 See Del Bo (ed.) 1964, pp. 81–8.

6 See Hunecke 1971.

imi a copy. It is true that Engels wrote that 'all of these' editions were 'badly and in part incorrectly translated',[7] but even so, this did mean that an important document of Marx's was circulating among a far from negligible section of Italy's democratic and socialist movements. The fact that Mazzinian newspapers played a prominent role in divulgating these texts is also an index of the relative permeability of the entire revolutionary ecosystem: a permeability that would continue to survive, within limits, even after Mazzini's 'excommunication' of Marx and the violent polemics that followed from this.

Rather, the existence of a broadly polyvalent *sovversivo* [subversive][8] ecosystem (and militants on both the democratic and socialist far Left would long use this adjective without any negative connotation) encouraged the formation and consolidation of a 'common sentiment': a weft of 'common reasoning' and 'common *topoi*' that endured as a substratum capable of enduring even profound doctrinal divisions. These horizontal stratifications provided the 'key ideas' that would, in determinate circumstances, later find a more complete formulation in the acceptance (or better, the composition) of a Marxist systematic, at least as much as did the vertical lineaments derived from the gradual expansion and increased awareness of Karl Marx's writings.

The 1865 *Il Dovere* edition of the *Inaugural Address* and the *Rules*[9] is of particular interest, in that it is highly emblematic of a problematic node that seems to have been the point of departure for a series of themes later destined to a long albeit contentious maturation.

First of all, because here the *Inaugural Address* and the *Rules* were published together, and they were effectively presented as something that should be read as a whole, as opposed to each text appearing separately of the other. Such a presentation was anything but commonplace in the publications of the time, barely a year after the meeting at St. Martin's Hall. Already upon a first approach, we can immediately see how this connection speaks to the new charge with which the question of the relation between democracy and socialism now tended to be posed: for Ernesto Ragionieri, 'the *Address* took account of the fracture provoked by the experiences of 1848, such as to invest the relation between socialism and democracy with the activity and initiative of a revolutionary historical subject'. At the same time, 'the *General Rules*' charac-

7 Engels to Cuno, 24 January 1872: *MECW*, Vol. 44, p. 306.

8 [In Italian this term may also have the rather pejorative connotation of a raw spirit of rebellion, lacking in political direction]

9 See Nicolò Lo Savio, 'La miseria delle classi operaie in Inghilterra', *Il Dovere*, Genoa, 29 July, 12 and 26 August 1865.

teristic element was 'their accentuation of the democratic moment, understood as the possibility of the full expression of a new movement and, together with this, the need to gather and unify a series of common experiences'.[10]

Next, because of the context in which this document was published: namely, Niccolò Lo Savio's reflection on the poverty of the very working class that was at the cutting edge of capitalist development. The historiography on the Italian socialist movement has made numerous references to both Lo Savio's precociousness and (in part) his maturity as a socialist. These traits of Lo Savio's – prompting Mazzini to direct his suspicious and far from well-disposed attentions toward him[11] – are certainly indicative of the democratic polyvalence that was then proving to be the cultural terrain most favourable to the development of the antithesis. Lo Savio would, for that matter, also find more rigorous analytical coordinates precisely thanks to his encounter with the *Inaugural Address* and the *General Rules*.

Lo Savio wrote one of his most significant 'socialist' interventions in August 1865 – that is, very shortly after the publication of these Marxian texts, whose influence on his own writing is plain to see. He sought to specify the meaning of 'emancipation', which he termed the 'fundamental dogma of socialism': for Lo Savio, emancipation was 'not an ephemeral, illusory equality like what is called equality before the law, but the real, effective equality of conditions among men. Without equality there can only be poverty and proletarianism. Socialism, therefore, is the *democratic formula par excellence*'.[12] Poverty was not a natural outcome; rather, 'poverty and … proletarianism are the consequence of so-called Capitalism'. Here we also see the echoes of the *incipit* of the *General Rules*, which ought to be held in renown 'as Marx's well-known judgement':[13] 'It is useless …, workers, to nurture the hope that others will come to salve your suffering; it is time to break out of this intellectual chaos …, choose a path, and yourselves take charge of securing your own wellbeing'. Marx's influence is similarly apparent in Lo Savio's definition of class consciousness and the meaning of class: 'You exist as a social class, distinct from other classes … [This class is] distinct from the bourgeois class because it has an *idea* of its own, has interests separate from those of the bourgeoisie; and

10 Ragionieri 1968, pp. 11, 13.

11 In September 1864 Mazzini noted that the word 'socialism' appeared in Lo Savio's articles on the workers' condition, and that 'a false solution to the problem' was thus present within them. See Santarelli's piece on Lo Savio in Andreucci and Detti (eds.) 1977, p. 166.

12 See Nicolò Lo Savio, 'Alla democrazia operaia', in *Il Proletario* ('an economic-socialist newspaper of workers' democracy'), Florence, 20 August 1865. My italics.

13 See *L'Italia del Popolo*, 11–12 August 1890.

in its social economics professes maxims wholly different from those of bourgeois economics'.[14] This last passage was directly inspired by a comparable one in the *Inaugural Address*. Moreover, Lo Savio's recourse to these Marxian texts brought him to a more analytically rigorous vision of how to define the bourgeoisie, as compared to one weighed down by the baggage of moral categories – and this latter problem was widespread not only in the democratic press of that time, but even in the democratic and socialist press of the decade following the Paris Commune.[15] Perhaps it is of some use to note Osvaldo Gnocchi-Viani's[16] identification with Lo Savio's framework – Gnocchi-Viani being a figure whose political and intellectual trajectory would be very much interlinked with the particular forms that Italian Marxism came to adopt, as we shall see later on.

The *Inaugural Address* and the *General Rules*, so opportunely published in combination, perfectly encapsulated all the themes that would in subsequent years – particularly in the 1870s – traverse the political and cultural process that led to both the rejection of 'Marx's party' and the progressive affirmation of 'Marxism' outside of 'Marx's party'. In particular, in their emphasis on the need for resistance and the necessity of the struggle to improve living and working conditions; that is, in their emphasis on the possibility of improvement within a framework of historically flexible limits. This possible improvement would also demonstrate the justified claim that this resistance had an *antithetical* logic, faced with the supposedly *natural* rigidities of the dominant economic relations. A fine example of this was the 'struggle, fought with most admirable perseverance' through which 'the English working classes' 'succeeded in carrying the Ten-Hours Bill'. As Marx wrote:

> This struggle about the legal restriction of the hours of labour ... told indeed upon the great contest between the blind rule of the laws of supply and demand which form the political economy of the bourgeoisie, and

14 The same concept reappeared in an article one month later 'The class of wage-earners and proletarians feels itself distinct from the Bourgeoisie, has an idea of its own, and in its social economy professes maxims wholly different from those of the bourgeois economy' – 'Le società cooperative di produzione', *Il Proletario*, Florence, 16 September 1865.

15 See 'Intraprenditori e lavoranti', *Il Proletario*, Florence, 7 January 1866. A few years previously Lo Savio had sketched out a rudimentary theory of surplus-value, defining poverty as 'the worker's deficit' and identifying the 'inequality between the product provided and the salary received' as the primary reason for this deficit. See Nicolò Lo Savio, 'L'operaio e il proprietario', *Il Dovere*, 25 July 1863.

16 See *Il Proletario*, Florence, 17 September 1865.

> social production controlled by social foresight, which forms the political economy of the working class. Hence the Ten Hours' Bill was not only a great practical success; it was the victory of a principle; it was the first time that in broad daylight the political economy of the bourgeoisie succumbed to the political economy of the working class.[17]

Thus there was a mutual correspondence between the practice of workers' demands, the practice of the class struggle in its varying degrees of consciousness, economic theory, and the theory of society – which Marx had elaborated even in the very year in which these lines first appeared in Italian translation. In the long term, this correspondence would be understood as essential for the total 'emancipation' that organised workers set as the ultimate goal of their struggle.

Hence the 'political question' that would soon become a terrain of very bitter clashes:

> the lords of land and the lords of capital will always use their political privileges for the defence and perpetuation of their economical monopolies. So far from promoting, they will continue to lay every possible impediment in the way of the emancipation of labour. Remember the sneer with which, last session, Lord Palmerston put down the advocates of the Irish Tenants' Right Bill. The House of Commons, cried he, is a house of landed proprietors. To conquer political power has therefore become the great duty of the working classes.[18]

The clarity with which the 'political question' was defined upon the moment of the International's foundation suggests that when we evaluate the polemics of 1871–2 over the unfaithful French translation of the words 'as a means' appearing in the fourth paragraph of the *General Rules*,[19] we ought to analyse

---

17 Quoted in Nicolò Lo Savio, 'La miseria delle classi operaie in Inghilterra', *Il Dovere*, Genoa, 29 July, 12 and 26 August 1865. English text taken from *MECW*, Vol. 21, p. 330.

18 Ibid.

19 As we shall see, an aspect of the controversy over the famous Resolution IX of the London Conference was also linked to the question of 'loyalty to the *Rules*' and in particular how the fourth paragraph ('Considering that the economical emancipation of the working classes is therefore the great end to which every political movement ought to be subordinate as a means') ought to be understood (and translated) in the most important European languages.

In the 1870s these were the most important editions of the *Rules*:

them in their specific and contingent character, and not extend them too far beyond this context. Indeed, before the violent eruption of the conflict between Bakunin and the General Council, the 'political question' was not at the centre of any particular enduring controversies.[20]

We have mentioned the fact that in the same year in which the *Address* and the *Rules* appeared in Italy, both in the *Il Dovere* edition and the *L'Unità Italiana* one,[21] Marx made an intervention in London – in the General Council, indeed –

1) Provisional Rules of the International Working Men's Association (1864)
2) Statuts et réglements de l'Association International des Travailleurs (1866)
3) Statuts et réglements de l'Association International des Travailleurs (1866)
4) Rules of the International Working Men's Association (1867)
5) Statuts généraux de l'Association International des Travailleurs (1870).

Their respective formulations regarding the disputed text were 1) 'as a means', 2) it went untranslated; 3) 'comme moyen'; 4) 'as a means', 5) 'comme un simple moyen'. In the German editions curated by Marx we find 'als Mittel'.

20 Engels was not mistaken when he indicated thusly Resolution IX's antecedents: 'The position of the General Council as regards the political action of the proletariat is sufficiently well defined.

'1) By the General Rules, in which the fourth paragraph of the preamble runs: "That the economical emancipation of the working classes is the great end to which every political movement ought to be subordinate as a means."

'2) By the text of the Inaugural Address of the Association (1864), this official and essential commentary on the Rules, which says: "The lords of land and the lords of capital will always use their political privileges for the defence and perpetuation of their economical monopolies. So far from promoting, they will continue to lay every possible impediment in the way of the emancipation of labour ... To conquer political power has therefore become the great duty of the working classes."

'3) By the resolution of the Congress of Lausanne (1867) to the effect that: "The social emancipation of the workmen is inseparable from their political emancipation."

'4) By Resolution IX ...' (*MECW*, Vol. 21, pp. 54–5).

21 The two versions of the *Rules* are not the same. The one that Lo Savio used came directly from those close to the General Council it was a translation by Giuseppe Fontana, a member of the London *Società Operaia Italiana*, on the basis of a text that Marx had given to him directly (see the Italian-language Marx-Engels collected works published by Riuniti: *MEOC*, Vol. XLII, p. 14). The text that appeared in *L'Unità Italiana* was instead based on a French translation from that same year, and it imitated its errors and important differences from the original. For example, the two versions clearly diverged on the famous fourth paragraph of the *Rules*. While the *Il Dovere* version read '[Considering] that the economical emancipation of the working classes is therefore the great end to which every political movement ought to be subordinate as a means', the *L'Unità Italiana* one read '[Considering] that for this reason the economical emancipation of the workers is the

with a speech seeking to establish a close connection between economic theory and the practice of fighting for demands. Though the text of this speech was unknown in Italy (and not only Italy) until the end of the nineteenth century,[22] the General Council had nonetheless established an analytical attitude and delineated an approach toward workers' organisation – the perspective of structuring it in a 'class-party' – that allowed the development and consolidation firstly of 'Marxism' outside of 'Marxism', and then 'practical Marxism' and 'working-class Marxism' *tout court*.

In spring 1865 the carpenter John Weston – 'a good old codger, an old Owenist',[23] had presented a theoretical-practical platform to the International's General Council, concerning the effects of trade-union struggles. Weston maintained that a general rise in wages would be immediately cancelled out by a general rise in prices, of similar proportion. The workers' conditions could not, therefore, be improved by way of fighting for increases: hence the strike actions to which the trade unions were so heavily committed were useless. These were arguments that would at other moments be attacked precisely for being 'Marxist'.

In his speech to the General Council, Marx refuted Weston's argument, closely conjugating the *theory* of wages with *historical* experience and the *actual* conditions of the English workers' wage situation. Even if in a didactic manner, here he did introduce some of the categories from the first volume of *Capital*, which was then nearing completion.[24] The theory of wages was

great end to which every political movement ought to be subordinate' (see its 18 February 1865 edition).

22 The first Italian edition of this text in fact came out in 1932 (the Edizioni di coltura sociale edition of *Salario, prezzo e profitto*, labelled 'Brussels' but in fact published in Paris) but English and French-language editions of it had appeared almost simultaneously in 1898 (*Value, Price and Profit*, edited by his daughter Eleanor Marx, and 'Salaire, prix et profits', in the *Devenir Social* of that same year, pp. 385–405, 439–525). As we shall see, this latter edition would immediately be used in Italy in the polemic over Marx's theory of wages, which was at that very moment beginning to develop.

23 John Weston had presented two arguments to the General Council: '1. that A GENERAL RATE IN THE RISE OF THE RATE OF WAGES would be of no benefit to the workers; 2. that the TRADES-UNIONS for that reason, etc., are harmful. If these two propositions, in which he alone in our SOCIETY believes, were to be accepted, we should be in a terrible mess, both in respect of the TRADES-UNIONS here and the INFECTION OF STRIKES now prevailing on the Continent': *MECW*, Vol. 42, p. 159.

24 Marx was not a 'populariser', even if 'the greater part of his economic teaching was given its first expression in lectures to working men: his exposition in these circumstances was by all accounts a model of lucidity and conciseness' (Berlin 1978, p. 2).

thus linked on the one hand to the theory of value, and on the other hand to the theory of accumulation, by way of a definition of the mechanisms of the rate of profit and the rate of surplus-value. So in terms of his strictly analytical categories, the wage level was limited only by the emergence of grave dangers for the continuation of the process of capital valorisation – far from the wage being bound to the minimum necessary for survival (and Marx particularly insisted on the historical, non-static character of such minimums). So it was not only or mainly the wage level that determined whether this limit had been reached, but all the multiple elements that influenced the dynamic of the profit rate. Moreover, the increase in labour productivity also brought an increase in the general wealth, and in the conditions of strong growth – particularly in the decade of 1849 to 1859 – there had been wage rises that were not absorbed by the increase in the cost of living. In that same period, the number of officially registered poor people also fell, even if not by a great amount. So what was the force capable of improving workers' conditions, within the context of the variations in the profit rate between the minimum and maximum limits of labour-power's price, apparent in each economic conjuncture? 'It is evident', Marx answered, 'that between the two limits of this *maximum rate of profit* an immense scale of variations is possible. The fixation of its actual degree is only settled by the *continuous struggle between capital and labour*'.[25]

Immediately after emphasising the centrality of the conflict on the factory-floor, Marx also stressed the need for the extension of this struggle, which must also have a political dimension:

> As to the limitation of the working day in England, as in all other countries, it has never been settled except by legislative interference. Without the working men's continuous pressure from without that interference would never have taken place. But at all events, the result was not to be attained by private settlement between the working men and the capitalists. This very necessity of general political action affords the proof that in its merely economic action capital is the stronger side.[26]

Workers' organisation to win better working conditions through a struggle at the site of production; *workers' organisation* to act on the political sphere, such as to give legislative ratification to the improvements that had been obtained and give a general substance and depth to the great task of 'emancipation'. These

25 *MECW*, Vol. 20, p. 146. My italics.

26 Ibid.

were the two closely interconnected paths that the International indicated to the workers of Europe – who had, in fact, in some places already begun down these roads – and which appear both in the official texts of the IWMA and in the theoretical analyses underlying them. These would be often-treacherous and meandering paths; sometimes these paths would disappear only then to reappear in a different landscape, with routes that it is only possible to identify a very weak trace of. But they were, nonetheless, paths that would prove over longer distances to be essential to the intersection of the multiple itineraries through which the problematic encounter between the workers' movement, socialism and Marxism would ultimately be concretised.

Conflict at the site of production almost always meant strikes. And engagement with the 'strike question', both on the plane of theory and on the terrain of the real development of strikes, would be a constant task of the International's throughout the 1860s. Moreover, the very foundation of the IWMA was in a sense linked to this question. Starting from the negative micro-cycle at the end of the decade, almost all of industrial Europe was affected by a powerful strike wave, with sometimes imposing struggles going beyond the workplace and sometimes arriving at sharp clashes with political authority, and thus repression. These strikes were not driven by the International, but in general they did ultimately lead to an encounter with the International. As Marx put it, 'In the Lyons case, it was not the International that threw the workmen into strikes, but, on the contrary, it was the strikes that threw the workmen into the International'.[27] This question appears in almost all the International's internal debates; we find it in the IWMA's internal documents as well as in the correspondence between Marx and Engels and with their other interlocutors; from the victorious strikes of 1866–7 – through which 'proof' of the International's 'immediate practical importance' had 'struck the practical English mind'[28] – to the Belgian tragedies and massacres of 1869. The importance of the strike problem for Marx, the General Council and the various expressions of the IWMA certainly also mirrored a reality that was extremely captivating at all levels. However, at the same time the strike seemed to show concretely that the actively practiced class struggle reinforced both trade-union demands and a vast range of meanings that ultimately transcended narrowly trade-union ones. Precisely for this reason, Marx considered it a priority task of the International's to mount an intense activity 'to give direct sustenance and impetus to the requirements of the class struggle and the organisation of the workers into a class', while also being aware

27 *MECW*, Vol. 21, p. 75.

28 *MECW*, Vol. 42, p. 272.

that 'every concentrated social movement, and therefore also that which can be achieved by *political means* (e.g., such as limitation of the working day *by law*)' could be defined revolutionary.[29] The reduction of the working day by law – obviously, considered within the context of the process of conflict that was necessary to achieving it – appeared as a revolutionary phenomenon, and thus so, too, did the regulation of women's and minors' labour, as well as all the normative mechanisms allowing the worker and the class to achieve the conditions and tools for *advancing along the road* leading to 'total emancipation'.

The International's platform was *revolutionary* yet in no sense 'catastrophist' or one-dimensional; rather, it was highly articulated and attentive to *all* the expressions of the class struggle. We can see as much in the very great precision of the 1866 Geneva Congress's *Instructions for the Delegates of the Provisional General Council – The Different Questions*. The key parts of these *Instructions* concerned the struggle for the reduction of the working day, 'a preliminary condition, without which all further attempts at improvement and emancipation must prove abortive'[30] (a formulation again approved by the 1868 Brussels Congress), the regulation of child labour, and the promotion of co-operative labour ('We acknowledge the co-operative movement as one of the transforming forces of the present society').[31] Naturally, the central question was that of promoting and supporting workers' resistance: 'the trades' unions ... must now learn to act deliberately as organising centres of the working class in the broad interest of its *complete emancipation*. They must aid every social and political movement tending in that direction'.[32] A resolution on the 'resistance societies' was approved at the Basle Congress, calling on Internationalists to support these bodies and to devote themselves to their struggles. Marx also indicated as a model of working-class conduct the Pressburg workmen's response to the interior ministry in Vienna, after months of being banned from any kind of political or trade-union demonstrations: 'Since state matters influence the workmen's condition, the workmen must occupy themselves with politics, and they will certainly do so'.[33]

In conclusion, the general line that was becoming prevalent in the International – before the devastating conflict between the Council in London and Bakunin put its very foundations in question – was constructed through a complex set of arguments that, taken together, were very much internally consis-

---

29 *MECW*, Vol. 42, p. 326. My italics.
30 *MECW*, Vol. 20, p. 187.
31 *MECW*, Vol. 20, p. 190.
32 *MECW*, Vol. 20, p. 192.
33 Quoted by Marx in *MECW*, Vol. 21, p. 79.

tent. Central to this line was class organisation, in its dual connotation as both a primary instrument of resistance and as a necessary projection into the political sphere. This was a conception that would later be summarised in Marx's famous definitional statement: 'every class movement as a class movement, is necessarily and was always a political movement'.[34] Hence its corollary commitments to work for social legislation that would 'ratify' the advances that had been made in changing the power relations between the classes, and to work in a cooperative movement that could give indications for how to construct labour relations different from the dominant ones. In an interview that Marx gave to *The World* on 18 July 1871, he summarised this IWMA platform with exemplary clarity:

> The workers ... have to change the relationships between themselves and the capitalists and landlords, and that means changing society. That is the common goal of every known workers' organization; the Land and Labour Leagues, the trade unions and the associations for mutual aid, the consumer and productive co-operatives are only means for achieving this end. The task of the International is to bring about a truly genuine solidarity between these organizations.[35]

Even if the International's task had been, and certainly still was, something more than the simple coordination of solidarity among existing organisations that Marx was here prepared to admit at a moment when the IWMA was suffering the full backlash following the Commune, there remains the fact that the working class that Marx faced when he made his *Inaugural Address* and all the others elaborated during the 1860s was in fact an organised working class in struggle;[36] a working class whose most advanced organisations had *founded* the International. Which implied that the needs of these organised structures and their struggle were decisive in the construction of the International's general line. And as we have seen, this was a line that could be defined as *revolutionary* in a sense no different from the *revolutionary* forms of the democratic and socialist tradition. A line that could easily have connected with the non-reductionist reformists of the early nineteenth century (and indeed, in part did so), a line that was maturing in the progressive unfolding of the *democratic antithesis*.

34 *MECW*, Vol. 43, p. 491.

35 Text not included in *MECW*. Interview republished in *The Red Menace*, Winter 1979, online at http://www.connexions.org/CxLibrary/Docs/CX5169-MarxInterview.htm.

36 Rosenberg 1939.

This line, whose coordinates Marx was now constructing on the basis of the real processes underway in the movement, can without doubt be considered to have been the line of the International itself. Naturally, such a consideration ought not be based on too-rigid parameters. Certainly, it was the General Council's line; it had come to prevail over the course of the 1860s, although in ways that were not simply linear, and sometimes by means of a gradual construction – as the line taken by the IWMA's congresses, before the fundamental statutory organs of the IWMA made it their own. But the International was something more than the aggregation of its institutional sites, however essential these were. Not only did the European workers' movements' varying levels of development and different cultural and political traditions imply diverse means of receiving and using this platform, indeed sometimes in a very fragmentary manner (even though this platform had itself been structured in an extremely coherent way). More than that, the very mechanisms of the individual sections' affiliation encouraged a form of participation that was anything but ideologically centred. Often the sections requested affiliation to the International on the basis of contingent motivations, even if they were important ones, as in the case of strikes. They knew very little of the International's (brief) history, or of its positions and the theses that the IWMA had produced. Sometimes it was even the myths of the London organisation's (widely overestimated) power, means and capacity to intervene that drove their affiliation. Marx and Engels were conscious of the existence and persistence of this panorama of discrepancies, and convinced that given 'the stage of development reached by different sections of the workers in the same country and by the working class in different countries necessarily varies considerably, the actual movement also necessarily expresses itself in very diverse theoretical forms'.[37] As they would very often have cause to repeat, the only binding request made of the affiliate sections was that they respect the *General Rules*. Yet even this proved to be no particular guarantee of homogeneity, given the different interpretations of this document, the question of whether or not it was read together with the *Inaugural Address*, the various poor translations of the original text, and its sometimes only-partial use.

The Italian situation of the 1860s particularly lent itself to an uncoordinated relationship with the International and the texts that Marx had endowed it with, since Italian connections with this body proved fragile not only on the organisational plane, but also in terms of knowledge of the IMWA's essential elaborations, which were used patchily if at all on the peninsula. These were

37 *MECW*, Vol. 43, p. 235.

years in which the 'social question' started to be forcefully and starkly posed in the consciousness of ever-wider strata of the subaltern classes, as well as among more attentive and clear-sighted ruling-class circles, who sometimes themselves adopted the 'social question' as a horizon, with varying perspectives. These were years in which there was a constant growth of workers' associationism, which while expressed in diverse political and cultural forms did nonetheless construct a web of relations; a largely common experience of the dimension of labour; and a complex set of values that slowly formed as a solid sedimentation. Beyond the (nonetheless important) scansions of Italy's *Società operaie*, as marked by their congress dates; the rhythms of the splits marking one period from another; paternalistic mutualism; Mazzini's *Patto di Fratellanza*; and the *società* aligned to the Bakuninite international – it is perhaps opportune to reflect more closely on the movements that deeply shaped the manner in which the working-class *antithesis* developed. Even the canonical congresses provided evidence of significant organisational 'survivals' from phases considered already to have been 'transcended'. In Naples in 1864, at the moment that the *Atto di Fratellanza* was approved, only 57 of the roughly six hundred *società operaie* existing in Italy were represented, and 12 of these were from Naples itself.[38] And even in 1877 (the mutual-aid societies' congress held in Bologna on 28–31 October), 377 *società* with 427 delegates were represented.[39] Notwithstanding the government measures to help the delegates (reductions on their travel costs) these numbers are worth dwelling on, given that they are generally much higher than the figures for the Mazzinian and Internationalist congresses. Even the 1871 split in the *Società Operaie Affratellate* at the Rome Congress, provoked by the Internationalists, was a minority affair. And 1872–73 would see a far from negligible flourishing of *società operaie* of Mazzinian inspiration,[40] without this being to the detriment of the mutual-aid societies, which were also on the rise.[41] But even beyond these (nonethe-

38 Romano 1966, pp. 100–1.

39 Manacorda 1963, p. 149.

40 Manacorda 1963, pp. 122–6.

41 The mutual-aid societies were 443 in number in 1862, with 111,608 associates, rising to 1447 with 218,822 associates in 1873. See Maic, Statistica delle Società di Mutuo soccorso, Rome, Tipografia Metastasio, 1888, pp. vi and ix. According to another source, the mutual-aid societies reached 1,600 in number that same year. See *Relazione della Commissione Direttiva sui quesiti proposti alla discussion del XIV Congresso Generale delle Società operaie affratellate*, Rome: Regia Tipografia, 1876, p. 4. Naturally these were not only *Società Operaie*. On the criteria according to which the statistics on the mutual-aid societies were gathered, see Marucco 1981, pp. 201–22.

less important) organisational 'survivals', which alone pose problems to any vision that sees the workers' movement's development in terms of 'stages', there remains the fact that as Sombart noted at the end of the nineteenth century,[42] Italian workers' associationism was strung together by threads of continuity that go some way to invalidating any 'stagist' reading. There was an obvious red thread running through the mutual-aid societies, the *Fasci Operai*, the *Partito operaio italiano*, and the *camere del lavoro* of the 1890s, namely the 'sense of solidarity ... that mutualism transmits to ... [workers'] resistance ... the continual flow of solidarity among the different trades'.[43] Underlying the succession of 'stages' there was an irresistible tendency for the progressive transformation of 'solidarity' into 'resistance',[44] through the *necessary* affirmation of class autonomy, which would ultimately emerge even within those mutual-aid societies that had remained 'paternalistic'.

> Our opposition has nothing to do with matters of democracy or aristocracy [stated the artisan Franceschini, a member of the Rovereto mutual-aid society, faced with the 'honorary' associates' attempt to influence its decision-making]. We artisans are men, too, intelligent men, and we would not want to be so arrogant as to refuse the good advice of those well-intentioned people with good advice for our society ... but on the other hand how can I, a worker and poor artisan, turn to these men to direct our society? There could never be such a confidence.

And immediately afterward, the worker more bluntly clarified the meaning of class belonging: 'Remember what I tell you: that you would be just so many imbeciles if you were not capable of leading yourselves; so I call on those who think like I do to come over to the left'.[45]

Indeed, when they voted on the proposal the workers did all come over to the left, except for one who abstained.

---

42 Sombart, 1893–5.

43 See Bonacchi and Pescarolo 1980, p. 40.

44 From the point of view of the history of trade-union organisation there is an evident discontinuity between mutualism and resistance. But here the problem is not so much that of the transformation of mutual-aid societies into resistance organisations – a transformation that had indeed in many cases taken place – as a consideration of the role that the extension of the solidarity activities typical of mutualism had in creating the 'preconditions' and 'depth' of the conditions for resistance. An exemplary analysis of this question appears in Tomassini 1984.

45 Quoted in Raffaelli 1955, p. 234.

As such, the roots of the plant that would branch out into the 'class-party' – a plant whose growth would be identified with an essential aspect of Italian Marxism – sank into a terrain whose nutrients filtered through deep layers that cannot be distinguished in terms of each single stratum's political-ideological 'maturity'.

The 1860s were, then, the years in which also in Italy 'the strike began to take on citizenship rights among the customs of workplace struggles'.[46] And yet the Mazzinian *Società affratellate* were against the strike, and the 'paternalistic' mutual-aid societies even more so.[47] The strikes of that decade – chronologically concentrated in 1863–4 and 1868–9, with the industrial ones concentrated in Lombardy and Piedmont (though there were also major strikes in Naples) and the agricultural ones in Lombardy and Veneto[48] – did not necessarily occur in separation from the workers' organisations, and in particular the mutual-aid societies, even if this was a far from direct relationship. When such a relationship did exist, this was almost always a case of mutual-aid societies organised according to trades, which 'presupposed, and at the same time encouraged, the consolidation of a different type of solidarity among the associates, more anchored in the structure of production itself'.[49] For example, the

46 See Rosselli 1967, p. 125.

47 It was thus possible that at a national mutual-aid societies' congress at which all those intervening hurried to exorcise the strike, one could hear the following words: 'Gentlemen! Each voice that has been raised from this tribune, and every order of the day that has been proposed, has let out a cry against strikes; they have condemned themselves, as with the most blustering words they have come to say "the worker must always work, always suffer and never rebel in defence of his cause". And yet, gentlemen, I take a contrary view: I will be alone – that does not bother me, but my conviction has formed through labour, through study, through suffering, and it is unshakeable. I will explain it to you in a few plain words. See Society as it is constituted, study the laws that govern it, they always present this fundamental character, which defend accumulated labour, capital, to which they accord an exercise of its own rights, whereas the worker has only the pure right. What use is the art that I cannot exercise? Well, gentleman, in this state of affairs what is the path that the poor worker must take when he feels that his inclinations are being thwarted? In my opinion he has only one path, to abandon the workshop and with this to show what he can do, and that the worker ceasing his labour knows his own dignity and his own right'. See *Congresso generale delle società operaie italiane tenuto in Roma nell'aprile del 1872*, Rome: Tipografia Barbera, 1873, p. 176.

48 See *Relazione presentata a S.E. il ministro dell'interno nel mese di marzo 1879 dalla commissione d'inchiesta sugli scioperi nominate col R. decreto 3 febbraio 1878*, Rome: Regia tipografia, 1885.

49 See Gianola 1988, p. 40.

bakers' assistants' society at the centre of the strike initiatives in Livorno of 1863 to 1864;[50] and likewise the dockers' society in the Genoa strikes of 1864 (which the Mazzinian *consociazione* was compelled to join notwithstanding its doctrinal opposition to strikes);[51] meanwhile, one of the most important strikes of this first two-year strike wave – the Biella textile workers' strike of 1863 – was promoted and sustained by the Croce Mosso weavers' mutual-aid society, 'a true and proper resistance league'.[52] The fact that this struggle may seem 'backward' in its objectives, insofar as it sought to safeguard the 'artisan' craft methods of workers of great professional capacity, takes nothing away from the fact that through their struggle and organisation a 'class sense' was taking form, which in most cases tended to assume various forms of 'consciousness'. As has been aptly observed

> The history of class organisation was ... firstly the complex set of attempts to stop capital from being able fully to develop and gradually to subordinate social condition to itself, before it was the history of working-class antagonism toward capitalist relations.[53]

As such, the history of working-class organisation appears to have been initially entirely 'bound up with that of the organisms devoted to protecting "artisan trade"',[54] and in substance to defending certain precapitalist labour customs. This was a link that 'also constituted one of the principal channels by which the democratic tradition of the *Risorgimento* flowed into socialist ideology and organisations'.[55] In 1868–9 the strikes movement deepened and extended, independently of the contemporary riots against the milling tax, and almost seems to have followed the tendency that was then underway in more industrially advanced countries, albeit at an inferior level. Again in this case, the link to existing organisation cannot be read as if there were a logical correspondence between the strikes and the 'advanced' *società operaie*. But here there was a substantial novelty, indeed a powerful catalysing factor: namely, the existence of the International. As an indication of the new climate (though without doubt distorting matters), in commenting on the 8 August 1868 strike in Bologna the conservative newspaper *La Nazione* identified what had changed:

---

50 See Badaloni 1951.
51 See Montale 1960, pp. 44–5.
52 See Foa 1973, p. 1785.
53 Berta 1979, p. 299.
54 Ibid.
55 Ibid.

> In their character and in their unfolding, the Bologna disorders appear to be a further episode in that sad drama that has for some time been developing in England, in France, in Belgium, in Switzerland and in Bavaria, and, now we might say, in every part of Europe. The revelations in the Geneva newssheets in recent days can perhaps shed some light on this episode. According to these papers, the strike in the canton continues, and they attribute it exclusively to the dark arts of the International Working Men's Association there established …[56]

As we know, there is no basis for claiming that the International was behind the strike movement spreading across Europe in that period, even if the IWMA did give its support in numerous episodes. As we have seen, it was, rather, the strike that threw the workers 'into the arms of the International', and this would prove to be of great importance. So it would be difficult indeed to maintain that the International was at the origin of the strike initiatives of the Italy of the 1860s, or even to attribute it interventions after the strikes broke out. Even so, here too the real movement expanded the IWMA's sphere of influence: not so much through the foundation of sections, at least at that moment (with the Naples and Girgenti ones unable to enter into direct relations), as through the fact that it became a point of reference, a point of convergence for proletarian layers' hopes in redemption and 'emancipation' that would ultimately fertilise the terrain of democracy.

It is symptomatic that the newspaper of the International's first section in Italy (in Naples) immediately published Marx's report to the 1869 Basle congress and at the same time took as its epigraph the very most Mazzinian of the expressions used in the *General Rules*, which Marx considered a pure concession to the Italians: 'No rights without duties, no duties without rights'.[57] This was an expression that would appear countless times in the 'subversive', Bakuninite, Mazzinian and 'experimental-socialist' publications of the 1870s, and somewhat even beyond that. These were so many signs of the threads

56 Cited in Rosselli 1967, p. 194.

57 Wolff had presented a proposal for the statutes that 'was EVIDENTLY a concoction of Mazzini's. The sub-committee charged Marx with revising it, as he explained in his letter to Engels of 4 November 1864: 'The Sub-Committee adopted all my proposals. I was, however, obliged to insert two sentences about 'DUTY' and 'RIGHT', and ditto about 'TRUTH, MORALITY AND JUSTICE' in the preamble to the rules, but these are so placed that they can do no harm. At the meeting of the General Committee my "ADDRESS", etc., was adopted with great enthusiasm (UNANIMOUSLY)': *MECW*, Vol. 42, pp. 17–18.

intersecting beneath a set of ideological divides that were themselves very deep, in a context in which Marx was spread via Mazzini and Mazzini via Marx. We can also take the example of the 1881 founding congress of the *Partito Socialista Rivoluzionario di Romagna*: perhaps when anarchist elements did not try to oppose the 'defector' Costa proposing the original *Rules* of the International for this new political formation, it was because of their deep conviction that Bakunin had written this document?[58]

Even in the incomplete version published by *L'Eguaglianza*,[59] Marx's report to the Basle congress remains a document that is very much representative of the central core of what we have called the IWMA's *general line*. Centring on the strikes question, it unfolds according to lines of argument that were designed to emphasise the political valence of this form of the class struggle.

In the 1860s, then, democratic and Internationalist newspapers published some of the basic documents of Marx's reflection. These documents had emerged from his encounter with the *real movement* that gave rise to the International, and whose further development would then itself receive fresh stimulus from the International. That is not to say in an absolute sense that these alignments became the point of reference for the variegated world of working-class organisation or for the likewise variegated democratic-socialist universe. The fact that even important texts of Marx's appeared in various periodicals is not enough to justify such a conclusion – particularly when we consider that they did not reappear in a continual or programmatic way, but as part of a publishing context that amounted to myriad rivulets of 'generic socialism'. Even as we leaf through the first few years of *La Plebe*, a paper that would later play an essential role in the development of a socialist culture in which Italian Marxism would sink thick roots, we can see that this earlier publication of important Marx texts had not made its mark. A 'republican, rationalist, socialist' paper, it did not feature a single line of Marx among 18 socialist 'Thoughts and phrases' published in a special issue.[60] This paper saw proletarians generically as the 'have-nots', as counterposed to the 'haves',[61] and saw the solution of 'equality among the social classes' as coming from 'the application of laws'

58 See Galassi 1989, p. 260.

59 See 'Rapporto del Consiglio generale del 4' Congresso dell'Associazione Internazionale degli operai: letto a Basilea il 7 settembre 1869', *L'Eguaglianza. Giornale degli Operai*, Naples, 24 and 31 December 1869. This remained the only translation of the report into Italian up till its republication in 1964 in *Rivista Storica del Socialismo*, no. 22.

60 'Pensieri e sentenze', *La Plebe*, 24 July 1868.

61 'I proletari', *La Plebe*, 11 May 1869.

through which 'work [would] be recognised as the poor man's right, proportionally connected to the rich man's fortune'.[62]

Nonetheless it would be mistaken to consider the presence of Marx texts in this paper as a merely chance episode, incapable of leaving sedimentations of some importance and visibility. Their presence in these years speaks to the breadth of reflection through which the *democratic antithesis* was being articulated. The *general line* of the International, so intimately linked to these texts, would through its underground journey ultimately re-emerge in a terrain liable to giving a positive reception to its vital residues.

2 The Anarchist Antithesis

The early 1870s – with the repercussions of events in France, Garibaldi's adventure with the Army of the Vosges, and, in particular the outcome of the Paris Commune – provoked a qualitative leap in both the International's presence and its echoes in Italy.

At the same time, this was also the period in which the divulgation of Marx and Engels's texts seems to have lost its episodic character. Now it would instead become a constitutive factor directly intervening in the Italian socialist and working-class movement, as well as a point of reference and identification for the great choices being made on the international level. We need only think of Marx's address on the civil war in France, a partial version of which was printed by Girgenti newspaper *Eguaglianza* in November and December 1871.[63]

The relatively abundant presence of Marx and Engels's texts in the Italian socialist and democratic press may seem to stand in contradiction with the fact that they did not have any manifest influence on the forms that the socialist movement was then taking. Indeed, studying these writings some have asked whether 'the delay in the formation of a class-struggle current in the Italian workers' movement was truly "inevitable"'.[64] Beyond this statement's implication – albeit a barely elaborated one – that we might reconsider the thesis that there is a direct relation between the belated development of modern capital-

62 'Del problema sociale', *La Plebe*, 2 July 1869.

63 Karl Marx, 'La guerra civile in Francia. Manifesto del Consiglio generale della Società Internazionale degli operai ai membri della Società in Europa e in America', *L'Eguaglianza*, Girgenti, 12 November 1871, no. 12; and nos. 21, 22, and 24, from 3, 10 and 27 December (translated by C. Cafiero).

64 Bosio 1955, p. 14.

ism and the 'natural' backwardness of the workers' movement, it probably also bears the conviction (a none-too-hidden one, indeed) that there is a necessary identification between a 'class-struggle current' and a 'Marxist current' of the workers' movement. We are now well aware how complex the formation processes of the dynamic reality called 'class consciousness' are, and how many multiple 'strata' there were in a continually redefined equilibrium feeding in to this formation. The influence of Marxian formulations – and not Marxism, which did not exist in the commonly-understood sense in the 1870s – was certainly not the only determining ideological factor, here; moreover, in this process the experience of Italian Bakuninism ought not be understood as if it stood in absolute contradiction with these formulations' influence.

It is well-known that Robert Michels considered the parabola of Bakuninite-inspired Italian Internationalists to have been a necessary 'intellectual preparation' for the 'Marxist' phase:

> The fundamentals of the International's programme, which were very widely known in Italy, were the intellectual property of their author Marx. A propaganda for modern socialism was conducted in Italy, and it had come by way of Marxism, even if the name of that theory did not appear there. We could say that the Italian workers, saturated with Bakuninist ideas, were *eo ipso* psychologically prepared to receive Marx's ideas.[65]

It was then necessary also to consider the fact that 'just as Lassalle was the pike in the carp pond of Prussian democracy, so Bakunin smashed open the fortress of Italian democracy with dynamite-like violence'.[66]

Michels's argument, later adopted by authoritative Italian scholars,[67] is far from groundless. At the same time, however, we ought also to underline its definitely partial dimension.

First of all, it would be mistaken directly to attribute the flourishing of the International in 1871–2 to Bakuninist activity and ideas. There had already been a series of initiatives in Naples at the end of the 1860s, such as that of the *Libertà e Giustizia* group, which was clearly the fruit of an internal evolution among the democrats:[68] if these initiatives did encounter Bakunin, they were not his own creation. There was no contradiction with the General Council

65 Michels 1926, p. 50.
66 Michels 1909, p. 62.
67 See Valiani 1973.
68 See Romano 1966, pp. 240–52.

at that time, with the group calling on workers to count on their own forces and publishing a declaration affirming its affiliation to that set of associations 'that [had] their permanent central committee in London'.[69] But even after the conflict between Marx and Bakunin was already engaged, before the Hague Congress, Italian Internationalism was anything but clearly aligned to either side, party as it was to the travails of Italian democracy.

The Internationalist papers of these two years faithfully mirrored this indeterminacy and the intrepid process that was then underway. 'It is said that if Karl Marx were to succumb, the Russian Bakunin ... would become head of the famous association', the important Girgenti section's organ tells us.[70] And a Berlin correspondent of *La Plebe* could even define the 'illustrious Karl Marx' as 'Germany's Bakunin'[71] (thus implying that Bakunin was Italy's Marx ...) as well as pointing out that 'portraits of Garibaldi, Marx, Bakunin and other civil redeemers are here ... venerated and admired in the windows of our press-stores, and similarly in the main Berlin halls and clubs'.[72] Ultimately this was not so different from what the Macerata *Associazione democratica* did when it proposed Marx as an 'honorary *triumvir* together with citizens Giuseppe Garibaldi and Giuseppe Mazzini',[73] a decision mocked by Engels, who had perhaps not deeply understood the complexity of the Italian situation, which though certainly displaying elements of 'backwardness' was at the same time rich in ferments with the potential for new and original developments.[74]

The travails of Italian democracy assumed an almost paradigmatic expression in the pages of Milan's *Il Gazzettino Rosa*. Radical in its anti-Mazzinian line – in particular through its positions on the Commune and the 'Apostle's' philosophical 'idealism' – and resolute in its internationalist orientation, Bizzoni remained wholly aloof from the Marx-Bakunin *querelle*. Again it was the *democratic antithesis* that was developed and amplified, here: democracy 'would be working contrary to its own principles if it did not ally with the

69 See 'Le associazioni operaie', *Libertà e Giustizia*, no. 17, August 1867.

70 See *L'Eguaglianza*, 17 September 1871.

71 See 'Lettere da Berlino', *La Plebe*, 5 January 1872.

72 See 'Lettere da Berlino', *La Plebe*, 4 February 1872.

73 See 'Associazione Democratica di Macerata a Marx', 22 December 1871, in Del Bo (ed.) 1964, p. 166.

74 'A society in Macerata, in the Romagna, has nominated as its 3 honorary presidents: Garibaldi, Marx and Mazzini. This confusion will show you very clearly the state of public opinion among the Italian workers. Only Bakunin's name is needed and the mess is complete': Engels to Liebknecht, 2 January 1872, *MECW*, Vol. 44, p. 289.

workers' movement'.[75] Certainly, the International's banner heralded 'the abolition of the classes' but only within the limits of the formula 'no rights without duties, no duties without rights'.[76] The 'Internationalist worker' polemicising with Alberto Mario from the columns of this paper – while showing full respect for his interlocutor's character – clearly delineated the coordinates of the democratic Internationalism of this *open* period, just before Internationalism in Italy became for some years almost synonymous with Bakuninism. Responding to the 'noble' figure Alberto Mario, who had, however, accused the International of fomenting class hatred, the Internationalist worker responded in the following terms:

> At the basis of its conduct and its activity, Internationalism has set down the principle that the emancipation of the workers must be the work of the workers themselves, and their goal the complete emancipation of the proletariat. The International only asks that it be left to develop freely. The revolution to which it aspires is a peaceful revolution that will come about through the necessity of things, when these principles are well established and the solution of the economic problem has reached maturation.[77]

Yet it still ought to be clear 'that the proletariat [could not] achieve its own emancipation if not through the abolition of classes'.[78] This worker said that he was not part of 'Marx's authoritarian school' – with certain of the stylistic idiosyncrasies of the political-ideological battle then underway obviously making their mark – but he nonetheless remained faithful to the International, an association 'without any leaders, whether a Marx or a Bakunin'.[79] Indeed, he would repeat that he was loyal 'not to Marx' but 'to the Provisional and General Rules' – thus also establishing a far from negligible loyalty to Marx, in some regards.[80] The rooting of Marxism in Italy would play out on the basis of both this apparently disjointed situation, and its gradual concordance with the further factor of Marxism's separation from the development of the real

---

75 See 'Questioni del giorno', *Il Gazzettino Rosa*, 26 November 1871.

76 See 'L'Internazionale e i suoi detrattori', *Il Gazzettino Rosa*, 20 November 1871.

77 Un operaio Internazionale, 'La confusione delle lingue', *Il Gazzettino Rosa*, 15 July 1872.

78 Ibid.

79 L'operaio internazionalista, 'L'internazionale. Risposta ad Alberto Mario', *Il Gazzettino Rosa*, 25 July 1872.

80 L'operaio internazionalista, 'L'internazionale. Risposta ad Alberto Mario', *Il Gazzettino Rosa*, 3 August 1872.

movement. That is, the basic elements of Marx's thinking became increasingly pervasive even as almost all of the Italian Internationalist scene rejected 'Marxism'.

The fluidity of the Italian situation in the two years in question is well-represented by an episode in which Theodor Cuno – the severe German engineer who was briefly at the cutting edge of the General Council's intervention in the peninsula – played a central role. Pezza invited Cuno to speak to the assembly of a workers' mutual-aid league. To his 'great amazement' Cuno found himself 'faced with an association of arch-Mazzinians of the conspiratorial school. They had no idea about the International, and did not even know that their statutes and proclamations were copied from our own'.[81] Cuno participated 'in the debates determinedly' and defended 'the cause with some success', indeed declaring himself certain that 'within a few weeks' this workers' association of 'arch-Mazzinians' would join the International.[82] But were episodes like this one – based on a fundamental permeability that was surely widespread in the extraordinarily vivacious associative climate that accompanied and followed the Paris Commune experience – only an index of these associations' 'confusion' and their condition as 'kids, whelps still struggling to find their feet', who had to be educated without treating them too 'brusquely'?[83] Or did these episodes also speak to their great readiness to listen to voices able to open up new perspectives, even if without forgetting the realities and, indeed, the originalities of the contexts with which they were concerned?

Papers like Mantua's *La Favilla*, Bologna's *Il Fascio Operaio*, Naples's *La Campana* (whose epigraph read 'No right without duty – No duty without right'), together with numerous others born or revived in this conjuncture, all of them rigorously anti-Mazzinian, continued to be coloured by Mazzinian motifs. Meanwhile, the question of choosing between Marx and Bakunin had still not entered into their considerations.

For certain, Marx had forcefully arrived on their horizon. He had not appeared in the guise of a 'scholar', since neither the socialists nor even Italian academic circles read him as such at the time. Without doubt, the brief commentary and translation of a small section of the introduction to *Capital*, appearing in *Libertà e Giustizia*[84] soon after the first volume was issued by Meissner in Hamburg, was not sufficient for a 'militant' reading, even if it probably did have some influence on Covelli and Cafiero. Nor were the news on

81 Cuno to Engels, 30 November 1871, in Del Bo (ed) 1964, p. 105.
82 Cuno to Engels, 30 November 1871, in Del Bo (ed) 1964, p. 106.
83 Cuno to Engels, 25 April 1872, in Del Bo (ed) 1964, p. 194.
84 See *Libertà e Giustizia*, Naples, 27 October 1867.

Capital in the non-socialist press[85] or even Di Menza's[86] or Martello's[87] more academic commentaries, sufficient to encourage a discussion in the 'scientific' community. On this level, the first true and proper qualitative leap came with Vito Cusumano's writings.[88]

As for militants reading Marx's scholarship, the Italian situation in these years was very different from the German one. In Germany, already before the publication of *Capital* Marx was a 'high culture' reference point, including for organised workers. 'There is no need to demonstrate the enormous respect with which his name is uttered even by the party's less committed militants, who have ultimately proven unable to ignore this scholarship', two workers explained on 13 November 1865.[89] We might also remember that at the Brussels Congress it was German workers' representatives who proposed a resolution – which was approved by the Congress – recommending 'Marx's work *Capital* to men of all nations' and calling on them 'to do everything possible such that this important work is translated into languages it has not already been [translated into]', further declaring that 'Karl Marx has the inestimable merit of being the first economist to have subjected capital to a scientific analysis and to have reduced it to its fundamental elements'.[90]

Nor should we forget the long review of *Capital* by the Lassallean Schweitzer, published in 12 parts in *Social-Demokrat* from 22 January to 6 May 1868. This review drew particular praise from Marx himself – despite his bitter fight with Schweitzer on the political terrain – as he compared it favourably to the weakness of a piece by the 'Marxist' Liebknecht.[91] So already in the 1860s, political Marxism and Marx's economic theory did not necessarily coincide.

Conversely, in Italy in 1871–2 Marx's fame was rather more connected to the role he was ascribed as 'founder and general leader of the International',

---

85 See Bravo 1992, pp. 83–5.

86 See Di Menza 1874a; 1874b, p. 5.

87 See Martello 1873, pp. 472–3.

88 Cusumano 1873, 1874 and particularly 1874 pp. 314–15; 1875.

89 Cited in Bravo 1979, p. 7.

90 Cited in Bravo (ed.) 1978, Vol. 1, p. 316.

91 'At the same time, I am sending you the Schweitzer, which please return [sic] to me after use. A few lines from Meissner, in which he notifies me of his stupidity in informing Schweitzer that he should not continue with his EXTRACTS until I have stated my views. Quelle bêtise! … Although he makes a MISTAKE here and there, he has studied the stuff really hard, and knows where the centres of gravity lie. Such a "base consciousness" is still preferable to the "honest consciousness" of a Heinzen or the "noble consciousness" of a Wilhelmchen': Marx to Engels, 23 March 1868, *MECW*, Vol. 42, p. 556.

sometimes accompanied by a certain mythologisation: 'Karl Marx is an astute and courageous man faced with every challenge. He rides from one state to another, continually changing his disguise, allowing him to escape the surveillance of every police spy in Europe'.[92] It is not that such fantastical claims – which did have a certain ability to spread, given Internationalist newspapers' habit of taking and republishing each others' articles[93] – bore any substantial influence on perceptions of Marx as a figure, and still less in relation to his conflict with Bakunin, which would soon become manifest even in Italy. However, what they do suggest is a tendency toward a *conspiratorial* understanding of the revolutionary imprecations coming from the IWMA, which is perfectly understandable in light of the experiences of the 'Italian revolution'. This attitude was not without importance to the coming decisions of the Italian Internationalist scene.

As 'leader of the International' Marx had attracted Mazzini's ire; and the Trier philosopher would thus play the role of anti-Mazzini in a context in which the internal division among democrats was now taking on the sharp bitterness typical of new identities' founding moments.[94] As *La Favilla* wrote in autumn 1871:

> Mazzini called Marx a man of *destructive ... genius, a dominating temperament etc.*, perhaps because Marx has been so well able to destroy the cabal working on Mazzini's orders to the detriment of the International ... If he is indeed correct, then the International must be glad indeed to have among its members a *genius* and a *temperament destroying* and *dominating* in this manner – keeping it on its feet for seven years and working more than any other man to bring it to its current superb position[95]

92 'Carlo Marx capo supremo dell'internazionale', *Il Proletario Italiano*, Turin, 27 July 1871.

93 See Zangheri 1993, Vol. I, pp. 234–6, on how this affected the circulation of Marx's biographical details.

94 This explains the enthusiastic applause for the journalist Luciani when he proposed a toast in honour of Marx in September 1871: 'Last week the revolutionary party in Rome held a banquet for Ricciotti Garibaldi, and a report on it in the Rome paper La Capitale has been sent to me. One speaker (il signore Luciani) proposed an enthusiastically received toast to the working class and 'a Carlo Marx che (qui) sé ne (en) é fatto (a fait) l'instancabile instrumento (l'instrument infatigable)': Marx to Jenny Marx, 23 September 1871, in *MECW*, Vol. 44, p. 220. Luciani had made a sharp anti-Mazzinian reference in calling for a 'hearty and very warm toast to Karl Marx, to the president of the International Association, to the man so vigorously stigmatised by Mazzini', and was applauded 'enthusiastically and rapturously': Zangheri 1993, p. 233.

95 'Associazione internazionale degli operai', *La Favilla*, Mantua, 7 September 1871.

Citing Marx, and partly paraphrasing the second of the *General Rules*, Milan's *Il Martello* made the following statement in order to emphasise its profound theoretical difference with respect to Mazzinianism: 'With the worker's economic dependence on capital lying at the bottom of every other slavery, be it material or moral, political or economic, we want the abolition of the current wage system'.[96]

In the information from the International appearing (often in rather repetitive fashion) throughout these papers, and sometimes regarding questions of small detail, Marx's name – the name 'citizen Marx' – took on exceptional significance. This resulted in a certain privileging of Marx, also through the reproduction of extracts from his interventions at the General Council and through the publication of this body's documents.[97] In short, it is impossible to find any negative prejudice against Marx or the London 'centre' in these papers.

Rather, it seems that it was Marx and Engels who had some difficulty understanding the process that was then underway on the Italian peninsula. They filtered what was happening in Italy through the logical prism of the simultaneous clash with Bakunin, and the use of the category 'backwardness' to characterise the country's socio-economic situation. Both of these elements were doubtless very real, but they ultimately overshadowed some significant aspects of what was in fact a rather more uneven situation. Engels was certainly right to say that Italy was a 'very difficult terrain' giving him 'a fiendish amount of work',[98] but at the same time he failed to note the significance of the *whole* range of these difficulties. The Italians expressing themselves through the sudden multiplication of International sections did not represent merely a 'backward', 'peasant people' 'mak[ing] itself ridiculous when it tries to prescribe

96 See the first issue of *Il Martello. Giornale democratico degli operai. Organo del circolo operaio di Milano*, 4 February 1872: it is in this edition that it professes its allegiance to the International.

97 For example, *Il Gazzettino Rosa* published numerous documents from the General Council, including Engels's 'L'intervento di Mazzini contro l'Internazionale' (13 September 1871), the 'Risoluzione del consiglio generale sulla espulsione di Durand' (20 October 1871) and the 'Dichiarazione del Consiglio generale sull'abuso del nome dell'Internazionale da parte di Neciaev', by Marx (3 November 1871).

98 Engels to Liebknecht, 18 January 1872: *MECW*, Vol. 44, p. 299. And as he wrote to another interlocutor 'These damned Italians make more work for me than the entire rest of the International put together makes for the General Council. And it is all the more infuriating as in all probability little will come of it as long as the Italian workers are content to allow a few doctrinaire journalists and lawyers to call the tune on their behalf' (Engels to Becker, 16 February 1872: *MECW*, Vol. 44, p. 321).

to the workers of big industrial nations',[99] but also a revolutionary tradition capable of transcending these conditions of backwardness; capable, at its high points, of shaking up the inflexibility to which this backwardness seemed to condemn it.

There was an indication of this already by the end of 1871, though Engels did not seem fully to understand it; indeed, it was an indication that was entirely independent of any Bakuninite influence. Ludovico Nabruzzi made contact with Engels, writing:

> In Italy in general and Romagna in particular, the Inter. will arrive at an essentially revolutionary organisation. Our working-class youth has in large part inherited the rebellious aspirations of our fathers who were conspirators their whole lives, and its desire is struggle in the public streets and to appear on the barricades like the heroic defenders of the Paris Commune.[100]

Reading Nabruzzi's lines, we should note not only the references to a conspiratorial and insurrectional dimension – though these are, indeed, explicit, and a fertile terrain for agreement with a Bakuninite outlook – but also the very strong and enduring link with the tradition of the 'Italian revolution'. This was a long-term factor, and at the beginning of the twentieth century Costa himself would recall the first important manifestations of socialism in Italy, and above all the influence of the International, by making reference to the roots of this continuity:

> If we add that the Italian people had just come out of a national revolution; that workers and bourgeois had conspired together, suffered and hoped together; that a good part of the youth and of the old popular parties had followed the people in its successive developments; then we can understand why upon its emergence the International was composed of such diverse elements: workers, proletarians, old *carbonari*, students, old soldiers of Garibaldi's, aspiring for better things, and ready to fight the battles of the social revolution with the same courage with which they had fought the battles for Italy's independence.[101]

99 Engels to Cuno, 10 June 1872, *MECW*, Vol. 44, p. 393.

100 Nabruzzi and Resta to Engels, 25 November 1871, in Del Bo (ed.) 1964, p. 80.

101 Costa 1900, p. 10. Costa gave a similar analysis in another turn-of-the-century text: 'It was a necessary and fruitful period, and it says it all when we say that it was inevitable; it

In substance, Costa was showing that in Italy the nascent socialist ideology could not seek to make workers a privileged referent. This owed not only to structural factors of economic and social 'backwardness' – an element that Engels had already particularly underlined in his polemic against Bakuninism – but also for particular reasons deriving from the way of understanding and living the inheritance of the 'Italian revolution'.

This was a 'foundational' aspect of Italian socialism, and it could scarcely be classified as a 'congenital defect'. Operating in various ways and in diverse contexts, the development of Marxism and socialism continued to unfold in a panorama distinguished by a plurality of social referents, even when the *Partito Socialista* (and later the *Partito Comunista*) officially defined itself the Marxist party of the working class. Marxist parties in Italy have never had the characteristics and mentality of the *parti ouvrier*; indeed, a particular – and highly significant – characteristic of Italian socialism has been the fact that it has also had an important political and organisational influence among social layers (peasants, for example) generally extraneous to the 'classic' models of Marxist parties' formation in Europe.

Naturally, it was precisely the gradual establishment of a working-class criterion at the heart of all socialist approaches – from the organisational plane to the cultural one – that allowed for the overcoming of the 'Bakuninist' phase and for the 'Marxist' phase to begin to take root, just as Engels had predicted. But the enduring continuity with earlier roots in the 'Italian revolution', through the filters of the *democratic antithesis* and the *anarchist antithesis*, had no little impact on this Marxism's characteristics.

'Do we not perhaps all belong to the so-called *bourgeois* class? After all, who among us is a worker in the true sense of the word? Who among us has ever had to put the shirt on the back of the respectable? Who among us ever sweated in the workshops?'[102] These words (probably by the young Costa) appearing in *Il Fascio Operaio* in early 1872, demonstrate that, in the formation of what would for some time be the leading part of Italian Internationalism, the category of 'the centrality of the working class' was something rather alien. They also show that this category's alien character was closely linked to a lack of conceptual

corresponded to our conditions of temperament, culture, and tradition, and the economic conditions that we faced. For better or worse, it could not have been otherwise. And it showed the extent of our enthusiasm, abnegation, virtue of sacrifice, and possibility of becoming – that is, among a new generation that was supposed to be tired, weak and exhausted after three generations of revolution' (Costa 1952 [1898], pp. 324–5: his memoirs, written in prison).

102 'Carte in Tavola', *Il Fascio Operaio. Periodico Democratico-Sociale*, Bologna, 2 March 1872.

rigour in analysing society, as we will go on to see. However, this perception of a 'bourgeois' element capable of causing political and cultural instability, and, above all, of an extremely vast social terrain beyond the organised working class – the subaltern layers who made the most sacrifices, the 'people who truly die of hunger, cold and fever'[103] – would remain a constant in the Italian way of being 'socialists' and 'Marxists'.

Also deriving from this is the need to read the Internationalist experience in Italy after the break with the General Council in a manner that does not reduce it to a simple schema of the struggle between Marxists and Bakuninites. Not least given that while it is relatively easy to identify the 'Bakuninite side' in the 1870s, the task of identifying the 'Marxist side' presents rather different problems, even if we do consider this possible at all.

The Italian Internationalists' polemic against Marx was certainly very severe, and often resentful and personalised, even resorting to overt calumnies; and more generally, the Bakunin-Marx clash was fought without any blows being spared. Nonetheless, it is at least doubtful that beyond certain contingent aspects this struggle could be considered *internal* to the logics of Italian socialism's development – that is, as if it thereby succeeded in marginalising or excluding an embryonic 'Marxism' from its real movement. Indeed, it seems inopportune to suggest that what we are used to identifying as 'Marxism' – on the basis of experiences that had barely begun to consolidate by the second half of the 1880s – could in any sense have fallen within the conceptual and political horizon of the Italian socialist movement of the 1870s and early 1880s.

The interest in Marx – the 'general leader of the International' – that developed in 1871–2 in no sense meant allegiance to a 'Marxian party', despite the more or less conscious uses of Marx texts. For cultural and structural reasons no such party could exist in Italy. The discussion of the '*partito marxido*'[104] – the array of '*marxidi*' mentioned in the polemic with Luigi Stefanoni – concerned a polemical dimension that only seems to have touched on the

103 'The International (and, yet further, all the workers' associations and parties) is composed of only a tiny fraction of the people, of those who are privileged in their intellect and indeed relatively so also in terms of their economic conditions. The great masses, the people who truly die of hunger, cold and fever, the people that has the greatest interest in the social revolution [succeeding], remains completely indifferent and ignorant of everything that socialist propaganda is doing; despite all its efforts, [this propagandising] never penetrates beneath this social crust, and there is no use hiding it': Andrea Costa, 'Il socialismo legale e il socialismo rivoluzionario', *Il Martello*, Jesi, 24 February 1877. Cited in part in Della Peruta 1965, p. 302.

104 See 'Lettera di Stefanoni', *Il Gazzettino Rosa*, 9 May 1872.

surface level of the Marx-Bakunin clash, namely that of personal calumny.[105] And yet even reading this polemic we can see that Italian Internationalism had a particular sensibility with respect to 'centralist' and/or 'authoritarian' practices. Already the '*operaio internazionale*' who had defended Marx's *Provisional Rules* and *General Rules* against Alberto Mario had referred (and clearly not positively) to 'Marx's authoritarian school'; and so, too, did the director of *Il Gazzettino Rosa*, defending Marx against Stefanoni, accuse the General Council of having committed 'a grave error in wanting to centralise – to use a fashionable word – the various sections, demanding that it should itself become leader in everything and for everything, paralysing their autonomy'.[106] Now, the tendencies toward 'centralisation' coming from London were not the ones that Bizzoni had outlined, but there remains the fact that even circles who were not hostile to the General Council were making reference to what was evidently a rather widespread image. To invoke a bureaucratic rationale, declaring that 'these people constitute[d] an International of their own, they ha[d] never applied for membership, ha[d] never paid dues, but [acted] as if they belonged to the International',[107] was in fact evidently a confession of a defeat that had been maturing over some time, in an Italian situation in which the 'battle between Bakuninists and Marxists [was] perhaps never openly joined'.[108]

It was Cafiero's shift of position that gave a clear signal that the great majority of Italian Internationalism was lost to the General Council. If the basic reasons for the split between Cafiero and Engels lay in the non-applicability of the *Manifesto*'s analysis to the situation of Southern *plebi* ('I suggest that you and Marx come along upon our populations' first social uprising, and propose

105 Notwithstanding this predominant aspect, the polemic that Stefanoni sparked did allow the emergence of a line in defence of the International and specifying its characteristics, through the interventions of Marx, Engels, Liebknecht and Cafiero: see Marx and Engels 1955, pp. 43–62.

106 See A. Bizzoni, 'A proposito della Lettera di Stefanoni', *Il Gazzettino Rosa*, 9 May 1872.

107 See Engels to Becker, 5 August 1872: *MECW*, Vol. 44, p. 419. And again, with reference to the sections present at the Rimini Conference: 'It should be pointed out that of the 21 sections whose delegates have signed this resolution, there is only one (Naples) which belongs to the International. None of the other 20 sections has ever fulfilled any of the conditions prescribed by our General Rules and Regulations for the admission of new sections. An Italian federation of the Working Men's Association therefore does not exist. Those who want to found it, form their own international outside the great Working Men's Association': *MECW*, Vol. 23, p. 217.

108 See Albonetti 1982, p. 42.

agricultural armies to our peasants in Calabria and Abruzzo'),[109] the framework in which he set this conviction was the very weighty framework of 'anti-authoritarianism', a particularly appealing category in Italian Internationalist circles.

Cafiero's attempt to read Resolution IX by way of the *Manifesto*, and above all his attempt to read the future 'communist' society by way of the *Manifesto* was largely miscued, even if the relation between this analytical dimension and the situation of backwardness was very real. Among other things, he did not grasp the changes in perspective that had taken place in Marx and Engels since the end of the 1840s, precisely as a consequence of the experience of the International. Moreover, in seeking to emphasise the 'authoritarian' character of this work Cafiero did not hesitate in voiding the work of its universalist inclination, on each occasion citing it as the 'Manifesto of the German Communist Party'.[110] It is certainly no chance thing that in the same period, at the moment of the final showdown, Bakunin used the same formulation,[111] even though he knew the *Manifesto* well, having been somewhat involved in its translation into Russian.[112] Guillaume also used this formulation, maintaining that the General Council had an official doctrine that had been published twenty years earlier in the *Manifest der deutschen Kommunisten-Partei*. Many years later he would admit that this was a polemical excess, but he would justify it with the barely-credible claim that since the text was written in German, published in German and the other editions translated from the German, 'It was natural enough that we were used to calling it the *Manifesto of the German Communist Party*'.[113]

The discussion and then the passing of the famous Resolution IX at the London Conference represented the culmination of a conflict that had already been underway for some time, and the point of no return for the splits that were then on the horizon. The fundamental issues at the centre of the discus-

109 Cafiero to Engels, 12 June 1872, in Del Bo (ed.) 1964, p. 220.

110 Del Bo (ed.) 1964, pp. 219, 221, 222.

111 See his letter to the Brussels paper *La Liberté*, 5 October 1872, quoted in Bravo (ed) 1978, pp. 857–880, referring (p. 874) to the 'Manifesto of the German communists'.

112 Guillaume 1905–7, I/1, p. 283, maintains that Bakunin was first to translate the *Manifesto* into Russian, though he does so on the basis of statements made in Marx and Engels's preface to the 1883 Russian edition. For his part, Bert Andréas maintains that Marx and Engels 'were ill-informed as to the precise circumstances in which the Russian edition of the *Manifesto* was produced', and is instead more willing to attribute it to Nechayev's initiative (Andréas 1963, pp. 49–53).

113 Guillaume 1905–7, I/2, p. 303.

sion were loyalty to the *General Rules* and the manner in which the 'political question' should be understood. Though the split ended up proposing entirely different interpretations of these problems, these interpretations themselves took on different meanings in specific situations, including in the Italian case.

During the discussion at the London conference, Marx repeatedly intervened on each of the – evidently interconnected – questions of the *General Rules* and political action. On the first topic, he maintained that it was urgently necessary 'to publish ... a true and literal translation of the International Rules', since the first French translation by Tolain was 'full of intentional mistakes' on several important points: for example referring to 'equal rights and duties' but leaving out the call 'for the abolition of class rule'; substituting 'the word "capital" for "the means of labour"'; and, most importantly, omitting the words 'as a means' from the reference to 'the great end to which every political movement ought to be subordinate as a means', thus lending the fourth paragraph of the *Rules* a wholly different meaning.[114] On the second topic, he wanted explicitly to emphasise that there was not any single way of doing politics, and that it was necessary to operate 'according to the conditions of each country'. Faced with the authorities' hostility it was necessary to 'respond with all possible means that we have available'.[115]

It was difficult indeed to maintain that Resolution IX stood in contradiction with the *Rules* and in particular with the International's history. Indeed, the opposition's reasoning on this score was weak or even untenable. Guillaume argued that up till that moment the *Rules* 'had been regarded as simply expressing the personal opinion of their author and the General Council members who approved them'.

Robin even claimed that the English version of 1864 was the one that had been 'changed' from the French-language text from Geneva. Guillaume corrected Robin's error and admitted that the English text was the original one, yet even so he maintained that the French, English and German versions were 'each equally authentic'.[116] The real answer had already been given two years previously, at the conclusion of the first true and significant split in the International, at the *Fédération Romande*'s April 1870 Chaux-de-Fonds congress. After the General Council called on the splitters to stick to the International's *General Rules*, they responded in the 24 July 1870 *La Solidarité* that the *Rules* said the political movement had to be subordinate to the economic one as a means,

114 *MECW*, Vol. 21, pp. 89–90.
115 Burgelin et al. 1962, Vol. II., pp. 162–3, 195–6.
116 Guillaume 1905–7, I/2, pp. 203, 205.

and they thought themselves 'wholly in conformity with this, in that we have subordinated the political movement to the economic movement so well that we have resolved no longer to occupy ourselves with politics at all'.[117]

So the point of distinction here was 'politics' and not the 'party', exactly as would also be the case at the London Conference and the Hague Congress, where the debate did not revolve so much around the problem of the workers' party as the justification of the necessity of the 'principle of the political struggle'.[118]

However, if we are to follow truly rigorous criteria, the 'political' dimension cannot itself be so immediately identified as the point of distinction. This was also a result of the fact that Bakunin understood the Alliance as a true and proper political party, complementing an International that must have more of the character of a social party: 'The International's [programme] ... contains the germ, but only the germ, of the Alliance's whole programme. The Alliance's programme is the last explanation of the International's [programme]'. According to Bakunin, the International had to bring together the workers of different trades and countries in an immense, compact phalanx. The Alliance would give them a revolutionary leadership, 'a positive and determined political and socialist programme'.[119] As Engels had mockingly noted, there would effectively have to be two General Councils, 'the practical council in London and the "idealist" theoretical one in Geneva'.[120] Paradoxically – if not entirely so – in the development of the International, the idea of a 'consciousness from the outside' serving as the vital germ for 'the class' was more part of Bakunin's vision than Marx's.[121]

So this was a question of the 'anti-authoritarians'' different vision of politics, rather than of their rejection of politics *tout court*. Bakunin tended to derive

117 Guillaume 1905–7, I/2, p. 58.

118 Haupt 2011, p. 7.

119 Bakounine 1974, p. xxxiv.

120 Appears untranslated from French in *MECW*, Vol. 43, p. 191 (Engels to Marx, 18 December 1868).

121 A man like De Paepe, who was certainly not well-disposed to the 'authoritarians', emphasised that according to Bakunin's approach the working-class base would become the object of an external political-ideological élite's ideological penetration. He would reproach Bakunin for his contradictory, mistaken wish to create 'utterly autonomously ... within the IWMA ... an initiative group that through the force of things could not but become a leadership group, a sort of ruling class, as we say today'. This article appeared in *L'Economie sociale* (Brussels) on 1 August 1876 upon Bakunin's death, and is quoted in Vuilleumier's introductory essay in the anastatic reproduction of Guillaume 1905–7: see Guillaume 1980, p. L.

their present differences in their conception of politics from their different conceptions of the future society, whereas 'Marx and Engels only dealt with the "future" in relation to present struggles, and in terms that already constituted practical interventions in these struggles'.[122] We absolutely should not underestimate the importance of expectations and of 'views of society's more or less distant future' as points of distinction among 'the two opposed parties';[123] and these considerations would take up much space in socialist publications over a long period. But in the last analysis, what would be decisive for the success of either one of these 'politics' was the correspondence between the general theory of economics and society and the real, actually-unfolding movement of organisation and struggle.

Carlo Cafiero also came to reject Resolution IX through a reading of the 'Manifesto of the German Communist Party' that was largely projected onto radical differences regarding the organisation of the future society. Through this type of reading, the category 'anti-authoritarianism' ended up being absolutised, drawing a veil over the specific analysis of real situations. A few months before his break with Engels, Cafiero had written the following comments on Resolution IX:

> We have never said that the working class and the International, which represents its highest inspiration, should break from any political notions, but on the contrary have maintained and continue to maintain that the working class must have a politics of its own that is in harmony with its class interests and responds to its legitimate aspirations; a politics that cannot in any way be that of bourgeois parties, all of which have an interest in conserving the existing institutions ... Resolution IX, then, far from pushing the proletariat to make common cause with bourgeois political dealers – in contradiction with the *General Rules* – essentially looks to hold the members of the International to a line of conduct that is wholly its own, and thus different and contrary to any existing politics.[124]

It is difficult to see this interpretation as an invalid one, in the light of the projection of 'authoritarian communism' onto the present and the future.

Cafiero's shifting position was certainly decisive in accelerating the process that would soon lead to the constitution of the *Federazione italiana della*

122 Balibar 1974, p. 83.

123 Bakounine 1974, p. 174.

124 Un internazionalista (Cafiero), 'L'Internazionale', *Il Gazzettino Rosa*, 20 December 1871.

Associazione Internazionale dei Lavoratori [Italian Federation of the International Workers' Association]. However, we should not consider the split with the General Council – officially decreed at the 1872 Rimini Conference, which has rather exaggeratedly been called the 'birth certificate of Italy's first modern political party'[125] – as a clear caesura in the spread of ideas of Marxian provenance in the socialist and proletarian scene on the Italian peninsula. That would have been impossible, also because within the 'anti-authoritarian' camp there continued to remain a firm attachment to the *General Rules*, even if with certain oscillations, as well as a general theory of society that had an unavoidable reference point in Marx, insofar as they were aware of his work.

Bakunin himself repeatedly made clear his views in this regard, even after he had declared war on the General Council. Marx's 'eternal honour' was that he had sought and found 'some practical ideas resulting from [the modern proletariat's] own historical traditions and daily experience, which we find in the sentiment and in the instinct – even not always as reflected thought – of the workers of all the countries of the civilised world, constituting the true catechism of the modern proletariat'. That is, Marx had not sought and found these ideas in just any economic and philosophical system, but in the modern proletariat's own universal consciousness. This was all magnificently expressed in the *Provisional Rules* and the *General Rules*, which formed 'the true, the only, constitutive, fundamental, obligatory principle of our Association'.[126] And again in the 'Letter to the Internationalists of Romagna' he turned his addressees' attention back to the *Provisional Rules*, reproducing the text in full in order to be sure that they were properly aware of it, as well as adding his own comments interpreting each of its points,[127] concluding that the *Provisional Rules* and the *General Rules* were 'absolutely compulsory' for all those individuals and clubs that wanted to be recognised as members of the International.[128]

125 Masini 1973.

126 Article for *La Révolution sociale*, January 1872, in Bakounine 1974, p. 175.

127 Naturally his personal exegesis sometimes forced the meaning of the text somewhat, (particularly the paragraph on economic emancipation, taking the translation 'as a simple means' and explaining that this 'means that the International repudiates any policy whose immediate and direct goal is not the economic and social revolution itself, which alone can bring the triumph of the complete freedom of each, founded on the real equality of all' – 'Lettre aux internationaux de la Romagne', 23–6 January 1872, in Bakounine 1974, p. 209) yet the full reproduction of the text, carrying all of Bakunin's authority, was nonetheless of very great importance.

128 Bakounine 1974, p. 210.

As for the fundaments of Marx's theory – meaning his historical materialism and economic theory, even if they were understood in a reductive and deterministic sense – Bakunin not only never tried to distance himself from these, but constantly pointed to them as the essential heritage of all socialism.

Already at the end of 1868, the Russian revolutionary wrote a letter to Marx that was rather telling in this regard:

> I have come to understand how right you are in following and inviting all of us to march along the great road of economic revolution ... I am now doing what you began to do more than twenty years ago ... My Fatherland today is the International of which you are one of the main founders. So you see, then, dear friend, that I am a disciple of yours – and am proud to be so ...[129]

It is possible that this letter as a whole was marked by tactical concerns, owing to the particular relationship that Bakunin wanted to cohere between the Alliance and the International. However, that was not the case of the statements that we mentioned above, since they were in harmony with other, even more committed judgements that Bakunin formulated even after 'war had been declared'.

Indeed, he had the following to say about *Capital*:

> This work should have been translated into French a long time ago, because no other work that I know of puts together such a profound, enlightening, scientific, decisive analysis that – if I may put it like this – so mercilessly unmasks the formation of bourgeois capital and the cruel, systematic exploitation that this capital continues to exert on the proletariat's labour.[130]

> Mr. Karl Marx is a bottomless pit of statistical and economic science. His work on capital – however unfortunately it is riddled with metaphysical subtleties and formulas, which make it impossible for the great mass

129 'Ein Brief Bakunins an Marx', 22 December 1868, in *Die Neue Zeit*, XIX, 1900–1, p. 7. He would further add on this point that when 'we were on friendly terms he was much more advanced than I was, just as today he is incomparably more knowledgeable than I, if not more advanced. Then I knew nothing of political economy ... and my socialism was but indistinct ... He called me a sentimental idealist, and he was right': Bakounine 1974, Vol. II, p. 123.

130 Bakounine 1974, Vol. III, p. 209.

> of readers to understand – is a positivist and realist work to the highest degree, in the sense that it can accept no logic except the logic of facts ...[131]

In sum, on the scientific plane it was impossible to deny who was incontestably 'the leading socialist and economic scholar of our time'.[132]

It is true that in 'anti-authoritarian' circles there were some who posed the question of producing 'a work that would be the counterpart to Marx's *Capital*';[133] yet such a task was evidently unrealisable. Guillaume, a proponent of such a plan, had reacted rather differently a few years beforehand at the International's Lausanne Congress, when he was introduced to Marx's theories by way of Eccarius. In an assembly that took place side-by-side with the Congress, the delegates clashed over the theoretical systems of Schultze-Delitzsch and Lassalle. One among the speakers was Büchner, the author of the very popular *Force and Matter*, which Marx had strongly criticised.[134] Then Eccarius intervened, initially speaking 'in a monotonous voice, and without grace' on the themes that Büchner had just addressed. He then expounded

> Karl Marx's great theory of history. Little by little his voice became more expressive, he lifted his gaze from the floor and became more animated, and his speech took on a familiar and picturesque eloquence of incomparable effect. We were captured by his charm, and the transformed Eccarius now held these hundreds of men hanging on his every word ... This lasted for almost two hours, and when he had finished the assembly, swept along, broke out in stormy applause ...[135]

Guillaume further commented on his relationship with Eccarius-Marx at the Congress: 'Eccarius interrupted his *Times* correspondence in order to expound

131 Bakounine 1974, Vol. IV, p. 63.

132 Bakounine 1974, Vol. II, p. 216.

133 See Guillaume 1905–7, Vol. II, p. 122.

134 'I have received Büchner's lectures on Darwinism. He is obviously a "book-maker" and probably for this reason is called "Büchner". His superficial babble about the history of materialism is obviously copied from Lange. The way such a whipper-snapper disposes of, e.g., Aristotle – quite a different sort of natural philosopher from Büchner – is really astonishing' – Marx to Kugelmann, 5 December 1868, *MECW*, Vol. 43, p. 173. Fifteen years later, 'Büchner was probably the most illustrious name to appear in the pages of *Die Neue Zeit* upon its first appearance': Ragionieri 1968, p. 85.

135 Guillaume 1905–7, Vol. I, p. 39.

Marx's theory for my benefit. What happy moments! I could fill a whole volume with what I learned in eight days with these venerable champions of right and justice'.[136]

This was a sign of the wholly particular effect that even an indirect relationship with fundamental aspects of Marx's thought (which had certainly been 'vulgarised') produced among Internationalist circles. Bakunin was extremely clear on this point, also with regard to the theory of history:

> Karl Marx has the honour of having established this idea: *that all evolutions, even the most ideal of evolutions in human history, always and everywhere have their first causes in the successive, inevitable transformations of the economic organisation of human societies* ...[137]

If, then, we consider that the fundamental watchwords that he suggested for the proletariat were 'Workers of all countries, unite!' (for its foreign policy) and 'The emancipation of the workers must be the work of the workers themselves' (for its domestic policy),[138] anarchist culture's landscape of Marxian references ultimately ended up taking on such importance as to become almost impossible to ignore.

Naturally, that is not to say that Bakunin's 'Marxism' – in terms of the theory of history and the theory of capitalism – was immediately able to influence the propensities of the young Italian Internationalists who gave rise to the Italian Federation of the International Workers' Association in 1872. However, what it does show is that at the moment at which these young militants were emphasising the need to complement their socialism with an economic and social theory, a relation with Marx's theories seemed wholly natural and not at all in contradiction with the traditions of their own anarchism.

The Bakunin that the young Italian Internationalists chose as their teacher in the early 1870s was a figure who had some familiarity with Marx's fundamental texts. He was also a figure who had had encounters with the most lively and important currents of European culture. This differed from the case of the 'old soldiers' and 'young materialists' – as Costa would define them – who lay the bases of the first *fasci operai* and the first sections of the International.[139] Their 'materialism' was substantially based on Büchner's popular and very well-

136 Guillaume 1905–7, Vol. I, p. 40.
137 Bakounine 1974, Vol. II, p. 185.
138 Bakounine 1974, Vol. II, p. 168.
139 *Égalité*, 18 March 1880, cited in Berselli (ed.) 1982, pp. 27–8.

fated *Force and Matter*, which had just appeared in Italian translation,[140] and their theory of history did not go far beyond a teleological-progressive vision, if certainly on a materialist basis. These views were so widespread in 'progressive' and/or 'revolutionary' (in various forms) common sense that we can even find traces of it in deepest Russia at the beginning of the second half of the nineteenth century, in the world of small proprietors and minor nobles that Turgenev showed to have been effected by the European long wave, even in their apparent situation of immobility.[141]

However, at the same time, the 'old soldiers' and 'young materialists' remained tenaciously committed to the *General Rules* and the 'old *Provisional Rules* of the International's programme',[142] precisely at the moment that they created an Italian federation openly breaking with Marx and the General Council. This was almost compulsory, even independently of Bakunin's suggestions, given the mass use of these documents among the *fasci* and *sezioni* from 1871 onward.[143] Sometimes the original texts of these documents were subjected to 'anti-authoritarian' and 'anarchist'[144] commentary, but they *were still*

140 Published in Italian in 1868 by Geatano Brigola Editore, Milan. Two years later Luigi Stefanoni, who edited and wrote the preface to the translation of *Force and Matter*, would curate the Italian edition of Büchner's *Man in the Past, Present and Future. A Popular Account of the Results of Recent Scientific Research as Regards the Origin, Position, and Prospects of the Human Race*.

141 'This morning I was sitting reading Pushkin ... I remember, it happened to be *The Gipsies* ... all of a sudden Arkady came up to me, and, without speaking, with such a kindly compassion on his face, as gently as if I were a baby, took the book away from me, and laid another before me – a German book ... smiled, and went away, carrying Pushkin off with him. "Upon my word! What book did he give you?" "This one here". And Nikolai Petrovitch pulled the famous treatise of Büchner, in the ninth edition, out of his coat-tail pocket'. Turgenev 1950, p. 53. And this was the response from one old member of the *odnodvortsy* (a freeholder-proprietor of a small piece of land, owned by one family) when asked whether he saw positive changes as compared to his own time: '"Things were better formerly, in your time, weren't they?" – "Some things really were better, I will tell you ... We lived more peacefully: there was greater ease, really ... But, nevertheless, things are better now; and they will be better still for our children"': Turgenev 1907, p. 101.

142 'Associazione Internazionale dei lavoratori. Federazione Regionale Italiana. Secondo Congresso Federale, 15 marzo 1873', in Masini (ed.) 1964, p. 62.

143 A particularly telling example is the 1872 *Statuto sociale della società l'Emancipazione del Proletariato*, published in Turin by the Tipografia Perrin.

144 A programme elaborated at the first Marche and Umbria congress of the Italian region of the IWMA was preceded by a set of *Provisional Rules* that were partly Marx's, but spliced together with arguments designed to justify anarchist positions. Hence 'the emancipation of the worker must be the work of the worker himself ... for this reason the worker is

used and circulated, becoming increasingly fundamental elements of socialist common sense. Not by chance, at the very moment that the Italian federation's crisis began to mature, it concluded by decisively and clearly stating that 'The International was founded in London and not in Geneva, and we here – adopting the line of conduct that we have adopted – stand precisely within the limits of London's original *Rules*'.[145] The *Provisional Rules and General Rules* ultimately became the fixed points of a system of variables that the development of the *real movement* altered according to its own fundamental needs.

The *real movement*, indeed, was decisive; and without this, it would have been much more difficult to propose the reconsideration of 'London's original *Rules*',[146] as Marx had seen them in 1864. And *real movement* still, above all, meant strikes and the organisation of resistance. In the 1870s, strikes increasingly proved to be the site where the decomposition and recomposition of the movement took place, even if such actions were discontinuous and very uneven geographically speaking, and developed in terms of parameters that did not directly depend upon ideological choices.[147]

The contemporaneity of the decade's most important strikes[148] and the foundation of the Italian Federation of the IWMA is, certainly, of strong symbolic value. The strikes in Milan and Turin in the summer of 1872 were linked to a particular conjunctural phase and a fluctuation in the availability of manpower that would not allow for the stabilisation of their results or of the organisation that they entailed; yet nonetheless they clearly took on the 'function of catalysing the dispersed forms of antagonistic working-class consciousness'.[149]

---

essentially anti-authoritarian and anarchist – that is, in not recognising any power above him that should drive or lead him along the road to emancipation or the struggle for it'; or considering 'that economic emancipation is the great end to which every political movement must be subordinate, this [economic emancipation] is impossible with the current organization of the state and property': Masini (ed.) 1964, pp. 80–2.

145 'Secondo Congresso della Federazione dell'Alta Italia e nuclei aderenti tenuto in Milanto nei giorni 17 e 18 febbraio 1877', in Masini (ed.) 1964, p. 191.

146 The significance of the Northern Italian Federation's congress vote did not escape Marx, who drew Engels's attention to 'the important declaration by the federation of Italia alta [sic] in which they state that they have always abided by the "original Rules" of the International': Marx to Engels, 3 March 1877, in *MECW*, Vol. 45, p. 203.

147 See *Relazione presentata a S.E. il ministro dell'interno nel mese di marzo 1879 dalla commissione d'inchiesta sugli scioperi nominate col R. decreto 3 febbraio 1878*, Roma: Regia tipografia, 1885.

148 See Civolani 1977.

149 Civolani 1977, p. 427.

The first wage demands were egalitarian in tendency, even if this orientation would come up against the resistance of some of the strongest and most professionalised categories. The achievement of an embryonic work contract, destined (among other things) to collapse once the conjunctural situation had changed, stimulated the birth of organisations for managing the contract, which had a tendency toward promoting worker-resistance. Nonetheless, the nascent Italian Federation was in substance indifferent to these important manifestations of the modern class struggle.

In truth, not all of the International's *sezioni* remained extraneous to the summer 1872 strikes. For example, in Turin the 'L'Emancipazione del Proletariato' club followed the movement's progress, and indeed participated in it directly. It addressed the bosses in the following terms: 'If in drawing up the contract you considered the manpower your own, something belonging to you, at the same price for the whole time the contract lasts, then your calculations are mistaken',[150] thus displaying an acute awareness of the ambivalent and particular character of labour-power as a commodity. As against those who denied the use of strike action, this Internationalist *sezione* noted that even if

> using this weapon the worker also himself takes a hit, we can say that without strikes not a single factory, building site or workshop in Italy would have fixed [a set number of] hours for those working there. Nor would the philanthropy of those enriched through the proletariat's labour have made them understand the insufficiency of the pay they gave the workers, and not a penny of increase would have been secured, had it not been for strikes ...[151]

The 'L'Emancipazione del Proletariato' *sezione* was not present at Rimini and in this period still maintained positive relations with the General Council. Its paper *Il Popolino*[152] was 'exclusively edited by workers' and its horizon was that of the 'class-party':

> One of the duties and goals of our association has been that of propagating these ideas among the working class, in this way creating a great independent party, the workers' party, which must be very much part of the struggle, set the workers' interests as its goal, and not be a simple weapon

150 'Gli scioperi', in *Il Popolino*, 'Monitore dei lavoratori' (Turin), July 1872.
151 'Qual è la potenza?', *Il Popolino*, 4 August 1872.
152 See the 1 June 1872 edition.

> in the hands of the bourgeoisie. That is the task to which the International has nobly committed itself ...[153]

The reasons for the Rimini Congress participants' [*riministi*'s] almost total lack of interest in strikes and working-class organisation should, without doubt, be identified (as they have been already) within the structural dimension of 1870s Italian industry and the type of social position that the Internationalists themselves occupied. It has been observed that the organisation of labour in manufactories, with a weak degree of interdependence among the branches of production, modest industrial concentration and a low level of growth in mechanisation 'made it rather difficult for collective experiences of struggle to become sedimented in workers' consciousness', instead encouraging 'the establishment of a personal type of relation between worker and employer', orienting 'the genesis of an antagonistic consciousness within the unilateral and reductive perspective of the fight against the boss'.[154] It has also been noted that the Internationalists themselves had greater implantation in sectors with a very limited tendency toward unionisation, whereas they were almost absent where traditional associationism was transforming into resistance; and that an organisational dualism dependent on economic dualism fed 'a substantial scepticism regarding the real possibility of winning over the majority of the labour force',[155] thus inhibiting any organisational effort in the workplace.

However, we ought not forget the vision that the 'anti-authoritarians' themselves displayed – precisely on the basis of their international congresses regarding the possibility of improving proletarians' living conditions, the characteristics of workplace struggle, and the use of organising resistance. The founding congress of the anarchist International at St. Imier gave very clear indications on these points:

> Already in many places there have been attempts to organise labour in order to improve the proletariat's condition, but even the slightest improvement has been quickly reabsorbed by the privileged class ... For

153 'Il partito operaio', *Il Popolino*, 29 June 1872. In the still-fluid situation of the spring of that year, Bologna's *Il Fascio Operaio* supported the station porters' strike, stating 'The Municipality must do its duty: we will be pleased if it succeeds in doing so: but we will not be contradicting ourselves, nor be held responsible, if it does not succeed and our Society is thus constrained to take to the road of resistance': see 'Resistenza', *Il Fascio Operaio*, 10 March 1872.

154 Civolani 1981, pp. 25, 27.

155 Civolani 1981, p. 43.

> us the strike is a precious means of struggle, but we in no way delude ourselves as to its economic results. We accept it as a product of the antagonism between labour and capital, which has as its necessary consequence ... the preparation of the proletariat, through simple economic struggles, for the great final revolutionary struggle ...[156]

Without doubt, the Italian Federation of the IWMA operated in a particular socio-economic environment that it also in some aspects expressed. However, it fully responded to St. Imier's logic, which as we have seen did not at all stand in contradiction with the tradition of the 'Italian revolution'.

The set of problems connected with the question of strikes and resistance were of such nature that we can see their echoes also within the Italian Federation milieu. Indeed, there were sections that posed the question of whether they 'should promote the organisation of the International through sections for trades and crafts'.[157] And in one congress debate, we can also read that it was 'urgently important that all Sections study all the means of resistance in all the relations between Capital and Labour; that in any case, it is useful to organise single Sections for trades and crafts and to federate them in unions for each trade and craft, such that resistance can more easily be exercised'.[158] However, in this field both the *riministi*'s activity and their elaborations were oriented in a wholly different direction, according to which 'any deviation from the mother-idea of the Revolution will hamper the proletariat',[159] and as such rather than 'undertaking and supporting the struggle against capital' in a 'partial struggle' the sections instead to 'prepare themselves for the supreme struggle'.[160]

Indeed, it would be the crisis of this outlook that would allow a new conjugation of Marx's indications in the *Provisional* and *General Rules* and his indications regarding the organisation of workers 'as a class'. This took place on the terrain of the *real movement*, independently, in this period, of any direct reference being made to Marx. This crisis saw the recomposition of a branch of Italian Internationalism that *riminismo* had broken apart. Gnocchi-Viani, who

156 See Bravo (ed.) 1978, pp. 840–1.

157 A query from the Naples section, July 1876, quoted in Masini (ed.) 1964, p. 130.

158 'Associazione Internazionale dei lavoratori. Federazione Regionale Italiana. Secondo Congresso Federale, 15 marzo 1873', in Masini (ed.) 1964, p. 66.

159 'Il [Terzo] Congress della Federazione italiana dell'Associazione Internazionale', November 1876, in Masini (ed.) 1964, p. 141.

160 'Mandato della Federazione di Firenze e delle Sezioni di Pomarance e di Cortona a Victor Cyrille delegato al Congresso Internazionale di Ginevra', August 1873, in Masini (ed.) 1964, p. 85.

had sought to create a resistance organisation within the Roman section, and then been ostracised when this section fell more into line with the Italian Federation,[161] now again insisted on the need to 'prepare societies of trades and crafts' – and he was listened to. 'These societies of trades and crafts are feared', he said, 'because they represent labour in struggle with its adversary. And since struggle is what best awakens solidarity, I believe that the Societies of trades and crafts encourage solidarity among workers better than other social forms do'.[162] The backdrop to this was the Italian socialists' task of building 'the great Workers' Party of Italy'.[163]

In this sense, part of Michels's argument is correct, where he maintains that it is mistaken to consider the parabola of Italian Bakuninism in terms of a total antithesis with respect to the spread of ideas inspired by Marxian formulations. However, the part concerning the 'pike' of Bakuninism is questionable if we shift our perspective from the level of ideological polemic to that of the *real movement*, whose development destroyed neither the Mazzinian societies nor the mutualist ones. Moreover, there can be little basis for overlooking the *crisis* of Bakuninism, which proved to be a factor of undoubted importance in accelerating this whole process.

This was all the truer given that the maturation of this *crisis* specifically concerned one of the aspects of decisive importance in the formation of the proletarian 'class-consciousness' that would later be defined in a Marxist sense in the 1890s: that is, the question of working-class organisation. Indeed, working-class organisation was the fundamental ring in this chain precisely because it was the *link* between external 'elaboration', 'socialist consciousness' and 'working class social consciousness' – that is, the set of informal practices and customs determined purely through their collocation within the production process.[164]

From this point of view, the crisis of Bakuninism began to come into view already by the mid-1870s, when the Internationalists grouped in the *Sezione del Ceresio* and papers like Palermo's *Il Povero* and above all *La Plebe* (now the Milan one), did not limit themselves to criticising the Bakuninites' 'ill-conceived uprisings',[165] but increasingly shifted their own attention to the prob-

---

161 Della Peruta 1952.

162 'Secondo Congresso della Federazione dell'Alta Italia e nuclei aderenti tenuto in Milano nei giorni 17 e 18 febbraio 1877', in Masini (ed.) 1964, p. 183.

163 'Associazione internazionale degli operai-Federazione Lombarda. Manifesto agli Operai, alle Operaie, alla gioventù d'Italia', 1876, in Masini (ed.) 1964, p. 259.

164 See, in this regard, the observations in Hobsbawm 1984.

165 See 'Ottavo congresso generale dell'Associazione internazionale dei lavoratori', *Il Povero*, 3, 23 October 1876.

lems of organising resistance. And at the same time they devoted themselves to bringing such organisation into existence, or strengthening it where it existed already. Between 1876 and 1877 socialist circles worked to link together such organisations, specifically focusing on the embryonic workers' movement as their privileged reference point and trying to become something more than propaganda groups of varying degrees of stability. Sometimes they succeeded in doing so, as in the case of the Associazione generale dei lavoratori di Mantova's affiliation to the Federazione dell'Alta Italia; this Mantua association counted some 1,982 associates in 1877, with 1,666 of them being agricultural labourers.[166]

As such, the crisis of Bakuninism matured precisely in the fastening of the *link* between 'socialist consciousness' and 'working-class social conciousness', and for these reasons its outcomes were of great importance to the future character of Italian socialism.

Certainly, neither the groups gathered around *La Plebe* or *Il Povero* or those united in the Federazione dell'Alta Italia could be defined as Marxists. Rather, they considered the Marxists and Bakuninites 'two churches of ambitious types, fighting among themselves',[167] and both responsible for the death of the International. However, the terrain of their determination to set socialism and the workers' movement on more solid footing proved particularly favourable for taking in the indications provided by Marx and Engels's framework; namely, the terrain where the *democratic antithesis* and *anarchist antithesis* were resolved in the *working-class antithesis*.

166 Della Peruta 1965, p. 262.

167 'Nostra corrispondenza', *Il Povero*, 5, 26 December 1876.

CHAPTER 2

The Marxism of the 1880s: The Characteristics of a Transition

1 Socialist Culture: Sociology

In *Primo maggio*, a novel that was in several aspects paradigmatic of many intellectuals' conversions to socialism in the 1890s, the protagonist gradually becomes conscious, with 'deep sadness', that his maturation as a socialist would entail definitive breaks with some of his oldest friends. 'The old friend he spoke with was still the same man; but he seemed distant from him, on the opposite shore of a wide river that neither of them was able to cross any more'.[1] Before his 'conversion' there may have been 'serious disagreements over politics, art and philosophy', yet it was nonetheless possible to save the friendship by agreeing to avoid too-contentious subjects. However, it was impossible to preserve this friendship if they were 'wholly in disagreement on the socialist idea, which since it embraces everything, creates a disagreement over everything'.[2]

This conception of an 'integral' socialism corresponds accurately enough to the self-image (more than the reality) constructed and promoted by 1890s socialism. This was the focal point in which the key elements of an intellectual construct would converge, and, at the same time, their point of departure; that is, an intellectual construct tending to embrace the processes of consciousness in a single set of relations structured according to a model of self-referential totality. Evidently this involved a particular emphasis on the movement's absolute cultural autonomy, sharply defining its boundaries with other cultures and proposing to use tools of analysis drawn from its *own* philosophy, its *own* political economy, its *own* sociology, and so on. This was a process of cultural separation, in short, that had been consciously planned and could now be considered to be passing through its concluding phases.

We could imagine this as a gradual process that had already been underway for some time: in a sense, inscribed in socialism's genetic inheritance, destined to reach maturation as its growth naturally progressed. And yet if we do want to speak of natural growth, we would struggle to argue that it was linear in

1 De Amicis 1980, p. 239.
2 Ibid.

character. If already at the beginning of the 1890s the need for self-sufficiency was increasingly becoming a particular element of socialist identity – the conscious assumption of the total horizon of Marxism being the most obvious aspect of this – the panorama of the decade that immediately preceded it was decidedly more uneven, and anything but one-dimensional.

Indeed, it was in the 1880s that the reasons for socialism's cultural autonomy – arguments that were also sometimes mentioned at the time – ultimately proved to be particular moments of the very thick web articulating the universe of positivisms; and they could not have been otherwise.

The well-established distinctions among positivism as a 'methodological direction', as a 'mental form' and as a 'doctrine'[3] directly concerned the socialist culture of this decade. This culture developed in a dimension symbiotic with both 'positive' needs and many of the 'isms' characteristic of positivist cultural accumulation, which had arrived in Italy during the first phase of the high point of its parabola.

Emile Durkheim had already very acutely pointed to some of the aspects of this symbiosis with positivism's principal social science – sociology – when he said that 'at more than one point [socialism's] history has mingled with that of sociology itself'.[4] Yet the degree of 'mingling' between the history of socialist culture and of positive culture had many other possible permutations. This owed not only to self-evident factors relating to the cultural climate of a given epoch, but also the fact that the 'social question' was the fundamental proving-ground in which political choices, states of mind, epistemologies and methodological experiments were put to the test. The 'social question' was the site of ambivalences *par excellence* – the ambivalence of political economy, the ambivalence of sociology, and the ambivalence of reforming policies, all revolving around the central ambivalence: the 'social question', whether of antagonism or of emptying out this antagonism. Socialism and its cultures – the child that foresaw, and prepared itself for, a future as giant of the century – posed itself as the privileged participant in this whole complex and far from homogeneous ensemble.

Naturally, socialism had its own structural peculiarities and particular *raisons d'être*, with which the positivisms of its specific cultures necessarily had to be conjugated. And in the development of two histories whose interlinking would concern a whole long and important period, it was socialist reasoning that would force open preconstituted systems and prepare the ground for

3 See Limentani 1924, p. 1.

4 Durkheim 1986, p. 98.

the mutation of general methodological coordinates and ideological reference points. Moreover, the Italian socialism of the 1870s had only made episodic references to the need for the already wide range of political and social choices now coming into definition to be founded on a 'philosophy' or even on ontological presuppositions. Only at the end of the decade did the question begin to be posed with greater emphasis and urgency, given that a movement and culture that considered themselves to have gone beyond their episodic initial phase now needed to find unifying 'scientific' reference points. The answer was clearly taken for given, in its most general characterisation: if socialism's adversaries denied that it had a philosophical principle, a great inspiring criterion, then 'how [could they] not see that socialism [was] a great anti-idealist current ... that socialism, overall [was] a positive, realist, materialist philosophy'?[5] This was a profession of philosophical faith that in its most ingenuous forms would even lead to an exposition of the theory of surplus-value being presented on 'the basis of the general distribution of energy in the universe'.[6]

Naturally, such a demanding philosophical choice – whatever its *de facto* necessity – could now begin with its own foundational experimentation, as a theoretical tool in a wide panorama of social analysis ranging from political economy to anthropology. In some cases in Europe, socialist culture and theory were first tested in the dimension of political economy,[7] but in Italy they instead first chose the paths of criminal sociology.

I believe that in this regard it is worth reflecting very carefully on the statement offered by one scholar of nineteenth-century democratic and socialist

5 'La filosofia del socialismo', *La Plebe*, 1 June 1879.

6 The author's intention was to prove, in light of the 'general distribution of energy in the universe', 'the theory of production formulated by Marx and accepted by socialists, according to which – expressing ourselves in the language of physics – human labour accumulates in its products a greater quantity of energy than has to be spent in the production of the workers' strength': see S. Podolinski, 'Il socialismo e l'unità delle forze fisiche', in *La Plebe* (monthly), 3–4, 1881. Engels read the article in question, writing to Marx that 'Podolinski went astray after his very valuable discovery, because he sought to find in the field of natural science fresh evidence of the rightness of socialism and hence has confused the physical with the economic', noting that 'All the economic conclusions he draws from this are wrong' (Engels to Marx 19 December 1882, in *MECW*, Vol. 46, pp. 409–12).

7 We can note that in very different contexts of 'industrial' and socio-political development such as the France and Germany of the early nineteenth century, the different consciousness and consideration of classical political economy among such figures as Comte and Hegel – particularly representative of these societies and their cultures – would later be reflected in the different relation between sociology and political economy and between socialism and sociology in these same countries in the second half of the century: see Negt 1964.

culture, Massimo Ganci, according to which 'Napoleone Colajanni's *Il Socialismo* was ... the first theoretical platform of the Italian workers' movement'.[8]

Il Socialismo explicitly presented itself, even in its title, as an essay of criminal sociology, the ambit within which 'Filippo Turati, Leonida Bissolati, Camillo Prampolini, [and] Napoleone Colajanni ... [had] subjected the European positivist experiences to revision in a socialist key'.[9] This meant adopting sociology as a general horizon and criminal sociology as a particular field of investigation.

The process that was then taking shape obviously did not allow the nineteenth-century sociological tradition any uniformity of conceptual systems. Indeed, even after more than a century of gradual disciplinary professionalisation, there were still clearly profound epistemological controversies and 'contradictory hypotheses'.[10] Yet this tradition's interest in the subaltern classes' living conditions and modes of action, and in the moral and criminal dimensions, was very widespread and itself informed empirical research. We could say that for a long time sociology's distinctive trait was that it 'interpret[ed] modern society as industrial society';[11] it was a knowledge deeply immersed in a new world, one generated by a new world, whose way of presenting an ancient evil – poverty – was also new. This type of poverty, the phenomena associated with it, and its physical and behavioural consequences, provided the most evident means of revealing the mechanisms through which social relations functioned – and this in a universe that was undergoing a gradual and irreversible transformation.

This systematic interest in the mechanisms of society – starting from phenomena that upset the established order – long remained the primary inspiration for studies into the subaltern classes. This was true even in contexts such as the American one, which had better integrated the hard core of Spencerian hyper-individualism than in the Italian case, and yet continued to explore the vagaries of poverty. Here we are still very far from the time when the term 'social' – even if conjugated with science – would itself be seen as too charged with ideological meaning and too linked to the descent into the infernos of industrial capitalist modernity, with the result that some would suggest replacing it with a supposedly more neutral word like 'behaviour'.[12] On the contrary, in this period Gnocchi-Viani could fully coherently think that sociology was

8 See Ganci 1968, p. 151.
9 Ganci (ed.) 1959, p. xx.
10 See Adorno 1976.
11 See Rossi 1982, p. 15.
12 See Seen 1966.

nothing other than a 'social chemistry', collectivism its 'perfect operation';[13] if when 'faced with science it [was] called *Sociology*, in activist life it [was] called *Socialism*'.[14] The *Rivista Internazionale del Socialismo* would write that 'socialism [would have] no *raison d'être* if it [were] not inspired by the works of social economy and the method followed by the other sciences', concluding that 'from this point of view, however, socialism becomes sociology'.[15] In our case, as we have said, this meant a criminal sociology.

Beyond its intrinsic merits, Napoleone Colajanni's book truly represents an epoch-defining moment in the culture of Italian socialism. The arguments that it works through were not necessarily any more original than what other socialists had already been producing. For example, as we shall see, Turati not only anticipated this work but was also a both more refined and restless analyst. However, the young Castrogiovanni republican-socialist's work was constructed in a manner totally in accordance with the precepts of the scientific publications of his time: it was a systematic volume, built around a series of branches, and, indeed, encyclopaedic in scope. Yet given that despite the book's substantial dimensions it was not as exhaustive as originally planned, it was considered only the first part of a monograph; and indeed the monumental *Sociologia criminale* published five years later[16] was advertised as the logical continuation of his 1884 work.

This was a book perfectly in accordance with the science of the era, up to date on the theoretical questions of its time, and fully positivist in character; but it simultaneously interpreted the fundamental aspects of positive science from the viewpoint of socialism. It cohered with science also because it demonstrated that socialism was the first element of scientific coherence.

An attitude that would later seem inscribed in the very DNA of socialist culture had now almost taken final form in this first Italian attempt at 'scientific

13 Gnocchi-Viani 1879a, p. 5.

14 As he put it in his *Il nostro ideale*; and again, in his *Il socialismo moderno* (Gnocchi-Viani 1886), '... Socialism is science, or, if you want to use another word for that, Socialism is Sociology. One cannot be a socialist without being a sociologist, and without studying social science. But you can be a sociologist without being a socialist'.

It is interesting to note that according to Montalbán, at one point Spanish revolutionary groups who called themselves Marxists felt strongly attracted by sociology – that is, in the 1950s, when the relations between sociology and Marxism were anything but simple: 'there was a lot of willingness [to conduct] sociological analysis, because sociology had begun to be fashionable as an intrinsically subversive science that could cast off the ideologisms of politics': Montalbán 1993.

15 See P., 'Socialismo e sociologia', *Rivista internazionale di socialismo*, 1880, II/2, p. 40.

16 Colajanni 1889.

socialism': an attitude that would at different times be either a point of strength or weakness for this culture. It was an attitude that favoured the assumption of 'Marxism' as a first, privileged horizon of reference – and then a total one – but which would then come, almost unchanged, deeply to mark the complicated experience of the relation among the different 'Marxisms'.

Socialism, then, could be considered *inevitable* only if it accorded with the general tendencies of a scientifically proven evolution. Hence it would evidently be nonsensical for socialist culture to be anything other than the protagonist and the mirror of the most rigorous paradigm for the interpretation of such tendencies. Moreover, the dimension of 'necessity' also presupposed the continual and progressive pervasiveness of 'socialist science', which would become ever more 'autonomous' and 'primary'. At the end of the century Antonio Labriola would both mockingly and critically refer to the 'mania that many people have to force whatever ... science they had in their grasp within the terms of socialism'; a mania owing to the fact that

> Those in Italy who commit[ted] themselves to socialism, and not as mere agitators, speech-makers and candidates, fe[lt] that it [was] impossible to make it scientifically persuasive if not by somehow attaching it to the existing genetic conception of things, which [was] more or less at the basis of all the other sciences.[17]

This mania, however, had deep roots, and did not only concern Italy. Nor would Labriola's sharp tones and rigorous method prevent its continuous and significant presence.

Any direct entrance into the 'upper echelon' of 'positive science' in Italy would have struggled to avoid recognising the centrality of criminal anthropology. Lombroso's anthropological school, the Italian school of criminal anthropology, was in fact particularly significant in the field of positivist culture, enjoying 'enormous success on the international scientific stage'.[18] We might almost think that it was in this specific field that it seemed easiest to overcome what would appear to be an element of contradiction between Comtian-derived positivism and socialism. That is, the contradiction between a culture that emphasised 'the harmonious interplay of classes, as determined by the overall economy of society',[19] and one that necessarily insisted on the antagonistic

17 Antonio Labriola, 'Marxismo, Darwinismo, eccetera', *Critica Sociale*, 1897, p. 190.

18 Papa 1985, p. 19.

19 Negt 1964.

characteristics – indeed, the irresolvable antagonism – present within the context of the existing relations. We will go on to see the different elements that would ultimately be disentangled from this contradictory knot.

The study of the 'criminal' allowed for an almost direct correspondence with all the positivist models of knowledge: from the statistical-classificatory model to the interactive biological-psychiatric one, with strong geographical-naturalist connections; moreover, the very concept of crime was 'forced to become the container for a number of highly disparate elements'.[20] At the base of this was the common anti-voluntaristic sentiment that was something of a distinctive trait of sociology during its long initial phase; an aspect of the anti-Jacobin inheritance, feeding into an already powerful tradition strongly tending to limit the role of politics in the processes of social evolution. The expression 'free will' often appeared in socialist periodicals, being understood as a residual moment that 'science [was] every day doing more to chase out of its nest';[21] and if the rejection of 'free will' was substantially a commonplace among both the protagonists and the followers of the 'Italian school' of criminal anthropology, there was no similar agreement as to the deeper causal factors behind this determinism. It is possible that in the specific ambit of this 'school' the dissent was limited to certain 'heretics'[22] (as Gabriel Tarde called them), such as Colajanni, Turati, and, we might add, Prampolini. They were rather marginal from the viewpoint of defining this discipline's scientific status, but they did pose questions that were of no little significance in terms of both how one could remain within the terms of positivist categories, and how it was possible to conjugate them with the needs of a more structured socialist culture.

There is probably some measure of exaggeration in the currently prevalent historiographical interpretation that sharply counterposes Lombroso and Ferri's rigidly naturalist determinism to the socio-historical determinism of Turati and Colajanni (as well as Prampolini), at least in part. That is particularly the case when this is considered the basis of a distinction between 'conservative socialism'[23] and socialism *tout court*. It has rightly been noted, with regard to naturalist categories, that Lombroso analysed man within a historical conception of biological nature, 'an ensemble of species and races in-becoming, an ensemble of phenomena of evolution and involution or degeneration to

20 Portigliatti-Barbos 1985, p. 428.
21 'Aspettiamo fiduciosi!', *Avanti!*, 20–21 May 1882.
22 Tarde 1887, p. 50.
23 Bulferetti 1951 uses this expression to define Lombroso's position.

which structures and types are reduced'.[24] Without doubt, the interpretation of the criminal as pathological represented a qualitative leap with respect to the previous schools of criminology; nonetheless, the 'heretics'' position marked a further extension of the sociological dimension, now openly heralded as an aspect of socialism itself.

Turati was well aware of his interlocutors' 'progressive' position ('We love to battle with those who, like us, are heading toward the future').[25] However, at the same time he accused them of not drawing the full consequences of the methodological mechanisms that had proven to be the true positive science, and which were ever more separate from a bourgeois common sense that was now 'dissolving with the complete collapse of all its prejudices'.[26] As such, Lombroso and Ferri needed to expand their horizon by using precisely the same potent tools that had already allowed them to advance science so considerably, and not stop 'at the immediate, accidental circumstance of the crime, neglecting its truer and deeper social causes'.[27] If this discussion could have remained limited to a question of method, Turati instead consciously introduced the question of conjugating the necessary methodological developments and the needs of socialism: 'Socialism's ideal, when it comes to criminal relations, is the following: to establish a social order where the criminal act is neither necessary nor of any use ... the penal question is first of all, and at its very roots, a question of social transformation'.[28] Turati defined his study as 'Positivist and sociological', an essay in 'radical sociology',[29] but doubtless also considered it a work of socialism, even if perhaps only *in nuce*, for now.

It was, indeed, Colajanni who transformed this outline of the question into the coherent work of 'scientific socialism' of which we have spoken, even if he was also stimulated by Turati's active, involved contribution. This produced a work with which a whole generation of young intellectuals destined to play a leading role in the history of Italian socialism could identify. Furthermore – in different roles and forms, and however directly or indirectly – some of them contributed to the gestation of this work, whose fundamental arguments had

24 Bulferetti 1975, p. xvii. From Lombroso's reading of Darwin came the tendency in Italy to use evolutionist determinism above all in its political dimension. See Landucci 1977 and Pancaldi 1983.

25 Turati, 'Appunti sulla questione penale', *La Plebe*, 5, 12, 19, 26 November and 3, 10, 24, 31 December 1882.

26 Ibid.

27 Ibid.

28 Ibid.

29 Ibid.

in part been discussed even before the volume was published. And first among them, without doubt, was Turati, who had urged Colajanni to produce this text, and looked 'with emotion and not without a certain sadness' upon the Castrogiovanni doctor, having 'supported [him] with great strength',[30] suggested the title and structure of the work, and provided far from negligible comments on the manuscript. They also included Prampolini – whom Colajanni sought to involve on account of some of his articles published in *Lo Scamiciato* – and also Bissolati and Candelari,[31] whom he kept informed of the work in progress throughout their correspondence and conversations. Thus a direct and immediate correspondence was established between the 'scientific' field, journalism, and the exchange of letters.[32]

These were, indeed, interconnected discussions: Turati posed himself the problem of the 'dangerous ambivalence of evolutionary positivism' and posed the same question to his friend Prampolini as he noted the unresolved difficulty of reconciling 'justice with the necessity of the struggle to live'.[33] In substance, this demanded an interpretation of Darwinism that did not contradict the aspirations of socialism. Turati matured his answer to this question by taking his cue from Mill, as he immediately explained in his correspondence with his friend Colajanni. This was a 'juridical, just, beneficial, contractual' interpretation 'with equal weapons' of a struggle for life translated into the terms of competition; a competition that gradually became more civilised as 'the duel' replaced the 'brawl, arbitration the duel, etc. etc.'; a 'transformation of the struggle' in which 'the desired point of conciliation between socialism and Darwinism [would] be found'.[34] For his part, Colajanni seemed to have a greater propensity for Prampolini's interpretation, to the point that the book

30 See the letter from Turati to Colajanni of 13 February 1884, in Ganci (ed.) 1959.

31 Candelari had, besides, already intervened on the question of the possibility of reconciling Darwinism and socialism, with orientations very close to those that would then be adopted by Prampolini and then developed by Colajanni. He had maintained that 'the positivist school has shown, in the animal field, a law of life-struggle owing to the disproportion between the generative forces and the capacities of the various environments'. If the circumstances in which such a law happened to operate were changed – which was possible, in human society – then 'there would begin to be realised a beneficial tendency toward equilibrium between vitality and environment': see R. Candelari, 'La legge di selezione e l'uguaglianza sociale', *La Plebe* (monthly), 3, 1881.

32 See for example Turati, 'Il delitto e la questione sociale', *La Favilla*, 1 April 1883.

33 Turati to Prampolini, 7 October 1883, in Marmiroli (ed.) 1966.

34 Turati to Colajanni, 13 February 1884, in Ganci (ed.) 1959. This was similar to the position transforming the struggle for existence into the 'struggle for vital competition': see 'Socialismo e Darwinismo', *La Favilla*, 27 January 1884.

included long passages from a letter of his. This was a Prampolini that opted for a 'sociological' and thus organicist Darwinism; the conditions of an organism's survival did not lie in the struggle among different sides, but rather 'association, solidarity … [and] the equality of rights and duties'. 'The struggle for existence' – Prampolini argued – 'is the law, or better, the force through which living beings reach their maximum force, their maximum resistance against a hostile nature; it is easy to show that this is the same force that drives the exploited to rebel, and which also, however, inevitably leads men to an ever-closer solidarity, an ever growing equity and an ever more extensive equality'.[35] Indeed, we can find aspects of this outlook in Colajanni's volume, where the conjugation between Darwinism and socialism is realised in a processual dimension: 'the more socialistic the organisation of humanity, the more the Darwinian struggle for existence among men is attenuated and diminished'.[36]

Putting all this together, Colajanni's first systemisation of this question was somewhat flexible. As against Italian Spencerism's seemingly complete identification of biological and sociological method[37] (which was in part also apparent in Prampolini), Colajanni clearly maintained that biology and sociology 'go hand in hand, but are never confused'.[38] Moreover, evolution itself foresaw qualitative leaps, and in the field of social evolution the *laws of the psyche* would exercise a progressive substitution effect over *physical laws*. Indeed, the socio-economic bases of political determinism developed through mechanisms that while certainly different to natural ones, did not stand in contradiction with them. The laws according to which society evolved were not written in any genetic code, but rather 'realised within certain limits and in certain conditions, and when these change, so too is the law itself altered'.[39] However, it does

---

35 Prampolini to Colajanni, 13 November 1883, in Ganci (ed.) 1959.

36 Colajanni 1899, Vol. II, p. 46.

37 The Italian socialists' Spencerism did not reach the extreme 'biologism' that we can find in several different contexts, which developed this biologism into a generalised common sense. We see this in the words of the protagonist of one popular novel of the early twentieth century: 'The evolution of the tool, of the harp, of music and song and dance, are all beautifully elaborated; but how about the evolution of the human himself … biology in its largest aspects … the biological factor, the very stuff out of which has been spun the fabric of all the arts, the warp and the woof of all human actions and achievements'; London 1982, p. 772.

38 Colajanni 1884, p. 59.

39 Colajanni 1884, p. 250. Five years later these coordinates remained unchanged: 'Determinism has received and continually receives new vigour from experience, from the observation of facts, from physiology and psychology and tries to make the widest possible use of these in the practical sciences … every *phenomenon* has a *cause*, and if this *cause* ceases

not seem that the rejection of determinism as 'fatalism' also implied denying that the historical process does have some orientation. As such, socialism had a 'character no less scientific than does sociology',[40] instead representing its 'greatest and most important chapter'[41] precisely because it could not be interpreted outside of the general law of evolution. These orientations would remain unchanged over the 1880s, and were re-asserted in full in 1889's *La sociologia criminale*. This work, indeed, was received as a work of science and at the same time 'a strenuous defence of socialism and humanity'.[42]

The picture drawn by Colajanni – a man whom Kautsky called a *Gesinnungsgenosse* (which has been translated into Italian as *compagno di fede* [comrade-in-faith], but more precisely refers to a *compagno di idee*: a comrade in sharing one's way of thinking) – was, therefore, largely a commonplace also among the other *compagni di idee* who had in various ways contributed to the political-cultural debate from which it emerged.

Certainly, it was no novelty that sociology and the tools of positivism in general were an integral part of the socialist culture that was now being constructed. The variegated world of 'progressives', from democratic republicans to socialist republicans, had been a fundamentally favourable context for the propagation of positivisms, including both the opening that it favoured for engagement with the high points of European positive philosophy (as in the case of Comte's correspondence with Benedetto Profumo),[43] and Cattaneo's indigenous tradition. In the less distant past, an attentive look through the pages of a republican-socialist periodical of relatively long tradition such as *La Plebe* would suffice to demonstrate the gradual definition of specifically socialist cultural elements, as well as their symbiotic relation with positivist categories.

However, something new was also happening in the early 1880s, as scattered arguments and positions now tended to cohere around an ideological centre endowed with a strong propensity toward autonomy, and which was responsive to its own logics. And these logics would do much to condition the relation that it was now establishing with 'science'.

---

to be active [the phenomenon itself] disappears; if it returns, the phenomenon will necessarily be reproduced. In identical conditions we have an identical phenomenon; when the conditions change the phenomenon changes in turn. This is *determinism*': Colajanni 1889, Vol. 1, p. 19.

40 Colajanni 1899, p. 275.

41 Colajanni 1899, p. 302.

42 See the long review by Romeo Candelari in 'Il sole dell'avvenire', 3 August 1890.

43 See Larizza Lolli 1985.

The *Lo Scamiciato* experience was in some senses exemplary in this regard, precisely because it was one of the many ephemeral publications without particular weight amidst the socialist press and which had no special or glorious traditions. However, one thing that did characterise this small-format paper, without any prior history, was the fact that it was born in 1882,[44] on the initiative of a group of young students and recent graduates – the most notable of their number being none other than Prampolini – and thus emerged at a time when what one great interpreter of our modernity has defined as 'the utopia of exact living' was becoming increasingly prevalent in socialist intellectual circles.[45] And not by chance, at this particular moment, the attempt to reach a 'theoretical' definition of one's own choices and political practice, was considered a fundamentally important task. It is even more significant if we consider that Camillo Prampolini's important role and long activism in the ranks of Italian socialism were never linked to any particular propensity for theory, and yet here he posed as his preliminary problem the extremely theoretical question (albeit one that also had evident practical consequences) of the relation between socialism and science. This was a theoretical matter, for certain, but he addressed it precisely in order to demonstrate 'the historical and scientific truth of socialist doctrine'.[46] There is no doubt that at that time Prampolini was, as has been noted, 'one of the few young people willing ... to address the question of the relation between scientific and human progress',[47] but it is much more problematic to say that the intellectual attitude with which he addressed these questions really afforded him an analytical 'capacity' that was up to this task.[48] In fact, Prampolini's almost axiomatic statement that 'there is an identity between our dreams and the future of humanity, according to science',[49] seems to have been the horizon conditioning his research. For certain, tension between 'epistemological positivism' and 'existential positivism'[50] did represent a constant across the history of this culture, and this 'existential socialist positivism' seems particularly relevant to the Prampolini, Colajanni and Turati of the beginning of the 1880s, if not in the same measure. It would have been difficult for this not also to affect the quality of 'epistemological positivism'. The very great density of the *existential* dimension, more-

44 Zavaroni 1979, pp. 85–107.
45 See Musil 1997, Part II, section 61.
46 Ursus (Prampolini), 'Scienza e socialismo', *Lo Scamiciato*, 15 January 1882.
47 Mascilli Migliorini 1979, pp. 62–3.
48 Mascilli Migliorini 1979, p. 62.
49 Prampolini to Colajanni, 13 November 1883, in Ganci (ed.) 1959.
50 An expression used in Sola 1983, p. 70.

over, would make its effects felt every time that the problem of the relation between socialism and science was posed, even beyond this long stage of development.

Criminal anthropology had been the sector in which a first systemisation openly promoting itself as a socialist sociology came to maturation, fully integrating these two terms. Yet the attitude that now characterised the developments of socialist culture also gave it a significant tendency to widen its horizons of intervention. What was being postulated, here, was a progressive convergence of active – innovative – cultural processes, together working toward the *inevitable* transformation of society. The young Candelari, who had taken on the modest role of a 'lowly propagandist' – in contrast to his more gifted friends like Prampolini, Turanti and Colajanni – particularly publicised this latter's book, which he described as 'one of the best [works] ... of social [socialist] doctrine ... written with all the science of the century'. He thus particularly clearly and effectively explained the tendency for socialist culture to annex all the ferments of the latest novelties. As Candelari wrote with regard to the growth and taking-root of realist literature:

> Realist literature can nowadays be considered one of Socialism's most powerful auxiliaries. That is, if by Socialism we mean not only the rising movement of the lower classes, but the whole ensemble of social phenomena that exercise a transformative action on institutions, customs and the arts, then realist literature can consider itself an integral part of the transformer *par excellence* that is socialism ... New concepts are emerging from every branch of the knowable; the builders of the new are advancing in every field of the arts and sciences.[51]

In sum, a thousand little streams were flowing into the great river of socialism, for which 'every scientific advance' thus became a 'fresh triumph'.[52] Not by chance, at the same time it was possible to read in *La Plebe* that socialism was nothing other than 'the mathematical corollary of modern scientific axioms, all taken as one' and that the discoverers of 'these axioms' were 'Galileo, Darwin and Marx ... each of them attracting the hatred of all reactionaries'.[53] The following year Engels himself would confer his prestige on this comparison between Marx and Darwin, as he spoke at Marx's graveside.

51 Candelari, 'La letterature verista e il socialismo', *Avanti!*, 4 June 1882.
52 'Una profezia', *Avanti!*, 26 March 1882.
53 See 'La nostra battaglia e il nostro ideale', *La Plebe*, 18 July 1882.

In general, we are used to thinking that formulations, commonplace sayings, key ideas, and mobilising elements that invoke Marx and Engels's authority, or the authority of Marx and Engels taken separately (or even in opposition to one another) are the initial and determining factors behind certain cultural and political processes. Of course, these elements – in particular after the assumption of 'Marxism' as a total ideological horizon for socialism – would almost always end up undergoing a process of separation and estrangement with respect to the cultural contexts in which they happened to emerge. These cultural contexts were sometimes profoundly transformed by the irruption of 'Marxism', while at other times they instead seemed to embrace it wholly naturally, without finding it at all extraneous. Moreover, this 'natural' embrace and the 'qualitative leap' that followed were not necessarily perceived as contradictory.

There was no need for Engels's speech at Marx's graveside for socialists to consider Darwin a scholar whose fundamental theory could give more solidly-grounded bases for their conviction that they were moving 'with the march of history', and thus for them to elaborate 'original' doctrinal systems that could defuse the 'bomb' of the 'struggle for life'. Since Marx was perceived as the scholar whose work on economics and theorisation of capitalist development had provided guarantees for the direction in which human history would unfold – just as solid as the ones that Darwin had provided for 'natural history' – the very force of things imposed the conjugation of Marx with Darwin. This force of things could be seen on a shared terrain[54] that Darwin had fertilised, and on which there met 'names such as Marx, Engels, Lassalle, Schäffle, Guesde, De Päpe, Kautsky, Hyndman, Morris, Gronlund and a hundred others'; a shared terrain that 'declare[d] the legitimacy of the workers' demands and unquestionably demonstrate[d] that the society they wanted ... [was] not only possible, but indeed the economic order that was being prepared by the law of nature and by the accomplishments of the bourgeoisie itself'.[55]

If through their various interpretations[56] of the 'struggle for existence' the Italian socialists thought that they had demonstrated the possibility of a 'social-

54 A common terrain on which Colajanni and Kautsky had met, and on which Kautsky had proposed a rigorously evolutionist vision of history to his Italian *Gesinnungsgenosse* – albeit one that had a 'spiral' movement, clearly evoking Vico. See Kautsky to Colajanni, 30 August 1884, in Ganci (ed.) 1959.

55 Dott C. (Prampolini), 'Evoluzione e rivoluzione', *La Giustizia*, 4 March 1888.

56 Together with Turati's reduction of the 'struggle for existence' to a progressively more equal competition, and Colajanni's (and in part Prampolini's) interpretation of the progressive extension of the human sphere over the animal sphere – the sphere of altruism

ist' Darwin, as opposed to the bourgeoisie's Darwin, they still needed to clarify the relation that they wanted to establish between 'evolution and revolution'. This was particularly the case for those socialists like Costa and his followers who had until very recently exalted the miraculous virtues of the revolutionary act itself, and even now did not want to renounce their title as 'revolutionaries'. This was a question that would continue to be re-posed also in subsequent periods characterised by the predominance of 'Marxism' – a re-proposition profoundly influenced by the ways in which 'socialist' Darwinism was discussed.

First and foremost, as a result of the obsessive insistence on conjugating the terms 'socialism' and 'science' it had now become customary closely to conjugate the 'scientific' dimension with contingent political choices. As such, it was not sufficient for 'science' to guarantee the longer-term course, that is, the direction of history; rather, it also had to guarantee the rightness of particular 'turns'. If the abstentionist tactic was now considered obsolete, it was possible to abandon it on the basis of the 'Darwinist' theory of adaptation to the environment:

> The secret of the organic victory of species, the modern biological sciences teach, lies in their capacity to adapt to the environment. Now, in a social environment in which the struggle is waged with all sorts of

over that of egoism – there also co-existed other parallel or complementary interpretations. There was the possibility of changing human behaviour by changing the environment, thus preserving a naturalistic framework: in the last analysis, 'the positivist school ha[d] shown, in the animal field, a law of life-struggle owing to the disproportion between the generative forces and the capacities of the various environments'. If the circumstances in which such a law happened to operate were changed – which was possible, in human society – then 'there would begin to be realised a beneficial tendency toward equilibrium between vitality and environment': see R. Candelari, 'La legge di selezione e l'uguaglianza sociale', *La Plebe* (monthly), 3, 1881. Other arguments that were upheld simultaneously had contradictory elements. Hence on the one hand, the historical environment was different from the natural one, and yet the natural environment itself provided a demonstration of the progressive character of altruism: the worker who produces everything is better adapted to the environment than the bourgeois who produces nothing and 'does nothing but squander what the worker has produced'; at the same time, there are socially-adapted species that develop, and other, poorly-adapted ones that decline. See 'Carlo Darwin' (obituary), *La Plebe* (monthly), 6, 1882. Loria also made an authoritative intervention on this question, refusing any schematic application of Darwinism to the sphere of human history. In social struggle the selection was often the inverse of that seen in the natural struggle: see 'Carlo Darwin e l'economia politica', *Rivista di filosofia scientifica*, May–June 1884.

> weapons, those parties who have renounced making use of this or that civil weapon simply because it is contaminated by privilege will never succeed, and will succumb. As such, the socialist workers' party will triumph if it proves able to make its strategic conduct conform to the special nature of the historical-civil field in which it today finds itself in combat.[57]

And if Andrea Costa and part of the socialists had at a certain moment chosen other 'terrains of struggle',

> Those who attribute this change of tactics on the part of most of the Socialists to the personal effectiveness of one or more men would show how very little they understand the fatal unfolding of the political forces and the times. These ingenuous types would be confusing form with content. No: this development among these socialists has taken place because it had to take place ... it was not anyone's personal deed, but the inevitable work of the times, of the environment, of changed conditions, of impersonal factors.[58]

Of 'evolution', in short.

Not only strategy, then, but also 'tactics' had to be guided by 'science'. This was a root that had profound ramifications for the subsequent development of socialism and Marxism, with very differentiated, controversial and even contradictory results. It produced a constant attention toward structural phenomena, a careful study of the general conditions within which political action had to unfold, a consideration of politics itself as a moment in a more complex set of interdependencies, and a consideration of culture as a primary and indispensible moment of this politics. At the same time, however, even in the best of cases the 'scientific' justification of 'tactics' tremendously impoverished the profundity of the epistemological problems that were necessarily connected to this, trapping the necessary flexibility of contingent political choices in rigid and

57 Candelari, 'Avanti con fiducia', *Avanti!*, 27 April 1884.

58 Candelari, 'Da un estremo all'altro', *Avanti!*, 15 June 1884. Here the author picks up on almost exactly the same arguments as Costa had used three years previously as he defended himself from critics of his 'turn': 'We say that man is not responsible for his actions, that he is the product of the environment in which he lives; that he does not create, but at most formulates, the laws of social phenomena; that judgement and condemnation are absurd and inhuman acts': Costa, 'Ai miei amici ed ai miei avversari', *Avanti!*, 15 September 1881.

doctrinaire schemas. In the worst cases, 'science' became only an instrumental appendage to tactics, reducing it to an ideology of immediacy. Indeed, the reduction of 'science' to ideology could almost be taken as read, given these premises. Ultimately, even an ideology could play a noble function, and not necessarily be transformed into something tawdry and instrumental. And in the reality of the historical process that concerned socialism and Marxism, there was, certainly, a place for science, and even for a noble use of ideology – but also a rather less noble one.

At the same time, in the transition period marking the late 1870s and early 1880s – in the climate leading up to and following the 'turn' – the question of the relation between 'evolution and revolution'[59] appeared as one of the main testing grounds of the functional capacity of a still-noble ideological dimension.

Could categories like 'evolution' and 'revolution' not prove contradictory, for those 'revolutionaries' whose Darwinian (and then Darwinian-Marxist) law of evolution indicated the certain road to palingenesis? In this case, too – as in the case of the 'struggle for life'-'social justice' binomial – the threads of a pattern designed to weave both terms together in one same fabric were continually being intertwined.

As we have said, it was in general the old Bakuninists who insisted on mechanisms of conciliation, precisely on account of the past identity that they wanted to conserve. It was impossible to deny revolution, and in particular its characteristics of 'struggle, irregular tremors ... [and] rapid and violent transformations'.[60] This revolution was not counterposed 'to the law of the evolution of the natural order': rather, it manifested itself 'when a force extraneous to nature's' intervened to challenge the free unfolding of this law itself. In truth, it was suggested, there existed two complementary laws, the evolutionary and the revolutionary.

> The first is methodical and slow because it is the effect of the unfolding of natural forces and their harmony. The second is intermittent and violent because it is the effect of the difference between man's science and nature's own way of acting. The one determines the natural selection of humanity, the other its artificial selection, and both combine in advancing human perfection, governed by a yet more general and com-

59 A truly impressive number of articles appeared under this title in the socialist papers of the era.

60 'Evoluzione e Rivoluzione', *Il sole dell'avvenire*, 7 October 1882.

> prehensive law – the law of progress – constantly driving man to make his own deeds as uniform as possible with nature's.[61]

'Evolution' and 'revolution', therefore, made up part of one same process, and evolution did not proceed without 'running into sudden shifts in its equilibrium'.[62] Moreover, the programme of the *Partito socialista rivoluzionario di Romagna* clearly stated that the revolution was a 'violent, material insurrection of the multitudes against the obstacles that the existing institutions oppose to the affirmation and realisation of popular will',[63] and in these same years some prophesied that with the accumulation of the same factors that had led to the French Revolution breaking out at the end of the previous century, by the end of the nineteenth century there would be 'a new social upheaval, which will be even more violent to the extent that the bourgeoisie is more fierce in its reaction'.[64] At the same time, it was noted that the development of the revolution would not depend 'on anyone's free will, but inevitable, having its *raison d'être* in the very nature of things'.[65] In substance, what counted, here, was Giovanni Rossi's sharp formula 'Prepare evolution, achieve revolution'.[66] This formula could bring together both the socialist circles around Costa and the 'pure' and 'experimental' evolutionists. After all, had Prampolini not argued that revolution was 'simply an inevitable phenomenon',[67] above all if the forces that evolution was accumulating '[found] the regular paths to be closed-off' and were thus compelled to throw themselves 'into disorders'?[68] And in his famous book – which had become a point of reference for all socialists – Colajanni had written that 'evolution' and 'revolution' could not be taken as 'distinct, opposed, antinomic' categories, 'when one is but a moment of the other, the beginning or the fulfilment of a historical phase, and not a capricious or accidental episode in this phase'.[69] This question of the relation between evolution and revolution was framed in the terms of the 'socialist science' of the era. One telling formulation provides a rather sharp image of the way in which this question was understood at the beginning of the 1880s: 'The rev-

61 Ibid.
62 Zirardini, 'Evoluzione e Rivoluzione', *Il sole dell'avvenire*, 20 July 1889.
63 The programme appears as a supplement to the 6 September 1881 *Avanti!*
64 'Risposta al corrispondente Imolese della Democrazia', *Avanti!*, 5–6 October 1882.
65 'Aspettiamo fiduciosi', *Avanti!*, 20–21 May 1882.
66 Cardias (Rossi), 'Accademia', *Avanti!*, 13 April 1884.
67 'L'ora della rivoluzione', *Il Scamiciato*, 19 August 1883.
68 'Evoluzione e rivoluzione', *Il Scamiciato*, 12 August 1883.
69 Colajanni 1899, p. 384.

olution is the ... triumph of reason and science'.[70] The fundamental question connected to this – the relation between determinism and voluntarism – would continually be presented anew throughout the history of socialist cultures, and addressed in diverse 'scientific contexts', sometimes at very refined theoretical levels.

The threads being arranged in a now largely composed pattern were the strings of a 'scientific socialism' deeply penetrating into the fundamental structures of a culture that had developed over a long period. In this case, too, the expression 'scientific socialism' had no need for Marx (or Engels, in this specific case) in order to become a naturally accepted and fully commonplace moment of the socialist universe. In this regard, I think that we should fully agree with the argument that a fundamental aspect of the effectiveness of Engels's constructions lay above all in his capacity 'to transmit elements of thinking and practice developed within the working-class movement itself in a form in which it could become an intrinsic part of the architecture of the new theory'.[71]

Moreover, Marx and Engels themselves did not pose the question of 'scientific socialism' in a univocal manner, based on any axiomatic conviction that they were founders of a 'scientific revolution'. This was in fact an expression widely in use among French socialist circles even before 1848;[72] an expression that Marx did not consider it necessary to dedicate any systematic reflection to, and only used occasionally after 1848; and which he picked up again in 1880, upon Lafargue's request, 'probably only as a concession to an expression used in the French language', and 'would not again use in German, up till his death'.[73] Marx was convinced that he was working on a 'revolutionary science', but this had nothing to do with the construction of a new systematic of 'scientific socialism'; rather, he was interested in the science produced by a real historical movement, finally glimpsing the other side of historical experience. As long as the proletarians 'look for science', Marx warned, 'they merely make systems'; only when they also see the 'side' of the overthrow of the existing social order – which cannot just happen arbitrarily – do we have 'the science produced by the historical movement and associating itself consciously with it' – a science that 'has ceased to be doctrinaire and has become revolutionary'.[74]

---

70 'Teoria rivoluzionaria', *La Favilla*, 17 June 1883.

71 Stedman Jones 1977, p. 103.

72 Pelger 1983.

73 Schieder 1983, p. 106.

74 *MECW*, Vol. 6, p. 178.

It was the polemic over Dühring that gave fresh impetus and meaning to the expression 'scientific socialism'. The fact that Dühring – considered a representative of science in German social-democratic circles in a period in which we can speak of a genuine 'social-democratic infatuation for Dühring'[75] – accused Marx of a lack of scientificity, led Engels to insist on the Trier philosopher's fully 'scientific socialism' and to retort by accusing the German professor of being the latest epigone of 'utopian socialism'. The transformation of this book, born in a specific context, into a true and proper 'encyclopaedia of Marxism' owed both to the way in which it was constructed (perhaps the first time that Engels had posed himself 'the problem of the consequences of a theory that becomes a material force, which it bears in its very form')[76] and the fact that it became an object of political struggle within the SPD itself, in conformity with this party's own practical needs.

It seems rather unlikely that the use of the expression 'scientific socialism' in Italy across the late 1870s and early 1880s can be attributed to the direct influence of the 'encyclopaedic' atmosphere – already marked by the 'will to distinguish' – driven by the *Anti-Dühring* and its echoes. First of all, on account of this book's publication history: the first Italian edition came out in 1901.[77] We should not over-exaggerate the importance of this fact; after all, some circles (however tiny) could in any case refer to the 1878 German original, and its intellectual legacy mainly came by way of a reduced version of the text, *Socialism: Utopian and Scientific*.[78] An Italian edition of this latter text, translated by Pasquale Martignetti, first appeared in 1883; printed at Martignetti's own expense in Benevento,[79] it had very little distribution, and the 1880 French edition was perhaps more readily available.[80]

Tellingly, however, the expression 'scientific socialism' appeared in *La Plebe* even in 1876,[81] in reference to Marx and his economic theory, albeit in a general context totally different to the slightly later scenario of *Anti-Dühring* and its various derivatives. Nor do the uses of this expression at the beginning of the 1880s seem much different, even though chronologically speaking, more direct influences would now have been possible. It is true that in 1882 it was said that

75 See Dowe and Tenfelde 1983, p. 196.

76 Negt 1979, p. 112.

77 Published in Milan and Palermo, with a preface by Enrico Ferri and an introduction by Bernstein.

78 There have been 26 Italian editions of this text, 9 of them before the Fascist period.

79 Engels 1883.

80 Engels 1880. Martignetti translated this version, published by Paul Lafargue, into Italian.

81 'Un trionfo del socialismo', *La Plebe*, 22 October 1876.

'scientific socialism' is 'a modern thing',[82] with Lassalle and Marx – and also Bebel – named as 'divulgers' of 'scientific socialism',[83] yet overall it seems that it was a sense of continuity that prevailed.

In substance, 'scientific socialism' seems rather to have been the product of the third stage of socialism's development, as Malon and Gnocchi Viani defined it; that is, from 'the scientific *or* experimental'[84] period, from which followed a 'scientific *and* experimental' socialism.[85] This was a science that had much in common with what Colajanni was elaborating in the same period: Ghisleri was, fundamentally, not mistaken when he recalled many years later that the young republican-socialist doctor had published 'the first book of scientific socialism in Italy'.[86] Indeed, a contemporary review in a paper without any scientific pretensions emphasised that Colajanni's volume had established 'the principles of scientific socialism ... and their relations with natural laws and society'.[87]

Above all, we should emphasise an element that was present even in an author as extraneous to Marx as Colajanni. Namely, that during this turn at the end of the 1870s and beginning of the 1880s, there was an increasing tendency to associate 'scientific socialism' with Marx's name. This association proceeded through paths that did not necessarily coincide with the systematisation that resulted from the polemic with Herr Dühring.

2 Socialist Culture: Political Economy

The various threads of socialist culture were thus brought together on the terrain of sociology – in its specific dimension of criminal anthropology – as the

82 'La questione sociale', *Avanti!*, 13 August 1882.

83 See the obituary appearing upon the (clearly false) news of Bebel's death, in *Il sole dell'avvenire*, 23 September 1882.

84 XXX (probably Gnocchi Viani), 'Lettere sul socialismo contemporaneo', *La Plebe*, 12 *fiorile* 87 (1 May 1875).

85 'Risposta di un socialista alle quattro conferenze del Senatore Rossi', *La Plebe*, 17 September 1882. My emphasis.

86 Letter from Ghisleri to Colajanni, 26 February 1898, in Ganci (ed.) 1959.

87 Colajanni explicitly attributed one of the bases for his 'scientific socialism' to Marx, who had 'established that social evolutions are not determined by sentimental considerations. Their causes are found in the economic structure, in the means of production of exchange that govern the distribution of wealth, and, in consequence, the formation of classes and their hierarchy; they take place not because they correspond to a higher ideal of justice, but because they accord with the economic order of the moment' – Colajanni 1899, p. 275.

attempt was made to coordinate them 'scientifically'. Sociology, understood as a general knowledge, allowed incursions into multiple sectorial disciplines, whose particular scientific statuses tended to be attributed to certain commonplace methods of cognition. Very probably it was this mechanism that allowed socialists gradually to approach a science whose modern genesis and contemporary development were perceived as hostile to the subaltern classes and the cultures representing them. In his *Crime and Punishment* Dostoyevsky depicted the ideological horizon of a 'modern' Russian proprietor of the 1860s, describing 'Mr. Lebeziatnikov who keeps up with modern ideas explained the other day that compassion is forbidden nowadays by science itself, and that that's what is done now in England, where there is political economy'.[88] At the same time, the great majority of socialists would have perfectly recognised themselves in this image of political economy coming from the mouth of the poor, oppressed Marmeladov.[89]

Indeed, no discipline seemed more marked by its symbiosis with its object of study – in this case, modern capitalism starting from the second half of the eighteenth century, a period in which the general use of the expression 'political economy' emerged, even if with a different meaning. During its genesis it was linked to a determinate social form, strongly anchored as it was in an aristocratic-bourgeois, or even solely bourgeois environment.

Before 1848, Marx himself had counterposed 'the economists[,] scientific representatives of the bourgeois class' to 'the socialists and the Communists[,] the theoreticians of the proletarian class'.[90] He had emphasised the fact that the economists 'express the relations of bourgeois production, the division of labour, credit, money, etc., as fixed, immutable, eternal categories'.[91] He had underlined that the 'Classics', Smith and Ricardo – 'historians' of the development of capitalism in their own time – had investigated 'how wealth is acquired in bourgeois production relations', formulating 'these relations into categories, into laws' and considering poverty 'merely the pang which accompanies every childbirth, in nature as in industry'.[92] At the same time, his scientific pro-

88 Dostoyevsky 1917, p. 13.

89 A socialist paper wrote a number of years later 'Political economy corrected feudal vices, developed the trades and industries, and increased the production of wealth; but its egoistical, anti-humanitarian theories and its antinomies conserving privilege and perpetuating misery must be replaced with a social science that is to the benefit of all humanity': 'Teoria rivoluzionaria', *La Favilla*, 17 June 1883.

90 *MECW*, Vol. 6, p. 177.

91 *MECW*, Vol. 6, p. 162.

92 *MECW*, Vol. 6, p. 176.

gramme – if also defined as a *critique of political economy* – did then enter into the dimension of economic categories, reformulated in such a way as to construct an analytical model capable of inserting the economy, history and society into one same cognitive panorama. Certainly it was not easy for the socialists to grasp *this* economic dimension of the *critique of political economy*: grasping Marx's own *quality* as an economist, within the terms of the professionalisation of this discipline. The sociological route to Marx-the-economist would end up appearing the natural, indeed almost compulsory one – that is, using parameters drawn from an accepted and familiar culture in order to make recognisable a scholar whose contours it would otherwise have been difficult to define with any clarity.

In post-unification Italy, socialists considered economists an essential part of the deployment of forces opposed to them. This ought not be surprising, if we consider that 'from the outset the caste of economists was an expert component of the post-unification ruling class, an indispensable link between the governing and the governed, between the state and civil society'.[93] Even less so, if we consider that faced with any signs of thinking that might translate into social legislation, the leading Italian economist of the period, Francesco Ferrara, would warn of looming socialism, threatening that 'socialism is not to be discussed, but to be crushed'.[94]

Still in 1875, socialists defined the economists as 'theologians of bourgeois society',[95] though they combined this evaluation with constant attention to economic disciplines and their developments in these years, taking an overall view that was much more problematic and uneven than this definition implies.

Already in 1874, *La Plebe* had highlighted the need for a study of the economy from the viewpoint of those whom the economists' analysis considered the 'inevitable' other side: those who suffered pain and poverty. The 'economists' had rightly noted that 'machinery and the division of labour [were] a great portent of modern industry'. This was perfectly true; and yet for proletarians this phenomenon had added fresh woes to their already deeply distressed condition. This was the central node that the socialists had to address, and from this emerged the need 'to throw themselves into studying economic questions and to struggle over them'; the need, indeed, to organise as a class, 'by workshops and by trades', and 'study the great question of machinery and

93 Faucci 1981, p. 19.

94 Ferrara 1975, p. 319.

95 xxx (probably Gnocchi Viani), 'Lettere sul socialismo contemporaneo', *La Plebe*, 12 *fiorile* 87 (1 May 1875).

the division of labour'.[96] 'Studying and resolving' these questions would 'thus be the same thing'. This latter expression was indicative for future approaches to a theoretical dimension in which these two terms already represented an original element of the proletariat's 'science'.

Moreover, it is hardly without significance that the interest in economic questions was focused on the Milan economists' conference that officially opened up both the question of 'the battle over method' and the question of *Kathedersozialismus* – barely a year after Francesco Ferrara had made violent attacks on 'economic Germanism'[97] in a 'dramatic, visceral' essay.[98] In this text, Ferrara sought to mash together the *Kathedersozialisten* and the true socialists, and to identify the spectres of the German author of *Capital* lurking behind the curtain of 'Germanism'. He thus warned that '[t]he penniless man who reads Marx's *Capital* from the start will inevitably succumb to the melodies of this ruinous siren, and crash into the cliffs'.[99] Also telling was a congress taking place this same year, inaugurating the third series of the *Biblioteca dell'Economista* [Economist's Library] – the series directed by Gerolamo Boccardo, specialising in 'the intersections of knowledges'.[100] In the first volume of this series, Boccardo published Roscher, the founder and champion of German economic historicism. *La Plebe* sent its own 'representative'[101] to the Congress, commenting on it in a manner that showed a capacity to distinguish between the different levels in which economics and politics were being articulated. The reporter particularly highlighted the theoretical novelties of the Lombardo-Venetians, in particular underlining the progressive character of an economic science that would make it possible to overcome the doctrinal abstractions of Italian Smithianism, also thanks to the widened horizons afforded by a correct application of the 'positive method'. As *La Plebe* noted, 'statistics is the new and growing organ of economic science in particular, bringing it many novel facts that had not hitherto been observed, and as such it is compelled to expand its doctrine in order to remain at the level of the times'.[102] The so-called Germanists' theoretical-methodological premises, and the sphere of observation that most interested them, were also considered worthy of note: indeed, 'hearing

96 'La divisione del lavoro e le macchine', *La Plebe*, 12 *pratile* 83 (7 June 1874).

97 'Il germanesimo economico in Italia', *Nuova Antologia*, 1874.

98 See Macchioro 1996.

99 'Il germanesimo economico in Italia', *Nuova Antologia*, 1874, p. 985.

100 An expression used by Macchioro 1995, p. 11.

101 The representative in question was Benoît Malon: see Briguglio 1979, p. 21.

102 XXX (Rappr. della PLEBE al congresso), 'Il Congresso degli economisti in Milano. Riassunto ed appunti di un socialista', *La Plebe*, 26 *nevoso* 87–15 January 1875.

the sweeping promises of the economists intervening in the first session, we might have believed that they wanted to throw themselves wholeheartedly into social reform'. Yet despite these positive premises, the Congress 'only managed to formulate three very modest proposals', and the report thus concluded:

> Before breaking up the Congress founded a Society for the *progress of economic studies*. Well, this Society will be of no interest to the workers; after all, in its own way the Congress had confirmed the truth that *the liberation of the workers must be the work of the workers themselves*.[103]

Certainly, the mountain had given birth to a mouse,[104] but this did not mean that socialists would give up looking everywhere – even in the elaborations of non-socialist economists – for the elements of theory and political economy with which they thought they could make their *own* edifice more robust.

From this point of view, relations with the multiform world of the Italian *Kathedersozialisten* – relations that were also long-term in character – tended to appear through a complex web of 'intersecting paths'. Ideological objections were but one aspect of the problem, and not even the most important one. At the same time, numerous threads would link socialist militants' economic interpretations to certain sections of *Kathedersozialismus*, even if these connections were not immediately apparent: and this was true both in terms of specifically economic questions, and in terms of the links among economic methodologies and, more generally, theories of social development. Not least among these, naturally, was the sociological reading of Marxian economic categories. It is certainly true that the rather different structural conditions of Germany and Italy make it difficult to establish a relation between the discussions in each country that is not only 'extrinsic and accidental in character', and that much of the debate on 'economic Germanism' was 'predominantly an aspect of the more general battle between free-traders and protectionists over

103 Ibid.

104 Note that in this period, together with 'maximum' positions that were meant to be theoretically founded on a teleological view of social development, there were also true and proper 'cries of pain' that simply needed a frame of reference different from the 'orthodox' one, in order to feed some sense of hope. 'You will have lots of trouble, with the sophisms of your economists' school [claiming that] *industrial phenomena are unchangeable and men must not try to change them*; do you know what they'll tell you in reply? *Any* labour has the right to a just payment; this is nature's law, and we want our toil to be at least recompensed with enough to sate our hunger'. 'Osservazioni d'un socialista all'economista del giornale Il Secolo', *La Plebe*, 19 *piovoso* 84 (7 February 1874).

Italy's capitalist development'.[105] All the more so given that the most representative figures of the Lombardo-Venetians like Lampertico and Cossa were far from linear in their theoretical vision:

> On the one hand they introduced the new theoretical-practical elaborations of the German historical school into Italy, and on the other hand they remained anchored to Italian liberalism's Anglophile tradition, proposing the English model as the highest example of balance and effectiveness in the resolution of social problems.[106]

This was only an apparent contradiction, with the ruling climate of 'mediation' allowing this and other such forms of co-existence.[107] At the same time, however, the long wave of certain sectors of *Kathedersozialismus*, which had been entirely minoritarian in 1875, also had its effects on the various periodic phases in which liberal Italy flirted with reform, in particular with regard to the 'taxation question'.[108] This was a terrain of encounters and clashes that the socialists could not simply forsake, and which also had implications for the definition of their theoretical-political identity (Marxist or otherwise), that were anything but taken for granted.

It is no chance thing that among the exponents of the Lombardo-Venetian school, Ferrara particularly targeted Vito Cusumano, in 1874 defining him as 'the most pure and resolute adherent'[109] of 'economic Germanism'. Indeed, his 'teacher' Cossa had also reproached him for what he considered his excessive socialist sympathies.[110] In his German experience the young Sicilian economist had in fact proved very sensitive to the theories of Wagner. This latter in a sense represented the 'left' wing of the German *Kathedersozialisten*, even to the extent that in a letter to Lampertico, Cusumano noted the spreading claims that he had drawn close to the socialists.[111] Nor is it any coincidence that Lampertico, who had some of Cusumano's 'reports' from Germany published in the *Giornale di Vicenza*, altered what he considered their most radical (and indeed, most telling) points, which would not have been accepted in the very moder-

105 Ragionieri 1961, pp. 34–5.

106 Scaldaferri 1992, p. 242. On the methodologically composite character of Italian *Kathedersozialismus*, see Gozzi 1989, Roversi 1986 and Schiera 1988.

107 See Macchioro 1996.

108 Favilli 1990.

109 'Il germanesimo economico in Italia', *Nuova Antologia*, 1874.

110 Cossa 1976.

111 Cusumano to Lampertico, 29 January 1873, cited in Salvo 1979, p. 61.

ate environment of the 'Lombardo-Venetian' reformers.[112] Indeed, following in Wagner's wake, already in the first half of the 1870s Cusuman conceived the system of free competition in *historical* terms, did not consider the right to property to be without its limits, and was a convinced upholder of the distributive and generally equalising character of fiscal policies. Moreover, next to the productive sphere of a free-trade economy, he hypothesised the existence of a '*common* and *collective* economy, which [must] not be an end in itself, like the private [economy], but a means of satisfying common needs'.[113] In substance, at the very moment at which he began his profession as an economist, Cusomano seemed to consider the 'social question' to be the main testing ground on which the discipline ought to prove itself. In his view, the 'optimists'' approach had already failed this test – namely, the stance of those who thought it sufficient to do everything possible to increase production and then leave the question of distribution to the free play of the market. Why, then – Cusumano asked himself – was 'the relative condition of the working class worsening' even though production had enormously increased over the course of the nineteenth century? And why, 'if increasing production [were] the only means for resolving the Social Question … has our century, famous for its inventions and discoveries, still not resolved it?'[114]

When he expressed these positions, Cusumano was absolutely not thinking about the possibility of a 'socialist system', and still less of encouraging notions of revolution; rather, he can be considered one of the first intellectuals 'devoted' to establishing a decisive counterposition between reform and revolution, insisting on the necessity of the former in order to ward off the latter. 'Reforms, reforms, and more reforms: that is the last word of our practical programme'.[115] And yet he came to represent an element of the fabric of relations in which certain socialist readings of economics and Marx himself would now mature, a fabric much of whose weft would henceforth be woven, as we shall see, by Achille Loria. This owed not so much to the possibility of the Sicilian

112 Cited in Salvo 1979, pp. 48–50.

113 Cusumano to Lampertico 6 June 1872, cited in Salvo 1979, p. 52.

114 See Cusumano 1873–4 (quote from 1874, pp. 314–15).

115 Cusumano 1875, p. 360. In the same period he had written to Léon Walras in the same terms, insisting on the economist's duty to 'breathe the living atmosphere of his time', which in his time revolved around the 'social question' and thus the need for state intervention to 'influence social facts'. 'Socialism today', he wrote, 'the so-called *Fourth Estate*, the *red spectre*, must be fought with *reforms, economic* and legislative *reforms*'. Letter to Walras of 3 January 1873, in Jaffé (ed.) 1965, Vol. I.

economist joining the PSLI in 1892[116] – even if this would not have been without significance – as to his insistence on a 'method' of economic analysis that was by no means extraneous to the general coordinates of the socialist culture now being constructed.

We can add a further piece of the mosaic to the ones mentioned above, even if not with the unrealisable goal of constructing a coherent image; namely, noting that the first widely expository interpretation of Marx 'the scholar' – the Marx of *Capital* – owed precisely to Cusumano, given that the previous works of reference by Covelli[117] and Di Menza[118] (if very different in nature), had more episodic and/or ideologically oriented characteristics. Cusumano's writings were of a whole different depth. Notwithstanding their rather controversial relation with the original sources,[119] he did manage to provide an image of the

116 See Spoto 1984.

117 Emilio Covelli concerned himself with *Capital* in the context of the Italian presentation of a work by Dühring, of whom he had been a pupil. The references to Marx's work were substantially accidental ones, even it is worth noting that he insisted on a 'positive' interpretation of *Capital* in line with the 'most rational and modern method of scientific socialism'. See E. Covelli, 'Storia critica dell'economia politica e del socialismo del dott. E. Dühring', *Rivista Partenopea*, no. 7–8, July–August 1871, 9–10, September–October, 1–2, January–February 1872, 3–4, March–April. Quotation from this last issue, p. 117. See also Masini 1951. In truth this was not the 'first news' of *Capital* in Italy, as Masini's title claims, for already in 1867 a passage from the preface accompanied by the news of a work, 'das Kapital', 'which after the books of Proudhon will mark a luminous era in the annals of social literature' had appeared in the Naples paper *Libertà e giustizia*. See Basso 1962. Again two years later, in a 23-page pamphlet, Covelli returned to *Capital's* 'positivism'. See Covelli 1874.

118 Giuseppe Di Menza, an 'advisor' and secretary to the Palermo Accademia delle Scienze accosted Marx – and not the original texts – with the open intention of opposing him, demonstrating the falseness of his 'supreme postulates'. His Marx is a substantially Proudhonian one: 'Marx's doctrines do not even have the merit of novelty, for among other things they are but a retailoring of his predecessor Proudhon, although almost always without reference': see Di Menza 'Le condizioni sociali dei nostril tempi', in *Atti della Accademia di Scienze, Lettere e Arti di Palermo*, n.s., Vol. IV, 1874, pp. 1–25; 'Evoluzione del socialismo. Carlo Marx e le sue dottrine. Memoria (Appendice alla memoria precedente), on pp. 1–18. Quotation from p. 5.

119 Bravo 1992, p. 91, has raised serious doubts as to whether Cusumano could 'have directly read this work'. Andréas 1963, p. 74, has noted that Cusumano's 1875 volume was 'based on Jäger's [work] from 1873'. Jäger's *Der moderne Sozialismus*, described by Bravo as an 'important and informative work', appeared in Berlin in January of 1873, at the same time that the young Sicilian economist was in the city, and there can be no doubt that he made great use of it, in particular in the first draft of his work appearing in *Archivio Giuridico*. However, after this first approach Cusumano did proceed to get his hands on a copy of the

'scientific' Marx and Marx the 'scientific-socialist'; an image that was not only unknown in Italian culture, including socialist culture, in the Italy of the early 1870s, but was in its own way linked to the battles of culture and ideas toward which the men of the 'new method' were now gravitating, by way of the 'social question'. Indeed, Cusumano sought to bring to light the 'method' of Marx's analysis, in particular the distinction between the *essence* and *form* of economic systems and the historical and thus relative validity of economic laws. On this aspect, he openly asserted that Marx and the 'historical school' shared a common territory, namely that 'although he takes care to find regularity in economic phenomena, he seems to attribute a different economic form to each different period of historical-economic development'.[120] The difference between the 'historical school' and Marx seemed less a matter of method than the fact that this school 'aspire[d] to a relative and not absolute good, the economic ideal that is so difficult to achieve'.[121] Notwithstanding his critique of aspects of Marx's theory (including far from marginal ones, like his theory of value and theory of profit) Cusumano seems particularly to have emphasised the political divide stemming from this counterposition of 'relative' and 'absolute': the separation between 'reform' and 'revolution'. All things considered, we could conclude from this that while he found Marx largely acceptable as an economist, he found 'Marx the revolutionary' unacceptable, and so too, evidently, the aspects of 'Marx the economist' that supplied the basic arguments for 'Marx the revolutionary'. This was not without significance, particularly in light of the fact that the 'reformist' reading of Marx in Italy did not only begin *after* the 'crisis' at the end of the century, upon the instigation of the 'Bernstein-Debatte'. As we shall see, at least on the political plane – but not only there – the 'non-revolutionary' interpretation of Marx was a non-negligible element of the shifting basis of his influence. This was an aspect of what has been called 'the struggle between the Social Question and Marxism to "swallow" the other';[122] and if it reached its

second German edition of *Capital* and to study it (letter to Lampertico, 9 June 1874, cited in Filippi 1984, p. 143). So it seems probable that though Jäger remained his 'basis', his reading could now be considered the fruit of an awareness strengthened by a direct relationship with the text. Spoto's propensity is to see his analysis as founded on the 'direct reading of the text' (Spoto 1984, p. 235).

120 See Cusumano 1875, p. 316.

121 Ibid.

122 The expression appears in Macchioro 1970, p. 501. He very opportunely shows the influence that Cusumano and the 'debates over the direction of the age' had for Loria and his generation. He cites a passage from Loria's memoirs (Loria 1927, pp. 13 et sqq.) in which the author of the *Analisi della proprietà capitalista* recalled that these discussions and read-

culmination in the 1890s, it had its roots in the mid-1870s, in a climate pregnant with new directions for state economic policy (the beginning of protectionist legislation) and changes internal to the governing class (the parliamentary revolution). Indeed, Cusumano was particularly hard on the Italian socialism in the 1870s, which in its majority had taken Bakuninist and not 'German' choices. His opinion of a socialism that was profoundly influenced by 'oddballs ... political intriguers ... [and] ten-a-penny journalists'[123] curiously seems to echo Engels's. Could there, then, be moments of encounter with a socialism whose 'science' would 'naturally' temper the dangerous extremes resulting from a 'free will' permeated with an ineffective revolutionism?

There did simultaneously remain the indubitable fact that at least part of socialist culture was interested in looking into 'bourgeois' political economy in order to find arguments that could be useful for strengthening its own perspective. The attention paid to the Milan economists' congress was but one symptom of this. And the question in which the 'naturalness' of economic laws should be understood made the orthodox economists a common enemy of both the socialists and the *Kathedersozialisten*.

The 'orthodox' Smithian economists declared that the present state of social and economic organisation was 'natural'. Conversely, 'thanks to the study of the natural sciences and history' the socialists had been able to discover the 'progressiveness' of human history, and thus formulate an assessment that was almost an appeal:

> You economists who speak of natural laws: are you sure that you've found them? Don't you think that a Kepler, a Galileo, a Descartes, a Newton of social science could emerge, and discover a natural law of the social dynamic, explaining the contradictory phenomena that you now take for unchangeable general laws as you confuse effect for cause, the particular with the general?[124]

---

ings 'suddenly ignited' his 'frenetic love for the new disciplines [Economics] ... it was a true lightning bolt, a thunderstorm of a passion' (cited in Macchioro 1970, p. 493).

123 See Cusumano 'La questione sociale in Europa con ispeciale riguardo all'Inghliterra, alla Germania e all'Italia', April 1875 lecture at the University of Palermo. The original text is lost, but Salvatore Ingenieros Napolitano provides an extensive account of the lecture in *La Lince* of 12, 19 and 26 April 1875. The quote appears in the 19 April edition. *La Plebe* also reported news of German socialism drawn from this lecture: see 'Il socialismo in Germania', 16 *fiorile* 87 (5 May 1875).

124 'Note e pensieri sull'economia sociale', *La Plebe*, 21 January 1876. The article had already been published the previous year.

This augured the coming arrival of a 'Newton [a Darwin?] of social science'; and we know that this urgently expressed need would indeed be materialised. Through the study of the natural sciences and history, the reasoning for the existence of a socialist future – and the expectations in it – would, certainly, be strengthened.

The search for arguments that could legitimise and consolidate the socialist perspective – also looking into the works of non-socialist economists – began to develop very early, and tended to be articulated around the theme of the possibility and/or inevitability of collective property. For example, in the Italy of 1873, the year of John Stuart Mill's death, the idea was circulating that

> the most illustrious of modern economists and publicists, after having in his golden book of *freedom* defended the boundless individualism of the economists with such knowledge and with such energy of logic and will, [Mill] end[ed] up changing his thinking in his last work, and accepting the collectivist theories that he had earlier so doggedly fought.[125]

This was a 'metaphorical'[126] Mill rather than a real one. This interpretation of him was particularly widespread among the socialists who Malon[127] and Gnocchi-Viani[128] had pointed in this direction, and one repeated in countless articles dedicated to the identity-defining question of collectivism.

Indeed, the model of collective property was becoming one of the discriminating parameters in the construction of a more precise socialist identity.[129] The very progress of socialism was often judged in terms of the (real or presumed) level of support for such a model, in particular on the part of 'bourgeois

125 'L'Internazionale', *La Plebe*, 4 *glaciale* 84 (11 October 1873).

126 Macchioro 1993, p. 242.

127 See Malon 1979.

128 'If Mill were alive today, he would be repudiated by the economists, and socialists would list his name among their precursors': Gnocchi Viani in his Preface to Mill 1880, p. 7.

129 In 1879 Gnocchi-Viani had insisted that this link between collectivism and socialism was indissoluble. This also meant re-proposing its connection to the relation between science and socialism. Indeed, before becoming the common element of all schools of socialism, collectivism had already been posed on the scientific plane, and certainly not starting with Marx: 'The first to baptise collectivism in rational science and give it its own place in the world was Colins, born five years before the famous epoch of 1789' (in fact six: Jean-Guillaume-César-Alexandre-Hippolite de Colins, a French economist of Belgian origin, was born in 1783 and died in 1859): see Gnocchi-Viani 1879a, pp. 4–6.

economists': for example, Laveleye, like 'the famous Stuart Mill, the most illustrious contemporary English thinker' already before him, was presented as a partisan of this model.[130] This was supposedly a 'natural process', that had persuaded

> other Stuart Mills to recognise that little by little the 'collectivism' [being discussed] in the crucible of experimental science [made it possible] to predict the architectonic lines of a social organisation whose public functions probably [would not be] either political or religious, but clearly social ...[131]

From the 1880s the discussion on land property, its origins and legitimacy became a very important moment of the debate among economists in Italy,[132] setting in confrontation all the different trends of the *Kathedersozialismus* universe. The socialists were also very much involved, seeking to grasp the 'natural' tendencies toward an increase in the number of Stuart Mills.

It was again Colajanni, now devoted to delineating all the coordinates of 'scientific socialism' who tried to draw the first conclusions from the international debate on collective management of land.

He affirmed that even if collectivism had 'become the common basis of all schools of socialism' it ought not therefore be considered as narrowly linked to this movement alone. The *facts* gave a clear indication of this – 'facts relating to the past and present existence of property systems that we can assimilate to collectivism; facts relating to the recent, purely *objective* studies, devoted to [this question] by many eminent writers not active among the ranks of socialists'. He named a great number of authors whose lowest common denominator was that they had not taken an *a priori* position against collective property over land: from Schäffle to De Laveleye, from Gide to Walras, from the late Mill to Spencer. Moreover, collective property over land still existed in many areas of the contemporary world, and was not only limited to the Russian *mir* – though this did also seem a most interesting element, charged with future possibilities. 'It [was] not, as some believe, some special inheritance of the Slavic world, and represents a *phase of development* and not of *stasis*'. What Colajanni called 'the return to collective property' did not at all imply contradicting or denying the

130 'Un economista borghese che encomia e predica la proprietà collettiva', *La Plebe*, 29 March 1876.

131 Gnocchi-Viani, 'Il trinomio sociale', *La Plebe*, 21 *germile* 87 (28 March 1875).

132 And not only them: see Grossi 1977.

theory of evolution, since the future order would not suffer all the impediments and hindrances of the past. Rather, it marked a phase of its progress.[133]

The socialists' interlocutors remained, necessarily, all those who moved within the atmosphere of *Kathedersozialismus*. The socialist attitude toward the *Kathedersozialisten*, from the Milan congress onward, remained the same: an appreciation of their attitude toward questions of method in economic science, and likewise appreciation of the centrality that the 'social question' had taken on in the context of their elaborations, but severe criticism of both the modesty of their social and political proposals and their lack of courage in taking to their full conclusion the principles associated with their consideration of economics.

Not by chance, a text produced at precisely this moment circulated among the workers of Milan in the early 1880s, together with Carlo Cafiero's *Compendio del Capitale* and Osvaldo Gnocchi-Viani's *Le tre internazionali*, almost symbolising the ideological references of the organised proletariat of Italy's most modern great city.[134] It was an open letter that Jules Guesde had written to Senator Lampertico, published in *La Plebe* in 1876[135] and then transformed into a 31 page pamphlet the following year; a publication that enjoyed wide distribution even among working-class circles.

In this letter Guesde addressed Lampertico, trying to grasp the contradiction between his purely economic-contingent justifications for private property over land – and not the 'right' to it – which were thus historical and relative in nature, and the absoluteness of his opposition to socialist collectivism. For Guesde, from a scientific point of view the theories of Lampertico and the *Kathedersozialisten* in general were fundamentally compatible with socialist evolution, but this conflicted with the logic of their interests as landowners. If it was not a question of immediate social interest, the logic of property was a matter of sentimental residues, destined to be transcended over the course of time.

Thus Pietro Ellero, another key figure concerned with 'mediation' and the 'social question' – and not in truth an economist, but a 'positive' jurist who denounced the apologetic economists on the basis of his own positions, critical toward capitalism – was effectively subsumed into the wide array of *in pectore* socialists 'given his critique of property, his interest in the social question, and his dissent from the optimistic economists'.[136] And if, in response to the

133 Colajanni 1887, quotes from pp. 3 and 16.

134 See Anzi 1917, p. 17.

135 'Della proprietà. Lettera al Senatore Lampertico', *La Plebe*, 19 September 1876.

136 XXX, 'La questione sociale per Pietro Ellero', *La Plebe*, 1 *piovoso* 87 (20 January 1875), 4

heightened appreciation of Ellero following a further volume of his,[137] some criticised the excessive enthusiasm for a book by a non-socialist, *La Plebe* counterposed the sentimental, not-yet socialist Ellero to the scholar Ellero, who had become a socialist.[138]

Naturally, someone who was a socialist *in potential* did not inevitably become an *actual* socialist, as De Laveleye's case (and many others) made clear. This did lead to disappointment; but at the same time, the reactions very clearly showed one of the key elements of the socialists' relationship with whatever kind of socialism might come from the 'university chair': it was said that 'we should be grateful to De Laveleye anyhow, for having clearly acknowledged the social question from his university chair, for having recognised that there is something – a lot – to be done. After all, it does set a good example for an economist to speak in the cause of the exploited'.[139]

We have seen that this was only one key – albeit a fundamental one – to explaining the ensemble of highly ambiguous relations that linked *Katheder-sozialismus* to militant socialism. This was a complex set of relations that also grew around the common conviction as to the 'historicity' of the great economic formations and thus of their 'laws' of functioning; and this would lead the socialists to a more mature consciousness of the need for a relationship with political economy that was not excessively filtered through the logics of subalternity, as expressed through the 'cry of pain'. A comment that Filippo Turati made with some emphasis during his rich exchanges with Colajanni over *Socialismo e Sociologia criminale* was highly indicative of the levels that this awareness had now reached. Responding to a Colajanni who seemed to have established a relationship between socialism and economics that lacked any particular depth, Turati posed the problem in the following terms:

> it seems to me that socialism is not only a *way of seeing economic development* (which is, moreover, an ugly and ambiguous phrase) but also a programme of action based on an interpretation of natural and historic laws that is rather different from that of orthodox economics: hence it is not only a *natural science* but also an *applied science* or *art*, and it does

---

piovoso 87 (23 January 1875), 8 *piovoso* 87 (27 January 1875), 12 *piovoso* 87 (31 January 1875), 16 *piovoso* 87 (4 February 1875), 22 *piovoso* 87 (10 February 1875), 26 *piovoso* 87 (14 February 1875) and 30 *piovoso* 87 (18 February 1875). The book here reviewed was Ellero 1874.

137 Ellero 1879.

138 'Diventerà socialista', *La Plebe*, 4 May 1879.

139 See A.P., 'Elementi di economia politica', *La Plebe*, (monthly), 2, 1883.

> not only *provide elements* to sociology, but also makes use of elements of sociology for its own deductions and proposals.[140]

From this we can see a consideration of economics that is structured according to various levels, open to different valences: a sharp distinction with respect to orthodox political economy; the translatability of theory into socialist economic policy, implicitly also meaning an accentuation of the socialist character of the theory itself; and a two-way interaction between sociology and economics. Of course, the very consideration of Marx 'the scholar', which as we will see was growing vigorously in the socialist milieu of the early 1880s, made no little contribution to the problem of political economy being posed in wider terms. It mattered little that he was extraneous to this type of economic sociology: the dominant cultural climate and the requirements of socialist activism allowed him to be effortlessly assimilated into this interpretation. More than sixty years ago, Luigi Bulferetti very effectively described this interactive ensemble:

> Sociology provided stimulus, also in an effectively socialistic sense, to the study of political and juridical questions under the name of social questions. It injected fresh vigour – even if also a polemical one – into economic studies. According a priority focus to nature, society as nature, man's needs, and the world of use, meant attributing maximal importance also to what had until then been called economics, and the greatest contribution to sociology ultimately came from economists, jurists, and political scientists, who, with their various names, in substance concerned themselves with the same phenomena. Indeed, [economists] managed to understand that political power is an economic good for those who hold it, and that that the only ones who can hold it are those who hold relatively greater amounts of economic goods; and they found the economic bases of political constitutions. [Jurists] found that the juridical system responds to the requirements of those who, as the [political scientists] demonstrated, had conquered power.[141]

Turati had demonstrated that he had the overall significance of this question in mind: political economy could not remain an occasional or only polemical moment of socialists' cultural elaboration. It instead had to become a knowl-

140 Turati to Colajanni, 13 February 1884, in Ganci (ed.) 1959.

141 Bulferetti 1951, pp. 35–6.

edge in which the various threads starting out from 'science' and the 'social question' could converge, and from which other threads able to nourish science could in turn depart, reinforcing its 'positive' character, as well as indicating the means through which the 'social question' could begin to be disentangled.

Turati had notable capacities of intuition, useful for grasping the 'socialist' sense (in its most general dimension, and in its system of relations) of political and cultural problems typical of the phase now being crossed. However, for contingent reasons (the youthful neurasthenia frequently mentioned in his correspondence), and on account of his life choices and intellectual structure, he was not able to translate the intuitive outlines at which he had arrived into the mammoth forms characteristic of the science of the era – and nor did he have any intention of doing so. This was the case also with regard to questions of criminal sociology – a sector that in many aspects tallied with his specific professional interests; and this in a certain sense demanded the further development of the primitive outline he provided to Colajanni. This would have been much more difficult with regard to his economic thinking, notwithstanding sociology's infinite integrative capacities.[142]

Turati's 1880s economic interests were rather considerable, even if they were also filtered through a very abundant sociological literature. A mass of economics texts from the period have been found in his library, and in particular the works of Luigi Cossa.[143] There is no need to emphasise the importance

---

142 That does not however mean thinking that Turati's 'intuitive' qualities prevented him from fully seriously measuring himself by the standard of the 'positive' approach, deriving from an epistemological conception tending to privilege facts, and demanding the development of cognitive orientations directed at research and the classification of the facts themselves. In 1885 he was charged – together with Anna Maria Mozzoni – with assisting Agostino Bertani, who was leading the inquiry into hygiene complementing Stefano Jacini's agricultural Inquiry.

Bertani's instructions were both interesting and modern in character: 'You have as your object: the *material life* of the workers on the land' (letter of 16 April 1885). He would go on to show his appreciation of Turati's work: 'I attentively read your report on Torre del Greco: it was precise, far-reaching, well posed and comprised everything that does and does not concern me: it is a singular monograph, a credit to you which will be of great use to me, and will make my desire to have similar ones for other localities ever greater' (9 May 1885). See Schiavi (ed.) 1947.

We could also consider the mass of data he collected through his research into criminal anthropology. Also on this terrain Turati would give precise indications to Colajanni, as is clear from the correspondence in Ganci (ed.) 1959.

143 See the fine analysis of his library in Monteleone 1987.

of the man who has been called the 'archimandrite of the new flock',[144] on account of his capillary divulgation of the cultural climate of *Kathedersozialismus* among the Italian economists. In particular (with more direct regard to the object of this work) it ought not be forgotten that Cossa was the common teacher, at least in part, of both Vito Cusumano and Achille Loria. At this point, and for some years still to come, the only Marx present in his library was Cafiero's *Compendio del Capitale*. This corresponds perfectly to what was already apparent from a list of 'Turati's books passed on to Leonida [Bissolati]' that Masini found among the Ghisleri papers at the Pisa Domus Mazziniana, a list mostly made up of works of political economy and texts by authors like Boccardo, Cossa, Lampertico and Errera ... to the extent that Masini himself could conclude that Marx was not detectable in these young men's reading 'except for Cafiero's compendium'.[145] At the same time, political economy itself increasingly became the privileged knowledge through which Marx's figure would gradually acquire greater centrality; and this would later prove essential to a long-term definition of socialist identity. Not by chance, one of the arguments that Costa provided in order to justify his 'turn' was explained in terms of the need for immersion 'in a cold bath of political economy'.[146]

In truth, notwithstanding this evidence that these young socialist intellectuals did not have Marx's main texts to hand, his presence did hover over their formative period. As we shall see, certain publications were already hypothesising paradigms inspired by the Trier philosopher; and yet the logics on which mechanisms of disciplinary analysis were being constructed (in this case, for political economy) directly depended on cultural contexts rather closer to home. The social question had often been hypothesised more than analysed. But if in mid-1880s Italy there was to be a theoretical construction able to hold together the multiple themes regarding this question that were now emerging in an often-heterogeneous manner from the *Kathedersozialismus* milieu (which notwithstanding its 'Germanism', did conserve typically endogenous characteristics) it could not come from Marx's operative presence. However, without a Marx who was far away, and yet in a sense an encumbrance upon them, there would perhaps not even have been an attempt at building such a construction.

When the very young Loria was writing his laureate dissertation, he was taken with a 'frenetic love' and 'thunderstorm of a passion' for the economic schools of Germany, and was fascinated by 'Ricardo-Thünen-Marx, the great

144 Macchioro 1970, p. 494.

145 Masini (ed.) 1961, pp. 7 and 20.

146 Costa 1952.

triumvirate at the peak of all learning',[147] as he addressed the problems of land property in their relation with law and economics. And now it was precisely the man who had been Ferrara's polemical target *par excellence* who suggested to him a possible development of his reflections. Vito Cusumano exhorted him to 'think through today's socialism and explain the theories of Marx, Lassalle and other renowned socialists', given that he had been 'dealing with property rights' he could easily move on to the '*theory of value* [which] is nothing but the theory of the origin of property'.[148]

In certain regards, the development of the thick volume[149] that Loria went on to construct, on the basis of intuitions that were already present in his laureate thesis, would preserve the watermark of the problem that Cusumano had raised; a problem that now corresponded to a common feeling among these young men, who seemed to discern with sufficient clarity the ideological dimension connected to supposedly neutral analytical categories. This was a feeling that Loria tried to transform into a more articulated consciousness, precisely by way of a declared Marxian inspiration.

The non-linearity of the brief exchange of letters between Marx and Loria (1880–3) and then the bitterness of Engels' reactions to him – first faced with the 'tiny mind'[150] who had accused Marx of fashioning a second volume of *Capital* as an 'ingenious expedient ... substituting for scientific arguments',[151] and then in the 1890s faced with the danger that Lorianism might establish itself as the Italian socialists' Marxism – has led the literature on this matter to underestimate the cultural connections between them, associated with the way in which the 22-year-old Italian economist had presented himself to 'the greatest thinker of the contemporary age'.[152]

Beyond the young Mantuan's hyperbolic style, his first letter to Marx – accompanied by a copy of his *La rendita fondaria* – immediately indicated the fundamental justification for the relationship that he sought, which was reasoned in such a way that it would be mistaken to consider it purely circumstantial.

Loria warned Marx that he was not 'a follower of communism's social theory', but justified sending him his book on the basis of his debt to the man to

147 Loria 1927, pp. 20–1.

148 Letter from Cusumano to Loria, 11 June 1877, in the Loria papers, until 1980 conserved at the Soprintendenza Archivi del Piemonte e della Valle d'Aosta.

149 Loria 1880.

150 Engels to Loria 20 May 1883, in *MECW*, Vol. 47, p. 25.

151 Loria 1902, p. 48.

152 Loria to Marx, 23 November 1879, in Del Bo (ed.) 1964.

whom he owed 'the true method of economic research, the method of analysis that [Marx] had introduced to political economy'. And immediately afterwards he offered a note of clarification with regard to a certain aspect of this method: Marx was the author of an 'epochal masterpiece' – albeit 'unfortunately, an incomplete one' – that had 'forever dispersed the unrelenting fantasies of apologetic science'.[153] Two years later, when Marx's relations with Loria had sharply worsened, and he provided Engels with a 'ruthless psychological portrait'[154] of the young scholar, he also recognised not only his 'talent', but also the fact that he had 'sought to make his own, in so far as in him lay [sic] and not always without success, the methods of research he had found in *Capital*'.[155]

The key to understanding what Loria wanted to suggest when he said that he had acquired Marx's 'true method of economic research' lies precisely in his explicit characterisation of *Capital* as a distinctly anti-ideological work. Even if he reduced this method to a rigid economic determinism with apparent naturalist traces, it would remain a constant of his immense intellectual production, in continual confrontation with Marx. Loria had identified two distinct components in Marx's work, 'the *vision* – the materialist conception of history – and the *analysis* – the theory of value and prices',[156] and considered it possible to take inspiration from the one without any necessary interference from the other. The fundamental motif that Loria claimed to have deduced from *Capital*'s method was already present in the weighty volume that he sent to Marx in 1880: namely, the attempt to demonstrate the true reality underlying the theory of rent and the theories of capitalist development that the 'orthodox' economists defended. Naturally this did not prevent him maintaining that the principal mechanisms of modern exploitation were not 'of a capitalist character, but a territorial one'.[157]

153 Ibid.

154 Faucci 1978, p. 601.

155 Marx to Engels, 3 August 1882, in *MECW*, Vol. 46, p. 298. A letter from the Russian Kablukov to Loria from 24 April 1886 also indirectly attests to the fact that his judgements were not simply linear. Saying that he had heard of Loria's work from Rusanov (also cited in Loria 1927, p. 42), Kablukov wrote 'K. Marx told me of your book "on rent" and talked to me about it at some length. Though he did not entirely agree with many of your arguments, his references to your work were of such interest as to awaken the keenest interest in me, which has only grown as my knowledge of your works has deepened': Archivio Feltrinelli, *Carte Loria*.

156 Faucci 1978, p. 601.

157 Loria 1880, p. 291.

The impression that reading *Capital* had on Loria was without doubt very considerable, and perhaps decisive for his future as an economist, independently of his system's high degree of autonomy. In the famous essay he wrote immediately after Marx's death, and which was the cause of his break with Engels, he expressed himself on this first (and for him, only) volume in the following terms:

> This work … marked … a true event in the field of social science. The influence that this work exercised was immense. The theorists of economic optimism saw their utopias destroyed by the statistical exposition of British conditions. The professors of political economy looked on with indignation as a dilettante, a sectarian, descended into the scientific arena with a prodigious doctrine, counterposing to their monotonous, inanimate, stitched-together treatises an organic, palpitating work alive with facts and ideas, with its thought breathing life into an immense and marvellously elaborated and coordinated scientific material.[158]

We know that the effect that *Capital* had on the economic community, in particularly when Marx was still alive, did not at all correspond to this description. Very probably, though, it does correspond to the effect that it had on Achille Loria.

If a 'left-wing' 'university-chair socialist' like Vito Cusumano, who otherwise presented Marx to the Italian scientific community very accurately, read him completely within the terms of 'economic Germanism' when it came to economic categories, Loria's case was a wholly different one. 'The relationship between Loria and Marx' – it has been commented – '[and] between Loria and Marxism was a relationship that in a first phase proceeded through Loria's own personal research: entering into the world of culture he came across Marx, and would settle accounts with him in a successive process of agreement, plagiarism and also rejection'.[159] This was, therefore, a true and proper qualitative leap in the Italian academic world's perception of Marx, and it took place by way of Loria. The young Mantuan economist's personality played a decisive role in this regard. But Loria also found himself becoming the intersection of a set of converging pressures coming from different terrains and directions. The current coming from *Kathedersozialismus* was mixed up with the strong and distinctly socialist ethico-political tendency pervading the milieu in which

158 Loria 1902, p. 21.

159 Allocati 1990, p. xviii.

he had been trained, which would also be the milieu of Turati, Ferri, Bissolati and Prampolini. Colajanni, too, would make his 'way of understanding the evolution and ... [the] interests of the bourgeoisie'[160] concord with the social evolution processes depicted by Loria. In certain respects the same process that had taken shape just a few years previously in reaction to Colajanni's *Il socialismo* would be repeated also in this latter's case, in particular with regard to the role that the key works of the 1880s[161] came to assume. The disciplinary context was not the same, with this being a work of political economy rather than one of criminal sociology (albeit with just as important a sociological framework); and the level of these works and the echoes they had both in the short and long term was very different. But they had the same function in bringing scattered elements back together, and expressed the same need for a systematic to find some adequate realisation.

Only the existence of a *diffuse Marxism* – that is, an atmosphere formed by a complex set of psychological factors, tools of analysis, visions of historical development, senses of identity and role, and doctrinal elements whose selection was the fruit of experiences coming from organisational reality and 'vanguard' struggles, which 'Marxism' would (largely *a posteriori*) be able to structure organically as a scientifically-underpinned whole – makes it rather easier to read a process in which it was possible to obtain a Marxist output from a non-Marxist input.

This *diffuse Marxism* – not all of whose component parts were necessarily consciously identified with this – was composed of scattered particle-cells, which, at a certain moment, experienced a rapid coagulation effect. It concerned *all* the levels in which the formation-process of Italian Marxism was articulated, high culture included. Even the Loria phenomenon can be considered an aspect of this diffuse Marxism.

A wide historiographical discussion has developed with regard to this phenomenon, in large part developing along lines of thinking derived from the very harsh judgements that Engels, Labriola, Croce and Gramsci passed on Loria. Clear traces of this controversy are still today present in the latest studies. Even if more than one person has today been led to ask who Achille Loria was,[162] in the last decade of the nineteenth century his figure as a positivist 'intellectual-type',[163] discussed in Italy and Europe, was the necessary crucible also for the development of Marxism.

---

160 Colajanni to Loria, 7 April 1886, *Carte Loria*.

161 See Loria 1886, 1889.

162 Notes in Gallino 1985.

163 Expression used in Ottaviano 1985.

The 'Loria question' – in relation to the modes of Marxism's spread in Italy, its taking-root, and its 'quality' – undoubtedly entails a sizeable range of meanings, though within this we can identify two fundamental components.

As concerns the 'quality' of the Italian Marxism of Lorian inspiration (which was of very great significance), the judgements expressed by Engels, Labriola and Croce in the midst of a political-cultural battle have substantially been confirmed. This certainly justifies the positions of those who have read the Loria phenomenon as one of both surrogating and emptying-out Marxism, with deleterious effects on its content, as 'deterministic sociologism' ended up falling into scientific discredit. Right at the beginning of the new century, in the moment of the 'revolution of the intellectuals', it would, in sum, become rather easy to strike against Marx by way of Loria.[164]

At the same time, starting from the second half of the 1880s Loria found himself (not necessarily willingly) to be a fundamental element of *diffuse Marxism* in the academic world. The near unanimous agreement that greeted his university career and his intellectual production from 1883 to the end of the century – with Turati defining him as 'in a certain sense the most socialist, the most Marxist of the Italian economists (overlooking certain minor distinctions that matter a lot to the scholar and little to the public)'[165] – played a front-rank role in the growth of Marxism's 'dignity' within the fortress of theories' 'scientific' recognition. Thus a stable connection was established between the different levels on which *diffuse Marxism* operated: within the workers' movement, consciousness of Marxism as a 'scientific' underpinning for *class* reasoning was slowly maturing; and this consciousness was further reinforced by the recognition that not even the bourgeois sanctuary of 'science' could fail to take into serious consideration the theory that brought the ultimate fate of capitalism together with the radiant proletarian dawn. Lorianism ought thus to be considered a non-secondary component of the ensemble that between the late 1880s and early 1890s facilitated the widening of Marxism's sphere of influence, behaving as a true and proper accelerator of different synergies.

An ambivalent and contradictory reality thus took form: one that cannot necessarily be made compatible with schemas assuming the complementarity of the two terms of the Loria problem.

As we have seen, the myth of a socialist movement that was the faithful interpreter of the 'general laws' of historical and social development – such as seemed to have been indicated by the latest discoveries of 'positive sci-

164 An argument advanced with particular lucidity in Macchioro 1970.

165 Turati to Loria 26 December 1890: appears as an appendix to Favilli 1980, pp. 181–2.

ence' – was, certainly, one of the cornerstones of the affirmation of Marxism and, at the same time, the privileged terrain for a Lorian reading to prevail. We would certainly not be risking much to say that *La teoria economica della costituzione politica*, a book that Turati considered an example of a 'perhaps even too-unilateral Marxist orthodoxy'[166] was the basic text for the reception of historical materialism by almost all the intellectuals/leaders of Italian socialism, from future reformists Filippo Turati to Emanuele Modigliani,[167] to future revolutionary syndicalists Arturo Labriola[168] and Enrico Leone,[169] to prestigious historians and heterodox politicians like Gaetano Salvemini.[170] Even Gnocchi-Viani would make use of it in order to strengthen his own determined efforts to refute not only the primacy but even the autonomy of the political sphere. This was a text perfectly in line with the precepts of positive science: it was naturalistic, deterministic, evolutionistic, and, at the same time, 'objectively' demonstrated the historical necessity of transcending the capitalist system. It could satisfy the demands of both 'scientific dignity' and 'social revolution', and in this sense, in the last fifteen years of the century it would play a front-rank role in defining the categories through which identification with Marxism could take place in Italy. This was the same role, in substance, that the *Anti-Dühring* played in other contexts.

The monumental *Analisi della proprietà capitalistica*[171] did not have effects within the field of socialist culture comparable to those of the slimmer and, above all, more 'sociological' 1886 text. Even if Loria had conceived of this work as an attempt to overcome 'the partial impulses of classical science and socialism', which in their study of profit had not covered 'the entire economic constitution',[172] the socialist intelligentsia did not at all see this work as standing in contradiction with *Capital*, either. And yet it would be difficult to doubt Loria's will to build his own theoretical autonomy with respect to Marx. The explicit references to Marx in this *Analisi* ... almost exclusively belonged to a critical dimension, criticising Marx using either Ricardian argumentation or – as con-

166 Turati to Ghisleri, 2 November 1886, in Masini (ed.) 1961.

167 See Arena 1962, Cherubini 1990.

168 See Labriola 1945.

169 See Leone, 'La difesa del sistema loriano', *Critica sociale*, 1901, pp. 221–2, 234–7.

170 See Artifoni 1981.

171 Loria 1889, Vol. I. The ambition with which Loria constructed this text and his open intention of placing himself on the same terrain as Marx also shines through from the way in which he referred to this text in his private correspondence. Pantaleoni spoke of it as his friend Loria's *Capital*: see Fiorot 1976, p. 473.

172 Loria 1889, pp. vii–viii.

cerned the theory of value – argumentation derived from Loria's own system. Moreover, the centrality of this system consisted in a 'land-tenure theory' – the theory of 'free land' – which Loria saw as a mechanics of social development without external influences, and wholly extraneous to Marx's categories. For certain, the evident guide of Loria's analytical outlook remained his 'historical materialism', which he had already fully set out, in its general terms, in 1886. In fact, the assumption that the juridical and political 'superstructure' was absolutely dependent on property relations, stated already in his 1886 work, would have to be completed with a theory of the natural evolution of these relations, and the theory of 'free land' would indeed be added to this as a complementary element. Thus it remains possible that the persistent aura of 'economic determinism' that pervaded both volumes of his work threw a veil over a precise perception of his position with regard to Marx's elaboration.

There were also other reasons for this 'incomprehension' on the part of the socialists. First of all, the context into which a work like the *Analisi ...* entered was different from that which could smoothly take on board a book like *La teoria economica della costituzione politica*. While the first was rigorously academic, the second was rather wider and more heterogeneous. Turati, for example, who had read, reflected and commented on *La teoria economica ...* almost certainly left the pages of the *Analisi ...* wholly untouched. At the same time, however, a work of this kind was decisive in marking out the image of Loria as the 'most famous of the Italian economists'; he who was also 'the most well-disposed toward socialism'.[173] If we reflect that even at the end of the 1880s Italian socialism had not ingested 'Marxism' as an overall ideological reference point, it is not difficult to imagine how 'the most famous of the Italian economists' could be placed side-by-side with the 'giant' Marx, both of them co-operating in giving a more secure definition of socialist economic science, notwithstanding the 'minor distinctions' between them.

3 Cultural Mediation in the World of Organised Workers

Leo Tolstoy portrayed in the following terms the image of the Marxist revolutionary worker of the late nineteenth century, as seen by his Prince Nekhlyudov on his journey to the living hell of Siberian exile

173 Labriola 1945, p. 51.

> He was ascetic through habit, contented himself with very little, and, like all those used to work from childhood and whose muscles have been developed, he could work much and easily, and was quick at any manual labour; but what he valued most was the leisure in prisons and halting stations, which enabled him to continue his studies. He was now studying the first volume of Karl Marx's, and carefully hid the book in his sack as if it were a great treasure.[174]

The worker, called Kondratieff, had 'a dense sense of being wronged', but only when a 'celebrated revolutionist' and intellectual came into his factory 'to work as a working girl' and provided him with the tools to account for his condition, did he develop his uncontainable passion for study: 'he believed that the knowledge that had shown him the injustice of the state in which he lived would also abolish that injustice itself'. This must, though, have been an exceptionally gifted worker, if '[i]n two years he had mastered algebra, geometry, history – which he was specially fond of – and made acquaintance with artistic and critical, and especially socialistic literature'.[175]

With difficulty could we think of any possibility of generalising the model that Tolstoy suggests. At the end of the 1880s in Milan – which was hardly backward – the *Partito operaio italiano* had difficulty circulating even Cafiero's *Compendio* among the 'conscious' workers.[176] It seems wholly unrealistic to hypothesise that Boccardo's edition of Volume I of *Capital* could have circulated among this same milieu.[177] That is not to say that the experience of autodidact workers managing to reach advanced levels of knowledge of socialist literature (and not only that) was unimportant to the history of socialism. Indeed, in some aspects the very close link that some sought to establish between the collective emancipation of the workers and individual improvement through cultural development was one of the most interesting aspects of this history. We need only think of working-class and POI leaders like Anzi and Lazzari who had a good knowledge of the texts concerning socialism and sociology that were most widespread in their times, including untranslated French-language ones. Or even men like Rigola and Verzi, who as we know played a very much front-rank role in the history of Italian socialism: the former had not continued beyond elementary school and already at 13 years of age worked as a carpenter's apprentice, while the latter had gone little further with his basic

174 Tolstoy 1899, pp. 208–9.

175 Ibid.

176 Anzi 1946, p. 62.

177 Published in Turin in 1886.

education, and all his socio-economic culture was the fruit of autodidactism. Not to mention the worker Benoît Malon, who not only rapidly mastered a significant part of the existing socialist literature, but was one of the exponents of that literature who had a far from marginal influence on both French and Italian socialism. And naturally together with or after these, there were also broad milieus of workers who shared and practiced this attitude and system of values, at different levels. But common to all these workers – even those who managed to break through to the highest levels of the movement – was the insurmountable difficulty of any analytical relationship with *Capital*. It could not have been otherwise, and indeed even a very large number of academics who also possessed quite different tools had these same difficulties.

In the ideal-type outlined by Tolstoy there appear almost all of the moments of the path that it was thought linked social positioning to awareness of this positioning and of the overall logics of socio-economic development deriving from it: an initial and confused class 'sense'; the encounter with a theory that came from the outside but which had to measure itself concretely with proletarian conditions in order to make the proletariat flesh and blood; the both naïve and conscious flash of awareness as to the powers of culture; the exertions and the joys of a not-only intellectual advance; and a relation with the text mediated simultaneously by both reason and a sense of its 'sacredness'. Faced with such a text, the worker could have directed the same words to the author as the obscure proofreader Nathanäel expressed to the great philosopher of his century:

> It seems to me that Mijnheer manages to join together and link up things – and by that I mean both objects and human thoughts – with words that are subtler and stronger than the things themselves are. And when words are inadequate, with numbers, letters and signs, as if with steel cables …[178]

Words, numbers, letters, signs, like taut steel cables forming the structure of an extremely solid conceptual construct, capable of giving order to the chaos of things, the guarantee of the correspondence between science and justice, between aspirations to a better future and the certainty of that same future: thus this text gradually began to appear in the sentiments shared by all those proletarians whose lives socialism entered into, filling the voids of violent caesuras with the hopes of rebirth.

178 Yourcenar 1987, p. 83.

The means, the paths through which this image gradually came to take on an evident, substantial form, were immersed in a rather blurred reality whose levels of articulation appear anything but rigid or determined aprioristically. Certainly, it materialised in many varied and dissimilar ways in high culture or in the proletarian environment, but there was also a vast and far from always seamless intermediate layer in between these.

In particular between the late 1870s and early 1880s, a publication like *La Plebe* truly represented a fundamental link communicating between the different levels in which socialist cultures were articulated. It was a socialist paper that distinguished its role with respect to the very few workers' papers 'in the strict sense of the word', but which did not, however, theorise any one-directional pedagogical operation, instead considering it necessary to mount a continued discussion and engagement for the sake of 'mutual strengthening and self-correction'.[179] It was a socialist paper that had for some time been very clear as to the fundamental distinction – one that is often ignored even today by interpreters held in esteem for their analytical refinement – between 'Marxism' as defined by its adversaries, as a political current in the International, and Marx's theory as a science of society, or more precisely as the science of capital. It was the socialist paper that published the first translation of a significant part of *Capital* Volume I: the sixth section of chapter twenty-four, on 'so-called original accumulation'.[180]

---

179 Underlying the distinction between workers' papers and socialist papers, and the ways in which the existing relation between them was identified, there was a conception of the socialism-working class relationship that certainly does not allow us to establish a *direct* connection between *La Plebe*'s culture and workerism, a link that some of the literature on this topic has emphasised: '*Workers*' papers, in the strict sense of the word, distinguish themselves through three very well determined qualities, namely: a practical sense that is difficult to derail, a clear and uncorrupted consciousness of the poor man's most urgent needs, and an instinctive and persistent attachment to the *economic question*. Which means that they are on the right path, just and good. They have a lot of affinity with the socialist papers, which also for their part are founded on the economic question, but beyond the urgent needs of the working class they likewise study men's remote needs, regenerated by social renewal. But studying these they often depart from the practical orbit of the worker in order to investigate the forms of the future Ideal. Both the one and the other [type of] papers, however, are destined mutually to strengthen and correct each other': 'Attraverso il 1881', *La Plebe* (monthly), 2, 1882.

180 See 'Genesi del capitalista industriale', *La Plebe*, 11, 16 and 23 February and 9 March 1879. This was not a direct translation from the German; rather, it was translated from a French edition. The true first translation of a section of *Capital* in Italy had in fact come only a few weeks after the 1867 Meissner edition was published in Hamburg. The

Faced with the greatness of Marx's *Capital*, it had no hesitation in fully welcoming its significance for science and for socialism:

> This is one of the most important works of our century, which heralds a new age in the history of social sciences. In his book (which is just one first part of the great work that Marx is thinking through and writing) the German writer has not invented a *system*, nor a *means* of arriving at the goal of socialism ... Anyone who looks for a new socialist school in this work will be disappointed: but if he instead looks for a work of devastating scientific critique, then he will be left fully contented. The historical necessity that is driving everyone toward socialism clearly does shine through from his critique. When the bourgeoisie reads Marx's work and properly digests it, and if it is acting in good faith, it will have to repudiate all its errors and kneel to the new social current. We salute this work of Marx's as an invincible precursor to the triumph of our cause.[181]

In Marx's overall elaborations – one could also read in the columns of Bignami and Gnocchi-Viani's paper – there were, certainly, political aspects that were the object of controversy among socialists, but there were no such controversies among 'any contemporary socialists' on economic theory, and in particular with regard to 'the definition of value, the law of wages and the formation of capital'. Moreover – it was further specified – 'Marx's economic theory ... [was] in its essential points nothing but the socialist programme accepted by the International as a whole ever since the day when, at the Basle Congress of 1869, it proclaimed the necessity to establish collective property'.[182]

Here we can see the increasingly clear definition of the relation that *La Plebe* saw being established between Marx and socialism: *Capital* placed Marx 'in the first position among the critical economists ... of the nineteenth century' and at the same time delineated a process determined by 'the laws of economic evolution', according to which the need for collective property was gradually maturing. As a 'critical economist' he completely belonged to the world of science, but given that the materials that he produced in this sphere justified both the workers' struggle and the ultimate perspectives of that same struggle, he also completely belonged to the revolution. Thus Marx ought to be consid-

Naples paper *Libertà e Giustizia*, organ of the similarly-named workers' club, published the central and final parts of Marx's introduction in its 27 October 1867 edition: see Basso 1962.

181 'Rec. a K. Marx, *Le Capital*, Paris, Lachâtre': *La Plebe*, 4 December 1877.

182 'Un trionfo del socialismo', *La Plebe*, 22 October 1876.

ered the 'scientific leader' of socialism, its 'most profound thinker',[183] and at the same time 'the greatest modern sociologist'.[184]

This did not at all imply that socialists had to define themselves as 'Marxists'. 'Marxists' had been a current in the International – the 'statolators', the 'authoritarian communists' – and still at the twilight of the 1870s they remained one of the fundamental terms of a laceration that was still far from being resolved. Conversely, Marx's deeper theoretical dimension proved in practice to be a structurally unifying element. The 'objective' scientific results that he had reached would gradually have to be accepted even by bourgeois economists and sociologists, or at least those whose intellectual activity developed free of the obfuscations of class interests and prejudice. And *La Plebe* showed itself particularly concerned to capture all the symptoms of the process that was then considered to be underway, from Laveleye to Schäffle. Beyond a direct reference to the analytical core of *Capital*, the socialists would thus derive from Marx 'a general socialistic idea, sufficiently widely accepted to unite the militant proletarians of the various civilised nations':[185] a socialistic idea developed from a common agreement over the 'economic' programme of the 1869 Basle Congress.

The socialists of *La Plebe* thus posed Marx as the primary reference point in the socio-economic sciences – as a general horizon for a long-term perspective – without that implying any potential translatability of the political forms that were then defined as 'Marxist'.[186] *La Plebe* saw the highest example of these forms in the political dialectic of the time in the 'German working-class world, which, following Marx's doctrines [saw] the possibility of emancipation only through the organisation of a people's state [*Volksstaat*] constructed through a parliamentary majority of democratic-socialist deputies chosen among the workers'.[187]

The attempt was made to keep these two levels distinct and perhaps parallel: but given their evident disparity, they ended up proceeding in a manner that made it impossible to avoid significant mutual interferences. The former,

183 'Carlo Marx', *La Plebe* (monthly), 4, 1883.

184 See Gnocchi-Viani 1886.

185 'Il socialismo di Marx', *La Plebe* (monthly), 5–6, 1883.

186 This phenomenon did not only concern *La Plebe*'s socialism or even the Italian experience. As Kolakowski has rightly noted, 'Apart from the conflict of influences in the International it may be said that from the 1860s Marxism was the most important of the rival socialist ideologies, in the sense that doctrines and programmes throughout the world defined their positions by reference to it': Kolakowski 1978, p. 257.

187 'Arbeiter-Zeitung', *Il Martello*, Fabriano, 26 August 1876.

indeed, manifested itself with a weight and a role that the latter was not fully able to compete with. If it was argued that the socialist movement could now refer to a theoretical framework capable of explaining the logics of capitalist development and, in the last analysis, also to explain the factors behind the immanent and future development of a society based on a different production relation, then it was difficult to avoid expanding the spaces in which that theoretical framework was used. That was particularly the case when the exploration of this analytical universe had barely begun, and new phases of exploration and the acceleration of the rhythms of industrial society seemed mutually to illuminate each others' explanation. As such, it was difficult to free oneself of the duty to construct a set of tools – and also a practical one – that was not in some sense derived from a system (as it was generally understood) held to be the highest point thus far reached in the science of society.

In substance, the relation that was effectively being established between the two levels was the relation between *necessity* and *contingency*. In the case in question, *contingency* was certainly of no little significance: it touched on the sphere of politics, not understood in a reductive sense, and concerned a way of feeling oneself a socialist and revolutionary, derived from a brief but intensely-lived Italian tradition that had already built up stratifications that were not just at surface-level. And yet faced with an economic and social theory that seemed to demonstrate ever greater capacities to account for the dynamic of the social relations from which socialism drew the very fundaments of its *raison d'être*, it does not seem impossible to imagine a *necessity* projected onto a reality that gradually came to require a different *contingency*.

In other words, 'Marxism' was without doubt wholly absent from *La Plebe*'s socialism in the late 1870s and early 1880s, toward the end of this publication's history. Marx, however, was very much present therein, and very evidently inserted into the deep analytical core of its socialism. So should this aspect be considered secondary to the effects of future developments?

The particular relation that almost naturally came to be established with the centrality of this analytical core would also now nourish the specificity of this socialism; its characteristics distinguishing it from other types of socialism with regard to the – certainly not marginal – questions of its propensity toward 'study' and 'moderation'. Indeed, those who were strongly convinced that the emancipation of the working classes and their moral and material redemption could not succeed without the maturation of 'a clear idea of the various bases and processes of socialism, as a scientific-economic movement'[188] evidently

188 Gnocchi-Viani 1875, p. 66.

considered 'study' an essential moment of the revolutionary process. At the same time, this had to be conjugated not so much with 'moderation' (a term more used by its opponents, with a clear pejorative cadence) as with a necessary attention to the levels reached by the development of the productive forces (even if this Marxist language was not used in the period here under consideration).

It may perhaps seem paradoxical, but it was a sign of how tortuous the paths of great and strongly pervasive cultures can be, that Marxism became the official ideology of socialism in a context of powerful radicalism, as the 'ideology of absolute opposition', while a decade previously, reworked 'Marxist' elements – or even ones labelled 'Marxist' by their opponents – had been transplanted precisely into a 'legalist' and gradualist perspective.[189]

Very sharp in denouncing 'legalism' and gradualism, the opponents of this perspective viewed it through the prism of the examples set by the German socialism based on 'the authoritarian theories of the People's State',[190] and they thus expressed their 'vote' for its 'complete defeat in the parliamentary elections'.[191] Naturally the men of *La Plebe* would (with good reason) have rejected any accusation of sympathy for the *Volksstaat*, but they would have struggled to deny their perfect consonance with fundamental aspects of a framework that was now being delineated as 'Marxist' in inspiration. The socialists who 'in Italy, too' put study before action were described in the following terms: 'They are socialists ... but only to impose the counterweight of political economy on socialism, or to force it to proceed little by little ... in the form of a purely economic movement through crafts and trades, they preach nothing except moderation'.[192] Indeed, 'legal socialism' was the socialism of those who wanted 'to study economic processes scientifically, concentrating on the organisation of workers', and for whom 'the revolution [had to come] before the organised forces of the proletariat [could] seriously believe in the possibility of peaceful emancipation'.[193]

From this perspective, revolution did not require the study of political economy: 'the Paris workers could create their Commune without even having

189 As Renato Zangheri notes: 'Even the police tended to connect dissident groups to a "legal" route that was ascribed to Marx. In Milan, for example, the "Partito internazionale" was termed "a follower of Marx's theories, which propound the achievement of social communism through evolution and propaganda"': Zangheri 1993, p. 486.

190 'Il socialismo in Italia', *L'Avvenire*, Modena, 27 July 1878.

191 'Le elezioni in Germania', *L'Avvenire*, Modena, 6 July 1878.

192 'Poco a poco', *Il Martello*, Jesi, 19 November 1876.

193 'Socialismo legale e socialismo rivoluzionario', *Il Martello*, Jesi, 24 February 1877.

heard of Marx's book *Das Kapital*'.[194] Not by chance, these 'Internationalist-anarchists' identified *Capital*[195] as the symbol of the scientific study of the economy that the 'legalist socialists' wanted to pose as the foundation of their 'experimental socialism' of Italian vintage.[196]

In substance, a large part of the connective tissue where ideals and perspectives of 'Marxist' derivation would most easily take root was in fact created by a non-'Marxist' cultural environment; and in its main personalities like Osvaldo Gnocchi-Viani and Enrico Bignami, it would continue not to be so, even when Marxism became the hegemonic ideology of Italian socialism.

If we reflect on what appeared as this landscape's immediate cultural product, the first 'programmatic platform'[197] of Andrea Costa's 'turn' – that is, the *Rivista Internazionale di Socailismo* – then we can very clearly identify some of its defining aspects.

Indeed, it was Gnocchi-Viani himself (and Costa was situated on his terrain – not that of any hypothetical Marxism) who took stock of the culture of Italian socialism by emphasising the central planks of the *overcoming* of Bakuninism.

Gnocchi-Viani referred to the close-to thirty Italian periodicals which from the Commune onward represented all hues of socialism 'from Marx to Bakunin, from Engels to Herzen, that is, from authoritarian socialism up to anarcho-communist socialism'.[198] However, when it came to indicating the modern character of Italian socialist literature, he cited only *La Plebe* and the *Rivista Internazionale di Socialismo*, the only publications that addressed 'the questions of Property with radical criteria and a *scientific* outlook'.[199] Enumerating the masters of European socialism, the only one whom he attributed the qualifier 'scholar' was Karl Marx: he characterised the others as philosophers or thinkers. Gnocchi-Viani would never change his opinion on this score, and still in the much later reflection appearing in his memoirs he would say that 'Bakunin was a man of faith, Marx a man of science'.[200]

Then proceeding to delineate the characteristics of Italian socialist literature, he expressed himself in the following terms:

---

194 'Il socialismo in Italia', *L'Avvenire*, Modena, 27 July 1878.

195 References to Marx's name in all contexts often cited *Capital* as a primary, immediate element of identification: for instance the reference to 'Mr. Karl Marx, author of the book *Capital*', 'Movimento sociale', *L'Avvenire*, Modena, 6 July 1878.

196 Angelini 1994.

197 See Della Peruta 1965, p. 333.

198 Gnocchi-Viani 1880, p. 12.

199 Ibid. (my italics).

200 Gnocchi-Viani 1974, p. 154.

> The arena where Italy is not poor is that of Outlines, Drafts, that is to say, fragments of social Science. Which makes us think ... that these fragments are less the effect of a complete, ready-made Science broken down into pieces in order to allow it to flow through all the veins of society, than they are partial attempts at science, which sow fruitful seeds here and there, and await the future synthetic critique that will correct, complete, develop and coordinate them in a *scientific* system.[201]

The need for a *scientific* reference point for the developing workers' movement's political horizon was something of a *leitmotiv* of the publishing effort that became the protagonist of Italian socialism's new course at the beginning of the 1880s. And this would, indeed, be one of the main paths through which the affirmation of 'Marxism' would find the highest point of its legitimation.

Obviously the milieux that gave rise to *La Plebe* and the *Rivista Internazionale di Socialismo* did not think of Marxism as a *scientific synthesis* also including the political projection of the various socialist experiences, and nor did they think of it as a privileged element among the other cultural elaborations that existed. Their cultural reference points remained multiple, and were often linked among themselves and combined with deft eclecticism 'with cultural ideas and projects and impulses that cannot be reduced to the "Germanic school"'.[202] Yet when it came to explaining the *economic* mechanisms of the social question, then the privileged reference to Marx became almost compulsory.

When he had to address the problem of 'Bourgeois Capital' and its internal modes of functioning, Gnocchi-Viani seems clearly to have been influenced by Marx's schemas, more than by those drawn from his beloved Malon. Yet this latter would reappear at the moment that these economic elements came to be explained in 'ideal' and 'moral' terms. So alongside what looks like a proper determination of the peculiar nature of labour-power, as well as a correct schematisation of the formation of absolute and relative surplus-value, at the same time he defined the process of capital valorisation as an 'ulcerous excrescence feeding on its own ulcerous humours'.[203] Meanwhile, he attributed the market determination of the exchange-value of labour-power a fraudulent character, an exchange 'using false scales'.[204]

201 Gnocchi-Viani 1880, p. 15 (my italics).

202 Giovannini 1984, p. 147.

203 Gnocchi-Viani 1879b, p. 6.

204 Gnocchi-Viani 1879b, p. 7.

The *Rivista Internazionale di Socialismo* would soon publish a rather interesting presentation of Marx's analysis of value.[205] This was in fact an interpretation – or better, the beginning of an interpretation – of the theory of value, and one that also seemed attentive to the multiplicity of 'value forms', not totally restricted to the *quantitative* terms of exchange-value alone. On this point, it was without doubt more perceptive than the reading that would become paradigmatic of the *Partito socialista*'s official popularisation from the 1890s onward.[206]

Without doubt, it was also more perceptive than the reading produced during the first polemic among socialists in Italy over the theory of value, which took place barely two years later. Even if 'this was, all in all, a rather modest episode',[207] it was indicative of the fact that the interest in Marx's economic theory was no longer an episodic moment or a purely external reference point, but a problematic element that had to be confronted within the terms of Marx's own analytical categories. For certain, the inadequacy of the instruments used by the protagonists[208] in this *querelle* seems to justify Marx's own dismissive attitude toward it;[209] but we ought to consider that up till that point 'the most peculiar opinions' on the theory of value had been expressed also in the international socialist movement, including where it had developed relatively early such as in *Vorwärts*.[210]

Moreover, we should note that in these Italian writings dedicated to aspects of Marx's economic theory – writings in which it is not easy to distinguish between the goal of popularising his work and of enriching socialist culture – there is an almost complete avoidance of Marx's own vocabulary. It is well known that the Marxist component of the socialist movement brought extremely novel and important contributions to the language that it used, and

205 A. Pistolesi, 'Carlo Marx e la sua "Analisi del valore"', *Rivista Internazionale di Socialismo*, 3, 1880, pp. 10–17.

206 See J. Stern, 'La teoria del valore di Carlo Marx', *Critica Sociale*, 1892, pp. 149–51, 170–2.

207 Cortesi 1971–2, p. 14.

208 See R. Candelari, 'La critica dell'economia radicale moderna', 'De Laveleye e Rodbertus' and 'La teoria del valore secondo Marx'; C. Cafiero, 'Polemica'; and R. Candelari, 'Polemica. Ancora sulla teoria del valore secondo Marx', in *La Plebe*, respectively, 8 October, 15 October, 22 and 28 October, 5 November, 12 November 1882.

209 'What is remarkable about the stuff in the *Plebe* concerning my theory of value is the rubbish talked by all 3, Laveleye, Cafiero and Candelari, in mutual opposition *l'un contre l'autre*. In the quotation concerning my aforementioned theory of value which Candelari adduced from Malon's *Histoire critique de l'économie politique*, Malon's superficiality is such that it actually surpasses that of all 3 smatterers' – *MECW*, Vol. 46, p. 392.

210 See Stephan 1977.

that the generalisation of these innovations is among the most interesting indices for determining the spread of Marxism.[211] And yet we almost get the impression that the writings in question are *translating* Marx's analytical categories into the then-widespread socialist language.

By six years later – if we continue following this same tendency of Italian socialism – the situation seemed to have changed in a far from negligible manner. The *Rivista italiana del socialismo* – a publication that can be considered the direct heir of the *Rivista internazionale di socialismo*, and again the fruit of Andrea Costa's milieu, an environment in which the possibility of a 'Marxist party' was still rather remote – shows signs of the changes that were then taking place in these socialists' cultural reference points. This review's programmatic article was the clearest manifestation of this.

This article,[212] conceived as a sort of manifesto of Italian socialism in the mid-1880s, clearly privileged an appeal to Marx's analysis, even if it remained wholly within the terms of the typical commonplaces of 'positive science', mechanicism and teleology. Its lexicon and language in general were enriched with the introduction of Marxian terminology and locutions, and the only quotation in the text is taken from Marx.

Moreover, in this review's short life (ceasing publication in 1887), it made a far from negligible contribution to the introduction of Marx and Engels's texts to Italy: it published *The Civil War in France*, 'The class struggle' (a page from *The Poverty of Philosophy*), Engels's 'The Labour Movement in America' (his 1887 preface to *The Condition of the Working Class in England*) and also a short section from Deville's compendium. These were the first texts of Marx and Engels's to be programmatically advanced from within the socialist culture *in the 1880s*. In fact, before then there had been publications of *Socialism: Utopian and Scientific* and *The Origin of Family, Private Property and the State*, in 1883 and 1885 respectively, wholly upon the individual initiative of Pasquale Martignetti, and the publication of the first volume of *Capital*, in 1886, as a splendidly academic initiative.

Naturally, this did not at all mean that the star of Marx shone so intensely in the sky of the Italian socialists' cultural reference points, even in the second half of the 1880s, as to make it hard to perceive also the light coming from other stars. For example, in this same *Rivista italiana del socialismo* a long epigraph taken from Schäffle's *Quintessence of Socialism* concerning the organisation of pro-

---

211 See the points in this regard in Lequin 1968 and Robin 1973.

212 See A. Lanzoni, 'Come intendiamo il socialismo', *Rivista internazionale di socialismo*, 1, 1886, pp. 3–9.

duction in a collectivist system followed immediately after the programmatic article mentioned above. This was a sign of the particular role that this well-fated pamphlet took on in these years, having been translated by Costa (from Malon's French edition) and immediately inserted into *La Plebe*'s 'library'. This true and proper encyclopaedic manual of socialism was continually recommended to all those who wanted a general and systematic vision of socialism, considering that, as Gnocchi-Viani himself later recounted, 'we were not able to find any better than Schäffle's volume'.[213] Schäffle, whom Costa presented as the author who had indicated 'the inevitable consequences of coming socialism' more radically even than Marx,[214] was considered as being *internal* to the socialist culture, to the extent that when he sharply distanced himself from German social democracy, he was bitterly reproached for an act standing wholly in contradiction with his scientific elaboration.[215]

It would thus be superfluous to emphasise once again the fact that Benoît Malon's star also shone in the 1880s, and far from weakly so;[216] rather, he appeared as a particularly macroscopic element of the dominant ideology, even in that part of the Italian socialist environment where the attention for Marx's work was most developed.

In 1886 Turati himself recommended Malon's *Revue socialiste* as the fundamental point of reference for the youth who wanted to begin their socialist studies, as he outlined a panorama of indications in which Marx and Engels were put together with Laveleye, Schäffle, Lange, Lassalle, Chernyshevsky, and so on.[217]

And yet even Malon's parabola was perfectly well inscribed within the gradual expansion of the Trier philosopher's prestige and influence among non-Marxists, or rather, in the case in question, among those whom the 'Marxists' had opposed to the last. Still in 1870, Malon did not even know Karl Marx's name. Guillaume recalls this curious episode that took place in March 1870:

> Malon later told me how Lafargue invited him for lunch, and having introduced him to his wife, said with some emphasis:

213 Gnocchi-Viani 1909, p. 135.

214 'La quintessenza del socialismo' (review), *Rivista internazionale di socialismo*, 2, 1880, p. 32.

215 N. Colajanni, 'Il socialismo e Schäffle', *Rivista italiana del socialismo*, 1, 1886.

216 Briguglio 1978.

217 F. Turati, 'Organizzazione, Studi, Propaganda (A un nucleo di giovani socialisti)', *Rivista italiana del socialismo*, 2, 1886.

– 'this is Karl Marx's daughter'.
– 'Karl Marx', Malon said, a little confused, not knowing who he was talking about, 'I think that I have heard that name. Is he not a German professor?'
– 'Well, no, he is the author of the book *Das Kapital*'.

And Lafargue went to find the weighty volume.

– 'You do not know this book?'
– 'No.'
– 'It's not possible, surely? You do not know Karl Marx, who leads the General Council?'[218]

Only during the 1870s, in close contact with the Italian socialist milieux of *Il Povero*, *La Lince* and then *La Plebe*, in a system of reciprocal influences, would Malon mature first a summary awareness and then a changed relation with regard to Marx's elaboration, to the extent of dedicating a chapter of his 1879 *Histoire du socialisme* to the author of *Capital*.[219] In 1892 he would speak of Marx as 'the author of the most knowledgeable and deeply considered book that present-day socialism has produced',[220] even though still then he was hardly familiar with this book, and still less its full version.[221]

Moreover, it is not the case that future Marxists' relation to Marx's theory was necessarily so different from Malon's. We need only think of Guesde, one of the principal popularisers of theoretical Marxism,[222] one of the main organisers of

218 Guillaume 1905, Vol. I, p. 285.

219 Malon 1879.

220 Malon 1892, p. 135.

221 All of the citations from *Capital* in Malon's short book were taken from Deville's *Compendium*.

222 I think that Willard was right to say that the *Parti Ouvrier Français* carried out 'the first clear, coherent diffusion of Marxism's fundamental ideas' in France, further adding that 'Following the example of German social-democracy, Guesde wanted to take on two great historic tasks: introducing scientific socialism among the proletariat, that is, a doctrine elaborated by intellectuals and which at first only intellectuals could divulgate; [and] to operate the fusion of the Marxist current and the spontaneous workers' movement': Willard 1965, pp. 13–14. The question of the 'quality' of this Marxism is certainly not without interest. But within the perspective of a historical analysis that is particularly attentive to the system of interdependencies among structural dimensions and cultures developing through never wholly defined relations of opposition and osmosis – I do not

political Marxism, and a tenacious political adversary of Malon's. Despite this Guesde confessed in a letter to Fournière (13 March 1912) that when he wrote his *Essai de Catéchisme socialiste* in Rome in 1872 he had 'still not read a line of Marx'.[223] In 1873 he moved to Milan, and his famous letter to Lampertico was, indeed, the fruit of the climate in Milan and his relation to that city's workers' movement and its culture.[224] Deville writes that even in 1876 Guesde 'knew Marxism only through Italian translations of Lassalle and Schæffle'. When he returned to France he was – again according to Deville – 'very well-disposed toward Marx', but he was full of enthusiasm for Schäffle's *Quintessence*, which he knew of thanks to Malon.[225] In terms of any greater awareness of theory, it was in 1877 that Guesde began to draw closer to Marx.

As such, there were not any particular differences in the paths taken by those who have – very appropriately – been called the *marxistes d'intention*, and those whose precise intention had been to distinguish themselves from the *marxistes* at the Saint-Étienne Congress, where the term *marxiste* was used perhaps for the first time in France.[226] During the 1870s, in particular in the second half of the decade, the figure of Marx and recognition of the centrally important dimension of his theory in *Capital* were the object of growing attention among the *whole* European socialist milieu, independently of the disaggregating effects that the traumatic end of the International entailed.

There can be no doubt that the Guesde-Lafargue-Deville *trinité* (and among the three it was without doubt this latter who displayed most familiarity with Marx's texts) had a determining role in giving the POF its Marxist coloration, starting with the phase preceding the Saint-Étienne split. All the same, it is well-known that Marx's highly renowned and very-often (sometimes overly so) cited phrase, '*je ne suis pas marxiste*', referred precisely to this Marxism (and particularly his son-in-law's), referring both to its contents and the sectarian branding that the use of that term inevitably assumed at that time.

At this point in our study, and given the analytical dimension that we have chosen, it is not of essential importance to measure the degree of correspondence between the Marxism of Guesde's *Égalité* or of Brousse's *Le Prolétaire* and the fundamental terms of Marx's theory. In any case it would be rather difficult to award either of these two socialist publications the prize for having

think that the precise determination of the boundaries between true and false Marxism is a priority question, here.

223 Cited in Dommanget 1969, p. 25.

224 See Willard 1965, p. 25.

225 Dommanget 1969, p. 156.

226 Dommanget 1969, pp. 122, 161.

the most consequential theoretical Marxism. In the middle of the controversy between the 'Marxists' and the 'possibilists' Paul Brousse expressed the following remarks in this regard, which we can wholly agree with: 'Marxism does not consist of being partisans of Marx's ideas ... In that sense, not a few of his current adversaries, and in particular the present writer, would be Marxists'.[227] For Brousse, Marxism instead represented the tendency to transfer the model of German social democracy into the organisational and political tradition of French socialism. That is, in short, a still-'political' Marxism, almost a re-proposition of the same spirit that led to the divides in the International, in a period when the development of the real movement and the development of the theoretical dimension itself had now made much further headway.

Even in German social democracy, before the anti-socialist laws, the question of taking on Marxism as a party ideology still had problematic aspects and was not posed in wholly definitive terms. Yet in Germany there were all the conditions for the rapid emergence of the conjugation of Marxism-as-theory and Marxism-as-party ideology. The formation of the Reich had found the German socialists wholly isolated, and the rapid industrialisation process that followed had reinforced the battalions of social democracy without changing their relationship with the rest of society. The separation of the socialist universe in Germany took place both at institutional levels and in social ones, through the mechanisms of what has been called a 'negative integration'.[228] The imperial authorities' rigid exclusion of the socialists from all the articulations of the state corresponded to the complete exclusion and discrimination against the working class as it formed and grew in symbiosis with the growth of industrial society. This was an exclusion that 'began in the workplace with employers' oft-reported disdain for their workers, clearly manifested in the fact of not greeting them, the way they spoke to them, their demand for the worker's submissiveness, and the repudiation of social contacts'.[229]

On the theoretical-ideological plane, moreover, there was a long and constant continuity in this movement's relation with Marx and Engels, with the 'masters' repeatedly intervening in the affairs of the workers' and socialist associations of Germany. Bebel and Liebknecht, who, notwithstanding their 'practical' approach, also believed some relation with theory to be essential, were considered the direct element of mediation between the German movement and the 'Londoners'. And, indeed, they did really play this role: even if both

227 Cited in Haupt 1978.

228 Roth 1963.

229 Quoted in Kocka 1871, p. 51.

Liebknecht and Bebel kept their autonomy intact, they did generally act in conformity with the Londoners' instructions when they corresponded to their own convictions, in what was 'not a one-way' system of influences.[230]

Engels's pained decision to intervene against Dühring is indicative enough of the fluidity of the theoretical references in German social democracy close to the end of the 1870s. And if it was in large part the *Anti-Dühring* itself that provided both the starting signal and the main instrument of what was a true and proper 'battle for Marxism', it was the anti-socialist laws that created yet more appropriate conditions for new modes and forms of ideological reception. And the coordinates of this battle consisted precisely in the construction of a doctrinal link able directly to translate *theory* into *politics* and party *identity*. And yet even in this context there were Marxist theorists who while directly engaged in social democracy's activities did not intend on fully digging themselves into the political Marxism that was now being defined in the radical contrasts of the 1880s. Such was the case, for example, of Carl August Schramm, who up to the end of the 1870s was considered 'after Marx and Engels, the most authoritative theorist of German social democracy in the economic field'[231] (as explicitly recognised by Kautsky, who would bitterly combat him during the following decade),[232] who not only did not recognise the seamless translation of economic theory into political radicalism, but also fought against the party adopting any precise ideological status.

Hence both in France in Germany – even given the profound socio-economic and cultural differences between these contexts – the logics that brought 'science' and 'socialism' to meld into 'ideological Marxism' responded to a mechanism of political conflict, a true and proper struggle for hegemony within the socialist movement. That does not mean that the role that Marx's economic and social theory was gradually assuming – and not only among militant socialists – was without effect on the results that then followed. Certainly the 'battle for Marxism' was of no little consequence in that regard, and yet even this did not manage to cancel out the existence of a 'Marxism' outside of 'Marxism'.

In Italy, as we have already partly seen, the process in question played out not only on a different timescale, but, most importantly, in very different ways. In the 1880s there was no important battle for Marxism, there was no group that defined itself as Marxist and that could have played even the role of

230 Longinotti 1974, p. 822.

231 Steinberg 1979, p. 16.

232 Kautsky 1960, p. 433.

the POF, never mind the more outlandish prospect of playing the role of the SPD. Yet precisely 'Marxism' outside of 'Marxism' was of decisive importance in determining the destinations of this process, in constant engagement – sometimes in symbiotic relation – with the forms assumed by the class struggle, which it intended to be both a consciousness of and a stimulus to.

The formation of an environment particularly receptive to parts of Marx's theoretical and ideal universe, to the extent that it can be defined Marxist, was also the fruit of the particular correspondence emerging between already-existing ways of feeling and thinking and the winds of systematisation that would ultimately derive from these Marx texts. This concerned both the popularisers of Marxism and those at whom this popularisation was directed.

In his correspondence with Marx at the end of the 1870s Guesde would tell his London-based interlocutor that he had 'always thought' the greater part of the theoretical doctrinal elements running through their correspondence, and later he would confide in Georges Diamandy, founder of the *Ère Nouvelle*, that 'he had conceived of Marxism before having known Marx's works'.[233] Just as the German social-democratic militant of working-class background, Adelheid Popp, maintained that in *Capital*, which she probably approached by way of a compendium, she had 'heard clearly and convincingly expressed that which I had instinctively felt'.[234] And again referring to *Capital* – a book whose fame now spread even among those who would never have read it, but who nonetheless ever more began to think of it as the scientific systematisation of their personal experience of the proletarian class struggle – one worker-organiser offered an unusually effective account of this phenomenon, as he gave a balance-sheet of the books borrowed from the Milan *Commissione di propaganda socialista* and the weak circulation of even Cafiero's *Compendio*, emphasising that 'Marx's *Capital* was explained and interpreted through everyday struggles at work'.[235] Beyond the difficulty in verifying such a statement through specific analysis of the correspondence between the Marxian theoretical dimension and the political and organisational processes of worker resistance, it is doubtless true that precisely this is the knot that we need to unravel in order to understand the mechanisms through which a system of

233 Cited in Dommanget 1969, p. 155. Willard has demonstrated – incontrovertibly so – how little the Marxism that Guesde had conceived before he knew Marx's works related to Marx's theory, in particular as concerned the economic sphere. The iron law of wages long remained a constant of his thinking, as it did, for the most part, among European Marxism generally.

234 Cited in Roth 1963, p. 207.

235 See Anzi 1946, p. 62.

connections between the different levels of a multidimensional and expanding culture was articulated.

Almost as if complementing Anzi's statement, another worker-organiser, Costantino Lazzari – who like Anzi also played a leading role in the *Partito operaio italiano* – would write that the primary task of this leadership group was to inspire in their workmates 'the will to know the causes of their misery, to make them appreciate the immense power of their solidarity, to make them desire an ideal future of justice and equality, and lay the bases for a methodical and continuous work for the improvement and emancipation of their class'. This would be done by applying 'the fundamental maxim that the emancipation of the workers must be the work of the workers themselves'.[236] A maxim, remember, that was becoming popular as 'Karl Marx's well-known saying'.

It was precisely on account of its capacity to give persuasive answers – no matter whether real or ideological – to the problems posed by Costatino Lazzari, that Italian Marxism would effectively be defined.

There is a common-sense saying, made back then as it is today, that fundamentally workers never read Marx, and Marxism in itself has never been of interest to them; if they joined trade union and political formations that defined themselves as Marxist, that was because they thought that they could defend their immediate interests through such organisations. However, that leaves us still to explain the reasons why in certain periods a *stronger* reference to Marx appeared to organised workers to be the instrument most adequate to defending their *immediate* (?) interests. In particular when the organisations that we are discussing were the almost exclusive fruit of workers' own direct initiative.

In any case, could there be a 'working-class movement' without 'philosophy'? In certain regards, its very awareness of being a 'working-class movement' was born from a strong theoretical foundation – and certainly it was *based* on that. This foundation was translated into a diffuse ideological consciousness through an organising structure rooted in the social fabric and capable of effectively linking concrete demands with more general perspectives for 'movement'. In this sense, 'philosophy' functioned as a powerful tool for the politicisation of the social, and was a point of strength and stability in the bitterest moments of the class struggle. Single struggles and single conquests – even the most immediate and elementary ones – were in fact configured as pieces of a historical process that conferred a universal value upon them. So it does not seem possible to separate 'working-class movement' from 'philoso-

236 Lazzari 1952, pp. 618–19.

phy': working-class organisation began thinking with more far-sighted theoretical reference points precisely when it started to define itself as a 'movement'. And that was true precisely because working-class history and the history of the working-class movement are non-coincidental. The famous question concerning the 'qualitative leap' that takes place in working-class organisation when 'consciousness from the outside' makes clear the contours of the passage from class-*in-itself* to class-*for-itself* – a question that has run through more than a century of the history of socialism – is very clearly affected by ideological projections. These ideological projections can only be tempered by an internal analysis of organisation itself, closely connected to the cultures it considered necessary for its development.

Marc Bloch reminds us that during the formation of feudal society, one far from secondary aspect of the particular web of relations of dependency holding together the variegated world of vassalage was determined by the 'importunate cry' that beat that society's rhythm: the 'importunate cry ... of the empty stomach'.[237] And this was not just a matter of the hunger of the peasant world, the endemic hunger of those without names and history – which could be taken for granted – but also the hunger of whoever in some sense entered into relations of vassalage.

Reading the workers' or socialist newspapers from the last three decades of the nineteenth century that featured workers' correspondence, this same obsessive appeal emerges: 'Hunger! Hunger! This is the immense and terrible spectre that knocks each hour at the door of our poor workers'.[238] And even in this case it was not just a matter of the hunger of the *plebs* in general, but rather of the industrial workers, of those who worked in the modern factory and were the motor of the modern economy. Of those who found themselves effectively forced to consider factory labour as 'an unbearable burden that nonetheless, as the only means of providing oneself bread and butter, for [maintaining one's] animal survival, must be considered the greater good'. This was work that could be lost at any moment; a 'labour ruled by fear'.[239] A cultural amalgam formed on the basis of the relation that workers established with *this labour*, in the inevitably interwoven searches for moments of explanation, of improvement and of prospective exit routes; and this amalgam was structurally ill-suited to being divided into an *internal* consciousness and a consciousness coming from the *outside*, coordinated in scales of ideological priority.

237 Bloch 2014, p. 173.

238 'Corrispondenza da Livorno', *L'avvenire*, Modena, 7 July 1878.

239 The cry of a German author of the nineteenth century, H. Bettziech, cited in Kuczynski 1967, p. 73.

This analytical dimension, then, absolutely cannot neglect the centrality of the factory and the *peculiarity* of the *new* social relations originating from the factory. And in Italy this means turning back to the 1880s, when the forms of workers' associationism 'in which the antagonisms between capital and labour still did not seem irreconcilable' truly entered into crisis, and the old forms of security derived from traditional mutualism seemed to have been 'disarmed faced with the power of capital'.[240] These were years in which a whole culture connected to a class identity and consciousness directly opposed to a contemporary employers' pedagogy truly began to take form among the workers. And all this means noting once again the central importance of the POI and all the organisational forms of *resistance* that were in some sense influenced by this party.

Moreover, even at the time there was perfect awareness of the novel characteristics that workers' organised presence in the 'socio-economic party' was introducing into the body of Italian socialism. In a parliamentary inquiry into the Interior Ministry over the arrest of workers' leaders in Milan in 1886, Andrea Costa emphasised that 'the emergence of the *Partito operaio* in Italy [was] not the work of chance or of anyone's whim ... [but rather] a necessary consequence of the conditions of production themselves ... [and of] capital's dominion over the labour force'. And he added that it was no chance thing that the POI had arisen in 'Lombardy, in Milan, where modern industry had penetrated more than it had elsewhere'.[241]

There was an interaction between the POI and industrial capitalism, and between the POI and the socio-economic environment produced by this type of development; and the effects of this interaction favoured a road to Marxism that no longer passed through the contest among 'socialist schools' and the residue of all their old *querelles*. Rather, the necessary attitude for the organisation of resistance, structured in a *class-party*, was one of 'describing a reality, not pronouncing laws on it';[242] of understanding the mechanisms of the production relation within which the class-party sought to operate with maximum effectiveness in both defending itself and entering onto the offensive.

Throughout much of the 1880s we can see certain far from marginal aspects of this itinerary *en bas*, by examining what has been termed 'the first true Milanese workers' paper',[243] *Il Fascio Operaio*. This was not the fruit of a 'backward' socio-economic situation but an expression of the 'Northern Italy' that, as

240 Brocchi 1907, p. xv.

241 See *Camera dei Diputati, Leg. XVI, Discussioni, Tornata del 2 luglio 1886, Vol. I*, pp. 433–6.

242 Julliard 1983, pp. 358–81.

243 Hunecke 1982, p. 346.

Engels put it, was 'decisive not only strategically, but also to the working men's movement throughout the whole length of the agrarian peninsula'.[244]

It is true that the editors of *Il Fascio Operaio* were a particular set of workers – and, first and foremost, specialised ones – exponents of a true and proper *élite* of 'cultured' (even if autodidact) workers. Some of them had learned foreign languages (almost always meaning French), and were able to read non-translated socialist literature. They thus knew the greater part of the socialist literature circulating in Italy at that time very well indeed. They cannot, for certain, be considered a representative sample of the northern Italian working class in general, nor even of that section which had acquired consciousness *of itself* – of its own separateness with respect to other classes and the need for resistance.

However, they were workers nonetheless, for the most part continuing to work in the same environment as their proletarian comrades. They were the *direct* expression of this environment, giving voice to its needs and demands; and at the same time they were capable – without any suspicion of ideological patronage – of introducing therein those elements of socialist culture that best responded to the needs of the *class struggle*, as it was both theorised and practiced.

And yet precisely this concept and expression – 'the class struggle' – was rather little used in the Italian workers' movement (or the French one)[245] at the beginning of the 1880s. For *Il Fascio Operaio*, rather, the logical-historical centre that all the activity of working-class organisation necessarily had to revolve around was the true key to reading social reality.

The class struggle was continually presented in this paper's columns as a central, non-eliminable element of a socio-economic relation that produced exploited and exploiters. 'If, then', it explained, 'up till now a certain peace existed between the class of workers and the class of exploiters, this was because the working class was ignorant of its own strength and its own value. In acquiring this knowledge and consciousness, it is certain that *peace* will be disturbed, [seeing that] *thinking things through we have come to know that our slavery is entirely unnecessary*'.[246]

Gnocchi-Viani would subsequently recall that the fundamental arguments 'scientifically' proving that this 'slavery' was 'unnecessary' were drawn from Marx himself:

244 Marx to Engels 23 February 1877, in *MECW*, Vol. 45, p. 200.

245 See Perrot 1974, Vol. II, pp. 625 et sqq.; Muller 1911.

246 'La lotta fra le classe', *Il Fascio Operaio*, 31 October–1 November 1885. My italics.

> It is a fact, denied by no-one and not even vaguely put in doubt, that the school of historical materialism, created and headed in erudite fashion, we might say, by Karl Marx, overturned all the barriers building up a wall around the economic problem. Not only that, but with the cutting and sharpened plough of a formidable critique, breaking up and fragmenting the century-old crust that prevented any investigation from getting down to the very bottom of the substrata of the economic world, he brought out into the open the parasitical origins and hypertrophic development of Capital, the baneful passions of servile Labour, either badly paid or not at all, and the route and method of a comforting economic redemption.
>
> The first cure was, through propaganda, to tear up the roots of the mortal belief in the poor man's heart that poverty is the unchangeable and providential decree of a God. Poverty is the deplorable work of man, and just as man brought it into existence, he can and must make it disappear.[247]

The forms in which the class struggle expressed itself were multiple, even if they were hierarchically ordered.

First and foremost was the strike; 'The worker ... must organise in Associations of crafts and trades with the objective of putting up *resistance* against the abuses and insidious deeds of the privileged capitalists. Strikes are his first weapons'.[248] The strike had the dual function of obtaining improvements in working conditions and at the same time of giving workers' organisation better consciousness of itself. It was not, however, a primitive weapon; rather, 'when the workers prove capable of mounting strikes it means that they have already achieved a certain progress, and that they are beginning to feel capable of fighting as men to secure other, more important advances'. In situations of backwardness, where 'poverty is deeper and ignorance greater ... there are headstrong impulses, albeit headless ones, and not strikes in the true sense of the word'.[249]

We know already that the question of strikes has been a central and at the same time defining element of working-class history, in the history of the working-class movement, in the history of socialism; a true and proper crossroads of itineraries, and the weft of many different threads. The strike, 'a rich, dense, object of the workers', 'a means of pressure and mode of expression',[250]

---

247 Gnocchi-Viani 1909, p. 115.

248 'Gli scioperi', *Il Fascio Operaio*, 18–19 October 1884.

249 Ibid.

250 Perrot 1984, pp. 13, 9.

was, in the period in which the working-class movement experimented with its first organisational forms, an essential moment of the 'extension of the individual worker's personality' that set in motion the first mechanisms of the full formation of a 'class consciousness'.[251]

When the workers of *Il Fascio Operaio* wrote the above comments, there had already been divisions and clarification over the strike question,[252] and they already had experiences of some importance behind them such as that of the 1871–2 *biennio*.[253] But only at that point, in the 1880s, would the strike movement in Italy – or more precisely, in the Italy now being industrialised – become a constant characteristic of the social panorama, albeit one remaining well below the level reached by this type of conflictuality in other European contexts. And it was, indeed, starting in 1883, contemporary to the sharp increase in the resistance leagues that would soon become the growth medium for the POI, that there arrived a qualitative leap in the strike movement in industry, with 12,900 participants as opposed to 5,854 the previous year. The number would not again fall under that level, and then rose – albeit with some oscillations – to 96,051 participants in 1896.[254] The strike had now stopped being an *extrema ratio* forced upon the workers; and even if they did only take recourse to strike action when the reasons to do so were truly very pressing, it had become both an *instrument* and a *value*. Strike victories came not only to represent the achievement of demands seeking the improvement of labour's conditions, but also to symbolise *labour*'s victory over *capital*. Strikes were, moreover, decisive moments in the construction of organisational structures transmitting both the *contingent* and *necessary* senses of the conflict between *labour* and *capital*, therefore transmitting both concreteness and utopian projections, a sense of community and the need to widen the sphere of this same community's action, 'a mixture of political, ideal and ethical moments that prefigure[d] a new humanity attached to a new society'.[255] Strikes, therefore, proved to be profoundly important accelerators of the 'process that leads from socialised labour's coming-to-consciousness to the organisation of the struggle against capitalist transformations and the encounter between this resistance

251 Hobsbawm 1984, p. 27.

252 In the documents approved by the Rimini Conference, reproduced in Masini (ed.) 1964, it is said that strikes 'are held to be of little use to the worker materially, but very fruitful in developing the sense of solidarity in labour's struggle against capital' (p. 34).

253 Civolani 1977, Valiani 1950.

254 Barbadoro 1979, reworking the Ministry of Agriculture, Industry and Commerce sources in its 1900 *Statistica scioperi*.

255 See Merli 1972, p. 614.

and political forces and ideas, *within a context of their mutual conditioning*'.[256] This was the connective process most favourable to what would become the working-class mode of understanding Marxism.

After the strike, there was politics. Politics had always been the monopoly of the ruling classes, who had so long 'whipped' and still now 'continue[d] to whip' the subaltern classes. Now, the worker-editors explained, 'We feel the need ... to see if we are able to hold this whip in hand as surely as we do the spool ... or other such instruments of labour'.[257]

In general, then, the class struggle would 'have to unfold in all possible fields. Why? Because the great paths of public life are closed off to the working class, or almost closed, or threatened even where they are open. So it is necessary either to break down the gates to these paths, or to chase off all the threats. And that is why it is necessary to act, and not stand with our arms crossed'.[258] Politics was the site in which 'public opinion becomes an immense melting pot of ideas', the crucible of 'the infamous pandemonium that has so long blinded and swept up the humanity of the oppressed'. As the workers of *Il Fascio Operaio* maintained, 'We have to be there, too'.[259]

Of course, the proletariat could not enter into politics like one of the traditional bourgeois parties, be they conservative, moderate, or radicals, but rather '*as a class* that demands its just rights'.[260]

This was, overall, a relatively articulated and also strongly radical conception of the class struggle, but it was certainly not beyond the bounds of what was maturing as the common sense among 'Marxists' at the end of the 1880s. Indeed, *Il Fascio Operaio* would offer readers explanatory notes from Arturo Labriola himself in this sense.[261]

As we know, the project of organising the working class into a political party has been considered the element of discrimination between 'Marxist' and 'non-Marxist' socialism. We have already seen that it would be more accurate to distinguish – in a relatively long-term comparison covering various different contexts – between 'political Marxists' and 'non-Marxists', within this specific field. Another not-necessarily correlated but also important aspect, here, was

256 Foa 1973, p. 1788.

257 'La Politica', *Il Fascio Operaio*, 13–14 September 1884. See also 'L'urna politica' in the 1–2 May edition of 1886 and 'Candidature operaie' on 8–9 May 1886.

258 Ibid.

259 'L'urna politica' in the 1–2 May edition of 1886.

260 'Per le prossime elezioni comunali', *Il Fascio Operaio*, 15 June 1890, my italics.

261 A. Labriola, 'La lotta di classe', *Il Fascio Operaio*, 15 June 1890. This was a set of passages from a letter of Labriola's appearing in the Reggio Emila *Giustizia*.

the expansive process of increased references to other nuclei of Marx's theory. Yet we can also note that even as directly concerned the question of the 'political party of the working class', the line of discrimination did not take on entirely sharp contours.

That was first and foremost true because, apart from Marx's constant theorisation of the necessity of the working class's political autonomy, and his theorisation of the class struggle as operating in a dimension that would *always* also entail political struggle, in his thought we cannot find any univocal orientation regarding the political party/external class-consciousness relation, nor – and these two aspects are evidently linked – a linear conceptual distinction between party and class. Although we would not accept *in toto* the claim that for Marx the concept of *party* corresponds to the concept of *class*,[262] it is a fact that there is a difference between the way in which he addressed this problem in his writings from 1848 and its immediate aftermath, and the way in which he dealt with it when working-class organisation began to become a structural element of the panorama of European industrial society. In the first period, Marx had identified the *communists* as the intellectual élite that had acquired a general consciousness of the real movement of the class, and thus the party would define itself and grow by means of the stimulus represented by their presence – which was, precisely, a consciousness 'from the outside' of the autonomy and real movement of the working class. In the second period, conversely, the stress no longer fell on the communists as the stimulus to autonomy, but on the 'organised class'. 'With all reference to intellectuals' specific function having been eliminated, the political movement has as its subject the organised class. The organised class is the party'.[263] We have seen that *Il Fascio Operaio* exhorted the workers to enter into the political struggle organised 'as a class', as the appropriate means of confronting the political question. At the Mantua Congress of the POI, the first article of its Statutes stating that the '*Partito operaio* is absolutely extraneous to any political or religious party', also featured this important corollary: 'the *Partito operaio* will participate in the public struggle as a class'.[264] In each case, exactly the same expression was used as had already been present in documents of the International, drawn up by Marx; the same expression, as neither the editors of *Il Fascio Operaio* or the participants at the POI congress could have known, that Marx had used in his critical

262 Rubel 1974.

263 Manacorda 1981, p. 259.

264 Perli 1972, p. 80.

interpretation of the Gotha Congress, in a text dedicated precisely to the politics of the proletarian party.[265]

The POI, the 'workers' party organised as a class', always refused to consider itself a 'political' party, preferring the title 'economic' or 'social' party. The concrete history of the POI clearly demonstrates the very powerful political valence of this 'economic' or 'social' characteristic. But one of the theoretical inspirers of the *Partito operaio* had already introduced some clarification in this regard a few years previously (and, moreover, would repeat these concepts on numerous further occasions) when he stated that 'the political question is not the economic question: but the economic question absorbs and annihilates the political question'.[266] It is difficult to deny that this conception (and practice) of the party in Italy was also a component of the 'diffuse Marxism' that did not take the name 'Marxist'. Of course, it is much more problematic to evaluate how far this corresponded with the 'orthodox canon of Marxist doctrine',[267] even if we accepted that it was possible to define the coordinates of 'Marxist orthodoxy' in the Italy of these years and to indicate which cultural and political forces and which organisations were its bearers.

As such, the conception of class struggle expressed in the columns of *Il Fascio Operaio* was an articulated and radical one. The radicalism of this conception was linked, on the one hand, to the conditions of wage-labour in the period of the 'great depression' (with the microcycle of 1887 to 1894 in Italy proving to be a particularly harsh part of the macrocycle of depression) and on the other hand the type of vision of capitalist society and its historical destiny that was increasingly tending to spread across the workers' movement. Naturally, this type of vision was itself also in part determined by the effects of the 'great depression'.

The cycle of the first great modern capitalist restructuring created more favourable conditions for the reception of the complex set of theoretical and/or ideological elements that we are accustomed to calling 'Marxism'.[268] This

265 'It is altogether self-evident that, to be able to fight at all, the working class must organise itself at home as a class and that its own country is the immediate arena of its struggle': *MECW*, Vol. 24, p. 89.

266 See O. Gnocchi-Viani, 'La questione economica e la questione politica', *La Plebe*, 20 June 1878.

267 Gnocchi-Viani 1989, p. 98; the citation is from Angelini's introductory essay.

268 The radicalism of the class battle that encouraged a particular type of reception of Marxism, providing *one* of the aspects of its reception, cannot be absolutely reduced to a cultural and political attitude favouring the 'civil war' that 'Marxism' declared on the effects

reception was not a univocal phenomenon, with the 'social, political and psychological disposition of those receiving it' also being of essential importance.[269] There is now a vast literature on the effects of the 'great depression' on the world of waged labour in Europe, analysing not only the structural changes it produced, but also cultural and psychological ones. For our present study, it is worth emphasising that in the Italian experience the impact of the system of relations between socialism and the workers' movement remained particularly evident. More precisely, it was the socialists who took political responsibility for the practical requirements stemming from the immediate interests of the world of labour, and even shaped its organisational forms. Wage issues, questions concerning the length of the working day, and working conditions in general, found ever greater space in the socialist press, with an evident change in the general culture of socialism; it was ever less interested in debates and *querelles* among 'schools of socialism', and the winds of 'resistance' increasingly blew through socialism itself. Working-class organisation, its struggles, its values, what Jaurès called its 'creative genius', its positioning itself in the political sphere 'as a class', constituted the densely-textured connective tissue that socialism found that it had to be *internal* to. Whatever remained outside of this context not only had no chance of influencing the real movement, but was destined to dry out, for want of life-blood. Even in European situations where the socialist parties were already by the 1880s relatively developed organisms, and even in the Germany of the SPD, the party deeply breathed in the air of the organised workers' movement. In Italy, where the *Partito socialista* was far from a key element of the political panorama (despite a significant local presence in some areas), what matured was not just the interdependency of the resistance leagues and the party (which was also important); rather, what was ripening was precisely the party organised 'as a class'.

The radicalism deriving from this had nothing to do with old rebellious impulses, but was instead the immediate fruit of 'modernity'; and it operated in relation to the categories of this modernity. It was enriched by the proletarians' attempts to understand the mechanisms of capitalism's functioning, their attempts to outline a clear role for the fundamental subjects of the modern pro-

---

of the industrial revolution. The viscous reality of historical processes provides little basis for those interpretive formulas that attempt to give a global account of more than a century of social struggles in terms of a continuity between the 'civil war' Marx declared on the 'modernity' of the industrial revolution and the 'civil war' that Lenin declared with the Bolshevik revolution in Russia. See Nolte 1983, 1987.

269 Dowe and Tenfelde 1983, p. 176.

duction relation, and in their attempts to give account of their condition and make out a path through which they might transcend it. If the very 'definitions of class' had at one time been 'imprecise and generic' among the socialists, with the *plebs* often standing 'for the working classes and privilege for capitalism',[270] now the organised working class directly took it upon itself to mount a more rigorous analysis – and this would also be reflected in its lexicon. All this took place in an atmosphere in which the correspondence between working conditions and the categories of thought appropriate to explaining them tended to be exalted.

We have mentioned the cry of 'Hunger!' appearing in every corner of the working-class universe, even within the most modern of social relations. This hunger affected not only the vast and fluctuating 'reserve army' that the worker could be forced into at any moment, but the overall dimension of the price of labour-power: the reality of the wage itself. The period of the 'great depression' aggravated what was already, structurally speaking, a very grave situation. Over the last three decades of the nineteenth century[271] the wages of the large majority of industrial workers remained below the minimum living standard established by doctors and sociologists, despite the fact that they often set this level using very restrictive parameters. In general, only skilled workers reached such a standard, but this was a rather precarious balance: any unforeseen occurrence – and there were plenty of them for working-class families lacking almost any safety net – forced them into the abyss of debt, which it was then extremely difficult to escape from. Organised workers, pressured by elementary needs, fought for the improvement of their wage conditions, but at the same time they accompanied this struggle with the search for the reasons for the poverty of their waged labour, and the search for a theory of wages able to give account of the factors behind it. The encounter with Marx's theory of wages was, then, almost obligatory; but as we shall see, the workers' 'Marxist theory' also incorporated elements of a psychological universe that had no particular overlap with 'Marx's theory'.

---

270 Zangheri 1979, p. xx.

271 In truth, notwithstanding certain sectional improvements, this structural situation remained the same through the expansive phase of the Giolittian era. This is apparent from the abundant literature on the incomes and outgoings of working-class families both in the last decades of the nineteenth century and into the 1900s. Many years ago the present writer reconstructed the finances of one working-class family – of skilled workers – in one of the most modern sectors of Italian industry, the strategically important steel industry, toward the end of the Giolittian period. The results only confirmed this picture: Favilli 1974, pp. 88–94.

This same mechanism also concerned the other key point of the worker's condition, namely the length and intensity of the working day, which together with the wage was the central object of the theory and practice of the class struggle. In the 1880s, indeed, much of Italian industry's competitive capacity owed to the fact that it disposed of an inexhaustible reserve workforce, and to its possibility of taking advantage of this in order to make up for its technological and organisational backwardness relative to the more advanced European industrial economies. Hence the dominant characteristic of the non-opposition between the goal of increasing 'absolute surplus-value' and that of increasing 'relative surplus-value': namely, that for a very long time, practically up until the end of the century, both the length of the working day and the intensity of labour increased.

Marx described this phenomenon in language in which *pathos* and realism were closely connected to the more properly analytical moment:

> in its blind unrestrainable passion, its were-wolf hunger for surplus-labour, capital oversteps not only the moral, but even the merely physical maximum bounds of the working-day. It usurps the time for growth, development, and healthy maintenance of the body. It steals the time required for the consumption of fresh air and sunlight. It higgles over a meal-time, incorporating it where possible with the process of production itself, so that food is given to the labourer as to a mere means of production, as coal is supplied to the boiler, grease and oil to the machinery. It reduces the sound sleep needed for the restoration, reparation, refreshment of the bodily powers to just so many hours of torpor as the revival of an organism, absolutely exhausted, renders essential. It is not the normal maintenance of the labour-power which is to determine the limits of the working-day; it is the greatest possible daily expenditure of labour-power, no matter how diseased, compulsory, and painful it may be, which is to determine the limits of the labourers' period of repose. Capital cares nothing for the length of life of labour-power. All that concerns it is simply and solely the maximum of labour-power, that can be rendered fluent in a working-day.[272]

The fundamental elements of this text were evoked on a continual basis, independently of any direct knowledge of its contents.[273] Was it not Marx who

272 *MECW*, Vol. 35, p. 271.

273 Probably the very few workers who had any direct relationship with Marx's text would,

had demonstrated that 'the real goal of capitalist production is the production of extra surplus value, the extortion of extra labour', from which derived 'capital's instinct to prolong the working day, without relent and without discretion'?[274] Was not this, then, the explanation of the working-class condition that made the worker 'raw material in the hands of capital, on account of too many hours of labour', which produced 'the most deplorable, powerful damage to the proletariat's intellect, mind and body'?[275] Here was a correspondence between economic analysis and the worker's lived experience, a correspondence now proving to be the essential component of a 'deep Marxism'.

It has been said that the question of the historic destiny of capitalism represented the other side of the radicalism of workers' conception of the class struggle. And yet the editors of *Il Fascio Operaio* directly attributed their image of capitalist society and its dynamic to the 'resplendent light of the social-economic sciences, which penetrating into the dark back-passages of the proletariat' awakened its consciousness, precisely because it allowed this class to move sure-footedly along the identified paths of social development, 'wholly unlike the capitalists, tenacious [in holding] to false theories'.[276] The contest among the different 'socialist schools', and the prospects of one or the other of them hegemonising the workers' movement, thus played out in terms – also at the immediate levels of workers' awareness – of their capacity to give 'scientific' guarantees to the proletariat.

Obviously the set of 'scientific' postulates to which they referred was as narrow as it was schematic, but at the same time it also took the form of a very coherent web of key ideas, with a notable capacity for aggregation.

One fundamental current, here, was the continually repeated conviction that the antagonism between workers and capitalists was wholly impossible to resolve within the terms of the existing social and political structures.[277] At the same time, the 'scientific' analysis of society's evolution hypothesised the

upon reading such passages, have had the impression of being 'lifted by the hair of the head' like the young Zurich humanist-manual worker Thomas Platter, when in 1519 he heard the 'complete and unadulterated word of God from the pulpit'; see Bainton 1952, pp. 82–3.

274 'Carlo Marx e la giornata normale di lavoro', *Il Fascio Operaio*, 1 May 1890.

275 'Il diritto umano e la riduzione delle ore di lavoro', *Il Fascio Operaio*, 1 May 1890.

276 'Il nuovo partito', *Il Fascio Operaio*, 13–14 December 1884.

277 This concept was formulated in multiple different ways in the paper's columns. For a more systematic version see 'Il capitalista', *Il Fascio Operaio*, 2–4 January/24–25 January 1885, 31 January–1 February 1885.

(catastrophic) end of these structures and the birth of a wholly different order. It identified the tendency toward the polarisation of society as the fundamental contradiction of capitalism, with 'the ever growing poverty of one side and the ever-increasing wealth of the other'.[278] Crises that were ever more ruinous in tendency – *inevitable* stages marking out capitalism's path – resulted from the anarchy inherent to this system of production as well as the constant underconsumption that resulted from *the iron law of wages*, which did not allow the workers' condition to rise above one of mere subsistence.[279]

It is interesting to note, however, that even *Il Fascio Operaio*'s full acceptance of a 'catastrophist' vision, within a perspective of capitalist 'collapse', did not prevent it from maintaining that struggles seeking to win wage rises and a reduction in working hours were both useful and just, including from a 'theoretical' point of view. In fact, the workers of *Il Fascio Operaio* did not hesitate in mounting a polemic (even if in rather polite terms) against Giovanni Rossi (Cardias), author of one of the 'socialist parables' most popular in the 1880s workers' movement,[280] contesting his argument that it was 'illusory' to think of attaining such improvements within the capitalist system. And they did so by taking recourse to Marx's authority, with what was perhaps the paper's only direct reference to the Trier thinker prior to 1890.[281] Marx, therefore, played the role of a 'scientific' authority *in the last instance*, even in a context where he was cited very little.

Il Fascio Operaio maintained that Marx had ascribed a relative, not absolute value to the minimal limits of subsistence that regulated the wage dynamic: the level of vital needs could be increased, translating into 'an immediate improvement of … [workers'] conditions'.[282] Therefore, they maintained that it was right to fight for wage increases and the reduction of working hours, even while remaining convinced that 'the worker question [continued] to exist and [demanded] its only possible solution, namely the complete emancipation of the workers from the capitalist yoke'. After all, the achievement of these partial objectives would simultaneously represent 'a rapid improvement in …

278 'Parole, parole, parole', *Il Fascio operaio*, 23–24 October 1885.

279 'Crisi e fallimento della moderna società', *Il Fascio Operaio*, 7–8 March 1885, 28 June 1885.

280 *Un comune socialista*, signed 'Cardias', published in Milan in 1878. One index of its popularity can be deduced from the fact that among the close to fifty books and pamphlets included in the Biblioteca di Propaganda Socialista in 1880, Rossi's text was the only one to sell out of copies.

281 See 'Ancora il nostro scopo finale', *Il Fascio Operaio*, 5–6 December 1885.

282 Ibid.

conditions and a powerful means for increasing ... the forces in struggle for the ... complete emancipation' of the workers.[283]

In sum, this was a set of propositions that a few years later would almost fully flow into the 'Marxist consciousness' of the political organisation of the proletariat, now coming to represent the hard core of a popularised, collective Marxism. As for its confusion between Lassalle's *iron law* and Marx's own conception of wages, this would in fact long remain a constant, and would not only regard Marxism *en bas*, but also the very flower of the academic economists, whether socialist or otherwise.[284] We might, indeed, ask if such elements of confusion in the workers' culture owed only to philological shortcomings and/or the difficulties of reading Marx's texts, or if they were, instead, linked to the overall 'catastrophist' interpretation – of which the theory of wages can be considered one aspect – that seemed almost a necessary phase in the early development of the workers' movement. Often we have an image of Marxism penetrating through a line of descent: from Marx to socialist political movements to workers' movements. This type of approach suggests a reception process that has a *subject* and then an *object*: Marx's *oeuvre* and the workers' movement, respectively. In reality, as we have seen already, the workers' movement was also itself a *subject* in this process. We need only think of the conception – held to be a corollary of the theory of wages – according to which the worker had a right to 'the full proceeds of his labour'. Despite the fact that we find no such argument in Marx – indeed, Marx explicitly combatted such a notion – this would long remain a 'Marxist' constant in the organised working class's modes of feeling and expressing itself.

The paths that we have followed thus far allow us better to understand the character assumed by the relation that *Il Fascio Operaio* now began to establish, from the start of 1890s, with the 'Marxist model' represented by the SPD.

A far-reaching literature has shed light on the role that the German social-democrats' 1890 electoral victory had in the decisive triumph of Marxism within the Italian workers' and socialist movement, with the German social-democrats' successes 'appearing to European public opinion as a ring in a chain apparently inevitable and necessary in its succession'.[285] This qualitative jump is immediately clear from *Il Fascio Operaio*, even though it had also shown previous interest in the SPD's electoral activities.[286]

---

283 'La riduzione delle ore di lavoro', *Il Fascio Operaio*, 21–2 November 1885.

284 Favilli 1980.

285 Ragionieri 1961, p. 159.

286 See 'Gli operai e le elezioni in Germania', *Il Fascio Operaio*, 25–6 October 1884.

Italy's most emblematic workers' paper thus greeted the German social democracy's electoral success by reporting that 'the workers of Germany, rallied in the Socialist Party, have brought our cause an immense, grandiose victory'.[287] From then onward it published (and gave prominent position to) numerous of Martignetti's translations of articles from the *Sozialdemokrat* dedicated to the Italian workers' movement, whose development the German paper followed by way of Marxist analytical categories.[288] Martignetti himself presented Marx's positions on the length of the working day by making use of a few citations from *Capital*, wholly naturally speaking of 'our Marx', who was now clearly accepted as *nume tutelare* of their common home.[289] And the editors now made use of Antonio Labriola's Marxism better to specify their own positions with regard to bourgeois radicalism.[290]

Although *Il Fascio Operaio* was the organ of the *Partito operaio italiano* – that is, of a party within which there was a long discussion of whether or not to adopt the label 'socialist' – it remained almost wholly governed by a socialist perspective. This experience and the themes that we have analysed thus far can, therefore, be read as an important aspect of the evolution of working-class socialism in the 1880s. And yet they did not concern the socialist milieu alone. Independently of their panorama of ideal references, over the course of the 1880s all the forces that were truly an expression of 'resistance' and fully accepted the logics of the class struggle in which it played a prominent role came to elaborate a relatively homogeneous culture and to share fundamentally similar goals.

Again in the industrial 'Upper Italy' to which Engels referred, another paper wholly produced by workers, *Il Lavoratore Comasco*, was printed from 1888 onward in a setting shaped by old manufacturing traditions. Indeed, the editors of *Il Lavoratore Comasco* deemed *Il Fascio Operaio* not 'a true workers' paper', given that 'teachers and lawyers' also collaborated in its production, and they added with pride 'we of the *Lavoratore* are all workers'.[291] The paper was Mazzinian and Garibaldian in inspiration, declaring itself open to social legislation and even traditional political forms, and rejecting only 'those who do politics

287 See 'Vittorie e Speranze', *Il Fascio Operaio*, 16 March 1890.

288 'Pel 18 marzo'; 'Il 1° maggio e il movimento operaio in Italia'; 'Quel che dicono i compagni tedeschi sulla situazione sociale d'Italia'; 'Come viene giudicato in Germania il movimento operaio-socialista italiano', *Il Fascio Operaio*, from the 23 March, 25 May, 29 June, and 17 August 1890 issues respectively.

289 'Carlo Marx e la giornata normale di lavoro', *Il Fascio Operaio*, 1 May 1890.

290 'Il radicalismo borghese e il partito operaio', *Il Fascio Operaio*, 18 May 1890.

291 'Meglio soli che male accompagnati', *Il Lavoratore Comasco*, 17 March 1888.

as a career ... or out of dilettanteism'.[292] There was no lack of polemics with the POI, often considered too socialist and not sufficiently working class. However, it did recognise that beyond their ideological distinctions it did have some common ground with the POI, and was completely in accordance as to their common 'watchword; *Resistance our means, emancipation our end*'. It was both radical and decisive in its choice to consider the 'organisation of the proletariat' the primary tool 'to bring the reign of social privilege inexorably to its end', together with what was very tellingly described as 'the exploitation of man by man'.[293]

Its radicalism consisted precisely in its indication of emancipation as its end goal and its rigid counterposition of class against class. At the same time, it was sharp in its condemnation of violence, verbose but hollow revolutionism, and eschatological expectations for the short term, such as were preached without distinction by both anarchists and 'the charlatans of socialism'.[294] Emancipation would instead come from a gradual process of objective growth in workers' self-education and self-government in their organisations. Yet once again, Marx was used as a scientific guarantor of a gradualist path to emancipation.

Only in one article in the first months of this paper's life – and in this period, also with some contradiction[295] – would Marx appear as the inspirer of a minority socialist current convinced 'that the emancipation of the proletariat will never come if not through violence, through force, through revolution'.[296] After that, Marx and the experiences of the SPD would become positive moments exemplifying the decisions of the resistance leagues inspired by *Il Lavoratore Comasco*.

If Liebknecht won at the polls, this was because he refused to be too 'exclusivist',[297] and his party could fly from success to success because it was truly the expression of the workers and did not breed internal feuds.[298] Of course there were also discords even among the German socialists, but Bebel, a front-rank figure, had 'for some years maintained a very moderate attitude ... Thus the

292 'Agli amici e agli avversari. Operai e politica. La legislazione internazionale del lavoro', *Il Lavoratore Comasco*, 18 February and 31 March 1888.

293 'Partito operaio o socialista', *Il Lavoratore Comasco*, 3 March 1888.

294 'I ciarlatani del socialismo', *Il Lavoratore Comasco*, 31 March 1888.

295 For example, the paper would always hold in high esteem the positions of Bebel and Liebknecht, defined as 'the two most audacious promoters of Marx's school in Germany': 'Bismark e la questione sociale', *Il Lavoratore Comasco*, 9 June 1888.

296 'Il movimento operaio Franco-Italo-Svizzero', *Il Lavoratore Comasco*, 21 July 1888.

297 'Le vittorie del socialismo in Germania', *Il Lavoratore Comasco*, 8 September 1888.

298 'L'esempio della Germania', *Il Lavoratore Comasco*, 1 March 1890.

fanatical revolutionaries truly have it in for Bebel, who has proven temperate in his ideas'.[299] And moreover, Bebel had won in a conflict at Halle opposing *the old to the young*, his victory being the victory of a non-extremist socialism attentive to the political dimension.[300] These German tendencies pointed the way to the international proletariat, which was already starting to draw its lessons; the Marxist international, which had proclaimed the objective of reducing working hours, was 'a legalist International ... destined to triumph'.[301]

There was thus a perfect continuity when two years later, in a climate of now changed political choices, the figure of Marx himself appeared as a surety to the claim that 'combatting capitalism is not worthwhile' since 'it combats itself, by itself';[302] this was a Marx who did not encourage 'class hatred' since 'both the capitalists and the exploited are necessary instruments of the present system'.[303]

This road to 'Marxism' – the road of 'gradualism' and 'legalism' – would be just one aspect, and perhaps the most externally evident one, of the 'transition' in the working-class world that found its voice in *Il Lavoratore Comasco*. The other, internal one – even for these workers who up till 1892 had not defined themselves as 'straightforwardly socialists'[304] – related to the fact that independently of their ideological reference point, they did end up organising in a party 'as a class'. While their original programme had seemed moderate, they immediately clashed with the very harsh reality of the bosses' 'resistance'.[305] They thus faced the need to take recourse to strike action 'because the proletariat has no weapons left';[306] the demystification of labour's freedom, 'since the worker has his law and it is a terrible one: the law of hunger, which does not allow him to go without working, at his pleasure like a delinquent';[307] and the primary necessity of an organisation not bound within corporatist limits.

299 'Le discordie dei socialisti tedeschi', *Il Lavoratore Comasco*, 30 August 1890.

300 'Il congresso dei socialisti tedeschi', 'Echi del congresso di Halle', 'Dopo il congresso di Halle', *Il Lavoratore Comasco*, 18 October, 25 October and 1 November 1890.

301 'Riflessioni', *Il Lavoratore Comasco*, 10 May 1890.

302 'Il Socialismo italiano', *Il Lavoratore Comasco*, 4 June 1892.

303 'Che cosa è il socialismo (leggendo Marx)', *Il Lavoratore Comasco*, 31 December 1892.

304 'Commiato', *Il Lavoratore Comasco*, 6 August 1892.

305 Its essential points on the socio-economic plane were 'labour sharing in the profits of production', the 'normal working day', and the limiting of women's and children's working hours; and on the political plane universal suffrage and payment for elected representatives: see 'Programma', *Il Lavoratore Comasco*, 26 May 1888.

306 'Il nostro sciopero', *Il Lavoratore Comasco*, 24 November 1888.

307 'La moralità dei licenziamenti', *Il Lavoratore Comasco*, 28 April 1888.

On this basis, they could not close themselves off from the POI, whatever their polemics. Yet it was necessary to arrive at the Party by starting 'from below', beginning by founding provincial resistance leagues 'such as then to arrive at the convocation of a mighty congress to decide upon the Federation of the *Partito operaio italiano*'.[308]

Through the highs and lows of its relation with the POI, the logic of day-to-day joint participation in the experience of the class struggle – with the foundation of leagues following successful strikes, their break-up after failed ones, and the search for a workers' unity that the Pact of Rome had proved wholly unable to secure – would end up leading the workers of *Il Lavoratore Comasco* and of the POI to construct a common *Partito dei lavoratori italiani*. Given the logic of this type of 'resistance', *Il Lavoratore Comasco* could not but meet together with *Il Fascio Operaio* and socialism. And the youth taking over from former editor Ariste Bari, a 'worker-radical', who left out of rejection of the paper's new 'straightforwardly socialist' positioning, could rightly remind him that fundamentally they were just the fruit of the way in which they had been 'raised and brought up' in the school that Bari himself had run.[309] Not by chance, then, the first writings of Marx's to appear in the socialist paper did not regard the political sphere, but rather the interwoven threads of the worker's labouring conditions that had always been at the centre of *Il Lavoratore Comasco*'s attention: the question of the length of the working day and the modes of labour-power's sale as a commodity.[310] And not by chance, they proposed to exemplify and test out Marx's analytical categories in light of the worker's practical experience.[311]

We can thus consider the outcomes of *Il Fascio Operaio* (and the *Partito operaio italiano* to which it gave voice) and *Il Lavoratore Comasco* to be in large measure 'Marxist', even if they matured in contiguity (and sometimes confusion) with other ideological themes within an atmosphere characterised by 'generic socialism'.[312] Many of these ideological motifs then continued to

---

308 'La resistenza', *Il Lavoratore Comasco*, 1 December 1888.

309 'Presentazione', *Il Lavoratore Comasco*, 13 August 1892.

310 'La giornata del lavoro', 'Valore del lavoro': *Il Lavoratore Comasco*, 10 September and 31 December 1892 respectively.

311 'Rivista sociale', *Il Lavoratore Comasco*, 15 October 1892.

312 The police informers must also have arrived at these conclusions, since in the Casati file the following could be said of the positions of one of the most 'exclusivist' POI members in the early 1890s: 'He is an admirer of the theories of Marx, but sometimes he has also exhibited anarchist ideas, too'. See the Casellario Politico Centrale file reproduced in the appendix to Briguglio 1971, p. 88.

accompany the development of Marxism, in parallel to or intersecting with it, even well beyond the outcomes of which we have spoken.

Obviously this was a particular, impoverished type of 'Marxism', whose schematic, deterministic character and mixing with other cultures an abundant historiography has repeatedly underlined. Yet it was a Marxism that would become a fundamental element of the ideological structure of the political organisation of the proletariat, of its socialist identity, and the object of a vast programme of *vulgarisation*.

It is important to note, however, that in this case such characteristics were not at all the effect of a conscious process of vulgarisation, and were in fact present *before* this process began. These elements were certainly present within the wider heritage of the various 'socialist schools', and it was sometimes difficult to distinguish which specific one they 'belonged' to, but they also directly corresponded to the cultural, political and organisational demands of strongly radicalised worker vanguards. In substance, here we are dealing with a sort of *diffuse Marxism*, a confused Marxism whose fundamental components had already tended to structure themselves in a largely organic system, under the impulse of the *practical* requirements of the most advanced part of the organised workers' movement. This already active tendency was sharply accelerated on account of the positive impact of an external event (the SPD electoral victory) in which an explicit 'Marxism', used as a banner and pointed to as a model, seemed to have played a fundamentally important role. This meant that the external influences, important as they were, met with an already active process that had distinctly autonomous characteristics, destined to leave a far from superficial mark on the peculiarities of Italian Marxism.

CHAPTER 3

The Marxism of the 1890s: Foundation – and Orthodoxy?

1 The 'Partito Marxista'

> The *Partito dei lavoratori*, conscious of its own mission, has developed, or is developing, only where the machine has already been very much at work, be that in cities like Milan, Como etc. or in the countryside like in [the provinces of] Mantua, Emilia and Polesine ... The workers' movement in Italy has arrived now, at a moment of historic evolution ...[1]

We are now in 1890, and the writer of these words, Antonio Labriola, would soon come to take a leading role in the foundation of the 'Partito marxista' in Italy. In the meantime, he indicated that such a party would be possible only where the conditions for a modern class struggle had matured, and that in the last decade of the 1890s it was possible to make out the signs of a turning point also for the workers' movement in the Italian peninsula.

So almost twenty years after the famous Resolution IX of the London Conference and the split in the International – which had divided at the Hague Congress with particular reference to this point – were the conditions now materialising for Marx's old indications to be operable also in Italy? And could the 'Partito marxista'[2] that would be born two years later, or the other 'Marxist parties in Europe' – almost all the fruits of the second half of the 1880s and the 1890s, and which the new 'Marxist international' was coordinating – truly be considered the direct heirs to Marx's elaboration in the times of the First International?

We have seen in the previous chapters that it is not possible to construct any systematic theory of the political party out of Marx's own elaborations, with the author of *Capital* having shown little interest 'in the problems of party structure, organisation or sociology, which were to preoccupy later theo-

1 Labriola 1973, Vol. I, p. 133.

2 This expression was used explicitly; see 'La Questione dei mezzi', in *La Lotta di Classe*, 7–8 January 1893. A few years later, the *Partito socialista* could readily be called 'a company with Marx's name above its door' or 'Marx's firm': 'Il bilancio', *Almanacco Socialista*, 1899, pp. 23–5.

rists'.[3] The two fundamental elements that did, however, represent the red thread of this elaboration, the *Selbständigkeit* – that is, the autonomy of the real movement of the working class – and the 'affirmation of the political character of the class struggle in capitalist society',[4] were still considered in relation to the historical processes then underway, which were thus decisive in determining the 'party form'.

In a period distinguished either by revolutions that are actually underway or by the hope in a rapid resumption of the revolutionary cycle, it is typical for conceptions of the party to confer a fundamental role on an élite in which 'consciousness' of the class's general interests has matured, together with the 'science' of the 'real movement' of the class and of society, even if this élite does not necessarily coincide with the class itself. Yet in a context marked by a long-term tendency of continued and rapid growth in the productive forces, seeming to delineate a fundamentally 'matured' historical time, there is a change in the coordinates of such an external consciousness's field of action. That is why political groups bearing an ideology, a 'philosophy' that does not directly spring from the heart of the *contradiction* inherent to the production process, and from a class that *autonomously* becomes conscious of the general significance of that contradiction, are no longer to be characterised as parties, but rather as 'sects', albeit 'socialist sects'. The International experience was fundamentally important in determining one particularly significant point of Marx's reflection on the 'political' party of the working class:

> The International was founded in order to replace the socialist or semi-socialist sects by a real organisation of the working class for struggle. The original Rules and the Inaugural Address show this at a glance. On the other hand, the International could not have asserted itself if the course of history had not already smashed sectarianism. The development of socialist sectarianism and that of the real labour movement always stand in indirect proportion to each other. So long as the sects are justified (historically), the working class is not yet ripe for an independent historical movement. As soon as it has attained this maturity all sects are essentially reactionary.[5]

3 Hobsbawm 1978, p. 260.

4 Manacorda 1992, p. 163.

5 Marx to Bolte, 23 November 1871, *MECW*, Vol. 44, p. 251.

And just the previous year, on the occasion of the founding of a new Paris section of the International, Marx had recommended to his daughter Laura and Lafargue:

> Let [Verlet] give to the new section he is about to establish no sectarian 'name' … *Il faut éviter les 'étiquettes' sectaires dans l'Association Internationale.* The general aspirations and tendencies of the working class emanate from the real conditions in which it finds itself placed. They are therefore common to the whole class although the movement reflects itself in their heads in the most diversified forms, more or less phantastical, more or less adequate.[6]

It would be a mistake to read this polemic against the 'sects' – a constant appearing throughout Marx and Engels's both private and public interventions in the 1860s and 1870s – mainly in terms of the logic of the controversy with Bakunin. This polemic preceded the beginning of the conflict with Bakunin and perfectly corresponded to Marx's way of considering the International experience, right from the moment of its foundation. Marx fully participated in this experience, in both the political and theoretical dimensions, with interventions in which action and reflection interacted on the basis of the real processes that were then underway. These were real processes in which class organisation and class struggle seemed to unfold in a manner characterised by the integration of the political and economic spheres. This was an integration that Marx very much wanted to see, considering it a primary index of the hoped-for – and actively sought – process forming the 'party as class'.

In the last chapter we saw that in the Italian case *this* 'Marxist' conception of the party – a conception according to which the two terms 'party' and 'class' could be used almost as synonyms – allowed the gradual taking root of what I called 'Marxism outside of Marxism'. But we also know that one of the fundamental elements of the ideology of the 'Marxist parties' of the Second (and also Third) International was the theorisation of the separation between economics and politics, between the dimension proper to the union and that proper to the party. The Italian 'Partito marxista', as *La Lotta di classe* explicitly called it, was no exception,[7] even if the contours of this separation were subject to continual adjustments. Nor were the other parties immune to discussions as to the fluidity of these boundaries, the SPD in Germany included.

---

6 Marx to Lafargue, 18 April 1870, *MECW*, Vol. 43, p. 485.

7 'La questione dei mezzi', *La Lotta di classe*, 7–8 January 1893.

The structural characteristics and political-cultural climate that encouraged such theories of 'separation' were not obviously the same as the ones in which Marx's own political initiatives and reflection developed. However, from the end of the 1880s and the early 1890s, when the 'Marxist party' in Europe began to lay down solid roots, the prevalent conditions – however homogeneous they were across different contexts – were still not such as to give any alien feel to Marx's ensemble of 1860s and 1870s indications on party and class. There persisted far from negligible aspects of a period in which 'the process of institutionalisation, the ritualisation of modes of action and the codification of means'[8] had not yet begun.

Even in Germany, where a commonplace long-cultivated by certain sections of the historiography has tried to represent the 'Marxist party' as a *primus* separate from workers' organisation – its near-dependent *offspring* – even at the beginning of the 1890s the question of the party-union relationship could still not be considered to have been defined in the fundamental terms that it would later assume.[9] Even in Germany, before the Gotha Congress the influence among the working-class world of what came to be defined as 'social-democratic' ideas principally advanced by way of organised labour – the current of ideas, capacity and experience of struggle matured within the *Arbeitervereine*.[10] Even in Germany, in particular in the period of the anti-socialist laws, it proceeded by way of the close connection between workers' organisation and the party, without any particular scale of priority, in a context in which economic crisis and political repression seemed to confirm the Marxist analysis of society and the state. This was a connection that Bernstein would later judge positively, on account of the lessons of realism and mobilising capacity that it would offer social democracy,[11] with notable effects even in the 1890s.[12] As the union leader Carl Legien explained at the 1893 Cologne Congress of the SPD, workers' organisation was:

> the best instrument of political agitation, and a school far better and much better-suited than political organisation in making the worker a comrade, firm in character and endowed with a spirit of sacrifice. Indeed, political organisation does not ask as much of its members as does trade-

8 Haupt 1981, p. 216.
9 Schröder 1975.
10 See Droz 1981, pp. 103–13.
11 Bernstein 1900.
12 Ritter 1959.

> union organisation … which demands that in battles over wages each member put his whole existence, his whole person on the line, for the good of the collective …[13]

Here were accents and elements that gave particular valence to the conception of the union as a 'school for socialism': a conception that was at that time widely accepted in the 'Marxist party'.

In Italy workers' organisation had been and continued to be considered a true and proper school, and not simply a preparatory class. Even at this stage Filippo Turati understood its fundamental nature, considering it an essential element of the construction of the *Partito socialista dei lavoratori italiani*. Certainly he was hardly familiar with *theoretical* Marxism in the late 1880s and early 1890s, and as we will see this lack of familiarity remained a constant even in subsequent years. Yet in this context he nonetheless proved an extraordinary interpreter of *political* Marxism, and the executor of Marx's Resolution IX in Italian conditions.

In the period immediately prior to the party's foundation, Turati was operating and reflecting in a context that was particularly favourable to the acceleration of the developmental tendencies already at work in the 'Upper Italian' workers' movement. 'The orientation toward doctrine' – Costantino Lazzari, one of the other protagonists of this operation, would write, 'was compulsory given the circumstances that we had found ourselves in'.[14] 1891–2 was distinguished by important moments of social and industrial crisis, with numerous, telling episodes of workers' resistance. The whole group of workers and intellectuals that had driven the *Congresso operaio italiano* of 1891 fully participated in this resistance movement, with the *Lega socialista* and the POI having demonstrated at the congress that real integration was possible. Moreover, the *Lega* had often operated in close contiguity with the POI, and often depended on its initiative, to the extent that this could hardly be considered simply a matter of 'outside consciousness'.

The experience of these strikes, in particular the 'Elvetica' strike – an exemplary display of workers' solidarity – profoundly connected Turati's reflection to the simultaneously both solid and potentially brittle processes of the organisation of the proletariat in the factories. They gradually consolidated his understanding of a *class* that was making itself a *party* precisely through the continuous practice of the 'class struggle'. This was a conflict that Turati would seek to

13 Cited in Benvenuti 1981, p. 69.

14 Lazzari 1952, p. 791.

intervene in directly, including by way of a text that he prepared as a preface to the *Statuto della Lega di resistenza fra gli operai metallurgici ed affini di Milano, votato nell'assemblea del 7 novembre 1891*, which can be considered the most mature argumentation produced by Italian socialist culture of the early 1890s concerning the complex morphology of the organisation of resistance and its role in the construction of the 'class-party'.

Resistance was the 'first step' in a 'revolution'; a 'revolution in which the workers cease to be the blind instruments of the upheavals of human history' and instead become 'conscious participants' in its development.[15] The relevant terrain remained the – wholly Marxian – one of the 'class struggle', conceived in a broad and articulated way. For certain, for Turati as for Marx the 'class struggle' was not entirely limited to the social dynamic of which the organised workers' movement is the protagonist; yet at the same time, without an organised workers' movement, without leagues and federations of trades, the class struggle would lose any depth, becoming merely evanescent and being reduced to a merely surface-level political project.

On the other hand, not only was it impossible for the workers' movement to do without a theory of its own role in the economy and society, but in practice its very development itself tended to become an essential function of that theory. Polemicising with Gnocchi-Viani on this point, the director of *La Critica Sociale* maintained that the objective situation in the factories provided for an 'instinctive' feeling of 'the mystery of capitalist accumulation and [the fact that this] cannot be anything other than the result of a spoliation', but the true qualitative leap in the class struggle would come only when 'scientific analysis [had posed] the precise formula of exploitation'.[16] Theory was thus presented as *necessary* for the workers' movement, at the same time that the development and extension of this movement and trade-union action were themselves considered *necessary* elements for both the construction and the confirmation of theory. In the Turati of the early 1890s we also find the conviction that this *confirmation* would be nothing other than the effective, necessarily realised proof of the theory's *scientific* character.

The resistance movement ultimately came to take on a multiplicity of meanings: it was not only a 'duty' on the workers for the sake of improving their own living conditions, and not only the 'salvation and very honour' of the class.[17] No; more importantly, it transcended the narrowly economic sphere, such as to

---

15 Turati 1898, p. 21.

16 'Postilla a O. Gnocchi-Viani, *La volatilizzazione della lotta di classe*', *Critica Sociale*, 1892, p. 200.

17 Turati 1898, p. 20.

play a role also in the sphere of social and juridical relations among the classes and their political expressions. Indeed, the precepts of 'Marxist science' held that the transition to socialism was now unfolding, and elements of it could already be seen in social struggles, above all in the more advanced countries. Turati followed the Carmaux[18] strikes with very keen interest (and we should also remember the importance that they had for Jaurès), which he saw as rich in lessons in the same sense that we have just described.

> In the regime of small industry the boss who shows the worker the door is not violating any law. Society does not even ask that he explain the reasons why he took away the bread of a man who sweated so much on his account ... In these conditions it is undoubtedly the worker who is in the weaker position. As industry develops, the right to sack workers begins to come up against limits: and it is limited to the exact extent that the power of the workers, in their solidarity with one another, grows: [this right] loses its absolute form when the workers are truly stronger than it. Hence there will be laws of regulation and prohibition, and in certain cases what is today considered a right will instead be considered a crime. Just as property ceased to be a usurpation the day that it became stronger than propertylessness. It again appears as usurpation, when propertylessness is enriched with social forces. The juridical and moral criterion exactly follows the deed, and the dimensions of the competing forces follow the pattern of what results.[19]

So in the Carmaux case, while the law that was in place allowed for the worker's sacking, the organised resistance forced the public authorities to resort to arbitration, which compelled the bosses' side to renounce its absolute right to hire and fire. Beyond the extent and the bitterness of this struggle, it produced a clarification and a new articulation of the political forces both within and outside of parliament. The bourgeois front had cracked, preventing the solidification

18 In the Carmaux mines in France, a sacking that was considered unjust gave rise to a long and sharp social conflict, which had a vast echo in the press and major repercussions for French political debate and, indeed, the country's political balance.

19 'Il conflitto di Carmaux ed il gioco dei partiti in Francia', *Critica Sociale*, 1892, p. 322. Antonio Labriola, engaged in a moment of sharp polemic with Turati as well as the work of founding 'Marxist party', aptly grasped the exemplary dimension of the Carmaux strikes: 'It seems to me that what is playing out in Carmaux is a typical example, which will serve as an education and as a drive', Turati to Engels 5 October 1892, in Labriola 1983, Vol. II, p. 391.

of the dreaded 'single reactionary mass', while the socialist front was enriched with more immediate and concrete class references.

Four years later, the same dynamic would again take hold in Carmaux – not in the mines this time, but in the glassmakers' workshops – and its repercussions were such as to unleash a governmental crisis. *In loco*, it encouraged the formation of a 'collectivist' nucleus with the idea of forming a workers' glass-making cooperative: doubtless a risky idea, but also one charged with positive novel elements.[20]

In short, the class struggle was not confined to the factory alone: it went out of the factory gates, concerning all levels of political and social organisation. The strike and the resistance leagues were essential elements of a circuit that was very much internal to the political dimension of socialism, the flesh and blood of its existence and vitality. In turn, socialism as a 'science', nourished by this real movement, gave the workers' movement the *Selbständigkeit* without which there was no possible way out of mere 'corporatism'.

The way in which the function and role of the workers' movement were conceived in the early 1890s thus directly derived from the way in which Marxism was used and understood, in an *organic* and *integral* vision of capitalist development and the transition to socialism. This was a conception of Marxism in which the trade-union and political dimensions were necessarily integrated, and not divided, and thus came to form the fundamental pillar guaranteeing the solidity of the whole structure. This conception reached its maturation and stabilisation in the period of the founding of the 'party'; and Turati's intention was to establish an indissoluble link between its core socialist *essence* and the reasons for its *diversity*. This entailed the delimitation of a territory, the deepening of a *consciousness*, and the foundation of an *ideology* – and the *Critica Sociale* of the 1890s was largely dedicated to these aims.[21] This was a programme that the director of *Critica Sociale* followed in a coherent and determined fashion, without any *ideological* eclecticism. Beyond the eclecticism of the line-up of writers appearing in this review,[22] we ought to follow the very

20 See F. Turati, 'Le grandi lotte moderne e il nuovo diritto proletario', and 'Il doppio versante della cooperazione. La vetreria operaia di Carmaux', *Critica Sociale*, 1896, pp. 341–3 and 354–6 respectively.

21 Explicitly stated in 'Rapporto presentato al congresso internazionale di Zurigo' (Report presented by the Italians at the Zurich congress), *Critica Sociale*, 1893, pp. 252–4.

22 Upon beginning publication Turati made sure immediately to clarify that the promised 'training ground' for debate should be understood as 'a training ground of struggle and thought, [aimed] toward a *designated end*', thus reserving himself a role in prudently yet decisively orienting the discussions. Indeed, right in the first issue, faced with a Bovio who

dense pattern of interventions by the Editors, by Turati, by Turati-Kuliscioff, the 'Marginal Notes' and 'Preface' pieces, pursuing a line that constantly unfolded in accordance with a precise project well permeated with a very deep internal coherence. The question of whether this line always succeeded in setting the overall tone of this publication – its image, as a review – has to be confirmed by way of a study of specific problems.

In any case, it would be hard to deny that Turati closely linked the possibility of a rigorous definition of the party's *diversity* with a full acceptance of Marxism as an *ideology*. Turati appeared as – and in large measure was – a promoter and 'master' of this programme.[23] For Turati, the *diversity* of socialism consisted in the fact that it was founded on a scientific analysis of the development of the capitalist productive forces and their historic antagonist: the working class. Socialism was socialism only if it was *scientific*, and *scientific* only if it was Marxist. It is no chance thing that the Turati of this period used the expressions *scientific socialism* and *Marxism* – and often even simply *socialism* – as synonyms.

What is today a historical problem – the question of the forms in which the encounter of Marxism, socialism and the workers' movement took place – would have not been a matter of any doubt for the Turati of that time: Marxism was but the point of arrival for the very idea of socialism, fertilised by the actual processes of the real movement.

He now accepted all the doctrinal components that defined the *corpus* of Marxism in the early 1890s. Prefacing Martignetti's translation of Engels's introduction to the popular re-edition of *Wage-Labour and Capital*, Turati showed that he had no doubts as to the fact that the 'labour theory of value' and the theory of the 'wage system' were 'the very basis of the Marxist critique of capitalism' and thus 'in a certain guise the foundation of scientific socialism'.

---

announced that being 'a Republican like Rosa, a naturalist like Ardigò, a socialist like you, I could not fail [to respond to the appeal to collaborate]' (letter, 4 January 1891), Turati took care to distinguish the socialism that this publication promoted from 'generic socialism': 'I partiti politici e il socialismo', *Critica Sociale*, 1891, p. 7.

23 Countless people recognised Turati as their 'teacher' in Marxism, and not only those who lived the whole history of Italian socialism in partnership with him, like Alessandro Schiavi, but also ones who became his 'Left' adversaries like Leone and Labriola, as well as 'right-wing' ones like Bonomi. In 1950, in his preface to the book edition of Turati's parliamentary interventions (published for discussion in the Chamber of Deputies), Bonomi recalled first having heard of him in the summer of 1893, when 'he was still not yet a deputy [in parliament], still not the leader of a great party; he was the director of *La Critica Sociale*, the most caustic of polemicists, and the most gifted and most acute of the young Italian Marxists': Turati 1950, p. xv.

'Marx's analysis', he added, 'appears to any attentive reader, not governed by prejudice, as so logical, so simple, so irrefutable, so obvious', while he accused 'official economics' of 'hiding the cardinal, guiding, basic idea of the system'. He continued:

> Marxist collectivism is the only truly scientific theory, the only impassable point of view, elevated and serene amidst the hubbub of purported social perspectives and solutions that the charlatans and dupes serve up to a suffering humanity, amidst so many useless good-will initiatives ... amidst so many awkward, hesitating, indecisive spirits, amidst so many miserable transactions between logic and interest and vanity, of corrupting philanthropy and more or less venerated impostures.[24]

---

24 F. Turati, 'Fra capitalista e lavoratore, Le ragioni intime del loro conflitto secondo Marx', *Critica Sociale*, 1891, p. 149.

A long comment on an article by Guglielmo Ferrero, 'Carlo Marx ucciso da Carlo Darwin secondo un nostro darwiniano' (*Critica Sociale*, 1891, pp. 133–5 – comment on pp. 135–8) allows us to grasp the fundamental elements of Turati's Marxist ideology at the beginning of the 1890s.

a) Marxism is the end of any utopian 'social romanticism'; 'the social romance is replaced by history, the true *natural history* of society. This is not simply a matter of erudition or political chronicling, but the informed search, based on natural facts, into the laws according to which the social organism evolves over time. This method gives Marxism its great superiority over any other contemporary socialist school. In other words, Marx is indeed the Darwin of the social sciences'.
b) 'Marx did not limit himself to noting the change taking place, over time, in species and beings, but also noted the changing of the laws that govern – or more precisely, express – the phenomena at the different levels of evolution ... The famous natural and immutable laws of the political economists, apologists for the bourgeois period, are but historical categories, born yesterday and left behind tomorrow. This is another of the cardinal points of Marxist materialism'.
c) All the tendencies of the present-day world 'from the threatening unemployment crisis to the ever more solid and conscious organisation of the proletariat, from the accelerated destruction of small property holders to the rise of militarism ... all these great phenomena, and with them trade wars ... colonial competition etc. etc. have their key in the Marxist formula, and are explained by it'.
d) Marx's discoveries will age 'like the discoveries of Newton, Galileo, Volta, aging like all that which – at least for a phase of history – is complete and definitive, not allowing any fundamental additions or tolerating any fiddling around with; aging like any masterpiece that nourishes generations' mentality across a whole period'.

Six years later, upon the eve of the 'crisis of Marxism', there had still been no change in his overall doctrine, notwithstanding some wavering on the labour theory of value, as we will explain later on in this chapter. Faced with a critic who asked him if he had not changed his ideas since the time when he was questioned for a 'psychical inquiry' on the five works that best satisfied a man's intellectual needs – and he replied, first Karl Marx's *Capital*, second Karl Marx's *Capital*, and so on up to number five – he insisted,

> ... the writer of these lines has not truly changed his opinion as to the value of Karl Marx in the few years that have passed since Tamburini's inquiry: or, he has changed it, in the sense that his admiration for the immeasurable genius of the great German has continued to increase the further he has been able to delve into its profundity and discern certain aspects that had previously still remained in the shadows, as he saw it. Marx's glory is one of those glories that grow with each passing year, because each new historical experience is like a key opening up a new drawer of this treasure chest of portentous intuitions, a chest of a thousand secrets and a thousand surprises, an inexhaustible mine of intellectual discoveries, which, for he who has just heard of it, makes the mania of those who strive to 'refute' it seem rather trivial.[25]

As such, in the process of the foundation and first taking-root of the 'Marxist party', Turati made use of Marxism by closely conjugating two moments that were not necessarily designed to be used in this symbiotic dimension. His cultural sensibility, the attention with which he participated wholly internally to the development of the workers' movement in both its organisation and its struggle, allowed him to grasp all the articulations of the complex relation that tended to be established between 'class' and 'party'. They allowed him, therefore, to guide the operation of the 'party's' foundation, while keeping intact and valorising a whole inheritance of *concrete consciousness* that would become a permanent wealth of riches for Italian socialism. This was the path of an open Marxism – which, as such, was not destined to the rigidities of an orthodoxy.

The need to build a party with a strong identity, sharply separated from all forms of *affinismo*[26] and equipped for an unpredictable period of 'absolute opposition', inevitably brought him to accentuate the 'systematic' and ideological dimension of Marx's theory. The 'political moment' certainly did favour a

25 F. Turati, 'Postilla a A. De Bella, *Socialismo antiscientifico*', *Critica Sociale*, 1897, pp. 167–9.

26 [That is, collaboration with superficially similar currents].

non-open Marxism, tendentially predisposed to presenting itself as orthodox, but the characteristics of this orthodoxy were also far from negligibly affected by Turati's weak familiarity with Marx's most demanding texts, such as we have already mentioned. This prevented him from fully exploiting all the potential of his cultural sensibility and political intelligence.

Turati's Marxism, during the work of founding the party, was certainly that of Resolution IX, though he was not able to take advantage of any deeper exploration of Marx's general theoretical hinterland. He could, instead, benefit from the solid background derived from experience of a real workers' movement.

During this same initiative, Antonio Labriola's Marxism was also that of Resolution IX, but in this case, conversely, it was firmly anchored in Marx's general theoretical hinterland. Labriola could not, however, benefit from the solid background derived from experience of a real workers' movement.

I believe that we should take account of these facts when we evaluate Turati and Labriola's 'Marxisms', as they faced the test of constructing a political organisation that they intended to be defined as a 'Marxist party'. This reality was barely perceived even by the protagonists of this collaboration/clash themselves, a contrast which ultimately made the political and personal relations between the director of *Critica Sociale* and the 'philosopher of socialism' very difficult indeed. It was not fully perceived even in the historiographical debate at the turn of the 1950s and 1960s. Though this debate did produce contributions that greatly contributed to our knowledge and were of considerable analytical finesse, it did not prove wholly able (and it would probably have been impossible in this context) to free itself of the various political and cultural traditions influencing its participants.

Labriola publicly described himself 'A Marxist, as I am', in 1892;[27] while not long previously Turati had proclaimed himself 'a Marxist … [and] enthusiast for the German model'.[28] Certainly, for the forty-nine year-old Neapolitan professor who had arrived at Marxism through a long and difficult experience of rigorous studies, indeed standing outside of the positivist cultural climate, being a 'Marxist' did not necessarily have the same meaning as it did for the thirty-five year-old Milan lawyer, who was fully part of 'positive' culture and who had arrived at Marxism through combining that culture with the ferment of a relatively advanced workers' movement. However, it is not without significance that both of them particularly insisted on *this* self-definition in *this* particular context – that of the party's foundation.

27 Labriola 1973, Vol. I, pp. 178–9.

28 Turati to Costa, 30 September 1890, in Manacorda (ed.) 1963, p. 403.

While Labriola doubtless ought to be considered more an 'outsider' to the real workers' movement and to organised socialism than was Turati, that does not mean that he lacked either information (indeed, detailed information) on the development of everything that identified with socialism, or the will – at least for a certain period – to assume a more immediate role in the process that was then underway. Beyond his very numerous personal and epistolary contacts with figures playing various roles within Italian socialism, he particularly attentively followed not only the most 'elevated' publications of the socialist universe, but also a very large number of the myriad of small local papers that it was also producing. His relations with Roman socialism, while reasonably close, remained within a largely pedagogical dimension, but in the late 1880s and early 1890s, when he thought it possible to build a socialist party that could receive and 'translate into Italian' the more advanced European experiences – the German social democracy first among them – he increasingly tended to behave almost as a political leader, in particular in the web of international connections. Italian socialism's important presence on the international scene, thanks to Labriola's address to the Halle Congress – an address confronting and clarifying in a Marxist sense questions including ones of major theoretical import, such as the slogan of the 'right to work' – was the fruit of his direct initiative, conceiving and writing this text in close collaboration and unity of intent with Filippo Turati.[29]

Notwithstanding its far from happy ultimate outcome, this collaboration made no little contribution to expanding the horizons of Turati's activity in what was a very delicate contingent situation. And it posed Labriola himself with cues to reflection. Both men acted as executors of Resolution IX, both considered a deep understanding of the SPD model essential, and both wanted to participate as protagonists in the construction of a strong and clear identity for Italian socialism. Right from the outset, however, we can also see different accents in their writings, liable to produce different paths of development – as would, indeed, happen. For the purposes of our study it is not so essential to bring out the disagreement between Labriola and Turati in the discussion on the Eritrean colony, with regard to the possibility of its 'socialist' use (also in light of Loria's theory of the *terra libera*) as to highlight the professor's responses to a Turati who insisted on the need to measure any socialist hypothesis by the yardstick of 'conscious workers' organisation'. 'I am entirely in agreement

29 Turati would write to Labriola on 21 September 1890, with regard to the Halle address – 'an embrace – and I will say nothing else – on your address. No one in Italy could have made it more elevated, more simple, more effective, more just than this'. In 'Lettere a Labriola', *Archivio Storio Per le Province Napoletane*, 1990–1, p. 615.

with you that the basis of socialism must be the proletariat', Labriola replied '… but I think that there are two things that cannot be neglected: the proletariat must be led by those who understand, and this understanding requires a full consciousness of the political forces in history'.[30] Labriola would return to this point several times better to clarify his thinking, such that there would be no doubt over his *anti-Jacobin* quality. 'We are not the *condottieri*', he would later say 'but the teachers of the workers' party. We mix in with the crowd, as soon as it seems educated in propaganda and sharpened by its own experience';[31] and furthermore 'the proletarians [need] to be habituated to this sentiment, that if *social democracy* excludes leaders, in the Jacobin sense of the word, it does not exclude teachers. Far from it!'[32]

This 'pedagogical' function that Labriola conferred upon himself and the 'learned members of our company'[33] in general derived from two different convictions that the Neapolitan professor conjugated in a wholly pessimistic basic vision of the overall conditions of Italian socialism. The first concerned the weakness of socialist culture, the almost insurmountable problems for the growth of a 'theoretical Marxism' that would be up to the demands of the time. As he wrote to Engels,

> Italy lacks a link able to join … spontaneous phenomena and developed consciousness of the proletarian revolution, and that missing link is socialist culture. Our workers will certainly not be the heirs to German philosophy, precisely because that philosophy struggles even to pass through the solitary head of any Italian professor. The new generation knows only the positivists, who for me are the representatives of a cretinous degeneration, bourgeois in type.[34]

And if 'the array of scientifically cultured Italian socialists' was a small one, the '*Partito operaio italiano*' was also of 'little strength'.[35] While Labriola recognised

30 Labriola 1973, Vol. I, pp. 113, 115.
31 Labriola 1973, Vol. I, p. 165.
32 Labriola 1983, Vol. II, p. 289.
33 Labriola 1983, Vol. II, p. 299.
34 Labriola 1983, Vol. II, p. 326.
35 Labriola 1973, Vol. I, p. 148. Labriola connected the two aspects, using this to explain the prevalent atmosphere of 'eclecticism'. 'Your eclecticism is certainly not the consequence of your intellect, or the immaturity of your cognition, but a necessary reflection of the world in which we live, where everything is subjective, arbitrary, accidental, and thus there is no place for organised science, for party discipline': letter to Turati of 4 August

that in some areas of 'Upper Italy' the 'machine [had] already been very much at work', he did not have a high opinion of the results achieved through that labour. He was wholly convinced, like Turati, that without '*the workers' party* socialism [was] an empty name',[36] and the party that he saw was not a *Partito operaio* worthy of such a title. Not the party that had thus far used that name, and that now, in its transformation process, called itself the *Partito dei lavoratori*. He saw its programme as only offering 'the spirit of third-class trade unionism'[37] and its behaviours as oscillating between 'politicking' and 'corporatism', disconsolately arriving at the conclusion that 'in Italy there [was] no workers' organisation'[38] and thus 'the class struggle and the worker-based political party [were] something premature'.[39]

This perception of the situation corresponded only partially to the reality of the development of the workers' movement in Italy (and Labriola extended this judgement also to Milan),[40] and shows how his position of an 'outsider' – even if a well-informed, attentive and analytically very lucid one – did not allow him to grasp the full wealth of what was now a long history of a far-from backward 'class struggle'. This was a history that had already produced several breaks from corporatist positions, a history that had already encountered politics – even if it wanted to define it in 'class' terms – and a history that had already encountered Marxism, even if it did not always define it as such, or defined 'Marxism' as a cultural atmosphere capable of strengthening the class in its struggles. Turati, 'from within' the movement, had a more accurate awareness of the processes that were underway, of a now-sedimented history, and of the possibility of the 'class-party' evolving in a positive manner, even within the short term. Hence also his decision to make use of favourable contingent circumstances in order rapidly to arrive at a definition of his relations with the other components of the socialist world, based on the 'need to produce a programme in accordance

1891, in Labriola 1983, Vol. II, p. 342. He wrote to Engels (p. 391; 5 October 1892) on the same theme: 'Eclecticism will not be going away any time soon. It is not only the effect of intellectual confusion, but the expression of a certain situation. When a *few* more or less socialist figures address themselves to an ignorant, impolitic proletariat, which is in good part reactionary, it is almost inevitable that they will reason like utopians and operate as demagogues'.

36 Letter to Prampolini, 1 June 1890, in Labriola 1983, Vol. II, p. 293.

37 Letter to Engels, 6 March 1892, in Labriola 1983, Vol. II, p. 357.

38 Letter to Engels, 16 September 1891, in Labriola 1983, Vol. II, p. 351.

39 Letter to Engels, 6 September 1891, in Labriola 1983, Vol. II, p. 350.

40 Ibid.

with the conclusions of scientific socialism';[41] he would not shrink from the task of responding to demands and requests coming from his interlocutor, but nor would he allow himself to be paralysed by them. Hence also, however, Labriola's verdict 'without appeal' on the foundation of the party at Genoa. There had been no true qualitative jump at the Congress: a party had not been created overnight 'through the mere fact that [Turati] had disagreed with the lawyer Gori and the worker Casati in a private meeting'.[42] What had, fundamentally, happened in Genoa? 'Those who had been *opportunists* right up till then suddenly became "Marxists and Germans enamoured with the logical line", abandoning their *own* programme to *their* adversaries and overnight becoming founders of the *Partito socialista*, by means of an *amendment*'.[43]

This party would ultimately become a point of reference that it was difficult even for Labriola himself to ignore, though this 'original sin' did continue to weigh on the almost always very harsh judgements that the Neapolitan passed on this party across the course of the 1890s. Above all, he stopped well short of considering the fruit of the Genoa Congress a 'Marxist party'. 'As for the *Partito socialista italiano*, this is a simple mystification',[44] he would write to Victor Adler even in 1895. In other contingent circumstances, the formulations that he used were not so definitive, and there would sometimes also appear certain moments of *sympátheia*; but there was never any shift in terms of his assessment of the quality of this political organisation's Marxism.

Paradoxically (to a limited extent), whereas a Turati previously very much lacking a theoretical orientation would emerge from the party's foundation seeking to anchor it in Marxist ideological postulates, in accordance with the model we saw in the last few pages – with a view to configuring a potential Marxist orthodoxy – Labriola, the rigorous theoretical Marxist, would end up denying the very possibility of orthodoxy.

Later in this study, we will see some of the characteristics of this 'professor of philosophy's' theoretical Marxism. For now, our concern is to note Labriola's

41 O. Malagodi, cited in Cortesi 1961, p. 147.

42 Letter to Turati, 22 August 1892, in Labriola 1983, Vol. II, p. 383.

43 Letter to Engels, 2 September 1892, in Labriola 1983, Vol. II, p. 385.

44 Letter to Adler, 5 March 1895, in Labriola 1983, Vol. II, p. 568. And furthermore, '[the] official Socialist Party headquartered in Milan, which has neither elasticity nor enthusiasm nor power of expansion and persuasion, will end up being a sect of pedants if it continues along the course it has taken. It will take years for the *Sozialdemokratie* to be born, which requires the conjunction of two elements, namely the most permanent and tenacious part of the proletariat in agitation and the most courageous and prudent groups of the official party'. Letter to Ellenbogen, 11 September 1894, pp. 511–12.

position on the possibility of constructing the 'Marxist party', a position that was particularly original, and, indeed, a countertendency to the Marxism of his era (and not only then).

There is no doubt that Labriola experienced the construction of the party, its outcomes, and its developments, as a truly personal defeat, a defeat of his own attempt to act directly as a teacher-militant, and he was not at all well-disposed to recognising the influence that he had also exercised on Turati. He felt that he was neither 'a soldier or a captain' of the political organisation now in the making, but 'just cut adrift'.[45] He was thus confirmed in the position that he had expressed some time previously: 'Practical action in Italy is impossible, now. What is needed is to write books to instruct those who want to be teachers. Italy is half a century behind the other countries' science and experience. We have to fill this void'.[46]

If he had 'resigned' from being 'a political citizen in Italy', he could not, however, 'resign from being an Italian';[47] and he did need to write. As we know, he would devote himself to filling this void, moreover remaining (as he was himself well-aware) a political citizen of both Italy and socialism.

Indeed, he introduced an important distinction in his first reflection on 'theoretical Marxism', in the same period in which others were trying to construct a Marxist ideology for the party. Citing the Italian case and the example of the Italian party (though his considerations also apply beyond this specific context), he expressed himself in the following terms:

> In recent years socialism has set off establishing and concretising the general type of *social democracy*, but with great uncertainty, that is, with little precision [continues in footnote:]. Many call this *Marxism*. Marxism is, and remains a *doctrine*. Parties do not draw their name and substance from doctrines.[48]

Labriola's reflection was of a general character, and did not regard only Italy's uncertain and imprecise *democrazia sociale*, but also the experience that had developed in contexts like in Germany where 'through special historical conditions'[49] the tendency to assume Marxism as a party ideology had found

45 Letter to Engels, 22 August 1893, in Labriola 1983, Vol. II, p. 430.
46 Letter to Engels, 3 August 1892, in Labriola 1983, Vol. II, p. 378.
47 Letter to Croce, 15 May 1895, Labriola 1983, Vol. II, p. 584.
48 Labriola 1977, p. 49.
49 Labriola 1965, p. 209.

'the most favourable terrain for taking root and growing'.[50] When it came to the question of the 'Marxist party', Labriola was re-proposing the positions that Marx had taken in the 1860s and 1870s. He had posed the problematic nature of any possibility of directly translating 'theory' into 'politics', rejecting the reduction of doctrine to ideology in a cultural-political context that in fact particularly favoured such an operation. This would remain a fundamental acquisition of the Italian 'theoretical Marxism' of the 1890s, bearing fruits (even if not immediately, and not in linear ways) also in the socialist political sphere.

2 Between Ideology, Science, Utopia and *religio*

The power with which the dominant horizon of 'scientific socialism' imposed itself, its pervasiveness – the effect both of the spread of its programme and of a terrain that was favourably prepared to receive it – came to form an essential connecting element, joining the needs of an ideology tending toward orthodox formulations together with the cultural tradition of the 'learned' members of the socialist 'company'. It represented the moment of closest continuity between the 'diffuse Marxism' phase and that of the 'Marxist party'.

Had the Genoa Congress not perhaps laid the bases for Italian socialism to become 'an active member of the Italian proletariat, fighting under the banners of scientific socialism'?[51] And was a review like *Critica Sociale* not perhaps born in order 'to commit Italian socialism to the scientific path'?[52] And could one, then, limit oneself to taking a 'sympathetic' attitude toward 'scientific socialism'? 'Karl Marx is to social science as Galileo is to astronomy, and Darwin to natural science. Would you ask us whether we take a more or less sympathetic attitude toward the rotation of the Earth or toward natural selection?'[53] No, it was not truly possible for the '*clear and scientific consciousness of the workers' movement* itself' to rouse this type of sentiment.[54]

Assuming these premises, it was obviously also necessary to 'give the class struggle an absolutely scientific foundation', which meant 'determining the facts of each time and each place, on which the sociological law of the class

50 Panaccione 1988, p. 196.

51 La C.S., 'Da Genova a Reggio Emilia. Il compito del congresso imminente', *Critica Sociale*, 1893, p. 257.

52 Turati to Engels, 23 February 1891, in Del Bo (ed.) 1964, p. 372.

53 F. Turati, 'Cosidetta inchiesta sul socialismo', *Critica Sociale*, 1894, p. 144.

54 'Congresso operaio', *Critica Sociale*, 1892, p. 242 (italics in the original).

struggle can base itself'.[55] And given that socialism advanced 'with the exaction of a mathematical formula, in the name of historic and cosmic inevitability',[56] why not even speak of a 'scientific party', within which 'socialists' scientific capital and their scientific force' would make it possible to identify precisely 'the social transformations [now] imposing themselves'?[57]

The early 1890s in particular were characterised by the programmatic spread of *this* Marxism upon each of the levels in which the socialist-inspired workers' movement articulated itself; a true and proper attempt at cultural homogenisation, directed at all the manifestations of Italian socialism.

Naturally the more 'elevated' referent remained *Critica Sociale*, but also emblematic from this point of view was the line maintained by the weekly *La Lotta di Classe* across its brief parabola (1892–8), coinciding with the period of the PSI's foundation and early consolidation. This publication is of interest on account of its position as a 'hinge' linking the socialist culture expressed in *Critica Sociale*, whose privileged reference point was the intellectual milieu, and the sphere of pure propaganda, of socialist 'evangelising' through local papers and 'penny pamphlets'. In short, it went some way to representing the feeling common among a socialist organisational landscape that was often working-class or in any case of very recent working-class origin, and it explicitly associated itself with the heritage of *Il Fascio Operaio*, maintaining that it wanted to resume work where the POI organ had left off. It thus allows us clearly to identify the elements of continuity and discontinuity across a long experience. It now bore as its epigraph the phrase 'Proletarians of all countries, unite – Karl Marx', however; it wanted proudly to speak in the name of the 'Partito marxista';[58] and it insisted on the need for close integration with socialism's intellectuals in order to avoid the risks of corporatism.

Right from the first issue it clearly indicated the relation that it intended to establish with Marxism: the worker-question was a social question, and its resolution demanded 'the full contribution of contemporary science', the 'great work of Marx – the most powerful sociological thinker of the century, as even his enemies admit … the illustration and analysis of the modern class struggle and its necessities'.[59]

---

55 B. Bertarelli, 'Spedizione alla ricerca del fondamento scientifico della lotta di classe', *Critica Sociale*, 1893, p. 107.

56 A. Zerboglio, 'L'attuabilità pratica del socialismo', *Critica Sociale*, 1893, p. 140.

57 O. Malagodi, 'Partiti scientifici', *Critica Sociale*, 1893, p. 341.

58 'La questione dei mezzi', *La Lotta di Classe*, 7–8 January 1893.

59 *La Lotta di Classe*, 30–31 July 1892.

A whole crescendo was based on this line: the socialists' particular positioning and *diversity* derived from their 'scientific conception of the workers' movement',[60] as did the radicalism of their position with regard to social reforms, seeing that 'science teaches that without this supreme reform [the socialisation of property] all the work of correcting and improvements will only achieve mediocre, uncertain and fragile results'.[61]

The phase that the workers' movement was advancing through was that of 'positive or scientific socialism',[62] and the events that were traversing Italy (the repression under Crispi) gave 'the widest confirmation of the accuracy of our doctrines, deduced from the positive investigation of historical phenomena'.[63] And indeed, 'only the *Partito socialista* sees the cause of the illness and offers the remedy',[64] principally because 'everywhere the variegated socialist factions are gradually disappearing to give way ... to the rigid doctrines of Karl Marx'.[65]

It presented the *Manifesto* as an 'essentially scientific work, though a rather popular one',[66] where 'all of our programme is briefly expounded, in a clear and profound way'.[67]

And finally, through the possession of these analytical tools it became possible to delineate certain perspectives for the future: 'we owe our intransigence not so much to our present – which is not much – as to our future'[68] and to 'the security of a future life'.[69]

This was an image that was projected with some force, both among the community of militants and beyond these 'oases in the great desert' – namely, the nuclei of socialists, totally occupied with the work of tilling and fertilising society's great spaces of hostility and indifference, through the use of all the tools typical of proselytism. One of the many allegorical iconographies widespread throughout this work (images were also used for painstaking explanation, in

60 'Il programma del partito', *La Lotta di Classe*, 6–7 August 1892.

61 *La Lotta di Classe*, 24–25 September 1892.

62 'Evoluzione del Partito socialista in Italia', *La Lotta di Classe*, 28–29 April 1893.

63 'L'uomo che muore, l'anno che nasce', *La Lotta di Classe*, 29–30 December 1894.

64 *La Lotta di Classe*, 30 June–1 July 1894.

65 'Socialismo pratico', *La Lotta di Classe*, 11–12 May 1895.

66 This appeared in its introduction to its publication of Bettini's edition in appendix form, presenting this as 'the first and only Italian translation loyal [to the original]'; *La Lotta di Classe*, 3–4 September 1892.

67 *La Lotta di Classe*, 10–11 August 1895.

68 'La nostra intransigenza', *Lotta di classe*, 18–19 March 1893.

69 C. Lazzari, 'Il nostro passato e il nostro avvenire', *La Lotta di Classe*, 28–9 April 1893.

an environment of poor literacy rates) was particularly telling in this regard. As the paper that had published this allegory described it[70]

> *Capitalism* – a wild and furious bull – had come across the path of the *Social Ideal*, which, like a lightning-fast train, advanced smashing through any obstacle, reducing any barrier to pieces, and flattening any force that tried to block its 'inevitable progress'. The train was made up of the locomotive – international socialism – and the wagons – the national socialisms, first among them the German one. The headlights of the train represented science, synonymous with Marxism in this context, the Marxism that – as was repeated in another popular context – meant the science bringing a solution to the conditions created by capitalist centralisation ...[71]

This way of understanding Marxism was of exceptional importance in the formation of socialist identity. The more *mythical-utopian* aspects of such theory in fact bore a decisively important influence in the creation of a *long-term mentality* particularly suitable to overcoming phases of repression, the hard lessons of history in general, and the socialists' self-proposition as a 'side' that inevitably had a 'universal' future precisely insofar as it nurtured the peculiar characteristics of its own *differentness*.

This mentality has allowed political and cultural forces that were sometimes decidedly unimportant on the quantitative plane nonetheless to play the role of a possible alternative, a privileged dialectical interlocutor with respect to the ruling classes, even when power relations, abstractly understood, could easily have confined them to marginality.

As we shall see, the type of Marxism that tended to take shape as a party ideology was only one aspect of 1890s Italian Marxism, with the rigidity of some of its coordinates also being dictated by its will/need for 'separation'. But did this not lend itself to risk of extraneousness, incomprehension, and an inability to make proposals for the country's economic and social development? This was a real risk, but one that was substantially avoided, even if there were some tumbles. This owed not only to the acute sensibility for reality present among the leadership group (in a broad sense) of Italian socialism, with Turati first among them – on account of their lack of doctrinairism, what-

---

70 'La allegoria socialista', published in *Socialismo Populare-Rivista Illustrata*, 6, 4 December 1892.

71 *Almanacco Socialista* 1896, p. 29.

ever their declamations – but also the ambivalent character that distinguished the whole formation process of this ideological Marxism. In substance, Marxism had meant opposition to an insurrectional-type conception of revolution, and this was one of the bases of its taking root. Revolution was built day-by-day through the growth of the objective and subjective forces, through the combination of voluntarism and determinism. Marxism also represented the will to separation, the affirmation of a sure identity. Fundamentally, it meant the coexistence within the same ideological construct of 'gradualism', with all that implied for socialist initiative, and 'absolute opposition'. While this former term was long destined to remain a constant, the latter would have to deal with the more changeable conditions of political experience. The 'Marxist party' now being constructed would, in sum, have to rise to the challenge of conjugating a projection with a strong dimension of futurity and the dynamic of immediate interests. This was not easy in a movement that privileged projecting its project into the future, and which used an ideological template through which it sought to 'delineate even the stages of this future's realisation'.[72]

This posed the question of how a 'catastrophist'[73] reading of Marxism could be made to coexist with the possible socialist initiatives to improve the living conditions of the subaltern classes, whether through the raising of wages and the reduction of the working day, or – and here, the theoretical and political problems became more complex – the use of tax reliefs, a more equitable distribution of the tax burden, a 'social legislation'.

The elements that came together in the definition of Marxist identity were particularly important when subjected to the strain of such a problem.

First and foremost, this related to the problem of what role was to be attributed to the state, its relation with the ruling class, and thus its positioning in the dynamic of the class struggle. Certainly, there was no doubt among the socialists as to the class nature of the state and its *structural* non-neutrality. However, the consideration that it was possible to achieve a more equal distribution of the tax burden, and that the socialists could work to obtain this, meant rejecting a rigidly mechanical conception of the state/ruling class relationship, in favour of the more articulated conception of a horizon rich in complex mediations. This meant recognising that 'the state could play the role of an apparent mediator precisely because it has a certain degree of autonomy with

72 M. Prospero, 'Il riformismo di lunga durata', *Rinascita*, 27 March 1990.

73 According to Michels 1922, p. 213, the greater part of the applied economics texts published between 1870 and 1900 brought up arguments that would have been called 'catastrophist', with growing poverty and the polarisation of the classes.

respect to the classes in struggle, [playing the role] of supreme protector of the social order in general';[74] an overall social order that could be endangered also by an 'extreme' faction within the ruling-class sphere itself. This also entailed the possibility of identifying lines of caesura and contradiction within the class in power, and the need to intervene directly in its internal conflicts, including by way of a politics of building alliances, or at least contiguity, with some of its fractions.

The interventions in this complex problematic entailed a continual redefinition of the difficult equilibrium between 'doctrine' and 'politics'. Precisely those people like Turati who had set themselves the goal of building the ideological edifice of the 'Marxist' party, were also very concerned with the rationales of politics. In the course of the 1890s the centrality of the 'tax question' represented the main terrain on which socialists would measure 'politics' up against 'Marxism', 'gradualism' and 'absolute opposition'.

Already in 1891–2 the lineaments of this 'question' began to be discussed in the socialist scene. It was principally Filippo Turati, the leading protagonist of that founding period, and a recognised teacher of Marxism and socialism, who tended to guide and select its features and, as far as possible, assimilate them to a certain framework of socialist identifiability. His greatest concern, at this point, was to define in a clear manner the borders of socialism's territory, emphasising its *diversity*, its complete autonomy with regard to all the democratic, humanitarian and social reformers' *affinismi*, its sharp differentiation from any kind of 'generic socialism', its peculiarity being guaranteed by its possession of a 'scientific' theory that all political proposals had to be brought back to.

The demands in favour of some intervention in the direction of fiscal reform, which were rather numerous in the socialist environment right at the beginning of the 1890s, appeared to Turati's eyes to be aimed precisely at blurring the differences between the socialist edifice and the variegated world of *affinismo*. As such, faced with all those who argued that progressive taxation, together with other reforms, would help 'raise the condition of the proletariat and allow it to fight against the capital tyrannising it, now at less of a disadvantage' and who thus did not 'disregard all reforms, when they improve[d] the worker's condition even if only a little', the *Critica Sociale* director's answer was to re-pose the fundamental question of the socialist *substance* of these proposals. 'Certainly', Turati maintained,

74 Guastini 1977, p. 199.

> The reforms that might improve the worker's condition, even if only a little, are all precious; but that leaves untouched the question of which [reforms] are to his advantage in a class and not only individual sense, which ones do not separate him from his comrades by dividing their forces, and are not only a mirage, a trifle, a waste of time: the ones which *socialism as such must encourage* [my italics]. After all, there are also reforms and trivial changes that may or may not help us in the harsh battle; in a sense, they are all useful, and above all the useless ones, because they prove their uselessness and thus do not come up again. But there are several that the bourgeoisie takes on itself, that it willingly grants, because it thinks that they will serve as a buffer, as padding against the blows [struck against it]; and it does not make sense for true socialism to get mixed up in these. All taken together, they constitute that 'reasonable' – a euphemism for 'innocuous' – socialism that we declare we have nothing to do with.[75]

This argument, which Turati here outlined with cutting clarity, remained the frame of reference for all hypotheses of tax reform. It was a frame within which there was evidently no room for a reform *considered in itself*. But it was also not closed off to the possibilities of reforms organically inserted within a complex set of variables, and that would thus strengthen rather than compromise the growth and autonomous characterisation of Italian socialism. It was not ruled-out – and indeed, at that moment it seemed almost a preference – that the proposed reforms could be used in an instrumental, agitational sense.

So when in the course of 1893 a tax-reform bill signed also by some of the party's deputies was tabled in Parliament, Turati called for a discussion among the socialists, since, as he put it, 'it was the first time that the party ... since it has truly been a party – has found itself wrestling with a concrete argument testing its character; not a solely theoretical question, but an essentially practical one, a subtle and complicated one. The attitude here taken would be indicative of its character, its nature and its leanings'.[76]

The discussion rapidly came undone with the reproposition of what was presented as a 'scientific axiom, for the socialists ... at least',[77] namely the existence

75 Siccardi-Turati, 'La storia di due code di cavallo ed il programma socialista', *Critica Sociale*, 1891, p. 155.

76 'Ed ora ammainiamo le vele! Replica al prof. Albertoni e ad Olindo Malagodi', *Critica Sociale*, 1893, p. 265.

77 La Critica Sociale-E. Gallavresi, 'Dissensi e critiche intorno al progetto Albertoni di riforme tributarie', *Critica Sociale*, 1893, p. 164.

of an *iron law of wages* that would, in any case, have kept the proletarians' conditions at a vital minimum, for which reason no tax reform could have been of any effect at this level. Even if, perversely, the ruling class had taken the full burden of taxation upon itself, this would nonetheless automatically still have translated into an equivalent overall mass of wages. If it was, indeed, necessary to operate on the level of reforms, it was better to fight for what would give the proletariat the tools to achieve effective improvements, like municipal autonomy and universal suffrage.

On the other hand – it was objected – the ruling classes were not a homogeneous bloc, and the socialist vanguards had ever more possibility and duty to take advantage of these classes' internal contradictions. Independent of whether or not the objectives of the proposal here being discussed did, indeed, have 'some small significance as a relief to the poor classes', the reform would in itself be of 'great significance, immense significance as a beginning of the subversion of the tax system applied ever since Italy's creation'.[78]

With specific regard to economics, an attempt was made to translate the concerns of a theoretical-doctrinal character raised by this question into the reality of Italy's social and economic conditions, albeit without denying the 'axiomatic' existence of the iron law of wages. In substance, it was said that the relation that existed between tax reform and the law regulating wage levels was anything but clear. Even if the iron law did serve as a law of physics, it would do so in conditions of perfect capitalism; that is, when there was a strong simplification of social relations due to the centralisation of wealth and property. This was not the case in Italy, a country of great backwardness in which numerous intermediate figures were present: that is, a context in which the general tendency of this law could thus easily be obstructed.

However, Turati launched a very severe attack against socialist support for this bill. At the doctrinal level, he challenged the interpretation offered by those who spoke of the 'wage law's' 'tendential' character, which he considered overly generic. And it had not at all been proven that this type of tax reform would truly act as a 'counter-tendency' to this law.

For Turati, in truth, the problem was not of a theoretical and doctrinal character; rather, it was a sublimely political problem: the struggle against *possibilism*. Turati was extremely frank in confessing this primacy of politics:

> There is not much point arguing whether the iron law of wages has a more or less absolute or relative influence ... At this moment in the life of our

78 O. Malagodi, 'Pel progetto Albertoni e pel metodo', *Critica Sociale*, 1893, p. 177.

> party, in which the upholding of the class struggle is still recent and its value not properly understood by everyone, and in which the ranks of our party are being arraigned for the great battle, this [move to] distract them with the mirage of small gains that the bourgeoisie might consent to with a little tax bill … with a little philanthropic bill that does not take on any of the great problems of socialism, but instead, with an all-too clever set of measures, touches on those parts of a minimum socialist programme that are most acceptable to our adversaries … distracting [the ranks] with such a mirage, seems to us, and more than ever, a backward turn.[79]

The qualitative leap that the foundation of the party had effectively provoked in the 'socialist universe' ensured that the new organisation would inevitably find itself at the centre of a political demand that was not measurable only in terms of 'palingenesis'. Moreover, the group at the centre of the Genoa Congress initiative was distinguished also by the centrality that it wanted to give to the political dimension, its programme having maintained the 'class' duty to 'do politics'. The construction of an ideology ought not contradict this primary need. The 'absolute opposition' that the ideology tended to reinforce was, certainly, a necessity in the period of the party's foundation and consolidation; but it was also determined by the persecution against workers' and socialist associationism, the state of semi-legality that the movement was forced into for almost all of that decade. Yet even in this context, this doctrinal emphasis did not prevent the socialists from 'doing politics' within the range of the possible. Turati insisted that every reform measure that the socialists upheld would have to '*be informed by the fundamental, scientific canons of the doctrine*'[80] but absolutely did not rule this out as a possible orientation for the party; and when cracks seemed to appear in the local authorities, the 'Marxist party' did fully commit itself to reform initiatives of 'a socialist character'.[81] The relation between Marxism and reform initiatives cannot be read exclusively in terms of counterposition, not even in a period in which the *fundamental, scientific canons of the doctrine* seemed to have taken on the function of regulating any 'reformist' hypothesis *in the last instance*.

---

79 'Ed ora ammainiamo le vele! Replica al prof. Albertoni e ad Olindo Malagodi', *Critica Sociale*, 1893, p. 267.

80 'Premessa' to Zolfanello, 'Il programma finanziara del governo e il Partito socialista', *Critica Sociale*, 1893, p. 371.

81 See Favilli 1990, pp. 176–201.

Not even the utopian projections connected to some of the *fundamental, scientific canons of the doctrine* appeared exclusively in terms of contradiction with the possibility of a reforms policy, even if in the abstract utopia privileged the absolute dimension and reform the relative one. Often enough, in reality utopia can appear as 'a sort of *perpetuum mobile* that activates various reform projects'.[82] In the history of Marxism this type of *perpetuum mobile* has often proved a factor, and, indeed, a non-episodic one, inspiring both political action and social imaginaries – namely, that system of representations that are essential elements of collective behaviours.[83] Utopia was one of the roads to be taken in the desperate search for meaning, given the suffering that a capitalist mechanism – 'irrational' from every point of view except the valorisation of capital – inflicted on the subaltern figures of the productive process. This demand for meaning strikingly emerges from even perhaps the least directly 'committed' of the great pre-revolutionary Russian writers, with one of his characters, doctor Koryolov, reflecting in the following terms as he crosses the factory district to go and cure Lisa Lyalikov in the boss's home:

> 'There is something baffling in it, of course …' he thought, looking at the crimson windows. 'Fifteen hundred or two thousand workpeople are working without rest in unhealthy surroundings, making bad cotton goods, living on the verge of starvation, and only waking from this nightmare at rare intervals in the tavern; a hundred people act as overseers, and the whole life of that hundred is spent in imposing fines, in abuse, in injustice, and only two or three so-called owners enjoy the profits, though they don't work at all, and despise the wretched cotton. But what are the profits, and how do they enjoy them? Madame Lyalikov and her daughter are unhappy – it makes one wretched to look at them; the only one who enjoys her life is Christina Dmitryevna, a stupid, middle-aged maiden lady in pince-nez. And so it appears that all these five blocks of buildings are at work, and inferior cotton is sold in the Eastern markets, simply that Christina Dmitryevna may eat sterlet and drink Madeira'.[84]

For certain, Marx and then (almost all) the Marxists of the 1890s would have sharply rejected any attempt to compare their production of ideas with the sphere of 'utopia', considering it scandalous. And, indeed, for the Marxists of

82 Baczko 1979, p. 47.
83 See Castoriadis 1975, Ansart 1977.
84 Chekhov 2003, pp. 178–9.

the late nineteenth century the tension between the two spheres could only have seemed wholly natural, given the role that a text like *Socialism: Utopian and Scientific* had played in determining their Marxism.[85]

Almost a century later, in the long end of the twentieth century, another negative assessment of utopia – this time referring to Marxism *in toto* – would establish itself as a fundamental component of the dominant political-cultural atmosphere. The collapse of what had been defined as Marxist utopia became the paradigm for utopia in itself, now considered almost exclusively as a *negative utopia*. It is true that this reading had only marginal effect on the world of utopia scholars, the heirs to a tradition of studies that is now well-established and has reached a very high level. Yet it did pervasively spread (and is prevalent still today) across all the other levels of cultural production and media in general, leading to a widely prevalent common sense in which utopian thought is simply identified with the realm of dangerous and unrealisable fantasies. As Günther Grass portrayed a philosophy student saying in 1990, 'We're taking Bloch apart. All that utopian shit. It's dead!'[86] – giving a perfect, immediate image of the widespread manner of considering the utopian dimension.

Robert Musil has argued that 'If there is a sense of reality there must also be a sense of possibility', and that it is reality that awakens possibility; the common sense to which we just referred considers reality irreconcilable with the type of possibility that feeds utopian thought.[87]

Yet even one of the great fathers of nineteenth-century liberalism, Alexis de Tocqueville, gifted with an acute 'sense of reality', came to discover the 'sense of possibility' precisely as he reflected on the destinies of socialism at a moment when it was considered defeated and discredited. After the revolutions of 1848, therefore, he investigated the destinies of those 'theories ..., very different among themselves, often contrary and sometimes enemies; but all of them aiming lower than at government, and trying to reach society itself, which serves as its basis'; theories that had taken the name 'socialism'. This was a

85 I believe that we still ought to reflect on Schumpeter's consideration on the relation between utopian socialism and scientific socialism: 'Thus, while it remains substantially true that, unlike most of his predecessors, Marx intended to rationalize an existing movement and not a dream, and also that he and his successors actually gained partial control of that movement, the difference is smaller than Marxists would have us believe. There was, as we have seen, more of realism in the thought of the utopists, and there was more of unrealistic dreaming in Marx's thought than they admit': Schumpeter 2003, p. 310.

86 Grass 1993, p. 151.

87 Musil 1997, p. 10.

socialism that wanted to 'change the immutable laws that constitute society itself'. For certain, immediately this struck Tocqueville as 'impracticable'; but upon further reflection, precisely starting out from what was called the right to property, he arrived at this conclusion: 'I am tempted to believe that what we call necessary institutions are often nothing but *the institutions to which we are accustomed*, and that as regards the constitution of society *the field of the possible* is much vaster than the men who live in each society imagine'.[88]

In short, even the aristocratic De Tocqueville – the realist, the disenchanted critic of a democracy that he saw as inevitable – seemed to have become convinced that 'the boundary between utopia and political realism is changeable and historically determined'.[89]

The science/utopia opposition in Marx and in nineteenth-century Marxism has rationales and meanings other than those of the reality/possibility opposition. If Bloch wrote that 'Reason cannot blossom without hope, and hope cannot speak without reason; both must operate within a Marxist unity; no other science has a future, no other future has science',[90] it is doubtful that Marx would have accepted this Marxist's formulation, his concepts of the *Docta spes* [learned hope] and 'being in possibility', or his conception of Marxism as the relation between 'hot' and 'cold' currents. Or rather, perhaps, he would have identified only as the 'sober detective'[91] impassively wielding the instruments of absolute analytical rigour.

Indeed, Marx's recognition of the positive values of the 'utopian' socialists' own utopian projections concerned only those aspects that expressed a certain consonance with the deep set of feelings that were developing among the world of the oppressed. So for Marx, utopian thought was only valuable as an 'anticipation' of a different, fundamentally important analytical phase, which would need to use scientific tools of cognition; ones that could be used only for analysing the (closely linked) past and the present, and certainly not the future.[92] The 'normative utopia'[93] that provided the basis for the images and constructs of *another* society, built on criteria of justice, would collapse when analysis proved able to supply knowledge of the deep mechanisms of social transformation. Only awareness of these mechanisms made it possible to identify some general guideline hypotheses for bringing this future closer –

88 De Tocqueville 1964, pp. 95–7, my italics.

89 Losurdo 1986, p. 436.

90 Bloch 1971, p. 33.

91 Bloch 1971, p. 36.

92 See Rota Ghibaudi 1987, p. 343.

93 Kolakowski 1974.

and certainly not a complete image of the society to come. 'Science', therefore, repudiated utopia, at least in the form of an imaginary that tried to design the features of the 'future city' on the basis of ethical or 'ideological'[94] parameters. But it did not repudiate a 'sense of possibility', as long as this latter was solidly anchored in the 'objective' tendencies of the historical process that scientific analysis had been able to unveil. This was a priority task for the revolutionary process: after all, 'he who is satisfied with the prevalent order has neither need nor interest in transforming society on account of scientific analysis',[95] but rather in covering it with ideological veils.

If this was, certainly, an aspect of Marx's programme, which he developed with exceptional analytical talent, then his overall *oeuvre*, combining real scientific knowledge, value judgements, calls to action, and also some measure of prophecy, cannot be considered extraneous to all threads of utopian thought. One of these threads has been defined as a 'Marxian eschatology',[96] but this is admissible only in a framework qualified by specific determinations. Even accepting that Marx really thought about socialism in terms of the logic of destiny and mankind's ultimate ends (and in Marx there often is a differentiation between underlying philosophical lineaments and the analysis of concrete processes of history,[97] if not an open contradiction), this destiny manifests itself

94 I believe that the term 'ideological' can be applied with regard to *these* tendencies of the both socialist and working-class collective imaginary in accordance with Marx's manner of considering such a form of intellectual production. It would be more difficult to maintain this consonance if we were to apply this term also in reference to the series of Marxist-inspired conceptions of history and society developed by the workers' movement itself, in particular given the lack of need for the revolutionary proletariat to pass through the sphere of the imaginary and the illusory. It is difficult to overestimate the importance that Marx's theory of ideology had for the *realistic* comprehension of the system of relations within which the production of ideas and the development of sociology itself were inserted. A critic of Marx like Schumpeter could speak of his 'great contribution to our insight into the processes of history and the meaning of social science' (Schumpeter 1986, p. 33). However, there remains the fact that Marx and, still more so, the Marxists, had serious difficulties recognising the 'ideological character' of marginal and sometimes substantial parts of their production of ideas.

95 Topitsch 1975, p. 40.

96 Fergnani 1969, p. 479.

97 Already in the first part of the *Manifesto* Marx had suggested that the proletariat's victory was 'inevitable', but at the same time – referring to the experience of history as a history of class struggles – he notes that this was 'a fight that each time ended, either in a revolutionary reconstitution of society at large, or in the common ruin of the contending classes'.

historically as the fruit of men's *will* within a structurally *determined* context. It is not possible to deduce such a 'Marxian eschatology' simply by assimilating a philosophy of history of Hegelian parentage to the conception of ultimate ends deriving from the tradition of Judeo-Christian messianism, metamorphosed through the 'secularisation of its eschatological model',[98] such as Karl Löwith suggestively proposes in an argument that would later be picked up by a very great number of interpretations, some of them of decidedly trivial value. 'Humanity in action'[99] does not meet with the absolute as it walks along the difficult paths of history, itself marked exclusively by humans, who can sometimes even be overcome by doubts as to the possibility of their 'future accomplishment'. We remain within the ambit of the 'relatively' rather than the 'absolutely' utopian, to follow Mannheim's old and still very relevant distinction.[100] Or even, the ambit of 'the effort to interlink the static utopia with history, providing a map of the barriers, bottlenecks and perverse consequences that all human projects of change run into, together with an indication of the possible paths for overcoming them'.[101] It is difficult, in short, to ascribe Marx's projection toward a totally different society – this utopian aspect of his – to the parameters of a long eschatological tradition.

Two further elements of Marx's thinking have been said to belong to a utopian dimension, if in a less immediately visible manner: the utopia of a perfect 'transparency',[102] and that relating to Marx's (and socialism in general's) own 'hunger for quality'.[103] This demand for quality is closely conjugated with the 'desire for a society in which men are not comparable to things, precisely on account of their qualitative difference'.[104] I think that we can feel free to emphasise the current-day relevance of this last point, and insist on the need for a life that constantly maintains this utopian dimension – an evident example of a

98 Löwith 1957, p. 2.

99 Bloch 1971, p. 23.

100 Absolute utopia is a matter of fantastical realities, and relative utopia a projection that is not actual today but in principle could be tomorrow. Mannheim 1954. Typifying this was the case, for example, of some of the reforming initiatives linked to the turn-of-the-century climate of 'municipal socialism' in Italy. 'They demonstrated that some of the suggestions for rationalising work, municipalising public services and introducing schooling and aid programmes were effectively to be ascribed to the realm of utopias at the beginnings of the [1890s], and would, however, a few years later become part of a programme to be realised'; Audenino 1955, p. 16.

101 Bodei 1995, p. 20.

102 Baczko 1979b.

103 Kolakowski 1974, p. 103.

104 Ibid.

positive utopia. The first point poses the problem of utopia partly in conjugation with the exposition of some of Marx's analytical mechanisms. Baczko has maintained that in the attempt to dig through the imaginary to reach the 'true' man, the 'true reality', and social agents 'naked, shorn of their masks, costumes, dreams, [and] representations', we paradoxically create another 'image', an image that is also a construct. 'The construction of the objects "*real* man" and "*true* social groups" – that is, shorn of their imaginary – was fully conjugated with the collective dream of a society and a history that would finally be transparent to the men who made them'.[105] Certainly, we cannot deny that the will to 'transparency' constantly runs throughout almost all of Marx's work, in different ways at different points, as the will to unveil the 'illusions' and 'ideologies' and as the will to grasp the reality of socio-economic relations lying beneath the *forms* in which they appeared. And nor can we deny that this journey into the *deep* also had the taste of a search for *essentiality*. Likewise, nor can we deny that following his analysis in *Capital* the dynamics of valorisation, the forms of the commodity and the relation between man and the productive process really were more *transparent*.

'We do not dogmatically anticipate the world, but only want to find the new world through criticism of the old one': this was how the young Marx had posed the problem of the relation between the *present* reality and the *other* society of the future, which could not be constructed by simply counterposing 'some ready-made system such as, for example, the *Voyage en Icarie*'. He added: 'we do not confront the world in a doctrinaire way with a new principle: Here is the truth, kneel!' His 'plan would answer a real need, and after all it must be possible for real needs to be fulfilled in reality'.[106] Marx's utopia would forever remained anchored to this awareness he had reached as a twenty-five year-old philosopher.

However, Marx's way of understanding utopia, and the utopian traits of his own elaboration, encountered a socialist movement totally projected onto the future, which fed on images of the future, and had developed a utopian dimension of its own independent of Marx's. Even in the 1890s, when Marxism was officially adopted as the social-democratic parties' doctrinal outlook, socialist utopia still had no lack of peculiar characteristics (even if in a 'Marxist' guise). These characteristics ought not necessarily be considered survivals of the old 'utopianism' that had now been transcended by 'science', but rather the expression of a deep need for a continual projection toward the future. This need

105 Baczko 1979b, p. 55.

106 Marx to Ruge, September 1843, in *MECW*, Vol. 3, pp. 142–4.

ensured that the now acquired certainties of science – a science that seemed to have demonstrated that this future was necessarily determined – were not substituted for the imaginary horizon that had been – and was still being – employed with regard to this future. Rather, these scientific certainties seemed capable of providing fresh light and colours to the complex set of hopes and expectations that had come to be crystallised in such images.

This relation between 'science' and the 'imaginary' appears particularly clearly from the indications given by one leading figure in the world of 'socialist propaganda' in the 1890s, with regard to the sources to which a 'propagandist of middling culture' ought to refer:

> First of all, a recap of the theories of Darwin and Spencer, which will inform the student of the directions of modern and scientific thought. Marx will complete the triad with his most famous and indispensable *Capital*, the Gospel of the contemporary socialists. In Ferri's recent volume *Socialismo e scienza positiva*, the student will see the accordance among these three colossi, who each complement the others ... Read also Bellamy's *Looking Backward*. It is a novel and we cannot swear by every part of it, but even so it does shed a ray of light on the unclear paths of our future.[107]

Even a socialism with a solid mastery of science,[108] then, could not do without a 'ray of light' that would make visible the features of the future that was to be built.

This same volume also indicated the journalistic source most useful to the propagandist of working-class background: *La Lotta di Classe*, the 'hinge' between the workers' and properly socialist publications that we mentioned earlier. This publication was particularly eager to insist on the definitive, solid conjugation – or rather, identification – of Marxism and science. Even in this context it was argued that 'scientific socialism' is guaranteed only by the 'security of a future life',[109] and that Bellamy's *Looking Backward* was able to shed light on some of its features.[110] Moreover, it was precisely at the level of pro-

---

107 Morgari 1896, p. 14.

108 In other parts of this study we saw the kind of 'science' that this triad represented, and we shall go on to discuss it further.

109 C. Lazzari, 'Il nostro passato, il nostro avvenire', *La Lotta di Classe*, 28–9 April 1893.

110 See 'I soliti errori', *La Lotta di Classe*, 27–8 February 1897. In truth, the same publication also featured those who warned against imagining socialism 'as it is represented by Bellamy in *Looking Backward*, a book more widely read and glorified than Spencer's *Principles*

paganda, the lowest level of divulgation of the message,[111] that there most often appeared descriptions of the future society's features, which were in general absent from more 'elevated' literature. The process of the true and proper construction of cultural institutions, in which the working class also played a leading role, offers sufficient demonstration of the pitfalls of claiming that it 'dreamed more than it thought'.[112] Certainly, though 'the dream' was also fully part of the 'titanic' task of working-class emancipation.[113]

Sometimes the utopian point of view seemed to have been almost consciously taken on board, as in a letter from De Amicis to Nitti:

> I have no need to be sure that the theories of socialism, as expressed in collectivist propaganda, are realisable. For me, it is enough to be sure that the *tendency* of socialism is moral, just, and necessary. I do not doubt this. For me, it is of secondary importance whether collectivism can or cannot be realised.[114]

Beyond the importance to socialism of ethical arguments, constantly explicit in De Amicis's thinking, the projection toward another society took on a value of its own, as a tension necessary for overcoming the *weight* of history, independent of the practical possibility of putting this project into effect. Precisely because getting to grips with De Amicis means 'getting to grips with the practical theoretical framework of [Italian] socialism' in the 1890s, the utopian dimension that appears in *Primo Maggio*, his most doctrinaire novel and thus the one of most interest within the logic of our study, seems to be strongly indicative of the way in which utopia entered into the cultural framework of 'average' intellectual production. That is, not the thinking of specialists, but one reflecting reasonably loyally the overall set of ideas circulating among the socialist universe. Even if there were also those, like Antonio Labriola, who con-

of Sociology or Marx's *Capital* itself': C. Treves, 'Strategia sociale', *La Lotta di Classe*, 5–6 November 1892.

111 Pisano 1986.

112 Lequin 1968, p. 16.

113 'The proletariat resembles Prometheus chained to the cliff face. Poverty, here a serpent, grasps him in his coil. Capitalism, represented by a vulture, sucks out the blood from his chest. In vain, bourgeois political economy offers palliatives and patches for the large wound. The unfortunate writhes and thrashes about, waiting for socialism to come and liberate him': 'Allegoria dell'emancipazione operaia', *Socialismo Popolare*, Venice, 3, 7 August 1892.

114 De Amicis to Nitti, 17 June 1893, in Bergami 1985, p. 367.

sidered attempts to delineate the future society to be like 'an objective satire of socialism, [portrayed] as the expectation of a fantasy'.[115]

What characteristics, then, would the future socialist society display? De Amicis has his protagonist Bianchini respond:

> I do not know. No one can predict, no one in any time has predicted what the future society would be twenty years later, because this depends on the conjunctures posed, which cannot be predicted. What does it matter to establish its precise forms? It suffices to ascertain its tendencies. Of course collectivism is an attractive and grandiose banner, one is necessary for rallying an army, for accelerating evolution, for exciting the energies that would otherwise long remain dormant. I do not think that is impossible. But perhaps the future will not look much like the plans of today's socialist reformers ... The future ... has in store social forms superior to the conceptions of even the boldest utopians[116]

The De Amicis who proposed utopia as an ultimate ideal, and who, loyal to Marx, rejected the recipes of the cookbooks of the future, was the same De Amicis who considered 'the weakest part of the doctrine' to be that relative to the features that 'the fundamental transformation of all orders',[117] as proposed by the socialists, would assume. After all, 'this Idea was not a dream, but a luminous counter-clairvoyance'.[118]

Hence he began to bring out the lineaments of the future, at the same time as he remained as cautious as possible. First of all, the modes of the revolution, which was to consist of a 'violent, but brief action' following a long period of 'evolution'. This revolution 'would not produce deep or lasting perturbations, because the people [would have] made immense progress in true civility'. And the revolution 'would be followed by a political dictatorship of the proletariat, a period of education in economic justice and gradual collectivism, from which even just the first benefits, being immense and evident, would keep the people composed and prudent'.[119] The new post-revolutionary state, following the brief period of the 'political dictatorship of the proletariat', would take on a role in service of society, abandoning any pretension to dominate. Moreover, it would be simplified through decentralisation, 'with its activity starting again

115 Letter to Croce, 23 July 1896, in Labriola 1983, Vol. II, p. 700.
116 De Amicis 1980, p. 402.
117 De Amicis 1980, p. 48.
118 De Amicis 1980, p. 194.
119 De Amicis 1980, pp. 96–7.

from secondary organs, local government bodies [emerging] out of necessity, little by little, under the new principle informing all social life'.[120] The capitalists would be expropriated, for certain, but through a form of redemption of their assets, through 'payment in instalments, in the form of means of enjoyment ... over an agreed timescale'.[121] The finally liberated world of labour and production would demonstrate unsuspected capacities of development:

> It would double the products of the land in virtue of its great rational culture, impossible for now on account of the fragmentation of property; it would greatly develop machinism, today limited by overproduction, the low price of human labour and the insufficiency of private capital; and there would be a greater number of workers on account of the suppression of parasites, intermediaries and the producers of useless items.[122]

Naturally, the distribution of the wealth produced would be regulated by the 'law of value' and inspired by the principle of equality. This equality was guaranteed by the collectivist society, which promised an austere and rational life. This was an image that sometimes also bore some signs of regret for less austere aspects of the old society.[123]

This was a widely shared image in the socialist common sense of the time; an image that can be considered the conjugation of the deeper demands of socialism's utopian tradition together with the brief references to the 'cookbooks of the future' present also in the Marxist tradition.

However, yet more solid, or even organic, was the conjugation between socialist utopia and Marxism regarding the 'scientific' direction of history, its 'guarantor role' whose gradual affirmation we have seen throughout this study.[124] One of the great figures of European social democracy, Otto Bauer, would express himself particularly effectively in this regard:

---

120 De Amicis 1980, p. 81.

121 De Amicis 1980, p. 90.

122 De Amicis 1980, p. 87.

123 '"Sometimes he even thought with sorrow that in the future society, subject to the rigid law of equality and work for all, there would be no more women like this one, with all those delicate graces of a creature grown up amidst idleness, with all those exquisite refinements that owed to her being accustomed to comfort and luxury, almost made and brought up for nothing other than pleasure, the quintessence of a lover": thus reflected, veiled with a soft melancholy, professor Bianchini – a rigorous socialist attentive to all the different hues of the doctrine': De Amicis 1980, p. 167.

124 See Panaccione 1995, p. 99.

> Confidence in the transformative power of a world-historic development that must triumph and flatten any obstacle, is the most precious thing that Marx's whole life of work has given us; this faith is the miraculous force that has kept thousands of simple workers standing in the worst of days ... Even for us, only faith – the faith, of course, that comes from science – provides the power to move mountains[125]

The importance of this aspect did not escape Vilfredo Pareto, who very sharply dealt with some of its most significant interpretative implications in his *I sistemi socialisti*. However, Pareto started out from the presupposition – upheld with great ideological vigour – that there is no scientific sphere in Marx's analytical categories,[126] for which reason this phenomenon ought to be read in a wholly one-dimensional manner, completely *sub specie religionis*.[127] Anti-Marxists or, in any case, non-Marxists have tended to highlight the religious character that Marxism as an ideology assumes, but that does not necessarily mean a similar judgement with regard to Marx's theory overall.

Almost at the same time as Pareto elaborated his *Sistemi ...*, within the socialist culture there were also very interesting comments on the eschatological hues pervading the socialist movement's psychology, its finalistic-providential interpretation of some of Marx's formulations, and also on the positive character of utopia:

---

125 O. Bauer, 'August Bebel', in *Der Kampf*, 1909, cited in Miller 1985, p. 41.

126 In this view, Marx's economic theory, 'is appropriate for bringing out sentiments favourable to class struggle, through its association of ideas. Everything essential in Marx's economic theory is expressed in John Stuart Mill's *Principles of Political Economy*; Marx only changed the terminology'. And he continues 'In reality, while *Capital* is Marx's most extensive work, it is in the *Communist Manifesto* that we find this central point [the theory of value/surplus value] and *Capital* is but an appendix, designed to clear the field of the objections that might be made to the doctrine, grounded in political economy': see Pareto 1974, pp. 695–6.

127 According to Robinson, who does not at all doubt the scientific character of Marx's theory or 'the scope and the penetration of his analysis of the "laws of motion of capitalism"', it was also the 'scientific aspect of Marxism' that 'had to give way to the need for a creed ... It was inevitable, and in a certain sense right, that Marxism should have developed into a faith rather than a science. The notion of a scientific revolution is delusory. Action has to be taken much faster than science can work out results. Marx made the first attempt to establish the laws of motion of capitalism. His hypotheses have been confirmed by events at some points and disproved at others. To check, revise, and establish them is a program for generations': see Robinson 1962, pp. 424–7.

> The world is cleansed with fresh tears, is re-baptised with fresh pains, makes itself a new faith and turns its eye toward a new light – and marches onward. Toward its earthly redemption? Towards other illusions? The supposed, hankered-after illusion, meanwhile, informs new life, itself replenishes the terrain, and is the most active force, making the new history.[128]

Unlike Pareto, Ciccotti had a creative experience of the heuristic capacities and profoundly innovative character of Marx's analytical categories. This inspired some of his pioneering historical works, among the most important studies of ancient history in the nineteenth century. Professor Ciccotti was at that time editing the first planned Italian edition of a relatively wide body of Marx and Engels's work. His observations were, therefore, based on the awareness that socialism's extraordinary capacity for expansion and wider influence were derived from a combination-system that was, certainly, informed by many elements typical of a 'mythical' reception of Marxism, but also conjugated these with the real and very robust presence of the most radical scientific revolution to take place in the course of the nineteenth century. In substance, certainty in the advent of socialism ended up reinforcing the eschatological and millenarian tendencies that were already present among the popular classes, as long-term mental structures. Yet the scientific dimension underlying this in any case remained a fact of fundamental cultural and practical importance.

128 Ciccotti 1903, p. 8. 'The conviction that the capitalist system is itself also a historical category, destined to transformation on account of its inner dissolution, means we can consider its last resistance with the same sentiment of superiority and compassion with which we look at the illusions, the whims and the malignity of an ill man now condemned to die. This feeling of certainty in the advent of socialism, made vivid by faith, pushes the centre of our own moral life into the future. … There is a reflection of this state of mind in the great certainty with which little-cultured people provoke disputes with adversaries more cultured than they, so much do they believe they possess the truth and find the most powerful of aids in this truth. Some of these states of minds invoke better periods – the heroic times of Christianity and of other young religions – but the comparison is wholly to the advantage of the socialist, for the future, which he thinks he can in someway contribute to, does not leave him inert. Moreover, because any egotistical motive is wiped away, as the socialist is – ordinarily – convinced that he will not personally reap the recompense for his own suffering, and will only see the promised land from afar. At most, the sun of the future will kiss his grave. The solidity of this sentiment is the first element of the party's cohesion and it translates not only into a principle of discipline, but moreover into a inclination to discipline, considered an indispensible condition of existence and victory'. (pp. 131–2)

3 'The Anatomy of Civil Society'

We have seen how during the 1880s socialists travelled a sort of 'sociological' route to 'political economy'. This afforded them a particular syntony with some of the tendencies of the Italian tradition of economics, which still in the 1890s – notwithstanding the progress of marginalism – would display a notable capacity to influence the peninsula's economic culture. However, at the moment that the 'Marxist party' was being constructed and Marxism was officially being taken on as the socialists' ideological horizon, it was clearly impossible to avoid the problem of an *autonomous* reading of Marx's economic categories. 'Reading *Capital*' has always been an operation particularly affected by the 'spirit of the time' and '*genius loci*'. The granite image of Marx, the scholar who 'in the last instance' represented the indestructible cornerstone of the guaranteed socialist destiny, had to be broken down along disciplinary lines, such as to be able to provide this same 'guarantee' in each branch of science. How, then, should Marx 'the economist' be cut into this granite?

In fact, it was not so simple (and not only in the 1890s) to provide any accurate delimitation of the sphere of Marx's economics, as a separate part of an *oeuvre* in which sociology, philosophy and history seemed indissolubly linked to the economic moment. Leszek Kolakowski decisively stated that 'Karl Marx was a German philosopher',[129] and on this basis read Marx's economic categories as substantially the fruit of a 'philosophical anthropology', insisting that *Capital* should be 'understood as a work of philosophy'. For Althusser, *Capital* constituted a genuine 'epistemological revolution' with respect to Marx's youthful philosophical works, the foundation of a 'science' sharply breaking with his previous 'philosophical' dimension.

Marx was certainly *also* a German philosopher, and some of the central philosophical problems of his youthful period certainly did not disappear from the horizon of his mature reflection – including, indeed, the question of alienation. But it is likewise significant that having arrived at political economy he 'studied this science, which was then a new science, for twenty years, with a level of interest that wholly prevailed over the other branches of knowledge'.[130] This evidently had some effect on his elaboration of new epistemological nodes; but that does not mean we have to arrive at a logic of opposites, such as is implicit in Althusser's interpretation.

129 Kolakowski 1978, p. 1.
130 Jossa 1987, p. 423.

The mature, *analytical* Marx was a *political economist*. The greater problem regards the peculiarity of his method and his conception of economics. Schumpeter underlined the 'chemical nature' of the fusion between history and economic theory in *Capital*, addressing the relation between economics and sociology in the following terms:

> Now, though Marx defines capitalism sociologically, i.e., by the institution of private control over means of production, the mechanics of capitalist society are provided by his economic theory. This economic theory is to show how the sociological data embodied in such conceptions as class, class interest, class behavior, exchange between classes, work out through the medium of economic values.[131]

It was a different matter in the case of philosophy, which – again according to Schumpeter – at most influenced Marx's 'vision', the 'preanalytic cognitive act', whereas it could be proven that 'every proposition of his, economic and sociological, as well as his vision of the capitalist process as a whole, may be either traced to sources other than philosophical – such as Ricardo's economic theory – or else understood as results of strictly empirical analysis of his own'.[132] This was an observation pregnant with cues to reflection, though it was not immune from the peevishness against philosophy – blamed for bringing its impurities into scientific paradigms – typical of a long tradition of economists for whom, in the best of cases, philosophy ought to be considered sharply separate from their discipline, and in the worst case, the site of a complicated but empty verbal rigmarole. This is a tradition that has only recently been put into question, by a certain group of economists.[133]

Philosophy plays a more important role in *Capital*'s argumentation than Schumpeter credits it with, though this does not mean that the economic analysis loses its specificity or that economic categories appear as mere shells for philosophical ones, as in Kolakowski's interpretation. First of all, the 'vision',

131 Schumpeter 2003, p. 20. And moreover, 'Marx's two "classes of participants in the economic process" capitalists and proletarians, are not mere categories but social classes. This feature is essential to the Marxist system. It unifies his sociology and his economics by making the same class concept fundamental for both. On the one hand, the social classes of sociology are ipso facto the categories of economic theory; on the other hand, the categories of economic theory are ipso facto the social classes', Schumpeter 1986, p. 525.

132 Schumpeter 1986, p. 390.

133 Zamagni 1994.

the 'pre-analytic cognitive act', has important effects on the direction of the analytical process. It is this that orients the components of the pre-established analytical model, which comes to be structured according to an order of dependencies rooted in the ensemble of principles considered 'pre-analytic'. In the second place – but certainly no less important – the 'vision' is directly reflected in more general decisions of method, and his way of confronting and resolving the epistemological problems of the discipline. We need only think of the explicit connection between method and object of analysis in Marx's analysis of the theory of value.[134]

Marx's 'critique of political economy' faces the 'vulgar' conception of economics first of all as a revolution of method, starting from an epistemological reflection on the foundations of economic science and the social sciences more generally. If science's task is to identify the 'inner connections' of phenomenal forms, and thus 'to resolve the visible, merely external movement into the true intrinsic movement'[135] then delving into research of these connections corresponds to the very logics of the analytical model, and has nothing to do with the search for any metaphysical 'essence'. Indeed, the author of a non-Marxian model of historical materialism, Leszek Nowak, has also constructed a non-metaphysical frame of reference for the 'essentialism' of the author of *Capital*. For Nowak, what Marx calls the method of abstraction is connected to the method of 'idealisation' that marks the passage from the stage of 'immature science' to the stage of 'theoretical science'.[136] The determination of an 'essential structure' explaining the system of relations among the phenomena under observation is grasped by introducing 'idealising' conceptual models that serve to isolate factors considered secondary from those that are considered most important. Once the deep regularities of the process under analysis have been established on the basis of 'idealising' hypotheses, a *progressive* concretisation of these 'deep regularities' is realised through the *progressive* comparison of 'the theoretical image of the phenomenon in question and the empirical phenomenon itself'.[137] Thus this 'essentialism', which is not definitive, but rather constructed on a hypothetical basis, is not an 'anti-empirical' essentialism.[138] For Nowak, precisely this is *Capital*'s main task: to construct an

134 Nowak 1980.

135 *MECW*, Vol. 37, p. 312.

136 Nowak 1983.

137 Ibid., p. 54.

138 Evidently this is a *positive essentialism*, something wholly different from the essentialism of 'ultimate explanations in the Popperian sense'. See Popper 2014, pp. 139 et sqq.

'idealizational theory' of bourgeois economics, and at the same time to introduce the method of idealisation into the social sciences; to be the 'Galileo of the social sciences'.[139]

This was a qualitatively complex reading of *Capital*, and while economic categories did not lose their specificity here, they were also held to be useful for explaining problems arising in other disciplinary sectors. This reading of course had very serious difficulties imposing itself in the last decade of the nineteenth century. This was not only because of the great – or even total – lack of knowledge of Marx's youthful philosophical works, only a small part of which had been published, and which were difficult to access,[140] but also because the necessary debate over political economy, including the latest acquisitions of 'economic science', effectively proposed a different typology of epistemological models.

In Italy, then, the intersections between academic economic science, socialism, and the early development of a 'Marxist economics', were of very particular significance. If the political operation of 'separating' 'scientific socialism' from any type of democratic-philanthropic *affinismo* and generic socialism, through the foundation of the 'Marxist party', could be considered to have arrived at a point of no return, the same could not be said of the 'separation' between 'Marxist economics' and other forms of *affinismo* in the realm of political economy. That is to say, it was one thing to define a 'political Marxism' with a sufficient degree of clarity, and quite another to define the scope of 'economic Marxism'. This was particularly the case considering that the development of the social sciences could naturally flow toward this latter, including a political economy

139 Nowak 1983. Even those like Kolakowski opposed to the so-called 'Poznan school', privileging Marx's youthful philosophical works and seeking to demonstrate that the mature Marx simply translated his philosophy into economic terms, did not manage entirely to refute the Marx-Galileo comparison: 'Certainly modern physics could develop only … by virtue of idealised models, some of whose defining conditions could not be confirmed in reality. This way of thinking can be found also in Marx himself, when he analyses certain imaginary situations and only later gradually includes other "disturbing factors"': Kolakowski 1974, p. 68.

140 Even Antonio Labriola had difficulty getting his hands on the *Holy Family*. He had advertisements placed in German newspapers declaring himself prepared to pay 'any price' for it. Conrad Schmidt had promised to lend him a copy, having only managed to get a single copy after long searches. He ended up making use of Engels's copy, and even that for one month only. See Labriola to Engels, 20 December 1893, 15 February and 14 March 1894, in Labriola 1983, Vol. II.

As for the unpublished ones, there is a well-known reflection critical of their supposed 'centrality', precisely given that Marx himself decided not to publish these works.

deeply infused with sociological categories and which was directly committed to making its own far from secondary contribution to solving the 'social question'.

The 'social question' had been an element of decisive importance in setting the coordinates that Italian economic science had adopted already in the 1870s with the triumph of the '*vincolisti*' over the *ferrariani*,[141] a victory that was not again put into doubt in the 1880s. Not only did this red thread of the social question not go away in the 1890s, but these years even saw it take a qualitative leap. The Sicilian *Fasci* and, albeit on a different scale, the Lunigiana riots sent a very different signal as compared to the 'flour mill' riots or even the ones in Romagna and the Matese region. Though the *Fasci* had very deep roots in a local terrain, they necessarily had to meet with the levels that socialist organisation had reached in Italy, including the fact that there now existed a 'Marxist party'. Perhaps 'the Sicilian movement [was] not the first act of proletarian socialism in Italy',[142] as Antonio Labriola recognised, but certainly it would provide Italian socialism with a rather wider horizon, and it did so very shortly after the party's foundation. Most importantly, however, it was 'the first time in Italy that a general political crisis spr[a]ng from the class struggle', even if not so much because of 'the *Fasci* movement considered in itself', as much as the way 'in which the ruling classes and the political class (the liberal class in its various articulations) reacted to the movement'.[143]

The 'great fear' brought with it two responses that at times cancelled each other out and at other times proved complementary. In this sense the 1890s cannot be read *only* in terms of the state of siege and repressive measures in general, though they did strike widely and deeply against the workers' movement, tearing holes in the fabric of the guarantees of the rule of law. No; theories of reform, as with the attempts at a reforming policy, were the other face of this repression – and this was not even hidden. They were hypotheses for a different response to the explosion of the 'social question', a positive response, in accordance with the fundamental tendencies of an evolving society, such as *science* was able to define them. So in terms of the culture of reforms, the 1890s represented a privileged exploratory terrain, whether as a 'decade of absorbing and concluding the whole process of "economic Germanism"',[144] or on account

141 [That is, the followers of Francesco Ferrara. These latter in turn termed 'vincolisti' all those who called for any kind of state role in the economy (putting *vincoli* [binds] upon the free play of economic forces), including protectionism]

142 Labriola to Ellenbogen, 11 September 1894, in Labriola 1983, Vol. II.

143 Manacorda 1992, p. 85.

144 Macchioro 1985, p. 151.

of an oppositional neo-utilitarianism's first attempts to test out certain points of its modernising radicalism.[145] Yet in certain fields – and not unimportant ones – the intellectuals' reforming tendency, the will to explore the *scientific* basis for normative hypotheses, to play with all the possibilities intrinsic to a period penetrated by both the 'aurora of hope' and the 'aurora of fear'[146] – so typical of the 1890s – ended up being significantly watered down, amidst the 'reforming' climate of the beginning of the 1900s. With difficulty would the Nitti of 1910 have repeated, as he had stated in 1894, that 'we are all socialists, we who accept that taxation must have not only a fiscal function, but above all a social one'.[147] And moreover, his *Riforma Sociale* was certainly not configured in the same terms, and would not come to play the same role, as Luigi Einaudi's.

In the 1890s, political economy would deal with the 'social question' no longer only within the terms of the 'scientific' paradigm that won out in 1875, but also with the 'vision' connected to another paradigm, that of 'pure economics', which in the course of this decade laid the bases for the transcendence and marginalisation of 'social economics'. Mathematisation as an analytical tool, but also (and often above all) mathematisation as an ideology, seemed no longer to find any obstacles at the same level as the challenge that was thus posed at very heart of economic science. This did not, however, mean that from the beginning of the decade the 'archangel with a flaming sword' had truly succeeded in seeing off all the false schools and 'proclaiming the sovereignty of pure economics'.[148] Indeed, precisely when we break out of Pantaleoni's approach, and do not concentrate on the islands of 'truth' in abstraction from the sea of 'errors',[149] we see that the panorama of the culture of 1890s Italian economics seems very variegated and far from one-dimensional, and the precious gem of 'pure economics' itself seems to need a skilful diamond-cutter in order to clean it of the spots tarnishing its luminosity. Moreover, as has aptly been observed, 'discourse on thinking about thought always leads to thinking about its civil effects', above all when 'we are in an era in which the economists are so dedicated to interventionism that we could turn our framework on its head, saying that the most important expressions of theory are found *outside* of their tomes, in the supposedly *sporadic* sphere of the papers and journals, since these tomes are nothing but the concentrate and scientification of what

145 Franzina 1976. See also Franzina 1974.

146 Macchioro 1985, p. 154.

147 Cited by Barbagallo 1984, p. 58.

148 Naturally, the archangel in question was Maffeo Pantaleoni: see Ricci 1939, p. 44.

149 Pantaleoni 1897–8.

is found outside of the tomes themselves'.[150] And this goes for the whole 'Italian tradition', very much including the pure economists.

The two journals corresponding to the protagonists of the 1890s clash were *La Riforma Sociale*, for the heirs of the *Kathedersozialisten*, and the *Giornale degli Economisti*, after the end of Zorli's period of control, for the bearers of the new marginalist paradigm. These were both theoretical reviews and publications that directly intervened in economic policy and politics *tout court*. In this period, themes relating to public finance were truly *central* to Italy's economic and political debate, with the 'financial question' – already a long-incumbent and pressing one, given the ways in which the Italian tax system had formed – having become the flesh and blood of the strategies (and sometimes even tactics) of counterposed formations (even if they did sometimes engage in the inevitable osmoses of *trasformismo*). As such, it hardly seems strange that the new schools immediately measured themselves up against this core problem. Moreover, another 'Italian tradition' – the socio-historical-'university chair' tradition – had also mostly addressed the financial question as a privileged aspect of state-interventionist policies. So it was almost natural that the marginalists' 'pure' and scientific methodologies set a priority on trying to address the high points of the very field with which they sought to reach a rapid day of reckoning.

There seems to be no doubt that the 'science of finances' was the privileged vehicle for marginalism's penetration into Italy,[151] even though this does also leave open questions of periodisation. Conversely, there is some doubt over the hypothesis that the foundation of the pure science of finances was capable – upon its appearance, at least up till the beginning of the twentieth century – of making *tabula rasa* of what already existed on the 'market' of financial thinking, or even of marginalising it.

The key years running from 1887 to 1891 saw the appearance of the foundational works of De Viti de Marco and Pantaleoni,[152] and through Ricca-Salerno's mediation, marginalism began to find its way into the historical-social-'university chair' environment.[153] In this context, the position of even some who would be considered rigid exponents of the school upholding the

150 Macchioro 1985, p. 6.

151 Barucci 1980, pp. 69–71.

152 See De Viti de Marco 1888; Pantaleoni 1889: on finance specifically in Pantaleoni see his earlier works Pantaleoni 1882 and 1883. Emilio Sax wrote, with regard to this latter study, that 'in 1883 [Pantaleoni] conceived the idea of applying the new theory of value to financial phenomena, without separating them out in a formal theory': Sax 1924, cited by Gallegati 1984.

153 Ricca-Salerno 1887.

economic theory of public finances would draw abundantly on analytical frameworks that were anything but immediately congruent with their own.

For example, in his approach to the questions of progressive taxation Augusto Graziani did not use hedonist postulates (in the manner of Sax) in order to arrive at a determination of the *reasons for* and *modes of* such taxation, but instead introduced arguments and mechanisms drawn from an evolutionist vision of economy and society, of clearly Lorian stamp.[154] Moreover, discussing progressive taxation Mazzola himself – who also subjected Loria's 'unilateral' vision to severe critique – maintained that this had only been posed as a question of current relevance when those on low and middle incomes had the political power (as a result of overall economic growth) to shift part of the fiscal burden onto other income groups.[155] In substance, as Griziotti would soon note, 'he had linked the problem of the distribution of public burdens to the same profound economic causes to which Loria referred, though explaining its interpretation by other means'.[156] An emblematic case, then, was that of the man who 'opened ... the doors to the divulgation of Sax's work'[157] in Italy: Giuseppe Ricca Salerno.[158] Ricca Salerno intervened in the discussion on progressive taxation with a long essay published in the *Nuova Antologia* in 1894,[159] whose outlook was a true and proper model of the combinatory logic that was the peculiar characteristic of a very great part of the Italian economic culture of the 1890s. And finally, there was Conigliani, who first appeared in the panorama of the studies of finance with a book that 'is a "little jewel" as a use of marginalist schemas', with an analytical structure 'deployed with a theoretical rigour that at certain moments recalls that of Pantaleoni's *Principii*';[160] who would then make abundant recourse to Lorian theoretical points;[161] and whose 'art' had results that Turati himself would consider 'very close [to the socialists] in many fundamental economic concepts'.[162] In short, we need to rethink the vision that sees 'great dichotomies' between the *Kathedersozialismus* paradigm spread in

154 Graziani 1891.

155 Mazzola 1895, pp. 61–83, 119–76.

156 Griziotti 1909, p. 490.

157 Barucci 1980, p. 84.

158 It is also interesting to note how Graziani, Mazzola and Ricca Salerno have recently been considered the most radical exponents of the economic theory of public finances inspired by Sax: see Petretto 1984.

159 Ricca Salerno 1894.

160 Barucci 1980. See Conigliani 1890.

161 See Favilli 1986.

162 See Turati, 'Necrologio di C.A. Conigliani', *Critica Sociale*, 1901, p. 380.

Italy by Vito Cusumano at the outset of the 1870s and incarnated by the most 'illustrious' of its representatives, Achille Loria, and the 'paradigm created by Sax and spread in Italy in 1887–1888 by Ricca Salerno'.[163]

If Loria continued to traverse – in a leading role – a context in which the currents still seemed rather mixed, why, then, should the nascent 'Marxist economics' not find 'the most socialist, the most Marxist ... of the Italian economists'[164] an essential reference point? Loria, moreover, 'transcended' (*transcendences* were his speciality) the Italian tradition of *Kathedersozialismus*, and projected his bold vision of society's future well beyond any timid state interventionism. And why, then, refuse also those aspects of the tradition of *Kathedersozialismus* that could demonstrate not only the injustice of the prevalent economic and social relations, but also the need to transcend those relations – looking beyond the often anti-socialist political propensities of the main exponents of *Kathedersozialismus*? The 'anatomy of civil society' could, then, pass by way of a multiplicity of instruments; and this did not in itself entail a need to break with such 'scientific' contiguities, when these latter flowed together in a thousand streams with the mighty river of Marxism, in clear demonstration of the historical necessity of socialism.

---

163 Spoto 1985, p. 32.

164 Having previously used this quotation from a letter of Turati's to Loria, I have been accused of being prejudiced against Turati, when I commented that the director of *Critica Sociale* had 'accredited' Loria's 'role as a socialist and Marxist economist'. See Degl'Innocenti 1995, p. 105. Here I do not want to discuss the question of this supposed 'prejudice' against Turati: the reader can judge that on the basis of the 1980 book as well as this one, which are wholly in harmony in this regard. The fact is, however, that Degl'Innocenti accuses me of having shown this prejudice by making use of a method that is gravely inappropriate on both the scientific and deontological plane: that of manipulating Turati's letter to Loria. Thus Degl'Innocenti writes: 'To justify his assertion ... Favilli has extrapolated the sole expression "most socialist, most Marxist" from its both literal and environmental context, *and together with that leaves aside the comparative reference to the "Italian economists"*, with the final result of changing the overall meaning' (p. 106). Now, it was I myself who published the letter in question *for the first time in full*, in that book, on pp. 181–2. It would be paradoxical, indeed, for an author to manipulate in the text a document that he then reproduces in full in the Appendix. But there is more. Let us look at the citation that I reproduced in the text, in a page in which I also reproduce other passages of the letter precisely in order to provide a better outline of the *environmental* context: 'Why would Achille Loria not come with us? Is he not in a certain sense the most socialist, the most Marxist of the Italian economists (overlooking certain minor distinctions that matter a lot to the scholar and little to the public)' (p. 56). Comparing this quotation and the page as a whole to what Degl'Innocenti says, we have all the necessary elements for determining where the scientific shortcomings lie. (My italics).

The scientific '*affinismi*' should not be put on the same plane as the political ones. In the early 1890s the socialists had constructed a precise system of clearly identifiable parameters for their political autonomy, while they were far from having done the same thing in terms of an autonomous economic theory.

The 'Luigi Cossa School in Pavia' was a typical example of the coexistence of a proclaimed political and theoretical anti-socialism with a cultural environment that had a significant polyvalence of political and theoretical orientations, which could even arrive at openly socialist results. This was a school inspired, according to those who frequented it, by a 'typically eclectic system', and by Cossa's innate sense of 'equilibrium' between 'Pantaleoni and Loria's extreme positions'.[165] This was a school in which the paths of Cusumano, Loria, De Viti de Marco, Graziani, Gobbi, Conigliani, Montemartini and others would at times cross. It expressed very well the climate of a culture that was still essentially impregnated with an 'economic Germanism', whose indigenous variants were pervaded by a profound sociological vein (and by way of the 'social question', a socialist one), and which was capable of coexisting and even in part feeding a contiguous *marxismus genericus*.[166] This was a culture that at the beginning of the 1890s gave the appearance of having reached its highest point, and seemed almost to celebrate its long continuity as it passed from the third to the fourth series of the 'Biblioteca dell'Economista', from Gerolamo Boccardo to Salvatore Cognetti de Martiis. This was a culture that explicitly entrusted political economy the task of 'promoting the *general well-being*'[167] by way of *applied* economics, 'hated' – as Cossa insisted – 'by the persons and classes who fear the *reforms* that it promotes or desire the *revolutions* that it combats'.[168] The economist was, then, a 'committed' intellectual, in the front line of the 'social question'. The master of the 'Pavia school', the 'living filing cabinet', whom Dal Pane termed the 'historian of doctrines in effect and being put into effect',[169]

---

165 Testimony of Coletti 1925 and Griziotti 1938.

166 Expression from Macchioro 1989, p. 89.

167 See Cossa 1892, p. 12. 'Political economy has a dual *remit*. It seeks the *essence*, the *causes* and the *laws* of the social order of wealth, and provides *directing principles* for the economic activity of *political bodies*. Hence the distinction between *rational* or *abstract* political economy (science) and its *applied* or *concrete* versions (as art) that seek the common *goal* of general prosperity. Different from *theory* (which includes science and art) is *practice* (action), which profits from the *truth* of science and the *principles* of art, combining them with the dictates of experience ... Science explains; art directs; practice executes'. See Cossa 1895, p. 8.

168 Cossa 1895, p. 10.

169 In Cossa 1963, p. vii.

gave moderate, 'balanced' suggestions that were also suited to marginalising socialist 'radicalism'.[170] Yet at the same time, the terrain of social commitment that he cultivated was particularly suited to coexisting with seeds liable to grow in different directions. Luigi Cossa together with his son Emilio sought to reconcile 'the historic school' and marginalists under the umbrella of a 'method of the classical economists', amplified beyond all proportion[171] (though not so much as to be able to include Marx's method). Yet he could not prevent elements of *marxismus genericus* coming also from his own school.

One of the economists who passed through Cossa's school, the same Augusto Graziani who sought to bring together aspects of marginalism and of *Kathedersozialismus* in his intellectual production, now attempted to separate the *Kathedersozialisten* from the socialists. Faced with the 'very powerful inequalities' apparent in society, which lacked any 'moral justification', the former proposed decisive state intervention for economic and social reforms 'protecting the working classes', whereas the latter pointed from afar to the 'collectivisation of the means of production'.[172] However, there was nothing stopping there from being significant convergences along the first part of the way. And at the level of *method*, there was no doubt that despite Marxism's 'exaggerated unilateralism' it had exerted 'a beneficial effect ... on the progress of economic science'. In particular, in

170 The study of political economy 'will prove very useful also to the workers, who through this will learn the true nature of their interests and the opportune ways of making them count, compatible with the rights of others. Political economy will teach them the need for capital and its true economic function, the advantages of saving, the dangers of freespending, the damage that strikes almost always cause, the utility of institutions of assurance and cooperation, and so on. A suitable lesson in political economy imparted in popular form to the working class ... will also bring society the incalculable benefit of preserving it from many crises and many dangers; for with this a barrier is set up against the breakthrough of subversive doctrines, which find a propitious terrain in uncultured minds and the excitable fantasy of persons belonging to the class of workers'. Here, then, we have political economy as a barrier against the 'dangerous doctrines of socialism': Cossa 1892, p. 112.

171 'The scope of the present work was to conciliate the various orientations today followed by the scholars of economic science, examining them with purely objective criteria and working to demonstrate that they can all be peaceably brought together, with notable benefit to science, under the banner of the classical school, which emerged through providence': Cossa 1895, p. vii.

172 'Il socialismo teorico e l'economia politica', lecture at the Circolo giuridico della R. Università di Siena, 9 March 1895, p. 6.

> taking up the critique of economic categories and institutions, [Marxism] compelled scholars to re-examine from new angles laws and principles that had seemed beyond discussion, and to explain the foundations of the economic system, which the classical economists had only briefly concerned themselves with. And thus socialism powerfully contributed to moving out of the splendid circle that the conquests of the classical school had been closed up in.[173]

The logic of this distinction did not mean building insuperable walls to the other logic that was also in play: the multiplication of points of contact between these milieux. This also spoke to the infinite mediating capacity of Achille Loria's system.

The same logic appeared in Cognetti de Martiis's 'Laboratorio di economia', a school that was in some aspects in continuation with and in other aspects contiguous with the 'Pavia school'. Here, too, there were no great walls dividing 'liberals', 'democratic socialists', and 'Christian socialists',[174] all of whom devoted their efforts to a 'science directed at resolving the problems of life, indicating the possible solution to the "great and numerous problems that agitate modern society"'.[175] The first, rather telling result of these efforts was, indeed, the review *Riforma Sociale*, whose editorial group in 1894 was 'in large part an emanation'[176] of the 'Laboratorio'. This was the *Riforma Sociale* of a 'socialist' and 'Lorian' Nitti. So what autonomous research exercise was there concerning the 'anatomy of civil society' in the columns of *Critica Sociale*?

There can be no doubt that the socialists did appreciate their 'contiguity' with the scientific tendencies that were now dominant in Italian economic culture. But there is also no doubt that they had no intention of identifying themselves with these latter. The usage of specifically socialist and Marxist categories brought almost insurmountable problems, in this context. Indeed, it was easy for *Critica Sociale* to respond to the violent attack that Pareto had levelled against Marx's economic theories, through the publication of his introduction to Guillaumin's edition of Lafargue's excerpts from *Capital*.[177] As even Pareto himself privately commented, his introduction was of 'no economic impor-

173 'Il socialismo teorico e l'economia politica', lecture at the Circolo giuridico della R. Università di Siena, 9 March 1895, p. 26.

174 See L. Einaudi, 'Salvatore Cognetti de Martiis', *Giornale degli Economisti*, 1901, II, p. 21.

175 See Pogliano 1976. On p. 148 he cites a 1901 eulogy of Cognetti by Ottolenghi.

176 Giva 1985, p. 325.

177 Marx 1893.

tance';[178] rather, it was an ideological treatise whose only goal was to strike a heavy blow against the doctrinal inheritance of the socialists, who did not want to break with the political movement that these excerpts represented.[179] In the abstract, then, it was possible to invoke a close connection between the proposals/identity of the socialists and an 'orthodox' interpretation of 'Marx's principal economic categories'.[180]

However, when it was necessary really to get to grips with some of these categories, *Critica Sociale* did not truly manage to establish the parameters by which this proclaimed 'orthodoxy' could be identified.

The discussion that began in the columns of *Critica Sociale* in 1894, regarding the problems of Marx's economic theory and in particular the labour theory of value, provides clear proof of these difficulties.

Certainly, Italian socialist economic culture was not sufficiently well-equipped to handle a question of such complexity in a competent fashion. Up till that point it had never been confronted with Marx's theory of value as a problem, and within this milieu there had been no take-up for Engels's 1885 invite for them to 'show in which way an equal average rate of profit can and must come about, not only without a violation of the law of value, but on the very basis of it'.[181] If in Germany this call was most importantly taken up by Conrad Schmidt (together with others),[182] who first posed, with notable originality,[183] what would then become the transformation problem, in the *socialisteggiante* environment in Italy it was still Loria's old position that prevailed,[184] while among the socialists there was no specialist with the scientific authority to be able to put it in question.

Could the Italian socialists of the first half of the 1890s have posed the problem of the role that the theory of value played in the overall context of the critique of political economy? Or been aware that the 'science of capital' con-

178 Letter to Walras, 22 January 1893, in Jaffé (ed.) 1965, pp. 208–9.

179 Letters to Pantaleoni, 23 February and 18 April 1893, in De Rosa (ed.) 1960, pp. 349, 364–5.

180 See 'Un cavaliere del libero capitalismo che si divora Marx in un boccone', and E. Guindani–L. Bissolati, 'Il sofismo del plusvalore in un economista liberista italiano', in *Critica Sociale*, 1893, pp. 285–8.

181 *MECW*, Vol. 37, p. 11.

182 Schmidt 1889.

183 Engels held Schmidt's study in great esteem, but reproached him for having 'strayed into [a] bypath when quite close to the solution'. *MECW*, Vol. 37, p. 15.

184 Loria had, among other things, also mounted a severe attack against Schmidt's arguments: see Bravo 1970, p. 542.

sisted of both 'political economy' and the 'critique of it',[185] and that the theory of value had emerged as the fundamental key to explaining this analytical duplicity? The socialists' system of cultural references in the economic sphere, such as we have thus far delineated, would seem to exclude them from doing so, even if they could not avoid dealing with the centrality that this theory nonetheless assumed.

If it is true that 'everything about Marx has been said already – and long ago, at that',[186] a major part of this 'everything' was a debate over the theory of value. This was a long-term process distinguished by the presence of numerous reiterated moments, again doubtless reflecting the 'centrality' of this theory.

Was the imposing body of literature produced across a century of research and often bitterly controversial discussions just the effect of a 'war of religion' over a theory that has ultimately proven rather more a case of 'sorcery'?[187] Certainly there were some elements of a war of religion, in an affair that sometimes showed faces at odds with the customary image of a chapter of the history of culture. But some of the problems that materialised in the discussion of the labour theory of value did not only regard the internal coherence of Marx's 'system'. Discussing this theory, and seeking to answer the questions over what type of knowledge it corresponded to (a philosophical knowledge? an economic one? what type of philosophy, or of economics?), was also to discuss the epistemological foundations of economic science. And when some deluded themselves that they had firmly established the final coordinates of a 'pure' economic science, because it definitively excluded the questions underlying the labour 'method' of value, they found that they possessed a 'toolbox' whose possible uses were exclusively self-referential in nature. The 'production of commodities by means of commodities' could not, in fact, be considered only a conundrum of algebraic analysis. Commodities are 'social things', the mirror of particular relations among humans. But is, then, the process of the 'production of commodities by means of commodities', in its overall, global significance, a question internal or external to economic science?

The temptation, in answering this question, to find a space *next to* but at the same time *separate* from economic theory, has constantly traversed a far from negligible part of the Marxist tradition. This temptation went as far as the point that the late Napoleoni ultimately reached,[188] considering labour-value-alienation the principal object of an autonomous philosophical evaluation,

185 Lunghini 1994, p. vii.
186 Salvati 1994, p. 69.
187 The expression is Joan Robinson's: see Robinson 1966, p. 22.
188 Napoleoni 1985, 1992.

naturally in a non-Paretian consideration of the philosophical sphere. Often there has been neither consciousness of nor a will to separation; but nonetheless, insistence on the dual significance of Marx's labour-value category has proven able to open the way to results that were not necessarily desired in advance. Rudolf Hilferding decisively repudiated any such separation, yet he was the first in the European Marxist tradition to argue that in Marx the labour theory of value did not only have the function of determining the profit rate and the prices of production, but also that of determining the *quality* of the capitalist social relation, to the extent that 'The fundamental economic idea is consequently identical with the fundamental idea of the materialist conception of history'.[189] Following in Hilferding's wake, Franz Petry was first[190] explicitly to shine a light on the 'methodological dualism' of the theory of value, while also explicitly speaking of a *quantitative* aspect of the theory of value *distinct from* its *qualitative* aspect. Implicit, here, was the conviction that the two levels of analysis could be used *separately*. But not even Petry considered Marx's analysis of the *what*, as opposed to the *how* of pure economics, something separate and apart from economic analysis.[191]

Western Marxism's change of horizon – with the works of Lukács and Korsch, which 'denied the very root of the idea of Marxism as scientific sociology'[192] – would particularly influence Marxist consideration of the limits of the economic sphere. This was not because the separation among spheres was openly theorised, but rather because economic categories were thought in philosophical terms.[193] Certainly, it no longer seemed possible to locate *Capital* within

189 Hilferding, 'Böhm-Bawerk's Criticism of Marx', text from marxists.org.

190 Hilferding and Petry were the 'first' of the Marxists to interpret Marx's fundamental economic categories in terms that were not exclusively Ricardian. And they were the 'first', in the sense that their framework then became a point of reference for a wide discussion on these themes. As we will see, however, at the turn of the century there was also an 'Italian tradition' that posed itself the problem of the 'quality' of these analytical categories.

191 Petry 1916.

192 Colletti, 1979, p. 43.

193 '*Commodities* and, in a still more conspicuous form … all further forms of capitalistic commodity production derived from those basic forms, such as capital, wage-labour, etc., are examples of that fetish form assumed by the social production-relations of the present epoch. What Marx here terms the *Fetishism of the World of Commodities* is only a scientific expression for the same thing that he had described earlier, in his Hegel-Feuerbach period, as "human self-alienation"': Karl Korsch's *Karl Marx*, text from https://www.marxists.org/archive/korsch/1938/karl-marx/ch02.htm.

the terms of the usual divisions among the sciences, and nor was it completely internal to 'economic science'.

We have referred to the frequent moments of repetition in the century-long discussion in which 'everything has been said' on Marx's labour theory of value. Indeed, the fundamental coordinates around which debate and research would develop had been posed already in 1900–15, the 1920s and the 1930s. The refined application of sophisticated mathematical techniques, used by Sraffa formally to resolve the transformation problem, clearly takes for granted the analytical apparatuses of Dimitriev and Bortkiewicz.[194] And, to limit ourselves to Italy, in recent years the whole range of problems from the first decades of the twentieth century has been proposed again, even if at what are undoubtedly much higher levels of analytical awareness. This was a labour theory of value wholly internal to economics and the classical tradition; a theory that had the role 'of allowing a determination of the rate of profit within the existing framework, in the only way that was concretely possible at that time'.[195] This was a theory articulated on two different levels: the *quantitative* one, resolved by Sraffa, and the *qualitative* one, linked to the concept of 'abstract labour'; the link that had to be smashed was that of the 'extraordinarily compact character of Marx's vision'.[196] Or even, grounded in a critical reflection on the positions of the late Napoleoni, the full recuperation of the labour theory of value into economic science – not on Ricardian premises, this time, but based on the recognition that the theory's fundamental core, 'the nexus among value, living labour, and social conflict ... the originality of capitalist exploitation',[197] defines a theoretical content whose validity is not confirmed, denied or demonstrated by any *a posteriori* mathematical formalisation.

Precisely because discussion of the labour theory of value has always been accompanied by discussion on the foundations of economic science, the most significant moments punctuating this debate have always been characterised by the echoes of a battle over method. And even in the mid-1890s[198] the echoes of this battle had still not died out. Rather, the battle was now entering into the decisive phase of a clash between the historical-sociological school and 'pure economics': in this specific case, between Lorian polymorphism and the aggressive vanguards of Italian marginalism.

194 Dmitriev 1974, Bortkiewicz 1952, 1984. These works originally date from 1904, 1906 and 1907 respectively.
195 Geregnani 1981, p. 56.
196 Vianello 1986, p. 163. See Vianello 1978.
197 Bellofiore 1993a, p. 133; 1993b.
198 I refer the reader to Favilli 1980, pp. 70–84, for an analytical discussion of this debate.

The 1894–5 debate marked both a first distancing of the socialists from Loria, seen as the noble father of an Italian socialist economic science, and the reaffirmation of a privileged relation with what was substantially a Lorian methodology. Francesco Coletti was a pupil of Loria's whose steps in this debate were in large part guided by his teacher. The two young socialists who were mounting their first efforts as economists in this context, Antonio Graziadei and Arturo Labriola, did arrive at conclusions different from those of 'the Illustrious one'. Yet they were themselves being trained in a Lorian environment, and at this moment they had in mind Loria's Marx rather more than they did the Marx of *Capital*. It was perhaps inevitable that the 'critique of political economy' was the great element missing from this debate, but the theory of the 'cost of production' was not necessarily the point of reference for all the participants' arguments. It was a rather uncertain line of defence in this phase of the *Methodenstreit*.

The debate was also a testing ground for the 'scientific socialism' that the director of *Critica Sociale* suggested was at the foundation of socialist identity, and of which this review presented itself as the most qualified interpreter in Italy. The results were not particularly positive. Turati, who had himself solicited this 'test', ended up seriously embarrassed. This was not only the embarrassment betrayed in the well-known affair over whether Engels's introduction to *Capital* Volume III – so severe in its polemic against Loria – should be published. It also reflected the much more serious question of Turati's incapacity to take account of the theoretical and political results of the themes in discussion, results that he thought that he could wish away using a few vague declarations of respect for the autonomy of science. There is good reason to believe that he had intended to intervene in the debate, and that only the publication of Volume III convinced him to hold off from any hasty decisions. However, we can find some elements that may give us an insight into what Turati's approach might have been like. Already in 1893, indeed, glossing an article of Coletti's that declared Marx's theory of value 'unsustainable', he maintained that he did not believe this theory 'essential' 'to the doctrines of scientific socialism'.[199]

Some highly authoritative Marxists have defended – and continue to defend – this point of view. The fact is that the protagonists of Italian socialism's most important theoretical review arrived at such conclusions (if they did do so) not on the basis of a rigorous critical analysis of the texts and a real engagement with the new terms of the theoretical discussion, but on the

---

199 La Direzione, 'Postilla', *Critica Sociale*, 1893, p. 9.

basis of *immediately* political considerations. To be clear, these were political questions wholly bound up with a contingent state of besiegement; and faced with this, it was not possible to show weaknesses in the ranks. However, this attitude also had another far deeper motivation: the habit of thinking the relation with determinate scientific and intellectual spheres in *a political way*. If it was held that preserving a relationship with certain circles – in this case, meaning the Lorian milieu – was of priority concern, then it was, indeed, possible to sacrifice a theory of value deemed 'not essential ... to the doctrines of scientific socialism'. The publication of Volume III and Engels's 'Introduction' certainly did make this question much more problematic, but it did not change this intellectual outlook.

The undoubtable weakness of some of the protagonists, the slapdash manner in which they dealt with some rather complex intellectual realities, and the somewhat equivocal climate created around the discussion – which Turati's suspicious character tended to exaggerate – all provided him sufficient reason to dismiss this question in such terms.

Antonio Labriola's attitude toward this debate was also essentially characterised by political concerns, because he started from the assumption that the discussion now underway lacked any scientific validity. 'This is not an intellectual and scientific question', he wrote to Engels, 'but an ethical question ... or rather one of manners ... or rather, of bad manners ... or rather, of charlatanism'.[200]

But the dimension of the problems raised – some of which were very real – went far beyond the inadequacy of the tools that the various different protagonists used. The searching attempt to understand and update 'critical communism's' economic theory – a need of which Labriola was very clearly aware – required a quite different response than his disdainful shrugging of the shoulders, faced with the only concrete results that Italian socialism had thus far proven capable of producing. Moreover, even though Antonio Labriola was not an economist, he would later express his view on the central points of the themes in discussion with notable originality and a wealth of articulations. However, the heavy consequences of his absence from the columns of *Critica Sociale*, in such a delicate moment for the growth of the Italian socialists' theoretical awareness, would remain an important missed opportunity.

Both the Party leader, who had so deeply internalised a sense of the primacy of politics, and the 'philosophy professor', so attentive to the (not merely 'inter-

200 Letter to Engels, 21 January 1895, in Labriola 1983, Vol. II, p. 549.

nal') logics of theory, were convinced that there could be no 'orthodoxy' in the scientific field guaranteed by the Party's authority.

Rather prudently, Turati held back from offering his own interpretation of the labour theory of value, and *Critica Sociale* stopped addressing a problematic of such density that it would have been difficult to manage using the 'toolbox' that it had at hand.[201] In certain aspects this theory would flow into the river of Italian socialist culture without joining its main current. The socialists that engaged in the economist's profession chose one or the other branch of the shifting delta of political economy in Italy; and Marx's labour theory of value was also either rejected or reinterpreted on the basis of these choices. The two young students who had intervened in the discussion of 1894–5, Antonio Graziadei and Arturo Labriola, operated precisely in these terms, as we will see, in a more analytic sense, in other chapters of this book.

Theory 'floated' over a milieu that was substantially incapable of addressing it in the terms of the critique of political economy; and this led to a more general tendency toward 'lightmindedness' in socialist attempts to use its explanatory capacities in analysing actually-existing capitalism, so far as was really possible. This was a 'lightmindedness' that was also identifiable in the ways in which the 'crisis of Marxism' played out in Italy.

This 'lightmindedness' further brings into relief – and it is a commonplace to notice this – Antonio Labriola's theoretical solidity. The 'professor of philosophy and socialism' was not an economist and never wrote specific essays on either value or pure economics. He did not consider Marx's economic thinking to be separate from the materialist analysis of history, and his interpretation always operated in terms of the global perspective that was one of the most important aspects of Marx's method. So Croce's claim that for Labriola 'the Marxist theory of "surplus-value" and "historical materialism" were above all important for socialism's practical purposes'[202] may in part be true; but not in the openly reductive sense that the Naples philosopher meant it, in suggesting that his interlocutor was clearly reluctant fully to work through those

201 Across 1895 and 1896 there was some trace of the discussion on this question: A. Groppali, 'Il principio della causalità economica secondo il Marx e secondo Loria', 1895, pp. 359–61; A. Marchi, *Ancora il principio della causalità economica secondo il Marx e secondo il Loria*, 1896, pp. 27–9; A. Groppali, 'Per chiudere la polemica sul principio della causalità economica', 1896, pp. 43–5. From a theoretical point of view this was of no significance, yet still here we see the struggle between the two giants, Marx and Loria. This battle moreover demonstrated that 'the legend that we socialists have also created a gospel for ourselves and a pontefix whom we credit with infallibility, is a false one'.

202 Croce 1961, p. 302.

scientific nodes that could create difficulties for the movement for workers' emancipation. It is also true that after 1899 the Labriola 'of the economic theory of surplus-value would not again open his mouth'[203] – but were the motivations for this the same ones that Croce implies?

Labriola did express himself on value – if not the law of value, given his disdain for both the positivist and formalist referents[204] – in a discussion of historical materialism, where he made a very general enunciation on the fundamental theme of *Capital*.

> Its very most important subject is the origin and process of *surplus-value* (of capitalist production, in this context), and then, after continuing from production into the circulation of capital, the division of *surplus-value* itself.
>
> This is the presupposition of the whole theory of value, brought to completion through its elaboration by economic science over a century and a half: a theory that never represents a *factum empirico* drawn from vulgar deduction, and does not express a simple *logical position* – as some have imagined – but the typical premise without which the rest is impossible.[205]

Thus here the theory of value was the *typical premise* of economic discourse. His friend Croce, mounting a polemical intervention regarding Labriola's own *Discorrendo di socialismo e filosofia*,[206] would raise objections to this position:

> ... you always speak of a theory of value according to Marx. I only know that there is a manner with which Marx deploys and uses the theory of value, which was an obvious one. The role that he assigns to that theory is different, yes – but not the theory itself. And to deal with this role, we have to enter into a whole historical and sociological critique. And moreover:

203 Croce 1961, p. 322.

204 'Verbalism always tends to box itself within purely formal definitions, leading to the erroneous conception that it is easy to reduce the intricate and enormous complex of nature and history into simple, palpable terms. It induces the belief that it is easy to get a direct view of the multiform and very complicated pattern of causes and effects, as if on a theatre stage. To put that in sharper terms, it obliterates the meaning of these problems, because it only sees denominations': Labriola 1965, p. 62.

205 Labriola 1965, p. 191.

206 Croce 1961, pp. 57–114.

> do you really want to convince yourself that this labour theory of value has a wider significance than it does for the economic current – that is, as a trivial, everyday explanation?

As has been said, these were extremely general statements, interested more in the labour theory of value's role with regard to capital's valorisation process than in the internal articulations of the theory itself. It should be understood that the 'obvious' way of using and deploying this theory was not specific to the classical economists.[207] Rather, it was only the recognition – which, too, was a very general one, and would later be theoretically systematised in the field of political economy – that labour stood at the origin of the process of capital valorisation. This recognition, brought down into the lived reality of social processes, and integrated into the concept of the mode of production, assumed the original *form* – completely detached from the classical tradition – that made it possible to explain the real and not only phenomenal movement of bourgeois economy and society, of which the formation of market- and production prices represented but one aspect.

The real need to safeguard the *unitary* central core of *Capital*'s cognitive complex, combined with a *philosophical* approach to this question ('philosophical' here only meaning a lack of mastery of some of the techniques specific to economic science) – and thus Labriola's refusal to get bogged down in a discourse of everyday empirical proofs using what he considered the typical premise of Marx's system – in part explain his failure to make any organic intervention regarding the theory of value. Indeed, given such premises, this was a task that he did not consider himself up to; but it was a task that he considered necessary in the continual process of critical rethinking and adapting to new problems, which he considered essential functions of a theoretically rigorous Marxism. Again, here, a letter to Croce bears witness to this:

> … I have come to be convinced that the formal principles of economics have to be entirely revisited: and since I will not be making this revision myself, I do not want to bore myself reading bad books. This sentiment has stayed with me throughout my life. Marx is the only man who tried to make economics a critical science, but he touched only part of the whole … and he, too, failed to provide a propaedeutics of the concepts with

207 See Napoleoni's clear and, indeed, exemplary framing of this problem in his *Lezioni sul capitolo IV inedito di Marx* (Napoleoni 1975). See also Grossmann 1977, Meek 1956, and chapters two, three and the second part of Faucci and Pesciarelli (eds.) 1976.

> which he operates: as if a physicist today did not provide a propaedeutics of the *energy* that he takes for his presupposition.[208]

This does not mean that Labriola thought that the way that he had hitherto posed the problem of value was erroneous, and numerous comments in his correspondence right up till his death also demonstrate that this was not his view. Rather, he was just arguing that given what he had said already, the only really rigorous manner of addressing this problem lay in a rethinking of some of the formal principles of economic theory. In this sense, 'he did not speak again'; and ultimately he had never spoken about it, in the sense that Croce implies.

Antonio Labriola's indications lend themselves to a dual order of consideration. His insistence on seeing the labour theory of value as a fundamental link in the analysis of the mode of production – as a concept that was, *in a first phase*, *per se* evident – exactly corresponds to the position that Marx himself had clearly expressed in his famous 11 July 1868 letter to Kugelmann.[209] Moreover, it corresponds to the fully Marxian way of defining the very object of social science by way of this theory, namely the 'Marxian project of studying society on the basis of the social relations that are established in production'.[210] In short, Labriola proved himself fully internal to the dimension of the critique of political economy. Moreover, '[i]t was also necessary to demonstrate that a theory of value erected on the basis of this particular concept was in fact capable of providing a real solution of the problems which were put before it'.[211] These included the problem of the coherence between a theory of value *qua*

208 Letter to Croce, 31 May 1898, in Labriola 1983, Vol. III, p. 865.

209 'The chatter about the need to prove the concept of value arises only from complete ignorance both of the subject under discussion and of the method of science. Every child knows that any nation that stopped working, not for a year, but let us say, just for a few weeks, would perish. And every child knows, too, that the amounts of products corresponding to the differing amounts of needs demand differing and quantitatively determined amounts of society's aggregate labour. It is SELF-EVIDENT that this necessity of the distribution of social labour in specific proportions is certainly not abolished by the specific form of social production; it can only change its form of manifestation. Natural laws cannot be abolished at all. The only thing that can change, under historically differing conditions, is the form in which those laws assert themselves ... Where science comes in is to show how the law of value asserts itself. So, if one wanted to 'explain' from the outset all phenomena that apparently contradict the law, one would have to provide the science before the science': Marx to Kugelmann 11 July 1868, *MECW*, Vol. 43, pp. 68–9.

210 See De Marchi, La Grassa and Turchetto 1994, p. 28.

211 Meek 1956, p. 164.

real basis of capitalist economic processes, and a theory of prices. Marx himself did not at all underestimate the significance of this consideration, convinced as he was that solving this 'transformation problem' would only require a few formal adjustments. The imposing critical literature that has continued, to this day, to address this question, demands a rather more problematised reflection.

Striking in the Italian (and not only Italian) Marxist literature of the late nineteenth and early twentieth century – even when Marx's economic object is properly understood – is the lack of consideration of the analytical problems posed by the progress of the economic sciences. These are questions of analysis that could not all be characterised as 'ideological' in character. Certainly the 'toolbox' cannot be taken in isolation from the object for which it has been prepared and on which it has to act, and thus 'analytical questions' are not independent of more general conceptions of 'economic science'. But at the same time, a science is gradually structured as it takes on ever more refined analytical techniques, which remain relatively autonomous of the wider, general processes of the object's definition. Notwithstanding the polemical character of such a large part of the debate on the 'neutrality' of analytical tools, it is a fact that even important Marxist writers, like Oskar Lange, for example, were acquainted with the pathways of 'econometrics' and above all 'praxeology', which, as a 'logic of rational activity',[212] was closely linked to questions of the 'neutrality' of techniques.

The undervaluation of this element – long a mainstay of Marxist economic literature, with extremely damaging effects to which Gramsci himself drew attention[213] – has often entailed a bifurcation between 'political economy' and 'economic' analysis.

Labriola did not pose the problem in these terms; or, more exactly, did not try to develop it in these terms – his 'scientific' formation being a quite different one – and addressed 'pure economics' at the level of method and of general principles. This did not mean that he 'did not know the critiques of

---

212 See Lange 1963. Think also of the neoclassical tendencies that tend almost to transform economic science into a branch of praxeology: Robbins 1972.

213 'Leaving on one side any judgement on the merits of the question, one may draw attention to what careful studies *modern* economists devote to their science in order continually to perfect the *logical instruments* of their science, so much so that one can say that a great deal of the *prestige* enjoyed by economists is due to their formal rigour, their exactness of expression etc. The same tendency is not present in *critical* economy, which all too often makes use of stereotyped expressions and expresses superior tones that are not warranted by the exposition: it gives the impression of tiresome arrogance and nothing else': Gramsci 1995, p. 175.

Marx that had matured in the neoclassical school, except insofar as they penetrated Croce's "revisionist" writings and Bernstein's work'.[214] Rather, precisely the fact that late nineteenth-century marginalism was not only an alternative to Marx's economic theory such as Labriola understood it, but also the object of a methodological confusion doing much to entangle a large part of Italian socialist culture, meant that he was necessarily an attentive critical observer of this school. Not only his comments in his *Postscriptum* and in *Discorrendo di socialismo e di filosofia* bear witness to this, but also certain among his letters to Croce. Naturally, he addressed it in the manner that we have mentioned – that is, as a matter of general principles, without getting to grips with its specific analytical articulations – but always with a first-hand knowledge of the most important literature on the question. We can see this, for example, in the long bibliographical note he attached to an outline for a study on the third volume of *Capital*, prepared in 1897, probably for his son Franz's use.[215]

At the end of the century the young Italian socialist economists – and, in his own way, so, too, Antonio Labriola – were continuing to discuss value. Antonio Graziadei, Arturo Labriola, and Enrico Leone were still talking about it in these years (and we will follow their trajectories later on in this book), but most importantly, as the 'battle over method' in Italy reached its decisive phase, the discussion on the labour theory of value became an element of the wider debate on the scientific status of 'political economy' and 'economics'.

In Italy, the discussion on value had displayed a strongly Lorian stamp. Fundamentally, it was 'the Illustrious one' who had anticipated some of the themes that would later be found in Böhm-Bawerk's *Zum Abschluss des Marxschen Systems*; but these would not be the particular elements debated in the Italian climate of the end of the century. Rather, we should note that authors as different in their political-cultural itineraries and capacity to use theoretical instruments as Sorel and Merlino – among the protagonists in this 'crisis of

214 Are 1974, p. 55. In this regard, Are also argues that Labriola knew Böhm-Bawerk's critique of *Capital* Volume III only in the 'extremely academic-bibliographical sense of "having heard of it", "knowing that it existed"': Are 1974, p. 56. In reality Labriola had got his hands on *Zum Abschluss des Marxschen Systems* in July 1896, immediately after its publication. The copy concerned – an edition that was not on sale – was lent to him by Mazzola, and it was Labriola who showed it to Croce (not the other way round) during this latter's visit to Perugia, probably that same month. Croce used it for his study of 'some of the concepts of Marxism'. See Labriola to Croce 9 July 1896; n.d. (but written between 2 and 28 October 1896); and 20 December 1896, in Labriola 1983, Vol. II, pp. 694–6, 725, 750–3.

215 Labriola 1946, pp. 34–7.

Marxism' context – also tended to read Marxian economic categories, including value, beyond the terms of the object for which they had been developed analytically.

In an important stage of Sorel's journey from considering the theory of value as an essential scientific element of Marx's 'new real metaphysics'[216] to considering it 'illuminated in a new light … full of juridical preoccupations',[217] in an essay that also wove together certain rather penetrating moments of interpretation, he added a note attempting to use theory as a link between what were two very analytically different spheres. In substance, Sorel maintained that Marx had introduced the notion of labour as a *measure* of value in order to establish a parallel with a hypothetical communist society in which labour-value would be the social norm of production and distribution. In particular, introducing this 'parallelism' hypothesis allowed him to avoid flights of fancy into a utopian imaginary of the future society, instead linking it to certain forms that were already present, albeit with different mechanisms of functioning, even in capitalist society.[218]

If for Sorel the link between the theory of value and the future socialist society was inserted within a vision of positive possibilities, Merlino's perspective was a different one.

Here we are not concerned with examining Merlino's 'internal' interpretation of Marx's labour theory of value – an interpretation whose theoretical depth remained well below that of other protagonists of the 'crisis of Marxism' – as much as its 'external' projection onto the universe of capitalist society. Already in *Pro e contro il socialismo*[219] we can discern a labour theory of value considered as a function of the 'collectivist society'; but this connection was even more clearly propounded during the brief but intense *Rivista Critica del Socialismo* experience. The fundamental and particular task of the theory of value was, in this view, to make 'the socialistic, or rather communistic argument' a plausible one. This argument was to be directly 'deduced' from the theory of value, for which reason 'Marx had to imagine the growing rise of profit and the gradual diminution of wages, the polarisation of wealth and poverty'.[220] The theory of value, then, was to be 'the key' to the collectivist 'new social order'. The 'Marxist utopia' consisted precisely of this mechanism.

216 Sorel 1894.

217 Sorel 1903, p. 196.

218 Sorel 1897.

219 Merlino 1897.

220 FS Merlino, 'Intorno alla teoria del plusvalore e al collettivismo', *Rivista Critica del Socialismo*, 1899, p. 109.

> The Marxist *utopia* is the supposition that the conditions of labour, capacities, tastes, and desires can be made equal, that all lands can be made equally fertile, all cities equally attractive, all hamlets into cities – or vice versa – all industries equally productive, taking away all the difficulty of labour with machines, reducing all labours to the average, social labour imagined by Marx, and all things to coagulates of this imaginary labour.[221]

Beyond the question of how far we can identify this type of utopia in *Capital*, the method here used in the overall consideration of the theory of value – bringing out its role in both capitalist society and in the 'collectivist society' – poses problems that have recently been the object of debates of considerable importance. In substance, according to one view it is possible to identify paths that, starting out from *Capital*'s analytical categories, directly and *necessarily* lead to the experience of 'actually-existing socialism'. That is to say, not only was this possibility proven *after* the experiences of 'actually-existing socialism' had unfolded, but these trajectories could be deduced even *before* they actually played out, as the far-sightedness of certain late-nineteenth-century authors supposedly already demonstrated. As such, the theory of value is itself here posed as one of the foundation stones of the now mighty edifice made out of Karl Marx's *responsibilities*.

This is not the place to get to grips with this *querelle* over Marx's responsibilities, now taking on the shape and characteristics of a war of religion – indeed, one meant to conclude with the extirpation of an original, malignant root. Certainly, this *querelle* seems rather thin when it comes to rigorous historical studies and evidence capable of attesting to the concreteness, the viscosity and the contradictions of complex historical processes that are supposedly *congruent* with determinate theoretical frameworks. Conversely, it abounds with a vast literature of a *deductive* character, where the rings in the chains of theoretical responsibility are easily linked together through mechanisms of a perfect logical coherence.

Taking the specific case of Saverio Merlino's intuition, the following type of chain of deduction can thus be established: the labour theory of value is, in substance, and independently of what Marx repeatedly argued, a theory of socialist planning, and planning always demands totalitarian political structures, and therefore …

I think that there is little doubt that we can reasonably deduce from Marx's few references to the 'cookshops of the future' that he was thinking of an econ-

221 FS Merlino, 'La mia eresia', *Rivista Critica del Socialismo*, 1899, p. 331.

omy that would be planned, in some sense. However, it is something quite different to say that we can draw from Marx's economic categories – and, in particular, from the labour theory of value – a given tool or, more simply, orientation on which basis a model of planning could be constructed. '[I]rony of Fate!' – one expert in socialist planning would ask – 'what can Marxian economics contribute to the problem of the optimum distribution of productive resources in a socialist economy?'[222] Certain parts of pure economics' analytical baggage may serve this purpose rather better than Marx. In any case, did one of the most lucid exponents of the Italian tradition of 'pure economics' not perhaps successfully address this very theoretical possibility at the beginning of the century?[223]

Even leaving aside – to use Petry's language – the 'qualitative aspect' of the theory of value, and remaining within the sphere of its 'quantitative aspect', the labour theory of value tends to be posed as a sort of theory of equilibrium for simple commodity production, a *deeper order* underlying the contingent fluctuations in the production and exchange of goods. And, therefore, if an *order of planning* were introduced controlling the flows of production and exchange, the 'law' guaranteeing equilibrium amidst a situation of 'anarchy' would lose its role. As Sweezy argues,

> In the economics of a *socialist society* the theory of *planning* should hold the same basic position as the theory of value in the economics of a capitalist society. Value and *planning* are as much opposed, and for the same reason, as capitalism and socialism.[224]

Marx's labour theory of value is a *theory of capitalism*, in both its qualitative and quantitative aspects. Not so much because Marx continually stated this, clouding his vision with an ideological veil, as because it perfectly corresponds to the deep analytical core of *Capital*, which not by chance begins with a study of the *forms* of the principal category of the capitalist process of production and distribution: the commodity.[225] Not by chance, it is precisely in the course of that

---

222 Lange 1935, p. 190.

223 See Barone, 'Il ministro della produzione nello stato collettivista', *Giornale degli Economisti*, 1908, pp. 267–93, 391–414.

224 Sweezy 1964, p. 54.

225 'The category "commodity" presupposes the prevalence of commodity relations. It disappears in the measure that central processes prevail, on condition of course that these do not have the function of ensuring the commodity character of labour power': see Bidet 1990, p. 68.

study that a first *form* of value comes into definition. The whole subsequent analytical dimension unfolds fully in coherence with these premises: a coherence that is not put into question by the difficulties that the formal solution of certain *transitions* also runs into, for example the key question of the *transformation* problem. If certain passages of *Capital* and the *Grundrisse* refer to the need for the accounting of a hypothetical society that has eliminated capitalism to *measure* labour time, this does not imply that it is possible to determine what socialism is using the overall labour theory of value.[226] These passages only demonstrate Marx's propensity for a planned economy and the suggestion that '[c]alculation and book-keeping also form the historical point of departure for the methodology of social economic planning'.[227]

However, as we have already noted, the end-of-the-century discussion on the theory of value was rather more centred on questions of 'method' than questions of 'merit': on the 'object' of economic analysis more than the internal aporias of an analytical tool. The processes defining an 'economic moment', which soon became the central element of the final phase of the 'battle over method', had the effect of rapidly precipitating the suspension that had been present in the Italian economic culture of the 1890s. And the part of that culture that was inspired in various ways by Marx's economics, and that had perhaps also begun operating in a critical manner within the Lorian climate, suddenly found itself faced with 'pure economics' as the only guarantor of the discipline's 'scientific' character – the only guarantor of its professionalisation. The socialist scholars of economics who were now emerging from Loria's influence did not arrive at the methodological indications provided by Labriola, but rather those of Pantaleoni and Pareto.

Benedetto Croce's role in this logic of transition was certainly an essential one. It is true that there were socialist economists like Montemartini who had always been marginalists. But Montemartini could not play the *general* cultural role that Croce did, and having always been a marginalist he had no transition to make or to propose to be made.

Was Croce's transition a move between a 'Marxist environment' and another, different one? Certainly the two great protagonists of this phase in the history of Italian culture, Labriola and Croce, decisively ruled that out. But Sorel, Merlino, Pantaleoni, Pareto, and Gentile himself – not to mention very many other

226 The author of an – in many ways laudable – recent book on Merlino offers a rather different interpretation. This book is, however, rather too belligerent in its desire to demonstrate a perfect correspondence between *all* of Marx's analytical categories, including those of *Capital*, and the absolutely *inevitable* results in the Gulag. See Berti 1993, pp. 291–4.

227 Lange 1963, p. 181.

protagonists and others with walk-on roles in this 'crisis of Marxism' – did at a certain moment explicitly make reference to such a move, or even speak of a 'conversion'. Labriola continually called on his friend Croce explicitly to state that he had never been either a Marxist or a socialist. In such an appeal we can see – beyond the philosopher's rigorous doctrinal dividing lines – also his political concerns over the characteristics that the 'crisis of Marxism' was now taking on. The professor sought, within the limits of the possible, to circumscribe the crisis to a substantially 'external' dimension. For his part, having collected his Marxological writings 'as if in a coffin' Croce would now instead refer to another milieu, doing so in different ways according to the historical time and the evolution of his thinking, all the while keenly asserting the coherence of his development – including as it related to these writings. And yet in the quasi-confession that was his *Contributo alla critica di me stesso*, he would clearly state that his first writings were intended as 'a defence and a rectification' of 'the concepts of Marxism'.[228] He would speak of a 'corroded faith', and set this 'defence' in temporal relation with the brief moment in which he had even been tempted by the socialist movement. The socialists' ideas and their passions, he explained,

> shook me up, for the first time awakening in me a semblance of political passion, giving me a strange taste of the new, like in the case of the no-longer young man who falls in love for the first time, and observes the mysterious process of the new passion within his own self … I came to breathe in faith and hope in the vision of mankind's palingenesis, redeemed by work and in work.[229]

Certainly, this is not enough to allow us to argue that Croce was a socialist and Marxist of 'revolutionary political faith',[230] even for a brief period; but it does suffice in allowing us to glimpse a border zone whose boundaries were not sharply defined. This was a border zone skirted by both *diffuse Marxism* and Labriola's rigorous, critical Marxism. Moreover, his 1896 essays – the first on historical materialism, and the other on Achille Loria – were perfectly inscribed within Labriola's programme of interventions regarding Marxism's theoretical substance, eliminating any 'concoction of scientific socialism'[231]

228 Croce 1989, p. 35.
229 Croce 1989, pp. 34–5.
230 Spirito 1965, p. 77.
231 Letter to Croce 24 December 1896, in Labriola 1983, Vol. III, p. 755.

and 'purify[ing] the air that socialism breathed in Italy'.[232] The questions on which Labriola and Croce agreed widely surpassed the ones on which they disagreed, such as we have just mentioned. These disagreements were in any case considered wholly internal to a common horizon, within the ambit of which – at the level at which their research unfolded – there was no orthodoxy to be respected or imposed. It is possible that Labriola was not aware of the 'venom of the argument';[233] but at that point, neither was Croce. The 'venom of the argument' would only become evident *after* the passage toward another horizon had come to be delineated. Moreover, the conceptual development through which this transition would unfold did not always wholly conform with the arguments that would naturally, gradually give rise to such venom. The denial – very much present in the first essay – that Marxism had the characteristics of a 'metaphysical materialism', of a teleological and fatalist conception of history, and of economic reductionism, would not survive these later developments.

The transition that the culture of the era had noted – and which both its protagonist and his most important interlocutor denied – really had taken place, but in times and forms that make its boundaries and its identifiability rather uncertain. The fact that another transition was also underway – that of another one-time interlocutor of Labriola's, Sorel – and that all this took place in the context of the 'crisis of Marxism', which could also be defined as a crucible of transitions, gave particular meaning and significance to an author from a 'Marxist environment' coming to encounter 'pure economics'. Indeed, this was an author capable of explaining at very refined analytical levels the meaning of the process that was now underway.

Maffeo Pantaleoni's position regarding Croce could be considered indicative of this process, its direction and the times in which it took place. Still after the appearance of the Italian edition of Croce's essay on Loria – where there was no noticeable prejudice against 'pure economics', but instead a somehow rather positive view of it – Pantaleoni continued to consider him a socialist writer who would have to clarify 'who [had] first and most clearly talked rubbish', Marx or Loria.[234] Two years later, in a long letter centring on questions of method in economics, he could write to this same author; 'In your dispute with Prof. Labriola I think that you are wholly in the right'.[235] And indeed, as con-

232 Croce 1961, p. 298.

233 Croce 1961, p. 304.

234 Pantaleoni, 'A proposito del Cours d'Economie Politique di Vilfredo Pareto', *Rivista Popolare*, 15 April 1897.

235 Pantaleoni to Croce, 30 May 1899, conserved in Croce's papers. I thank Luca Michelini –

cerned problems of economic method, Croce had now entirely absorbed the marginalists' conceptual apparatus, on which basis he operated together with his own analytical determinations, even if these latter were elaborated in philosophical terms. It was on this terrain – that of the 'economic principle' – that he would also confront the great figures of pure economics like Pareto,[236] who 'left the philosophy of economics to Croce, instead more modestly contenting himself with economic axioms'.[237] But *Capital* no longer had any right of way on the road of 'economic categories' and the general science of economics. Its object was something else; perhaps also an important one (and the importance that Croce attributed to it would vary as his thinking evolved), but all the same an object extraneous to economic science.

The combination of the outcomes of Croce's transition and the epistemic paradigm of 'pure economics' would – as we have said – have very significant effects on the young socialist economists of the 'Marxist environment', who now found themselves in a crucial phase of their scientific formation and professional aspirations. In another chapter of this book we will look at the itineraries of those like Arturo Labriola and Enrico Leone who wanted to remain 'Marxists' and at the same time – albeit in a very different way – to be 'pure economists'. At the moment at which this connection was sealed in Italy, only a non-economist Marxist would prove able to intervene at the levels of analysis that this set of problems demanded: and once again, it was Antonio Labriola. Indeed, he was the only person able to set himself in front of pure economics' conceptual system and deploy an explanatory approach capable of distinguishing between the 'epistemic' and 'epistemological' levels of discourse.[238]

Naturally, given the philosophy professor's formation, his interventions would take on particular importance above all at this second level. And indeed, faced with the paradigm of 'pure economics', he explicitly posed the question

---

who is using Pantaleoni's unpublished letters to Croce, in his possession, for his monograph on Pantaleoni – for allowing me to see this text.

236 Croce 1961, pp. 219–63; Pareto, 'Sul fenomeno economico. Lettera a Benedetto Croce' – *Giornale degli Economisti*, August 1900, pp. 139–62 – and 'Sul principio economico' – *Giornale degli Economisti*, 1901, pp. 131–8.

237 Busino 1974, p. 143.

238 The analysis of Marx and Marxism on the basis of the distinction between two levels of inquiry – the 'epistemic', proper to directly scientific, immediately objective knowledge, and the 'epistemological', the level of the 'theory of science' – was at the centre of the Polish philosopher Siemek's works, and has recently been reprised in Italy by Emilio Agazzi: see Agazzi 1987, 1987b.

of the reoccurrence of 'difficulties in the preliminary conception of any scientific problem', difficulties 'for which reason not only Marx but three quarters of contemporary thought remain beyond comprehensibility'.[239] The return of 'formal logic' as the 'arbiter of knowledge' did not necessarily mean proposing abstract tools of analysis, and the processes of abstraction and isolation were in any case those 'proper to any science that seeks the road of principles starting from the empirical base'.[240] This specific case, however, was a matter not so much of *determinate abstraction* as of *indeterminate abstraction*, an abstraction wholly neglecting those historical processes of which economics, too, was the flesh and blood. 'In this kind of abstract atomism', Labriola noted, 'we no longer know what history is, and progress is limited to a mere semblance'.[241] An ever sharper separation thus emerged between 'critically reasonable thought' and 'the matter of knowledge'[242] and the impossibility of 'thinking in the concrete, and also being able to reflect in the abstract on the data and the conditions of thinkability'.[243] What resulted from this was a tendentially self-referential science – a science unable to take into account the fundamental questions emerging from the socio-economic tissue, and a science with no answers to such questions. The new systematic did not consider it worthwhile for economic science to study why in determinate economic circumstances 'organised poverty' was necessary 'for the production of wealth'[244] and how this process came about.

Even just a few days before his death, when the defeat of his project had already been consummated for some time, Labriola returned to the problems of the object of scientific analysis. As he wrote to Croce,

> Your philosophising consists of simple analytical judgements. Faced with these purest of judgements (and I would argue that they are not pure, since they are not synthetic!) stand the infinite, disaggregated things of nature and the social world. For example (and they are your examples!): in the philosophy of right there is no class struggle, but in life there is: in economics there is no surplus-value, but there is in society – ... [and why]

239 Labriola 1977, p. 289.

240 Labriola 1977, p. 288.

241 Labriola 1977, p. 222. As concerns the relationship between 'pure economics' and 'progress', we need only think of the important conclusions at which almost all theories of economic development arrived.

242 Labriola 1977, p. 217.

243 Labriola 1977, p. 224.

244 Labriola 1977, p. 241.

> go and look for the *causa* [lawsuit] in penal law, when the *causa* [cause] is a logical concept! ... and so on and so forth ... Have you ever thought about the implications and the consequences of this way of thinking? The simplest of its consequences is this: that there is no empirically given science, only the science of so-called pure concepts[245]

These were questions that, despite everything, could not easily be shaken off, and which would soon re-appear – even if in an underground manner – also on the terrain of Italian scientific culture, both Marxist and otherwise.

If faced with the rise of 'pure economics' some young socialist economists opted for logics that in various ways combined a neoclassical modality with the modalities of their own tradition, others refused such logics, either accepting the new paradigm in its entirety or else completely refusing it. Such were the cases of Giovanni Montemartini and Antonio Graziadei, who came to represent these opposite stances: the former was a 'pure economist', and indeed an authoritative one, while the latter was a determined adversary of marginalism. Both were front-rank figures in Italian reformist socialism, both theoretically and practically speaking. Later in this volume we will see how a theoretical and practical reformism was defined also in relation to the economic themes concerning the 'collapse' of capitalism. For now, we should note that accepting the marginalist theoretical horizon, whether in part or in full, was not in itself an index of a predetermined choice in favour of either reformist or revolutionary socialism.

Graziadei was certainly the only one of the young socialist economists to refuse both marginalism and these 'combinatory' logics, even if he was not wholly immune to the fascination of 'pure economics' and in particular its Paretian version. Returning to these themes in his late maturity, he would fully accept the argument that saw marginalism as an apologetic theory of capitalism and an effective weapon in fighting Marxism.[246] Yet in his youthful polemic[247] there was no trace of such an argument.

At the centre of Graziadei's analysis was not pure economics as an overall theory, or its method, but exclusively the *hedonistic* theory of value. He was consistent on this point, holding that the results reached by the positive sciences, like psycho-physiology and physiology, were contradictory, or

245 Letter to Croce of 2 January 1904, in Labriola 1983, Vol. III, pp. 1002–3.

246 Graziadei 1943.

247 Graziadei 1901: 'Intorno alla teoria edonistica del valore', *La Riforma Sociale*, 1900, pp. 875–83. The first of the two studies was published as a pamphlet in 1900 by Roux in Turin.

at least indicated processes rather less linear than what the hedonists supposed in their theory of value. As such, no scientific base could sustain a theory of value founded on the 'principle of decreasing enjoyment'.[248] For this reason, Graziadei looked with very great interest upon the gradual break with hedonism of which Pareto had made himself the protagonist. He had a telling exchange of letters with the 'hermit of Céligny' in this regard.[249] However, while this exchange of letters allows us to see his interest in and even admiration for the way in which Pareto addressed the themes of economic equilibrium autonomously of the principles of marginalist theory, there remained the marginalist *supposition*[250] that the curve of market demand could not be considered wholly independently of the degree of utility. For Graziadei, such a supposition derived from the new school's fundamental error, namely that of 'having believed in an innate tendency to buy things. This error derive[d] from the individualistic method'.[251] And to insist on the individual character of the exchange relation meant denying the possibility of understanding the *social* character of economic phenomena. Even given his profound admiration for Pareto's work, this element would be decisive in the divarication of their different perspectives. The 'original sin' of marginalism, in Graziadei's view, did not allow the greatest Italian theorist of pure economics to break out of a model in which 'the profound differences between layers and classes disappear ... behind ... overly simplistic figurations'.[252] Here there seemed to be an echo of the notes in which Achille Loria had rejected the *economic* so many years previously, as he posed the questions of *political economy*:

> Why can the capitalist exempt himself from labour and thus take up a position in which the anticipation of capital has no sense or purpose if not taking in profit? Why does the worker go to beg the capitalist to front him the money for the necessities of life, and why can he not produce them himself? Why, in short, do we have the happy proprietors of 'present goods', who can live without working, and as against these, a multitude of

248 'Intorno alla teoria edonistica del valore', *La Riforma Sociale*, 1900, p. 871.

249 Busino published Pareto's letters to Graziadei in the *Rivista Storica Italiana* in 1971, and they then appeared in his *Correspondance*. I have used the originals conserved in the Fondazione Feltrinelli archive, since there are some marginal notes written in Graziadei's own hand.

250 From his letter of 29 March 1904.

251 Note by Graziadei in the margin of the 10 January 1901 letter.

252 Graziadei 1948, p. 19.

> men forced to seek capital from these former and to work for them to the point of complete exhaustion, in order to live?[253]

Montemartini, conversely, had barely broken out of the pervasive Lorian atmosphere, which did, in any case, leave certain traces here and there in his writings. When his main theoretical work came out in 1899, Léon Walras would judge the author

> one of the half-dozen men who ... have the complete insight into the economic system according to which *marginal unity* is the basis of the supply of services and demand for products by the consumers – financiers, capitalists, workers – and marginal productivity the basis of the demand for services and supply by producer-entrepreneurs

and counted him 'in the first rank of this small group, on account of his erudition, his gifts of invention and exposition'.[254] Indeed, this short volume was a successful attempt to apply categories of marginal utility already widely used in the sphere of exchange to the sphere of production, an attempt that Barone had begun in Italy a few years previously.[255] Here he gave proof not only of his perfect mastery of marginalist analytical techniques (with an evident slippage from early Mengerian hedonism to the Walras-Paretian framework of a general economic equilibrium) but also of his considerable intellectual autonomy.

Such a complete and conscious allegiance to pure economics' conceptual apparatus posed him – like the other socialist economics scholars who accepted this method in whole or in part, in its various formulations – with problems of theoretical conciliation that were anything but easily resolvable.

Indeed, these scholars did not get to grips with the economic and social reality only in order to study it and define the 'laws' of exchange, but also to change it in a deep or even revolutionary sense. Their point of view on the existing social reality was thus structurally and not only marginally critical, and all of them without distinction accepted Marx's reference to the class struggle both as theory and as fact. This meant being able to pose the appropriate questions on the link between choices of scientific method and the knowledge of a reality with a view to its transformation. It meant finding an acceptable definition of the relation between a theoretical construction that at that time generally

253 Loria 1901, p. 11.

254 Letter from Walras to Montemartini, 19 September 1899, in Jaffé (ed) 1965, Vol. III, p. 87.

255 See Barone, 'Studi sulla distribuzione', *Giornale degli Economisti*, 1896, pp. 107–55, 235–52.

tended to portray the economic equilibrium statically, and the dynamic, non-formal demands of a socialist perspective: investigating if, or in what way, the roots of the class struggle sank into the *humus* of the economic phenomena that were the object of scientific analysis; fully interrogating how far the methodology used was coherent with the intended use of the knowledge thus acquired; and posing the problem of how to recuperate the possibility of translating theory into historical and political terms.

What role would economic theory come to assume in a project of social transformation, if one no longer accepted a method implying the absolute co-penetration of economic and socio-historical analysis? It was, naturally, possible to beat the path that Pareto had indicated, and arrive at a definitive separation between the sphere of science and the sphere of politics, but such a path was of difficult viability for those who necessarily had to hold on to the hypothesis of the scientific rationality of their own political project, even though this latter could not neglect an anatomical study of civil society. And more specifically, for those like Montemartini who posed themselves the problem of method, the recuperation of the socio-historical dimension took place not so much by way of political economy, as through the history of economic doctrines.[256]

It was during the debate on economic science, originating from Pantaleoni's 'provocations', that Montemartini would have the opportunity to clarify a socialist economist's view of this question.

As we know, Pantaleoni had, in two immediately successive and closely linked phases,[257] a) denied that there could be different schools in economics, since the only fundamental division was that between those who understood economics and those who did not, b) denied, as a consequence, that there could be a history of doctrines, since if there existed only one *truth* and this was the object of the economist's investigations, it was thus completely useless from the standpoint of economic science to study a history of *errors*.

256 Even in Montemartini's more properly theoretical works, there is no lack of attempts to recuperate some of Marx's categories within the new theoretical system, but these are purely scholastic exercises. 'The class struggle [could be] considered the struggle among factors of production and over the distribution of wealth'; and moreover, 'It is the law of asymmetry that explains the whole history of society, [and] all the economic struggles made manifest in the principle of the class struggle. And it is from this law that we must expect the advent of the future, progressive forms of organisation that will mark the dawn of the more equitable, more elevated well-being of all the groups in human history'. See Montemartini 1896, pp. xxviii–xxix; 1899.

257 See Pantaleoni 1897, 1898.

Conversely, while Montemartini asserted with conviction the truth of certain theorems concerning the final degree of utility and the theory of marginal productivities, he refused to attribute them any absolute value, since they were theories elaborated on the basis of determinate conditions, and thus very much relative with regard to the economic phenomenon considered as a whole.[258] He insisted on the relativism of science's points of arrival – a relativism of standpoints as well as a historical relativism. 'We have had the economics of the capitalists, workers, consumers, etc.' – he would write in a *counter-thesis* – 'dealing not with different objects, for it was economics that were of interest, but the economics of a class or a nation or an individual, with the generalisations that flowed from this'.[259]

What, then, was the interest of a history of economic doctrines? It was the fact that '[t]he degree of cognition that the most elevated, preponderant classes in a determinate society at a given moment have of the economic phenomenon *can influence a whole series of conceptions, able completely to change the face of the society in question*'.[260]

The history of economic science was thus something substantially different from studying science itself. In this latter case the analytical process above all consisted of making sure that exclusively economic relations were clearly distinguished from others with which they were tied in reality; but – and here even Montemartini seemed affected by some doubts – was it possible to define any precise delimitation between 'exclusively economic relations' and the others? And, moreover, was it possible for the *truths* thus acquired to be true once and for all time?

The history of economic doctrines, conversely, made it possible to 'penetrate into the secret of social actions', and it thus became an essential tool in welding together pure concepts and the operative needs of a politics of social transformation.

4 The End-of-Century Marxist Corpus

Being able to refer to a sufficiently well-defined body of texts is a necessary but not sufficient condition of defining an 'orthodoxy'. Indeed, one of the very characteristics of an 'orthodoxy' concerns the controlled way through which

258 Montemartini 1899, republished in Griziotti 1938.

259 Reproduced in Griziotti 1938, p. 234.

260 Reproduced in Griziotti 1938, p. 240. My italics.

theoretical and political discussion develops, and through which its outcomes are determined. Decisive, here, is the appeal to the authority of what are considered 'classic' texts, selected in order to play such a role. This is an operation that structurally assumes notable difficulties and continual redefinitions. That is not just a result of the immediacy of politics and the instrumental use of these same 'classic' works when they are subordinated to this immediacy – a subordination that has marked far from brief periods of the history of Marxism. For even when the questions posed have had a hermeneutic *prius* substantially internal to the texts' own logic (if never wholly so, given that in historical Marxism it has been impossible wholly to overlook projections into the political sphere), the identification of the privileged *corpus* in question has often become the object of controversy. We need only think of the events surrounding the first Marx and Engels *Gesamtausgabe*, or the *querelle* concerning what place Marx's unpublished works should occupy relative to his published ones.

At the end of the nineteenth century, these problems had a different significance to the one that they would assume over the course of the twentieth, in particular after the Russian Revolution. That was particularly the case in that the characteristics of what has been called Second International 'orthodoxy', for which 'at least in the 1890–1905 period a free and pluralist definition of Marxism was justifiable',[261] were certainly not the same as those which later manifested themselves in Third International 'orthodoxy', and which long survived the dissolution of that body. Moreover, because it was then that the question of Marx's unpublished texts began to be posed, and it did not concern works of such theoretical content as to prefigure 'epistemological breaks'.

Nonetheless, a *corpus* of Marx and Engels's works was taking shape at the end of the nineteenth century, in many aspects more on account of the 'masters'' own choices than those of the socialist parties and movements. In the first place, because of the decision to leave certain writings 'to the gnawing criticism of the mice', and later, after Marx's death, the way in which Engels posed the problem of publishing both Marx's and his own texts. We will go on to see the characteristics of the set of works that late nineteenth-century socialism considered to be 'classics'. In the meantime, we might note that

> in Italy, admittedly a country with an unusually lively interest in Marxism among intellectuals during the 1890s, virtually the whole corpus as selected by Engels was available by 1900 (except for the later volumes of

261 Hobsbawm 1974, p. 243.

> *Capital*), and the *Scritti* of Marx, Engels and Lassalle edited by Ciccotti (from 1899) also included a number of further works.[262]

However, the history of the Italian editions of Marx and Engels's texts had not been a linear one, and it did not necessarily prefigure what ultimately resulted by the end of the nineteenth century.

The translation of fundamentally important works like the *Manifesto* and the first volume of *Capital*, or of works key to the economics-philosophy relationship like *The Poverty of Philosophy*, for example, had come relatively belatedly. Obviously likewise belated, given the events surrounding the 'Partito marxista', was any programmatic initiative made by a socialist political organisation. Such an initiative moreover concerned only part of the translation activity being realised in this period. This, too, was a sign of the wholly particular 1890s definition of 'orthodoxy'. Such orthodoxy was completely non-existent when it came to scientific questions. Antonio Labriola had denied that there could be any political authority in this regard, or that the proletarian party could adjudicate questions of science:

> I accept the *comrades* being rigid and even tyrannical with regard to the party's political conduct. But as for comrades having the authority to pronounce as arbiters of questions of science ... no, science will never be put to the vote, even in the so-called society of the future![263]

As we know, Antonio Labriola was mistaken in such a prophecy. But even political 'orthodoxy' – or at least the orthodoxy dependent on a programmed selection of texts – would also, by all accounts, take the form of a net with rather wide holes.

In the two years 1871–2 we can identify the far from negligible presence of texts by Marx and Engels (above all Engels) in the Italian democratic-socialist press. As we saw in the first chapter, all that had been published before then were various versions of the *Provisional Rules* and *Inaugural Address*, texts whose distribution and discussion – as we have also seen – would continue throughout the 1870s even during the prevalence of the *anarchist antithesis*. These were militant texts without immediately identifiable theoretical determinations. They were interventions seeking to delimit a territory, to make clear the terms of the International's General Council's outlook firstly as compared

262 Hobsbawm 2011, p. 181.

263 Antonio Labriola, 'Marxismo, Darwinismo, eccetera', *Critica Sociale*, 1897, p. 189.

to the Mazzinian tradition, and then faced with the Bakuninite international. It is no surprise that it was above all Engels, in his role as a delegate to the General Council from Italy, who was the protagonist of this phase of publications, and that in the period in which Cafiero was moving in harmony with the General Council, it was he who indicated to Engels the targets and horizons with which to operate, and who took care to ensure these texts' maximum possible resonance among the socialist and democratic milieu.[264]

44 Marx and Engels texts were published over these two years – taking into account the fact that some were reproduced across different papers –, 30 of them in 1871 and 14 in 1872.[265] In 1873 only 3 such texts were published, one of them as part of Tullio Martello's book on the International,[266] and then no others up till 1877. If the two 1873 works *On Authority* and *Political Indifferentism*,[267] both written soon after the Hague Congress, were also militant texts in that they directly intervened in the Italian situation at a moment in which the

264 See 'Associazione internazionale degli operai', *Il Libero Pensiero*, Florence, 1871, 31 August, one of the central texts of the General Council's polemic with Mazzini, which near-simultaneously appeared in *La Favilla*, Mantua, 6 September 1871; *Il Romagnolo*, Ravenna, 9 September 1871; *Gazzettino Rosa*, Milan, 13 September 1871; *Il Motto d'ordine*, Naples, 20 September 1871.

Another important text of Marx's, *The Civil War in France*, edited and translated by Cafiero, appeared in *L'Eguaglianza*, Girgenti, in no. 18 (12 November 1871), and nos. 21, 22 and 24 (3, 10, 27 December 1871).

265 Our references include not only Bosio 1955 and the first bibliography of the Italian editions of Marx and Engels (Bravo 1962) but also the supplementary efforts of Basso, Hunecke and others in research whose results appeared in various journals over subsequent years. A new bibliography of the Italian editions of Marx and Engels is currently being prepared, updated as far as 1985. This volume is edited by Dr. Beatrice de Gerloni, whom I thank for kindly allowing me to make use of the typescript. I myself conducted research into the Italian editions of Marx and Engels for an exhibition I curated for the Fondazione G.G. Feltrinelli and the Friedrich Ebert Stiftung, held in Trier from 20 September to 20 November 1987: see Favilli (ed.) 1989, pp. 89–117.

266 A partial publication of *The Civil War in France*, signed 'General Council of the International', appeared in Martello 1873, pp. 134–51. This volume, whose author would soon become one of the most well-known Italian academic economists of the free-trader milieu, and who was vehemently, bitingly anti-socialist, was nonetheless a balanced and relatively well-informed text with often-original documentation. This was a far from secondary contribution to spreading information on the International's affairs, also in a non-socialist environment.

267 *Dell'Autorità*, by Engels, and *L'indifferenza in materia politica*, by Marx, appeared in the *Almanacco repubblicano per l'anno 1874*, Lodi, III, 1873, on pp. 33–7 and 144–8 respectively.

peninsula's internationalist movement was completely aligned with Bakunin, they were in some aspects different from those of the previous two years. The development of a polemic at the level of general principles allowed the use of these articles in contexts very different from those in which they had been put together, accentuating their theoretical-political character.[268]

The 1877 texts[269] were more the marker of resumed contacts with Italy than a qualitative leap in Marx and Engels' intellectual presence in Italy. However, 1879 would see the appearance of publications that allowed an engagement with the fundamental theoretical nodes of Marx's theory, namely the first Italian translation of an important part of *Capital* Volume I,[270] and Cafiero's 'compendium'.

In the course of the 1870s there had been some attempts at an Italian-language edition of *Capital* Volume I, but without any positive results. The socialist environment from which such initiatives had emerged was not capable of bringing such a venture to a successful conclusion. Certainly it was not easy – and nor would it be even in future – to find a translator able to combine the necessary mastery of the German language with a first-hand understanding of social and economic theory. It was rather easier to make recourse to the French edition. The most important constraints, here, were weaknesses of editorial organisation and participation, which were, moreover, the symptom of wider weaknesses. In a certain sense, Cafiero's compendium well represented the extent to which the Italian socialism of this era was able to engage with a book of such characteristics as *Capital*.

This was, indeed, a well-produced condensation of *Capital*, loyal to the argumentation of the original and – in Marx's own opinion – superior to other such volumes of the 1870s, including Most's, particularly on account of an

268 Since the 1873 editions there have been eight versions of *On Authority* in Italy and nine of *Political Indifferentism*.

269 See Engels, 'Da Londra', *La Plebe*, Milan, 26 February 1877. This letter to Enrico Bignami marked the resumption of Engels's collaboration with *La Plebe* after having suspended it in 1872. This kind of 'international correspondence', which lasted until 1879, is particularly interesting. Six Engels texts appeared in *La Plebe* from 1877 to 1879, three of them dedicated to the British workers' movement, two to the German workers' movement, and one to a panoramic view of Germany, France, the United States and Russia.

270 The section translated for *Libertà e giustizia* in 1867 was in fact all too brief: Basso 1962. See also 'Genesi del capitalista industriale', *La Plebe*, Milan, 1879, nos. 5, 11 February; 6, 16 February: 7, 23 February; 9, 9 March. This was an edition of Chapter Thirty-One, on so-called primitive accumulation, not directly translated from the German but from a French edition.

engaging format rendering it particularly suitable to wider divulgation.[271] It is true that the text was filtered through a rather too fatalistic conception of social development. Marx did not fail to note this, writing to underline the role of class consciousness and class struggle;[272] but nonetheless, this short volume could be considered a good starting point.

Within a few years, Italy would have a full edition of *Capital* Volume I available; yet it was the result not of socialist endeavour, but rather a 'bourgeois' initiative taken at the highest levels of academia and publishing.

We should reflect further on the characteristics of the economic culture that made it possible for *Capital* to appear in such an official and even prestigious setting, when the greater part of the European academic establishment considered this book wholly extraneous to its own scientific paradigm. What Tullio Martello called the new 'anthropo-technical' economics was a multifaceted phenomenon, one with integration mechanisms that tended to make the new visible while simultaneously voiding it of its power, in an atmosphere of gelatinous contiguities. Indeed, it was in the gluey fluidity of 'isms' – in particular 'evolutionism', 'historicism' ('historical method') and 'sociologism' – that there would appear the first attentive reading and exposition of *Capital* (Vito Cusumano's) and so, too, Gerolamo Boccardo's first full version of this volume.

Boccardo perhaps lacked Cusumano's interpretative rigour, but he played an institutional role in Italian economic culture that the young Sicilian scholar was very far away from. As well as an ordinary professor of political economy, Boccardo was a senator, a member of the Accademia dei Lincei, a member of the Council of State, and most importantly, from 1876 onward, director of the third series of the 'Biblioteca dell'economista'. This was Italy's most prestigious economics book series, published by a well-established and also rather prestigious publishing house, the Unione Tipografico-Editrice di Torino (formerly Pomba). 'With Ferrara, in the first two series of the Biblioteca dell'economista, we are dealing with critical method and the *choice* of perspective. With Boccardo we have an eclectic descriptivism'.[273] This is doubtless a fair assessment, but certainly *Capital* Volume I would have struggled to feature among Ferrara's *choices*. In any case, Boccardo's 'eclectic descriptivism' *was* situated within the context of a *choice*, namely that of the 'isms' mentioned above. This would ultimately also include a dilution of the 'very great amount' that this '*faiseur des*

---

271 Marx to Cafiero, 29 July 1879, in Del Bo (ed.) 1964.

272 Ibid.

273 Macchioro 1970, p. 498.

livres' said that he had learned 'from the works of Karl Marx'.[274] But there would also remain an editorial presence that was substantial in its own right, beyond the framing of the texts and the exorcisms in their prefaces.

The translation of the book, based on Roy's French edition and edited by Boccardo himself,[275] probably began in 1879. Its 43 component instalments were published between 1882 and 1884, and were sold separately. Finally in 1886 they were brought together in a single volume[276] together with Leopold Jacoby's *Die Idee der Entwicklung* and Nikolay Chernyshevsky's *Critical Observations* on John Stuart Mill, all of them being framed as 'heretics of economics'.

This was the only Italian translation of *Capital* available to scholars, militant scholars and militants *tout court* until after World War II. The Turin publisher would reprint this edition between 1916 and 1924 and again after 1945 – now updated with an introduction by Luigi Firpo – another seven times by 1960. Only in 1974 would Utet devote itself to a new edition, the current version translated by Bruno Maffi and edited by Aurelio Macchioro.

The 1886 edition was wholly internal to official culture, and yet also indicated a certain permeability between 'the academy' and 'socialism' by way of 'science' and 'the social question'. This was a characteristic particular to the history of Italian culture. In this case, the socialists were certainly extraneous to the initiative, and indeed were surprised by it. Marx happened to become aware of it soon before his death,[277] and Engels only in 1893.[278] Probably, however, given the socialists' constant difficulties in producing their own full edition of the text, they ended up using Boccardo's translation, in an editorial vision that seemed almost to indulge a division of labour. The Boccardo edition in substance served Italian socialism's 'high' culture, while compendiums were ever more used for wider divulgation.[279] Indeed, Deville's compendium also came out in 1893,[280] and Lafargue's extracts the following year.[281] This latter

---

274 See Boccardo 1878, p. xlvi.

275 Bravo 1992, pp. 110–13.

276 *Il Capitale. Critica dell'economia politica*, published by Utet in Turin in 1886, in Vol. IX/2 of the third series of the 'Biblioteca dell'economista'.

277 See Tullio Martello to Marx, 5 January 1883, in Del Bo (ed.) 1964, p. 294.

278 See Turati to Engels, 1 June 1893, in Del Bo (ed.) 1964, pp. 479–80.

279 On the other hand, Turati's own copy, which he sent to Engels in order to allow this latter to see it, was still 'wholly intact, [with its pages] still not yet cut': see Turati to Engels, 9 June 1893, in Del Bo (ed.) 1964, p. 484.

280 *Il Capitale riassunto da Gabriele Deville e preceduto da brevi cenni sul socialismo scientifico*, published in 1893 by Cremona's Tipografia sociale.

281 *Il capitale/Estratti di Paolo Lafargue*, published by Sandron in Palermo in 1894. Pareto's

was accompanied by Pareto's famous introduction, which the socialists judged particularly severely,[282] but also Lafargue's own 'counter-introduction'. After Cafiero's compendium there would be no second Italian vulgarisation of *Capital* until after the turn of the century, with Ettore Fabietti's 1902 volume.[283]

In the 1880s, the publication of other Marx and Engels texts very important to historical reflection and as theoretical-ideological references would also be incidental in character, with no structured socialist circles taking forward such an editorial project. The first Italian editions of *Socialism: Utopian and Scientific*[284] and of *The Origin of Family, Private Property and the State*[285] (published barely a year after the original German edition) were, indeed, the fruit of socialist initiative – yet this was the initiative of *one* socialist, the commendable yet obscure provincial translator Pasquale Martignetti, who often financed the publication of the Marx and Engels texts that he translated out of his own (rather scarce) means. The relation that the proud 'general' Engels was able to establish with this humble soldier of the socialist revolution was exemplary for its level of intellectual rigour, its warm humanity, and the sense of belonging to a common ideal universe.

The texts published in more 'institutional' socialist settings in these same years were, however, of a different weight, and far from numerous.[286]

---

introduction appeared on pp. lx–lxxxv and Lafargue's 'counter-introduction' on pp. 183–224. A reprint followed in 1894.

282 See 'Un cavaliere del libero capitalismo che si divora Marx in un boccone', and E. Guindani–L. Bissolati, 'Il sofismo del plusvalore in un economista liberista italiano', in *Critica Sociale*, 1893, pp. 285–8.

283 *Il Capitale volgarizzato da Ettore Fabietti*, published by G. Nerbine Editore in Florence in 1902.

284 *Il socialismo utopico e il socialismo scientifico*, published by the Stabilimento tipografico F. De Gennaro in Benevento in 1883. Translated by Pasquale Martignetti.

285 *L'origine della famiglia, della proprietà privata e dello Stato, in relazione alle ricerche di Luigi H. Morgan*, revised by the author, published by the Stabilimento tipografico F. De Gennaro in Benevento in 1885. Translated by Pasquale Martignetti. In the first months of 1886 Martignetti had also translated *Wage Labour and Capital* (see Martignetti's letter to Engels of 8 February 1886, in Del Bo (ed.) 1964, pp. 310–11), but as we will see this translation would only be published in 1893.

286 'Discorso di Engels sulla tomba di Marx', *La Plebe*, Milan, April 1883; 'La lotta delle classi' (some pages from *The Poverty of Philosophy*) in *Rivista italiana di Socialismo*, Imola-Lugo, I, 1886, pp. 37–40; 'Dal Rapporto al Consiglio generale dell'Associazione Internazionale sulla guerra civile in Francia (1871)', *La Giustizia*, Reggio Emilia, 3 April 1887: 'La guerra civile del 1871 in Francia (rapporto del Consiglio generale della Associazione Internazionale dei Lavoratori)', in *Rivista italiana del socialismo*, Imola-Lugo, II, 1887, pp. 129–34, 166–

The end of that decade and the 1890s saw a true and proper qualitative leap. The turning point – and one particularly symbolic in character – was linked to the Italian edition of the *Manifesto*.

The most immediately identifiable aspect of the history of the Italian editions of the *Manifesto* was the very notable delay with which it first appeared on the peninsula. The first translation – whose features we will go on to take a look at – appeared in 1889. By that date there were twenty-one German, eight English, seven French, twelve Russian, two Swedish, three Danish, four Spanish, two Serbian, one Portuguese, one Czech, one Polish, and one Bulgarian editions.[287] From 1891 to 1902 there would be four translations and two reprints of this text in Italy.

However, the *Manifesto*'s 1889 debut, appearing in instalments in Cremona's *L'Eco del popolo*, was not a very happy one.[288] Based on the German original, the translation (rather dubiously attributed to Leonida Bissolati)[289] nevertheless suffered from contamination by a French edition. Not only did it feature considerable holes, but it seemed almost to have been adapted to the requirements of a compendium. 'It has all the linguistic characteristics of a compendium, consisting of a simplification of the original's syntactical and argumentative structure, the complete loss of its stylistic value and the reduction of its lexical richness and semantic complexity'.[290]

The first edition of the *Manifesto* as a separate volume, Pietro Gori's edition, was only an improvement on the *L'Eco del popolo* version in terms of its greater completeness.[291] Again in this edition, we can note numerous errors, linguistic inaccuracies, and difficulties in reproducing the rigour of Marx and Engels's language.

The true turning point in the Italian editions of the *Manifesto* came when the party's central publishing operation began to take over responsibility for this work. Pompeo Bettini's edition appearing in *La Lotta di Classe* in 1892 and as a pamphlet the following year was both a good translation and a complete

71, 202–5, 251–5, 272–6, 306–7, III, 1888, pp. 328–32; Engels, 'Il movimento operaio di America', *Rivista italiana del socialismo*, II, 1887, pp. 244–50; Engels, 'Libero scambio e protezionismo', *Cuore e Critica*, Savona, II, 1888, p. 229, III, p. 7.

287 See Andréas 1963, pp. 380–3.

288 'Il manifesto del Partito comunista', *L'Eco del popolo*, Cremona, 1889, nos. 35, 30–31 August; 36, 37, 38, 39, September; 40, 41, 42, 43, October: 44, November.

289 Bosio 1951, pp. 446–7.

290 See Cortellazzo 1981, p. 95.

291 *Il manifesto del Partito comunista. 1847*, published by Fantuzzi in Milan in 1891.

one.[292] These characteristics, combined by the fact that it was published by the Uffici della Critica Sociale, ordained it as Italian socialism's canonical translation of the *Manifesto*, and it would be reprinted a further six times by 1914.

Nonetheless, this official – almost 'party' – version did not take on the characteristics of an 'orthodoxy'. In the 1890s another edition appeared in Diano Marina, in the 'Biblioteca' promoted by the Ligurian socialist paper *Era Nuova*.[293] This was again a direct translation from the German, taking account of Bettini's version but not imitating it. This translation was 'faithful to the letter of the original, which it scrupulously followed in every detail, even where this led to certain elements of opacity'.[294] This edition would not be reprinted, but even so it is estimated that around 8,000 copies were distributed.

Finally came Labriola's version,[295] the 'most original and least passive' translation, which showed 'a certain tendency to amplify the text, rather than simplify it by reducing it',[296] also marking its relative autonomy from the German original. Perhaps for precisely these reasons it would not supplant Bettini's canonical translation, but it did have a particularly widespread distribution among scholars.

This was, then, a rather articulated panorama, in which even an implicitly 'official' status did not transform into uniformity.

The history of the *Manifesto*'s publication in Italy can be considered indicative of the way in which the *corpus* of the Italian editions of Marx and Engels came to be defined in the 1890s. Indeed, apart from 'militant' writings with a periodisation of their own, and which had lent themselves to immediate use, we could not truly say that Italian socialism had up till that point proceeded very far in piecing together the fundamental 'skeleton' of this body of texts. The Italian edition of *Capital* Volume I had been the fruit of a terrain external to socialism; and of the three works that Martignetti translated in the 1880s with the greatest theoretical valences, one had not been published and the other two had remained confined as if in exile in Benevento, finding little response

292 'Il Manifesto del Partito comunista di Marx ed Engels (1848). Traduzione dal tedesco di Pompeo Bettini', *La Lotta di Classe*, I, 1892, nos. 8, 10, 12, 13, 15, 16, 17, 19, 20, 21, 22; *Il Manifesto del Partito comunista. Con un nuovo proemio al lettore italiano di Federico Engels*, published by Uffici della Critica Sociale in Milan in 1903.

293 *Il Manifesto del Partito comunista. Con prefazione*, published by the Premiata tipografia Artistica in Diano Marina in 1897.

294 Cortellazzo 1981, p. 98.

295 *Il Manifesto del Partito comunista*, appearing in Labriola's *In memoria del Manifesto dei Comunisti*, third edition, published by Loescher in Rome in 1902, pp. 75–118.

296 Cortellazzo 1981, pp. 100, 103.

among the scattered forces of the socialist movement. In the final decade of the century this picture would change rapidly; but we should not suppose that there existed any specific, articulated plan for the construction of such a *corpus*, or that it was the Milan centre that laid all the bases for this.

The works that Martignetti proposed for publication were now more readily received, at least until the public emergence of the Engels-Loria split. *Socialism: Utopian and Scientific* was reissued (though not by *Critica Sociale*),[297] its first version having remained almost a secret. *Wage Labour and Capital*[298] was thus finally published in 1893 – Martignetti had translated it already in 1886 – but a second edition of *The Origin of the Family, Private Property and the State* would have to wait until 1901.

Whereas Marx's *Class Struggles in France* was published,[299] a text as key to the discussion on Marx's economic theory and the clarification of the Marx-Loria relationship as Engels's preface to *Capital* Volume III did not immediately find a place among *Critica Sociale*'s plans. If it first appeared as a non-'official' choice, this was again thanks to Pasquale Martignetti's initiative.[300]

Critica Sociale and connected publications were, without doubt, the sites in which Marx and Engels's texts appeared in greatest number; but as we have already observed, their publication did not correspond to a logically structured plan covering a determinate period. Often the choices made were fortuitous in character, originating in favourable contingent circumstances or sometimes in connection to the 'political moment'. Given the numerous options that the 'Partito marxista' – the party doing politics – had in front of it, it needed a 'North Star' to orient its choices and the secure anchorings that were necessary to what was naturally a 'strong' conception of politics. Reference to the texts written by

297 *Socialismo utopistico e socialismo scientifico*, published by F. Fantuzzi, Milan, in 1892.

298 *Capitale e salario, colla bibliografia dell'autore e con una Introduzione di Federico Engels*, published by the Uffici della Critica Sociale in Milan in 1893. A contemporary edition missing the first section appeared in *La Lotta di Classe* that same year. Engels's introduction to this work, again translated by Martignetti, had already been published in 1891: 'Fra capitalista e lavoratore. La ragione intima del loro conflitto secondo Marx', *Critica Sociale*, 1891, p. 148.

299 *Le lotte di classe in Francia dal 1848 al 1850, con prefazione di Federigo Engels*, published by the Uffici della Critica Sociale in Milan in 1896.

300 'Prefazione al volume III del Capitale', *La Rassegna*, Naples, 1895, 1–2, pp. 72–100. The complete edition was published by the Tipografia Editrice Romana in 1896, as *Dal terzo volume del Capitale di Carlo Marx. Prefazione e commenti di Federico Engels*. After Engels's death, Turati would also choose to publish a part of the text expressing the second phase of Engels's polemic with Loria: 'L'ultimo lavoro di F. Engels. Complementi e aggiunte al III libro del Capitale', *Critica Sociale*, 1895, nos. 21, 22, 23, 24.

the 'masters', often published in connection to some particular occasion, was almost compulsory.

In any case, there were also numerous 1890s editions of Marx and Engels that were not directly linked to the most important centre of the elaboration of socialist culture. *The Eighteenth Brumaire* was published on the initiative of Rome's *L'Asino*[301] and *The Poverty of Philosophy* by Bologna's 'Biblioteca socialista', while that city's socialist section took care of the printing of *The Civil War in France*.[302] Still other writings would appear in weeklies or dailies, almost as if to take on a directly militant function.[303]

While in these years the number of Italian versions of Marx and Engels's texts increased considerably, even at the beginning of 1899 not all the titles of the Marx-Engels *corpus* selected in the years between the two men's deaths had been translated on the peninsula. Take for example *Anti-Dühring*, which came out in 1901,[304] *Ludwig Feuerbach* and the *Theses on Feuerbach*, in 1902,[305] or the *Critique of the Gotha Programme*, again in 1901.[306]

Indeed, 1899 would mark a further qualitative leap in the publication of Marx and Engels's texts, reaching a particular peak in the years between 1899 and 1902.[307] This was the most important attempt thus far to provide socialism and Italian culture with the greater part of the works by Marx and Engels that were then available.[308] The publication in instalments of Marx, Engels and Lassalle's

---

301 *Il diciotto brumaio di Luigi Bonaparte, con prefazione di Federigo Engels*, published in Rome in 1896.

302 *La Guerra civile in Francia del 1870–71 o la Comune rivendicata*, published in Bologna in 1894 by the Società tipografica Azzoguidi.

303 Note for example the republication of *On Authority* and *Political Indifferentism* by Milan's *La Battaglia* on 14 July and 11 August 1894, respectively.

304 *Il socialismo scientifico contro E. Dühring*, published by Sandron in Milan and Palermo in 1901.

305 *Ludovico Feuerbach e il punto d'approdo della filosofia classica tedesca*, published by Mongini in Rome in 1902, with Marx's *Theses* on pp. 41–2.

306 *Per la critica del programma della democrazia socialista – scritto postumo (1875)*, published by Mongini in Rome in 1901.

307 Of the 36 titles published in the *corpus* edited by Ciccotti before 1914, some 23 came out between 1899 and 1902.

308 The titles published were 1) Marx, *The Proceedings of the Sixth Rhine Province Assembly* (1899, first Italian edition); 2) the *Critique of Hegel's Philosophy of Law* and *On the Jewish Question* (1899, first Italian edition, translation by Ciccotti); 3) Engels's *The Condition of England* (first Italian edition) – *Outlines of a Critique of Political Economy* (1899, translation by Ciccotti); 4) Engels's *The Condition of the Working Class in England* (1899); 5) Marx, *Revolution and Counter Revolution; Or Germany in 1848* (1899, first Italian edition); 6) Marx,

Works (later appearing as a collection), thanks to the collaboration of important ancient historian Ettore Ciccotti and socialist publisher Luigi Mongini, would doubtless represent 'Italian culture's only true and substantial approach to Marx ... until after the Second World War'.[309] The fruit of the conjugation of the most alert elements of Italian academic culture and an organisational effort coming from within the party itself – and yet for a long time not coinciding with the party – this publishing output represented a high point of the mediation between the requirements of scientific autonomy and the cultural representation and legitimation of a political movement. But could it be considered the fruit of an 'orthodox' conception of a *corpus of the* 'masters'' works?

Contribution to the Critique of Political Economy (1899, first Italian edition); 7) Engels, *Force and Economics in the Establishment of the New German Empire* (1899, first Italian edition, translation by Ciccotti); 8) Marx, *Revelations Concerning the Communist Trial in Cologne* (1900, first Italian edition); 9) Marx, *The Poverty of Philosophy* (1901); 10) Marx, *Two Political Trials* (1901, first Italian edition); 11) Marx, *Inaugural Address of the International Workingmen's Association* (1901, translation by Ciccotti); 12) Engels, *International Questions in the Volkstaat* (1901, first Italian edition); 13) Engels, *On the Housing Question* (1901, first Italian edition); 14) Marx, *The International Workingmen's Association and the international Alliance of Socialist Democracy* (1901, first Italian edition); 15) Marx, *Critique of the Gotha Programme* (1901, first Italian edition, translation by Ciccotti); 16) Engels, *Can Europe Disarm?* (1901, first Italian edition, translation by Ciccotti); 17), Engels, *Ludwig Feuerbach and the End of Classical German Philosophy* (1901, first Italian edition, translation by Ciccotti. Gentile had published fragments in 1899); 18) Marx, *Class Struggles in France, 1848–1850* (1902); 19) Marx, *The Eighteenth Brumaire of Louis Bonaparte* (1902); 20) Marx, *The Civil War in France* (1902); 21) Engels, *Socialism: Utopian and Scientific* (1902); 22) Engels, *Reply to Mr. Paul Ernst* (1902, first Italian edition); 23) Engels, *In the Case of Brentano vs. Marx Regarding Alleged Falsifications of Quotations. The Story and Documents* (1902, first Italian edition); 24) Engels, *The Campaign for the German Imperial Constitution – The English Ten Hours' Bill* (1903, first Italian edition); 25) Marx, *The Eastern Question: A Reprint of Letters Written 1853–1856* (1903, first Italian edition); 26) Engels, *The Peasant War in Germany* (1904, first Italian edition); 27) Engels, *Po and Rhine* (1906, first Italian edition); 28) Engels, *Two Letters on Historical Materialism* (1906); 29) Engels, *Speeches in Elberfeld – The Festival of Nations in London – A Fragment of Fourier's On Trade – The Civil War in Switzerland* (1908, first Italian edition); 30) Marx and Engels, *Circular against Kriege* (1908, first Italian edition); 31) Engels, *Savoy, Nice and the Rhine* (1908, first Italian edition); 32) Marx and Engels, *The Holy Family, or Critique of Critical Criticism. Against Bruno Bauer and Company* (1909, first Italian edition); 33) Marx, *Herr Vogt* (1910, first Italian edition); 34) Engels, *Herr Eugen Dühring's Revolution in Science* (1911); 35) Marx and Engels, *Manifesto of the Communist Party* (1914); 36) *Capital. Critique of Political Economy*, Volume I, new popular edition edited by Karl Kautsky (1915, translation by E. Marchioli, first Italian edition).

309 Bravo 1992, p. 79.

CHAPTER 4

Historical Materialism

1 What Philosophy? What Philosophy of History?

The itineraries of Italian Marxism that we have so far dealt with unfolded across multiple universes, with different levels of theoretical identifiability. As we have seen, sometimes a non-Marxism proved to be the other face – the often necessary condition – of Marxism taking root in society. *Diffuse Marxism* corresponded to Marxism's *diffuse* identifiability or near-lack of identifiability. At the same time, *diffuse Marxism* did not make lofty demands for theoretical rigour; it could not have done so. Conversely, the terrain of historical materialism in itself contained the essential parameters for the identification of theoretical Marxism. This was the privileged terrain for the elaborations of those scholars who placed Marxism's 'philosophical' problem at the centre of their concerns.

In 1983 – a year of Marx studies that now seems so distant, following the much-invoked 'death of Marxism', and yet which was itself already immersed in the last 'crisis of Marxism' – it was a historian always extraneous to any form of interpretative doctrinairism, Eric Hobsbawm, who re-posed the problem of the identity-connotation of some of the specifics of Marxism. And in particular, of historical materialism. Faced with the question 'When are we Marxists?', Hobsbawm brought to light the non-essential character of numerous 'Marxist' categorisations, which can often even be misleading. However, he did note the possibility of identifying a point of distinction, maintaining to this end it is necessary 'to return to the basic principles of Marxism as they were formulated at the end of the nineteenth century' as a point of reference, and to their kernel which consists 'less in a body of doctrine, results and texts' than in a '*method that arises from the application of the materialist conception of history*'. This obviously

> leaves room for a very wide range of interpretations – indeed, at times contrasting ones – that can nonetheless all boast of being 'Marxist'. None of them can be refuted simply by saying that 'it is not Marxist' ... yet certain ways of thinking or points of view can be classified as non-Marxist, independently of whether or not they are represented by people who define themselves Marxists. *This is the case of analyses that are difficult to attribute to the materialist conception of history.*[1]

1 Hobsbawm 1983, p. 169, my italics.

This paradigm of Hobsbawm's seems to have notable capacities for explanation on the level of historical interpretation. Yet while it is solidly founded on Marxist assumptions, it continues to pose no few problems in the theoretical domain – just like those that were already posed at the end of the nineteenth century.

The themes of historical materialism appear in the form of a complex aggregate, in which it is nonetheless possible to distinguish the unfolding of a theory, the concrete production of historical works, and the development of a socialist workers' movement that in various 'scientific' or 'ideological' forms (or both at once) came to establish relations with that theory. These were non-secondary aspects of the more general process of the encounter between socialism and Marxism, its modalities and characteristics. Sometimes they were more diffusely spread, and at other times they were grasped and/or theorised in a much 'tighter' sense. Spread generically, they were the substance of the countless 'battles over method' fought in the open field of historiography and social sciences across the last three decades of the nineteenth century, expanding the influence of Marxian and Marxist theory in diverse cultural contexts, while also allowing an osmosis among the different cultures, blurring the separations between them. When held more tightly, they confirmed the militant intellectual in his often recently acquired inclination toward theoretical solidity. Notwithstanding their sometimes contrasting statements, these two elements should not always be seen as separate and contradictory. Indeed, the new clothes of Marxist-socialist militant activity in this period were, inevitably, to a significant extent fashioned out of the cultural fabric of the era.

This was again, in part, a *diffuse Marxism*; one that was also active in a context different from that of the 1880s process of the formation of the 'party-as-class'. The thousand threads tying historical materialism to such a large part of Italian culture, as well as the very high level that the elaboration of this theory reached in the 1890s, gave the materialist conception of history an entirely special place among the different components of theoretical Marxism. In the general context of the *fin de siècle* 'intellectual revolution'[2] – so full of epochal grandeur, and of totalising breakthroughs that were heralded more often than they were analytically founded – the 'crisis of Marxism' implicated historical materialism – that is, the central element of Marx's method – in a wholly particular way. Economics was more in the line of fire: the labour theory of value, the themes of 'capitalist collapse' – in short, questions that could implicate both the very foundations of a sacred 'scientificity' and socialism's

2 The expression is from Stuart Hughes 1977, p. 33.

more modest 'new paths'. These were questions that could not be recuperated within other cultures.

Conversely, 'the bitter secretions of the dialectic' feeding historiography and philosophy through a thousand streams, 'albeit masked by the "sweet liquor" of materialism',[3] may have seemed rather less implicated in the destinies of socialism and of the class struggle. Moreover, even Croce, who had now left his interest in Marxology behind him, addressed this dimension of Marxism in a manner wholly different to the conclusions that he had reached regarding Marxist economic categories as he sought out and defined the pure 'economic principle'.

In numerous passages of his work, and in various forms, Croce expressed a positive evaluation of historical materialism's role in his own intellectual maturation, as well as in Italian historical and philosophical culture. In his *Storia d'Italia dal 1871 al 1915*, written in 1927, he devoted careful consideration to 'Marxistic' socialism and its central kernel, the materialist conception of history. These were not new observations, but the fact that he re-posed them in a text that was not designed for specialists – a text with an explicit ethical-civil function in a very grave moment of Italy's history – gave them particular significance. Moreover, Croce was here tracing an organic path internal to the development of Italian culture over a long period; the stages of a presence capable of changing this culture's course and breathing life into it.

His starting point was his negative evaluation (and that could be taken for granted) of the positivism of Italian culture, particularly in the 1871–90 period. This was the period when 'the name "philosopher", the word "philosophy" … became terms of discredit'. When historiography 'moved not (as they say) among particulars – and historiography must always move among particulars, knowing no details or determinations extraneous to it – but among particulars that were not related to their centre'. And when what was most missing was any 'powerful thought'.[4] Socialism had put itself forward as such a thought. But before the emergence of Marxism in Italy, a socialism indistinct from humanitarianism and generic revolutionism had played no role in the country's culture; notwithstanding the generosity and the enthusiasm of its exponents' efforts to spread the word, they remained 'standing on the margins of national and cultural life: the bizarre, fanatical or deranged, without any discipline in their studies, insufficient in their self-education, trained unevenly, or else the students of those who had not studied very much'.[5]

---

3 Croce 1921, Vol. II, p. 233.

4 Croce 1967, pp. 124, 125, 133.

5 Croce 1967, p. 139.

Then, however, Labriola had truly discovered the Marx of whom he had earlier caught wind, and now 'university students of every faculty, those of the most alert intelligence, and many teachers of economics, and also of law and history and the sciences' now passed over to socialism, or were strongly influenced by it. Now 'Marxistic socialism [came] to fill the void that tore through Italians' thought and ideals'.[6]

For Croce, there was no doubt that

> the reception of Marxistic socialism in Italy and the ferment to which it gave rise were … a complex set of corrections, restitutions and restorations of better foundations and deeper insights, that gave fresh content to Italian culture, *picking it up limp and flaccid and laying it over a structure made of bones*.[7]

As such, the 'philosophical reawakening in Italy … was realised … in the first place through Marxism and its historical materialism' and thus '… all Italian culture and thought were penetrated by Marxistic socialism and reinvigorated'.[8]

Labriola had initiated this period, and given that 'his critical mind did not allow him to be orthodox', the best of his lesson passed on to 'a pupil of his' who 'advancing along the path that [Labriola] had opened up' subjected 'all of Marx's principal theses to critique'.[9] This allowed the most nourishing juices of Marxism, purified of exaggerations and evident falsities, to enter into the circuit of Italian culture and national life in a lasting manner.

Certainly, this schema of Croce's corresponded rather well to what the Naples philosopher thought of his own intellectual experience and his own role in Italian culture, but at the same time it also succeeded in accurately giving account of the climate in which there developed an almost necessary encounter between a generation of young students' concern for cultural renewal and Marx's historical materialism.

Moreover, themes and problematics of historical materialism had a significance and pervasiveness in the Italian culture of the 1890s that can certainly not be seen only by looking at the high points of theory.

---

6 Croce 1967, p. 142.

7 Croce 1967, p. 143, my italics.

8 Croce 1967, pp. 146, 148.

9 Croce 1967, p. 153.

In the bibliography published in an appendix to his *Storia del marxismo in Italia*,[10] Robert Michels notes 79 'Monographs on historical materialism' in the 1890s, and 59 for the first eight years of the following decade. Michels's bibliography is certainly built on extensive criteria, seeing that it contains '*all* those writings, whether books, pamphlets, essays in reviews and articles in newspapers that revolve around Marx and his ideas, for better or worse, for or against'.[11] But as concerns historical materialism, the number of titles could be greater than this. In fact, Michels divides his bibliography into 'Monographs on historical materialism', 'Monographs on "Capital"', 'Theory of Value', 'Monographs on the Theory of Concentration and Accumulation', 'Monographs on growing Poverty and on crisis', 'Works on Marxism in general', 'Writings on the agrarian question, in relation to Marxism' and 'Writings on the so-called Crisis of Marxism'. Historical materialism is the transversal thematic, *par excellence*. For example, even among the 'Monographs on "Capital"' or the 'Writings on the so-called Crisis of Marxism' there are contributions by Croce, Giuffrida, Arturo Labriola, Antonio Labriola, Loria and others who also intervened in the debate on the materialist conception of history, even if in different ways. But it is particularly the 'Works on Marxism in general' that clearly evidence this transversality. The titles cited in this part of the bibliography are 155 in number for the 1890s and 125 for the first eight years of the twentieth century, and it seems that a truly vast number of these works dealt with questions of historical materialism. We need only look at the example of Gentile's writings on Marx; while one of them, *Una critica del materialismo storico*, does appear among the 'Monographs on historical materialism', the other, *La filosofia di Marx*, appears among the 'Works on Marxism in general'. Yet this is a text in which the centrality of historical materialism is hardly difficult to notice.

The publications offering these titles were not limited to the socialist or socialistic press alone. Almost all the main Italian journals took an interest in this theme, from the *Archivio Giuridico* to *Studii storici*, from *L'Economista* to the *Giornale degli Economisti*, from *Nuova Antologia* to *La Riforma Sociale*, and from the *Rivisita Filosofica Scientifica* to the *Rivisita Italiana di Sociologia*. Also here we see a transversality across disciplines, which necessarily reflected on the breadth of terrains that absorbed the 'juices' of historical materialism, even if to very different degrees.

Certainly, positivism did in very large part provide the cultural 'stock' for this extensive proliferation of moments of historical materialism. However, we

10 Michels 1909, pp. i–lv.

11 Michels 1909, p. i.

should be careful not to consider in negative terms a phenomenon that had such differentiated analytical approaches and results. This was a phenomenon in which we can find contributions capable of mounting a 'critical reflection on the fundaments of the social and moral sciences',[12] in a manner that does not fit with the commonplace view of the positivists' historiographical 'scientism'.

Indeed, Pasquale Villari's early 1890s text,[13] which would play a key role in Croce's polemical reflection on positivist historiography, cannot so easily be flattened into the one-dimensional plane that such constrictive interpretative approaches suggest. Rather, Villari's methodological positivism proved able to offer a discourse on history that was intelligently balanced across a vast range of articulations. First of all, it refused to fetishise facts, instead underlining the need for interpretative models – *hypotheses* to *play with*. Moreover, an anti-systemic, non-totalising spirit pervaded the whole of this long essay, with its explicit rejection of deterministic rigidities, exoteric philosophies of history and also, clearly, esoteric ones. This was, in sum, the outline of a non-teleological, integral historicism; a consummate split with any image of positivism's historiographical 'scientism', even though this latter image was not without substance. Moreover, in Villari's essay there remained a nomothetic structure, based on many lines of argumentation that were evidently the reflection of a certain culture. Yet this did not invalidate the substance of what was an essentially open methodological orientation.[14]

The terrain on which Villari was operating was certainly contiguous and in some areas overlapped with the ground simultaneously being tilled by those scholars who sought to conjugate 'history as science' with socialist militancy, precisely by way of the privileged reference to the materialist conception of history.

Symptomatic, in this regard, is the near-simultaneous appearance of Villari's essay and a text by Ettore Ciccotti,[15] conceived as an introduction to the ancient history course at Milan's Accademia Scientifico-Letteraria. Ettore Ciccotti was an activist, socialist professor, and a protagonist of the renewal of Italian studies of the ancient world, deploying a methodological framework that explicitly harked back to historical materialism. Neither Ciccotti nor, indeed, any of the young intellectuals living through that cultural climate could avoid engagement with the pressing questions that were now posed to both history and philosophy.

12 Garin 1983, p. 87.
13 Villari 1894.
14 See Moretti 1980, 1981.
15 E. Ciccotti, 'Perché studiamo storia antica?', *La Cultura*, 1892, pp. 132–41.

The ethical-cultural tension of Ciccotti's work was analogous to that of Villari's contemporary text, even in its rather less felicitous aspects concerning the determination of the immanent 'laws' governing how history and social life unfolded. He put a rather greater emphasis on 'practical and moral *telos*',[16] closely linked to a rather blurry set of interpretative criteria. He was explicit in his reference to the centrality of the economy, even if within the terms of an overt critique of Lorian determinism,[17] reaffirming the 'inseparability of the various manifestations of life' and of 'the reciprocal action of diverse factors'.[18]

Ciccotti was here grafting certain elements inspired by the materialist conception of history onto *a certain* branch of positivism, within *a certain mental framework* shared with positivism 'as a methodical orientation'.[19] This would prove an important factor in the history of Italian culture, and, indeed, one with a long future, even if it took uneven paths across this culture's many underground terrains.

By no means was Italian culture's encounter with historical materialism an accidental one. These themes emerged almost naturally from the vast, deep sea of positivism, from its most blurred and problematic currents – that is, from *methodical* positivism – and from its least flexible and most rigidly scholastic currents – that is, from *philosophical* positivism. Various different ways of addressing historical materialism resulted from this, with some of them being consciously critical of determinate positivist presuppositions, and others tending to subdue its methodological novelties by way of processes that absorbed it into a deterministic tradition made all the more rigid through the abnormally significant role exercised by this interpretive model's 'materialist' pole: the 'economic factor'. There necessarily also resulted different modalities corresponding to different levels of theoretical awareness and theoretical rigour.

Also at the higher levels of theory, therefore, the encounter with Marxism-historical materialism was 'neither casual nor accidental'.[20] It was not so for a figure like Croce who considered himself a protagonist of the very limited

16 The expression is from Treves 1962, p. 239.

17 Indeed, reaffirming the centrality of the economy, Ciccoti declared that it was 'an exaggeration [to say], as some economists have sought to demonstrate, that the economic element is the only factor in the constitution of politics'; E. Ciccotti, 'Perché studiamo storia antica?', *La Cultura*, 1892, p. 139.

18 Ibid.

19 Limentani 1924, p. 1.

20 The expression is from Garin 1991, p. 37. Spirito 1965, p. 77, instead argues that 'Gentile's interest [in historical materialism] owed to chance factors'. This argument is also advanced, in part, by Bruno 1979, p. 65.

circle (the three or four people?) among whom the discussion on 'theoretical Marxism' was being articulated in Italy; and nor was it for Gentile, who considered himself the restorer and guardian of the speculative-philosophical spirit in Italy, and for that reason felt compelled to try to bare the 'roots [of that] philosophy propounded by Labriola, by Croce, and by all the socialists'.[21]

Croce, moreover, never argued that his Marxist studies were of an accidental character; rather, he considered them a *necessary* site of his own intellectual maturation, in the context of Italian culture's renewal-process.

If already reading Labriola's work on Herbartian ethics had 'unexpectedly responded to [Croce's] anxious need for a rational form inspiring faith in life and its ends and duties',[22] the Neapolitan philosopher's lesson would have a very different impact on Croce's need to give rational form to the consciousness of history and to philosophy, more specifically.

This latter need – which Croce says he first felt as he wrote his essay 'La storia ridotta sotto il concetto generale dell'arte' – returned with overwhelming force when Labriola sent him the first of his essays on the materialist conception of history, 'which [Croce] read and re-read, feeling [his] mind being turned on again, [unable] to look away from these thoughts and problems, which spread and expanded in [his] mind'.

> And studying economics, which Marxism identified with the general conception of reality, that is, with philosophy, gave [Croce] cause to turn to the problems of philosophy … all those mediations that, like economic studies, always had as their ultimate end History, to which [he] planned to return for some time, armed with economics and historical materialism.[23]

At the centre of Croce's interests

> Were, first of all, problems of a historiographical and methodological order. It was no mere chance or arbitrary thing that his attention … was focused … on an interest in nature and essence of historiography; on studying the relations between historiography and the history of art (aesthetics); on the problem of whether there could be a philosophy of history distinct from historiography, and, if there could be one, if and within what limits it had scientific validity.[24]

21 Letter from Gentile to Jaia, 5 February 1899, in Sandirocco (ed.) 1969, p. 264.
22 Croce 1989, p. 24.
23 Croce 1989, p. 33.
24 See Oldrini 1986, p. 239.

Already elsewhere in this book, we substantially arrived at an interpretation holding that it is possible to locate a phase within Croce's intellectual biography that was not extraneous to the Marxist dimension.[25] His 1896 writings on historical materialism were fully situated within this 'internal' phase, and so, too, without doubt, was his essay on 'Professor Loria's theories of history', which Labriola had insistently requested, and which was the object of a collaborative discussion between the two – almost a necessary staging post in a joint project. Labriola identified this joint project when, considering that Croce – struck by an 'onslaught of ingenuity' – was conferring excessive importance on some of Enrico Ferri's observations, he expressed himself in the following terms: 'I think that *we* have something better to do – *spreading scientific socialism* – and then will follow the people who are capable of making use of it'.[26]

As for his essay 'On the scientific form of historical materialism',[27] we could not, of course, say that this expressed a point of view common to both Labriola and Croce, even if this latter did argue that 'it [did] not seem that the divergence between Labriola and [him could have been] a substantial one'.[28] We will later have space to reflect on this 'divergence'. Labriola highlighted the existence of a '*formal* presupposition' in Croce's 'lecture'[29] that sometimes led the author to stretch the texts in order to 'know more than he effectively did know', and yet he also confirmed that all of Croce's 'observations and reservations' were 'well-founded'; that is, they had a 'basis in the thing itself' and were not 'purely subjective or only in his head'.[30] And after a second reading of Croce's text he adjudged his friend's 'observations' to be of yet 'greater significance' than he had first considered them.[31] Croce's reading was, then, an acceptable one, wholly legitimately *internal* to the 'thing itself'. In subsequent months Labriola would only return to the essay in question in passing, noting that it had 'made an excellent impression on many people'.[32] We know that Labriola made determined and also severe interventions in those cases where the interpretations offered by interlocutors with whom he felt involved in a common project proved *exter-*

25 I would struggle to agree with the claim that 'Croce's work does not enter into the history of Italian Marxism. It does not enter therein, because he limited himself to criticising Marx from the outside': Corradini 1983, p. 56.

26 Letter from Labriola to Croce, 24 December 1896, in Labriola 1983, Vol. III, p. 755. My italics.

27 Croce 1961, pp. 1–21.

28 Croce 1961, p. 18.

29 The essay had in fact originated as a 'lecture' at Naples's Accademia Pontaniana.

30 Labriola to Croce, 24 May 1896, in Labriola 1983, Vol. III, p. 668.

31 Labriola to Croce, 25 May 1896, in Labriola 1983, Vol. III, p. 669.

32 Labriola to Croce, 6 June 1896, in Labriola 1983, Vol. III, p. 675.

nal to a conceptual universe that was partly to be delimited and partly to be constructed. Sorel was a case in point. Indeed, Labriola had remarked to Croce himself – in the period of their common project of 'spreading scientific socialism', and precisely with regard to the text most coherently inserted within this project, 'Professor Loria's theories of history' – on the inopportune nature of a note on the theory of value that 'truly [did] something to spoil its effect'.[33] And he had addressed the question of *pure economics* without diplomatically holding fire, deploying a welter of arguments.[34] The fact that Labriola instead took a rather detached attitude toward Croce's interpretation of his first essay on historical materialism is, then, a matter of no little importance, also in terms of better defining the oft-discussed relationship that Croce himself and Gentile[35] had with Labriola's theory – a theory that would so deeply affect the itinerary of 'theoretical Marxism' in Italy.

> Gentile's approach to Marx's theory was less favourably disposed toward understanding it – we could even say that he approached it with a preconceived hostility, politically determined by an indifference toward the social question and philosophically determined by an anti-materialist interpretation of Hegel.[36]

I believe that we can fully share in this judgement of Ugo Spirito's, which also serves better to bring into relief the apparent paradox of a young scholar who, despite being 'structurally' anti-Marxist, in the Italy of the 1890s necessarily had to encounter Marx and more precisely Labriola's reading of Marx, in the interests of a speculative philosophy of a theoretically high level.

Croce and Gentile thus discovered Marx by way of Labriola. The difference between their interpretation of Marx and Labriola's represents a point of comparison difficult to overlook for Italian historical-philosophical culture of either Marxist or non-Marxist varieties.

Naturally, the paths through which Croce and Gentile encountered Marx were different ones, as were the results of their journeys through Marxism, even if at some points their trajectories did seem to come close to one another.

---

33 Labriola to Croce, 25 December 1896, in Labriola 1983, Vol. III, p. 757.

34 Labriola to Croce, 1 and 5 January 1897, Labriola 1983, Vol. III, pp. 759–62, 762–3.

35 For Oldrini 1994, p. 206, both men also looked at Labriola, 'not without justification, as the continuation and authentic heir of the tradition of classical thought, of the Neapolitan philosophy of the masters'.

36 Spirito 1965, p. 78.

As we have already seen, Croce started out from the need to found his own *discourse* of history on more theoretically rigorous bases; and in Labriola he found a response that he considered – for a certain period – fully able to satisfy this demand for a theoretically-founded heuristics. Even when this consonance became blurred and then dispersed, substantial traces of this cultural experience remained components of his intellectual universe. He would at times claim the inheritance of those elements that he considered to have had a positive effect in nourishing Italian culture. Moreover, his encounter with Labriola also transformed into a *direct* encounter with Marx. He truly engaged with some of Marx's fundamental texts; from *Die heilige Familie* – and his copy of this extremely scarce work had been signalled to him by Labriola himself – to *Capital* and other, lesser texts, which he was predisposed to research on account of the theoretical and philological-scholarly interests that, taken together, represented the best aspect of Crocean historiography. This direct relation resulted in the dual development of Croce's reading of Marxism: on the one hand the understanding, explanation, analysis and critique of Marx's propositions, and on the other hand the comparison of these propositions and the Marxists' writings, in order to bring out the 'true' Marx. Even in 1899, when his disagreement with Labriola had already exploded in all its radical extent, and the divarication between their perspectives had become a very wide one, he would nonetheless still write the following words to his old teacher; 'The *crisis of Marxism*, in its doctrinal aspect, almost always requires providing a more correct and realistic interpretation of Marx's propositions, as against the shoddy mix-ups and exaggerations of his followers'.[37] Gentile – who had recently finished his second essay on *La filosofia di Marx* – could never have concurred with such a view.

If Giovanni Gentile's encounter with Labriola's Marx was the effect – in the broad sense – of the same cultural climate as Croce's, his case was a very different one in his relation to both a certain Italian philosophical tradition – Spaventa's – and the social question and socialism. Croce had for a moment 'breathed in' the 'faith and hope in the vision of mankind's palingenesis, redeemed by labour and in labour';[38] Gentile would forever remain extraneous to such a moment.[39] Indeed, having matured his reading of Spaventa's

37 Croce to Labriola, 27 March 1899, in Croce (ed.) 1987–8, pp. 317 et sqq.

38 Croce 1989, p. 35.

39 His first essay on historical materialism began, indeed, with a proud assertion of the preeminence of speculative-philosophical reflection over 'social questions'. 'Science certainly can and must refer to the real conditions of society, which it takes as a special object of its investigations: but it can and must not mix [these conditions] with and identify them with what is proper to its own essence. [Its essence] is, properly speaking, a product of

Hegelianism, Croce like Labriola considered it something that he had left behind – what he called 'vetero-Hegelianism' – whereas for Gentile, Spaventa's lesson remained central to a programme of renewing Italian philosophy. For this reason, Gentile's approach to historical materialism would always remain wholly internal to an entirely speculative dimension, to a philosophy understood 'as *the necessary knowledge of what is necessary*'.[40] His real knowledge of Marx's texts – in particular in the former of his two essays – proved 'close to nil'.[41] His principal reference points were secondary sources – the essays of Labriola, Croce, and Chiappelli; almost all of his citations were second-hand.

There is no doubt that 'Gentile's ingenuity and sharpness – something he certainly did not lack – were greatly superior to his philological and critical information'.[42] Indeed, even given his aforementioned lack of direct textual citations and use of a dubious, stilted translation of certain passages of the *Theses on Feuerbach*, he was able to set out the discourse 'on praxis' through which a very great part of the itinerary of Marx-the-philosopher would pass in Italy: that of 'the "Italian" Marx, the Marx constructed on a philosophical-political *sunolon*, which often had a problematic relationship with Marx's "materialism"'.[43]

This is a node that a great number of interpreters have tried to get to grips with, in general ones of a philosophical culture: it is a node that also concerns Croce and Gentile's readings of Labriola's (and Marx's) historical materialism. In substance the question is whether Gentile's reading – even if one less well-founded in an 'internal' knowledge, and one more limited in its *sympàtheia* for the object of analysis than in Croce's case – was not closer to Marx and Labriola's *philosophical* conception of historical materialism.

Gentile, certainly, considered historical materialism a philosophy: a philosophy of history in the full sense that *his* Hegelian tradition attributed to such terms.[44] This was an intimately contradictory philosophy, and one that was

---

the formal elaboration of the spirit, where [these conditions] are destined to provide the mere contents': see Gentile 1955, p. 14.

40 Vigna 1977, p. 10.

41 Turi 1996, p. 60.

42 Agazzi 1962, p. 235.

43 De Giovanni 1983, p. 14.

44 Croce had asked his view regarding the 'concept of philosophy' and he replied: 'I think that my historical concept of philosophy – which is not my own, but that of our century – can be resolved by reflecting on the concept of the human spirit ... For if spirit is not something fine and finished, operating according to innate activities, but a progressive formation – that is, a perpetual development of itself – it is evident that e.g. the spirit of the nineteenth century must be different to that of the eighteenth century, but developed and at a further

thus very fragile in its foundations, but all the same a philosophy, and a philosophy of history.

Already in his first essay, Gentile introduced his distinction between the *form* of historical materialism, the dialectic, and its *content*, materialism – this being the distinction that would allow him to uphold the thesis that this was a fundamentally contradictory philosophy. Of the two versions of historical materialism circulating in Italy – Loria's and Labriola's – he maintained that it was this latter that illustrated 'the doctrine of historical materialism in its most genuine and complete form, such as it was proposed by Marx and such as can be logically developed according to the master's general visions and particular understandings and applications of it'.[45] It was Labriola who 'perceived its theoretical requirements better than anyone, through the philosophical inclination of his thinking';[46] and for Labriola, as for Marx, 'the materialist conception of history can only be said to be a true and proper philosophy of history, given the *form* in which it presents itself to us'.[47] But if 'formally considered'[48] the materialist conception of history had a philosophical character, it also contained an unresolvable 'internal contradiction'. A philosophy of history must necessarily have an 'immanent absolute' as its object, and the 'immanent absolute' did not belong to the sphere of materialism.[49]

The fact that the second essay was a little better-equipped in terms of its direct references to Marx's texts and, most importantly, got to grips with a theme so important to 'Marx-the-philosopher' as the philosophy of praxis – a theme that would persist throughout a significant part of Italian philosophy, and not only that of Marxist inspiration – did not change the underlying 'fundamental contradiction' highlighted earlier.

Gentile identified as the 'keystone' of Marx's philosophical construction 'the concept of "praxis"',[50] made explicit in the *Theses on Feuerbach* which – as he

degree of formation ... Thus the modern spirit of our century cannot but comprise all the degrees of the spirit of the previous centuries. ... This is the necessary condition of life, and this is also the necessary condition for history, that is, of the history of the spirit – which has no other history'. 'The modern concept of philosophy is [the concept] of the awareness the spirit has of itself ... The historical is what is objectively, realistically necessary in its own time, in a given moment of the spirit's development'. Letters from Croce to Gentile, 29 June 1899 and from Gentile to Croce, 30 June 1899, in Croce 1981 and Gentile 1972.

45 Gentile 1955, p. 22.

46 Gentile 1955, p. 34.

47 Gentile 1955, p. 40, my italics.

48 Gentile 1955, p. 52.

49 Gentile 1955, p. 56.

50 Gentile 1955, p. 72.

put it – he had translated 'as best [he] could' especially for this text. While done 'as best [he] could', this translation stilted an important formulation of Marx's in an idealist vein. *Umwälzende Praxis* – a revolutionary or transformative praxis – became a transformed praxis (a self-transformed one?), with the evident disappearance of something that was of very real significance for Marx, namely the *object* external to thought that had to be transformed. This *contrived* translation was in truth only the most evident symptom of a *contrived* interpretation of Marx wholly boxed into the canons of Hegelian ontology, at least in the measure – and this was of no little significance to Gentile – that the Trier thinker was producing 'good philosophy'. Conversely, the Marx who roamed outside of Hegel was producing 'bad philosophy', or rather a 'non-philosophy'.

> Praxis is creative activity, for which *verum et factum convertuntur*. It is a necessary development of activity because it proceeds from its nature, and it is honed in the object, the correlate and product of activity. But this object that comes about by virtue of the subject, is but a duplication of this latter, a projection of itself, its *Selbstentfremdung*.[51]

Even some Marxists – perhaps in certain rather too 'Gentilian' passages – have interpreted Marx's philosophy of praxis as a 'theory that entails its own practice', as a theory in which 'the object connected to praxis is entirely contained within it'. But they have not been able to avoid posing themselves the question '*when* does material praxis become history? *Who* translates praxis into effective historical life?' Moreover, they have also had to identify in the *dynamis* of the 'labour-power' that 'makes abstract labour real' the principle of Marx's *praxis* that allows its rooting in a 'concrete body' posing itself the tasks of *transforming* a likewise concrete reality.[52]

For Gentile, conversely, Marx remains a philosopher only insofar as he is a 'born idealist'.[53] The conclusions that he reaches regarding Marx's historical materialism do not leave any room for doubt in this regard:

> This philosophy of Marx's is generally characterised by its eclecticism, its contradictory elements; today some of his disciples do not know what to do with this, and they are perhaps not so much at fault for that. There are many fertile ideas at its basis, which taken separately are worth meditat-

51 Gentile 1955, p. 87.
52 De Giovanni 1986, pp. 32, 33, 35, 43.
53 Gentile 1955, p. 164.

> ing on; but as has been proven, in isolation they do not belong to Marx and cannot justify the word 'Marxism', which is meant to be synonymous with sharply realistic philosophy. It is, however, true that science's interest is not a matter of names; and if some among Hegelianism's most important ideas can penetrate certain minds thanks to the attraction of Marx's name, then good luck to 'Marxism', too![54]

So even if historical materialism was founded on an absolutely insuperable contradiction, it was a 'philosophy' and a 'philosophy of history', exactly – Gentile tells us – in the sense that Karl Marx's most faithful interpreter Labriola considered it.

Can this be enough to maintain that Gentile's reading of Labriola grasped the deep *philosophical* red thread of his essays on historical materialism better than did Croce's reading? Did 'philosophy' and 'philosophy of history' mean the same thing for Gentile as for Labriola?

Certainly, Labriola could never have accepted – and did not accept – the reduction of historical materialism to a 'simple canon of historical interpretation',[55] but his relationship with Croce's interpretation cannot be read only in terms of a question that Labriola would himself in some aspects define as a 'verbalist' one. Moreover, this expression did not appear in the first of the essays Croce dedicated to historical materialism, but only in the November 1897 text when the elements of a divarication between their perspectives were now starting to become evident. Still remaining to be explained are the reasons why Labriola in a sense benevolently suspended judgement on the first of these essays, from May 1896, as well as recognising the well-foundedness of Croce's 'observations and reservations'.

There were themes running through the essay that the Naples philosopher certainly could not have considered extraneous. If this text denied that historical materialism was a philosophy of history, it nonetheless emphasised the fact that it did have to do with 'philosophising on history'; an expression that Labriola would himself repeatedly come to use, with analogous meanings. It made reference to the open character of a doctrine that was 'barely at its beginnings and still needed a great deal of development'.[56] Croce considered particularly significant the anti-theological polemic against 'abstract theology' as well as the anti-systematic spirit and anti-scholasticism running through Labriola's writ-

54 Gentile 1955, p. 165.
55 Croce 1961, p. 112.
56 Croce 1961, p. 9.

ings.[57] For Labriola, as we shall see, historical materialism certainly had broader dimensions and greater depth than the features marked out by Croce in this first essay would suggest. But considering Croce's reading in its *partiality*, it must not have seemed to Labriola to be wholly different to the logics of his arguments.

For Labriola, then, historical materialism was a 'philosophy' and also a 'philosophy of history', even if in this second aspect the problem cannot be resolved with reference to any *one* statement of Labriola's.

The question of Labriola's 'style' is not at all, then, an element external to the contents of his discourse; his 'style' perfectly conforms to the purpose of his philosophy, and is a structuring element of it. Kolakowski understood this well, explaining that the supposed generality of his style brings us

> to the conclusion that the generality of his style is not due merely to a preference for rhetoric over precision of thought, but to a *distrust of cut-and-dried formulas* and a conviction that Marxism is not a 'final', self-sufficient rationalization and schematization of history, but rather a collection of pointers to the understanding of human affairs; these must be imprecise if they are not to degenerate into a dogmatic contempt for the multiplicity and diversity of the forces that act in history ... From this viewpoint also, Labriola instilled into Italian Marxism a sceptical attitude towards comprehensive explanations of universal history.[58]

'There is no "philosophy" of Labriola's that can be classified with precise labels, expounded chapter and verse, and which is coherent in its unfolding and in its singular affirmations';[59] and this does not owe only to the aforementioned factors inherent to his 'style', important though they are. Rather, his was a continual engagement, across several decades, with a 'philosophy' whose fundamental questions he reformulated and specified through a series of encounters with the key figures of the development of philosophy and as new knowledges posed new problems on which to 'philosophise'. And even in the presence of

---

57 Only in 1898 would he distance himself from this mode of exposition: 'disdaining ... as scholasticism any work of formal elaboration, he effectively comes to use imprecise concepts, which are more *overall impressions*'. And the year afterward he would even speak of his 'confused and contradictory way of writing'. See Croce to Gentile, 4 February 1898 and 14 June 1899 in Croce 1981.

58 Kolakowski 1978b, pp. 183–4.

59 Garin 1983, p. 159.

very solid theoretical coordinates – and a fundamental coherence that also persisted across his long intellectual adventure – all this forbade any philosophical systematisation.

Labriola's encounter with Marxism and his becoming a Marxist were and still are at the centre of a wide historiographical discussion – one that is often rather polemical – regarding precisely the question of his continuity or caesura with the previous way of considering philosophy and the philosophy of history. This is an important node of historiography and one that cannot easily be unravelled. Sometimes it is overly simplified in a battlefield in which Hegelianism and Herbartianism (or perhaps Spinozism) and their infinite combinations run the risk of becoming purely markers of the clash among improbable 'orthodoxies', the 'closed' and the 'open', among various 'critical' degrees of 'communism'.

Not even in the relatively brief chronological arc in which Labriola elaborated his essays on historical materialism could we identify any systematic 'philosophy' of his. Nonetheless, we can clearly grasp the rough characteristics of Labriola's consideration of philosophical knowledge in this particular period.

In November 1896, when Labriola's reflection was still centred on the *Saggi sul materialismo storico*, the philosophy professor wrote a text specifically dedicated to the academy and his own profession; a text that served as a speech marking the beginning of the academic year. This was a text in which even if he did not define the object of his teaching – philosophy – he did at least contextualise it in the sphere of the scientific knowledge institutionalised in the University.[60]

Indeed, in his speech on 'The University and the freedom of science' we can immediately pick out the difficulties of giving any such definition of Labriola's object. He taught three disciplines, namely ethics, pedagogy and the philosophy of history: 'three chapters', he said, 'of what *through ancient tradition we call philosophy*'. These were disciplines 'that have for a while – together with all aspects of what else remains of philosophy – found themselves *in a period of deep crisis*, whose resolution cannot be seen or foreseen *without a precise examination of all the fundamental problems of the single sciences*'.[61]

---

60 'L'università e la libertà della scienza' – Labriola 1973, Vol. II, pp. 868–910. Benedetto Croce, who published the speech a few months later, would write 'There is nothing else for me to say for my part, except that I am proud to present the public with this speech, which in its thinking and its sentiments is one of the most elevated ever to have been heard in the halls of Italy's universities' (p. 869).

61 Labriola 1973, p. 871. My italics.

The professor's lectures on the three disciplines would increasingly roam 'through particular research within the context of determinate questions' and no longer encompassed 'the philosophy that would attempt to embrace with definitions and categories, as if in fine perspective, the totality of the real and all the forms of knowledge'.[62]

The crisis of philosophy was the consequence of the exhaustion of what Labriola defined as '*classical* philosophy'; that is, 'the systems of Herbart and Hegel', 'grand systems' under the 'direct and genuine influence of which' he proudly said he had been trained. These were, he added,

> Systems in which the antithesis – between realism and idealism, pluralism and monism, scientific psychology and phenomenology of the spirit, the specification of methods and the anticipation of all method in the omniscient dialectic – had arrived at its extreme consequences. Already Hegel's philosophy had given rise to Karl Marx's historical materialism, and Herbart's to ...[63]

As such, no 'new philosophical systematic' was possible any more, since the present state of philosophy – and here Labriola did almost seem to let himself head toward a definition – 'consist[ed] of the immanence of thought in the really known; that is, it consist[ed] of the opposite of any anticipation of thought on the known'.[64] This was a definition that did not define philosophy *in itself*; and nor would he later provide such a definition even in another context: 'For twenty years I have had a distaste for systematic philosophy, and this mental disposition has made it easier for me to access Marxism, which is one of the ways in which the scientific spirit has liberated itself from a "self-standing" philosophy'.[65]

Aside from the question of the philosophical dimension of historical materialism – to which we will return – Labriola's *Saggi sul materialismo storico* addressed philosophy as a specific knowledge in a manner conforming to what he had argued in his speech on 'The University and the freedom of science'.

Labriola indicated as the principal tendency of his time 'the perfect identification of philosophy, or *conscious critical thought*, with the material of knowledge; the complete elimination of the traditional gap between science and

62 Labriola 1973, p. 872.
63 Labriola 1973, p. 873.
64 Labriola 1973, p. 875.
65 Labriola 1977, p. 230.

philosophy'.[66] This was a tendency, a *desideratum*, more than a reality; but it was a tendency that ruled out any possibility of speaking of *classical* and systematic philosophy.

And furthermore:

> Making an exception for those ways of philosophising that are mixed up with the mystical or with theology, *philosophy* never means science or a doctrine apart, with its own particular objects, but simply a degree, a form, a stage of thinking with regard to those same things that enter into the field of experience. Philosophy is, for this reason, either a generic anticipation of problems that science still has to elaborate specifically, or it is the summary and conceptual elaboration of the results that science has already arrived at.[67]

Moreover, the notable characteristic of this philosophy was its 'methodical doubt'.[68]

The conception of philosophy as a knowledge with a highly epistemological content[69] and a great degree of systemic instability could not have been further from Giovani Gentile's conception, which, as we know, had maintained that 'the modern concept of philosophy' was the concept 'of the knowledge that the spirit has of itself'.[70]

As concerns the question of defining the 'philosophy of history', this was in a certain sense posed in the same terms as the definition of 'philosophy'. Moreover, it is wholly evident that a determinate conception of 'philosophy' was tied by a thousand threads to a conception of the 'philosophy of history'. At the same time, however, even a 'philosophy of history' intimately connected to historical materialism *as a philosophy* also maintained a substantial dimension as a methodology of historical research (methodology not being reducible to technique). This had been part of Labriola's reflection even before his encounter with the materialist conception of history.

66 Labriola 1977, p. 217. My italics.

67 Labriola 1977, p. 145.

68 Labriola 1977, p. 208.

69 Sbarberi overly reductively defined it as 'philosophy-as-epistemology'. See Sbarberi 1986, p. 82. The late Agazzi also emphasised this aspect, maintaining that Labriola's 'dialectical thought', like Marx's, was not an epistemic thought but rather an epistemological one; not a scientific theory but a critical theory. See Agazzi 1987.

70 See note 42.

It is true that for Labriola historical materialism 'appeared as something new, unknown to Italian science',[71] and this also entailed the partial reformulation and repositioning in a different perspective of some of the moments of his reflection. But with regard to the methodology of historical research he elaborated lineaments of a very long-term duration, based on deep convictions. Already before the famous 1887 text, in a constant engagement with the highest points of European (in particularly German) epistemological discussion, he 'showed that he had come to mature a strong perplexity with regard to any systematic construction of the philosophy of history'.[72]

The fundamental themes present in his 1887 introduction certainly would not go away after his encounter with historical materialism, even if they would in part be contextualised differently in what was not always a linear trajectory. When this itinerary reached its conclusion,[73] it was possible better to grasp the long-term solidity of the convictions that he matured with regard to the philosophy of history.

How could one define the philosophy of history?

> [As for] the precise concept of the philosophy of history; I would respond, without doubt, that I cannot even do so ... With this – that is, not being able to define it – ... I mean precisely that the name of philosophy, in this particular application, does not designate a body of doctrine ... but rather a more or less explicit tendency, albeit one that is always general to the spirit of our times, and latent in the presuppositions and conclusions of those historical disciplines that have reached a higher level of scientific exactness.[74]

Here was an attempt not to produce a philosophy of history, but to 'philosophise' on history. It was an attempt definitively to break from what is traditionally[75] understood by philosophy of history, namely a 'general outline or schema

---

71 Dal Pane 1975, p. 342.

72 Poggi 1978, p. 67.

73 Labriola 1977, pp. 320 et sqq.

74 Labriola 1973, pp. 5–6.

75 '... the greater part of the books a few years ago whose covers bore the title "philosophy of history" – and not rightly so, given what we are now saying – were thought up and written with the presupposition of [a] real unity that thought had to penetrate in order to reproduce, in full if at all': Labriola 1973, p. 22. And moreover 'Because when we want to neglect the place that the likes of Hegel or other philosophers who we want to place side by side wished to attribute to the concept of the unity of history, in the totality of their view of

of universal philosophical history'; a history that gives 'rise to the concept of a spirit operating only on the impulse of its internal formation, like a phantasm that moves through nature, free of obstacles or influences'.[76]

The reflection on history that Labriola expressed in his 1887 essay remained very much internal to a methodological dimension, but did not go so far as to identify itself with this completely. The '*philosophy of history* cannot and must not be a universal history narrated philosophically, but rather a simple research on method, on the principles and the system of historical knowledges',[77] Labriola asserted. But research 'on the principles and the system of knowledges', the reasoned refusal to consider the metaphysical 'as a totalising view of method' but rather 'as a critique and correction of the concepts necessary for thinking experience', the refusal of any mechanism of deduction *ab extra*, necessarily implied a conception of philosophy as a 'critique of the principles of knowledge'.[78]

One last aspect that we can already identify in this introduction would, as we will see, remain an important aspect of his interpretation of historical materialism as a philosophy of history, namely the critique of an idea of progress[79] that would ultimately give direction and meaning to the course of human collective experience.

In the first of his *Saggi* appears the exacting expression 'new and definitive philosophy of history', which Croce would work to minimise while Gentile (and others) considered it the explicit proof of a historical materialism understood as a philosophy of history. In what measure should we take account of Croce's observations, according to which numerous propositions and above all the

the nature of things, it always remains true that in our minds there lives a presupposition latent in any research; that is, if thought remakes history, that [history] must in some sense either conceal a thought or be so fashioned such as to lend itself to its reduction to thought. And for this reason – the questioner might add – one would rightly again attempt this same test that failed under the influence of other ways of philosophising, on account of an excess of ideology, [but this time] with a realistic understanding or a greater critical caution': Labriola 1973, pp. 25–6.

76 Labriola 1973, pp. 23, 30.

77 Labriola 1973, p. 32.

78 Labriola 1973, pp. 20, 29.

79 '… the study of human affairs necessarily brings us to recognise not only progress but also regress … When the idea of progress, of the perfection and completion of attitudes and aspirations, is erroneously transmuted from a criterion of appreciation into a rule of interpretation, we are ultimately unable to tell if the study of history should predispose us to optimism and not instead to pessimism': Labriola 1973, p. 28.

spirit of the text contradicted such a definition, almost as if it had slipped from Labriola's pen rather rashly? Or the observations of those scholars who see the subsequent development of his reflection in his other essays as entailing a process of 'revising' some of the assumptions of this first text?

We can certainly identify what could be considered a line of *development* of his essays, notwithstanding the relatively brief period in which they were written. Labriola was a highly attentive observer with antennae very sensitive to changes in the cultural and political climate. Though this did not bring him to change the deeper characteristics of his own elaborations, there is no doubt that certain adjustments can be seen, some of them of some importance.

The expression 'philosophy of history' appears just once in relation to historical materialism in the first essay. In the others it would not appear at all. This should not necessarily lead us to the conclusion that Labriola used this expression somehow inadvertently. Nor did he mean anything different with this expression than he had previously elaborated and clearly explicated in this regard in his 1887 introduction. A 'definitive philosophy of history' – the conception whose 'very first elements' the 'critical communists' had 'devised and discovered'[80] – 'was not, in effect, but the extreme development of realistic thought, in the field of history, and thus of the conception that he had been elaborating for some time'.[81]

This was, then, a 'philosophy of history' understood in a sense wholly different to that of the traditional 'systems'; a 'philosophy of history' that though doubtless a central moment of the 'new' doctrine nonetheless did not come to define historical materialism *in toto*.

Labriola, moreover, would express himself on 'historical materialism as a whole' in the following terms, structured in 'three orders of studies':

> The first responds to the socialistic parties' practical need to proceed in acquiring an adequate knowledge of the specific condition of the proletariat in each country, and to tailor socialism's activity to the causes, promises and dangers of political complications. The second can lead, and surely will lead, to renewing the orientations of historiography ... The third consists of dealing with directive principles, the understanding and development of which necessitates [a] general orientation.

80 Labriola 1977, p. 62.
81 Dal Pane 1975, p. 372.

Not long before this he had circumscribed the *metaphysics* of historical materialism within the ambit of 'those general problems' that revolve around 'the limits and forms of knowledge'.[82]

We will later see what model Labriola would point to as the representation that fully corresponded to historical materialism as a *whole*. As concerns the interpretation of history, there is truly nothing in the *Saggi* in any sense analogous to the 'ancient philosophy of history'.[83]

The 'philosophy of history' innate to historical materialism would be specified through an ever more open and problematic approach as Labriola's reflection in the *Saggi* developed. If in 1895 his 'morphological outlook' seemed to be in part guided by considerations of 'necessity' – even if a historical necessity founded on 'awareness of the means of its genesis'[84] – two years later 'the society of the future, the one into which we will project ourselves with our hopes, and, rather more, with certain illusions' – this same 'morphological outlook' – seemed 'uncertain, taking account of the enormous complication and extension of capitalism'.[85] It would be specified as a 'means of orientation' that could not limit itself to 'theorising' presumed immanent tendencies of the course of history, but instead had to descend into the determinacy of a history that was 'infinitely uneven and multifaceted'.[86] This was a history whose continuity 'in the empirical sense, circumstantiated by the transmission of the means of civilisation' was a fact, but one in which '*the idea of progress* ... implied nothing categorical'.[87] A history in which this thread of continuity had often been interrupted, a history that had also known *regress*, and a history that was unable to offer any guarantees in the face of new forms of regress.[88]

> And for this reason, our doctrine cannot be directed at representing the whole history of mankind in a prospective or unitary outlook, which repeats, *mutatis mutandis*, *a patterned historical philosophy* ... Our doctrine does not claim to be the *intellectual vision* of a grand plan or design, but is only a *method* of research and conception.[89]

82 Labriola 1977, p. 217.
83 Croce to Gentile, 9 February 1897, in Croce 1981.
84 Labriola 1977, pp. 22, 23, 35.
85 Labriola 1977, pp. 172, 272.
86 Labriola 1977, pp. 148, 155.
87 Labriola 1977, p. 158.
88 'The most sensible and most pressing of the objections that have ever been levelled against any *systematic* philosophy of history is that made by Wundt: that we do not know where history will finish': Labriola 1977, p. 345.
89 Labriola 1977, p. 98.

Of some significance is the fact that Labriola indicated two *different* sites in Marx's *oeuvre* as models of reference for the different structural dimensions of historical materialism. As concerned the philosophy of history *qua* 'method of research and conception', it was in *The Eighteenth Brumaire of Louis Bonaparte* that Labriola identified the 'first attempt to model the new conception of history into an account at the level of facts'. Conversely, the 'three orders of studies' innate to 'historical materialism as a whole' were to be found in *Capital*.[90]

Historical materialism 'as a whole' was, therefore, both recomposed and recognised in the analytical structure of *Capital*. This was an analytical model in which 'politics appeared as the practice of ... historical materialism, and philosophy as being inherent to the ... critique of economics, which was [Marx's] ... way of dealing with history'.[91] I think that we seriously have to consider the notion that the 'philosophical' self-sufficiency of historical materialism, which Labriola particularly emphasised, rested on the solidity of this analytical model.

This deeper understanding of *Capital*'s method – of its mechanism of negation of/conjugation with the classical philosophical tradition – ended up establishing almost a sort of parallel between Marx and Labriola in considering the relationship between this model and the dialectic of Hegelian derivation.

In Marx's still-'philosophical' works, from *The Holy Family* to *The German Ideology* and *The Poverty of Philosophy*, there was a gradual and radical break from a speculative historical dialectic in favour of a dialectical procedure that 'directly investigate[d] the material movement of history in its determinacy and "empirical verifiability", and consider[ed] categories only in function of this'.[92] He radically broke from such a philosophy, though later he would reprise certain Hegelian logical schemas in the determination of functional models of abstraction.

Equally, Labriola's relation with Hegelian philosophy was a constant and never definitively resolved one. There was a 'bad Hegel, the philosopher of history, or even a "theologist" of history, the philosopher of a linear and progressive time internal to the monism of the great Judeo-Christian eschatologies'. There was a 'Hegel suffering the burden of the bad interpretations made of him'.[93] There was a Hegel who had to be studied anew when the 'crisis of Marxism'

90 Labriola 1977, p. 217.

91 Ibid.

92 Dal Pra 1965, p. 408.

93 De Giovanni 1983, p. 40.

appeared on the horizon, and the 'irrational' appeared as the 'contradiction … within the process's very *raison d'être*'.[94]

In such a blurred and problematic context, for Marx as for Labriola measuring the 'level of Hegelianism' – considered a variable inverse to the 'level of scientificity' – did not seem the best way of giving account of the overall depth of historical materialism. Labriola truly demonstrated in his relationship with Hegelianism that overcoming it meant understanding it in full and assimilating it completely.

Also in this sense, Antonio Labriola was the only great Italian intellectual – and one of very few in Europe – capable of positioning himself, as an interpreter, at the level of the object of his analysis: Karl Marx. He was a great interpreter precisely because he had fully understood that 'a young Marx in 1898 [would have] humbly [set himself] to studying Wundt's logic'.[95] His was, therefore, an interpretative construct that was able to resolve the essential moment of historical-philological understanding, brought out with peerless analytical depth, in a philosophy/non-philosophy capable of getting to grips with what was new in culture and history. Through Labriola's reading of historical materialism, Italian Marxism not only became the privileged site of the renewal of late nineteenth-century Italian philosophical culture, but, beyond the ups and downs of this reading's 'fortunes', also endowed itself with tools with which it could measure up to the high points of European philosophy.

2 Materialism and 'Philosophy for Socialism'

'… [A] certain antipathy toward the materialist interpretation of Marx's *oeuvre* has always been one of the characteristics of Italian Marxism (which has also been termed "Italo-Marxism")'.[96] In saying this, Norberto Bobbio clearly grasped the basic elements of a philosophical reading present in 'macroscopic' form across the whole experience of twentieth-century Italian Marxism. However, this statement does not seem to have the same interpretative validity when it is applied – not that this seems to be Bobbio's intention – to the found-

94 'When the irrational, considered as a moment of the process itself, liberates us from the simplicity of abstract reason, at the same time it shows us the presence of revolutionary negativity in the very womb of the relatively necessary historical form': Labriola 1977, p. 186.

95 Letter to Kautsky, 8 October 1898, in Labriola 1983, Vol. III, p. 882.

96 Bobbio 1994, p. 79.

ing moment of theoretical (philosophical) Marxism in Italy; that is, to Antonio Labriola's elaborations.

For quite some time, a number of studies have critically questioned the linearity of the Labriola-Mondolfo-Gramsci genealogy, which rapidly appeared a rather problematic one. I believe, however, that in this regard we ought to accept the radicalism of Cesare Luporini's stance speaking of a 'deep fracture' in Italian theoretical (philosophical) Marxism's line of development.[97] This 'deep fracture' directly concerns the 'materialist' interpretation of Marx and also, in part – and in evident correspondence with the question of materialism – the conception and use of the dialectic.

Generally – though certainly not exclusively or principally – reflections on the *Anti-Dühring* have represented a particular moment in the evaluation of the connections between the dialectic and materialism, as well as the consequent choice of a negative or positive view regarding the 'philosophy of socialism'. Efforts to downplay the significance of the *Anti-Dühring*, and sometimes the claim that it is extraneous to the 'critical', 'open', 'non-encyclopaedic' dimension of Marx's theory, are almost always accompanied by a reading seeking to reduce this theory's 'level' of materialism, or at least to redefine its 'quality'.

It is a strange paradox, though not an inexplicable one, that a text that was expressly conceived as an attempt to combat the catechisms and encyclopaedisms circulating in social-democratic circles, based on the materialisms of the likes of Vogt and Büchner, would end up enjoying extraordinary success precisely as a '*Lehrbuch des Sozialismus*'. Certainly, this 'cannot be explained only in terms of the influence of an external cultural environment',[98] on account of the predominant 'tastes of the time'; rather, it also conformed to evident mechanisms internal to the book's own construction. And yet nor can this book be considered, in itself, the archetype of the notorious 'Diamat' of future years. This book suggests and brings into coexistence various different interpretative keys. Not by chance, a both rigorous and critical reader like Antonio Labriola was also an explicit admirer of this work.

He defined *Anti-Dühring* 'medicine for the mind of the intellectual youth',[99] recommending it to Benedetto Croce at the moment at which he and his young 'pupil' seemed committed to a common project.[100] Offering this recommendation to Croce, he counterposed this volume to the negative example of

97 Luporini 1973, p. 1587.
98 Gerratana 1972, p. 123.
99 Labriola 1977, p. 203.
100 Letter to Croce of 16 May 1895, in Labriola 1983, Vol. II, p. 585.

Plekhanov's materialism in his essays on Holbach, Helvètius and Marx, remarking that they seemed to have been written by 'a journalist trying his hand at science'.[101]

This was not because this text represented a philosophical 'monograph' or an 'encyclopaedia' of socialism; rather, it was a matter of 'fragments of a science and a politics that [were] in continual development'. It was not the 'book of a thesis'; rather, it was 'antithetical. Apart from a few isolated passages, like those that gave rise to a self-contained pamphlet (*Socialism: Utopian and scientific*) ...'[102]

Labriola's reading was, then, a methodological one, but as has rightly been noted, it was not a matter of 'abstract methodologism'. 'The methodological reading that he proposed was internal to a specific thematic, in relation to determinate contents, and cannot be understood outside of this context'.[103] And the determinate contents in question also concerned the dialectic, materialism, and their connections with science and philosophy.

When many years later Sebastiano Timparano produced a series of stimulating essays that had the merit of reposing the question of the hard kernel of 'materialism' – and this to an Italian Marxist philosophical culture that was very sensitive to the a-materialist appeal of a 'praxism' interpreted according to ideas of distant Gentilian ancestry – he also emphasised Antonio Labriola's 'materialist' dimension.[104] Naturally, as he did so, he privileged the aspect that was also the central moment of his own analytical approach, above all bringing into relief the importance that the Cassino-born philosopher attributed to the 'natural terrain', and its determining influence on humans' individual and collective history.[105]

We should not underestimate the importance that Labriola attributed to the 'natural terrain' and in general to all those physical-biological elements that remained irreducible to the subject's activity, and we will have cause to return

101 Letter to Croce of 28 January 1896, in Labriola 1983, Vol. III, p. 638.

102 Labriola 1977, pp. 183, 203.

103 Gerratana 1972, p. 121.

104 Timpanaro 1970, pp. 24–9.

105 For Labriola 'nature's influence on culture remained very real, in the triple sense of the influence of each individual's biological constitution on their psycho-intellectual character; nature as a stimulus to scientific-philosophical and artistic activity; and as an object of these same activities. And while Labriola explicitly recognised the mediation exercised by social context, he also very clearly denied that this mediation cancelled out the impulses and conditioning coming from nature, or that it rendered them negligible': Timpanaro 1970, pp. 28–9.

to this point. But at the same time, his materialism was not restricted to this dimension alone. In Labriola, the '*philosophy of praxis* ..., the core of historical materialism'[106] – that is, the 'philosophy of praxis' that would later become the privileged site for idealistic incursions – very much preserved its materialist contents. Timpanaro maintained an attitude of constant diffidence toward this 'philosophy of praxis', to the point of arguing that Marxism itself 'especially in its first phase (up to and including the *German Ideology*) was not, properly speaking, materialism'.[107] Conversely, for Labriola there was no doubt on this score: Marx was a *materialist* 'from 1845',[108] and the *German Ideology* and the *Theses on Feuerbach* were thus materialist works.[109]

'Man is doubtless an animal, and is linked to other animals by relations of descent and affinity'; and even if today his activity unfolds on 'an artificial terrain', the 'natural terrain' continues to condition it in a profound manner.[110]

Labriola showed no lack of certainty on this question:

> ... men living socially continue also to live in nature. They are not bound to it as animals are, of course, because they live on an artificial terrain. But still, nature is the immediate subsoil of the artificial terrain ... And just as we are naturally born as males and females, we almost always die unwillingly, and we are dominated by the instinct of generation. Thus in our temperament we bear specific conditions that education in the broad sense of the term – social adaptation – can, indeed, change within certain limits, but can never destroy ... For all these reasons our dependence on nature, however diminished from the times of prehistory onward, continues in our social life.[111]

And when his own 'spirit' – the very high level reached by his intellectual elaboration – had to face the wholly physical imminence of death, he would write to his friend Croce 'This letter has been interrupted by the attempt that I made to swallow cream, or cocoa, which I did not succeed in doing. As you see,

106 Labriola 1977, p. 207.
107 Timpanaro 1970, p. 16.
108 Labriola 1977, p. 233.
109 Labriola was aware of the *German Ideology*'s existence although it had not yet been published. See his letter to Engels, 21 February 1891, in Labriola 1983, Vol. II, p. 323, and Engels's 27 February 1891 letter to Labriola in *MECW*, Vol. 49, p. 136.
110 Labriola 1965, pp. 86, 88.
111 Labriola 1965, p. 148, also cited by Timpanaro.

there is something to be thankful for. A pity that your neoidealism cannot do anything against an obdurate matter'.[112]

This same letter, however, also displayed explicit traces of another, methodological materialism. He reproached Croce, whom he ironically (but not too much so) accused of presenting himself as an 'anti-development, anti-history, anti-evolution, anti-empirical, anti-genesis, anti-nineteenth-century [thinker] *par excellence*', of not doing science 'with anything empirically given', but instead limiting himself to a 'science of so-called pure concepts'. Three days later, in the last letter that he sent to his friend, he would again repeat that 'the *Spirit* that has nothing to do with *Nature* ... and with *History* ... must be a fine "Mamozio".[113] Send it to me as a gift for Epiphany Eve'.[114]

Materialism was thus very much inherent to the analytical models that Labriola had come to elaborate as distinctive moments of his own 'philosophy', of his own 'philosophy of history'. And in particular, 'since 1845' Marx's 'philosophy of praxis' had represented the centre in which the different levels of a conception of nature and history would have to converge – a conception no less materialist for its explicit rejection of any 'general law' of dialectical movement for nature, for history and for thought.

> ... historical materialism, the *philosophy of praxis*, insofar as it concerns the whole of historical and social mankind, as it puts an end to any form of idealism considering empirically existent things as the reflection, reproduction, imitation, consequence or likewise of a somehow presupposed thought, is thus the end of naturalistic materialism such as the word was traditionally understood until a few years ago. The intellectual revolution that has led to the processes of human history being considered absolutely objective appears at such a time as to correspond to the other intellectual revolution that has succeeded in *historicising* physical nature.[115]

If historical materialism was 'no longer the subjective critique applied to things, but the rediscovery of the *self-critique* that is in the things themselves',[116] the 'materiality' of the 'things' positioned on the 'artificial terrain' was just as dense

112 Letter to Croce, 2 January 1904, in Labriola 1983, Vol. II, p. 1003.

113 [An imaginary character in Pozzuoli folklore, based around a statue of the ancient-Roman counsel Mavorzio, unearthed in 1704 with the head missing.]

114 [Literally a gift of 'Befana', a mythical old woman who delivers presents on Epiphany Eve, 5 January – the date of this letter, in Labriola 1983, Vol. III, p. 1004.]

115 Labriola 1977, p. 208.

116 Labriola 1965, p. 118.

as that of the 'things' positioned on the 'natural terrain'. 'The miserable material thing that is economic exploitation' – the material ensemble represented by 'a harsh and powerful system of factual things: poverty organised in order to produce wealth' – was a 'thing' wholly irreducible to the activity of thought alone. The rejection of the two aspects of idealism – whether the 'metaphysical-subjective' or the 'metaphysical-objective'[117] – applied to the 'artificial' as well as the 'natural' terrain. Labriola also displayed his appreciation of the *Anti-Dühring* for having posed the problem of a common reading of these two 'terrains', independently of the provisional and questionable nature of the solutions provided.

Did a dialectic immanent to the two 'terrains' guarantee ways through them, and the possibility of understanding them? Or did the 'difficulties' of the dialectic necessitate further fine-tuning of one's analytical tools?[118]

In the *Anti-Dühring*, a work that Labriola 'use[d] continually',[119] and even more so in the *Dialectics of Nature* – a work that Labriola evidently could not have been familiar with – the 'difficulties' of the dialectic emerged particularly starkly.

Engels oscillated between two conceptions of the dialectic in the *Anti-Dühring*. The first consisted of reducing it to a method of thought: 'That which still survives, independently, of all earlier philosophy is the science of thought and its laws – formal logic and dialectics. Everything else is subsumed in the positive science of nature and history'.[120]

The second extended it, making it a general law of motion:

> An extremely general – and for this reason extremely far-reaching and important – law of development of nature, history, and thought; a law which ... holds good in the animal and plant kingdoms, in geology, in mathematics, in history and in philosophy ...[121]

Thus it was through the dialectical law of the negation of the negation, the law to which this passage referred, that the dialectic of thought was combined with the dialectic of reality; the 'artificial terrain' with the 'natural terrain'.

Notwithstanding Labriola's profound admiration for the *Anti-Dühring*, he would not develop his own elaboration of 'materialism' and the materialist

---

117 Havemann 1965, p. 26.

118 Letter to Karl Kautsky, 10 August 1897, in Labriola 1983, Vol. III, p. 797.

119 Letter to Engels, 13 June 1894, in Labriola 1983, vol. II, p. 492.

120 *MECW*, Vol. 25, p. 26.

121 *MECW*, Vol. 25, p. 131.

philosophy of *praxis* on the basis of this second conception. First of all, he suggested that when he highlighted the 'difficulties' of the dialectic itself he was referring precisely to the unresolved tension between the two formulations of the dialectic.

In his famous 13 June 1894 letter to Engels, we can identify not only the distinction we will later see between the 'dialectical conception' and the 'genetic conception' – which was not a merely 'verbal' distinction, but one of far from secondary importance, notwithstanding Labriola's deliberate use of understatement – but also a clear choice in favour of one of the conceptions of the dialectic that had been outlined in the *Anti-Dühring*.

Labriola only referred to one of Engels's two formulations, namely the dialectic as 'the form of thought that does not conceive things just as they are (as a factum, a fixed type, a category, etc.): and for this reason it must itself, as thought, be in ongoing movement'.[122] The dimension of the dialectic was, then, that which related to the *forms* of consciousness: that is, 'the formal consciousness of the act and the process of knowledge and thinking, in relation to experience and observation'. For this reason, the 'genetic conception' was neither a substitute for nor synonymous with the 'dialectical conception'; rather, as Labriola explained, it was 'more comprehensive'. Indeed, it 'embraced both the *real content* of things in becoming, and the formal-logical virtuosity of understanding them as being in becoming', whereas 'with the word dialectical only the *formal aspect* is represented'.[123]

The importance of the distinction that Labriola makes is even more evident when we consider that he would forever deny any *specular* relation between the (dialectical) way with which thought perceives real becoming, and the concrete logics of the becoming of things.

There is a passage of his *Discorrendo* ... that is of exemplary clarity in this regard. In *Capital* Marx had not used an all-embracing dialectical method; rather, 'It is the antithetical conditions of capitalist production, enunciated in formulas, that themselves *appear to the thinking mind as contradictions* ... These antitheses ... this vast system of economic contradictions ... are *concrete antinomies*'.[124]

The 'dialectical contradiction' thus pertained to 'the ways in which thought proceeds', and the 'concrete antinomy' to the real process of history. Not by chance, at the end of the century 'the greatest difficulty in understanding and

---

122 Letter to Engels, 13 June 1894, in Labriola 1983, vol. II, pp. 492–3. My italics.

123 Ibid.

124 Labriola 1977, pp. 185–6. My italics.

developing historical materialism [did] not lie in the mastery of the formal aspects of Marxism, but rather in grasping the things in which these forms are immanent'.[125]

These 'concrete antinomies' had the substance of the antithesis of 'rich and poor, those who live well and those who suffer, oppressors and oppressed' in a world where 'wealth has generated poverty ... [and] progress has generated regress'.[126]

Labriola's distinction between 'dialectical contradictions' – in forms of thought – and 'concrete antinomies' – the oppositions in reality – allowed him to emphasise the irreducibility of being to thought, and to do so within the terms of the analytical tools that he had employed. Likewise, it invoked the deep scientific materialism of the young philosophical Marx – officially not yet a materialist – who had also pointed to 'empirical singularity' and '*true* opposites'[127] as moments that could not be combined through any Hegelian *mediation*.

Counter to Benedetto Croce's claim, not even in liberal Italy would 'theoretical Marxism' 'die' at the end of the century. Indeed, Marxist theory was not limited to the philosophical dimension alone, but – as we will see in subsequent chapters – also engaged with Marx the economist, even if in a very problematic manner. The results of Croce's interest in Marx's economic categories would, conversely, end up taking the form of the elaboration of substantially philosophical categories.

Nor, however, did 'theoretical Marxism' on the philosophical plane run out of steam with the beginning of the new century. Rather, precisely in the period in which Croce proclaimed the death not only of Marxism (as having taken place ten years previously) but also of socialism, an operation of far from irrelevant theoretical significance was underway, indeed one aimed at the 'reconstruction' of Marxism as a 'philosophy of socialism'. This operation, of which Rodolfo Mondolfo was the leading figure, cannot just be considered the development of the theoretical framework that Antonio Labriola had elaborated over the course of the 1890s. The differences between the two figures, who were of different generations and different formation and operated in different political and cultural climates – and (why not) were also of different intellectual stature, notwithstanding the undoubtable significance of Mondolfo's 'philosophical' interpretation – were concretised precisely in the difference between the theoretical frameworks that they used.

---

125 Labriola 1977, p. 265.

126 Labriola 1902, pp. 27, 57.

127 *MECW*, Vol. 3, p. 83. Colletti 1974 particularly emphasised this type of 'real opposition'.

Up until a month before his death Labriola had reasserted his interpretation of Marxism as 'materialism' and continued his battle against an incipient 'neo-idealism'. Conversely, at the centre of Mondolfo's 'reconstruction' was the denial that Marxism was a materialism; and, together with this, something going far beyond the influence of neo-idealism, which was no longer only incipient.

> In his diligent re-elaboration of Marxist doctrine, Mondolfo arrives at a voluntarist philosophy, which *perhaps* does not correspond to the two founders of socialism's intention, but is certainly a perfectly logical and fitting construct, because it develops and connects the thought of two great thinkers effortlessly and without alterations. Mondolfo's superiority over the German neo-Kantian commentators consists precisely in the fact that he does not want to correct or complete or, still less, partly reject Marxist doctrine, but only to develop the fruitful elements that it entails but which, for various reasons, it did not know that it had, or did not want to develop ... Gentile, in his study on Karl Marx's philosophy – which the Neo-Kantians beyond the Alps wrongly ignore – brought to light the true finalistic meaning of Marxist praxis, in which the individual makes Society, which in turn reacts on the individual, making him social. Mondolfo has not only developed this concept, but demonstrated it with arguments taken from Marx and Engels's own writings. The importance of Mondolfo's exegesis also results from the fact that he does not separate socialism from Marxism, practice from theory; but rather, he puts the philosophy of praxis, which he has taken from the two communist thinkers' own works to the test in a fitting critique of political action, evaluating revolutionism, reformism, syndicalism and maximalism.[128]

A former student of Labriola's,[129] Antonio Poggi, a protagonist together with Mondolfo, Baratono, Basso and others in the early 1920s discussion on 'ethical

128 Poggi 1925, pp. 202, 205.

129 Poggi, who had been interested in ethical socialism since the beginning of the century, had asked Labriola for advice on a laureate thesis whose central thread was to be the *conciliation* of Marxism and ethics, and Labriola replied, 'I believe that the first of the theses that you suggest is preferable; but you ought to conceive it thusly: in terms of *the moral ideal in relation to historical materialism* (it is not a matter of *conciliating* them – as you say – but of considering two facts that really exist, in their relations with one another)'. Letter to Alfredo Poggi, 30 December 1902, in Labriola 1983, Vol. III, p. 980.

socialism', provided this image of Mondolfo's 'reconstruction' on the very eve of the definitive triumph of Fascism. Even in a context where the 'philosophy of socialism' was still a hot topic of political and cultural debate,[130] Poggi here aptly emphasised the fundamental elements of Mondolfo's 'reconstruction': namely, its voluntaristic idealism, the importance that it attributed to Gentile's analytical approach, and also its character as an 'integral' Marxism.

Was this, then, the influence of idealism? Without doubt yes, but this was certainly not a one-dimensional process. Moreover, already many years ago Garin warned against any simplistic use of numerous twentieth-century 'isms', pointing to the 'vital needs that were at the basis of both the "rebirth of idealism" and the "revisions of positivism"',[131] implying frequent osmoses that ultimately confuse any 'orders set in hierarchies'.[132] And more recent studies have demonstrated how in the first decade of the twentieth century the 'rebirth of idealism' co-existed with other currents of thinking, for some time in a minoritarian position with respect to these others: 'still in 1910 Croce and Gentile's neoidealism had not established itself as the hegemonic philosophy that it is widely believed to have been'.[133] Certainly, next to 'high' idealism, or rather Croce and Gentile's high idealisms, which were not the same thing, there was also a 'vulgar idealism' whose presence in the public press did not have the same logics as 'rigorous philosophy' did in the 'scientific world'. And when Mondolfo began his reflection on Marxism as the 'philosophy of socialism' not so much within the ambit of positivism, as within an atmosphere marked by the crisis of positivism, 'vulgar idealism' already gave the impression of having

---

130 I am here referring not only to the question of 'ethical socialism', but rather – and above all – to the use of Mondolfo's Marxist philosophy of socialism in analysing the new historical phase that had opened up with the Russian Revolution. Mondolfo very closely held together the reading of Marx that he had elaborated from 1909 to 1912 and his interpretation of the new phase. Faced with those who accused him of excessively wanting to follow 'in Marx's footsteps' [*Sulle orme di Marx*, the title of one of his main works], he replied, 'I had to … clear the terrain of the deformations of Marxist doctrine and restore its true line, in order then to be able to proceed to the dispassionate examination and direct critique of the present historical moment'. See his 'Risposte ai Critici', Preface to the second edition of *Sulle orme di Marx* (Mondolfo 1920, p. 9). Moreover, in the different editions of this book that he published between 1919 and 1923, he modulated his more decisively theoretical pre-WWI texts with his more immediately political-polemical postwar writings, also by way of certain textual changes. See the 1919 edition and the 1923 third edition, in two volumes: each published by Cappelli in Bologna.

131 See Garin 1966, Vol. I, p. 169.

132 Garin 1966, Vol. I, p. 184.

133 Di Giovanni 1996, p. 5.

achieved hegemony in the public press – including much of the socialist press – independently of the viscosity and set of interdependencies that continued to characterise academic circles. As Garin further notes,

> For Mondolfo the journey from Enlightenment thought to Marxism, from Hobbes to Engels, was not a peaceful stroll through the world of ideas under the guidance of Roberto Ardigò. It was a demand emerging from political struggles and the socialists' travails on the eve of the Italo-Turkish war that led him to engage in theoretically clarifying Feuerbach, Marx, Engels and Lassalle's positions – and he did so amidst the now shared atmosphere of the crisis of positivism, which was everywhere widespread …[134]

Certain aspects of this journey – at least insofar as it did pass through the 'world of ideas' – can provide us with useful pointers regarding the quality of Mondolfo's 'integral' Marxism. It was his reference point, the 'guide' Ardigò, who allowed him to 'integrate' idealism and positivism in a 'realism' serving as a response to the duplicity of knowledge; 'In consciousness, the "me" and the "outside of me" form an indivisible real whole. We can mentally distinguish the one side of a cloth from the other, but not separate them without destroying the cloth; and the same is also true of the "me" and the "outside of me" in consciousness'.[135] This was the Ardigò whom he particularly appreciated, already as he began his voyage within Marxism in 1908, for having 'got rid of the dualism of relative and absolute'. Likewise he considered it possible to 'integrate' natural law and Marxism by arguing that fundamentally 'the logical consequence of the principles that Locke establishes is common property over the means of production'[136] – independently of how well-founded such a reading of Locke really was.[137]

---

134 Garin 1983, p. 223.

135 Mondolfo 1991, p. 164.

136 Mondolfo 1991, p. 46.

137 Mondolfo conducted his analysis of Locke's concept of property with a view to proving the essay's fundamental assumption, of which this latter was a decisively important part: namely, that there was no 'antagonism' between the 'theoretical principles' at the basis of the French Revolution and of socialism, but rather a 'concatenation and historical continuity' (Mondolfo 1991, pp. 32–3). Since Locke's juridical-political philosophy constituted the 'theoretical preparation' for the 'Declaration of the Rights of Man', it was necessary to show that his philosophy logically led to 'property over the means of production, the social duty to secure the right to work for all, and the distribution of produce to each man

Mondolfo would use this 'integration' mechanism in the construction of his 'philosophy of socialism', which not by chance had a compact, systematic character[138] largely absent from Antonio Labriola's elaborations. Would Mondolfo's 'reconstruction' of Marxism not perhaps begin with the 'integration' into this process of the 'true' Feuerbach, taken away from materialism? And even if in the *Anti-Dühring* Engels had used 'the most absolute expressions of materialist monism',[139] could he truly be considered a materialist when in all his prior works he had only used a materialist 'terminology', and his opposition to 'speculative idealism' was specified by way of the 'philosophy of praxis' that was the negation of any materialist philosophy? And, most importantly, if the dialectic was also for Engels the 'form and condition of intelligibility of the real',[140] notwithstanding the *Anti-Dühring*'s indulgence of a 'dialectical materialism' tending to expunge philosophy from the ambit of the natural sciences, was this dialectic perhaps not itself the main antidote against any form of materialism?

---

according to his labours' (p. 46) – in a word, to demonstrate that Locke had laid the bases of communism, despite himself. This assertion of continuity demanded a significant 'correction' of Locke's theory, since in Mondolfo's view Locke had failed to introduce a distinction between the means of consumption and the means of production.

The analytical weakness of Mondolfo's interpretation is fully evident precisely on this point, since Locke had not in fact failed to note the distinction between *goods* (or means of consumption) and *resources* (or means of production): between 'the fruits [the earth] naturally produces and animals that it feeds' and 'the earth and *everything in it*' (*Second Treatise*, §26, my italics). This notwithstanding, the philosopher moved to justify the enclosures, which were real historical processes of land appropriation that endangered the freedom of appropriation that was formally recognised for each man; so what Mondolfo considered a contradiction was in fact Locke's very *problem* – to demonstrate the compatibility of the capitalist form of appropriation with the inalienable natural rights of each economic subject.

Mondolfo seems not to have grasped the complexity of Locke's notion of labour: certainly it was the juridical title of legitimate appropriation, but it was also a fundamental factor of production: 'the property of labour should be able to outweigh the community of land' (*Second Treatise*, §40; Haslett [ed.] 1970, p. 314; my italics.) – that is, of the land that was still available for appropriation. In other words, what was decisive to Locke's perspective was the creation of the conditions for a full deployment of each man's labour: which, unlike the earth, was an unlimited resource able to procure the 'necessaries and conveniences' of life to whoever pursued – as one must – the divine imperative of self-preservation. See Farina 1996.

138 Mondolfo would explicitly characterise historical materialism as a 'system'. See Mondolfo 1952, p. 9.

139 Mondolfo 1952, p. 206.

140 Mondolfo 1952, p. 400.

Here, 'integration' was an element of 'systematic construction', and the 'dialectic' the negation of 'materialism': and these elements would characterise a philosophical project seeking to give answers to the problems posed by a certain cycle of the history of socialism as it related to Italian society and culture.

It is certainly true that the period running from 1908 to 1912, in which Mondolfo elaborated the central core of his own Marxist readings, cannot be considered wholly homogenous. It saw a turn from the prospect of growth (in 1908) to the prospect of crisis (1911); and this at least in part explains Mondolfo's oscillation between a theory of socialism based on 'socio-economic analysis and historical-empirical analysis' and reflection based on a 'purely philosophical consciousness', with this latter ultimately prevailing.[141] However, there was also an element of 'homogeneity' that also transcended the period in question, and which allows us better to understand Rodolfo Mondolfo's project and its realisation. When he contributed to *Critica Sociale* in 1908, after the Florence Congress had confirmed the reformists' hegemony over the party, he was intervening in order to dispel the 'end of Marxism' that was now not only being evoked in the *Corriere della Sera* but also – and most importantly – *tacitly* accepted among many reformist circles.[142] We will take a closer look at the relations between reformism and the theoretical dimension in the next chapter. But there remains the fact that toward the end of the first decade of the twentieth century, some theory of reformist inspiration was developing elements extraneous to Marxism, and the founding fathers of reformism appeared to be struck by indifference toward this. So when three years later Mondolfo found himself directly involved in a debate with 'vulgar idealism', in a climate in which the death of both Marxism and socialism was being proclaimed, this was not a matter of confronting a new cultural atmosphere, but a kind of idealism and anti-Marxism that had already been circulating in the columns of *Critica Sociale* for some time.

Conversely, the revolutionary syndicalists particularly busied themselves with Marx and his theory; and in Mondolfo's pages there was a constant engagement with the books of both Arturo Labriola and Enrico Leone. Norberto Bobbio was thus quite right to argue that 'for Mondolfo the study of Marx and Engels's theoretical thinking was a way of settling accounts with revisionism, in both of its dimensions', and that 'from the theoretical point of view, Mon-

141 Zanardo 1979, pp. 185, 193.

142 Mondolfo 1968, pp. 5–7.

dolfo does not belong to the history of revisionism'.[143] Perhaps Mondolfo's philosophy would be better defined as the 'philosophy of reformism';[144] but precisely the 'integral' Marxism mentioned above, which was so characteristic of his 'philosophy of socialism', also makes this definition rather problematic.

Mondolfo saw socialism as lacking 'a theoretical soul ... a theoretical directive', and it thus 'needed a philosophical orientation'.[145] He made this clear programmatic statement in 1911, but there is little doubt that this framework also stood at the basis of his first important study 'reconstructing' a Marxist 'philosophical' orientation: namely, his 1909 essay on Feuerbach. This 'philosophical orientation' had to be 'reconstructed' in 'the mentality of both the reformists and the revolutionaries'; a mentality 'formed within what was for many years called *scientific socialism* ...'. In considering 'theory to have been transcended in practice [the reformists] had renounced ever settling accounts with philosophy', whereas the revolutionaries had never truly reflected on the 'voluntaristic philosophy'[146] from which they nonetheless claimed to draw inspiration. But

> no tendency, old or new, emerging in the socialist party, can ever neglect the primary need first felt by Marx and Engels: the need to settle accounts with philosophy. Until the voluntarism of praxis is substituted for materialist philosophy, historical realism will be interpreted upside down, with dead and inert things put in the place of living, operative men; the class will be fragmented, due to the lack of understanding of psychological reality; and there will be no recognition of fact that social activity depends on the attitude of consciousnesses and wills, and that the *social environment* is itself made up of men and not objects.[147]

Mondolfo's methodological 'integralism' also responded to the need to reposition the 'traditional' tendencies, faced with the new demand for a theory that could inform philosophy for *all* socialism.

Even if 'rigorous idealism' could still not be considered hegemonic – in particular in the university world – when Mondolfo began his philosophical reflection on Marxism, his 'reconstruction' would nonetheless take place in

143 See Bobbio's introduction to Mondolfo 1968, pp. xxx, xxxii.
144 Marramao 1971, p. 213.
145 Mondolfo 1968, p. 80.
146 Mondolfo 1968, p. 120.
147 Mondolfo 1968, p. 127.

the climate of the tumultuous development of 'vulgar idealism', the gradual, programmatic definition of a 'militant idealism' of a Gentilian imprint,[148] and the 'detachment of intellectual youth'[149] from socialism and its culture. His 'reconstruction' was proposed as a positive response to these tendencies that were now underway.

Mondolfo would delineate the analytical structure of the 'philosophy of socialism' in the brief arc of time between 1909 and 1912, bounded by his most significant theoretical works: his essays on Feuerbach and on Engels. The fundamental lineaments of this analytical structure were evidently conceived 'as a whole', with his entire construction characterised by an extreme internal coherence.

The first element of the work of 'integration' that Mondolfo outlined would be that of recovering Feuerbach, given a place within the analytical chain of the philosophy of praxis. Indeed, for Mondolfo it was precisely Marx's *Theses on Feuerbach*, written in opposition to Feuerbach's presumed naturalist materialism, that had demonstrated that 'the theories of the true Feuerbach, though in certain points far from achieving the precision and concatenation of those so vigorously sketched out by Marx in these brief notes of his, in large part presaged them, showing a close affinity [with them]'.[150] Certainly, Marx had written these notes with a quite different intent; but it was well-known that when he 'and Engels wanted to differentiate their doctrines from others', they 'used the hatchet more than the chisel'. In substance, however, their opposition to Feuerbach was 'but a dialectical opposition, transcending and also containing within itself the moment that it negates'.[151] For Mondolfo, indeed, if we look at the deeper aspects of the philosophy of praxis – with the dialectic first among them – then both Marx and Feuerbach's common Hegelian inheritance – beyond their 'frequent expressions of … [their] rejection of it'[152] – shows evident signs of *continuity*. The Feuerbachian 'need-of-life', the foundation of an existence with a sense of itself, was the fundamental principle capable of opening up a dialectically oriented process of activity. Need and consciousness of need became principles of dialectical activity, when it was asked 'what consciousness of need could come from, if not from the consciousness of an opposition or a limit to our being?'[153] Could this principle of

148 The expression is taken from Di Giovanni 1996, p. 52.
149 Santarelli 1977, p. 173.
150 Mondolfo 1968, p. 13.
151 Mondolfo 1952, p. 101.
152 Mondolfo 1968, p. 56.
153 Mondolfo 1968, p. 37.

'dialectical identity' – of need-consciousness of need, 'corresponding, in the dynamic value that it is ascribed, to the dialectical identity of the rational and the real as posed by Hegel'[154] – be considered a moment of a naturalist-materialist philosophy? Certainly not. It was rather more a matter of a 'real humanism', which Marx completed by providing it with a sociological and historical dimension, missing in Feuerbach.[155] Feuerbach did not, then, deserve to be 'considered a materialist'; rather, he was 'the founder of the voluntarism of praxis'.[156]

In support of this argument, Mondolfo produced an analytical framework of Gentilian inspiration, which, as Eugenio Garin rightly notes, preserved a striking 'overall symmetry' with that of Gentile's *La filosofia di Marx*.[157] From Gentile's reading of the *Theses on Feuerbach* Mondolfo also adopted the mistaken translation of *umwälzende Praxis*. This error so well served a construct whose keystone was, indeed, the 'praxis that is transformed', that even having recognised the mistake, Mondolfo considered it a *felix culpa*, better corresponding to the spirit of a Marxian interpretation.[158]

The second element of his 'integration' effort concerned Friedrich Engels. Mondolfo would produce what could be considered one of the first critiques of Engels's dialectical materialism in Europe, and he would do so at the very same time as he recuperated Engels himself into a voluntaristic philosophy of praxis.

The Engels of the *Anti-Dühring*, or of part of the *Anti-Dühring*, had differentiated himself from Marx 'both in terms of [their] conception of the universe, a problem to which Engels presents *dialectical materialism* as the solution, and

154 Ibid.

155 How could history be grasped and understood in all its fullness? 'Feuerbach was almost completely unaware of this; he sometimes alludes to it, with fleeting references ... but could not explain it, because it transcends the limits of his framework, [since] man's combat with nature is essentially the only [aspect] of history that enters into it. And thus it was here that Marx made the immensely important next step; namely, that as he and Engels saw, the step from naturalism to historicism could be considered in this aspect. In substance, he transported Feuerbach's essential view of humanism onto the terrain of history, developing and organically drawing out the consequences of the concept – already stated by Feuerbach – that human activity ought to be sought not in the abstract individual but in social man, in his associated collectivity'. Mondolfo 1968, p. 59.

156 Mondolfo 1968, p. 83.

157 Garin 1983, p. 225.

158 '[T]ranslating the expression *umwälzende Praxis* as "praxis that is transformed" does not alter the genuine Marxist concept but, instead, expresses it more fully, also including its essential element – no mere detail – of *Selbstveränderung*'. He wrote this, even while admitting that this expression was 'grammatically incorrect'. Mondolfo 1952, p. 403.

Marx the *philosophy of praxis*; and, in part, also as regards the conception of history itself, which is also meant to reconnect to a general philosophy: so much so that where Marx once used the expression "realistic conception of history", Engels instead introduced the name – which would then endure – "historical materialism"'.[159] 'The dialectical method has become one proper to natural science, and, as a method of scientific truth, it tends to eliminate [the method] of philosophy'.[160] Sometimes, Engels even seemed to let himself slide toward conceptions that considered thought and consciousness products of a 'material organ'.[161] Despite this, for Mondolfo not even the *Anti-Dühring* could be considered a 'materialist' work. Often its materialism was only 'terminological'. For example, in many passages Engels seemed to indulge a purely 'economic' conception of the social process. But when he came to look at the real components of the part of the economy standing at the basis of social change, then concrete men – the class – did appear. And 'as Engels tells us, the class exists as a historical reality, as an active and effective force, only when it has achieved consciousness of the need to struggle against the real circumstances, in its will to rebel against subjection'.[162] Was this not, perhaps, the *umwälzende Praxis* based on human action stimulated by need? What *praxis* was it? 'For Marx, thought is *praxis* and *praxis* is his object; that is to say, both these terms appear in praxis, and it is thus in praxis that *thought and reality coincide*'.[163]

This was certainly not, then, Gentile's 'auto-praxis', a praxis that was completely *thought*, but it certainly was a praxis leaving little space to the autonomy of the real. Moreover, although Mondolfo did often seek elements of consensus with Labriola's positions – agreements which, as we have seen, were rather weakly founded – in this case he counterposed the 'transformation of praxis' to the '*self-critique of things*, of which Antonio Labriola himself has spoken'.[164]

A praxism that nonetheless remained *wholly philosophical* could steal a march on both the 'vulgar idealist' – or 'absolute idealist' – and the 'metaphys-

159 Mondolfo 1952, p. ix. And moreover: 'Engels, above all on the basis of natural philosophy, tends – often, moreover, in verbal expression more than in the reality of thought – rather more toward materialism, where Marx, starting from the critique of knowledge, arrives at a philosophy of praxis, which would be very ill-defined as "materialist", if we want to preserve words' proper meaning': Mondolfo 1952, pp. 3–4.

160 Mondolfo 1952, p. 17.

161 Mondolfo 1952, p. 37.

162 Mondolfo 1952, p. 257.

163 Mondolfo 1952, p. 5. My italics.

164 Mondolfo 1952, p. 388.

ical determinist' young socialist intellectuals. But at the same time, this left wholly unresolved the problem of the relation between Marxism and scientific knowledge: a question to which Labriola had devoted a very great part of his own reflection. And it was also the problem of the *Anti-Dühring*, notwithstanding its 'dialectical materialism'.

CHAPTER 5

Marxism and Reformism

1 What were the Theoretical Roots of Reformism? The Tangled Web of 'Catastrophism'[1]

The two terms that appear in the title of this chapter, *Marxism* and *reformism*, have the singular characteristic of having long lost their specificity in what they denote, and yet also of being used as almost universal categories, as if to designate unambiguous contents whose meaning is generally taken for granted. And the qualities of reformism (reasonableness, pragmatism, gradualism), as counterposed to the corresponding lack of such qualities in Marxism (dogmatism, abstractness, revolutionism) are thus fixed in a spatial-temporal dimension in which they always appear the same.

Generally, the journalistic-political field has been the privileged terrain for this semantic slippage. But given its weak scientific status, and the inevitable strains coming from themes still running very hot on the political terrain, a far from virtuous circle arises between these political expressions and the institutional spheres meant to be responsible for cool analysis.

There are two particular elements that characterise the ways in which this circle tends to be activated: the embryonic-genetic approach, and the absolute counterposition of the terms in question.

1 The 'catastrophism' dealt with in this part of the chapter concerns the conceptual whole made to derive (or not) from Marx's *economic* categories. As well as this way of considering catastrophism, a not-necessarily-connected and wholly *political* conception also had a wide circulation, in particular in the Giolittian era. In this latter case 'catastrophism' did not consist of the natural result of a process of 'gradual immiseration', but of the *violent contractions* of the passage from the old society to the new one, a passage that would not be without pain. A revolutionary socialist at the beginning of the century, later a revolutionary syndicalist, accused the reformists of 'especially' fighting 'Marx's theory of catastrophe, that is, the revolutionary conception of socialism' but presented the 'catastrophe' as the final point of a long period of growth in proletarians' living conditions. 'For years and years we have expressed and repeated in all kinds of tones the idea that socialism must be expected to follow from living conditions superior to the current ones, to be created by the evolution of capitalism on the one hand and proletarian resistance on the other ... The triumph of socialism is subordinate to the technical development of the instruments of labour and the economic and moral improvement of the proletariat'; Allevi 1901, pp. 29–30, 38–9.

The embryonic-genetic type vision presupposes the existence of an embryonic Marxism in which the signs of its future development were already present, and indeed dominant. Its whole experience can thus be seen both at the beginning – in the embryo in which the signs of the end are supposedly already evident – and in the results that ultimately make these same signs more intelligible. Like Macbeth's witches, the upholders of the genetic approach think that they can 'look into the seeds of time/And say which grain will grow and which will not'.

However, the signs present in the first growth phases are very numerous. The different development of each of these signs is determined by a complex set of combinations, realised through the course of the general process of history. Each of these phases demands a specific analysis of its own, and, moreover, the phases that come afterward in chronological terms should not necessarily be considered the development of those that went before.

If, instead, looking at Marxism's relations with reformism, we privilege a reading in which the end is already inscribed in the beginning, yet the old signs of a gradual necrosis are only clear from the end, it would be natural to privilege the periods in which these characteristics tended to be more extreme, and thus simplified. Hence we will get a proof that 'Marxism' and 'reformism' are, and always have been, opposed and irreconcilable.

In truth, this latter consideration seems to find greater support in works of philosophy and political science, seeing that in general it is expressed through the use of a modelling system characterised by the 'paradigm'. However, certain historiographical efforts to revisit the question have also been influenced by this consideration.

This interpretative slant partly found justification in Marxist literature's propensity – and not only at the turn of the twentieth century – to propose a link between the theorisation of capitalism and prediction of the future. We can see large traces of this – even if the question is turned on its head – in today's debate on the 'death of Marxism'. This attitude certainly is rooted in the ground prepared by Marx himself, given that he considered it a scientific task to delineate processes that could – and must – become a point of reference for socialism and the workers' movement. Here, we are certainly not talking about *Capital*'s analytical core itself. But given the complex combination of science, political passion, ethical tension[2] and, as has been said, also of 'cynicism', 'utopi-

2 Croce's observation in this regard seems very much relevant still today: 'do we want to completely ignore the part that moral idealism played in Marx and Engels's thought, in homage to their rejection of moral values? I think this is another case in which we have to distinguish between apparent thought and real thought': Croce 1961, p. 172.

anism' and 'realism'[3] that Marx's overall theoretical construction represented, the currents resulting from it could hardly avoid a projection into the political sphere, whether in the long or short term. So we need to find different ways of addressing this problem. On the terrain of a 'history of analysis', the levels of Marx's approach can be rigorously distinguished from one another, and considered separately. In this logical field, the quality of a theory of capitalism is not put into question by the practical effectuation of its author's hypotheses (or hopes) regarding the collapse of capitalism and/or its transformation into a superior civilisation. Marx's extended model of reproduction and its tried and tested use in theories of crisis did not fall together with the Berlin Wall. As Joan Robinson aptly notes, 'Marx's analysis of capitalism shows its strong points, although his purpose was to attack it. Marshall's argument inadvertently shows the wastefulness of capitalism, although he meant to recommend it'.[4]

At the level of the 'history of culture', conversely, the validity of its analytical paradigms ceases to be a value in itself, finds itself inserted within a thick web of different meanings, and becomes the resultant of a complex field of forces. In this sense, Marx's extended schemas of reproduction could, indeed, fall with the Berlin Wall.

In a perspective with a programme of avoiding the reductionism of constructing processes in linear fashion *a posteriori*, it is also necessary to distinguish 'reformism' from 'revisionism' as elements of the history of European socialism. Nonetheless, the *Bernstein-Debatte* certainly was the site in which the mechanisms that doubtless did relate 'reformism' and 'revisionism' acquired particular relevance and meaning. The Italian discussion on the point of arrival of Bernstein's late nineteenth-century reflection was, however, wholly particular in character. From the viewpoint of 'theoretical Marxism' the voice of Kautsky's antagonist was one of the elements – but certainly not the main one – of a revisionist climate that had its highest reference points in Antonio Labriola, Benedetto Croce, and Giovanni Gentile in the philosophical dimension, and Vilfredo Pareto and Maffeo Pantaleoni in the economic one.

From the viewpoint of political interpretation, ideas of Bernsteinian inspiration had very few epigones within the context of Italian socialism, and were very widely repudiated. However, reformism was far from a marginal phenom-

---

3 'Cynicism led them never to ask history for remorse, utopianism allowed them to hold that it was possible to direct the future, and realism allowed them to hold that it was possible to direct the future *if* the class responsible for Utopia had, indeed, proven able, or could ... draw the Absolute down into the Relative, and make Utopia a programme of practical-intellectual realisation': Macchioro 1991, p. 169.

4 Robinson 1978, p. 71.

enon in the early twentieth century. Hence the tendency to define this experience as a 'practical revisionism', a reading common among attentive observers and scholars like Robert Michels as well as leading political figures like Ivanoe Bonomi or even Filippo Turati, albeit in particular circumstances.

In truth, Italian reformism had such depth and such valences that an expression like 'practical revisionism' is inadequate to defining it. The fact that Bernstein got little hearing in Italian socialism at the end of the century does not exclusively owe to a contingent political factor like the need for 'absolute opposition'; in any case, the characteristics of this 'absolute opposition', during the key moment in which socialism's Marxist identity was established, did not develop in exactly the same way in Italy as in Germany.

Kautsky certainly hit the nail on the head when he argued that the forced separation between socialism and the rest of German society had proven an exceptionally positive context for its full assumption of a 'scientific' core (Marxism) capable of orienting not only strategy, but also political tactics.

Like the SPD leadership group in general, Bernstein did not at all stand apart from this Kautskyan vision of the relation between theory and politics, according to which Marx had not so much constructed a theory of capitalism as provided the tools for identifying the stages of – and thus for building – the path through capitalism to the establishment of socialism. Hence the proposition of a relation between theory and the effective unfolding of history that lacked almost any mediation: they were a bloc in which one part changing *necessarily* and *directly* produced a corresponding change in the other part.

This genuinely *foundational* mechanism concerned not only the history of the Marxist SPD, but was also evidently a peculiar characteristic of the whole history of socialism across all its components, far beyond the Second International itself. The atmosphere of the Third International encouraged its use in a both tragic and caricatured fashion. Even an intellectual-politician as attentive to distinctions as Togliatti could believe that the victories of Joseph Stalin provided a conformation of Marxism. Not by chance, also in this case history and ideology seemed to concord in determining a state of 'total counterposition'.

In the last two decades of the nineteenth century – the crucial period for the formation of Italian socialism's Marxist identity – there was no 'forced separation' with society as a whole, whatever the numerous elements of 'total counterposition'. Filippo Turati was himself certainly an intransigent proponent of socialism's complete 'political' separation with respect to all the 'other' organisations. But it was very difficult indeed to bring out such a sharp demarcation line with regard to 'other' cultures, particularly in the university milieu.

This meant that (together with its many, persistent scholastic 'contaminations') socialist culture developed also by way of a continual engagement-contamination with scientific production of the highest level, actively inserted into the conjuncture of the European debate. Thus it was rather difficult to establish a self-sufficient *theoretical* bloc that could assert an *orthodoxy* of its own. At the point that the *Bernstein-Debatte* also came to take hold of Italian socialism, the theoretical aspects of the 'revision' were already being widely discussed within and outside of socialist culture, with evident areas of osmosis, and the various possible theoretical choices were not held to imply immediate political decisions. In fact, the practice that we can see here gave the theoretical sphere a far from secondary form of autonomy.

Was it really possible to elaborate a theory of reformism closely corresponding to the 'general theory', the economic theory in its macroeconomic dimension, and the plenitude of socio-economics? And did reformism display any particularities, on this terrain?

In a weighty volume written during a high point of the reformist experience, it was, paradoxically, the eclectic Lorian Arturo Labriola – now on the margins of the revolutionary syndicalist tendency – who re-proposed the fundamental questions of 'socialist' political economy by way of a historical analysis of the capitalist mode of production. In substance, these questions all revolved around the relation between the supposedly 'natural' unfolding of 'economic laws' and the reality of determinate social relations. Labriola's work was a latest attempt to mediate the connections between the theories of the time and the processes that were then underway, and to read the *raisons d'être* and the tasks of the socialist movement within an extremely general dynamic. Its horizons included both the development of capitalism and the mechanics of its transcendence.[5]

Within the socialist universe of the first decade of the new century, this type of approach to economic questions seems to have been a particularity almost wholly exclusive to certain among the revolutionary syndicalists. Certainly, their responses were in large part inadequate to the ambitions that they had set for their projects; yet even so, they did seek to place themselves within the economic dimension that the classics of socialism had indicated.

In the same period, reformism's economic culture was oriented according to wholly different guidelines. The great investigations, the methodological alternatives and microanalyses now seem to have been relegated into an ever more distant background. It is almost as if the end-of-the-century discussion on the 'crisis of Marxism' should be considered a decisive point of arrival, a finish line beyond which the tangled knots of Marx's theory were definitively

5 Labriola 1910.

unravelled and the unsolvable ones simply cut loose. That is to say, this was a point of departure for a reformism completely free of hindrances, and free to apply itself, without theoretical complexes, in explicating the whole array of practical possibilities. Applied economics, the reduction of 'science' to an 'art', seemed the most appropriate field for the socialist economists directly engaged in the political strategy of 'great reforms'.

Gaetano Salvemini had already clearly understood this aspect of reformist publications, which he related to its entire theoretical production, and not only that of an economic character

> The species of intellectual aridness that seems to have struck the Socialist Party, the difficulties that *Critica Sociale* is experiencing as it tries to remain as varied and rich in its ideas as it once was, derive from this fact: almost the whole group of writers that gathered around Turati between 1892 and 1901, guided by him, and which made his review such a fervid and lively centre of culture, has now broken up. Each has given up on theory and set to work, and no longer has any time to study whether evolution rules out revolution, whether Karl Marx was a Marxist, and whether the Darwin-Marx-Spencer-Ferri and co. operetta company is still playing. *Critica Sociale* could not remain a review of ideas, in the good sense, but sometimes also in the bad sense, and it had to become a review of facts, in the sense that facts are the actuation of ideas, and the elements of new ideas can only come from new facts.[6]

This evaluation was ungenerous toward the Southern intellectuals accused of being left the only ones still producing ideas – in that they now had nothing to do. Yet it does accurately give account of the truly exceptional effort that reformist culture was making to study the complex set of *new* tasks that the *new* political climate – and the choices that had been made – posed to those who identified with this long-term political-cultural operation.

Certainly, the internal, more properly analytical logics of this mass transition from 'science' to 'art' are far from obvious, and in many cases we would have good reason to doubt that these categories could be used in the way Francesco Ferrara thought they could – that is, in a manner not implying any sharp separation between these different spheres.

Was there, perhaps, a caesura between the 1890s theoretical writings of Montemartini, the brilliant theorist, in the field of pure economics, of savings and

6 Tre Stelle (Salvemini), 'Spettri e realtà. La malattia del partito', *Critica Sociale*, 1907, p. 68.

marginal productivities, and his activity as director of the new and important institution that was the *Ufficio del lavoro*? Between the rigour of the scholar delineating the laws of the *economic*, and the political *impresario* wrapped up in the twists and turns of social legislation and microeconomics? Or is it possible to identify threads that somehow tie the two moments together?

The debate exploding in 1901–2 on the criteria for the socialist *comuni*'s balance-sheets and municipal initiatives was, perhaps, a singular attempt to inform concrete political-administrative activity in a manner immediately coherent with the economic theory that socialist culture had elaborated. Thus 'pure finance' and the 'political *impresario*' Montemartini; Enrico Leone's 'harmonic balance-sheet' embodying the 'maximum collective hedonistic interest'; Arturo Labriola's wholly Lorian caution in applying 'the canons of Marxian categories' to municipal balance-sheets; and finally Luigi Negri's use of the 'North Star' of Marx's categories of 'value' and 'production prices', directly corresponded to everything that these individual authors had elaborated in the final moment of the nineteenth century.

Besides that, the difficulties in identifying such immediate correspondences did not only concern the spheres of 'theoretical' and 'applied' economics. They also regarded the question of what links did or did not exist between (i) the positions that had clashed in the 'crisis of Marxism' discussion on the definition of an 'orthodoxy' (which, as we have seen, could not be found on the theoretical terrain) and a 'revisionism', and (ii) the identification with one or another of the tendencies into which socialism would divide at the dawn of the new century. In short, a stance taken within the 'crisis' of Marxism did not determine one's allegiance to 'reformism' or 'revolutionism'. This was also because the delineation of a 'Left' and a 'Right' – seeking to distinguish the various currents within 'revisionism' – is more an *a posteriori* characterisation deduced from the political outcome, rather than an analytical key appropriate to distinguishing among different theoretical trends.

In upholding the need to identify a set of (often non-linear) mediations between the site of theoretical elaboration and that of political choices, we are certainly not denying that some such relation does, indeed, exist. But for a more precise determination of this question, we need specific analyses and not generalising ones. To limit ourselves to accepting this or that protagonist's claimed motivations of a theoretical order can even mean completely collapsing theory into ideology. And that is not our approach.

The end-of-the-century discussion on Marxist 'catastrophism' was particularly telling, in this regard. Another commonplace – both historiographical and otherwise – holds that there was a direct relation between critique, the rejection of Marxist 'catastrophism', reformism, and the latent or explicit abandonment of Marxism. Not only does such a linear view lack a basis in the real development of Italian Marxist culture, but we even find different political conclusions being drawn from shared positions on 'catastrophism'.

Themes concerning the 'collapse' of capitalism were addressed in late-nineteenth-century Italy following two different currents of analysis. One of them was wholly internal to the theoretical dimension, while the other, though starting out from theoretical nodes, could more directly be translated into political choices. The former directly addressed a chapter of Marx's analysis – the tendency of the rate of profit to fall – while the second played out within the themes of the wage question and the possibility of improving the workers' conditions within the context of capitalism.

It was Benedetto Croce's intellectual and organisational initiative that led to a series of specific contributions on the fourteenth chapter of *Capital* Volume III. He proposed to the Accademia Pontaniana that the subject of entries to the Premio Tenore contest should be the 'Critical exposition of the economic theories contained in the third volume of Karl Marx's *Capital*' – a volume whose third section was, indeed, dedicated to the tendency of the rate of profit to fall. In this same period, Croce published his critique pinning down the method and results of Marx's exposition of this law.[7]

Croce's reading of what appeared to Marx as 'the synthesis of the capitalist mode of production's contradictions'[8] now resounded of the concluding phase of what had clearly been, all things considered, a 'transition'. Croce did maintain that his examination was conducted 'on the self-same basis as Marx's doctrine',[9] but in reality the mechanisms of his argumentation reflected only partial aspects of Marx's analytical framework, and sometimes in an only formal manner.

The 'countertendencies' to this long-term 'tendency' of the rate of profit to fall are so significant to Marx's overall theory as to raise doubts that it could be considered 'catastrophist'. Investment in technology, in constant capital, tended to push down the rate of profit by increasing the organic composition of capital, but in increasing the rate of surplus-value it tended to raise it. Naturally, Marx thought that this second tendency was destined to prevail, but the development of 'antagonistic causes' in an overall system of 'intrinsic contradictions of this law' – the very possibility of other 'countertendencies' that were not yet visible – ultimately gave this theoretical whole an open dimension.

7 In Croce 1961, pp. 151–64.

8 Potier 1986, p. 172.

9 Croce 1961, p. 151.

Croce, instead, overlooked these fundamental aspects of the theoretical whole in order to concentrate exclusively on a particular case of technical progress.

Even if Croce's analysis was thus incapable of really getting to grips with Marx's theory of capitalism, all the same it allowed a more attentive consideration of the relation between investment in technology and the costs of production. The other contributors, intervening upon Croce's initiative, were not, however, operating at the same level.

The winner of the Premio Tenore, Vincenzo Giuffrida, did not go beyond settling for discerning the link that existed between the irregularities of the *trend* for the rate of profit to fall and the periodic crises of falling demand.[10] Apart from this, Giuffrida's book can be considered a work of scholastic exposition, whose critical part was there only to satisfy the conditions of the contest question.

As for the other competitors, Arturo Labriola only fleetingly addressed the theme of the tendency for the rate of profit to fall. His book,[11] as we will see better in the next chapter, was rather more concerned with the relation between Marx's analytical categories and pure economics.

This type of discussion was thus unable to produce any important contributions to a theory of reformism constructed on the basis of the critique of 'catastrophism'.

The discussion on wages was a rather different matter, getting to the heart of the reasons for 'absolute opposition'. It is a fact that on the eve of the crisis of Marxism, the prevalent view in socialist culture was that there was a Marxist theory of wages so similar to Lassalle's 'iron law of wages' that they were practically indistinguishable. But at the same time, there was an ever-spreading awareness that real wage phenomena were gradually diverging from such a prognosis. Antonio Graziadei's book *La produzione capitalistica*, which simultaneously dealt with the critical themes of Marx's theory of value and the tendency of real wages to increase, necessarily took on particular significance in this context. Graziadei's theoretical reflection on political economy – from which he would derive the *vie maestre* of his reformism – was wholly contained within the brief arc of time between his first interventions in the 1894 discussion on the labour theory of value, and his 1901 polemic on wages with Luigi Negro. The socialist scholar's return to the great themes of economics, with partial but significant changes with respect to his youthful elaborations, would have to wait for the great postwar crisis and the consequent changes also in his

10 Giuffrida 1899, pp. 111–12.

11 Labriola 1899.

political perspective. This did not mean that from the turn of the century up till the First World War Graziadei's output lacked any specifically theoretical reflection; rather, his ambition was to elaborate a rigorous economic theory *of* and *for* the workers' movement, a foundational theory of reformism. However, while on the one hand its purpose and emphases were eminently practical, on the other hand the structuring elements of his theory – at least as concerns our study's perspective – had reached maturation already by the end of the 1890s.[12]

The features of Graziadei's early formation were the object of studies in the late 1960s. Yet this did not provide the disaggregated vision able to give particular account of certain aspects essential to understanding the young economics professor's role in his long period apparently devoid of theory, covering almost all of the pre-war liberal period. Such disaggregation would also have allowed an analysis of the different moments in Graziadei, some of which were particularly linked to the time of their elaboration and their short-term results, while others instead had a long-term content and a long-term projection.

The 1894–5 discussion on the labour theory of value, a discussion in which Graziadei also took part, had a very much 'internal' character: it was a debate among specialists, notwithstanding the modest capacities of many of the participants. The damage to the 'Marxist party's' ideological edifice was thus reduced to a minimum. If both Filippo Turati and Antonio Labriola expressed concerns in this regard (with different tones, different concerns, and, at this moment, from decidedly different shores), the political climate in Italy – which still forced the party into the 'unity of the besieged fortress' – contributed to organisers' and militants' sense of extraneousness from a theoretical question that was above all known for its abstract characteristics.

Very different to this was the political and cultural context into which *La produzione capitalistica* entered at the end of the century. This also owed to the fact that this book itself identified and sought out relations with existing cultural and organisational reference points, attempting an aggregation among

12 As concerns his more general reflection, it was, indeed, from late 1899 to the early 1900s that he began his approach toward pure economics. He announced as much in a letter to Einaudi: 'I have set myself reading the Austrians. I am buried in Pareto, whom I like a lot'. Graziadei to Einaudi, Bari, 14 January 1900, Archivio della Fondazione Einaudi, Carte Graziadei. The first results of this would be concretised in the essays cited in Chapter Three.

Moreover, in another study of these same years that long busied Graziadei, we can see a partial re-evaluation of Marxist crisis theories in line with the widespread underconsumptionist literature. See Graziadei 1909.

all those forces interested in a socialist 'new course'. As such, a much more direct relation between theory and politics came to be established than had been present in the 1894–5 debate. If Graziadei's interventions in that period had presented a theory of surplus value independent of value – such as to make it a self-governing, autonomous element of theory in itself – four years later it would become a foundational structure of a productivist and un-conflictual theory of the workers' movement. These outcomes were not necessarily to be taken for granted, and indeed Graziadei the communist would seek to separate the two moments. Yet at the turn of the century, they could only have been of considerable political impact if they were considered as an organic whole.

The book was put together within the atmosphere of the so-called 'laboratory of political economy' founded and directed by the 'integral positivist'[13] Cognetti de Martiis. This is worth noting not so much in order to emphasise any supposed direct interference by Cognetti and Loria – as according to Antonio Labriola's wholly unjust claims[14] – as to bring into relief the influences of the surrounding milieu. Namely, the influences that a shared confidence in a direct correspondence between observing the 'fact' and registering the 'truth' had on Antonio Graziadei's rigidly positivist training, which would remain the most evident peculiarity of his scientific methodology.

When we analyse the rich exchanges between Graziadei and Einaudi[15] we cannot only confirm the existence of such influences, but also ascribe them a more organic character than might otherwise be assumed, given the young socialist economist's only brief period of work at the political-economy section of Turin University's institute of juridical-political sciences.

Certainly, the 'question of method' was posed *in primis*: 'the method that you have up there is truly the only one with which Economics can be made a science'. Such complete allegiance to the most rigorous positivism meant viewing with suspicion even the great socio-economic elaborations of Loria

13 The expression is from Faucci 1995, p. 601.

14 Letter to Croce, 29 January 1899, in Labriola 1983, Vol. III, p. 907.

15 Around two hundred letters by Graziadei are conserved in the Fondazione Einaudi's archives, providing precious sources for a more precise definition of a cultural climate that proved able, in the economic field, to place a common stamp on what were, in themselves, rather different political institutions. They are also valuable for studying the economics-centred institutions of Italy's university chairs – long recognised as a necessary field of inquiry, but one that is yet to find its historian. The corresponding letters by Einaudi are not available in the Imola *Biblioteca Comunale*'s historical archive, where Graziadei's incoming correspondence is conserved, but only from 1918 onward.

himself,[16] and opting – rather tellingly – for Schultze-Gävernitz's models.[17] Graziadei would also owe much to Schultze-Gävernitz's statistical material, much of which he used in both *La produzione capitalistica* and in his polemic with Negro on wages and Marxist theory.

The relationship between Einaudi and Graziadei was a very intense one: they diligently read and commented on the manuscripts for each others' studies, in an exchange of scientific experiences and bibliographical points of reference that was anything but formalistic.[18] But this is not just a matter of questions of method, important though these are. We get the impression that Graziadei was part of a cultural operation and political project largely shared by both

16 Such was his opinion of Loria, which we find in a letter: 'I greatly enjoyed reading your views on Loria. I find myself perfectly in agreement with you. Unfortunately, while he is a great genius, he is an anti-positive genius *par excellence*. In this aspect he will be very damaging, because instead of hurrying the solid progress of Economics, he will serve to take us back, in Italy at least, to *a priori* approaches. Many ... are already beginning to speak of a *signora terra* that boxes men's ears in; social formations that emerge because this is necessary *for some given end* that must happen, etc. etc. It seems to me that the only point on which Loria's genius coincides with the real interests of Science is in the way that he poses problems; that is, saying in what terms a given question must be posed, and what conditions its solution must fulfill in order for us to be able to consider it a definitive one. Do you remember, for example, how clearly he demonstrated in his first volume that the theories of interest given thus far are insufficient, and in what sense a theory of such a phenomenon could be considered a true one? As such, he gave value's role a much more exact concept than did all the other economists'. (Graziadei to Einaudi, Bologna, 28 October 1896, in Archivio Fondazione Einaudi, Carte Graziadei).

17 Again in this same letter, he offered these comments on Schultze-Gävernitz: 'I have read the Schultze-Gävernitz and I have found it a very fine book. I had still not read anything in economics in which the positive method was employed with such marvelous precision. I have changed my way of thinking a lot, since finishing the volume'. See Schultze-Gävernitz 1900. This Italian edition had appeared within the context of the 'laboratory'. Cognetti de Martiis included it in the fourth series of his *Biblioteca dell'Economista*, which he directed, and it was translated and edited by Jannaccone. Graziadei had already read the 1895 English edition. The volume was composed as a refutation of the theory of the iron law of wages, held to be a Marxist law propagated by Lassalle (see p. 121). Schultze-Gävernitz's privileged sources were the 'practitioners of economists', industrialists like Atkinson, also very much used by Graziadei in both *La produzione capitalistica* and the polemic on wages with Luigi Negro.

18 It is interesting to note that it was Luigi Einaudi who signalled the Webbs' *History of Trade Unionism* to Graziadei, a work that would have a far from secondary influence on the theory of the workers' movement in Italy. See Graziadei to Einaudi, 8 March 1899, Carte Graziadei.

the 'laboratory of political economy' and *La Riforma Sociale* circles, tending toward the affirmation of a socialism and above all, of a workers' movement, that would be of compatible, reasonable character. That is to say, toward the affirmation of a culture and a way of conducting the class struggle purged of essential aspects of Marxism, in both its revolutionary dimension and in the dimension of economic theory. The 'Marxists', in sum, were the *others*; a reality that the scientific school of which Graziadei felt himself part defined itself against; at times *indulgent* adversaries,[19] at other times aggressive and dogmatic ones that had to be 'unmasked',[20] or outflanked by destroying their weakest defences.[21]

---

19 'I was pleased by the correspondence in *Avanti!* about your lecturing; as you will have seen, they were rather good also in my case. Poor Marxists! Are they, at root, less fierce than we had believed?' – Graziadei to Einaudi, 12 November 1898.

20 Graziadei to Einaudi, 5 March and 6 November 1899. Seeking to demonstrate the theoretical continuity between his reformist and Communist periods Graziadei argued in his intervention at the Livorno Congress that his critique 'of the economic part of Karl Marx, certainly the most precarious' substantially remained the same as twenty years previously. So, too, remained alive his awareness that 'the vital essence of Marxism [lay] in the *Communist Manifesto*'. He argued that 'What prevails in the shaping of Marx's works is not his strictly economic conception, but the philosophical, social, political part ... It was in the period that wealth was growing, capitals were rapidly accumulating, the working classes could impose very considerable improvements and bourgeois democracy seemed to be opening the doors to power for the proletariat, that men of very great value – who I do appreciate, and will appreciate – believed they could interpret the spirit of the *Communist Manifesto* in terms of a passing historical conjuncture'. See the *Resoconto stenografico del XVII Congresso Nazionale del Partito socialista italiano*, published by Avanti! in Milan in 1962, pp. 36–7. He evidently forgot to include himself among these 'men of very great genius'. In reality through the whole period preceding the First World War he had had a very acute perception of the relation existing between economic theory, the modes of class struggle and forms of workers' organization. As for the *Manifesto*, it is worth noting his dissatisfaction with the 'excessive' concessions Vandervelde made to the logic of the class struggle in an article commemorating the *Manifesto*. This article – which, moreover, was already of a 'revisionist' stamp – however saw in the *Manifesto* the parting of ways between 'bourgeois socialism and the socialism whose fundamental axis is the class struggle'. See E. Vandervelde 'A propos du Manifeste du Parti Communiste', *Revue Socialiste*, 1898, I, pp. 327–41. As he wrote to Einaudi on 26 March 1898 (letter in the Carte Graziadei): 'Have you seen Vandervelde's article on the *Communist Manifesto* in the *Revue Socialiste*? What concessions he makes!'

21 'I have found a socialist who is very reasonable, despite his intransigence, and who is ready to admit Marx's fallibility. This Ferri is a bit of a brat, but he has a good mind and secure intuitions': Graziadei to Einaudi, 5 March 1899.

We can clearly identify the themes around which Antonio Graziadei would construct the ultimate logics of his book as standing within the political and cultural line of Nitti and Loria's review.[22] First of all, this meant attributing theoretical research a practical purpose; and, more specifically, directing research toward studying the conditions and compatibilities necessary for a politics of social reform.[23] Next – and to this end – it meant making use of all potentially reforming forces, and in particular socialism and the workers' movement, once its ideology had been cleared of pessimistic and 'catastrophist' tendencies. Moreover, the theory of 'high wages' and of the workers' movement's progressive role in capitalist development had already appeared in *La Riforma Sociale* – indeed, representing the foundation of a certain political choice – before it appeared in Graziadei's texts and certain socialist publications.[24] And as concerned the specific position of workers' organisation in the country's modernisation process, 'economic science' infallibly indicated that the union – *qua* 'hedonistic subject' – could play a positive function only if it was capable of matching its 'expectations of utility' with the needs of a general – albeit dynamic – economic balance.[25]

La Riforma Sociale's view of industrial relations tended to be defined in the following terms:

> May the workers give up on useless complaints, violent language, Jacobin behaviour and revolutionary tendencies, and associate themselves with the proposal to protect their social interests with ordered steadfastness and virile constancy. May the bosses and owners give up fearing every rustle of leaves and always invoking their authority, and may they and their associates also assert their economic power with just temperance, treat employees as equals, discuss their common interests with them,

---

22 A few years later Loria would organise his theories on the union in a single volume. Although he was fully part of the ideology of modernisation, underlining the role of the workers' movement therein, he also warned that only socialism as a whole – of which the union was the 'primary school', but the party 'the guide and consciousness' – could accelerate the natural movement of capitalism's disintegration. See Loria 1902b, 1901.

23 Loria, 'Scienza sociale e riforma sociale', *La Riforma Sociale*, 1894, pp. 13–17.

24 See (all in *La Riforma Sociale*); F.S. Nitti, 'L'economia degli alti salari', 1895, pp. 481–97, 557–81, 740–63, 824–37; 'Il lavoro', 1895, pp. 5–23, 101–15, 176–92; C. Supino, 'Scienza economica e realtà economica', 1896, I, pp. 397–415; A. Chiappelli, 'Socialismo e pessimismo', 1896, I, pp. 5–10; C.A. Conigliani, 'I pronostici del futuro sociale', 1896, II, pp. 827–44.

25 E. Sella, 'Alcuni appunti teorici sui sindacati operai', *La Riforma Sociale*, 1900, pp. 449–57.

> and show themselves well-disposed and determined in always working for conciliation.[26]

Even the proposal – also energetically advanced by *La Riforma Sociale* – for legal recognition of workers' associationism, with the intention of granting it its autonomy, assumed a meaning that was not exactly favourable to socialism and to what had been the prevalent conception of the class struggle up to that point. Moreover, these arguments were clearly being expressed by the same man who was then very close to Graziadei and would soon become the new director of *La Riforma Sociale*: Luigi Einaudi.[27]

In this context, Graziadei's book came to take on the specific value of a theoretical clarification of the need for a radical change in Italian socialism's culture and political activity, above all in relation to the radical logic of the workers' movement – a logic that had had very few opportunities to manifest itself in a generalised manner over the course of the 1890s. That notwithstanding, his book could not be entirely ascribed to this dimension alone.

La produzione capitalista would, in fact, be structured in two distinct albeit inter-related parts. The first corresponded to the articles that the author had already published in *La Critica Sociale* up till 1897, in which he had developed a theory of surplus independent of the labour theory of value. The second, for its part, was the statistical-empirical and analytically reasoned demonstration of the contemporary rise in wages and profits in the countries whose industrial development was most advanced.

The two parts were doubtless linked. Indeed, in Graziadei's view only a representation of the results of the productive process in 'physical' terms could properly give account of the phenomenon of distribution. Yet in Graziadei's overall production, these two components – and also the different analytical keys that could be deduced from them – came to take on very different levels

26 C.F. Ferrari, 'Socialismo e riforma sociale nel morente e nel nascente secolo', *La Riforma Sociale*, 1900, pp. 719–52; the quotation is from p. 751.

27 Einaudi would write, commenting on the great strikes in Genoa that started the new century's cycle of trade-unionism: 'A strike like the one in Genoa is the index of a morbid social condition … Give such a working class the possibility of freely addressing labour matters through its own associations, dealing with them together with the owners and the government, and within ten years you will no longer hear talk of strikes, since all of us will be conscious of the duty to remain united against foreign competition, and you will no longer see socialist tribunes at the head of the workers, because these latter will have learned to deal with their own interests and will no longer need tutors': see L. Einaudi, 'Lo sciopero di Genova', *La Riforma Sociale*, 1901, quotations from pp. 91 and 93.

of importance. 'Economics without value' would remain a constant of his theory, and when in the 1920s he resumed his reflection on the general themes of political economy, this element went substantially unchanged. Conversely, the theory of high wages and of 'compatibility' would remain irremediably connected to the peculiarity of a moment in which democracy, socialism, and social and economic development seemed to be inextricably linked – when they appeared as different aspects of a path whose limits it had not been possible to discern.

At the end of the century the socialist scholar's interest was clearly titled toward the problem that had emerged from the second part of the volume: that is, toward the development of the themes to which he would dedicate the greater part of his writings in the subsequent fifteen years. At the end of the century, then, the author of this highly controversial book was clear as to what path had to be followed. Namely, that of clearing the socialist movement of 'catastrophist Marxism' (and in his view, Marxism could not be anything other than catastrophist), demonstrating that it was completely possible for the conditions for the improvement of working-class living standards harmlessly to coexist with the process of capital valorisation and thus with capitalist development. Or rather, to demonstrate that in a certain sense the one could be considered functional to the other. On this basis a solid alliance could be established with social forces with liberal-progressive cultural reference points, and thus promote an effective policy of 'great reforms', guided by the compass of 'compatibility' and of the country's general interests.

As we have said already, in the more properly analytical parts of the volume there was no lack of elements liable to producing such results. Graziadei had abandoned the Marxian approach that, starting from the supply of labour-power and the formation of surplus-value, 'transforms' the rate of surplus value into a general average profit rate (leaving aside the question of the formal correctness of this transformation). This abandonment meant not only operating a break between the sphere of production and the sphere of distribution, but also excluding the category 'profit' from the modes of capital valorisation, thus dispelling it from the horizon of economic analysis. This was not only an economics without 'value', but also an economics without 'profit', at least in the Marxian understanding of that concept; an economics where the surplus, or rather surplus product, was determined and distributed outside of the production process. 'For me,' Graziadei had written to Loria, 'profit is a social and historical fact',[28] as he thus relegated the causes of capitalist 'exploitation' to the

28 Graziadei to Loria, 14 February 1899, in the Carte Loria at the Soprintendenza Archivi del Piemonte e della Valle d'Aosta.

sphere of juridical property relations, within a fully Lorian perspective. Thus no substantial change in the distribution of wealth could result from changes internal to the mode of social wealth's formation.

Variables of distribution here came to depend on the functional relationship between labour productivity and wage levels; a functional relationship that would ultimately mark specific limits around the 'high wages' dynamic. Here, there was a direct and explicit reference to the Webbs' books and in particular to *Industrial Democracy* – books that very closely held Graziadei and Einaudi's attentions. It is not hard to understand what pointers for the 'new' orientations of socialism and the workers' movement could be drawn from this theoretical vision.

Indeed, this message was immediately welcomed by liberal friends in the *laboratorio* as well as by *La Riforma Sociale* – by Luigi Einaudi, who hurried to underline that 'while the Marxists raced to cast modern capitalism in a harsh light, the theorist of the new socialism [gave] a highly sympathetic and historically equanimous evaluation of this capitalism'.[29] Moreover, directly intervening in the debate that had opened up among the socialists, he further called on them seriously and deeply to reflect on 'Graziadei's original and evocative book':

> It is the forerunner of a movement in socialist opinion, toward a more practicable and calm contemplation of the phenomena of contemporary economics. It draws up the main theoretical lines of the new programme to which the socialists will have to conform in their practical economic and political action.

France and Italy, Einaudi continued, both had socialist movements inspired by old ideas and by a class struggle in which no quarter had been given. Now, the economic and social conditions were changing, 'following a calmer and more pacific path of struggle'; and as such, it could be hoped that French and Italian socialism would begin to refashion the social struggle 'in the English sense'. Graziadei's book was a 'sure guarantee' that such a transformation would take place. 'The struggle between two different principles, two different systems of

29 L. Einaudi, '*La produzione capitalistica*, rec.', *La Riforma Sociale*, 1898, pp. 1173–6. Einaudi considered Graziadei the greatest Socialist theorist of the new tendencies. More cautious was Jannaccone, who found certain points of uncertainty in the book, but nonetheless positively emphasised Graziadei's insistence on the productivity of both labour and capital. See his '*La produzione capitalistica*, rec.', *Rivista Italiana di Sociologia*, 1899, pp. 82–93.

action always begins in the field of ideas, and then subsequently has a profound repercussion on real, living action'.[30]

Einaudi could not have been clearer, as he demonstrated his deep awareness of both the importance of a theory that broke through socialism's ideological tradition – and yet had matured internally to it – and the effects that it would necessarily have on the socialist way of considering the class struggle and social conflict.

The book's reception in the socialist milieu was rather more complex and articulated. In the pages of *La Critica Sociale*, responses varied between Treves's outpourings of enthusiasm and[31] Negro's sharp critique. That said, this latter was focused not so much on the political perspectives opened up by Graziadei's 'optimism' regarding the wage dynamic, as on asserting that even given his premises, Marx's analytical categories did offer the possibility of correctly interpreting the tendencies under consideration in advanced capitalist countries. We will soon go on to take a closer look at Luigi Negro's critical argument; in the meantime we will note that in the more immediately political context – in the columns of the party daily – the task of guarding the party's ideological inheritance would fall on Bonomi; that is, the man who would a few years later be one of the most exacting and consequential interpreters – and, at the same time, a convinced defender – of Graziadei's theories on trade unionism. At the level of theoretical argumentation, Bonomi's defence was a weak and embarrassed one, deliberately downplaying the dispute in question, as he accused the author of *La produzione capitalista* of limiting himself to substituting commodities for the hours of labour necessary for producing them, and thus of wanting to pass as an innovator at all costs, when the terrain of his analysis in fact remained a Marxist one.[32]

---

30 See L. Einaudi, 'Une nouvelle thèorie du profit et de la production capitaliste', *Revue Socialiste*, 1899, I, pp. 163–75, citations from pp. 174–5.

31 'It is possible to be socialists without being *piagnoni* [the devotees of Girolamo Savonarola], without bearing the exorcisms of Jonathan [the son of King Saul in the Hebrew Bible], the pyrotechnic lightning bolts of an Ezekiel ... Back on that May morning, as Tonino [diminutive of Antonio] spoke, just like now as I read his book, I felt that these ideas, true in their historical objectivity and false in the subjectivity of their principles, would meet with all the excommunications [issued by] the scholastic and the regimented. But I also felt that it would be useful to spread [these ideas] among the people, as a valuable social hygiene, as a healthy diet for the mind of our time – which is too horribly sad and desperate; and in the place of the "crisis of Marxism" I was struck by the idea of a socialist palingenesis'; Treves, 'Il socialismo ottimista: le idee di Antonio Graziadei', *Critica Sociale*, 1899, pp. 200–1.

32 See Bonomi's 'Un libro di Antonio Graziadei. Marx superato?', *Avanti!*, 3 January 1899, and 'La risposta d'un critico criticato', *Avanti!*, 20 January 1899.

Graziadei's response to this was both clear and specific, further demonstrating his awareness of the role that his theory – in its proposed break with the party's 'Marxist tradition' – was taking on in the debate that was now underway. He specified that Marx's theory of value and surplus-value was 'the original secret of the pessimism characteristic of the whole Marxist discussion of big industry, and of the resultant distrust in the possibility of the working class improving – today – its own conditions'. With the theory of the surplus-product, conversely, the accent was placed on labour productivity, and thus on a less rigid and contradictory relation between wages and profit. He concluded, 'So if my theory of surplus-product – necessarily – leads to a socio-economic conception that, even if it may be mistaken, is certainly different from Marx's, then how can Bonomi accuse me of playing with words?'[33]

However, *Avanti!* also wanted to have the 'scientific' last word in this debate, and it published a review by Montemartini that was strongly dismissive of the book; a review in which Graziadei was even accused of 'ignorance of political economy' and of having without a glimmer of critical insight slavishly followed the framework set out by Loria. This latter author was deemed – in his welter of arguments – 'very dangerous for the young' readers still unable to master the vast amount of material that the *Illustre* was working with. *Avanti!* prefaced this sharp dismissal with a note emphasising the strictly 'scientific' character of the text that it was publishing and the fact that its author did not belong to the 'Marxist school'.[34] It did so as if to say that it was not only 'the political' who rejected Graziadei's analysis for reasons of 'Marxist dogmatism', but also professional economists who could not be suspected of Marxism. It is not without importance to note that the marginalist Montemartini just like the 'orthodox' Negro would take up positions within the reformist universe. In substance, then, a large part of socialist culture and the official PSI organ received Graziadei's text in a manner that was anything but friendly to the young socialist economist.[35] This was both a defensive attitude and one

33 See Graziadei's, 'Pro domo mea', *Avanti!*, 15 January 1899. Graziadei wrote to Einaudi with regard to Bonomi's article and a possible response in the PSI organ: 'Would you agree to defend me in *Avanti!*, demonstrating how absurd it is to attack a book for not believing in Marx's theory of value, when it tries to demonstrate with facts that there is no need for this theory, and more generally that Bonomi's attack is a byzantine and scholastic one [?]': Graziadei to Einaudi, 6 January 1899, in the Carte Graziadei at the Archivio della Fondazione Einaudi.

34 Eos (Montemartini), 'A proposito di una critica del marxismo', *Avanti!*, 21 February 1899.

35 Paradoxically, one revolutionary did not consider Graziadei's strictly analytical categories a negation of Marx's theories, but a development of them: 'The disagreement that exists

underestimating[36] the role that *La produzione capitalistica* was coming to play in the debate on 'revisionism' and the theories of an emerging reformism.

As Michels wrote in 1909

> Such a book, written by a party socialist, was bound to stir up a lot of dust, and indeed it did. But in Italy as elsewhere, practice in history always precedes theory. If already in the past the Italian revisionists had broken with and cast aside much of Marx's theory in their everyday politics, they had nonetheless still not matured enough as to accept without opposition the theoretical critique that their comrade had levelled against Marx. Indeed, the party organs' reception of Graziadei's book was certainly not a very cordial one, and still today, even if the reformist revisionists have long since caught up with him, in their writings they do not like to give too much weight to the work he carried out in destroying one of the fundamental concepts of Marxist theory.[37]

In this assessment, Michels takes for granted the conjugation of 'reformism' with 'revisionism', which was in reality a far more problematic question. But at the same time, it does correctly identify an attitude that was very much present in the history of Italian reformism in the era of liberal Italy.

A number of scholars have rightly noted that this hard-fought theoretical battle against 'catastrophism' was being fought against what was only a rather pale spectre of the author of *Capital*. Luigi Negro noted this at the time, in his very accurate textual interpretation. Yet certainly this spectre was very real in

---

between the Marxist school and Graziadei is more apparent than real. For the Marxists ... profit originates from surplus-labour, and for Graziadei from the products of surplus-labour, which he labels the surplus-product. But our friend does not repudiate the Marxist doctrine; for he accepts "the existence of an antagonism between wage and profit, in the sense that the wage is something other than part of the worker's product" ... Moreover, he maintains – and this is the whole point – that profit comes from surplus-labour, though he differentiates himself from the "classic-Marxist school with regard to the meaning and limits of this surplus-labour". In order better to bring out the difference between the two theories, I will add that while for the Marxists profit continues to be the difference between the total and necessary labour of the individual worker, for Graziadei it becomes "the difference between the total product and the necessary product of the entire working class". Overall, then, Graziadei has done nothing other than extend, and I would almost say, complete Marx's theory of profit': Allevi 1901, p. 43.

36 For example, in a letter to his mother Turati defined Graziadei as 'a great fellow, but too much of a doctrinaire': see Turati and Kuliscioff 1977, letter of 5 March 1899.

37 Michels 1909, p. 113.

the socialist culture of the time, and as we saw in the previous chapter Turati did not hesitate in using 'catastrophist' categories when he opposed the tax reform project advanced by the democratic socialist Albertoni.[38]

If such positions could have an aggregating logic in the period of the formation of the party's 'Marxist' identity, or given the prospect of very severe socio-political clashes with revolutionary implications, they became a force for paralysis when faced with a more mobile political panorama. This demanded the difficult conjugation of its ideological inheritance with operational choices that would serve to increase the movement's overall weight and influence in society. At the end of the century important sections of Italian socialism were convinced of this, but they did, indeed, come up against the considerable difficulties of effecting such a conjugation. Graziadei's theory did, certainly, offer a way out of this impasse, but radical and coherent as it was, it also meant privileging elements of rupture over those of continuity. It meant paying a significant price at the level of the image and identity that had been constructed in a foundational period: a price that even those like Turati who would go on wholly to associate their political and personal selves with 'reformist' arguments were not at that moment prepared to pay. Indeed, nor would they be prepared to do so in the subsequent period, either. Perhaps here, too, the *Critica Sociale* director underestimated the importance of the explicit theoretical revision present within Graziadei's work. Indeed, even in 1902 Turati sharply denied that the division of the PSI into tendencies could be justified with the 'fig leaves'[39] of theoretical questions, in the manner of the *Bernstein-Debatte*.

---

38 Moreover, a few years later Turati would clearly explain the reasons for the socialist opposition to Albertoni's project. In 1893, Turati argued, 'there had not been principled grounds for opposing it, but rather tactical ones'. The party was weak and was barely beginning to take form, 'and if the newborn organism of the class socialist party had then fornicated with the social or 'socialistoid' democracy ... that was then eyeing it up, and of which Albertoni was then as now one of the most gifted and illustrious representatives, it would thus have stopped developing and growing: it would quickly have been absorbed ... Today', he continued, 'it is not our soul but the effective conditions that have changed, like night into day. The *Partito socialista italiano* has taken on bone-structure and been tempered in very many tests, and now rather than a tendency that might get confused it might, perhaps, be accused of excessive rigidity'. See 'La Critica, premessa a P. Albertoni, *Riforme tributarie e sociali*', in *Critica Sociale*, 1901, pp. 5–7, 19–21. Citation from p. 5. All of Turati's explanations were very good ones, though he did not mention that 'Karl Marx's iron law of wages' had specifically been invoked in opposition to socialist support for Albertoni's proposals.

39 'A true and proper division', Turati argued 'requires, if not a reason, at least a doctrinal pretext that serves, for decency's sake, as a fig leaf. See, for example, in Germany, where

If some time later he would become seriously concerned with the direct, mass influence of the Imola professor's elaborations, this was with regard to questions inherent to the 'party of labour'.

Yet even though Turati denied it, it was precisely in the years 1899–1901 that the bases had been laid for a particular reformism that was certainly not of any less theoretical dignity than Bernstein's. From the moment of his choice to join the Communist Party onward, Antonio Graziadei would repeatedly deny that he had ever had any relation with Bernstein's 'social-democratic revisionism', counterposing to this his own 'Marxist criticism'. If the reasons for his taking such a position are easy to understand, his argument is, however, hardly convincing for the period in question. Even given that the Italian scholar's theoretical journey was doubtless a completely autonomous one, the analogies with Engels's former pupil's point of arrival are striking. Fundamentally, they were seeking to respond to one same problem: reconciling socialist culture with the latest tendencies in capitalist development – tendencies that seemed to diverge completely from the analytical models suggested by Marx's theory.

Hence their analogous positions on the whole doctrinal edifice functional to the theory of 'collapse', the impoverishment of the theory of 'exploitation',[40] and the more general disappearance of the whole panorama of 'contradictions'. And, moreover, in their common privileging of an analysis bearing on the 'totality of enterprises' and the importance they attributed to the market as the chosen site for quantifying 'exploitation'. On this point Graziadei would

they tried to get to grips with the great questions making up the so called *crisis of Marxism*, and where the Kautsky-Bernstein duel could seem the index of a nascent and impossible-to-suppress heresy. But in our ranks? Here our doctrine is still so scarce, the party still so little impassioned by questions of substance (for example the theory of immiseration, the – inevitable or otherwise – concentration of property, the Marxist theory of value, etc.) that we do not even have big enough fig leaves, so if we want to be schismatic we grab onto such miserable, purely verbal little questions, which are truly just blades of grass': See Turati 1902, p. 2, Quoted in Santarelli 1977, p. 63.

40 Note the many analogies between Graziadei's many statements concerning the sharing of the 'surplus' among the different social classes, and this formulation of Bernstein's: 'the numbers of people living off ... the total labour contained in production are considerably greater than the numbers actively co-operating therein; and, additionally, income statistics show us that the social strata who are not active in production appropriate a part of the total product much greater than their effective numerical weight, as compared to those who are active in production. Their surplus-labour is an empirical fact that can be experimentally proven ... Whether Marx's theory of value is accurate or not is a matter of complete indifference, when it comes to recognising the existence of surplus-labour': Bernstein 1968, pp. 80–1.

go further than Bernstein, considering the play of supply and demand in the factors of production essential to the formation of 'surplus' and not only its distribution.

The relation between Graziadei and Bernstein was considered with some attention even at the beginning of the century. Writing in the columns of *Le Mouvement Socialiste*, Jaurès identified in the German and the Italian's theories a decisive contribution to rendering the boundary between social democracy and liberal democracy fluid and, indeed, unknowable.[41] Certainly, Jaurès's own intention was not to deny the correspondence between the development of the workers' movement and the interests of capitalist production, nor even the possibility of alliances with progressive wings of the bourgeoisie; but this was to be within the terms of 'a democratic bloc hegemonised by the proletariat and its party'.[42] As such, he emphasised the continuity of the socialist tradition rather than the rupture that he saw as clearly emerging from Bernstein and Graziadei's texts.

At root, the disagreement between those who would share the reformist perspective and even many of those who did not[43] revolved not so much around the possibilities of some improvement in working-class living standards under the capitalist system, as the way in which this should be interpreted and anal-

41 See J. Jaurès, 'Bernstein et l'évolution de la méthode socialiste', *Le Mouvement Socialiste*, 1900, pp. 257–73, 353–68, and also in *Critica Sociale* that same year. See also Graziadei's response, 'Risposta a Jaurès', in *Critica Sociale*, 1900, pp. 267–71, 280, 289–302, and subsequently in *Le Mouvement Socialiste* that same year.

A few years later Arturo Labriola would write in this same French review, drawing further comparisons between Bernstein and Graziadei. He maintained that revolutionary socialism was deeply connected to the theories of 'catastrophism' and 'collapse', and that for this reason the revisionists Bernstein and Graziadei had concentrated their critique against 'the most spontaneously revolutionary' ideas. They had upheld this theory of surplus in order to allow them to propagandise 'for reforms, as so many means of demanding for the workers a portion of their unpaid labour'. See his 'Plus Value et reformisme', *Le Mouvement Socialiste*, 1905, pp. 213–29. Fundamentally, we might note, this reading was only *politically* the mirror-image of Graziadei's.

42 Pinzani 1970, p. 302.

43 As one revolutionary put it, '... with the disappearance of the old forms of production, we see the tendency toward a progressive rise in wages, just as it is also true that workers' overall living standards are improving; but the wage rises have a limit set by the very nature of profit, beyond which they will never be able to go without the destruction of profit itself; and if there remains ... a continued antithesis between wages and profits, the much-vaunted coming-together of the classes will constantly remain a pious wish': Allevi 1901, p. 40.

ysed. Was it possible, in substance, to give account of this phenomenon within the terms of Marx's analysis of capitalist development? Neither an answer in the negative or in the affirmative necessarily meant disagreement as to the proper interpretation of the 'holy texts'. Rather, it was a question of whether or not to accept the historic tendency of capitalist accumulation such as Marx had studied it, taking into consideration not only the growth of the forces of production and of wealth, and the improvement – if a non-homogeneous one, within certain limits – of the proletariat's living and working conditions, but also its crises and its fundamental contradictions. On the political terrain, as Jaurès identified, there was a choice between a reformism substantiated by socialist reasoning, or a reformism that gradually took its distance from such arguments.

In Italy, the best-founded objections to Graziadei's way of addressing one of the essential moments of 'catastrophist' theory – that of the wage dynamic – came from a rather more 'minor' exponent of political socialism and socialist culture. We ought to reflect on the capacities that Marxist culture then had to awaken impassioned interest within people who sometimes stood very far from the figure of the professional intellectual. The autodidact-translator Pasquale Martignetti, the geometrist Luigi Negro, the lawyer Tullio Colucci and many others completely dedicated part of their lives to the divulgation or interpretation of Marx and Engels's works. Some of them reached very high levels of insight and knowledge, often superior to that of many of those considered almost institutionally deputised to discussing Marxism.

One such figure, the obscure Alessandria scholar[44] Luigi Negro, would both competently and accurately determine some of the theoretical roots of Marxist reformism, in a direct polemic with the most consequential and culturally well-endowed exponent of a non-Marxist reformism.

Negro made clear that the theory of wages could not be hived off from the other categories of Marx's economic theory. Beyond this context, it would transform into a 'metaphysical conception of wages',[45] thus obscuring any full understanding of the capitalist mode of production – the first condition, for a socialist scholar, of working toward a reasoned conception of social change. When considered as part of a system of relations with Marx's other categories, the wage

44 Negro's standing as a non-academic interlocutor would weigh on the esteem in which Graziadei held him. He was only mentioned in the Graziadei-Einaudi correspondence in the pejorative terms reserved for the unknown and unimportant – 'that Negro'. See Graziadei to Einaudi, 10 January 1901, Carte Graziadei.

45 See L. Negro, 'Antonio Graziadei e la crisi marxista', *Critica Sociale*, 1899, pp. 301–3.

necessarily lost its connection – that some had tried to privilege – to the 'catastrophist' dimension, instead assuming its natural dynamic within capitalist production relations and capitalist development. It was not an independent variable, but one closely correlated to technical conditions, market situations, power relations among social antagonists, and so on. However, beneath all these factors it was possible to discern its 'general tendency'.

'Ultimately', Negro maintained 'we see that according to the Marxist conception, as the bourgeois economy develops, the value of labour-power, both as a physical element and as a social-historical one, must gradually increase with the progressive increase of the productive forces and the intensity of labour'.[46]

This was an argument that the Graziadei of that time absolutely could not agree with, and he devoted himself to a response, in order once and for all to cut the umbilical cord linking Marxian categories to the new tendencies of capitalism. Firstly, he sought to demonstrate that the impossibility of real wages increasing within a capitalist society was a fundamental point of Marx's and Marxists' analysis. However much he declared his hatred for 'Talmudic discussions of holy texts of any kind', he had been compelled to devote himself to 'a monkish … consultation of the sacred books'.[47] In truth, his consultation of these texts had been a very brief one, limited to two works conceived and written between 1847 and 1849 – the *Manifesto* and *Wage Labour and Capital* – for which reason he did anything but prove his mastery of Marx's work. His task was, however, a rather easier one as concerned the Marxists themselves, who offered an embarrassment of choices.

Secondly, he wanted to make more explicit not only the proven *absolute* increase in wages, but also to the tendency for the overall mass of wages to increase relative to the overall mass of profit. To this end he wanted 'to set before theory the facts in their simplest form', integrating the statistics that had already been published in *La produzione capitalistica* – from which it was possible to understand only the absolute wage levels – with other figures drawn from the 'very conscientious and competent' studies of the American industrialist Atkinson and the usual reference point, Schultze-Gävernitz.

His analysis of the data in his possession led him fully to share in Atkinson's conclusions that 'as capital increases in quantity and productivity, the rate

---

46 See L. Negro, 'La teoria del valore di Carlo Marx e la grandezza dei salarii', *Rivista Critica del Socialismo*, 1899, pp. 530–46. Quotation from p. 542. See also his review of *La produzione capitalistica*, in *Rivista Critica del Socialismo*, 1899, pp. 187–90; and his *La centralizzazione capitalistica* (Negro 1900).

47 See A. Graziadei, 'Un aumento assoluto del salario è compatibile con la teoria marxista?', *Critica Sociale*, 1901, pp. 58–61, 88–90.

it takes from the product increases absolutely, but diminishes proportionally. Conversely, labour's share increases both absolutely and relatively. As labour continually increases, labour takes for itself an ever greater share'.[48] Graziadei himself confirmed the difficulties getting hold of a precise calculation taking account of both the purchasing power corresponding to these wages and the reduction of physical volumes apparent in these revenue statistics. Paradoxically, then, Atkinson and Graziadei's conclusions were hardly decisive in proving their point: rather, they could become useful examples in support of the theory of the tendency of the rate of profit to fall.

Negro's response proved much closer to both the letter and method of Marx's analysis, and was also considerably articulated on the historical plane, thus escaping the 'Talmudic' dimension that his interlocutor rightly disdained. His references were both precise and specifically contextualised,[49] but still today bear useful elements for explicating Marx's theory of wages. However, his overall position remained overly attached to the conviction that Graziadei and the 'crisis-ists' in general had made no real effort to understand Marx in his entirety – which often was true – and that grasping this dimension would alone be necessary to overcoming the theoretical and political reasons for the crisis.

As for the precise question in dispute (was Marxian theory able to give account of the phenomena of the absolute and relative rise in wages?) Graziadei would himself in the 1920s broadly recognise the justness Negro's argu-

---

48 A. Graziadei, 'Un aumento assoluto del salario è compatibile con la teoria marxista?', *Critica Sociale*, 1901, p. 89.

49 L. Negro, 'L'aumento assoluto del salario nella teoria marxista', *Critica Sociale*, 1901, pp. 108–9, 124–7. For the continuing polemic, see: A. Graziadei, 'Ancora dell'aumento assoluto del salario nella teoria marxista', *Critica Sociale*, 1901, pp. 173–6; A. Graziadei, 'Sempre intorno al massimo salario compatibile coll'interesse dell'industriale', *Critica Sociale*, 1901, pp. 200–3; L. Negro, 'Ultima replica al prof. Graziadei sull'aumento del salario nella teoria marxista', *Critica Sociale*, 1901, pp. 218–20, 253–5.

Negro's references to Marx's theory of wages were principally taken from *Capital* – a work that Graziadei had declared himself unwilling to address because it was too easily used for 'ambushes' – and were also inspired by an awareness of the changes in Marx's thinking on this question between the late 1840s, the International experience and his great theoretical works of the 1860s. Negro also particularly cited *Wages, Price and Profit*, a text that – as we saw in the first chapter – was written precisely in order to respond to the arguments of those who, starting from the hypothesis that real wages could not possibly increase within the capitalist system, attempted to deny the effectiveness of trade-union organisation and struggle. Negro quoted from the 1898 French edition. As such I think it is wholly baseless to speak of the 'inaccuracy of the references to Marx' in Negro's writings (Are 1974, p. 76).

ments, albeit without naming him specifically.[50] At the beginning of the century the justifications for a non-Marxist reformism would largely predominate over arguments based on a rigorous textual analysis.

So were there two 'reformisms' at the beginning of the century? It is obviously not possible, within the sole perspective of the history of culture, to give persuasive answers to a question concerning such a complex reality as reformism, in which – as we well know – the 'practical' dimension occupied such extremely wide spaces. However, we can agree on the fact that the theoretical roots of two different attitudes toward the party's 'tradition' – and, in consequence, its perspectives – were present within a political and cultural field now being defined with the features typical of reformism.

Indeed, Graziadei himself – in the second part of his political and theoretical development – provides us with an insight into how to read this process, in attempting to establish a distinction between the supposed 'gradualism' he had asserted in the Giolittian era and the 'reformism' that had proven a historical failure.[51]

As Luxemburg put it in one intervention in the *Bernstein-Debatte*, 'gradualism' was the recognition that if 'the march of capitalist development is slower than was thought before', this meant 'a slowing up of the pace of the struggle', and even partial alliances with the more advanced parts of the antagonist classes. Reformism, conversely, questioned 'not the rapidity of the development of capitalist society, but the march of the development itself and, consequently, the very possibility of a change to socialism'.[52]

It seems highly doubtful that Graziadei's positions could be considered 'gradualist' in this sense. Yet I think that it should be uncontroversial to say that already at the beginning of the century there existed the elements for one reformist culture 'internal' to socialism and another one that was extremely

50 'In *Capital* Volume I – the very volume in which he most expressly concerned himself with the problems of labour – Marx did not even vaguely consider the permanent reduction of wages a reality of the capitalist economy ... What is more, Marx explicitly accepted the possibility of an absolute increase in money-wages, and not their absolute reduction ... As concerned money-wages, Marx rejected – even in *Capital*, albeit in a less widespread form than in the repeatedly cited text [*Wages, Price and Profit*, unknown to him at the moment of the polemic with Negro, but now repeatedly cited, using Longuet's 1912 French edition] the belief that even many so-called Marxists wanted to attribute to him: namely, that in the capitalist economy the absolute level of money-wages tends in all cases to fall, and, moreover, toward a fixed minimum'. Graziadei 1928, pp. 9–11; identical arguments appear in Graziadei 1927, pp. 36–7, and 1929.

51 Graziadei, 1921, pp. 4–5.

52 From her *Reform or Revolution*: text from www.marxists.org.

liable to blur into 'other' cultures, and that these perspectives were gradually defined as 'Marxist reformism' and 'non-Marxist reformism', respectively.

As such, it seems no exaggeration to argue that Graziadei was the Italian Bernstein. This is all the more significant given the fact that he reached conclusions analogous to those of the German 'revisionist' wholly autonomously and yet in almost exactly the same period.[53]

We thus understand that the theoretical and practical stakes in dispute in turn-of-the-century Italian socialism were anything but negligible. In Graziadei's perspective, the 'crisis of Marxism' had to result in the official declaration of the death of theoretical Marxism, and, in consequence, its elimination as a characteristic of socialism's 'identity', 'differentness' and autonomy. This would mean elimination of a characteristic that had been at the basis of the foundation of the *Partito operaio italiano*, and which had been understood as the substance, the very essence, of socialism.

It is, then, rather striking that there was no *Graziadei-Debatte* in Italy: only Negro and later Longobardi would get to grips with the theoretical kernel of Graziadei's arguments. Aside from that, the reactions were either ones of superficial irritation or of indifference.

Perhaps this was because Turati was not Karl Kautsky – at least with regard to these specific problems – and could thus consider the young Graziadei a 'doctrinaire' without having well understood the true significance of his theory. Perhaps it was because, all things considered, the 'crisis-ists' thought that pure economics provided more modern and better-developed weapons for revising Marxism than did a discourse like Graziadei's, which they considered still too traditional and Lorian. But certainly Graziadeism's impact and penetration had to proceed by way of less immediately evident paths, less scorched by the fire of political and scientific discussion.

At the same time, the outline of the Graziadei-question, which emerged at the turn of the century in a little-favourable and immediately drying-up terrain, would ultimately reappear a few years later in a more vigorous and branched-out manner. Its forms would be different this time, with theory now tending to be translated into politics and organisational demands. Nonetheless, the

53 In his *Wie is Wissenschsftlicher Sozialismus Möglich?* (Bernstein 1901, p. 40) the German thinker had himself pointed to Antonio Graziadei as the other head of the two-headed eagle of revisionism. For his part, in a 26 June 1900 letter to Einaudi, Graziadei would write 'I learned many years ago that wages rise: but from Einaudi, in the *laboratorio* in Turin' (Carte Graziadei).

Falea di Calcedonia, 'La morte del socialismo (Discorrendo con Benedetto Croce)', *La Voce*, 9 February 1911.

discussion on the workers' movement concerned, to which Graziadei devoted a great part of his theoretical content, would continue to centre – even if in mediated fashion – on questions relating to the foundations and the strategies of socialism: the class struggle, Marxism, and the development or 'collapse' of capitalism.

2 Turati, the 'Marxist' and 'Reformist'

1911 can be considered a key year in the experience of Italian socialism: almost a chemical solution in which the introduction of a new element very rapidly produces a precipitate. It was the year in which the hitherto missing encounter between Turatism and Giolittism finally seemed possible – yet also the year in which the separation between the two perspectives would suddenly take off again. And in the backdrop of the action on the political stage – and with the full significance of a structural node – was a fundamental stage in the formation of Italian monopoly capitalism: namely, the concentration in the 'modern', strategic steel sector. This was marked on the social plane by the very harsh clash with workers' organisation, and the workers' movement's clear defeat. At the same time there was the external dimension of imperialism: the war in Libya.

Did Italian socialism still have an autonomous capacity to interpret such processes – a set of categories to give account of what was now happening, within the perspective of the analysis of capitalist development? That is, a Marxist reading?

Giovanni Giolitti had already given a response to this question early in 1911, in his famous 8 April speech. He made this intervention at the end of the parliamentary debate on the government's statements, at the moment in which this likewise famous 'encounter' was supposedly meant to have taken full form. Giolitti was clear in his assertion that 'Eight years have passed [since the first proposal for the socialists' collaboration in government], the country has marched forward, the socialist party has rather moderated its programme, and Karl Marx has been put up in the attic'. Equally authoritatively, barely a month before this Benedetto Croce had announced 'the death of socialism'.

Moreover, leafing through the socialist (and particularly reformist) literature of the turn of the 1910s, the terms 'crisis', 'decadence', and 'death' very often recur in reference to the party and to socialism in general – these now being 'branches running dry' of the 'sap' of life. At the same time, however, there was a will to *renewal* or even *rebirth*, which could not but mean a complete separation from a cultural tradition and a series of ideological reference points that the *renovators* moreover now considered entirely exhausted and residual.

Symptomatic of this context was a debate held in the first half of 1911 in *La Critica Sociale*, which some have ventured to discuss in terms of a 'second revisionism'.[54] Although the quality of the discussion and its outcomes do not seem fully to justify such a statement, it is nonetheless an interesting pointer for understanding how one of the privileged vehicles of the formation of Italian Marxism now considered Marxism at the moment that the reformist hegemony over the party was drawing to a close.

It was a young philosophy scholar, Tullio Colucci, who opened up the debate on the 'crisis of socialism'. He was profoundly influenced by the idealist cultural climate that had began to become dominant. His argumentation, developed across various different articles, was articulated according to the same mechanisms as those who sought to 'turn the page' – both *distruens* and *costruens*. The first made *tabula rasa* of Marxism, and the second pointed to the shining paths of an essentially ethically-based 'proletarian reformism'. According to Colucci, Marx's *Capital* was an 'archaeological remnant ... a book of the past', and in consequence socialism could no longer refer to any scientific substance. However, even if the 'greater part of Marxist doctrines' had now been 'destroyed', there nonetheless remained 'the practical activities of the proletariat'. These latter would be developed all the more effectively as the Socialist Party ideologically reconciled itself with 'its *de facto* status', by definitively ceasing to have 'any relation with the ideal that its name evokes'. Colucci thus suggested changing its name from 'Socialist' to 'Proletarian Reformist Party'.[55] He did nonetheless preserve the 'reality' of the class struggle, though it was now voided of any theoretical reference. Much more drastically, during the course of this same discussion another young socialist intellectual asked himself, 'if the class struggle ... as an instrument of political struggle and social transformation is the consequence of a Marxist theoretical premise, what is left of the consequence now that the premise has collapsed?'[56]

It is true that these were not the debate's only contents. It also featured the appearance of Rodolfo Mondolfo's[57] 'professorial Marxism',[58] with all his rigorous, intelligent interpretative capacity. But this did not alter the general 'tone' of the debate, and what remained in the forefront was the *de profundis*

54 Santarelli 1977, p. 172.

55 See Colucci's 'Rileggendo Marx', 'Il nuovo socialismo', 'La riconquista dell'Ideale', 'Grandezza e decadenza del socialismo' and 'L'erede', in *Critica Sociale*, 1911, pp. 145–7, 167–8, 182–3, 226–33 and 242–5 respectively.

56 See E. Marchioli, 'Oltre la lotta di classe', *Critica Sociale*, 1911, pp. 165–7.

57 See R. Mondolfo, 'Rovistando in soffitta', *Critica Sociale*, 1911, pp. 210–12.

58 This expression is taken from Asor Rosa 1975, p. 1163.

now decreed for Marxism, and which would soon be decreed for the socialism that had maintained an even vague analytical inheritance from *Capital*.

Filippo Turati's interventions were an element of far from secondary importance in ensuring the prevalence of such a 'tone'. As is well known, faced with articles that did not fully correspond to *Critica Sociale*'s line, Turati would often intervene with short introductory notes and commentaries, representing the 'red thread' of what continued to be the most prestigious of Italian socialist publications. Marxism's old master continued to defend some of the postulates of his own formation dating to the late 1880s and early 1890s: confidence in a collectivist future, the central role of the class struggle, and economic determinism. But he lacked the theoretical determinations that would have allowed him to work these postulates into a 'body' of theory, beyond simply asserting their existence. What really interested Turati in the cultural battle of the moment was to combat the rise of idealism, reaffirming that 'social justice' would be a highly abstract and indeterminate concept unless 'the proletarian soul, proletarian pain, will and energy had marked it with its own stamp, its own character'.[59]

Beyond that, he could almost agree with his interlocutors in stating that 'reformism ... [had] already recognised, in theory and in practice ... the relativity of Marxism's fundamental concepts' and that 'the class struggle itself [had] become far more complicated than it was in its initial conception'. Moreover, he considered Colucci and Marchioli's positions as being fundamentally 'internal' to socialism, indeed a proof of its vitality: 'You do not speak, reason or tremble like that from beyond the grave ... these are not the troubles of the dead'.[60] And he pointed to *action* as the privileged exit route from theoretical and cultural impasses in general.

So in 1911 did even Turati fully accept Bernsteinian revisionism, but in a strongly reductive sense? And how could this be the case, a few months after he had suddenly returned to Marx when it had been necessary to redefine the party's identity and 'differentness' with respect to even the most democratic shades of the bourgeois universe? Why were the socialists again 'reformists because they were revolutionaries';[61] and why the new and direct reference to 'the man we keep up in the attic'?[62]

59 See Ille Ego, 'Vi è veramente contraddizione? A proposito dei due articoli che seguono', *Critica Sociale*, 1911, p. 164.

60 See La C.S., 'Contravveleno', *Critica Sociale*, 1911, p. 225.

61 See Noi, 'L'accordo dei contrari', *Critica Sociale*, 1911, pp. 340–1.

62 See T-K, 'Colui che confinammo in soffitta', *Critica Sociale*, 1913, pp. 73–4.

Evidently the process through which a reformist culture took form – a process in which Turati played an essential role – cannot be read in the linear terms of the equation reformism = revisionism.

Over the first ten years of the twentieth century, Filippo Turati was often called on to make his reformism a more coherent one by taking on theoretical reference points that were clearly revisionist and explicitly non-Marxist. He would always refuse to do so, in a first phase for strongly ideological reasons, and in a second phase – when the 'facts' seemed to have proven decisive – for essentially political reasons. Even Turati's very considerable sense of political opportunities is not alone sufficient to explaining the reasons for what many have considered a long obstinacy often in contradiction with reformism's own practices. As such, we have to examine the 'hard kernel' of his 1890s Marxism, as it faced the test of the double crisis at the end of the century.

The turn of the new century was truly a turning point for the Italian socialist movement as a whole. That was not so much because of the new way in which its relations with the most advanced and liberal-progressive democratic forces – and, in the background, even the government – were posed. Rather, because for the first time in the history of Italian socialism it seemed really possible for it to have an impact on the development of the processes that were now underway – that is, to accelerate the country's modernisation, and thus also create the objective conditions for socialism's growth, by way of the party's own advancement. However, bearing such an impact would mean settling accounts with an industrial development that was difficult to conjugate with democracy in general and 'industrial democracy' in particular; with a state that had anything but linear relations with the working class and its organisations; with the most powerful, battle-hardened groups of industrialists, who were also the backbone of Italy's 'take-off'; and, finally, with the agrarian situation and the peasant world in general, whose conditions were themselves the fruit of very strong imbalances with respect to any strategy of 'harmonisation'.

This was an arduous task. The problems now starting to be confronted were vast in dimension, and sometimes even beyond the real capacities of the socialists' activity: problems that would in any case demand robust analytical equipment, a capacious toolbox, and a set of theoretical referents that was both dynamic and coherent with the movement's end goals and *raisons d'être*. And all this in a moment that the conditions for a vacuum of theory also appeared to be emerging. Or better, a moment in which a so-called 'revisionist' theory, determined to be a protagonist in indicating the workers' movement's and reformist socialism's 'new paths', was confronted not by a dialectical-alternative pole of discussion but rather an environment that absorbed and muffled contrasts. It had emerged amidst a context of substantial disinterest for theoretical concerns, downgrading them to 'doctrinal' affairs. An awareness of the risks inherent to such a situation did appear here and there in the discussion, in the dialogues among those like Turati and Kuliscioff who had been more convinced and tenacious propagators of a 'socialist consciousness'. But even their apparent doubts were combined with confidence in the inner rationality of what was in becoming, the possibility of reading things in 'socialist' terms, albeit in light of ever more general and even generic theoretical assumptions. 'What Italy saw in the last year has been anything other than a *crisis of science*',[63] Antonio Labriola commented as he welcomed the resumption of *Critica Sociale*'s publications after the long interlude owing to Kuliscioff and Turati's arrests. Yet the events of these terrible two years, the 'crisis of Marxism' included, seem not to have changed the terms of Turati's particular relation with Marxism, such as it had been posed since the times of the *Lega socialista milanese*.

Turati had begun 1898 commenting on the fifty-year anniversary of both the *Manifesto* and the bourgeois revolutions of 1848 in the following terms:

> If anyone had dared, in that year, to pair and compare – never mind draw an equivalence between – the two events, they would soon have been deemed mad: the great social-political earthquake that shook all Europe, and the little book that emerged from semi-secret London meetings of the League of the Just, without any clamour of publicity, and which was due to remain almost unknown for another twenty years and more ... Yet half-a-century later, the great, clamorous, universal fact seems flattened and reduced ... whereas that neglected and negligible book has become a bible, and is considered and venerated as a milestone of humanity's onward march. We can say that 'the new history began with this'.[64]

Explicitly declaring himself a disciple of Turati's, Bonomi intervened in defence of 'scientific socialism' in his comments on Merlino's works,[65] just as he soon did also with regard to Graziadei's. And Turati himself, addressing Croce and Sombart's publications, would further state that 'in history it will be as understandable to speak of "Marx's century" as of "Dante's century"'.[66]

They had absolutely no intention of putting in question the definition of socialism as 'scientific' socialism, since at that moment that would have meant

63 See A. Labriola, 'Il nostro compito', *Critica Sociale*, 1899, pp. 147–8.

64 See F. Turati, 'L'incontro di due giubilei', *Critica Sociale*, 1898, pp. 1–3. Quotation from p. 1.

65 See I. Bonomi, 'Due libri sul socialismo di Saverio Merlino', *Critica Sociale*, pp. 91–2, 103–5.

66 See Ille Ego, 'La recentissima letteratura marxista', *Critica Sociale*, pp. 126–127.

denying the very bases of their own political existence. Yet at the same time it did begin gradually losing its specific determinations.

What, then, remained, after all the critiques and 'revisions' of 'scientific socialism'? Turati argued:

> it still has … its great innovative spirit – hence its image of the social world, stood on its head and then put back on its feet; most importantly, it still has its capacity to revise itself, its power of self-critique and of assiduous perfection, so vaunted by those who declare a state of crisis and call for its dissolution. It still has the talisman that Marx gave it, allowing it to defend itself from all the eclectics, the confusionaries, all those who yearn for a new party, the latest bearers of all-purpose intermediate theories. It is still living and active.[67]

The emphasis was thus shifted onto 'living and acting', in accordance with the practical concern always so characteristic of Filippo Turati's sense of socialism.[68] But according to the Turati of the 1890s, this practice had to be rooted in a *corpus* of theoretical propositions, which were then considered self-contained and in any case capable of guaranteeing the young *Partito operaio italiano*'s total autonomy of inspiration and praxis. However, with the blurring of these determinations, leading to the reduction of Marxism – as we will see – to its 'basic elements' of collectivism and class struggle, a theoretical indifference would instead come to take form. This would make it more difficult to elaborate any 'socialist' reading of the processes now underway, the class struggle included.

In the Italy of the start of the twentieth century, this class struggle was taking unforeseen forms. The turn of the century brought elements of novelty for the

---

67 See. F. Turati, 'Postilla a G. Sorel, *La crisi del socialismo scientifico*', *Critica Sociale*, 1899, pp. 134–8, 139–41. Quotation from p. 141.

68 Turati was very early in posing the need for a 'practical programme', though he started out from the conviction that 'as for socialism's theoretical foundation, its positive premises can be said to be a *scientific* dogma'; at the same time, it was essential for the 'scientific party' to indicate the road that would bring it to its proposed end goal. See F. Turati, 'Necessità di un programma pratico', *Critica Sociale*, 1892, pp. 228–9. In the preparations for the Reggio Emilia Congress he would further say that now 'the time for theoretical congresses is over, and the time for practical congresses must begin', given that at the Genoa Congress the Party had definitively adopted a stance 'under the banners of scientific socialism'. See La C.S., 'Da Genova a Reggio Emilia. Il compito del congresso imminente', *Critica Sociale*, 1893, pp. 257–8.

workers' movement that were decidedly macroscopic in character. Without fear of exaggeration, we can speak of a true and proper 'explosion' of the workers' movement.

Certainly, the history of Italian trade unionism did not begin with the Genoa strike. Rather, the characteristics of radicalism and autonomy that had taken form in earlier years would continue to play a non-secondary role in the social dynamic of the Giolittian era. Yet only the rapid growth and very strong potential for struggle demonstrated in 1900–2 would make it one of the undoubted protagonists of the social and political panorama.

Multiple expectations that were not always compatible among themselves – and so, too theoretical systematisations and political initiatives that were anything but convergent – would now be focused on this workers' movement. Hitherto it had often been evoked and sometimes considered something of an encumbrance, but now it was finally becoming a substantial reality. In substance, the fundamental problem that the Socialist Party intended (and needed) to measure up to was now coming to be projected onto the trade union: namely, that of being a primary element in the country's development and modernisation, while keeping intact its function of working for the transition to socialism. Moreover, the trade union, which operated in the heart of the system, within the production relation, found itself being charged with wholly particular responsibilities with regard to both the first and the second horns of this problem. The manner in which they were combined, and the proportions that each of them assumed in the overall 'composite', could change the pitch of the workers' movement's essential relations – with the socialist movement as a whole, with the Marxist culture and tradition, and with the class struggle itself. Filippo Turati intensely and even dramatically felt the need – and, together with this, the difficulty – of conjugating these two terms.

The *heri dicebamus* beginning the first 1900 issue of *Critica Sociale* – an *heri dicebamus* that would recur on other occasions through this publication's long experience, working to underline the elements of continuity of its political history and the mark of a socialist 'essence' that could not be changed over time – also prefaced an article defending the basis for an alliance with the popular parties aiming at 'a work of political land-reclamation'.[69] The hard kernel of 'scientific socialism' and the 'economic materialism' on which it was founded could not be altered; yet the conditions in which 'the general concepts of the class struggle and collectivism take on life and content, and formulas

69 See T-K, 'Dichiarazioni necessarie', *Critica Sociale*, 1900, pp. 1–4. Quotation from p. 2.

become real' did change.[70] Moreover, was this explosion of trade unionism, the most important novelty of the moment, not perhaps the proof of the doctrine that made socialism scientific? With the Genoa strike, even backward Italy began to respond to the 'call of history'.

'Oh, the objections to socialism', Turati exclaimed,

> the theoretical objections of the salaried professors. Tell us how come this lowly people of dockers, to whom no one has read *Capital* or spelled out the *Manifesto*, came to make itself a single heart and soul ...? If you lose your agenda the tanned people of the Genoa docks will appear before your eyes. And Balilla[71] shouts – 'shall I begin?' Balilla, son of his time, become a Marxist, because the times are Marxist, making Marxist prose without knowing it, precisely now that the professors have so dismissed Marx.[72]

The situation that had opened up in the movement, far from diluting the hard core of 'scientific socialism', instead served as a guarantee of its 'differentness', ensuring that it could be surely and definitely identified. Only this guarantee could permit the openings suiting a wide range of tactical choices. Hence Turati's obstinate defence, in these first years of the century, of the 'fundamental unity of doctrine' – the very synonym of the 'unity of the party';[73] the constant revisiting of socialism's peculiarity and the precise delimitation of its territory. Yet this terrain, which was ever-renewed and ever less worked on, had ended up becoming little-productive and its boundaries had themselves shrunk like shagreen.

In the meantime, however, the fundamentals of 'doctrine', 'collectivism' and 'class struggle' were reaffirmed. And Turati also did this in the article that was considered the true and proper manifesto of reformism.[74] He made a profession of faith with regard to collectivism:

---

70 See F. Turati, 'In vista del congresso', *Critica Sociale*, 1900, p. 258.

71 [A hero of Italian patriotic mythology, 'Balilla' was a Genoese boy who began his home city's 1746 rebellion against the Habsburgs, supposedly shouting these words as he threw a stone at an Austrian soldier.]

72 See La C.S., 'Fra due secoli', *Critica Sociale*, 1901, p. 2.

73 See F. Turati, 'In vista del congresso', *Critica Sociale*, 1901, p. 258.

74 See F. Turati, 'Il partito socialista e l'attuale momento politico', *Critica Sociale*, 1901, pp. 209–15.

> I believe not only possible, but inevitable (and if I did not believe this, I would not declare myself a socialist) the unitary organisation of the great branches of production, with the consequent determination of values not in a 'bureaucratic' sense (with administrative functionaries establishing themselves and their authority), but scientifically and democratically, on the basis of the dual criterion of the socially necessary time for creating the unity of the product and social needs ...[75]

Here was a particular emphasis on the *end goal*, in a transition process where the movement was only socialist in character if it was congruous with that end. The motives for such an attitude, characterised by arguments posed in terms of continuity, explain Turati's detached – if not even hostile – position with regard to Bernstein, at least in the moment in which the 'Bernstein question' was placed on the order of the day of European socialism's internal discussion. The fact is that Bernstein was taking on an image placing him ever closer to Schultze-Gävernitz than to Marx.[76] As such, he could not easily be used within a perspective seeking to conjugate socialist identity, such as it had formed in the 1880s and 1890s, with the movement's new tasks at the beginning of the twentieth century.

In this regard, Turati's comment on the SPD's Hanover Congress was rather telling. This was the congress at which Bebel's 'orthodox' resolution was passed by 216 votes to 21. The Italian socialist leader expressed his satisfaction that theoretical disputes had not weakened the substantial unity of the German party, but above all because it had not been possible to declare 'the end of Marxism, that is, the end of positive modern socialism'. Here there was no rejection of reforms, but they could only fit into a context delineated as follows: 'the party's revolutionary character does not rule out support for all gradual reforms, useful to the improvement of the proletariat. But on one condition: that the effort to achieve reforms does not at all wipe out the revolutionary character of the party'. In short, it was necessary 'to be different each day, and always to remain essentially the same'.[77] Ivanoe Bonomi would soon again emphasise this concept of change in continuity, in open polemic with Bernstein. This was the same Bonomi who would a few years later fully welcome the German revisionist's positions; but at this point he declared, 'Exactly measuring the movement to the end goal: that is where the socialist parties' true insight lies. Neither forget

75 See F. Turati, 'Le confessioni di Saverio Merlino', *Critica Sociale*, 1901, p. 291.

76 An observation of Plekhanov's, welcomed by Kautsky: see Waldenberg 1972.

77 See La C.S., 'Il congresso socialista tedesco', *Critica Sociale*, 1899, pp. 257–9.

the end goal in favour of gradual advance, nor vice versa. Bernstein is mistaken when he says that the movement is everything and the end goal is nothing. No, the end goal is not nothing, since only this end goal can give the movement direction, and only with this can the proletariat spread a consciousness of its own'.[78] At the same time, however, the international point of reference for the Italians' rejection of Bernsteinism was not the one represented by Kautsky – something that would have been wholly normal in this particular moment. Yet the fact remains that for Turati, Kautsky was a too-cumbersome, overly theoretically determinate figure, who was excessively internal to a *strong* conception of the relationship between Marxism/socialism/political choices. In short, he was the bearer of excessively rigid assumptions. It is no chance thing that his correspondence with Kautsky ended in 1901, and that the German 'orthodox' writer's name would not again appear on a *Critica Sociale* article before 1914.

The 'response to Bernstein' that *Critica Sociale* offered – with all the trappings of an official position was that written by Jean Jaurès[79] – expressing his great affinity with Turati's way of considering the demands of *action*, tactical elasticity, and leaving oneself open a vast range of possible choices, at the same time as being careful not to introduce deep fractures in socialism's already-consolidated tradition. Indeed, Jaurès's argument, which Turati could also have signed up to from start to finish, was as impassioned in emphasising the political and ideal reasons for socialism's need for autonomy and unity, as it was vague and indeterminate on the substance of the theoretical problems that the *'Bernstein-Debatte'* had raised.

However, at this point the two leaders had no doubts on what direction to take. This was an orientation that both Turati and Jaurès would attempt to explore in full: that of the Marxist legitimation of gradualism, the policy of alliances with democratic forces, and the policy of social reforms.

Certainly, this was a difficult road given the conditions of the time, and the protagonists perhaps proved that they were not entirely prepared for it; but certainly it was a practicable road, full in its Marxist legitimacy. A historical analysis of whether or not a political and cultural path was *possible* ought not necessarily be deduced from its ultimate results.

It has been argued that 'Marx's doctrine was an ideology of the absolute opposition of the workers' movement against the existing social and political

78 See I. Bonomi, 'La nuova tattica', *Critica Sociale*, 1899, pp. 326–8.

79 J. Jaurès, 'Bernstein et l'évolution de la méthode socialiste', *Le Mouvement Socialiste*, 1900, pp. 257–73, 353–68, and also in *Critica Sociale* that same year.

structures', and it was received as such by the socialist movement of the 1880s and early 1890s. Like Marx's analysis of capitalism, the principal elements of his philosophy of history and sociology justified the politics of absolute opposition.[80] There is no doubt that the reception of Marxism as the 'theory of absolute opposition' was widespread throughout the history of the socialist workers' movement, and not only at the end of the century or in the period of the Second International in general. Likewise, there is no doubt that there are elements in Marx – including far from secondary ones – justifying such an interpretation. However, it is equally true that Marx's principal analytical categories concerning economic theory were not configured in such a manner as to rule out a gradualist and reforming political horizon.

Certainly Turati did not master the complexity of these theoretical nodes, and the difficulties – indeed, ones that still exist – of translating them into political economy. He was, of course, not alone in that regard, even within the European socialist milieu. He only argued that it was possible to break out of the 'ideology of absolute opposition', making socialist policy for expanding the sphere of freedoms and demanding social justice, while remaining loyal to the masters' lesson. And, in the specific Italian case, making continuous reference to Engels's famous 1894 letter.

In asserting this possibility, he could also draw comfort from the support of Antonio Labriola, who had earlier been one of the most severe critics of his way of understanding the relationship between theory and politics.

We ought to add that Labriola's critiques could have been re-asserted, and with much greater force, precisely in the moment of the experience that was beginning together with the new century. If, as we have said, there was no question of the Marxist legitimacy of an adaptable, non-intransigent policy – a politics at the level of the reformist challenge that Giolitti had posed to the socialists – then it was all the more necessary to pose the problem of 'mastering' that challenge politically and culturally. As such, what seemed to be the surest bases of the gradual de-theorisation of socialist political action were surely – and proved to be – the least appropriate responses.

Therefore, at the beginning of the new century Turati sought to set off on his own navigation of an open sea, but without abandoning the old nautical charts.

Precisely because the party 'tree' was so solidly rooted in the *humus* nourished by Marxism's 'essential principles', and the only possible novelty was the development of its branches, leaves and fruits, in Turati's view there was little sense in speaking of multiple socialist tendencies. A tendency struggle would

80 Waldenberg 1985, p. 99.

have been nothing other than the re-appearance, in none-too changed forms, of the old Marx-Bakunin conflict. For Turati, there was just one socialism: and on either side, the slip into anarchism or bourgeois radicalism. Turati had great difficulty accepting the term '"reformism" which he thought not only an overly reductive take on his elaborations, but even a mystification. It was a term that would only become an acceptable designation of his politics and his vision of socialism starting in late 1905'.[81] As he argued,

> In De Marinis's jargon the reforming tendency becomes reformism, and the legalist tendency a pacific one. Yet reformism is to socialist reform, and peace is to the legalist socialist struggle, exactly what the bourgeois programmes – however radical – are to our own one. Reformism means reforms made as ends in themselves, raised up as a movement's pillars of Hercules, conceded in the dose immediately necessary for diverting, containing and impeding the revolution, rather than easing its path. Peace and harmony between the classes is the ideal of those who rule, and is in their interest. But the oppressed, the ruled-over need struggle, reforms that are conquests, ones that ease further [such reforms], prepare the social and economic revolution, and are revolutions in themselves.[82]

Reflection on reforms was thus posed as an aspect of reflection on revolution. Yet revolution was not the end point of a seamless course from bourgeois democracy to socialist democracy, 'because although socialism does erupt from capitalism, it does so as its Hegelian negation and antithesis'.[83]

As such, in these years revolution was still at the centre of the *Critica Sociale* leadership group's strategic vision.[84] The revolution could absolutely not do

81 See Turati's letter to Bonomi of 22 September 1905, in Turati and Kuliscioff 1959: 'And the reformists should be admitted ... You will be amazed by this, knowing my aversion for the *word*. But now that is the only point of distinction. If we speak of reforms, everyone will come along: especially those who do not want them, and who will do whatever is possible to see them run aground'.

82 See F. Turati, 'Alla scoperta del socialismo. Riformismo radicale e rivoluzione proletaria', *Critica Sociale*, 1901, p. 324. And again in 1903: 'We longed for a revolution nourished by facts, not camped out on airy words, and a tendency was created to fasten it together, with the adorable little epithet "reformism"': C.S., 'La direzione risponde', *Critica Sociale*, 1903, p. 56.

83 See La Critica, 'Postilla a Bonardi-De Luca, *Ultime schermaglie intorno a Mazzini e al socialismo*', *Critica Sociale*, 1903, p. 148.

84 See, for example, Kuliscioff's important 14 August 1901 letter to Turati, in Turati and Kuliscioff 1977, Vol II/1.

without two processes and their mutual interaction: that of the gradual growth of the self-consciousness of the class *for itself*, and that of the growth of the material productive forces. In the last analysis, these same growth processes would very much depend on what characteristics the second of the fundaments of Turati's Marxism took on: namely, the characteristics of the class struggle. And the class struggle was a mass reality in the Italy of the early twentieth century, as a social struggle in the factories and fields.

Even in circumstances so different from those of the 1890s, Turati sought to remain loyal to the theoretical framework that he had earlier produced with regard to the party-union-class struggle relationship. As such, right from 1901, after the Bologna congress of the peasant organisations had deliberated the 'socialist character' of these same organisations, and Treves writing in the columns of *Critica Sociale* questioned whether this initiative was an opportune one[85] – essentially re-asserting the division between economic action and political action, in contrast to Bonomi[86] – Turati turned to widen the question, giving it a systematisation more in keeping with the way in which the movement as a whole had now come to be defined.

The question of the *Camere del Lavoro* and of union organisation in general found an implicit response in what Turati called 'our doctrine'. If every political struggle was a class struggle, then essentially the inverse was also true. He thus argued:

> The workers' resistance is not only – as some socialists unfortunately think, failing to penetrate into its deeply revolutionary soul – a mechanical struggle connected to the immediate defence of wages and hours, and whose tasks are limited to this immediate defence alone. It is a fulcrum around which circulates a whole atmosphere of eminently political questions and agitations – like an inseparable aura – ... which, taken as a whole, embracing all the relations between labour's interests and the specific activity of the state ... can be summarised in one phrase: proletarian politics.[87]

85 See C. Treves, 'Debbono le CdL diventare socialiste?', *Critica Sociale*, 1901, pp. 352–5.

86 See I. Bonomi, 'Le affermazioni socialiste del congresso di Bologna', *Critica Sociale*, pp. 369–71. Within just two years Bonomi began to shift emphasis from the party to the union, explicitly declaring himself Bernsteinian. See his 'La crisi del movimento socialista', *Critica Sociale*, 1903, pp. 305–8, 323–5.

87 See F. Turati, 'Variazioni sul tema dell'articolo precedente', *Critica Sociale*, 1901, p. 356.

The day-to-day conflict between labour and capital expressed a permanent class conflict, a conflict 'that will find its ultimate solutions in socialism, just as it is on the socialist road that it can find its immediate and partial solutions'.[88] The struggle in the factory was *proletarian politics*, a class struggle whose whole horizon of possibilities still remained unknown.

We can thus understand why Turati attributed only tactical importance to the question of whether or not the *leghe* should join party circles, or whether the trade federations and *Camere del Lavoro* should proclaim socialist end-goals. From the theoretical point of view – that is, according to theory that Turati did not yet see as being contradicted in fact – unionism was an aspect of socialism, of a socialism that was in-the-making, but an aspect that remained essential and inseparable from the organism as a whole. This held true independently of the levels of consciousness reached in each phase of the workers' movement's development.[89]

It has been said that Turati's vision rejected 'any Jacobin conception of the party' and placed the party and union on the same plane, without the one being prioritised over or hegemonising the other. Rather, he instead emphasised their mutual interdependence. Yet the party nonetheless remained the privileged site of 'consciousness', the motor of an indispensable activity of political pedagogy, even if within the terms of the relation that 'existed between the emergence-process of the class struggle and its final point of arrival, prefigured in doctrine and the party that incarnated it. [These latter were] the hypothesis that would have to be proven in the development of social struggles.[90] Indeed, already at the beginning of the century it was the party – or better, its reformist leadership, reluctant to declare itself such – that had elaborated a general frame of reference for socialist activity. This was a complex and fragile panorama of political and economic balances;[91] a frame of reference to

88 See F. Turati, 'Variazioni sul tema dell'articolo precedente', *Critica Sociale*, 1901, p. 357.

89 'As socialists we are subjectively convinced that every proletarian movement is tendentially and thus implicitly a socialist movement, but it does not at all result from this that [the movement in question] must – or, indeed, can – be conscious of that'. See C.S., 'Misticismo socialista', *Critica Sociale*, 1901, p. 375.

90 See Riosa 1983, p. 324.

91 Turati was particularly concerned with the radicalism of social struggles, and the possibility that serious incidents would put into question the now-begun – and little-consolidated – democratisation process. In this perspective, even 'the apostle of Molinella' could become dangerous: 'Yesterday Giolitti called me to talk to me about Molinella. The prefect tells him that the owners were offering reasonable amounts ... Massarenti must be a little fanatical': see Turati's 25 May 1901 letter to Kuliscioff in Turati and Kuliscioff 1977, Vol. II/1.

which trade unionism would have to adapt, and whose consolidation it would in some sense also assist.

It is true that even when, as in the Italian case, this framework was too restrictive to contain the multiplicity of trade-union experiences, these initial theoretical presuppositions would not be forgotten. However, the preoccupation with the immediate became a prevalent one, posing a priority need to 'discipline' the movement (given the difficulties and encumbrances of relations with the masses). On this condition – and also as a consequence of the bitter political-theoretical battle with the revolutionary syndicalists that was soon to open up – a wide reformist front could be created, formed of elements with divergent theoretical reference points and elaborations, and in the long term even ones of different political inspiration.

The need to 'discipline' the 'anarchist' forms that seemed to characterise so much of the social dynamic protagonised by workers' and peasants' organisations did not only concern the problem of general political equilibria, but also the logic of the development of the productive forces. Again on this point, Turati sought precedents in the Marxian tradition. He reasserted, 'following Karl Marx's imperious thinking', that 'industry [was] the essential condition of socialism', and thus there 'were certain areas of common interests between industrialists and proletarians'.[92] But given the difficulty (or impossibility?) of deriving a Marxist economic policy from Marx's economic theory,[93] he ultimately accepted (or gave in to) the productivist theories then present on the intellectual market. The early twentieth-century Turati thus wanted solidly to anchor his own trajectory in the reasoning that had ten years earlier seen him play a leading role in the formation of the 'Marxist party'.

However, alongside this proclamation of the Marxist reasoning behind the political journey that now seemed to be beginning, there was also the sense that it would have to find its own justifications above all within itself, through the engagement with things and not theories. As Turati argued 'today we have reached a point in which socialism, translated from the minds of its trailblazers

92 See F. Turati, 'Gli agenti dello Stato e le Camere del Lavoro', *Critica Sociale*, 1902, p. 227.

93 See the observations in Macchioro 1982. The man who happened to begin the 1894–5 discussion on the labour theory of value, Romeo Soldi, noted this difficulty when he argued that 'an orientation with regard to economic policy' was 'the most important question, in that it [must] represent the point of differentiation between our party and all the others'. However, Soldi limited himself to declaring his opposition to 'state socialism', favouring a completely free-trade economic policy. See his 'La politica economica del partito socialista', *Critica Sociale*, 1900, p. 200.

... into the immanent reality of life, no longer needs doctrinal justifications and theoretical illustrations: it is alive in things, and like the Greek philosopher, proves that it moves by moving'.[94]

It was precisely the test of facts – the harshness and complexity of the class struggle in the Giolittian era – that would demonstrate the difficulty of holding together the two elements inspiring Turati's strategic vision at the beginning of the century.

3 The Economic Theory of the Workers' Movement

In the first years of the 1900s Graziadei's 'productivist' programme entered without difficulty – indeed, without any great disharmonies – into the panorama of appeals for reform that the socialists were now carrying forward as they proceeded along their new course. In that period *Critica Sociale* seemed to have become the privileged site for the encounter between proletarian socialism and 'high-bourgeois socialism'[95] – the second *Kathedersozialismus*.

Reviewing Nitti's book *L'Italia all'alba del secolo XX*, Graziadei fully agreed with the author that the country's greatest problem was that of 'increasing production'. Yet he added an important additional comment:

> I would almost say that the whole effort with which our working classes have managed to increase their wages in recent months should not be measured so much in terms of its useful effects – the immediate material advantage it has brought them in terms of distribution – but its possible consequences for increasing production[96]

Almost at the same time Einaudi seemed almost to paraphrase his friend, again writing in Turati's magazine:

> It should be understood that if the workers want to earn a lot, they should do their best to ensure that capital is employed in the most productive and economical sense possible. This will seem paradoxical, but without doubt it is then that Italians will manage to improve their conditions in

94 See La C.S., 'Dodicennio', *Critica Sociale*, 1902, p. 369.

95 Expression taken from Lanaro 1979, p. 212.

96 See A. Graziadei, 'La nuova Italia, (a proposito di un libro del prof. Nitti)', in *Critica Sociale*, 1901, p. 34.

> a lasting matter – that is, when they become more jealous defenders of capital's interests than are the capitalists themselves[97]

In substance, what was here being re-proposed – this time in a truly favourable climate – was the very same perspective that Nitti, Loria and their entourage had long worked on in the 1890s. Even the names were the same: Einaudi, Cabiati, Sella, Supino, and Conigliani.

This latter contributed writing under the pseudonym 'l'Economista', and insisted on the need to combine the workers' movement's 'reasonable' action with the benefits of progressive social legislation, and *in primis* tax reform.[98] It was precisely on this point that illusions in 'the great reform' were repeatedly shattered.

Upon Conigliani's early death Turati published an incomplete article of his that had been conceived as the preparatory material for a university course.[99] He defined him 'very close to socialism' and took care to add that 'the ideas [that he] brought into relief in that seminar match with those that we defend in these pages on the same theme, which draw no little comfort and authority from professor Conigliani's agreement'.[100]

The ideas elaborated by professor Conigliani – 'a high-bourgeois socialist'[101] – with regard to the role of the workers' movement, 'high wages', and productivism were carefully inserted into the perspective that we have discussed thus far. So, too, were the very many reviews, analyses and references to foreign publications supposedly offering effective proof of the tendencies now underway on the world scale. The section 'Fra libre e riviste' was far from frugal in its output, though it did not find space to review the contribution that Ernesto Cesare Longobardi had made to the theory of wages.[102]

---

97 See L. Einaudi, 'L'ora degli spropositi', *Critica Sociale*, 1902, p. 34.

98 See L'Economista, 'La riforma tributaria e il ministero Zanardelli', *Critica Sociale*, 1901, pp. 251–252.

99 See C. Conigliani, 'Movimento operaio e produzione nazionale', *Critica Sociale*, 1903, pp. 105–10.

100 See Turati's introduction to the article.

101 Lanaro 1979, p. 212.

102 At the moment in which the theory of 'high wages' seemed to be becoming dominant within socialist economic culture, the future revolutionary syndicalist – one of the intellectuals most linked to the antagonistic vision of socialism – tried to analyse this phenomenon within the autonomous perspective that he considered underpinned by Marx's theory. Longobardi worked to offer an analysis in terms of the labour theory of value, with an explicit polemic against Graziadei. 'Graziadei is perfectly right to regret that some

Whatever its internal articulations, the 'reformist' front seemed still to be advancing with all its components moving in close connection, if we do not count the more slowly developing polemic on the relation between the road now being taken and the 'Marxist tradition'. Notwithstanding its lack of theoretical depth, this polemic could not simplistically be reduced to the tactical motives of a knowing 'false consciousness'.

Again here, one of the nodes of discussion was economic theory and the possibility of translating it into economic policy. There were substantially two positions coming into definition: on the one hand, that which argued that Marx's economic theory was not translatable into economic policy, and thus sought and proposed a form of cohering the two spheres that stood entirely outside of Marx's analysis. On the other hand, that which remained determined to preserve the inseparability of the Marxism-socialism pair, but at the same time sought to overcome the undeniable difficulties of such a translation by accepting a *de facto* caesura between the two moments.

In a first phase the 'reformist' front proved to be a compact one because the hypothesis at the basis of its operations – facilitating the rapid formation of a homogeneous and modern industrial society, and ensuring the widening of the spaces of democracy, such as to allow a true and proper democratic revolution – was sufficiently broad as to give productivist theory more the sense of a perspective, a general indication, rather than a specific norm of social and political behaviour. When the moment arrived – and it would come very soon – for the general perspective to be translated into concrete choices regarding the role of the trade union both in the country's modernisation and, above all, within the socialist movement as a whole, there would be no lack of sharp contradictions among the forces deployed on this front.

Already in 1904–5 Graziadei began advancing a theoretical-political offensive seeking a definitive clarification and more precise definition of 'reformism'. He did so through two essays, one of an academic character (a preparatory text

---

would try to reduce his dissension from the Marxist school to a simple game of words ... Marxists look to the value of commodities, Graziadei to their mass: and since their value and mass do not always increase together, the two ways of looking at them lead to often-opposite attitudes towards economic phenomena'. The relation that he sought to establish was not so much that between the mass of wages and the mass of profits, but that between wages and the rate of profit. He moreover distinguished between labour *intensity* and labour *productivity*, linking the possibility of wage increases to an increase in labour *intensity*, which would thus demonstrate the continued survival of 'the general sense of opposition between wages and profits'. See Longobardi 1903.

for a political economy course at the University of Cagliari), and the second of a more immediately political stamp.

This was the clear and coherent development of the arguments that he had elaborated at the turn of the century. The central theme at the centre of the preparatory text was that of giving 'scientific' rigour to explaining the forms of class struggle that were compatible with the greater efficiency of the economic system. The workers' movement's political and above all economic action were here closely correlated with the rhythms of industrial development, its setbacks and crises. Within this framework, strikes themselves were considered a 'primitive' element that had to be cast off in order to suit the logic of the country's 'general economic interest'.[103] Left free to play its role, the market's regulating mechanism was in the last instance the arbiter of the volume of wages, because it was able to establish a functional relationship between this variable and labour productivity. As Graziadei argued, 'since in a system of free competition the entrepreneur's role is of very great importance and corresponds to a true and proper social utility, it follows that ... it is in the workers' own interest not to touch, or still less to go beyond the limits'.[104]

Moreover – and this is no longer any surprise – writing at the same time in the same place Attilio Cabiati was theorising the role of workers' organisation in encouraging free market competition.[105]

Graziadei had to ask himself whether it was realistically possible for Italian trade unionism to take on such behavioural norms at the same time as maintaining close links with a party like the *Partito socialista*, a volatile force whose leading personnel were intellectuals liable to being drawn to the sirens

103 'In Italy, where the workers' movement is still a child and where, therefore, above all in 1900–2 there was a very great amount of lost working days, for the greater part of those involved and in public opinion workers' organisation still seems synonymous with strikes. Yet one of the most heartening manifestations of progress is this: that workers' organisation can become stronger even as it resorts ever less – or in a certain sense, to the degree that it resorts ever less – to a weapon of struggle that in itself always means a loss for society as a whole'. See A. Graziadei, 'Il Movimento Operaio. Prelezione al corso di economia politica nella Università di Cagliari', *Critica Sociale*, 1904, citation from p. 170.

104 A. Graziadei, 'Il Movimento Operaio. Prelezione al corso di economia politica nella Università di Cagliari', *Critica Sociale*, 1904, p. 202.

105 'Far from blocking the free play of competition, workers' organisation brings the maximal conditions for allowing it to play out, realising the hypotheses connected to this economic state. Organisation is, then, more than something of direct utility for the worker, a powerful means of general economic progress'. See A. Cabiati, 'Le basi teoriche dell'organizzazione operaia', *Critica Sociale*, 1904, pp. 42–7.

of 'Marxist revolutionism' (and lest we forget, this was in the climate following the 'intransigent turn' at the Bologna Congress). Of course, there could be no lack of effort to make sure that a real reformism did establish itself in the party – and this would be an unequivocal reformism, because it would be founded on solid, non-Marxist theoretical bases. Yet it was above all in the union that 'trade-unionist'[106] tendencies – which were, fortunately enough, already spontaneously present in the workers' organisation, by its very nature – had to be underpinned by a rigorous theory that would be developed wholly autonomously of the political institution.

The inherent spirit that animated unionism's policy was, in Graziadei's view, a utilitarian and practical one; that is, one based on essentially economic contents. As he argued:

> [U]nionism is the working class that directly concerns itself with its own interests, above all from the economic point of view. It is, therefore, the working class in immediate contact with the most complex and multifaced of realities: with the reality that automatically inflicts the most severe, serious sanctions on those unable to evaluate it properly.[107]

As such, only a union completely autonomous of the *Partito socialista* would be able to root the working masses in reformism in a deep and lasting manner – a reformism that defined itself above all as the elastic capacity to adapt to automatic economic mechanisms.

> *Every class struggle is a political struggle* – so the *Communist Manifesto* told us back in 1847. But it would take a few decades for the vanguards of the proletariat to delve deeper into the meaning of this phrase. Naturally, it will take a few decades more for the professors also finally to do so.[108]

Such was the sharp and severe response given by Filippo Turati – the man who still thought himself the staunch inheritor of the encounter between the *Lega Socialista* and the *Partito Operaio Italiano*; the man who like his antagonist at that moment, Enrico Ferri, thought himself the bearer of a 'socialist consciousness' that transcended – even if it did not ignore – the sociological fact of his

---

106 [That is, in the English sense]

107 See A. Graziadei, 'Sindacalismo, riformismo, rivoluzionarismo', *Critica Sociale*, 1905, p. 196.

108 See La C.S., 'Postilla a A. Graziadei, *Sindacalismo riformista*', *Critica Sociale*, p. 214.

class position. Yet his new adversary had little in common with the POI of the late 1880s, with his stance barely even being superficially analogous. The economic union that was now being proposed – the production union – was the fruit of a wholly particular relation with economic theory. Turati did not seem fully to have understand this.

For this reason, in his polemic with Graziadei he lay greater stress on the elements of the opposing argument that he considered regressive and neo-corporative. On this plane he accepted an open battle, without any desire for compromise, returning to cite Marxian sources. He here in large part accepted Engels's definition of 'class', though he made its conception of the arrival of 'consciousness' from the outside even more rigid in nature. And as concerned the party-class relation, he went much further than he had done with his positions at the moment of the foundation of the 'Marxist party'.[109]

Moreover, such positions seem to have had little effect on the overall elaborations of the unions' reformist leaders, and in particular the engineering federation (FIOM) and the Confederazione Generale del Lavoro (CGL). The fact is that the policies here being suggested to the unions, deriving either from a theory of the workers' movement's economic role that reduced it to a mere factor of production, or else from a vision of the gradual extension of 'socialist consciousness' among the proletariat, ended up converging: 'reasonableness' and respect for a very well-defined frame of possible conflict. Indeed, in this context even the 'socialist consciousness' that Turati here invoked seemed to be reduced to the one-dimensional role of disciplining the forms in which social struggle was expressed.

The relation that Turati sought to establish with the proletarian protagonists of the workplace class struggle was a difficult and complex one. A deep diffidence toward the 'proletariat devoid of consciousness' or of 'education' – easily visible in fleeting insurrectionism as in hopeless depression – pervaded a large part of not only the *Critica Sociale* director's interventions, but so, too, those of a

109 'Politically speaking, the class as a class is nothing. Worse, the proletarian class *qua* proletarian – subject – class, is the tool of the bosses' policy … The proletariat is and remains what it is, insofar as its condition and consciousness are modelled to suit the bosses' interest. Only when the proletariat begins to understand this (which, as a rule, will result from teaching by intellectuals, men from another class) … will it become an imposing force. But then, also … it becomes a party. The socialist party is nothing if not the proletariat – or a part of it – that has gained consciousness of its condition and is convinced that its emancipation will be achieved by way of socialism': see La C.S., 'Postilla a A. Graziadei, *Politica di partito e politica di classe*', *Critica Sociale*, 1905, p. 248.

large part of the socialist leadership group,[110] including many union organisers of working-class backgrounds like Verzi and Rigola.

At the same time, Turati was convinced that without active proletarian participation no socialist political programme would be able to develop. Rather, this participation was presented as the fundamental discriminating factor for distinguishing so-called socialist 'reformism' – a term that Turati would slowly get used to, in a particularly troubled way and not without sudden about-turns – from bourgeois 'reformism'. In Turati's framework there was no contradiction, here: the slow and gradual advance of 'socialist consciousness' among the proletariat, an important element in the growth of the productive forces themselves, would allow the further connection and ultimately the total conjugation of these two aspects.

However, in the reality of historical process 'things' followed rather different paths. This was a country where not only the 'feudal' propertied classes but also a large part of the modern ones had a notable predisposition toward direct relations with the industrial and agrarian proletariat, without the institutional mediations of the workers' movement, where social divisions were very strong, and where the elements of crisis were almost permanent. This lent itself poorly to the possibility of applying a conceptual framework that was wholly built on the basis of hypothesising long-term continuities.

One long, well-documented and rigorous study has argued that the Italian workers' movement's cycles of conflict were not exceptional as compared to other European experiences of industrialisation. In this view, this movement's cycles demonstrated a substantial correspondence between economic development and the order of magnitude of the manifestations of class struggle. It follows that there was no Italian anomaly in this field – and that reformist socialism's difficulties in broadly, deeply taking root among the proletariat and workers' movement should be located within a culture that had a totally unconflictual vision of development, rather than in the characteristics of social conflict in Italy and a presumed 'excess of conflictuality'.[111]

---

110 Indicative in this regard is a letter written by Kuliscioff with regard to strikes: 'They are declared light-heartedly, supported by the drunk, and finished by children who soon tire of any diversion. The way to handle it is by stringing them along, as you do with children. Do not take them from the front, maintain an air of following them, but try to give indication. This kind of hypocrisy, which offends our consciences, is however necessary when we come into contact with brute, drunken masses, often set off by those who have an interest in rising to the top, for want of any other means of distinguishing themselves'. Kuliscioff to Turati, 17 August 1901, in Turati and Kuliscioff 1977, Vol. II/1.

111 See Lay and Pesante 1981.

In truth, long-term quantitative analyses on the frequency and concentration of strikes, as they concern the relation between workers' struggle and the economic cycle, are certainly important elements, but they are just part of a multi-dimensional landscape.

The union as an institution and its activity were not reducible to functions purely corresponding to the logics of particular conjunctural phases. They were also a cultural moment, the expression of values, of ways of being and wanting to be, modes of action based on the projection of a certain identity. They were moments linked to the drives and needs of class unity and of the general re-composition of the movement. Functional theories serve only rather partially to explain the ever-composite nature of worker-conflictuality. Only if the hypothesis on which Graziadei worked so intensely – that of making the union's activity really a function (even an essential one) of the cycle – were truly well-suited to the overall reality of Italian unionism, would such theories display their capacities of explanation.

Moreover, we ought to consider – and this is without doubt a peculiarity of the Italian case – that such a great part of the conflict in question, in general meaning a highly episodic series of 'incidents', played out in the countryside, both in the advanced areas of Po Valley agrarian capitalism as in the 'feudal' *latifundia* of the South. The quantitative dimensions of this conflict without doubt increase starkly if we also take into account peasant struggles – indeed, we could not do otherwise.

This is true independently of the possibility of objectively determining an 'excess of conflict'. But this 'excess' would in any case be ascribed to multiple variables other than a rigidly quantative dimension, including ones relating to the ways in which this conflict was understood. That is to say, both how it was received in the country in general, and in particular in the sphere of those cultures then theorising the forms of class conflict.

In this sense, there is no doubt that for both Graziadei's functionalism and the parameters deriving from Turati's balanced 'socialist reformism' strategy, the social conflict expressed by the industrial and agricultural proletariat was certainly excessive, in terms of both the quantity of strikes and the means in which this conflict was expressed.

Moreover, the tendency struggle that played out between 1903 and the exclusion of the revolutionary syndicalists – which came to take on extremely bitter tones – would come deeply to shape Turati's attitude toward the union initatives now developing that had no possibility of being conditioned by reformism, instead being in some sense inspired by syndicalist revolutionism. For example, his diffidence – or rather, open hostility – toward the railworkers' federation owed both to his lack of sympathy toward strikes in the public services, and the fact that this federation was at that time one of revolutionary syndicalism's strongholds in industrial unionism.

Indeed, during the wage dispute of 1905, when the railworkers used the tactic of obstruction (the work-to-rule), and the government took the opportunity to resign, Turati proved unable to contain himself, reacting in a clearly over-the-top manner:

> I am destroyed. I believe that it would be difficult to conceive of a crime of high treason greater than this. They have made Branconi the king of Italy and Labriola the prime minister, and put Braccialarghe in charge of foreign affairs. The abdication of the state and the treason perpetrated against the King, parliament, and democracy is enough to cast the republics of South America in a good light. Note that the ministers knew very well not only from the railworkers' union, and not only from the spies that they have everywhere, but also from us, that this obstructionism was bound to end today, or at worst within a few days[112]

Even Kuliscioff, while sharing Turati's diffidence toward uncontrollable social movements, sometimes found his reactions wholly inadequate to the very policy of which the reformist leader had made himself the proponent, posing arguments to Turati that he himself could have been making.[113]

However, faced with forms of class struggle that could not be disciplined from the outside, Turati's reactions were something more than a matter of private disturbance. His concern to promote the disciplining of the forms of social conflict – through the establishment of court-recognised compulsory arbitration commissions – gradually led him to adopt theoretical assumptions typical of the 'bourgeois reformism' that he in other fields continued to fight with no little tenacity. As such, some of his formulations illustrating the need

112 Turati to Kuliscioff, 21 May 1905, in Turati and Kuliscioff 1977.

113 'I truly do not know why you are so bothered by the strike in the Vercellese. Now the owners are desperate because of the abandonment of the livestock, and for their concern for the livestock they will become a bit less fierce with the human livestock. You follow the legal path, and let the proletariat express its desires as best it can. I think that the two activities complement one another, and that such a vast movement can only strengthen you. It is ridiculous to attribute a movement of such breadth and solidarity to the likes of Cugnolio: those like Lucca and Giolitti can say this because the provocateur does much to serve the conservative spirit. But certainly we cannot in good conscience think the same ourselves'. Kuliscioff to Turati, 2 March 1907, in Turati and Kuliscioff 1977.

for compulsory arbitration seemed to express the idea of collective bargaining essentially being reduced to a merely technical function:

> We reach the gradual solution to social disputes – and there can be no other – by putting around a little table a few intelligent and responsible people who have been entrusted with authority ... Evaluating the forces concerned, the capacity and the interests of those represented [and] the conditions of the industry ... *a mathematically certain and invariable solution* can be found for every disagreement in every time and place: it is the only [solution] in that time and place, the one most useful and most just for all concerned.[114]

Turati's theorisation of pragmatism, as well as the pressures of immediate political demands, thus led him gradually to disarticulate the pair of factors that he had previously considered it essential to combine: namely, openness to the new problems of Italian society, and, at the same time, the maintenance of the socialist tradition's peculiar characteristics and its fundamental theoretical reference points.

As such, it was no chance thing that at the end of 1908, when reformism seemed triumphant, Turati referred to a conjugation between reformism and revisionism that he had always previously denied and combatted. It seemed that reformism would be sure to guide the party and, in time, the workers' movement, for a long period; and Turati wrote 'Reformism as a theoretical assumption can now be taken for a given ... Through a slower path, with more practical steps, and in closer connection to circumstances, it will nonetheless arrive at the same end goal'.[115]

In Turati's perspective, then, the Italian road to revisionism followed the course that pragmatism had opened up with such great effort. This was, however, true only from his own point of view. After all, there was also a solid, rigorous and theoretically established Italian revisionism that, even if unable to boast of giving rise to its German counterpart, was at least autonomous of it.

Turati, however, was keen to point to the practical aspect of Italian revisionism. It is important to emphasise this, because he had no intention, here, of wholly renouncing his old convictions. His recent path was one not lacking in uncertainties, aporiai and even contradictions.

---

114 See La C.S., 'I ferrovieri e il governo', *Critica Sociale*, 1905, p. 51.

115 La C.S., 'Quel che insegna uno sciopero che non esiste', *Critica Sociale*, 1908, p. 209.

Yet in this moment it was the figures closest to him – Schiavi, as we will see, and Kuliscioff – who countered him using his own previous argumentation. As Kuliscioff argued,

> The man who best recalls the 'reformists because we are revolutionaries' of the Imola Congress may appear to offer himself up to easy syndicalist and bourgeois mockery in this quarrel, but he was in fact the same man who provided a lucid synthesis of the difference in character between our reformism and radical, philanthropic, bourgeois reformism.[116]

It was not that references to this framework had wholly disappeared from Turati's writings. He still spoke of reforms as 'the revolution on the march', and of 'the true fundaments of Marxism'; but these were episodic statements, a consciousness external to specific and determinate choices.

It would, all the same, be mistaken to reduce these elements to mere 'false consciousness'. Arguments linked to a given stage of Italian socialism and to the decisions supposed to provide the basis for Italian democracy seem to have counted for more than did the oft-cited arguments for continuity. That is true independently of any errors of calculation that were made; and there were not a few of them. Yet the red thread supposedly derived from Engels's 1894 letter was not completely broken. Other conditions would favour attempts to tie back into it. Yet it was severely worn-out, and Turati himself would come to look at it with no little discomfort.

This can help us understand the reasons why Turati's interventions in these years – attempting to combat the 'labourist' project and the workers' movement's 'corporatist' tendencies, also by referring to the old Marxist Resolution IX – ran the risk of appearing strongly reductivist. That is, they were limited to a specific battle for hegemony, directed at asserting the pure and simple priority of the party over the union.

Turati sharply depicted this question: 'Socialism is to the workers' movement as the brain is to the spinal cord in animals – that is, it tends to replace simply reflex actions with the action of reflection, which is counter to these actions and a brake on them, even if it is but their evolved product'.[117] But what tended to go missing in these years was the socialist character of the impulses that the brain was meant to transmit through the spinal cord, at least in the sense of

116 See Schiavi, Kuliscioff, Turati, 'Il voto dei socialisti per ministero. Errore o degenerazione?', *Critica Sociale*, 1910, p. 147.

117 La C.S., 'Quel che insegna uno sciopero che non esiste', *Critica Sociale*, 1908, p. 209.

the 'party-as-class' that had been one of the most creative elements of Filippo Turati's Marxism.

If we expand our perspective to take into account the signals given out by Italian socialism's most important review, we can get an even better grasp of the weakness of the defences that Turati was trying to build in opposition to the 'trade-unionist'[118] offensive. His appeal to Bonomi to combat this offensive – an appeal to the man now becoming its cutting edge – was almost pathetic.[119] *Critica Sociale* continued to point to models of industrial relations based on 'class collaboration'; and if intellectuals-organisers of such considerable prestige and influence as Schiavi and Pagliari pointed to its problematic elements (whatever their own differences of perspective), others like Crespi and Marchioli who were foreign to organisational concerns instead produced an 'extreme' and ossified version of this model. Given these latters' continued presence in this review's pages over many years – being the curators of some of its sections and correspondents from London and Berlin – they did much to shape this publication's general 'tone'.

Already in 1904 Marchioli had insisted on the need to separate Marxism from socialism, and he now arrived at the conclusion that socialism also needed to be separated from the fate of the proletariat.[120] He long insisted that reformism must follow the entire 'revisionist' path, breaking with tradition, relativising

118 [That is, in the English sense]

119 It is true that in 1905 Bonomi's 'revisionism' was not fully explicated, but Turati and Kuliscioff considered the Mantua socialist to be to their 'extreme Right'. Moreover, when Bonomi published *Le vie nuove del socialismo*, Turati seemed not immediately to grasp the elements in which it broke with the socialist tradition. He published a section of this book in *Critica Sociale*, prefaced by a brief note commenting that this volume was 'the deepest and most courageous test of conscience that we have been able to read in all the contemporary socialist [literature] ... It is also to some extent our book'; *Critica Sociale*, 1907, p. 340. One year earlier he had written '[Bonomi] will prepare our new *Manifesto*' (letter to Kuliscioff, 17 March 1906). Conversely, Graziadei had tried to underline its elements of discontinuity. He did say that the book 'has not tried to delve into the economic problems most intensely connected to Marxist theory', thus suggesting that reformism's fundamental theoretical reference must necessarily attach itself to this past elaboration. But from this he drew conclusions rather different to Turati's: 'Twenty years of continuous propaganda and action have now enabled the *leghe*, the cooperatives, and the workers' unions to make their own policy, without the need still to remain under the protection of a party made up of Marx-loyalists'. See A. Graziadei, 'Le vie nuove del socialismo' (review), *Avanti!*, 25 November 1907.

120 See E. Marchioli, 'L'ultimo critico di Carlo Marx', and 'Dalle elezioni tedesche ai socialisti italiani', *Critica Sociale*, 1904, pp. 203–5 and 1907, pp. 71–4 respectively.

what he called 'the class's interest', and making 'class collaboration' an organic part of the party's and the union's activity, rather than a merely occasional one.[121] As he wrote:

> As a general line, we must seek ... to make the conditions of the economic balance as advantageous as possible to the workers and the trade organisations, these conditions (as illustrious economists like Pareto and Marshall have demonstrated) being subject to a perennial rhythm.[122]

Here we see that pragmatism did not at all mean disdain for precise theoretical reference points: it was simply a question of choosing between differently-grounded theories. Naturally, Marchioli did not spare the so-called 'fundaments' of Turati's Marxism, either. As he further wrote:

> if the class struggle ... as an instrument of political struggle and social transformation is the consequence of a Marxist theoretical premise, what is left of the consequence now that the premise has collapsed? ... The socialist party has an idealistic purpose, and its means must also be idealistic. The class struggle is inappropriate for two reasons: because it is based on false premises and because it derives from a mechanical-materialist philosophy ...[123]

Beyond adding a further call for the complete abandonment of Marxist culture[124] and paying tribute to the British ruling classes' contribution to socialism,[125] Crespi ended up calling for the 'right to blacklegging' [crumiraggio]. This cohered with a free-trade theory saving the company from any possible 'monopoly of workers' organisation'.[126] He thus touched on one of the socialist sensibility's most sensitive nerve endings.

121 See E. Marchioli, 'Tentativi di rinnovamento. Sulla crisi del movimento socialista', *Critica Sociale*, 1907, pp. 71–4.

122 See E. Marchioli, 'Filosofia della vittoria socialista nelle elezioni politiche', *Critica Sociale*, 1909, p. 69.

123 See E. Marchioli, 'Oltre la lotta di classe' and 'Lotta di classe e giustizia sociale', *Critica Sociale*, 1911, pp. 165–7 and 179–82 respectively. Quotations from pp. 165 and 167.

124 See A. Crespi, 'Intorno alla crisi attuale del partito socialista italiano', *Critica Sociale*, 1907, pp. 292–4.

125 See A. Crespi, 'Socialismo inglese e socialismo continentale', *Critica Sociale*, 1907, pp. 86–9.

126 See A. Crespi, 'L'organizzazione operaia e la libertà di lavoro', *Critica Sociale*, 1907, pp. 354–8.

These positions on the 'right to blacklegging' were not shared by the *Critica Sociale*'s editors, and Marchioli himself had to put up his shields. Yet Turati's marginal notes, edits and explanations do not seem to have been able radically to alter the atmosphere that built up around the review. Indeed, with the exception of the truly extreme points of Marchioli and Crespi's interventions – like the question of blacklegging – they were always considered *internal* to reformist socialism, and critical contributions to its enrichment.

The confines of the territory that the 'Marxist and reformist' Turati had wanted clearly to define were now gradually becoming more blurred. Turati even had doubts over excluding Angelo Crespi from the columns of *Critica Sociale*, not withstanding Anna Kuliscioff's calls for him to do so.[127]

It was Cabiati who gave the 'scientific' response – in syntony with 'economic theory' – to the question of the 'freedom of labour' and the possibility of a monopoly of workers' organisation. His theory of reference was that of the 'theory of the general economic equilibrium', with particular reference to labour as a factor of production and the relation between pure economics and the 'frictions' appearing on the real market. Cabiati's goal was to determine the maximum collective economic utility in the production process. The union could not represent a monopolistic element of imbalance, in that 'potential competition is always kept alive by the imbalance between the population and the means of subsistence, a continuous imbalance across a long period of time and that depends on capitalists in order to maintain it as a constant'.[128] So long as 'unions always remain[ed] a minority', workers' organisation would serve to eliminate the 'frictions' caused by the inequality in the starting points of the different factors of production, and prove the truth of Walras and Pareto's mathematical demonstration of the fact that 'in the system of free competition, prices are fixed in such a manner as to provide the maximum utility in each permutation'.[129]

Turati had called for this 'scientific' response, but for him it must nonetheless have remained difficult to conjugate the vision of the union that emerged, here, with his old conviction that 'every class movement *as a* class move-

127 Kuliscioff described Crespi's articles as an 'individualist-free trader mush, and above all an anti-socialist one', and proposed that their author be ostracised from *Critica Sociale*. Turati was, however, very much perplexed by this, writing 'We have too few friends and collaborators ... I fear that with such methods we would end up surrounded by a void'. See their 20 and 21 February 1908 letters in Turati and Kuliscioff 1977.

128 See. A. Cabiati, 'I sofismi economici di Angelo Crespi a difesa della libertà di lavoro e di krumiraggio', *Critica Sociale*, 1908, p. 24.

129 Ibid.

ment is necessarily a *political* movement'; another of the 'fundaments' of his Marxism.

This union discussion was the game being played by a modern reformism, and one lacking any Marxist equivocations. The 'revisionists' were perfectly convinced of this, and Graziadei was absolutely unprepared to give ground on the clarity of his theoretical discourse, even if this would prove tactically inopportune in the tendency struggle playing out within the party. In his view it was better to be a steady cultural reference point for workers' organisation than to acquire positions of authority within a socialist party whose tasks were destined to be drastically reshaped by the development of the workers' movement.

For this reason, Graziadei was sharply opposed to the operation leading to an alliance between reformists and 'fundamentalists' at the Rome Congress, both for the reasons mentioned already and – more importantly from the standpoint of his theoretical clarity – because this operation's success relied on it appearing to follow in the groove of the party's 'tradition': re-asserting the identity that had been 'violated' – as it was said at the time – by the foreign body of revolutionary-syndicalist culture. This thus meant the complete overturning of the perspective that held reformism to be the *new* socialism. For this reason, Graziadei's intervention on this question was brutal in its frankness.

For him, the tradition of socialism to which some sought re-attachment was 'sharply Marxist'. The revolutionary syndicalists were right in laying claim to this tradition, he argued:

> Whoever objectively examines the ensemble of Marxist doctrines must recognise that the revolutionary syndicalists are, in sum, rather closer to the letter of Marxism than are the reformists; we should conclude that these latter – we might say, thanks to their modernity – have lost the melancholic right to speak in that tradition's name.[130]

In his view, the Marxist tradition could be summarised in the following points: gradual immiseration, b) capitalist centralisation, c) an absolute antagonism of wages and profit, d) the illusory nature of the working class making gains within the capitalist system, and e) the conviction that only the working class's labour produced value.

Graziadei countered each of these points with the results of his own theory, as principally contained in his *La produzione capitalistica*. He asserted the

130 A. Graziadei, 'Riformismo e riformisti', *Avanti!*, 3 September 1906.

essential role of 'revisionism' – both his own and Bernstein's – ever since the discussions on the 'crisis of Marxism', this being the only theoretical orientation 'that could have prepared the intellectual and moral justification' for the reformist tendency. 'The real truth', he concluded

> Is that in its general terms Marxism is gloomily pessimistic, and thus catastrophic, and thus revolutionary. It is not in favour of reformism, but against it ... For many reformism will only cease to appear as degeneration or personal accommodation the day that they are able to bring their doctrine into accord with their practice, words with deeds ...[131]

And what better teacher of 'facts' could there be – as against ideological abstractions – than the long experience of organising and making demands that unionism had built up in the organised workers' movement? Indeed, 'being in direct contact with the reality of economic facts and laws – facts and laws that cannot be misunderstood or violated with impunity – union action finds in the very field in which it plays out a ready and inexorable endorsement of its own operation'.[132] In this view, union action played out in the context of forces that developed 'naturally'; its success would ultimately be determined by a precise identification of what tendencies were underway, and in adequating a demand-making policy to these tendencies.

Here Pantaleoni was almost echoing Graziadei, as he denied that there could be different 'schools' within the union: as he put it, it was instead a question of 'being capable or not'.[133] In this view, tendencies were typical of the party-political sphere; clashes over choices of a 'philosophical' character often emerged where there was a broad scope for subjectivity, and not in the world of those who had to face up to the 'objectivity' of the process of production and distribution and the 'objectivity' of the market.

The revolutionary syndicalists' error, then, was that they were political far more than they were syndicalist; that is, they were revolutionary because they were political, responding to doctrinal influences. Yet given that syndicalism was meant to operate in the economic sphere – in one dimension, a dimension that was by nature wholly removed from the improvisations of revolutionary voluntarism – it must necessarily be reformist, if it was not to negate its own syndicalist character.

---

131 Ibid.

132 Graziadei 1909b, p. 63.

133 Graziadei 1909b, p. 65.

If syndicalism was to be decisive and combative in assuring the equitable repartition of income, then it must be convinced that 'only class collaboration can solve the problems of production'.[134] It could be taken for granted that even such 'class struggle' as could freely unfold in the sphere of distribution, and social legislation itself, would necessarily meet an insurmountable limit in the 'natural' logic of capital accumulation and in the general social interest.[135]

In short, the Graziadei who sought, at the end of the 1900s, to define the relations between socialism, syndicalism, Marxism, and economic theory, displayed a deep trust in capitalism's capacity gradually to regulate itself, once freed of 'traps and snares'. This was a mature capitalism that, faced with a likewise mature workers' movement capable of 'freeing itself of the various mistaken economic ideas' – sowed 'amidst the working class'[136] by political socialism (Marxism) – would be able to guarantee a modern industrial democracy. It would thus be the bearer of an uninterrupted series of material and moral improvements.

Ultimately, then, socialism was certainly not the fruit of the contradictory dynamic of capitalist development. Rather, it derived from the fact that 'human needs, whether economic, intellectual, or moral, are by their very nature unlimited'.[137]

---

134 Graziadei 1909b, p. 45.

135 'From this point of view', Graziadei noted, 'perhaps it is fair to say that not a few Italian reformists have suffered from over-optimism, in the sense of maintaining that we can today achieve legislative measures superior to our true potential': Graziadei 1909b, p. 88. Writing to his friend Einaudi, he provided further assurances as to his moderation and his particular concern to seek solutions compatible with the system: 'I am glad that my pamphlet on *Socialismo e sindacalismo* was not to your displeasure. As for the danger that you note – namely that the reformist union might become "organised brigandage to rob money from others by way of the state" – believe me, that is not at all my intention. I think that a *certain minimum* social legislation represents a … natural and necessary phenomenon … I think that we must not want this certain minimum – in each moment relative to many factors, the very most important of which is the level of social wealth – to be artificially increased by the Jacobin mania to legislate': Graziadei to Einaudi, 8 July 1909, Fondazione Luigi Einaudi, Carte Graziadei.

136 Graziadei 1909b, p. 31.

137 Graziadei 1909b, p. 61.

4 The Articulations of Non-Marxist Reformism, the Returns of History, and Again on Reformist Marxism

How far was the 'economic theory' of the workers' movement able to impact the movement's culture and practical outlook?

According to the first great Italian study offering a synthesis of the CGdL's history, a large part of the platform providing the basis for the union confederation's activity after the 1908 Modena Congress was fundamentally inspired by Graziadei's elaboration.[138]

Without doubt, even a brief survey of the immense available material gives the impression of a figure deeply rooted in a terrain that he himself had helped to fertilise. This was not only the field later defined as 'right-wing reformism', though he did provide a considerable part of their theoretical baggage,[139] but also that of unionism. A common Graziadeian link united organisers like Verzi and Rigola to 'external' intellectuals strongly committed to the trade-unionist project such as Pagliari.

In his reflection on the Italian workers' movement, writing as both memoirist and historian, Rinaldo Rigola strongly insisted that the climate of 'revisionism' was the fundamental reference point for reformist syndicalism's culture: naturally meaning Bernstein, and, in the case of Italian revisionism, also Francesco Saverio Merlino.[140] It is possible that Graziadei's journey into communism in some way affected Rigola's memory. Conversely, in a private text – a 1949 letter – Fausto Pagliari declared himself a 'disciple' (suggesting a conscious relationship) not only of Graziadei's writings on the union, but above all *La produzione capitalistica*, which he defined, with delightful irony, as the socialist economics professor's 'first *pisello*[141] book'.

Beyond individuals' memories, we can find many substantial traces that evidence the influence of the 'economic theory' of the union. Some of them make explicit references to this theory, as an element of the culture in which the reformist union leadership found many sources of inspiration.

---

138 Pepe 1972, pp. 313–15, 437–9.

139 Neo-reformism's book-manifesto *Le vie nuove del socialismo* – and in particular its final chapters – owed a lot to Graziadei's analysis, even in its chosen vocabulary.

140 See Rigola 1946, pp. 203–9.

141 'Piselli' (Italian for 'peas', also echoing the acronym PSLI) was also the nickname attributed to the Saragatians (anti-communist social-democrats) after the post-World War II 'Palazzo Barbarini' split from the Socialist Party. See Pagliari's 1949 letter to Graziadei, Archivio Storico della Biblioteca Comunale di Imola. Carte Graziadei.

It is no chance thing that the FIOM was so early in taking an interest in Antonio Graziadei's positions. This engineering workers' federation was the union that made the most determined effort to build a model of industrial organisation inspired by a project of 'industrial democracy', based on solid productivist and pro-industrial foundations. It may be true that the lucid coherence with which this plan was carried forward appeared more as the 'image'[142] than the organisational reality of the engineering workers' movement taken as a whole (and above all in the case of Italian industry). Yet nothing takes away from the fact that as the pieces of the mosaic of a culture were coming together – as an 'image', indeed – they were taking on the substance of a reality, or in any case were sure to influence reality.

The 'economic' conception of union activity, such as we have outlined it – a conception conditioning the choice and use of the tools of industrial relations themselves, from collective bargaining to the closed shop – was necessarily reflected in the hypothesis of a more directly union-oriented use of the party itself. And, indeed, already in August 1905 (Graziadei's first essay on the economic theory of the union had appeared in May 1904) comments began to appear in the FIOM's official organ regarding the fact that 'whatever its economic aims, an essentially political organisation cannot … much accelerate the emancipation of the proletariat'.[143]

As signals pointing in this direction became ever more numerous in the course of 1906–7, and the argumentation behind them more extensive, there were also ever-more specific references to Graziadei. Reference was made to the 'two splendid talks' he had given 'on the initiative of the Milan *Camera del Lavoro*', and the 'concepts that he expressed in masterly fashion, regarding the fact that economic organisations fulfil their *raison d'être* without a hoard of rival tendencies impeding the free unfolding of their activity'.[144] Subsequently the FIOM's paper published 'Sindacalismo riformista e sindacalismo rivoluzionario',[145] the very text that had provoked Filippo Turati's first worried reactions.

Evidently a trade-based federation is not a single scholar or a laboratory of political and union economy. So the linear progress of any position often came up against obstacles and the rethinking demanded by tactical concerns. Even so, there did remain a clearly identifiable red thread, and the proof of

142 See Antonioli 1983.

143 See *Il Metallurgico*, 1 August 1905.

144 'Il sindacalismo di buona marca', *Il Metallurgico*, 1 May 1906.

145 *Il Metallurgico*, 1 October 1906.

this appeared in the arguments advanced in the book most paradigmatic of the FIOM union's culture, written by its secretary, Ernesto Verzi.[146]

If we think of the role that Verzi himself played in the formation process of the Confederazione Generale del Lavoro, it is no surprise that both the CGdL's programmatic platform and his immediately subsequent elaborations also contained theoretical elements that could develop according to a vision functional to a union-centred logic. They could develop through what another reformist, Modigliani, later defined as the 'small' working-class politics characteristic of 'trade-unionist reformism'.[147] 'Given these premises', it has been written, 'what necessarily now emerged was a plan to get rid of any socialist perspective, and replace the class-party with "the party of labour" ... a tool for negotiating a *quid pro quo* also at the governmental level'.[148]

Perhaps there was never any such conscious, subjective decision, and moreover we also have to account for the rather articulated panorama of positions that existed within reformist syndicalism. But certainly even the most articulated view cannot overlook the fact that this culture was now internalising one of the fundamental principles of the dominant economic theory; namely, that the workers' movement could not present itself as anything other than a factor of production. Even if Graziadei was the only socialist to give a rigorous theoretical systematisation of this assumption, his theory was nonetheless immediately received, metabolised and used, precisely because it corresponded well to tendencies and organisational models that were already being put into effect.

We have said that factors emerging from the struggle against revolutionism bore notable influence on Turati's gradually increasing 'compatability' with theoretical positions whose origins and development were different from his own manner of 'giving into' reformism as a tendency. Yet these same factors also pushed others to seek out a reformism with *other* solid theoretical roots,[149] as well as a place where this plant could grow strongly without any particular impediments.

Similarly, ever since 1905 Graziadei had argued that the only suitable terrain for the growth of the reformist tree was the union. Subsequently, and with some

146 Verzi 1907.

147 That is, in the English sense. Cited in Cherubini 1990 – for more general considerations, see pp. 357–71.

148 See Barbadoro 1979, p. 382.

149 Not by chance, when Turati sought to pin down Marchioli by explicitly asking him what his so-weakly 'socialist' reformism consisted of, this latter took care to portray himself as being in the company of the likes of Graziadei, Pagliari, and Bonomi. See E. Marchioli, 'Il mio riformismo', *Critica Sociale*, 1909, pp. 108–11.

degree of hesitation and equivocation, some of the most prestigious CGdL leaders would come to agree with him.

That is not to suggest that the 'party of labour' question was only an epiphenomenon of the more general battle to found an organically structured reformism on the basis of a non-Marxist revisionist framework (first of all in the economic field). But certainly, this backdrop was essential. Without that, the question of the party-union relationship and the trade-unionist model would have been a far less deep one.

It was in this perspective that a figure like Fausto Pagliari – who linked such a great part of his infatigable activity precisely to the construction of a reformist edifice solidly based on 'revisionist' foundations – made use not only of Graziadei's aforementioned '*pisello*' book, but also his *Socialismo e sindacalismo*. He presented this latter as a 'major contribution to reformist theory', adding 'It came at a good moment. The socialist party suffers above all from a poverty of theory and having to grope around in the dark. Books like Graziadei's are a powerful antidote to the "crisis of socialism"'.[150]

So well-nourished on the juices of Graziadei, the Webbs and Bernstein, Pagliari would make a far from insignificant contribution to the 'trade-unionist' offensive, precisely because he thought that only the union could fully take on board the lesson that each of these figures had provided. Here, in short, the 'party of labour' was conceived as a tool allowing the culture that had been better-elaborated by European revisionism to take root in Italian socialism; a culture that the PSI had proven little-able to take on board and still less to promote. Pagliari's presence in the socialist press was particularly substantial, and in some cases excessive and repetitive; for years he remained an editor in charge of columns like the 'Cronaca Sociale' in *Critica Sociale* and the 'Cronaca Operaia' in *Confederazione del Lavoro*, and his many interventions invariably overlapped.

While the greater part of this output was inspired by the theoretical guidelines of which we have spoken, it would be mistaken to understand them as having been extremely coherent or rigid. In reality, contingent motivations arising from the tendency struggle often also influenced strategic concerns, meaning that in any given moment particular stress could be placed on this or that underlying theoretical theme. For example, the parameters of the project of centralising the union confederation were more or less rigid in different peri-

150 See F. Pagliari, 'Il sindacalismo riformista', *Critica Sociale*, 1908, p. 266. There were also hints of Graziadei in his 'Le organizzazioni dei funzionari e il sindacalismo riformista', *Critica Sociale*, 1908, pp. 215–18.

ods, in accordance with the demands and urgency of the battle against the revolutionaries. Hence at the beginning of 1907 his polemic against the localism of the *Camere del Lavoro* was a very bitter one, as he referred to these latter as the fruit of 'socialist propaganda' more than the industrial development of an advanced country, and thus particularly liable to make 'the organs of the resistance movement degenerate into mainly political organisms'.[151] And precisely because 'mainly political' organisms could not be reduced to functions of more general socio-economic mechanisms, in his view they were inevitably subject to the revolutionaries' influences. Rather, it was necessary to follow the model provided by Germany, where that very year it had been possible to defeat revolutionary syndicalism by allowing ever less room for this kind of localism.

Certainly, this had been possible in Germany because even authoritative members of the SPD (like Bebel) had supported the unions' positions, thus isolating the intransigent wing (as represented by Kautsky). In Italy's PSI, conversely, there was still a widespread propensity to consider revolutionary syndicalism and reformist-trade-unionist syndicalism as two opposed 'exaggerations'.[152] Hence the CGdL had to use all means at its disposal in order to sterilise the terrain in which the plant of revolutionism might flourish – and centralisation was necessarily fundamental to this effort.

When, conversely, the demands of this struggle seemed less urgent, the centralisation model appeared in a less rigid and more realistically-articulated form.[153]

Again in the case of the question of the party-union relationship, Pagliari's positions did not develop in an entirely linear fashion. It is true that the fundamental factor, here, was the often-invoked inspiration provided by the model of British Labourism.[154] But at the same time, his considerations on the state of the Italian workers' and socialist movement even led him to hypothesising

---

151 See. F. Pagliari, 'L'organizzazione di resistenza in Italia', *Critica Sociale*, 1907, pp. 113–25. Citation from p. 124.

152 See. F. Pagliari, 'La fine del sindacalismo in Germania. Annotazioni e confronti', *Critica Sociale*, 1908, pp. 77–9.

153 See Pagliari's letter to Rigola, 20 March 1909, in Favilli 1983.

154 'The socialist party must become ever more the expression and the political tool of the organised working class ... The party must be considered not an organism more evolved than and superior to organisation ... but a tool of organisation, because socialism and socialist power lie in workers' organisation and in its politics': see F. Pagliari, 'Il Partito socialista e l'organizzazione operaia', *Confederazione del Lavoro*, 25 April 1908. Statements of the same kind appear very frequently in Pagliari's interventions between 1907 and 1909.

the party playing the role of a 'catalyst'[155] for union organisation – a role that was certainly not entirely compatible with the models being suggested more generally.

The culture of reformist unionism – and also of trade-unionist and non-Marxist reformism – was a culture that Pagliari did much to spread (and for which he at some moments also provided original inspiration). It must be read in a manner attentive to the multiplicity of themes running through this culture; its different levels of elaboration, analysis and divulgation; and the different moments and scansions of the phases through which it was advanced.

Rigola was a partly different case on account of his formation as well as his position as the main leader of the CGdL, which also meant a certain elasticity in his behaviour. A complex figure, central to the 'party of labour' experience, but at the same time one attentive not to get locked up in any corporatist cages, he was in those years a sure defender of a model of unionism that 'must take the form of a counterpart of capital, and not that of a radical antagonist'.[156] Yet it was also a model underpinned by a very robust sense of class. He was also very liable to invoking Antonio Graziadei as a theoretical reference point.

Rigola had earlier had a veiled *querelle* with Graziadei over the question of the autonomous organisation of the rural labourers' leagues. If the two men did essentially agree on this question, the *querelle* derived from the Confederation secretary's greater sensibility to the delicate nature of the CGdL's relations with its internal Federations, in this case meaning the powerful Federterra.[157] Yet when the often-cited little volume *Socialismo e sindicalismo* appeared, Rigola's references to it were particularly telling. As he wrote:

> in the pages of this valorous economist and socialist, who once passed for a heretic ... it is not difficult to find the scientific formulation of the

155 'Perhaps the workers' movement is too practical and not idealist enough to make the party's absorption within the class advisable; perhaps the party, which is necessarily a minority, despite its defects serves as a catalyst among the amorphous part of the working class'. Pagliari writing to Rigola, 15 May 1911, in Favilli 1983.

156 See Cartiglia 1967, p. 28.

157 See A. Graziadei, 'Mezzadri e salariati. Un grave problema di organizzazione', *Avanti!*, 27 May 1908 and R. Rigola, 'La LDN e la CGdL', *La Confederazione del Lavoro*, 5 December 1908. Graziadei and Rigola had a far-reaching exchange of letters throughout this period, which had an accelerator effect on Graziadei while moderating Rigola somewhat. The letters are held in the della Fondazione Feltrinelli, Carte Rigola. This episode also allows us to see that Graziadei did not well conform to the figure of a 'doctrinaire theorist', instead proving well able to translate theory using the tools of politics.

> syndical postulates that the proletariat's emancipation movement has now reached ... Compare Graziadei's ideas with the ideas and conclusions that we have been expounding in these pages in fragmentary form, solely on the basis of everyday experience; and [those expounded by] other valiant friends and collaborators, on the basis of doctrine, and we see how much they correspond with the happy synthesis that Graziadei has made of them.[158]

Naturally, passages from the book in question were reproduced in various issues of *La Confederazione del Lavoro*.[159]

Even after Costa's death, when Graziadei was looking to stand as a candidate in Imola, Rigola spoke of him in the following terms:

> We recognise him as one of the most lucid interpreters of the contemporary union movement, the theorist *par excellence* of the union activity ... that our Confederation pursues. With Graziadei's election ... there will be a place [in parliament] for a tone that is more directly in contact with class organisation, him having long familiarised himself with it through his studies.[160]

These brief insights may suffice to offer a glimpse of Graziadei's relations with what were centrally important Italian socialist and syndicalist milieux, and the characteristics of these relations. But where, then, did the image emerge – one that has often accompanied considerations of his reformist theory – that he was a *vox clamans in deserto*?

Perhaps this vision of Graziadei as an isolated 'heretic' lacking major impact on the real development of Italian socialism in fact resulted precisely from the coherence of which we have spoken. Namely, the fact that he boasted of his will

158 See R. Rigola, 'Socialismo e Sindacalismo', *La Confederazione del Lavoro*, 5 June 1909. Well aware of the significance of Rigola's public declaration of affinity with his own elaborations, Graziadei responded in the following terms: 'I deeply thank you ... for your complete adherence to the set of opinions that I have considered it opportune to publish. Your agreement offers me great comfort, both on account of the official position that you occupy, and most of all because of the very great esteem in which I hold you. This is the best prize that I could have hoped for, for my love for the workers' movement as a scholar and a socialist', Graziadei to Rigola, 10 June 1909, in the Carte Rigola at the Fondazione Feltrinelli.

159 See the 12 June, 22 June, 17 July and 25 September 1909 issues.

160 See *La Confederazione del Lavoro*, 12 February 1910.

to break with a certain history and tradition – consolidated images and ways of being – while showing little regard for the 'viscosity' of the moment.

For example, the conflict that emerged between sharecroppers and day labourers over the management of threshing machines served Graziadei in his production of an essay on the agrarian question, in which this episode was considered in the context of the general tendencies of agricultural development. In his view, these were tendencies that provided a further demonstration of the inapplicability of the supposed 'Marxist tendency' of progressive immiseration. And there is no doubt, in this regard, that his analysis better suited the real articulation of the processes then underway than did a Marxist vulgate certain that it could discern the mass proletarianisation of the different social figures who existed in the countryside. The political-organisational proposal that he drew from this – distinct associations for casual labourers, sharecroppers and petty proprietors, coordinated by a confederal-type body tying them together – doubtless had the merit of conjugating this articulation with the need for a unitary perspective. At the same time, however, such suggestions ran the risk of remaining in the background, because the overly productivist tailoring of Graziadei's arguments tended to cast doubt over the strongholds of Socialist-inspired union organisation in the countryside. His exaltation of forms of co-participation in management, which he considered the best economic measure for agricultural activity, in fact led him not only to mythologise the significance and historic endurance of sharecropping as an institution, but also to elaborate positions on political-union conduct that were decidedly opposed to the day labourers' interests. Indeed, he judged wage-labour – by its very nature 'disinterested' in the end produce – totally unsuitable for profitable use in agriuculture. The perspective for the future instead had to be that of encouraging the growth of 'co-interested' management, thus giving rise 'to a much more conscious and responsible supply of labour than that coming from pure wage-labour alone, whose ultimate tendency is for each worker to take no interest either in the quality of produce or its price'.[161] Faced with the rise of various forms of colony, the category of rural labourers operating outside of any 'economic balance' – the day-labourers – would gradually disappear.[162]

The economic theory of the union, as well as the political initiative characterised by the search for 'compatibility' at all levels, ran into their limit when – as we have already noted – the tendencies of Italian 'real capitalism' seemed

161 See Graziadei 1913. This text had appeared in *Critica Sociale* across the course of 1911–12: this citation is from *Critica Sociale*, 1911, p. 25.

162 *Critica Sociale*, 1911, p. 87.

to have run out of any capacity or will to find mediation. Reformist syndicalism and revolutionary syndicalism were confronted with a conflict dynamic often resulting in heavy defeats for the whole workers' movement. Moreover, beyond their different theoretical and ideological perspectives, it is not always possible to find substantial differences in the platforms of demands advanced by local 'reformist' or 'revolutionary' unionism. There was a very gloomy horizon for the reforms 'of a socialist stamp' on which the reformists – whether clearly or more vaguely Marxist, or not at all – had built a whole political perspective. The war in Libya now came to show how high the barriers still were between the 'socialist world' and the 'bourgeois world', including even its most advanced fringes. If the thread of reformism that wanted to preserve its Marxist ancestry and the thread that wanted to reject it were in part mixed up again in some of the curves of the river fed by the 'economic theory of the workers' movement', now the harsh returns of history demanded renewed clarification.

In truth there had been figures wholly internal to reformism who had long worked to maintain a clear path for a gradualist, reforming approach moving in accordance with the fundamental elements of socialist identity. One such case was Alessandro Schiavi, so close to Turati that he remained a Turatian even when the 'master' seemed to be oscillating toward forms of generic reformism.

Schiavi and Pagliari were moving on the same thematic horizon, and both worked in a key institution of Italian reformist socialism, the *Società Umanitaria*; yet the frameworks of their reformisms were nonetheless different ones. Their different readings of Marx's lessons were a far from secondary factor in explaining this difference between them.

Schiavi was a translator and divulgator of Marx's work from the 1890s into the Giolittian period, and he also entered into a certain form of collaboration with the first attempt to provide Italy with a broad, organic *corpus* of Marx and Engels's writings: namely, the initiative driven by Ettore Ciccotti.

But at the beginning of the century, his function as a translator-divulgator took on a specific characterisation directly relating to reformist practice. The passages of Marx and Engels that Schiavi selected and translated for a volume entitled *Pagine socialiste*,[163] and which was aimed at 'young propagandists', were programmatically inserted within what was a rather interesting pedagogical operation. He considered a 'philologically' correct relation with the texts necessary for any non-'simplistic' understanding of the masters, and, therefore, for the full use of their lessons in the war of movement that was now underway.

163 Marx and Engels 1902.

For Schiavi, indeed, young propagandists mounting 'an attentive examination of Marxist literature' and grasping its 'theoretical core' – essential for 'acquiring a sense of reality' – would emerge bearing 'the convinction that far from being trapped in the narrowness of dogma and simplistic little formulas, far from recommending one preferred method as the only good one for finding the solution to the problem occupying their minds ... these formidable theorists ... keeping their eyes fixed on the multiform, complex, organic manifestations of life and nature, suggested the most varied means, as demanded by the struggle, which is itself multiform and complex'.[164]

His choice of Marx and Engels texts not only conformed to this general objective, but seemed almost to anticipate the political and intellectual attitude that Schiavi would later maintain across the whole early twentieth century.

He chose passages from the *Critique of the Gotha Programme* that sought to debunk the commonplace that the worker had the right to the full product of his labour, as well as the notion that the bourgeoisie was a 'single reactionary mass'. He drew on the *Critique of the Gotha Programme* and the *Inaugural Address* in order to underline Marx's realism, not his ideological prejudice: cooperatives were neither the road to socialism nor mere crumbs. There were passages of Engels's writing in *Volksstaat*, which did not mythologise the general strike as a universal means of struggle. He also drew on Engels for what appeared to be one of the most practical questions facing reformism: *The Housing Question*. Such an approach inevitably enjoyed the support of Antonio Labriola, who advised his former pupil to proceed further down this path, mounting 'a more extensive work'.[165]

Strongly involved in reformism's day-to-day praxis, Schiavi never managed to engage in the type of work that Labriola had suggested to him. Nonetheless, throughout his rich and multi-form output during these years he would remain loyal to this method. In substance, he always sought to keep up with new realities, on the basis of the concreteness of effective facts, a patient study of experiences, and a comparative examination of the processes underway in Europe, as he consistently rejected the explanatory key of what he called 'theoretical doctrinairism'.[166] He thus remained wholly internal – partaking fully and with absolute convinction – to the essence of the 'reformist method'. At the same time, the tools of Marxist analysis ought to play the role of a

164 From Schiavi's preface to Marx and Engels 1902, pp. x–xi.

165 Labriola 1983, vol. III, letter of 4 October 1902.

166 See A. Schiavi, 'Il movimento contadino in Francia', *Critica Sociale*, 1904, pp. 25–8. Citation p. 28. In this article we can see his original positions on the 'agrarian question', as they related to 'Marxist doctrinairism'.

flexible and articulated interpretative web, and the sense of 'socialist identity' provide a general framework of orientation. For Schiavi, this was not so much a matter of conjugating reformism with Marxism, as of making the former naturally emerge from the latter, in perfect coherence with the claim that 'the fundamental outlines' of international socialism were still 'the same as those established around halfway into the last century, albeit assimilating all the vital elements that the evolution of the times and of things continually germinate'.[167] Naturally Schiavi like Turati had to deal with the difficulty of drawing Marx's categories down into his analytical procedure. The effect was that sometimes these two moments appeared to be juxtaposed, or else the only explanatory capacities assumed by the Marxist dimension were those of a first approximation. Yet overall, the pattern that the student designed to hold these two moments together suffered from less holes than did the teacher's own work.

The true and proper explosion of the workers' movement at the beginning of the century, including in Italy, posed unprecedented problems for socialism as a whole. It was in this same moment that Schiavi embarked on his engagement with the experiences of syndicalism internationally. Here he showed the maximum possible openness to what seemed to be the most advanced situations, but without falling into any submissive provincial mentality. Moreover, he felt guided by the awareness that amidst the vastness and complexity of this international phenomenon, it was always necessary to identify the paths through which proletarian organisation would increase its own capacities to control the processes that were now underway.

Schiavi's attentive study of the conditions of industrial production and of market outlets was not only aimed at a clear identification of the limits of 'compatibility', and thus avoiding either painful defeats or crises in given industrial sectors. Rather, it was also a matter of making workers used to considering themselves the primary subject of the development of production, feeling that this development was in their own collective interest, and thinking of themselves as a ruling class in the making.[168] To this end, it was necessary to avoid being boxed into the economic struggle alone – even at the higher, more 'scientific' levels of organisation achieved by the British trade unions – but instead consider 'immediate economic and parliamentary achievements' 'means for the realisation of a higher objective'.[169] The precise identification of this objec-

167 See Sticus, 'Da Gotha a Tours', *Critica Sociale*, 1902, p. 84.

168 See A. Schiavi, 'Gli scioperi e la produzione', *Critica Sociale*, 1902, pp. 71–5, 106–10, 123–4, 134–6, 156–7, 167–9, 186–8, 211–14.

169 See A. Schiavi, 'Gli scioperi e la produzione', *Critica Sociale*, 1902, p. 214.

tive – and that of the articulated, non-linear path to it – was linked to the levels that the consciousness of theory had reached.

The non-linearity of this path allowed Schiavi to say that 'the dreams of the elimination of crises through trusts, the peaceable conquest of political power thanks to experiments *à la* Millerand, and the penetration of the socialist spirit among the British ruling classes' had now 'vanished' and that in the coming years 'the dream that flashed before our eyes, that war and catastrophes are a matter of the past and only a path of peaceable, tranquil progress lies before us' would also disappear.[170] However, such a perspective absolutely should not stand in the way of the patient and day-to-day work of encouraging economic growth and, simultaneously, the strengthening of socialism in all its different contexts: the party, parliament, the union, cooperatives, municipal administrations, and in the socialists' multiple initiatives for cultural and civil pedagogy.

In the climate of reformism's 'socialist' turn, Schiavi would reflect on the difficulty of filling this day-to-day work with a theoretical consciousness, together with reformism's overall lack of progress in this sense. It was not by chance that apart from his political initiatives (he was one of the protagonists of this turn, having long been one of those who most called for it) he particularly devoted himself to 'Per la cultura socialista', the aptly named section of *Critica Sociale* that he curated. Here he pointedly complained that the socialists in Italy had overlooked 'the study of socialist theory, of Marxist economics'.[171] In this effort, seeking the tools most adequate to understanding a rather dense moment of history, the boundaries of identity would soon collapse. When Marx's categories served the purposes of explanation, they could be used – or at least, redeployed – even by the revolutionary syndicalists. Hence Enrico Leone's analysis of the 'colonial war' – an analysis moving on Marx's terrain, 'the historical and economic terrain' – was preferred to that produced by the party leadership, 'elaborated from a too-exclusively ethical and sentimental point of view'.[172] Similarly, for a continued programme of reflecting on socialist culture one could turn to Robert Michels, who had published his *Storia del Marxismo in Italia* only a few months previously.[173]

Given the early-1910s situation putting into question the ways in which reformism defined itself, the threads woven by Schiavi could be used in the difficult work of reconstructing a general pattern of this culture. This is the

170 See Sticus, 'La teoria delle crisi', *Critica Sociale*, 1902, pp. 217–18.
171 See A. Schiavi, 'Per la cultura socialista', *Critica Sociale*, 1912, pp. 147–9. Citation from p. 148.
172 See A. Schiavi, 'Espansionismo e colonie', *Critica Sociale*, 1912, pp. 40–3. Citation from p. 40.
173 See Michels's letter to Schiavi, 2 March 1911, Archivio Fondazione Feltrinelli, (microfilm).

same pattern that we have described as severely worn-out; the pattern that left Turati himself feeling dismayed.

This was the dismay of a man who suddenly felt the disappearance – and not wilfully so – of all the parameters on which he had built his own political strategy, and who became aware that he did not have the tools for reading all that was new and unforeseen. Moreover, this took place even after he had abandoned, or stopped cultivating, certain analytical criteria precisely because he considered them unsuitable for understanding the 'new'. The man who had sought to follow the 'new' was now left betrayed by it.

Turati's reaction was, indeed, that of a man who felt betrayed, as he explicitly stated in a parliamentary intervention directed at the Giolittian benches: 'It is this democracy's abdication that forces us, despite ourselves, to break from it in order to remain loyal to ourselves'.[174] This was an almost-instinctive reaction, which Turati represented in the following terms:

> At the most decisive moments for parties and classes, we have something abler than ability, more profoundly reasonable than syllogism, more useful than a skilful calculation of utility. There is this instinctive, intuitive rebellion, the unbending, intransigent protest that truly and visibly distinguishes one responsibility from another: one that clearly separates interests, classes, and spirits – and sets them before a battlefield. There is a party of revolution and of the future that the easy flattery of secondary successes has attracted too far into the enemy trenches, and has suddenly realised that it is being held prisoner there. There is this instinct for life that makes it jump up again, proudly taking back control over itself and withdrawing at once. It thus recovers, fully intact, its whole ardour for battle, concerned by nothing more than distinguishing itself, reasserting itself, being itself again.[175]

These words were, without doubt, testament to a way of living politics that was always permeated by ethical values, references to a deeply felt system of principles, and renewed faith in the reasons for becoming a socialist. But they were likewise testament to the failure of a certain kind of politics, an underestimation of the necessarily 'high' stakes of the reformist challenge, and an incapacity to master its phases, including on account of a lack of appropriate cultural tools.

174 See F. Turati, 'Discorso pronunciato alla Camera dei deputati', 23 February 1912.

175 See F. Turati, 'Il miraggio della pace', *Critica Sociale*, 1912, pp. 1–4.

Turati had also hoped that the socialists' proclaimed 'return to themselves' – the attempt at a direct return to their Marxist roots – would be able to give an immediate key for reading the processes now underway, and thus allow a socialist policy appropriate for the challenges of the times. Yet this hope, too, would remain substantially illusory, and for many reasons. Even when Turati proclaimed himself 'orthodox' and 'German' in his Marxism, this was always more a Marxism of principles than of analyses. Faced with the need to develop this culture – this *whole* culture – in order to ready it to confront the new – and this was a need that the rigorous, non-'orthodox' Marxist Antonio Labriola had aptly noted – Turati responded by reducing principles to their 'first elements', leaving to the unfolding of *events* the fundamental role of providing a *positive* response.

Once again, now socialism appeared as a 'differentness' – even if this differentness was not posed in terms of separation – and the socialists were again 'reformists because they were revolutionaries'.[176] Again there was renewed and direct reference to 'the man we keep up in the attic'.[177]

But in the context in which the return of 'the man we keep up in the attic' took place, it necessarily had to take the form of a proud assertion of identity. This was not nothing, and nor was it wholly taken for granted. Another proud assertion derived from this, and Turati almost shouted it in the face of his democratic interlocutors as war appeared on the horizon, insisting that '[o]nly we socialists know the *how* and *why* of things'.[178] Yet this was purely declamatory, a dream of the possibilities that could be discerned. Turati himself was

176 See Noi, 'L'accordo dei contrari', *Critica Sociale*, 1911, pp. 340–1.

177 'Only thanks to Marx's work was this miracle achieved: the ideal came down to Earth … making itself life, action, destiny, history, reality … The speculators, the pedants, the critics who never see the wood for the trees, all came along, pointing their fingers at the disproven phrase, the fragment negated by events; disproven, negated by some passing episode. The minister who reduces the whole world to the chamber, the nation to the assembly, history to the legislature, has told us of his Marx, held hostage in the attic. But Marx's creations, his proofs, cannot be confined within the passing moment, but only in the century as it slowly unfolds. The titan in this supposed attic resists, gets up on his feet, and leaves the crowd of Myrmidons in his vast shadow. Each day that comes, each economic fact that unfolds, each new position of a changing society, minute-by-minute realises a fragment of his thinking. What Marx saw germinating thus becomes a tree, a wood. The industry growing gigantic, the increasingly dominant trusts, the finance absorbing politics, the imperialism that overwhelms whole peoples and states, the proletariat moving forward, the extending class struggle, becomes consciousness, and, getting rid of classes, ineluctably prepares a humanity based on solidarity': see T.K., 'Colui che confinammo in soffitta', *Critica Sociale*, 1913, p. 74.

178 See Noi, 'Gli insegnamenti di una polemica', *Critica Sociale*, 1914, pp. 7–8.

ultimately convinced of this, as we see in his disconsolate comments in his correspondence with Anna Kuliscioff, noting the almost total lack of any analysis of reality or of any proposals that could define the socialists' *differentness*.

It has rightly been noted that one of the main characteristics of the leaders of Second-International socialism was their lack of any sharp division between political, theoretical or simply ideological activity. Naturally among these leaders there were various different gradations of the relation between theory and politics, whether placing greater emphasis on the theoretical or the political dimensions.

Doubtless Turati was one of the leaders who particularly displayed a more immediately political sensibility, such that at certain moments he appeared as a true *totus politicus*. That is not meant to be a reductive observation; but his was a gift of no little importance when it came to fighting a war of movement like the one that had begun at the beginning at the century.

In this war Turati confidently made use of both the workers' movement and Marxism. The need for discipline did not always prevail in the Giolittian era: at times he invoked the spectre of the workers' movement in order to make the parliamentary struggle less 'lifeless', as he himself repeatedly stated. Similarly, at certain moments he used Marxism, or reference to Marxism, as a sporadic injection of energy. But neither social movements nor *cultures* in the strong sense could easily be deployed to meet contingent opportunities.

At the same time, the reformism that sought to define itself in sharp contrast with *heri dicebamus* showed all its limits, as 'socialist reformism' in parliament dealt with socio-economic problems, the 'great reforms', and *in primis* the tax reform.

Already in his first parliamentary speech of March 1910, Graziadei had made clear the cornerstones of a framework to which he would remain loyal until the 'catastrophe' of the European war. Namely, a state budget aimed at balancing the books, and tax reforms above all aimed at substantially lifting the burden on consumers. Essentially this meant no real change in a tax system that was both regressive and left very major holes encouraging tax evasion.

The reasonableness with which Graziadei expounded such arguments and his constant attention to budgetary concerns – a rigid concern for balancing the books, to which the demands of social legislation would have to conform – drew the embarrassing praise of the treasury minister Salandra. This latter said that Graziadei's speech was so much in line with his ministry's views, that he thought that the socialists must have joined his own parliamentary group.[179]

179 See *Atti Parlamentari*, Leg. XXIII, Camera dei Deputati, 3 March 1910.

Filippo Turati bitterly responded that Graziadei had 'made a speech that was felicitous in its form, but everything about which was ever less socialist ... Fundamentally he was speaking as a free-trader *à la* Nitti ... It all stood outside both socialism and reality'.[180]

Moreover, in the parliamentary chamber Graziadei would also make explicit his convinctions regarding the economic concepts that were key to the socialist perspective. He insisted that the workers' movement needed to remain wholly internal to 'today's economic laws'[181] and that only in a marginal sense was 'exploitation' a phenomenon produced by the production relation, instead being produced by the contours of a market now lacking a proper balance of distribution among the different 'factors of production'.[182] Reflecting on the weakness of socialist economic culture – as if it had gone on the run – Anna Kuliscioff, writing to Filippo Turati, lamented that this serious deficiency forced the party to entrust in men who 'consider[ed] economic phenomena from the viewpoint of purely bourgeois political economy'. 'Alas', she concluded disconsolately, 'neither the old nor the young will produce the true socialist discourse – attacking all the fundaments on which bourgeois society is based using science, consciousness and conviction – because their minds have now lost their socialist orientation'.[183]

Kuliscioff and Turati could not even expect the man who had a few years earlier wanted to open up 'new paths for socialism' to provide this 'true socialist discourse'. Indeed, in 1907 Bonomi had produced a volume putting itself forward as a theoretical-programmatic manifesto of reformism: *Le vie nuove del socialismo*.[184]

In truth the results did not match up to such ambitions, both for reasons concerning the 'quality' of this study, and because of the objective barriers to it achieving any positive reception. As we shall see, this latter aspect was the more important one.

The whole book moved between two closely connected poles, seeking to demonstrate (i) the irremediably revolutionary – *stricto sensu* – nature of Marxism, and (ii) the revolutionary nature – tendentially – of democracy. Overall, however, this work seemed deeply conditioned by the contingent

---

180 Turati and Kuliscioff 1977, Vol. III, letter of 4 March 1910.

181 Graziadei's intervention in Disegno di legge: Stato di previsione dell'entrata per l'esercizio 1910–11, *Atti Parlamentari*, Leg. XXIII, Discussioni, 24 February 1911.

182 Graziadei's intervention on a motion made on the Confederation's initiative. *Atti Parlamentari*, Leg. XXIII, Discussioni, 28 January 1911.

183 Kuliscioff to Turati, 1 February 1910, in Turati and Kuliscioff 1977, Vol. III.

184 Bonomi 1907.

polemic with revolutionary syndicalism, with the effect that the general tone was more that of a political intervention than a study setting itself the objective of founding, or at least systematising, a 'new road'.

Perhaps for this reason, the image that Bonomi gave of Marx's view of the revolutionary process seemed rather rigidly posed; indeed, it was posed in the very terms that the syndicalists themselves had attributed to the Marxist elements of their revolutionism. Not by chance, the expression 'revolutionary gymnastics' often recurs throughout Bonomi's argumentation, referring to the attitude that Marx supposedly prescribed to the 'communists' for all favourable conjunctures.

Though a fundamental question, the problem of the connection between socialism and democracy ultimately itself also lost something of its depth. Here it was devoid of any concrete analytical dimension, instead being projected into the linear terms of a process whereby economic growth, social growth and the widening of the spaces for the subaltern classes' participation in managing public affairs were necessary functions of an unlimited historical dynamic. Bonomi's perspective was that of a 'creation in continual becoming',[185] in which the succession of legislative gains would assume the characteristics of *irreversibility* and *necessity*.[186]

This 1907 text was reprinted in 1992,[187] again being offered to readers' attention on the occasion of the one-hundredth anniversary of the *Partito Socialista Italiano*'s foundation. Noting this volume's poor reception, the author of the preface to the 1992 edition posed an extremely interesting question, which I think is a necessary point of departure in order to arrive at some concluding remarks.[188] He asked himself for what reasons the only 'possible socialism, democratic socialism' – that is, reformist socialism, for which the '*Vie nuove* was meant to become a holy text'[189] – was almost up to our own time unable to establish itself, and required such harsh returns of history to put its status beyond further doubts.

Certainly, we should accept his suggestion that the answer is not mainly to be found within the history of the workers' movement, its ideological projections and its antagonistic tendencies. We should, instead, look at the mechanisms that in the last instance determine the integration of the subaltern classes, which in our case means taking into account the precise cultural and symbolic

185 Bonomi 1907, p. 105.
186 Bonomi 1907, p. 135.
187 Bonomi 1992.
188 See Chiarini's introduction in Bonomi 1992, pp. 11–29.
189 Chiarini in Bonomi 1992, p. 15.

reference points of the urban and rural proletariat. We need to look at *all* these mechanisms, meaning not only institutional ones or those that in some way attach to the political dimension, but also those that – on the basis of the peculiarities of the production relation – determine material living conditions and the ways in which they are felt: in short, the sphere of lived experience.

From this point of view, anyone who has some familiarity with studies of the dynamics of unionism in the Giolittian period and the now-abundant body of social history regarding the subaltern classes in this period, knows perfectly well that the spaces for the possibility of integration were very limited and substantially impracticable. Moreover, beyond the reformist and revolutionary syndicalists' differing general perspectives, it is well-known that their respective logics of resistance were practically analogous.

Holding closely to this perspective should not, however, mean ruling out the possibility of taking a wider view. The risk is that of merely re-proposing the category 'backwardness' as explaining the peculiarity of the Italian case. Yet across all of the major countries of continental Western Europe on the eve of the catastrophe, including France and Germany, almost all of the reformists in the socialist parties would have struggled to sign up to the 'holy text' of the *Vie nuove*, and above all to identify with its author's own trajectory. Their number include not only Turati but also Jaures and even Bernstein; indeed, in 1914 this latter returned to reflect on the experience of fifteen years of 'revisionism'.

Though not rejecting the fundamental framework that had been at the origins of revisionism, Bernstein here critically reviewed certain of its passageways. He returned to question both the possibility of democracy and welfare expanding uninterruptedly, and the progressive reduction of the divide between the incomes received by capital and wage-labour respectively. At the same time, he recuperated essential parts of Marx's analytical baggage.[190]

Faced with this dimension of the problem, it would evidently not be possible to say that 'programmatic political manifesto' that was so isolated by both objective and subjective immaturities, and that was of such modest level, prophesied the 'only possible socialism'. So we get back to the original question: why did 'the only possible socialism, democratic socialism', not establish its authority? The counterposition of 'democratic socialism' and 'un-democratic socialism', which in some regards runs throughout the whole history of socialism, has different valences when it is considered *before* or *after* the *great catastrophe*, and, indeed, the Russian Revolution that was one of the effects of this

190 'Das Bleibende des Marxismus', *Der Kampf*, VII, 1913–14, pp. 224–5.

catastrophe. Indeed, the experience of twentieth-century communism colours the 'democratic question' with characteristics lying beyond the thought-horizons of even the anti-democratic revolutionaries of the turn of the twentieth century.

The end of this twentieth-century experience certainly does ask questions of the history of socialism; but it is not self-evident what these questions are. We could leave behind the communist experience convinced not only that its outcome represents an epoch shift – a genuine, period-defining macrocrisis – but even that it represents the end of the history of socialism *tout court*. That is, the end of the socialism whose roots lay in the terrain of the *critique* of the capitalist mode of production and a commonly-accepted consciousness of its *historical* character. The branches of that plant were very numerous and produced rather different fruits, some of them very bitter – but socialism *only* as the aspiration to social justice, in separation from the dynamics unfolding in the depths of the economy and social relations, did not make up part of this terrain. And it is perfectly legitimate to think that if this plant has now been uprooted and is thus totally lifeless, a new plant taking the same name (which is itself no longer necessary) would have to grow on another terrain, or needs no terrain because it can instead draw on above-ground roots. But it would, then, be wholly pointless to ask questions of the vital logics of another organism, in the name of understanding the vital logics of this new one.

It is possible that this rather modest 1907 book, and all the more so its author's subsequent evolution, were the anticipation of this new organism, with generic reformism serving as the only possible socialism. Yet in the crucial years in which theorisations of the 'death of socialism' were intersecting with the resumed offensive of real capitalism both at home and abroad, it was the reformists themselves who saw this 'anticipation' as a foreign body.

Yet the division in question was not determined by different conceptions of 'democratic centralism' or disagreement over the absolute priority of reforming gradualism. Rather, the central issue was that of the party's socialist identity, and thus the question of relating to the cultural tradition that had up to that point been best able to guarantee that identity.

This was not only a question of making recourse to the reassuring resources of an ideological *corpus* – a rediscovered syntony with a symbolic universe that had proven and very considerable capacities of aggregation – but also the possibility of using the heuristic and cognoscitive capacities proper to the theory itself. As we well know, the ideological and scientific aspects of this question were closely interlinked. Utopian projections and rigorous, innovative analytical capacities made up (and make up) part of the same *logos*, having direct repercussions on the way of being and doing politics – the *quality* – of the reforming hypothesis.

The experience of Bonomi as a socialist proponent of the 'great reform' – tax reform – across the first decade of the new century can be considered paradigmatic, from this point of view.

In *objective* terms, the spaces for a *strong* socialist initiative for tax reform in the Giolittian era were decidedly broad ones. Growing budget surpluses over a series of consecutive years, extemporaneous legislative mechanisms accentuating the already-pronounced regressive character of the tax system, and authoritative interlocutors across the 'other shore' who seemed to be sending signals showing their decided readiness to reach an agreement. Bonomi thus made the 'great reform' the central point of his own intellectual elaboration and political involvement in this first decade of the century.

In 1903 he had presented an overall study-project that aptly presented the socialist position as standing side-by-side with the radical and progressive-liberal positions of Giulio Alessio and Leone Wollemborg. Though Bonomi declared that he was aware of the problems of 'compatibility', his programmatic exclusion of any 'socialist specificity' was deeply inserted in a cultural climate that posed the reform question as a profound – albeit gradual – change of Italy's tax structures. These latter were themselves considered the epiphenomenon of balances in society that were as deeply unjust as they were inadequate to modern economic and industrial development.

But as Bonomi's relations with the central core of socialist identity began to change – and not just particular elements of it – the *quality* of his tax reform proposal gradually deteriorated. In 1910 he presented the Milan Congress with a platform accepting that the Ministry's budget-balancing mechanisms were untouchable, and proposing marginal retouches wholly similar to those that the finance minister had declared himself open to. These were the same retouches that Bonomi had a few years earlier declared 'a caricature of reforms'. The year later he agreed with Nitti that in a speech applauded triumphally by the majority in parliament, he had buried any initiative seeking reform in a redistributive sense. Nitti had argued that 'in Italy everyone, rich and poor pays too much', for which reason it was instead necessary to take measures 'in defence of the taxpayer against the continual rate-rises'.[191]

In these extremely concrete aspects – important markers of 'reformism put under test' – the noble fathers of Italian reformism became ever more distant. This was far from the Kuliscioff who had placed many hopes in the young

191 Nitti 1973, speech of 28 January 1911.

Mantuan Bonomi, and now commented on his lash-up with Nitti by saying that 'Finally democratic conservatism has found its scientific interpreter (!!?) … not that it is any surprise to me that Nitti is what he is. But the fact Bonomi is writing just the same as what Nitti says, except in form – grey in the one and phosphoric in the other – is truly the limit for any socialist …'[192]

Socialism was thus reasserted as an element qualifying reformism. If even Turati and Kuliscioff would now struggle to use the knowledge categories of this cultural tradition in a creative sense, they had no doubt as to its capacities of connotation and inspiration: its mobilising capacities. They could have made the same claim that the Polish philosopher Kolakowski did, when he was very far along his 'revisionist journey', some decades later:

> nobody knows if Colchis really exists, but one can be certain that on the way to it there are better countries than the one we are living in.[193]

---

192 Kuliscioff to Turati, 29 January 1911, in Turati and Kuliscioff 1977, Vol. III.

193 Kolakowski 1969, p. 2.

CHAPTER 6

Marxism and Revolutionary Syndicalism

1 Did Syndicalism Have Roots in Turn-of-the-Century 'Revisionism'?

Robert Michels interpreted the formation of a revolutionary syndicalist culture that was constantly engaged with Marxist themes – in its *Debatte* with the reformist Marxists – through the lens of the specificity of the Italian situation. As he wrote:

> In Italy ... there was no struggle between orthodox Marxism and critical Marxism ... such as was fought ... in the ranks of social democracy in Germany ... There were, at root, two impure Marxisms disputing the terrain. Generally we could say, without fear of paradox, that of the two principal currents of Italian scientific socialism, one was simply occupied with practically revising Marx, without too much invading the master's theoretical field, whereas the other, while retaining all its criticisms on the theoretical front, in practice carried out a rather Marxist theory. Particularly in the years 1906–8 the syndicalists occupied themselves with Marx with great fervour.[1]

This is an argument that has had rather discontinuous success across the historiography of Italian socialism. It was subsequently picked up by Norberto Bobbio, albeit with a rather less favourable judgement regarding the syndicalists.[2]

As we saw in the last chapter, the problem of reducing reformism to its 'practical' dimension alone, devaluing its theoretical bases, is in truth a rather complex and controversial question. Conversely, Michels's conclusion regarding the difficulty of finding a major 'orthodox' current in Italy – that is, a current that truly represented a mainstay of dialectical theory – is immediately apparent when we browse the socialist literature of the time, of either tendency. This is a conclusion that, upon a first approach, takes us back to the moment at which the very concept of revisionism began to be defined: that is, the Italian dimension of the 'crisis of Marxism' at the end of the century.

1 Michels 1979, pp. 332–3.
2 Bobbio 1987, Vol. I, pp. 58–63.

It is true that the object of this chapter, revolutionary syndicalism, was inexistent at that point. But nonetheless, I think that we need to start from there in order to identify some of the important categories of this revisionism.

Some scholars pose the *terminus a quo* of syndicalism as beginning with the first Italian general strike, in September 1904; others identify it as starting with a peculiar case of the revolutionary tendency, namely the Milan periodical *Avanguardia Socialista*; still others date it to the moment that Georges Sorel's thought began to be received in full among certain Italian intellectual elites. These latter often reduce revolutionary syndicalism to an Italian Sorelianism. In the course of this work, we will see a different perspective maturing, and one that helps us better to understand the periodisation of revolutionary syndicalism. Yet given the more specific focus of this study – that is, analysing how a culture formed and developed – the fluidity of our subject certainly does not allow us to remain within too rigid periodisations. For example, intellectual figures like Arturo Labriola and Enrico Leone, who would become eminent points of reference for syndicalism, had already at the end of the century played a far from secondary role in the discussions that were then underway, despite their young age. Indeed, it was precisely within this context that they had matured analytical categories that were certainly not of merely conjunctural importance.[3] Georges Sorel also played a leading role in this same context, having 'militarily occupied three or four reviews';[4] and for this reason this period can be considered a privileged observatory not only for understanding revisionism's genesis among the most important figures inspiring the revolutionary syndicalist intellectual milieu, but also for confirming what relation did or did not exist between this type of revisionism and the growth of syndicalism itself. Georges Sorel, Arturo Labriola, and Enrico Leone would, then, be very much internal to the 'crisis' of Marxism – even if not linked among themselves, or all involved to the same measure –, determining some of its coordinates and in part absorbing others.

As we know, the themes addressed in the debate at the end of the nineteenth century combined in a rather thick web. Philosophy, economics, sociology, epistemology and politics proved to be far from separate and self-sufficient spheres. As such, the protagonists in the discussion often intervened outside of what might be considered their own particular areas of competence. In

3 While Leone's explicitly revisionist book *La revisione del marxismo* was published in 1910, it was in part composed of material written in 1900–1, even if this was subsequently revised and updated.

4 The expression is from Antonio Labriola's 5 April 1899 letter to Luise Kautsky, in Labriola 1899, Vol. III, p. 915.

part – and *only in part* – this was due to the fact that the professionalisation of the different disciplines had still not yet appeared in finished form, even if the acceleration of this process was one of the components of the cultural climate that provided the context for the unfolding 'crisis of Marxism'. This was an atmosphere well-suited to a genius of a dilettante like Sorel to move freely in refusing disciplinary limits and, notwithstanding certain excessive interventions (and this was no slander on Antonio Labriola's part), appear as a connecting element among diverse cultural experiences.

Independently of the deep differences in their intellectual personae, Leone and Labriola could not but have moved in a rather different environment, determined by the fact that they had chosen to be economists precisely in the period in which the 'economist's profession' was increasingly tending to define its terms of belonging (and thus of exclusion) in more rigorous terms. But precisely in this 'strait' leading towards professionalisation – the bitterness of the *Methodenstreit* – the contentious paths around the foundation of the 'economic moment' necessarily ended up significantly widening the boundaries of discourse on political economy. A far from negligible part of the fundamental axis of the 'crisis of Marxism' would pass through this very dimension. Moreover, at the end of the century 'pure economics', which had appeared in Italy right at the start of the 1890s with very great theoretical authority, had entered into the final phase of its definitive settling of accounts with the prevalent Lorian 'economic sociologism'. Only then did marginalism truly start to become economics.[5] And the marginalisation of 'Lorianism' did not only mean the end of the 'determinisms', 'sociologisms', 'historicisms' and 'all the "strange peculiarities" that Loria's work is undoubtedly rich in' but also, as has rightly been noted, the disappearance of Marx's name from economics journals, the deepening of the divide between historians and economists, and the decline of 'the attempt to study history on a "materialist" – that is, structural – basis'.[6] The establishment of 'economics' thus in itself constituted a fundamental element of the 'crisis' in question, and compelled the 'Marxist' economists who wanted somehow to remain internal to both spheres to adopt 'revisionist' conceptualisations.

The two young economists Labriola and Leone may have been almost the same age, but they appeared at this end of the century 'appointment' with rather different intellectual histories: the former already had behind him a

5 For a different periodisation see Barucci 1980.

6 Faucci 1978, p. 675. Obviously the ease with which it was possible to strike against Marx by way of Loria is another question, which we have dealt with elsewhere.

whole baggage of interventions concerning Marxism and economics, which meant he was now an emerging protagonist among the new generation of socialists, whereas the latter would define himself for the first time in this determinate context.

Up till 1898 Arturo Labriola had distinguished himself with the positions he took against both the 'Lorian' critics of Marx (notwithstanding his own more than evident Lorian genealogy) and 'pure economics'. Still a student (he graduated this same year), he had replied to the first Italian critics of the theory of value by propounding, almost as a scholastic exercise, a simple and not very articulated version of his interpretation of Volume III of *Capital*, which he had read recently.[7] As against rising marginalism – which, to ease his polemic, he reduced to a simple matter of hedonist psychologism – he counterposed the complexity of a society divided into classes, the reality of a capitalism in a precise historic phase of which the analytical tools of pure economics had barely scratched the surface. And also here, faced with the demand – deeply felt by the marginalists – 'to group all parties under singular principles, to construct an organic whole of logically deduced laws', he responded that this was possible precisely on the basis of Marx's labour theory of value: 'the third volume of *Capital* has placed it beyond any doubt'.[8]

These first attempts of Labriola's were thus wholly programmatically internal to the Marxism of the time; they showed no particular originality,[9] but were certainly an attentive reading. This was itself of far from negligible importance in the dominant cultural climate (including in the academic sphere),[10] and he

7 Arturo Labriola, 'La teoria marxista del valore e il saggio medio del profitto', *Critica Sociale*, 1895, pp. 43–6; 'Le conclusioni postume di Marx sulla teoria del valore', *Critica Sociale*, 1895, pp. 76–9.

8 Arturo Labriola, 'La conception hédoniste de l'économie politique', *Le Devenir Social*, 1895, p. 868.

9 Engels was certainly right to refuse his consent to Labriola's project for a compendium of the third volume of *Capital*, on such a precarious basis. It was Turati who had made the request, but Engels drily responded that there were only 'half a dozen men capable of doing it' in all of Europe, and that on the basis of the articles published in *Critica Sociale*, 'Labriolino' could not consider himself one of them. Apart from any objective appraisal, Antonio Labriola had given Engels a very bad impression of Arturo Labriola only a couple of months previously, and this doubtless had some bearing on his attitude. See the correspondence: Antonio Labriola to Engels, 15 February 1895; Turati to Engels, 19 June 1895; Engels to Turati, 28 June 1895; Turati to Engels, 1 July 1895, in Del Bo (ed.) 1964.

10 One of the protagonists in the discussion of the labour theory of value in 1894–5, Francesco Coletti, a pupil of Achille Loria's, had considered transforming his contributions into an overall study of Marx's theory of value. He had difficulties with Volume II of *Capital*, and

expressed a clear recognition of the most significant element of the themes being discussed. Not by chance, in the two subsequent years he continued to deepen the reflection that he had begun upon the publication of *Capital* Volume III, convinced that the conditions for an overall evaluation of the theory of value, taking account of the different levels of articulation of Marx's analysis, had now presented themselves. And the point of arrival of this reflection would constitute a true and proper qualitative leap with respect to his earlier output: a more mature approach, with extremely interesting intuitions, some of which would remain a constant of his thinking even as he developed it in non-linear ways.

The essay that Labriola published in *La Riforma Sociale* in 1897 is pervaded by the – partly successful – attempt to remain within the field of the critique of political economy. It does so by way of an interpretation seeking clearly to shed light on the difference of perspective between classical theories (particularly Ricardo's) and Marx's, with regard to the function of value within economic theory as a whole and in the processes of actually-existing capitalism. The Ricardians as well as Loria in Italy had privileged the quantitative dimension of economic variables, and according to Labriola this had not allowed them to understand the distinction between labour and labour-power, which was essential to the specific historical relation of value production. Labriola thus particularly insisted on criticising the interpretation of Marx's economic categories – particularly those relating to value – in pure terms of 'physicality'. He attributed the greater part of the simplistic refutations of Marx to this approach, which was extremely widespread at that time. His comments on the problem of the value *form*, which were rather unusual in the literature of the day, further strengthened a framework that was not limited to searching for the 'extent' and defining the 'substance' of value, and which made it possible to see that the 'transformation problem' in *Capital* was not limited to the question of the transformation of values into prices.[11]

If in Volume I Marx's theoretical argumentation operated on the terrain of *values*, and in the third volume the terrain of *prices of production*, Labriola con-

turned for his teacher's help in the following terms: 'The study of K.M.'s theory of value is proceeding slowly … I am translating the most important passages, relating to the third volume (first part); and it is a difficult job. I would be thankful if you could specify for me in which passages M. recaps and condenses his *new* theory or explanation of the general average rate of profit; then I would be able to proceed more rapidly'; Coletti to Loria, 28 May 1895, appears as an appendix in Favilli 1980.

11 On the non-coincidence of the transformation problem and the transformation of values into the prices of production, see Veca 1973 and 1975, pp. 169–75.

sidered this not a logical contradiction, but rather a cornerstone of his whole analytical development. In fact, only such an approach allowed a coherent recomposition of the sphere of production with the sphere of circulation by way of an *internal* link. Prices appeared as an epiphenomenon, expressing the relations among commodities in capitalist society, as mediated by the general equivalent, money; but prices were but a *form* of value, and it was necessary to go back to value and hence attach the modes of functioning of the social relations of production and exchange to the real-concrete level. Certainly, it was necessary that values *really* were transformed into prices, and here Labriola obviously ran into analytical difficulties that he barely perceived;[12] but in substance his intervention remained an open and problematised critical contribution, which, at the same time, was still wholly internal to Marx's parameters.

Labriola would run into the problem of the 'revision' of some of Marx's approaches, and subsequently even an overall rethinking of the socialism-Marxism relationship, through his encounter/clash with Francesco Saverio Merlino. Through Merlino he also came into contact with the problematics that Sorel and Bernstein were currently developing, and thus now entered into the very heart of the 'crisis of Marxism'. He dedicated two different articles, a few months apart, to Merlino,[13] which while different in part also had numerous far from secondary elements in common. In both he sharply refuted Merlino's more directly analytical arguments; in the first he defined his critique of Marxism as 'insufficient, one-dimensional, erroneous' and declared that the only admissible part of his discourse was that relating to 'the *positive* programme of socialism'.[14] Similarly in the second article, he maintained that he did not share 'any of Merlino's fundamental arguments', accepting only his suggestion of directing research toward defining 'the ideal and material content of socialism'; but the context in which these statements were inserted was far more open to the hypothesis of a 'revision'.[15]

12 '... we think that it is possible to determine the average rate of profit with methods even more precise than those Marx proposed, naturally respecting its base and setting it in accordance with the phenomena of competition'. See Arturo Labriola, 'La teoria marxistica del valore', *La Riforma Sociale*, p. 256.

13 Arturo Labriola, 'Pro e contro il socialismo', *Critica Sociale*, 1897, pp. 213–14; 'La crisi della teoria socialistica', *La Riforma Sociale*, 1898, pp. 1150–62.

14 Sorel gave a distorted reading of this article – and likely had some interest in doing so – as he claimed that Arturo Labriola had invited Marxists to take advantage of Merlino's ideas in order to develop Marxism while keeping its substance intact. See Sorel 1898, p. iv, a preface to a work of Merlino's.

15 Arturo Labriola, 'La crisi della teoria socialistica', *La Riforma Sociale*, 1898, pp. 1161–62.

Certainly, Marxism remained 'the official theory of socialism', and the 'most complete, integral and perfected' one *thus far*. Moreover, a socialist theory that did not base itself on a conception of social revolution as a *necessary* process condemned itself to regression toward utopian subjectivisms. 'The Marxist conception ... is essentially economic. Sorel is thus mistaken when he writes that "Marx's communism must not be interpreted in a purely economic sense; it is, before anything else, juridical"'.[16] Behind Merlino, then, appeared Sorel, whom he clearly distanced himself from, but recognised as an interlocutor gifted with greater theoretical solidity and, in a certain sense, one who was internal to the Marxist dimension, whereas the former anarchist from Naples was wholly external to it. As we have already said, this piece also clearly rejected Merlino's theses critical of what Labriola called 'the law of capitalist accumulation'.[17] However, it is worth noting that the *economic* arguments demonstrating the 'virtual movement' of the 'law of capitalist concentration', and denying that the social question was 'a juridical question, in the sense that its solution might owe to the realisation of principles of distributive justice'[18] – in short, the arguments used to refute the kernel of Merlino's theory – were all taken from Pareto's *Cours* ... and in part from Pantaleoni's 1898 *Principii teorici della cooperazione*.

In this phase of opening up to 'revisionist' arguments, then, Labriola unlike Sorel remained attached to a vision of 'social becoming' that had economic and not juridical and ethical foundations, even if he did not deny that the proletariat must become the bearer of a higher morality; he seemed to be orienting himself toward a conception of the *neutrality of scientific economics*; and held that there needed to be a work of 'revision' above all for reasons of a psychological order, as against dogmatic mental attitudes, 'in order to get rid of a faith in Marxist arguments that are already blindly accepted in advance'.[19]

The literature on this argument tends to consider the mooring point of Labriola's 'revision' the far-reaching study that he presented on the occasion of the Premio Tenore competition announced by the Accademia Pontaniana in 1899, on the theme – suggested by Benedetto Croce – 'Critical exposition of the economic theories contained in the third volume of Karl Marx's *Capital*'. And indeed, this was a key book, a prognosis both for Arturo Labriola's own intellectual development and for the clash between Marxism and pure economics as academic economics became an ever more professionalised discipline in late 1890s Italy.

---

16 Arturo Labriola, 'La crisi della teoria socialistica', *La Riforma Sociale*, 1898, p. 1153.

17 Ibid.

18 Arturo Labriola, 'La crisi della teoria socialistica', *La Riforma Sociale*, 1898, p. 1156.

19 Arturo Labriola, 'La crisi della teoria socialistica', *La Riforma Sociale*, 1898, p. 1161.

In general, this book has been read as an attempt – perhaps a confused and substantially unsuccessful one – to combine two different analytical apparatuses. I believe that excessive weight has been given to the concluding statements of this volume, which rather display the character of an 'academic profession of faith'. But if we instead consider the study in its overall dimension, we see that this work provides not so much an integration or combination, as the juxtaposition of a fragile ideological enunciation and a way of considering economic problems that was now deeply rooted in Labriola, and which, in substance, was destined not to change.

The intellectual tension running throughout the book was explicated through a continual confrontation between classical economics – which, for Labriola, reached full maturity only in Marx – and pure economics. For the author, there was no doubt: the classical economists' and Marx's method had such a capacity to explain the ensemble of socio-economic phenomena that it brought into relief the restrictedness of pure economics' viewpoint, which was fundamentally reducible to a simple 'theory of exchange'. Certainly, it could be argued that Marx's work is divided into an economic part and a sociological part, but in reality each of the two parts strongly penetrates the other, and it could not be otherwise: the 'object of seeing into men's static relations, so to speak, of understanding what are the social relations under which they live, of explaining the way in which men effectively produce their material life – this is the proper [object] of economic science, which … results in a science of social relations'.[20] Marx had, indeed, presented his 'Böhm-Bawerk and company' trying to discover the laws of 'human nature's' behaviour, which yesterday realised its greatest well-being in the slave system and today did so in the capitalist one. But the true task of a social science is that of studying social man, man as he is given in a determinate society; and political economy is not a science of nature, but a social science. Moreover, it is precisely capitalist economics that transforms human capacity into an economic category. In this context, hedonistic economics could only be defined as a 'science apart, not to be confused with political economy true and proper'.[21]

Having restricted the field of pure economics' possible operation, Labriola imposed strong limits on its autonomy. The phenomena of the market and of competition could not, indeed, be explained 'on their own terms'; rather, it was necessary to turn to analysing the social relations from which they derived as organic moments. 'Any doctrine that does not manage to break the

20 Labriola 1899, p. 11.

21 Labriola 1899, p. 16.

symbols of the market down ... into the realities being symbolised (quantities of labour) will remain mere phraseology. Marx began precisely from here; the others who have taken the destination for the starting point have got lost along the way, doubling back on themselves'.[22] Precisely for this reason, Marx's procedure for calculating the prices of production remained valid, in that the fluctuation of market prices always revolved around a centre of gravitational pull: labour-value '... the price-form is one of the expressions of the value-form'.[23]

The polemic against the 'hedonists' on this fundamental analytical element, a direct consequence of a profound divarication in the conception of economic science, was constant throughout the book. It was a polemic against those hedonists who obliterated the bodily reality of labour producing value in the 'tranquilising sphere of price'. 'Even the people of Israel forgot its Jehovah and made itself a golden calf' – Labriola noted – 'and it is true, moreover, that punishment was not slow in coming'.[24] And in the whole volume, the only apparent departure from the terrain of 'objectivism' regarded the evaluation of abstract labour at the moment of exchange – an exchange that cannot take place in terms of 'the effective quantities of labour' contained in the commodity. Naturally, this was all in accordance with Marx, and perhaps in disagreement with Engels's (ill-understood) interpretation.[25]

In this same concluding chapter, Labriola's final conclusions did not seem to follow from his initial framework. He stated that 'the goal of Marx's *Capital* is to study the laws of the normal formation of profit', specifying that the 'normal' process of profit formation concerns reproducible goods, not irreproducible ones. Marx, in short, had circumscribed his analysis to the capitalist mode of production *alone*. He had examined *only* the 'normal' production of profit, overlooking its 'peculiar inflexions, distortions and transfigurations'. In Labriola's view, these latter corresponded to the way in which single capitalists distributed profits among themselves. Since Marx had treated the question of distribution among the various sectors of production in exhaustive fashion, the problem that remained related to analysis of 'the laws that govern the distribution of single capitalists' individual profits'.

This meant a logical jump that seems wholly external to the general context of his argument. Pure economics had to occupy itself with the problem that *Capital* had not interested itself in; but since only the solution of this problem

22 Labriola 1899, p. 46.
23 Labriola 1899, p. 117.
24 Labriola 1899, p. 198.
25 Labriola 1899, pp. 169–70.

would allow an understanding of the real laws of the economy, insofar as 'all the conditions for economic equilibrium' would thus finally be present, the task facing pure economics was a 'colossal' one. Given this analysis, Labriola could thus arrive at the well-known conclusion that science would have to 'definitively adopt this approach, [whose] results will not at all be in contrast with Marxist laws, since these latter refer to an order of facts that form the substrate but not the object of the psychological-mathematical school's research'.[26] He thus jumped from the need to insert into economic analysis themes that were not limited to the multiplicity of commodity *forms*, to an acceptance of a new scientific status for the discipline: clearly a wholly contrived move. The pervasive atmosphere of the 'economic moment' – an atmosphere that the aspiring young professor of political economy would fully breathe in, at a time when political economy *as a whole* tended to be identified with marginalism – is explanation enough of this contradiction.[27]

We must, in any case, rule out the idea that the book in question could be considered the sign of a 'turn' either in Arturo Labriola's Marxism or in his conception of economic science.[28]

There is, rather, another aspect that we ought to emphasise, which while in part strengthening the argumentation that we have elaborated thus far, on the other hand allows us to identify an element of evident continuity between Labriola's Marxism at the end of the century and a far from marginal moment of revolutionary syndicalist ideology.

The question concerns the problem – very much discussed in the economic literature of the time (and not only that time) – of the productivity of capital. Its mutual implications with one of the numerous readings of the theory of exploitation are self-evident. Labriola was highly categorical in denying capital in the formation of profit. For him, the theories of the time regarding circulation, capitalists' abstinence, productive services, and marginal productivity, were merely ideological expressions in defence of a particular interest. Labour

26 Labriola 1899, pp. 291–95.

27 All of Labriola's subsequent scientific development was testament to the extent to which this volume's extreme conclusions were linked to this specific moment in his professional life. Moreover, in a passage from the preface to the second edition of 1908's *Marx nell'economia e come teorico del socialismo*, appearing in 1926 under the title *Studio su Marx*, he referred to this earlier 1899 text, noting that it 'was exclusively dedicated to seeking the terrain of an accord between Marx's theory of value and the theory of prices', without making any reference to the 'fundamentally' important function of 'pure economics'.

28 A turn did not occur even to an attentive observer like Pareto, who reviewing the book noted that 'to criticise this book would be to criticise the theories of Marx'.

was the only *active* element, the element that produced *transformations*. Production was, precisely, the production of transformations, the production of value. At the beginning of the process was only labour producing two incomes, wages and profit; the origin of profit, then, was entirely in its nature as labour. 'Profit as a social necessity' – Labriola could thus conclude – is historically justified by the existence of a class that consumes without producing. Surplus value is 'the tax for the maintenance of the capitalist class'.[29] Here Labriola was combining and reaffirming two cornerstones of the Marxist tradition, a tradition that he had no intention of renouncing: firstly, that of considering capitalist representations not as a given but as a problem in themselves (the mystery of capitalist 'retribution'), and secondly, the recognition that every human operation can be considered economically, insofar as it is a product of labour – and this in perfect accordance with the most profound truth of the classical theory of value.

The impossibility of thinking socialism without Marx, for Labriola, and the difficult – but, all things considered, external – relation with 'official economics' are amply documented in a contemporary intervention of his aimed at the political heart of the crisis of Marxism: an intervention on the *Bernstein-Debatte*.[30]

In this essay, Labriola considered Bernstein the most important representative of a shared attitude toward Marxism that also brought together Sorel, Merlino and even Croce. Labriola considered this group of intellectuals' common stance to be interesting only from a psychological point of view, and certainly not from a scientific one. From this latter point of view, the 'crisis-ists' had done nothing but return, via tortuous paths, to the 'bourgeois point of view' and 'official science'. That did not mean that it was right pre-emptively to reject all 'official science', like the German social-democrats had done, considering Marxism a separate knowledge. Economic science had made progress since Marx's time, which it was impossible not to take account of; but overall it was necessary to continue to have a critical view of it, and in any case to evaluate it in its specific field of application, which was not that of Marxism. Bernstein, conversely, ended up accepting all the viewpoints of this 'official science', including in his incomprehension of the function that the theory of value had in Marx. Moreover, Engels's former disciple argued that social surplus-value was not the product of the workers only, but the cooperation of all classes

29 See Labriola 1899, p. 94. For the way in which Marx addresses the problem of capital's productivity specifically, see Maffi (ed.) 1969, p. 92. See also the observations in Napoleoni 1972, pp. 120–1.

30 Arturo Labriola, 'Bernstein et le socialisme', *La Revue Socialiste*, 1899, pp. 663–79.

in society. This meant striking a lethal blow against the very idea of socialism, in that profit now became only the wage for the capitalists' labour, and the abolition of classes was transformed into a substitution of the individuals at the top of society.

Bernstein, like Merlino, Sorel and Croce, in reality stood wholly outside of socialism. In this sense, 'what is commonly called the crisis of Marxism is, then, nothing other than the abandonment of socialism by certain socialists'.[31] At root, Berstein had ceased to be a socialist because he had abandoned some of the cornerstones of Marx. His horizon was not that of the class struggle and collectivism, but rather that of cooperation and democracy. This meant shifting everything onto the terrain of capitalist society.

These observations on Bernstein's revision also help us understand easily enough that the young Naples economist's way of addressing the 'crisis of Marxism' was not reducible to the lowest common denominator that to some degree united – whatever their differences – the variegated world of the 'crisis-ists'. It is doubtful that the results of this phase of Arturo Labriola's intellectual itinerary could correctly be termed 'revisionism', at least in the generally accepted use of the word. Yet notwithstanding his and Leone's common problems related to the professionalisation of the discipline, his stance toward Marxism at the end of the century certainly did not coincide with that of his friend and fellow Neapolitan.

'Having set out armed against hedonism, the inverse has happened to Enrico Leone – above all a speculative thinker – who has himself converted to the new economic doctrines'. So wrote Giuseppe Calvino, presenting the text of a lecture on the *Communist Manifesto* that the young Neapolitan socialist gave while still a student in early 1898.[32]

Certainly, Enrico Leone's battle was not a long one, if it was, indeed, a battle. In 1898 he spoke of Marxism as

> the conscious theory of a spontaneous movement that is transforming the social world … Not … only the consciousness of a party, but … the science of society. Not the programme of a class, but the analysis of the historic movement of the classes, which weave the pattern of social development.[33]

---

31 Arturo Labriola, 'Bernstein et le socialisme', *La Revue Socialiste*, 1899, p. 677.

32 See Leone 1901, p. 5. Caivano dates the lecture to January of 1898, whereas more recent studies date it to 27 February: see Volpe 1966, pp. 413 et sqq.

33 Leone 1901, p. 14.

By the following year, the fundamental science of society, which for Leone still meant economics, had taken on the paradigmatic characteristics of 'hedonism'. One important sign of this: in 1899 he became immersed in his economics studies, frequenting Maffeo Pantaleoni's classes and beginning to work on his laureate dissertation under the supervision of Augusto Graziani, a Lorian who was an expert in combinatory logics and who was open to using marginalism (even if in a sectorial way) from the 1880s onward.[34] In 1899–1900 Enrico Leone began his *profession* as an economist.

Though some themes of Leone's 1898 text, beyond the *economic* field, would remain constants of his elaboration, his experience as a revolutionary syndicalist would end up giving new light and new perspectives to these themes. In this conception, the socialist political party and the organised workers' movement could not but coincide, at the moment that the self-consciousness of the *necessity* of the historical process, in which the working class was gradually becoming the main protagonist, came to maturation. Had the most important workers' organisations not perhaps 'been compelled to frame their practical action within the theoretical schema of the *Manifesto*, almost without noticing it', even at this point? And this because 'the communist parties [could] have no function other than that of the workers' movements … [as] a general expression of a spontaneous historical movement unfolding before our very eyes'.[35] As we will have plenty more occasions to see, well-rooted deterministic substrata and strongly stated professions of voluntarism coexisted very well not only within the same movement, but even within the same person.

From 1899, then, Leone appeared as an *economist* and revealed himself to be a crisis-ist.

If Arturo Labriola (like, moreover, his namesake Antonio, though with a different level of authority) could state that much of the 'crisis of Marxism' was determined by nothing other than the defection of a group of intellectual-activists from socialist ranks, Enrico Leone turned this framework on its head. He instead argued that it was precisely these intellectuals who had posed the now impossible to defer task of providing contemporary socialism with a 'more satisfactory theory',[36] now that the old theoretical edifice was head-

34 See Graziani 1887, 1897. Some years later he would give a highly positive view of the fact that not a few socialists had maintained that 'the theories of final utility' were conciliable with 'Marxist ones': see Graziani 1908, p. 15.

35 Leone 1901, pp. 30, 33.

36 E. Leone, 'Nuovi orizzonti socialisti', *Critica Sociale*, 1899, p. 252. See also its 'enrolment' by Merlino: 'Nuovi orizzonti socialisti', *Rivista Critica del Socialismo*, 1899, pp. 906–8.

ing toward ruin. The 'crisis-ists', then, not only did not abandon their old home, but opened up new horizons and thus new future perspectives for socialism.

Leone's collaboration with Merlino's *Rivista Critica del Socialismo* seems far from coincidental, in this regard; for this was a continual and particularly significant collaboration, in contrast to Arturo Labriola's episodic appearance in its pages.[37] Having made contributions regarding the fundamental nodes of Marx's economic theory,[38] Leone now for the first time proposed his own vision of economic science, in relation to the overall theory of *Capital*.[39]

He, too, like Labriola, considered Marx the 'perfecter and the definitive, greatest theorist of the classical concept of value', albeit at a moment in which the 'methodological revolution' offered by hedonism had now radically and definitively changed the discipline's analytical parameters. There was no more space in the field of economic science for an approach that wanted to investigate the *causes* of value, that posed itself the problem of value within a social dynamic, that posed itself the problem of the difference between the *formal* and *substantial* levels of value. The only dimension of value that was of importance to economics – and here form and substance coincided – was that which could be picked out at the moment of exchange, in the sphere of the market; and 'the word market must mean not only the stage of exchange, but the entire economic reality taken as a whole'.[40] 'The Marxist system', conversely, 'studies the social side of wealth, relating to the original attribute of its existence, labour'.[41] Hence a sharp division between the spheres of inquiry proper to both 'hedonism' and the 'Marxist system'. Economics, in the proper sense of the word, was the former's specific field, while the latter explained phenomena 'of a sociological order'. This corresponded to the use of two different methods: the 'mathematical-mechanical' method, grounding economic theory in its own internal and organic laws (now 'it can be said that political economy is

37 Arturo Labriola limited himself to a review explaining the themes of a work by Pareto: see 'V. Pareto, *Comment se pose le problème de l'Economie pure*', *Rivista Critica del Socialismo*, 1899, pp. 761–3.

38 E. Leone, 'Intorno alle teorie economiche di Marx. La legge marxista della caduta del saggio di profitto', *Rivista Critica del Socialismo*, 1899, pp. 521–37, 733–46, a critical exposition of the contributions of Benedetto Croce, Arturo Labriola and Vincenzo Giuffrida regarding the tendency of the rate of profit to fall.

39 E. Leone, 'Il metodo nel "Capitale" di Karl Marx', *Rivista Critica del Socialismo*, 1899, pp. 993–1004.

40 E. Leone, 'Il metodo nel "Capitale" di Karl Marx', *Rivista Critica del Socialismo*, 1899, p. 1001.

41 Ibid.

entirely internal to this method')[42] and the 'etiological' one of 'causal origination' proper to 'economic sociology'.

The echoes of the 'controversy on method' were very much present in this argumentation, echoes closely associated with the frequently recalled need for a clear definition of the spheres of disciplinary professionalisation. Nonetheless, in Leone's end-of-the-century output (and not only his) there continued to be difficulties in precisely delimiting these different terrains. In particular, scholars specialising in economics had difficulties fully going along with the likes of Pareto and Pantaleoni in their work of rigorously excluding the '"social question" from the horizon of the social sciences', relegating it to the separate sphere of what Durkheim called the 'cry of pain'.[43] Could a 'revolutionary' intellectual, who wanted to remain a 'scholar' within the cultural climate of the time, perhaps renounce having a 'scientific' theory of social development?

Leone used the locution 'economic sociology' to refer to the field of Marx's research, the same expression that Benedetto Croce had applied to the same order of problems two years previously. However, Croce had had the insight to warn that 'the word "sociological" [was] one of those used in the most varied and arbitrary ways'.[44] In 1897 not even Croce truly managed to make entirely clear what was the role of this 'economic sociology' – which in the course of his essay became 'comparative economic sociology'[45] – in constructing a science of society. He told us that it was a 'legitimate' research approach, which could be placed alongside (parallel to?) economic science proper; but he did not tell us what specific function he assigned to it, nor in what dynamic field of knowledge Marx's parameters could have been used. In 1899, when his relations with Marxism had developed further, 'economic sociology' – or at least Marx's – perhaps came to find a more precise location in Croce's vision: he explained that this research served 'strongly [to bring] to consciousness the *social conditionality* of profit: the tears and blood that this profit oozes out of, a profit that in the unilateral and formalistic expositions ... [of the] travelling salesmen of *laissez-faire*, appeared almost to arise from the miraculous virtue inherent to capital. *To bring this to consciousness* is not to *discover a scientific law*: it is – to bring it to consciousness.[46] 'To bring to consciousness' a history and a reality of 'tears and blood' was not 'doing science', but 'bringing a cry of pain to consciousness'; so here we are not far from Émile Durkheim's framework.

42 E. Leone, 'Il metodo nel "Capitale" di Karl Marx', *Rivista Critica del Socialismo*, 1899, p. 1004.
43 Durkheim 1986, p. 99.
44 Croce 1961, pp. 72–3.
45 Croce 1961, p. 111.
46 Croce 1961, p. 167.

Enrico Leone certainly had Croce's approach to this question in mind, following him almost obsequiously throughout much of his own argumentation. Yet even if he, too, demonstrated aporiai and uncertainties in giving a more precise definition of the sphere of Marx's 'economic sociology', he did not arrive at the same conclusions as Croce. For him, a study of the twists and turns of the formation of capitalist profit did not just mean a descent into the underworld of the proletarian condition, but also (and perhaps above all) the necessary starting point for a theory of social classes. This aspect of Marx's interpretation would prove to be of particular importance to the revolutionary syndicalist experience.

Closely linked to this dimension was Leone's consideration of the research in *Capital* as a foundational element of a 'science of the universal laws of society, in its very composition and functioning';[47] and this, in turn, was the presupposition of a theory of capitalist development, and perhaps of possibly predicting its outcomes.

Now, it is certainly possible – or rather, necessary – to make rigorous distinctions between the more directly analytical aspects of Marx's theory and the historic destinies of 'Marxisms' and 'socialisms'. Yet we know that it is precisely the particular status that Marxism has enjoyed that makes this operation a far from simple one. Indeed, it is very difficult to separate a wilfully 'combatant' theory from the outcomes of the combat itself.

The fact that Leone wanted to keep these two levels of discourse close together (the theory of capitalism and the prediction of capitalism's future) corresponds to a need that was second nature to the socialist movement as a whole, in particular in the long foundational period that was perhaps still ongoing even at the end of the century. Certainly, at the higher levels of cultural elaboration, reflection surrounding the autonomy of determinate analytical tools had reached considerable levels of awareness – we need only think of the discussion between Benedetto Croce and Antonio Labriola on the relationship between historical materialism and socialism. But in general, it was osmosis that tended to prevail. As was very much evident among the revolutionary syndicalists, sometimes the 'prophetic' part of discourse would tend to develop wholly to the detriment of its analytical side, and the historical hardships of the former aspect would negatively reflect on the latter, which it had already previously served to impoverish.

Leone's full acceptance of Croce's outlook regarding the exclusion of *Capital*'s method from the field of economics was based on the development of

47 E. Leone, 'Il metodo nel "Capitale" di Karl Marx', *Rivista Critica del Socialismo*, 1899, p. 1004.

an interpretative approach toward the labour theory of value that had began, after the publication of Volume III, with the interventions by Schmidt[48] and Sombart[49] followed not only by Croce's but also by Sorel's.[50] However, the interpretation of the theory of value as a 'logical fact' (Sombart), or as a 'scientific hypothesis, (Schmidt) did not necessarily have to lead to it being considered an 'extra-economic fact'. Engels's attentive consideration of Schmidt and Sombart in a discussion that was almost 'internal' to Marxist parameters obviously wholly ruled out such conclusions – and not only for himself, but also for his interlocutors' part. The old patriarch of socialism's observations on a theory of value that could not be reduced to a 'purely logical process', but could be understood as internal to 'a historical process and its explanatory reflection in thought, the logical pursuance of its inner connections',[51] took it for granted that Schmidt and Sombart shared some of his fundamental categories of judgement, including in relation to the historical-social character of political economy. As compared to this problematic field, the positions of Croce, Sorel and Leone were not a natural development, but at the very least the prefiguration of a 'qualitative leap'.

If for Croce these results could be considered definitive ones, in particular after the collection of some of his essays on Marxism in a single volume ('as if in a coffin'), the same cannot be said of Sorel and Leone. Despite their common revolutionary syndicalism, their itineraries certainly did not coincide. Nor would the exclusion of the theory of value from the realm of economic facts simply result in its marginalisation. Rather, it would repeatedly lead them to reflect on the epistemological status of this theory, and to ask what type of 'knowledge' it concerned. A sociological one? A philosophical one? What type of sociology? What type of philosophy? And, moreover: what type of relationship did it have with economics? In sum, reflection on a key point of Marxism would become an integral part of a rather broader and truly long-term epistemological reflection; one which was, in many respects, never exhausted.

Meanwhile, in this crucial turn of the century, Leone explored all of pure economics' possibilities of giving a response to the problems left unresolved by the prevalent Marxism's theoretical barrenness, which had led to the discrediting of what had previously been accepted as analytical categories but turned

48 C. Schmidt, 'Der dritte Band des "Kapital"', *Sozialpolitisches Zentralblatt*, 22, 1895, and then in *Le Devenir Social*, 1895, pp. 181–93.

49 Sombart 1894.

50 Sorel 1897.

51 *MECW*, Vol. 37, p. 882.

out to be merely agitational slogans. His consequent total immersion in hedonism would produce the materials that would be at the basis of the particular 'revision of Marxism' that became one of the components of the syndicalist theoretical universe. Leone – as we will go on to see – would in a sense combine the materials he had produced in 1900–1 with the need for a 'return to Marx' as demanded by the revolutionary syndicalists' choices. The result was a consideration of Marxism's weight and permanent influence that was partly different from his view at the moment of his first elaboration. The middle term that allowed the *formal* consistency of this operation was apparent in the central role that even the 'crisis-ist' Leone assigned to the class struggle in the processes of the formation of reality, a field where the 'greatest collective hedonist' could impose itself. The 'class struggle', in fact, was the essential instrument of the 'revolution in social relations' without which the conditions 'effectively producing the maximum utility' would never be fulfilled.[52]

We know well the almost sacralised centrality that the 'class struggle' would assume within the syndicalist ideological construct a few years later. Is it possible that at the end of the century a particular reading of this aspect of Marx's theory brought together the future syndicalist intellectual elite, from Leone to Sorel?

> Once the critical realist method, applied to economics, had disappeared from Sorel [Enrico Leone would say many years later] he lost the possibility of grasping the antagonism, by way of the rivalry between capitalist revenue and the wage in its deep economic sense. The class struggle thus assumed a particular meaning in [Sorel], richer in confidence but deprived of rationality.[53]

Sorel, then, had not understood the 'rational' meaning of the class struggle – *susceptible to being a fundamental element of a theory* – precisely because of his lack of 'Marxism' and lack of care for 'its economic foundation'. After all, Sorel's elimination of 'concepts relating to the fact of surplus-value den[ied] him the possibility of thinking working-class questions economically'.[54]

In reality, this *a posteriori* reading seems to refer to a later Sorel, rather than the Sorel of the *Avvenire socialista dei sindacati*, even if in this case it is not possible to establish any sharp caesura between these two moments.

---

52 E. Leone, 'Gli studi economici nel XX secolo', *Critica Sociale*, 1901, pp. 57, 58.

53 Leone 1923, p. 24.

54 Leone 1923, p. 68, 71.

There is no need to underline the importance of the 'Italian' Sorel. This has been the object of attentive interest across a wide literature, particularly the Sorel who was the joint protagonist of end-of-the-century 'revisionism', an interlocutor of Croce, Antonio Labriola and partly also Gentile on the fundamental questions of 'historical materialism', and Marxism as 'philosophy' and as a 'science'. Rather, in this part of our work it is necessary to confirm whether or not there was a common theoretical reference point among those who would in future be the main inspirers of syndicalist theory, on the terrain of the revision of Marxism and the aspects of this revision that revolutionary syndicalism might develop. Indeed, while it is certainly right to recognise that 'syndicalism moved on the same terrain as "revisionism", [and] was a chapter of its historical-ideological experience', this is insufficient to understanding the internal mechanisms of this specific revision, either in their uniformity or in their diversity.[55]

In the discussion on the 'crisis of Marxism', Leone and Arturo Labriola were evidently neither interlocutors nor associates of Sorel's. He first saw a text by Leone in *Rivista Critica del Socialismo* in 1899. He does not seem to have held this 'student' in much esteem, a view further aggravated by Leone demonstrating a certain admiration for Arturo Labriola.[56] Sorel's remarks with regard to this latter were very severe, and sometimes contemptuous. They passed from an initial judgement on 'this young man [who] has an easy way with words but does not delve deeper into anything and only sees the surface of things',[57] to constant and ever more negative references, through which he gradually came to see Labriola as at the spearhead of the Italian 'orthodox' thinkers, almost Turati's hand in the scientific field. Hence while Arturo Labriola 'blathers' 'the Italian socialists consider him a luminary' and Turati considered him 'the hope of socialist science'. Pareto, for his part, wrote to Sorel that Labriola 'knows nothing about the theory of value and can make nothing other than literary objections',[58] so much so that the former roads and bridges engineering chief could declare himself not 'displeased that orthodox social-democracy has similar defenders in Italy', thanks to which this current 'placed itself outside of any scientific discussion'.[59] Moreover, as we have already been able to see, Arturo Labriola's positions on the 'crisis of Marxism' were wholly different from Sorel's.

---

55 De Clementi 1983, p. 11.

56 Sorel to Croce 23 August 1899, in Sorel 1980.

57 Sorel to Croce, 30 November 1897, in Sorel 1980.

58 Sorel to Croce, 19 October 1898, in Sorel 1980.

59 Sorel to Croce, 11 November 1898, in Sorel 1980.

While taking very different positions during 'the crisis of Marxism', Labriola and Leone did both continue to maintain that the justification for socialism had to stand on 'economic' bases, and furthermore their 'revisionism' (and there are doubts as to whether Labriola was a 'revisionist' in the usually accepted sense of the term) had no particular affinity with Bernstein's. That is not to say that the Sorel of the end of the century could be considered a Bernsteinian, but certainly throughout the nearly fifty articles with which he flooded the journals of France, Italy and Germany between 1898 and 1900 in the context of the Bernstein-Debatte, he appears to have been a determined supporter of Engels's former disciple. In his view, Bernstein represented the future of socialism. Just like Marx he had lived in England, and like the great master thought in terms of modernity, the continuity in the development of the productive forces from capitalism to its inheritors. 'With Bernstein we get the pleasure of imagining that Marxism constitutes a philosophical doctrine destined to a bright future', once its unsustainable parts had been removed and it had been confronted with recent developments. Fundamentally, Bernstein 'appeal[ed] to the same spirit as Marx: this mean[t] a *return to the Marxist spirit*',[60] while if Kautsky were to prevail this would mean the definitive ruination of Marxism, now shorn of any scientific interest. He emphasised to his friend Croce that 'Socialism has to travel down the road that Bernstein understands so well, or else it will become a simply scholastic exercise'.[61] Moreover, even Bernstein himself did not deny that he had received stimuli from Sorel as he formed some of his own critical hypotheses regarding Marx's theory.[62] In certain aspects, we could argue that Sorel was stepping forward to play the same role in Latin Europe as Bernstein was in Germanic Europe.

It was, however, this latter who would lay stress on the limits to his agreement with the French 'revisionist', when he wrote to him – probably after having been sent *Avenir socialiste des syndicats* – explaining that he did not believe that they were in agreement 'on all the points of Marxist practice and theory', but believed that both addressed 'these questions with the same state of mind'. He continued thusly:

> [This is a] state of mind that we could characterise as follows: accepting the fundamental principles of the theory, repudiating hasty and simplistic conclusions. For me, the use of 'scientific' as a prefix to 'socialism' is a

---

60 Sorel 1903, p. 326.

61 Sorel to Croce, 9 May 1898, in Sorel 1980.

62 Gustafsson 1972, pp. 224–90.

> demand or an obligation, more than it is the recognition of a reality. Socialism is scientific only on condition that it refuses to set down any final truth, that is, so long as it remains *research*.[63]

If this 'state of mind' were truly the same as Marx's, then Bernstein did not feel it right to say as much, seeing that the Trier philosopher had not been 'the same in different times'; like everyone, he had evolutions and passions of his own. It was not possible to determine with any certainty what his position may have been amidst the climate of a capitalism preparing to face the new century. Even if in his mature works he had distanced himself from the 'revolutionary Blanquism' typical of his youth, it was perhaps possible also to hypothesise him taking a 'crisis-ist' path.

Bernstein, however, was interested in highlighting – albeit with all the necessary prudence – the fundamental disagreement between them, relating to the anti-political conception of the union movement that Sorel was developing on the basis of the example of British trade-unionism. The German 'revisionist' emphasised that despite all the risks inherent to the political dimension it remained 'a powerful means of intellectual education and a wake-up call to public consciousness'.[64] Union organisations certainly could prove able to remedy 'the corrupting tendencies of politics', but they, too, were subject 'to many errors and seductions'.[65]

At this moment Sorel chose to overlook this telling point of clarification in his German interlocutor's response, instead concentrating on the elements they held in common in the battle against 'orthodoxy'. Even many years later, when the two 'revisionisms' had proven sharply counterposed, Sorel continued to attribute Bernstein an 'important and positive' role in his work of separating Marx from the 'Marxist school' and in seeking 'new, always unstable and provisional balances among the fundamental tendencies of modern socialism';[66] and, therefore, in restoring vitality to a doctrine hitherto condemned to sterility. It acquired vitality through the *decomposition* of Marxism.

Even so, beneath the veneer of this lowest common denominator, the political outcomes of the 'crisis of Marxism' were clearly visible, as rather different articulations destined to produce profound divisions now took shape. They could be prefigured even at this stage, as Bernstein lucidly theorised the democracy-socialism nexus.

---

63 Letter reproduced in Prat 1983, this citation on p. 131.

64 Ibid.

65 Prat 1983, pp. 132–3.

66 Sorel 1971, p. 744.

However, in the years from 1898 to 1900 Sorel's fortunes in Italy were not linked to the echoes of *Avenir socialiste des syndicats*, and nor was any project of constructing the 'book on wage-labour' that circumstances had prevented Marx from finishing yet looming on the horizon.[67]

If from the viewpoint of 'theoretical Marxism' Sorel, together with Croce and Labriola, represented one of the sides of a triangle (or a quadrangle, if we also include Giovanni Gentile) that managed, by way of a bitter internal dynamic, to express itself at very high levels of theory, from the viewpoint of 'political translatability' other juxtapositions tended to prevail. The Sorel-Bernstein binomial made great headway in an Italian press that seemed not to notice the existence, *in nuce*, of a parting of the ways between their perspectives. What it instead particularly valued was a reading of 'crisis' that starting from the demystification of all the categories of 'catastrophism' (gradual impoverishment, capitalist centralisation, tendency for the rate of profit to fall) led to an attenuation of the 'absolute opposition' syndrome. Francesco Saverio Merlino wrote in black and white that socialism as he understood it – that is, as a result of the workers' struggle for their emancipation, but also of the small bourgeoisie's struggle for emancipation from the middle bourgeoisie and the middle for emancipation from the big – was the same socialism as 'Sorel, Bernstein, [and] Vandervelde' meant it.[68] In short, Merlino grouped Sorel together with Bernstein and Vandervelde, and also with Graziadei and Van Kol (a leading exponent of a revisionism that some time later could take the name 'transigent' socialism) such that Turati, too, could argue that Sorel 'in agreement with Merlino manage[d] to confine socialism within the Procrustean possibilism of minimum programmes'.[69] Not only did Turati do so, but also those like Bonomi and Bissolati who would later proclaim themselves direct heirs of Bernstein's reformism-revisionism, and also almost all of 'political' Italian socialism. None of these showed any willingness to indulge a movement of ideas that seemed to them to be directed against the very *raison d'être* of the Socialist Party, its justifying basis as an expression of a 'class of wage-earners' with its own specific interests, 'the supreme one being to free itself of the yoke of wage-labour'.[70]

The dominant climate in Italian socialism, both in terms of the way that the Marxist identity of the party was constructed in the 1890s, and in terms

---

67 Rubel 1983.

68 Merlino, letter to *Avanti!*, 2 January 1899. In another letter to this socialist daily (11 January 1899), polemicising with Bissolati, Merlino maintained that the 'ideas [that he had] expressed were welcomed by the most capable writers, like Sorel [and] Bernstein'.

69 Turati, 'Postilla a G. Sorel, *La crisi del socialismo scientifico*', *Critica Sociale*, 1898, p. 140.

70 Expression used by Leonida Bissolati in a polemic against Merlino, *Avanti!*, 8 May 1899.

of the very difficult conjuncture that it was then going through, was not particularly favourable to a 'transigent' revisionism taking root, including the one that Georges Sorel was advancing. Certainly neither Enrico Leone nor Arturo Labriola stood outside of this climate, though it remains difficult to define what an 'intransigent revisionism', a 'Left revisionism', could have consisted of at this moment. This latter expression, sanctified by later use, does not seem absolutely able to explain the second term's relation to the first, even apart from its inadequacy in defining itself a 'revisionism' (in relation to what 'orthodoxy'?). It was of the *Left* 'not so much for its revisionist contribution in itself, as for having conserved, beside this, revolutionary postulates inherited from previous political and theoretical experiences, as if in an airtight container'.[71]

Beyond their participation – in different measure and with positions that certainly did not coincide – in the complex political-cultural phenomenon that was the first 'crisis of Marxism', it does not seem that we can identify a theoretical and/or political kernel common among Leone, Labriola, and Sorel, such as could *in itself* indicate their future *common* role in inspiring revolutionary syndicalism. Or, at least, even if there were traces of one, they did not appear absolutely clearly in the consciousness of the protagonists themselves.

'For our contemporaries, science is first and foremost a methodical means for acting on the world, for directing its forces in a useful way. This notion is no different from Marx's, demanding not that thought [sic] "interpret the world, but that it change it"'.[72] Focusing on this brief remark as he subjected certain hardly secondary aspects of Marx's science to critique, Sorel seemed to be indicating a precise thread of continuity between the refinement of the scientific tools tested during the 'crisis' and the new political deployments that were now being proposed. Could, then, social science's renewed analytical system provide an outline of the pattern commonly marked out by the future syndicalist intellectuals?

As we have seen, in Italy at this point the redefinition of social science's analytical tools largely took place on the terrain of the economic disciplines. This also meant that many socialist economists were seeking the very bases of socialism, and of the processes of the transition to socialism, within the paradigms of their own disciplines. As such, Leone saw 'a society where capital gets a reward' as 'a society in which the natural hedonistic law is violated',[73]

71 Gianinazzi 1989, p. 49.

72 Sorel 1903, p. 181.

73 Leone, 'Gli studi economici del XX secolo', *Critica Sociale*, 1901, p. 58.

and posed the problem of socialism as the question of 'the achievement of distributive justice'.[74] As Arturo Labriola stated, 'Socialism, as an attempt to secure human happiness, implies the need to put at men's disposition a mass of material and ideal (intellectual, moral, imaginary) goods greater than what the capitalist system does. And this is a problem of the most vulgar economics'.[75]

It was not only the future Italian revolutionary syndicalists who looked to certain economic categories for evidence of the social dynamic justifying their own political perspectives; so, too, did future reformists like Montemartini, who explained the class struggle as the permanent antagonism among the different factors of production and their counterposed evaluations. Its resolution would be the logical outcome of the 'law of asymmetry'.[76]

While Sorel stuck to the postulates of 'pure economics' – as a decision favouring 'modern science' – from the end-of-century 'crisis' onward he identified the future of socialism not so much in a (more or less inevitable) process of the resolution of economic antimonies, as in its resolute transformation into a 'metaphysics of customs'.[77] As such, the point he made on Marx's theory of value in 1899, when he saw it as 'illuminated in a new light', because it was 'full of juridical preoccupations', certainly did serve him in separating this analytical approach from the economic sphere. This now seems to have become a truism, but also and above all the basis for a non-economic theory of exploitation.[78] Indeed, the theory of value became the site where Marx 'allows us to see the juridical process that accompanies the production process' – the site where two 'rights' necessarily entered into conflict, even though they were born on the basis of a 'proper' economic transaction, namely a contract for buying and selling labour-power according to liberal principles respecting the rights of man and the citizen. Hence this was a 'Marxist solution' that was no longer in any sense teleological, and that 'did not inevitably derive from the economic evolution directed by modern capitalism', but could be realised 'under the influence of certain juridical ideas that may develop among the proletariat'.[79]

74 Leone, 'Le coalizione operaie e il liberismo', *Critica Sociale*, 1900, p. 235.
75 Labriola, 'La crisi della teoria socialista', *Nuova Antologia*, 1898, p. 1160.
76 Montemartini 1899, pp. 221–2.
77 Sorel 1903, p. 188.
78 In a wholly different context and using a quite different analytical toolbox, in his last studies Claudio Napoleoni posed himself the same problem, namely that of completely freeing Marx's concept of exploitation not only of the labour-theory of value, but also of economic theory as such. See Napoleoni 1992, pp. 171–92.
79 Sorel 1903, pp. 195, 196, 220.

Could the results of this theoretical 'renewal' have some effect on the protagonists' political positioning, the quality of their proposals, and ultimately the party line?

I believe that we can rule out any affirmative response to either the first or third question. The second poses rather more problematic questions.

Immediately after the 'crisis of Marxism', a political phase seems to have opened up in which it was possible to experiment with certain 'elements of socialism' *in loco*, through conquering and administering the *comuni*, in particular through a 'different' use of the praxes of municipalisation. This phenomenon, which came to be widely termed 'municipal socialism',[80] has been the object of attentive critical study, on account of its importance in multiple spheres. Here our interest is to highlight the link among some of the analytical products of the 'crisis', and a particular way of understanding the politics of 'municipal socialism'.

Arturo Labriola and Enrico Leone were rather isolated voices in the 1900–1 debate on the function of municipalised companies in the definition of 'municipal socialism'. The prevalent tendency among the socialists was to conjugate municipalisation and financial reform of the *comuni* in a logic of redistributing monopolies' profits.

Precisely this point sparked the profound disagreement of those socialists – economists by profession – who fully accepted the liberal paradigm of municipalisation regarding not only the factors that drove its genesis – namely, the need for a better allocation of resources in an imperfectly competitive market – but also the narrowly *economic* dimension of this programmatic choice. That was the common reaction of both Arturo Labriola and Enrico Leone, despite their far from negligible differences.

Arturo Labriola openly spoke of the decision to municipalise as a 'formally socialist' one, seeing that it was a response that economic rationality demanded in a situation where 'the artificial monopoly takes on all the characteristics of a natural monopoly'.[81] Hence the role of the local body managing the munici-

80 Generally there is no direct relation between the theme of municipalisations and 'municipal socialism'. Liberal economists like Einaudi, Pareto, and Pantaleoni were not against a selective policy of municipalisations, given their recognition that in certain sectors of production tending toward monopoly the private owner's 'natural' predisposition toward profit maximisation would prevent the best equilibrium for a more efficient allocation of resources and the achievement of the greatest possible collective well-being. Obviously they doggedly rejected any link being made between this *purely economic* choice and 'municipal socialism'.

81 Labriola, 'Sul socialismo municipale', *Critica Sociale*, 1900, pp. 139–41 (I, 'Socialismo munic-

palised company had to be that of restoring, as far as possible, the conditions of a competitive market, in which the prices at which the rendered service was sold would tend to be pushed down toward the prices of production.[82] This would, then, produce a reduction of 'the ills that strike the consumer', through a 'reliefs' policy that did not directly proceed from changing the tax system.

Municipalisation thus had to maintain rigorously *economic* characteristics, and absolutely not become a 'fiscal expedient' that would inevitably have transferred 'part of the tax burden onto the poor'.[83]

Labriola's interventions in fact remained internal to a generally free-market outlook, without this latter necessarily being explicated in the terms of 'pure economics'.

Conversely, Enrico Leone tried to make the question of municipalisation and its relation with local finance a question that closely descended from a constellation of general principles whose extreme points were Bentham and Sax, in a rigid conjugation of utilitarianism with the 'pure science' of finance.

For Leone, the total application of the postulates of pure economics – in its hedonistic dimension – to the criteria informing local finance was the only solution that made it possible to break out of the relativism of ideological subjectivism and to follow the reliable tracks of 'science'. In this view, socialist humanitarianism was mistaken in its typical outlook of seeking to draw on an abstract idea of justice in determining its local tax policy: since, in fact, 'every economic-financial appreciation' is based on utility, 'every estimation of justice in budget allocations is an estimation of utility'.[84] This entailed the need to substitute the principle of the *maximum collective hedonistic* interest for the egotistical-sectional visions that had always previously informed local finances. This meant that in socialist *comuni* the administration should try and construct a *harmonious* balance sheet, 'whose overall sum corresponds to the quantity of public wealth that is necessary to securing the maximum collective advantage, or the *maximum social hedonistic*' interest.[85] Only the *harmonious*

ipale e socialismo di Stato), pp. 155–6 (II, 'La riforma fiscale') and pp. 170–2 (III, 'Le imprese municipali debbono dare un profitto?'); citation from p. 140.

82 '... a municipal company must seek to realise the advantages of free competition, on a different basis of property. Free competition approaches cost price and eliminates profit only deliberately and gradually; the municipal company can get there directly and immediately': Labriola, 'Sul socialismo municipale', *Critica Sociale*, 1900, p. 171.

83 Labriola, 'Imprese municipale e profitto', *Critica Sociale*, 1900, p. 350.

84 Leone, 'I criteri socialisti per i bilanci comunali', *Critica Sociale*, 1900, p. 315.

85 Ibid.

balance sheet could be a *just* one; and as such, socialist councils should not worry if they had to increase taxation levels up to the point at which this balance sheet was, indeed, harmonious. As Leone argued:

> We are convinced that socialism must, irresistibly, bathe in realism and wipe itself clean of its old metaphysical-sociological covering. [Socialism] must not consist of a formulation of its own, but of *science*. It will not have a body of doctrines of its own, because it must cease to be a theoretical school, instead becoming the very reflection of science ... That is why this writer has no hesitation in accepting these results at which science has arrived: namely, *that there is nothing other than the individual*.[86]

Satisfying public needs meant nothing other than satisfying individual needs through collective means, in the most economic way possible. Anything that broke with this principle in honour of empty ideological formulas, like those promoting the socialisation of municipal services at all costs, worked against individual utility, and thus against justice, and thus against socialism. Had not Pareto also maintained that the maximum hedonistic interest of a hypothetical socialist organisation of the economy would, in the last analysis, coincide with that deriving from a system of perfect competition? And for Enrico Leone the most realistically coherent path seemed to be the one affirming that 'the scientific soul of socialism is represented by pure economics in its most rigid hedonistic formulation', and in particular establishing a close link between 'the criteria of socialist administration and modern financial outlooks, especially Sax's'.[87]

As in Labriola's case, we could say that this elaboration by Leone was certainly indicative of the complex web of influences in the difficult relation with economic theory now making itself felt in the formation of those young socialists who wanted to become professional economists. But again, it had no practicability as a concrete proposal for reforming the local tax system.

Moreover, it is worth noting that Leone – with the lack of flexibility typical of the neophyte – took no account of the important scientific debate that had also particularly emphasised the problematic character of the logical passage from *individual hedonistic maximums* and *the maximum collective hedonistic* interest. This lack of any 'bridge' was in fact a problematic that had drawn the

86 Leone, 'I criteri socialisti per i bilanci comunali', *Critica Sociale*, 1900, p. 316.

87 Leone, 'I "criteri socialisti" nei bilanci comunali. Replica a Ivanoe Bonomi', *Critica Sociale*, 1901, p. 143.

attention of the very people who had been, and still were, the greatest Italian exponents of the 'pure science of finance'.

As compared with positions like Arturo Labriola's and Enrico Leone's, the interventions in the debate by the likes of Caldara, Bonomi and Montemartini not only appear much more realistically articulated, attentive as they were – independently of the success of this operation – to conjugating socialism's strategic prospects with the specificity of the social-political moment that the country was living through. They also appear much more 'scientifically' grounded.

It does not seem that the positions that emerged in the discussion can be reduced to any counterposition of reformists and revolutionaries, which would instead be rather more deduced from the decisions that the protagonists in this debate would take in later times (even if not long after). That is true even if we can certainly find some roots of these future choices even in this debate. Labriola's and particularly Leone's arguments seem to be rather more the fruit of the 'flash of inspiration' that a culture of very strong Lorian inheritance had when it was faced with the panorama of greater scientific 'certainties' that arose from the paradigm of the economic school now becoming hegemonic in the academic world. An economist like Montemartini who was completely trained in the marginalist school, with which he had a first-hand connection, was able to move on the terrain of the necessary analytical distinctions with a very different grasp of the problem than the 'masters', and without any reverential subordination toward them. Hence there was an articulation of pure economics, municipalisations, and the fiscal system of local bodies, that could not absolutely be defined as 'moderate' compared to the presumed 'radicalism' of the future revolutionary syndicalists.

Italian revolutionary syndicalism has assumed many forms over the course of its history; it has been many 'things', including, among others, the instrument through which a rather broad group of intellectuals became conscious that they had a separate function of their own, and which offered itself as a reference point for them to maintain an active and distinct role in the political equilibria of Italian society. A large proportion of them were not able to participate in the end-of-the century cultural climate – in the discussion on the crisis of Marxism – purely because they were too young. The likes of Panunzio, Lanzillo, De Pietri Tonelli and Weiss were all born in the 1880s, and thus faced their first political-intellectual tests in the very climate in which revolutionary syndicalism was being formed and defined. Partially different were the cases of Olivetti, Orano, Soldi, and Longobardi, even if this latter – born in 1877 – was only slightly affected by the winds of the 'crisis'. Romeo Soldi and Ernesto Cesare Longobardi were economists, and obviously for them the 'revision' could not but proceed by way of the specificity of their discipline. Even in this situation, each of this pair made clearly different choices. Soldi,[88] who in his time had been the 'orthodox' figure who provoked the first Italian discussion on Marx's labour theory of value, had by the end of the century completely accepted Montemartini's thesis of a pure economics transcending, from a superior point of view – indeed, the only scientific one – the particular vision *from the workers' standpoint* that Marxist economics ultimately amounted to.[89] Longobardi, however, was the author just after the 'crisis' of a study in which the theory of exploitation was re-elaborated in Marxian terms, precisely on the basis of the labour theory of value.[90] Also in this case, we see no link between the use of determinate analytical tools and 'revolutionary' political choices.

Orano and Olivetti can be considered typical representatives of the milieu of 'generic', non-specialist intellectuals that characterised a certain dimension of Italian revolutionary syndicalism, particularly within the elitist, aristocratic, voluntaristic, aestheticising tone of Italian culture in general at the start of the twentieth century. Even at the end of the nineteenth century, Orano and Olivetti had been wholly internal to a certain culture, namely the culture of a less analytically-informed positivism. The former stood on the terrain of a crudely deterministic sociological psychology; the latter on the terrain of a typically Lorian brand of historical materialism.[91]

Indeed, Olivetti's laureate thesis was posed as an attempt to apply historical materialism to the study of some of the juridical institutions of ancient Rome. Its explanatory structure was almost wholly drawn from the method of *Analisi della proprietà capitalistica*. Fundamentally, it sought to demonstrate that 'the history of Roman colonisation was a fine proof of the exactness of Loria's law of history'; a proof, among other things, of 'its general applicability, its very value as a law, in the positive meaning of the word'.[92] Another text of the same time emphasised that 'the new evolutionist doctrine' had 'an absolute methodological value', applying to all branches of science, even if up till now the most significant examples were to be found in political economy, 'to which

88 To be precise, Soldi cannot be considered a syndicalist, in the sense that his political activity abruptly came to a stop before an organic theoretical-ideological vision of this kind was fully elaborated, and thus his 'revolutionism' would always remain internal to the logics of the PSI.

89 See R. Soldi, 'Nuove tendenze dell'economia politica', *Critica Sociale*, 1899, pp. 300–1.

90 Longobardi 1903.

91 See Orano 1895, 1896.

92 Olivetti 1898, p. 12. For a different reading of this work see Perfetti 1984, pp. 11–12.

Karl Marx applied himself, followed by a scholar who [was] the honour of the Italian nation ... Achille Loria'.[93]

If, then, the 'law of universal evolution', far from proving to be 'one of the three great scientific facts of the century', instead proved to be discordant with the 'science' of the new century, then the 'modern social protest that [did] not raise its voice in the name of mere needs or coarse appetites, or crude, brutal arguments, but in the name of science',[94] would have to find other cultural reference points in order to continue standing apart from the miserable 'brutality' of needs.

2 Early Definitions of a 'Left'-Marxism

In a moment in which he reflected on revolutionary syndicalism's difficulty in expanding its own sphere of influence, Arturo Labriola – who was also beginning to mature his 'crisis' with regard to the movement – returned to his past *L'Avanguardia Socialista* experience, which he considered the true genesis of the movement itself. This also meant a particular interpretation of revolutionary syndicalism. Indeed, it meant placing the accent on the now apparent need to 'start over: to get back to first principles', faced with a Socialist Party that had travelled so far from its lineage that its culture 'was a mix of bureaucratic conceptions and archaic philanthropism'. It was necessary to initiate an effort to rebuild socialism as a revolutionary political phenomenon, on the one hand recuperating a reading of Marx that justified this kind of socialism, and on the other hand injecting theories into the movement – 'as a pedagogical means' – such as would excite an 'appeal to the energies of revolt, the shock of insurrectionism'. 'Any means would do', Labriola warned, for the purposes of 'breaking through this immobile and suffocating ice over the pond'.[95]

Syndicalism, then, was not born with a theoretical corpus of its own, distinct from that of the socialist tradition; as such, it could not be considered an *Italian Sorelianism*. As well as serving as a revolutionary catalyst, Sorel's indications had also enriched the panorama of considerations on the development of the workers' movement. Yet this did not necessarily have to mean syndicalism separating itself so sharply from the tree of socialism; and it was, fundamentally,

93 Olivetti 1899, p. 12.

94 Olivetti 1899, p. 22.

95 Art. Labriola, 'La crisi dei partiti in Italia. I sindacalisti', *Il Viandante*, 1909, p. 210.

no more than an important branch of this tree. Only the political and moral degeneration of the Italian Socialist Party had led to these effects, which were not necessarily inscribed in the genesis and development of the movement itself.

Another syndicalist intellectual – he, too, an economist – had in this same period positively appraised Sorel's contribution to socialist culture and politics, but only in the sense that he had rendered 'the socialist idea more heroic', which for him was no small thing. As for the role of 'myth' in the proletariat's fight for emancipation, it was right that the 'great ideal figuration' of the actions underway should not be undervalued; yet this should be tempered with a 'representation of the struggle' that took 'account of the proportions of the forces in combat and the means at their disposal'. In conclusion, one had to be clear that 'Marxism ... [was] a school that was even truer and more profound in its realism'.[96]

In the *Avanguardia Socialista* experience the lesson of Marxian 'realism' did not, in truth, appear such as to give substance to this publication's 'tone', while Labriola's 1909 remarks seem to correspond to the reality.

Indeed, the pages of the Milan review saw the beginning of an operation that would attempt to provide the proletariat with the most rigorous coordinates for defining its identification with socialism. This was the same operation that Turati had mounted many years previously in order definitively to separate 'generic socialism' from 'scientific socialism', and which was now being conducted in opposition to Turati – the supposed protagonist of a collapse into philanthropic socialism – in the name not so much of 'science', as of 'revolution'. Moreover, Arturo Labriola had been very clear in defining the terms in which he sought to pose the question, explaining that 'the present disagreement burning up the Socialist Party is but the sudden resumption of a duel that critical communism took up against vague petty-bourgeois philanthropy masked as reformist socialism with Marx's text against Proudhon in 1846'.[97]

The separation between 'science' and 'revolution' had notable side-effects on the type of Marxist framework that would serve as the basis for revolutionary socialism's political culture. Labriola here evoked the method of *The Poverty of Philosophy*, but this was certainly not the central theme of the political Marxism proposed in this period.

By comparison, Turati's foundation of political Marxism in Italy in the late 1880s and early 1890s was of an incomparably higher calibre, and posed at a

---

96 E.C. Longobardi, 'Giorgio Sorel. Il teorico della violenza', *Il Viandante*, 1909, p. 27.

97 Art. Labriola, 'Duello Antico', *Avanguardia Socialista*, 16 August 1903.

wholly different level. Its constant intellectual tension, derived from its attempt to hold 'science' together with 'revolution', also resulted in an abundant production that was conditioned by doctrinal schematism and often characterised by scholastic positivism more than by positive knowledge; yet that was only one aspect of this process. Together with this, there was also a continual engagement with the various disciplines' scientific status, with the results that they had reached, and at the same time, an attempt to read reality in the light of the renewal of the tools of knowledge. This led to a Marxist framework that was sometimes incoherent and had evident imbalances in its interpretative parameters, but which was nonetheless certainly articulated and polyvalent.

The same cannot be said of the choice made by the *Avanguardia Socialista* group at the end of 1902. The lineaments of its Marxism were of a predominantly simplified and one-dimensional character. The thread that set the tone of this publication ended up reattaching itself to the never-defeated 'catastrophic' conception. Its approach to Marx and Engels's theses was in general characterised by the method of reciting catechisms. The citation, upon repetition, was transformed into a 'postulate'. The ensemble of these postulates came to form a web of identification with socialism, and thus it was argued that 'destroying these postulates [would be to destroy] all socialist theory of any kind'.[98]

What they wanted to recuperate was Marx 'the sarcastic and tremendous philosopher of social revolutions, the satanic theorist of historical catastrophes', the author of a theory whose 'indestructible vitality' lay in its '*being understood as a doctrine of proletarian action*'.[99] This was the Marx in whose 'system – more than any other – violence occup[ied] *first place* among the means of social transformation'.[100]

This Marx was presented as the only Marx who could legitimise socialism, and as such the revolutionary tendency was posed as the only 'heir to the intransigent socialist tradition ... the non-bastard progeny of the ... socialism ... of the *Communist Manifesto*',[101] of the 'sarcastic, aggressive, resolute and unashamed socialism of Karl Marx'.[102] This was a 'Marxist school' that it

98 U.F., 'Lo Stato', *Avanguardia Socialista*, 9 August 1903.

99 Art. Labriola, 'Carlo Marx', *Avanguardia Socialista*, 15 March 1903. Italics in the original.

100 S. Panunzio, 'Socialismo legalitario e socialismo rivoluzionario', *Avanguardia Socialista*, 3 January 1904. Italics in the original.

101 A. Polledro, 'Per un paradosso di Filippo Turati', *Avanguardia Socialista*, 10 January 1904.

102 'Dopo la vittoria', *Avanguardia Socialista*, 14–17 April 1904.

claimed 'to strictly belong to',[103] from which arose the 'Marxist programme' that it did not intend 'to renounce in any way'.[104]

This proprietary claim to Marx's inheritance ought to be considered also in terms of the logics of the very sharp political clash that had recently begun among the different tendencies. Reformism had to be 'crushed' into revisionism, into Bernstein, who in turn had to be seen as wholly extraneous to the culture of the socialist tradition. At the most, there was some readiness to recognise Bernstein's intellectual and moral coherence, which was not, conversely, granted to those reformists not prepared to consider themselves 'revisionists'.[105] The same mechanism was evidently at work in the reformist milieu's equation revolutionaries = anarchists.

The need for international recognition of their own role, and the fact that various important figures of European socialism gave their (actively requested) support to the agenda that revolutionaries presented at the Lombard Socialist congress held in Brescia,[106] led the *Avanguardia* group to define themselves – with some exaggeration – as standing on the positions of these authoritative interlocutors, and sometimes to ossify their stances. They presented such figures as 'the most authoritative and authorised interpreters of the Marxist doctrine', 'best [capable of] interpreting the thought' of the 'great masters of socialism', also on account of the 'personal relations' that they had entertained.[107] Kautsky was 'the most faithful continuer of Marxist thinking that exist[ed] in Europe', and Guesde 'the leader of the *parti ouvrier* that realise[d] Marx's thought among the French proletariat'. Sorel was he who 'combated Marxism, but who had also read him with triumphant effectiveness', hence his 'return to Marx'.[108]

Was this, then, a rigid Marxism, delimited by easily recognisable parameters strongly anchored in the international milieu that was now commonly called 'orthodox'. A Marxism consciously used (at least by a very small core of intellectuals) as a revolutionary pedagogy, aimed at a proletariat considered 'pacifist [sic]' and a socialism considered still affected by 'bourgeois philanthropy', was necessarily a highly unstable product, and it would be difficult

103 S. Panunzio, 'Socialisti e anarchici', *Avanguardia Socialista*, 23 July 1904.

104 'Corrispondenza di Parma', *Avanguardia Socialista*, 24 July 1904.

105 Art. Labriola, 'Riformismo e ipocrisia', *Avanguardia Socialista*, 27 September 1903; and in the 18 October edition, 'Il socialismo di Jaurès'.

106 See Kautsky's letter specifying the extent and the limits of his support for the Brescia agenda, published in the 20 March 1904 *Avànguardia Socialista*.

107 E.C. Longobardi, 'Il ritorno a Marx', *Avanguardia Socialista*, 9 April 1904.

108 *Avanguardia Socialista*, 7–8 April 1904.

to conjugate it with the overall solidity of Kautsky's construction. Moreover, even in the brief period in which this operation seems to have unfolded within these pre-established guidelines (1902–4), there was a magmatic fluid under the surface whose rivulets fed the 'Marxisms' of revolutionary syndicalism. The oft-mentioned 'spirit of Marxism' had proven an inspiration that was simultaneously both too specific and too generic not to feed a tension between the two poles; a tension that was never fully resolved.

Could an entirely political Marxism have long avoided addressing the problem of its relation with the 'scientific' dimension of its cultural assumptions? Some of the most conscious intellectuals tried to dispel this question by emphasising a (temporary?) separation of these spheres. As Longobardi asked,

> Should Italian socialism still take its inspiration from the political thought of the great Trier thinker, or should it transform into something else? ... His political thought, we said. Among us there are men who still fully accept the economic system as theorised by the great German socialist, and there are others who think it necessary [to make] revisions and innovations [regarding] its technical part. But that is not the issue. It is to the spirit of Marxism that we must return.[109]

Others with much lesser awareness portrayed the predicted imminent and *inevitable* catastrophe from which 'socialist reality ... would violently emerge' as directly deriving from Marx, the 'scholar who [had studied] the laws of historical becoming', which had the same mechanisms as 'cosmic becoming'.[110] Also in this case, as in many others – both ones we have seen already, and others yet to come – the oscillations between rigid determinism and extreme voluntarism unfolded without any apparatus for mediation.

Sorel's appearance among the Italian revolutionary socialists' points of reference ought to be considered internal to this 'Marxist pedagogy' operation. Sorel was one of the 'crisis-ists' who had forcefully maintained the need for the 'return to Marx', and that was what truly counted, more than the characteristics that Sorel himself ascribed to this 'return'. 'We have researched only that part of Sorel that contains the immortal and ever-renascent spirit of Karl Marx', *Avanguardia Socialista* explained; this was no Sorelian Marxism, but rather another pillar in support of the construction of their 'Karl Marx', built on 'his soul, his

109 E.C. Longobardi, 'Il ritorno a Marx', *Avanguardia Socialista*, 9 April 1904.

110 See S. Panunzio, 'L'unità del socialismo', *Avanguardia Socialista*, 11 October 1904. For more on Panunzio's rigid determinism in this period, see also his 'Lotte di classi e solidarietà umana', in the 1 May 1904 issue.

conception, his end goal, his permanently revolutionary method'.[111] And, moreover, *Avanguardia Socialista* published *L'avenir socialiste des syndicats* as an appendix in parallel with its publication of Kautsky's *Die soziale Revolution*.[112]

The highest, and in certain aspects emblematic, point that was reached in weaving together the lineaments of this revolutionary Marxism between 1902 and 1904 was represented by Arturo Labriola's volume published in Milan at the beginning of 1904.[113] Some historiographical tendencies have considered *Riforme e rivoluzione sociale* to be the first theoretical text of revolutionary syndicalism in Italy; a work in which Sorel's influence is supposedly particularly evident. This interpretation may have been influenced by the fact that the edition that had the greatest circulation was the 1906 one, revised (particularly its introductory chapter) in light of the experience of the general strike and the syndicalist theories now being defined in a rather precise manner.

Labriola's book represented, more than this, an attempt to provide a systematic character, as well as the dignity of theory, to the set of Marxist 'postulates' that formed the rather fragile and inorganic grid pattern on which *Avanguardia Socialista*'s operation of 'revolutionary pedagogy' was based – what the reformists, not without some justification, called its *latinetto*.[114]

The distinction that Labriola introduced in order to draw an insuperable line of differentiation from the reformists was formidably and completely political in character, just like the Marxism that was meant to underpin it. For Labriola, a political party was not revolutionary in character on account of its ends or its 'ideals' – even if this meant the socialist ideal – but rather the 'formal and technical method' of its activity. The state is the political guarantor *par excellence* of class domination; and as such, any social transformation that is not simultaneously directed at first the weakening of the state and then its transcendence will be an illusory one. 'A party that seeks to reach its ends by revolutionary means is naturally a party that attacks the existing form of the state. Conversely, a party that respects the existing forms of the state will never be a revolutionary party'.[115]

Anti-statism would be one of the fundamental themes of this volume, and Labriola treated the question of violence in correlation with this argument. The

111 See W. Mocchi, 'L'ultima mascherata', *Avanguardia Socialista*, 30 September 1904.

112 It published Kautsky's text starting from 11 January 1903, and Sorel's from 21 June of that same year.

113 Labriola 1904.

114 [This untranslatable expression refers to learning Latin grammar at school; the implication is that it is learnt by rote but also inaccurate]

115 Labriola 1904, p. 61.

manner in which he addressed the issue of violence – a political theme *par excellence* – itself demonstrated the difficulties of remaining wholly internal to this dimension. It would have been risky indeed to emphasise to an extreme extent the voluntaristic vein that was already powerfully circulating among *Avanguardia Socialista*'s political-cultural milieu, and Labriola was not ready to run these risks. Certainly, he did use the reference to Marx's eleventh thesis on Feuerbach in a voluntaristic manner, as was now common in Italian culture (and not only Marxist culture): he understood this less as 'philosophy of praxis' than as 'philosophy of action'. He rejected 'Engels's latter-day positions on violence', which he considered to stand at odds with 'the spirit of Marxism'; but at the same time, he very much had in mind the problem 'of combining collective and individual voluntary effort with the immanent laws of a social system'.[116] He considered this the source of one of historical materialism's greatest difficulties.

Labriola tried to give a response of his own that could link the voluntarism inherently arising from the problems of violence to a series of referents that would limit its subjective element. Moreover, it was taken for granted that violence could not 'be deployed capriciously',[117] but instead had to respond to the very specific demands of the subjective maturation of proletarian organisation and to the particular configurations of economic equilibria.

It was in this particular regard that the impact of the 'moment of violence' would find a solid anchoring in the 'economic moment'. '*The economic moment is an act of violence, become necessity*', Labriola argued, adding '*It is conditioned violence that generates the initial arrangement of the economy*. This is Marxism'.[118]

His logical passages toward clarifying the terms of this relation did not, however, go beyond the recognition that particular socio-economic conditions – like for example those concerning the hours of the working day – were the fruit of the changing power relations among the counterposed forces, and that the new 'economic' equilibria reached on the basis of a given 'compulsion' would then be codified in social legislation.

But these were not the most characteristic aspects of this volume's argumentation, even if they can be considered indicative of the conscious and functional 'partiality' with which the author elaborated his text. More characteristic were those that ultimately flowed together in the message that 'Marx-

116 Labriola 1904, p. 145.

117 Labriola 1904, p. 154.

118 Labriola 1904, pp. 149–50. Italics in the original.

ism [had been] and remain[ed] a great philosophy of force, a genial theory of intelligent violence as a factor for social progress'.[119] Arturo Labriola's relation with Marx's theory was certainly not limited to formulations regarding the 'philosophy of force' and the 'genial theory of intelligent violence'. We have seen – and we shall see further still – the complex, weighty set of links that was now gradually being stratified. The substantially one-dimensional character of his 1904 approach remained wholly internal to the justifications for the 'revolutionary' choice of the very first years of the new century. This was a choice that would lead the socialist militant to an existential condition pervaded with a continual ethical-political tension. Indeed, the fundamental economic relation of capitalism had proven 'infinitely more rigid, more heavy and more tenacious'[120] than could have been imagined. Hence the need to keep the level of revolutionary tension at a constantly high level – something that Labriola saw reformism as unable to guarantee over long periods, by its very nature.

If Labriola as an intellectual and political figure, and his Marxism itself, would far transcend the experience of both *Avanguardia Socialista* and *Riforme e rivoluzione sociale*, the Marxism to which this experience gave substance nonetheless left a deep imprint both on the culture of revolutionary syndicalism itself and on the cultures that intersected in various ways with revolutionary syndicalism. It is no coincidence that the young revolutionary socialist Benito Mussolini collaborated with *Avanguardia Socialista* in 1903 and 1904, contributing articles and correspondence. Nor, perhaps, is it any chance thing that a 1908 essay of his on Nietzsche – which has been considered 'the first concrete manifestation of Mussolinian "ideology"'[121] – was titled 'Filosofia della forza', just as Labriola had defined Marx's philosophy four years previously.

Between the final third of 1901 (with the publication of the revolutionary tendency's programmatic manifesto)[122] and the final third of 1904 (the first general strike in Italy) there was no system elaborated in the peninsula that could be defined, from either a doctrinal or an organisational point of view, as revolutionary syndicalist. As such, we cannot identify, here, any specific 'revolutionary syndicalist' reading of Marxism. Rather, what was taking shape was an attitude that progressively converged with Marxism, making use of it in a political-ideological sense – an attitude common among the whole variegated

119 Labriola 1904, p. 163.
120 Labriola 1904, p. 198.
121 De Felice 1965, p. 60.
122 See Labriola 1901.

and fluid milieu that could be considered as a 'socialist Left', a milieu that arrived at a momentary aggregation (indeed, as the majority) at the Bologna Congress.

This was, indeed, a heterogeneous aggregation whose parts would soon be decomposed and recomposed on different fundamental axes. Yet they were grouped together at this moment on account of the fact that they represented geographical areas and fragments of the subaltern classes and of the workers' movement that were excluded from the seemingly compact, coherent form in which the reformist project presented itself. The *Avanguardia Socialista* group, old POIers, and sections of unions that were struggling to deal with the reversals underway in both the number and results of struggles, almost naturally found their point of mediation in the ephemeral experience of *ferrismo*.

This experience has given rise to evaluations that mostly descend from the severe critical judgement usually made against the moral and intellectual personality of the man who for a time stood forth as Turati's greatest antagonist. The profound difference between the two men, both morally and intellectually, has often been taken as a discriminating factor also for historical judgement. I believe that Enrico Ferri's own personality and cultural-political *iter* can and should be distinguished from something else, namely the needs, deeply rooted within the socialist and workers' movement, that found cause for coagulation around the function that this figure played during a certain period of his life.

Il Socialismo – the fortnightly paper that Ferri brought out from 1902 onward, and which explicitly sought to be an alternative to the reflection in *Critica Sociale* – stated in its inside cover page that it wanted to discuss 'the problems and the doctrines of socialism in their fundamental terms and in their particular attitudes, *keeping alive and predominant the revolutionary spirit of the Partito socialista*'.[123] This was a project whose *ferrismo* remained sufficiently fluid that it did not rule out either possible openings to reformist projects or the most severe opposition to *turatismo*; and it would become a point of aggregation for forces whose lowest common denominator was represented by commitment to revolutionary pedagogy among the masses. In this phase, this inevitably meant taking for granted a strongly conflictual interpretation of Marxism.

Particularly telling, in this regard, was Enrico Leone's itinerary in the years from 1902 to 1904. In some regards, Leone played the role of *ferrismo*'s 'theoretical consciousness', and this led him to clash – also severely – with the

123 My italics.

Avanguardia Socialista group, which he considered to be a deviation from – one of the 'two opposite exaggerations' of – 'the common consciousness of socialist principles'.[124]

At the same time, the attempt to give substance and depth to the 'socialist spirt' without which any partial attempt at struggle and resistance was doomed to lack 'vital and continuing persistence' – whatever its momentary victories – led him to emphasise the need always to bear in mind 'awareness of the antagonistic character of ... capitalist production'.[125] This led to a gradual reconsideration of the results of the 'crisis of Marxism' and the role that 'revisionism' had played in shifting the 'traditional theoretical and practical bases of socialist activity from the *Marxist* terrain to that of *democracy*',[126] as well as an insistence on the need for a 'rigid Marxist conception of the process of history, understood as the rhythm of class clashes and class struggles' to prevail.[127] The political line indicated by Enrico Leone at this moment was different from *Avanguardia Socialista*'s, but they had the same way of using Marxism, corresponding to the same reasoning.

The brief and intense experience of the September 1904 general strike brought a sudden acceleration of certain tendencies that were already present in the political culture of the 'socialist Left', which had with many difficulties formed a deployment of its own between the congresses at Imola and Bologna. Only through reflection on such an event, so important to the history of the Italian workers' movement – that is, reflection on the 'new and greatly effective instrument' that now seemed destined to establish itself – could cultural themes that had until then been confused in the fluid whole of the revolutionary amalgam begin to acquire an autonomous dimension of their own, now being structured in terms that we could define as 'revolutionary syndicalist'.

Moreover, this was a structuration process that continued to maintain a high degree of fluidity. Nothing would be more inaccurate than to imagine a revolutionary syndicalist theory being organically delineated as a body of doctrine across late 1904 and the early months of 1905. Revolutionary syndicalism would never be an organically complete doctrine. It may appear easily understandable that revolutionary syndicalism expressed itself in decidedly different

124 E. Leone, 'Da Imola a Bologna', *Il Socialismo*, 1904, pp. 17–20.

125 Ibid.

126 E. Leone, 'La crisi del socialismo italiano e il Congresso di Bologna', *Rivista popolare di politica, lettere e scienze sociale*, 1904, pp. 175–6.

127 E. Leone, 'A congresso finito. I "revisionisti" a Bologna', *Avanti!*, 15 April 1904.

forms in the period in which it remained a component of the PSI, and the period in which it organised and defined itself externally. However, it seems rather more problematic to explain some of its sudden changes of perspective, if we consider it in terms of a presumed autonomous maturation of its theoretical themes. More often, the motives of a battle among tendencies unfolding in a climate of particular bitterness would encourage both moments of radical and incurable contradiction, and its tactical adjustments. They would also be partly responsible for the outcomes of the revolutionary syndicalist experience, results that certainly could not have seemed solidly determined after the September 1904 general strike.

During the aforementioned process specifying the features of revolutionary syndicalism, even the very idea of the general strike had far from the same meanings in the elaborations of Leone and Labriola – both of them clearly central figures. Moreover, in the first years of the 1900s, before the international congress at Amsterdam – and in some regards, also afterward – there was no absolutely univocal conception of the general strike. This was not, then, the discriminating factor among different conceptions of socialism.[128]

Leone, perhaps the intellectual who was more internal to the union dimension, would have struggled to agree with the position upheld by Arturo Labriola – which, for that matter, was not a long-term one – claiming that 'all of working-class socialism [was] to be found in the general strike, considered ... the shorthand formula for the social revolution'.[129] Though in agreement with his friend on the 'new era'[130] of union politics that had begun with the general strike, which proved to be of incomparable (and not only symbolic) value in the acquisition of ever more advanced levels of 'class consciousness', he ultimately attributed it a less decisive role in the overall revolutionary syndicalist vision.

But the simultaneous and particular emphasis on the role of the general strike as an accelerator for the process of the working class's total autonomisation, and its unmediated counterposition to 'all the rest of society',[131] could only make the revolutionaries' ways of using Marxism yet more rigid. This was a horizon that both Labriola and Leone certainly shared, but that they cannot have felt themselves limited by.

128 Lagardelle (ed.) 1905.

129 From Arturo Labrola's intervention at the 1906 Rome Congress, appearing in Labriola 1911, pp. 169 et sqq.

130 Intervention by Leone cited in Lagardelle (ed.) 1905, p. 355.

131 Intervention by Leone cited in Lagardelle (ed.) 1905, p. 351.

Economists by profession, and participants in the epistemological discussion on the social sciences, their familiarity with Marxism was clearly of a quite different depth. And it is no chance thing that precisely as their political Marxism was being ossified into an ever more intensified 'total counterposition', they felt the need to redefine their relation with Marx's overall theory in the very same problematic dimensions that the end-of-the-century 'crisis' had shown to be anything other than resolved.

3 Enrico Leone's and Arturo Labriola's Marx in the 'High' Period of Syndicalist Theory

Enrico Leone's life was much more deeply marked – and for a longer time – by the experience of revolutionary syndicalism than was Arturo Labriola's. We can consider this latter's syndicalist experience to have substantially come to a close in the course of 1911. That same year Labriola collected in a single volume, 'like in a grave' (as had Croce ten years previously), some of the texts that he had published in syndicalist reviews in the preceding years, almost as if he wanted to give a personal sense of a journey in which he had sought to combine both 'science and revolution'; a journey at the end of which it seemed possible to make out the gloomy symptoms of failure.[132] And in the second edition two years later he added a newly written essay,[133] making wholly explicit what had only been suggested in the 1911 one. Even more clearly, in a book printed without any further additions or explanation in September 1943 – but put together during the crisis of the liberal state and completed in 1926 – he referred to this type of experience 'of combination' and his subsequent 'scientific' return to Marx, using the metaphor of the traveller who

> after reaching some distance from his homeland, having travelled through unknown lands and shared in the lives of other peoples, ends up thinking that his own homeland's sky is clearer, its air finer, its people more agreeable and its customs more tolerable. Ultimately we see that there are questions and answers in [Marx's] theory that we sought in vain in other authors, and that if it is not necessary to give it up, we must return to this theory.[134]

---

132 See Labriola 1911.

133 Labriola 1913, pp. 225–55.

134 Labriola 1943, p. 10.

We have seen that this journey through 'unknown lands' had set out from the end-of-the-century 'crisis'; and we have also seen the controversial and in some aspects contradictory set of tools that the traveller prepared to take with him as his baggage. This was precisely the point[135] at which the conviction matured in him – one which he never abandoned during his syndicalist period – 'that every socialist doctrine [was] ultimately the critique or development of the prevalent doctrine'.[136] And so now, at the moment that he was faced was the task of giving a doctrinal structure to the intellectual and organisational whole that took the name 'revolutionary syndicalism', Labriola, together with others, tried to unpack the 'kernel of the new ideas' precisely on the basis 'of determining the principles of the *exact* economics of very recent times'.[137]

In truth, it does not seem that Labriola's approach to Walrasian-Paretian categories, and the relation that he tried to establish between the use of this theory and Marx's, saw particular developments in his revolutionary syndicalist years, as compared to the point that he had arrived at with his 1899 *Studio sul III volume del Capitale*. Even when he tried to pin down 'The current moment of economic science in Italy',[138] explicitly seeking to demonstrate the coincidence between the economic sphere and pure economics, his arguments were not, in truth, convincing for those who really were marginalists.

Beyond his homages to a Pareto who had the merit of 'sweeping away' any 'sophisms' regarding value, and of having given pure economics 'a more vigorous and systematic representation', the spaces that Labriola ultimately assigned to this type of study were much more restricted than those considered by the 'hermit of Celigny'.

The young Naples economist limited himself to defining it as a pure 'mechanics of egoism': 'Economics distinguishes [egoist] actions from others and makes them the object of its own investigations, insofar as they are logical and rational actions. Economics, in other terms, studies a fragment of man'.

135 Merlino recounts that in 1899 Arturo Labriola (clearly identifiable as such, though Merlino does not refer to him by name) had written the following lines to a friend: 'Theoretical socialism has always been the shadow of Political Economy. Now that political economy is taking on the prevalent hedonistic-mathematical tendency, the socialist doctrine must – *on pain of death* – radically change its orientation'. See F.S. Merlino, 'Altre polemiche', *Rivista Critica del Socialismo*.

136 Labriola 1911, p. vi.

137 Ibid.

138 'Sul Momento attuale della scienza economica', written 1907, appears in Labriola 1911, pp. 3–32.

In this brief analytical segment he could be in agreement with even Pantaleoni as to the non-existence of 'schools' within economics, but at the same time it could not be denied 'that men and social facts feel economic … processes in different ways'. The worker, the entrepreneur, the stock-market speculator and the banker had different points of view: hence the different theories of profits as 'unpaid labour, abstention from consumption, the product of capital', and so on. In this sense it was possible to speak of economics as a 'class science'. These were legitimate, but partial points of view. Economics in general did not occupy itself with the origin of profit. Fundamentally, the most important questions concerning the relations among aggregates of humans in production were explained more by sociologists, historians and jurists than by economists. Mathematics left 'the laws of demand and social income in complete darkness'.[139]

The fact is that Labriola never managed to overcome his basic hostility toward pure economics, revolving around the very epistemological coordinates that the discipline had set itself. Cleansed of statements linked to the particular social climate, and to the oft-mentioned demands of academic professionalisation, his position would make openings to it only in terms of limited technical tools that could be used with regard to 'fragments' of human activity. He did not recognise it as having any explanatory potential on the terrain of the social dynamic.

Not by coincidence, in the same period in which he wrote these Paretian panegyrics, when he thought that he could make out symptoms of an improbable 'return to Ricardo', he went so far as to express his 'repugnance' for the system of 'pyschological-mathematical doctrines'. He thus launched into the following statements:

> I believe that the foundation of this repugnance lies in the difficulty accepting all the imaginary [measures of] quantity with which the new economic sciences have populated economic science … The new Economics' complicated hedonimetry and the dynamic concept at its basis – be they true or false – turn attention away from the reality of work, as a substratum, condition and element of economics – or rather a *hypostasis*, to put it in scholastic terms, but which in this case says it all. The new economics would willingly gladly all the manifestations of the economic process into the sphere of exchange. Exchange is the night in which all cats are grey. From the viewpoint of exchange, all economic acts are equal.[140]

139 Labriola 1911, pp. 7, 8, 10, 11, 31.

140 Labriola, 'Il ritorno a Ricardo', *Pagine Libere*, 1907, 11, p. 80.

As such, if Labriola thought he could make out symptoms of a 'return to Ricardo' in economic culture, he considered this to be extremely positive for understanding the real mechanisms of capitalism. Obviously the economic categories re-entering the field, here, were Marx's ones, read in the context of classical methodology, and the method common to Marx and Ricardo that 'brings proof that each single fact (at the same time both subjective and objective) is determined by the existence of society, by the social condition of men and things'.[141]

Reading the action of the working-class revolutionary syndicalist organisations in the terms of 'political economy' – the only way, for a culture like the one Labriola participated in, to give it the dignity of 'theory' – he declared that he could not really use the distinctions proper to 'pure economics', with all their 'mathematical metaphysics'. He instead introduced the category of the 'extra-economic', a category that should absolutely not be confused with the 'non-economic'. In substance, this was a matter of expanding the sphere of the pure 'mechanics of egoism',[142] in order to make into objects of economic analysis phenomena that pure economics considered rigorously extraneous to its own sphere.

Labriola, therefore, defined the terrain of economics as 'the terrain of the "contractable"', a terrain on which the social and historical *status quo* was defined.[143]

The terrain of the 'contractable' is pervaded by associations, which, naturally, are organised in tendentially monopolistic terms, in order to achieve their maximum hedonistic interest. Even accepting, however, that workers' organisations are capable of truly achieving a monopoly in the labour market, ultimately they will inevitably crash up against the limits of the companies' capacities, at that specific moment. Hence the failure of marginal companies and the consequent constriction of the labour market.

As such, if the workers' union remains on the terrain of the 'contractable' – that is, the terrain of 'the economic' – it will not be able to achieve the complete fulfilment of its objectives. So at a certain moment (of objective and subjective maturity) it must break out of this terrain, and thus enter into the sphere of the 'extra-economic', out of which it will build a new economic state, a new economy. Between the one and the other moment of the 'economic' there is,

141 Labriola, 'Il ritorno a Ricardo', *Pagine Libere*, 1907, II, p. 92.

142 Labriola, 'L'economico e l'extra-economico', *Pagine Libere*, 1908, pp. 1357–72; 1909, I, 297–311.

143 Labriola, 'L'economico e l'extra-economico', *Pagine Libere*, 1908, p. 1361.

wedged in, an 'extra-economic' moment. It should not be forgotten that this transition is realised under the impulse of purely economic forces. Competition gives birth to monopoly, and the need to escape the 'recoil' of monopoly gives birth to 'the extra-economic moment'.[144] For Labriola, therefore, there is no seamless continuity between the two moments – the 'economic' naturally being understood 'in the broad sense of everything that concerns our material life', and not in the restrictive sense of 'mathematical metaphysics'.[145]

Attempting better to specify the contiguity of the 'economic' and the 'extra-economic', and the lack of 'qualitative' difference between them, Labriola defined this latter as 'the submarginal stratum of the economic, that is, the stratum in which a class's effort to change the present economic form in a manner conforming to its vital needs unconsciously develops'. And he pointed to revolutionary syndicalism as the element that would discipline the 'sub-economic and extra-economic' energies 'of the working-classes'.[146]

If the social revolution was possible only at the end of a long period of growth in the collective wealth, the revolutionary syndicalists declared themselves conscious that the highest factor of wealth remained man himself. This man would produce greater wealth the more he felt 'energetic, free, "individual"'; a quality that would tend to develop precisely through his activity in the particularly 'extra-economic' sphere.

The 'extra-economic' category thus lent itself to a dual need: the already mentioned one of reasoning in terms of political economy, and that of not privileging the ethical-voluntaristic dimensions of the revolutionary process, which were here seen as very closely related to the processes of economic development. This corresponded to the deeper themes of Labriola's reading of Marx, and as we will see, also Leone's, while another current of revolutionary syndicalism would take a different position in this regard.

The fact that Labriola could not stop continually re-posing the problem of the relation between Marxism's cognitive tools and the reality of the development of capitalism – and not only as an eternal redefinition of the boundaries of the economic sphere – clearly demonstrates the deliberate partiality of the Marxist approach in both the early *Avanguardia* experience and in its inevitable corollary in *Riforme e rivoluzione sociale*. Even at the height of his syndicalist period, Labriola almost naturally posed the need to return to addressing the theme of the relations among Marxism, science, and 'new'

144 Labriola, 'L'economico e l'extra-economico', *Pagine Libere*, 1908, pp. 1369–70.
145 Labriola, 'L'economico e l'extra-economico', *Pagine Libere*, 1908, p. 1370.
146 Labriola, 'L'economico e l'extra-economico', *Pagine Libere*; 1909, I, pp. 306–7.

socialist theory. And he did so precisely because he had never thought that they could be reduced to the scholastic-voluntaristic schema of the 'philosophy of force'.

Labriola seemingly returned anew to delimiting the territory of the economic – this time to defend Marx, the philosopher, from the 'bourgeois' economists' critiques – in order to 'prove that economics will get to the bottom of the economic part of Marxism only when it studies it with a philosophical spirit'.[147] In reality, this was a more complex discourse, with many valences. It was partly concerned to make revolutionary syndicalism's Marxist reasoning more articulated and less superficial, and it was also very much internal to the climate of the Italian Marxism that had arisen from the end-of-century discussion among Croce, Gentile and the other, older Labriola.

For the younger Labriola, then, Marx the philosopher and Marx the economist could not be separated. Indeed, Marx's methodological framework had distant roots: in his youthful works, in particular his theses on Feuerbach; and historical materialism was the true link conjugating a general philosophical research with political economy. Only a close familiarity with the terrain of Marx's philosophical work could allow a full understanding of the 'density' of his economic categories.

In a context in which pure economics now appeared as economics *tout court*, to qualify an economic category as 'philosophical' was effectively to take away its 'scientific' dignity. We need only think of Pareto, for whom 'philosophy' was synonymous with 'metaphysics', and by which last term – beyond any specific meaning it might have – he simply meant something with its head in the clouds.

The book also featured indications regarding the analysis of the Marx who was not *stricto sensu* 'economic', seeing as he had wanted 'to arrive at the substance of the economy itself' and thus had posed himself a problem 'that was not located within an economic science'.[148] It might almost seem that the general thrust of the study was to demonstrate the separation – clouded in the title – between Marx the short-lived economist and Marx the eternally young theorist of socialism. But here, too, as in the 1899 book, it is important to be wary of those formulations that seem to make too much of a concession to the then widespread conception of economic science. The overall logic of the argumentation would ultimately contradict them; and, moreover, there were also other formulations that fitted the book's fundamental analytical approach in a more coherent manner. 'The eternal youth of Marx lies in his intelligent

147 Labriola 1908, p. 104.
148 Labriola 1908, p. 131.

understanding of capitalist society', Labriola declared, further specifying 'the essence proper to capitalist society lies in its economic character'.[149] So it was perhaps, then, Marx the theorist of capitalism who was 'eternally young', rather than the theorist of socialism. And if the essence of capitalism lay 'in its economic character', was it possible to construct a theory of capitalism that neglected a correct – and centrally important – use of 'economic categories'?

A great part of the volume was, in fact, devoted to illustrating Marx's 'intelligent understanding' of capitalism.

First of all, this meant taking capitalism as a *problem*; it was a system in which phenomenon did not correspond to reality, and Marx's theory was posed as an attempt to 'explain both reality and the explanations of the reality', to explain both the mechanisms of capitalism's functioning and ideologies.[150] Its very narrative method was functional to this objective; its historicism had nothing to do with that of the historical school, being 'a means of research, not a means of exposition':[151] fundamentally, a historical-logical method.

What was the tie binding all of capitalist society? The commodity. The commodity 'does serve to satisfy concrete needs, but also serves as an equivalent of exchange. The thing has an internal split: the material substance remains something capable of fulfilling a need, but its ideal phantasm, value, takes on a socially-connective function'.[152] For Labriola, within this logic it was not so important that the transformation of values into prices, attempted in *Capital* Volume III, had not worked out in quantitative terms. The substance of exchange remained value, and the price just a form: and Marx had, indeed, sought to demonstrate the non-coincidence of value and price, and the fact that the second was but a 'transformation' of the first.

For Labriola, the fundamental reasons for the revolutionary syndicalist choice arose precisely from this method of constructing a theory of capitalism – the only method that had proven capable of giving account of its 'essence' and its distinctive 'laws of movement'. If the 'essence' of capitalism consisted in the distinction – and sometimes counterposition – between 'value' and 'price', and if the technical and social means through which labour was provided were the constitutive element of the creation of value, then 'to explain the wage-relation is, in large part, to explain the capitalist system itself'.[153] Only one

149 Labriola 1908, pp. 161, 167.
150 Labriola 1908, p. 19.
151 Labriola 1908, p. 26.
152 Labriola 1908, p. 56.
153 Labriola 1908, p. 167.

coherently Marxist political position could be derived from a shared acceptance of this theoretical crux. It was the one that centred its own analysis and its own 'practical-Marxist' activity on the problem of the wage-relation, the antagonism deriving from the subordination of the worker's labour, and the 'irreconcilable antagonism' that remained the primary element 'identifying' the capitalist mode of production. The wage-relation was not a purely economic relation: wages could also grow within certain limits, and working conditions could improve. Catastrophism was here expunged from the socialists' cultural and political horizon, insofar as it was almost impossible to determine the limits of capitalism's capacity for development. Society as a whole could be reformed, but the hard core of a 'substantial' counterposition was destined to last, so long as the existing mode of production remained. What differentiated the 'revolutionaries' from the 'reformists' was not, then, a rejection of 'reforms', of 'social legislation', of the possibility of improving the subaltern classes' living conditions. Rather, it was a question of whether all this could really change the nature of capitalism. Labriola argued:

> Making changes and reforms in capitalist society does not mean reforming or changing capitalist society. The Marxists' anti-reformism results from their conviction as to the impossibility of modifying and directing capitalism's essence in a different manner. But they do not claim that if the kernel does not change, then nor can the texture, the colour or the fragrance of the surrounding fruit.[154]

The awareness gradually growing in the union that the only solution to the problem of workers' emancipation was to remove this 'kernel' itself meant that 'Marxism [was] the definitive theory of the workers' movement'.[155]

The differences could not have been deeper between Labriola's own wholly political use of Marxism in the first definition of the revolutionary Left, and this 'practical Marxism' wholly internal to the 'economic' categories of *Capital*. Yet in revolutionary syndicalist ideology the one was not posed as the negation of the other: they both persisted, and were often posed in complementary terms.

The *Communist Manifesto* itself, which had also been the privileged source for the formulas of the 'revolutionary Marxist *latinetto*', could be used to claim that syndicalist arguments had a quite different theoretical weight. The passages in Marx regarding the coincidence between the progress of the proletariat

154 Labriola 1908, p. 168.

155 Labriola 1908, p. 216.

as a class and the progress of workers' organisation were taken as the basis for demonstrating the union's essential role in the process of social revolution, 'an internal, indissoluble link that tie[d] "syndicalism" to the *Communist Manifesto*'.[156] And this also allowed for the strengthening of the Marxist conception, common across all tendencies of socialism, that revolution was possible only at the high points of capitalist development. In this view, only the gradual and indefinite improvement of the capacity to control production – one of the functions particular to the union – could prepare the conditions favourable to substituting the *classes* who ruled over the productive processes and society as a whole. This was, then, not an exclusively *party* solution, which Labriola predicted would bring a wholly political dictatorship; 'There is an old history of this', he warned, 'The regime established through this process can have only one name: capitalist spoliation. It is the regime of Roman imperialism and the *Convention nationale*. Our compliments to "scientific" socialism …'[157]

The revolutionary syndicalist Labriola wanted, then, to remain substantially internal to Marxism, both in its political dimension and in its fundamental theoretical features, and this notwithstanding his proclaimed 'revisionism'. For this reason, his reaction faced with the characteristics of Plekhanov's attack against him was both disconcerted and very violent.

Plekhanov had begun publishing anti-revisionist articles in *Sovremenny Mir* in 1907, and, indeed, the first of them was directed against Arturo Labriola. Angelica Balabanoff translated these texts into Italian in the context of the sharp political battle opposing the 'intransigents' to the 'syndicalists', with the precise intention of denying these latter any Marxist legitimacy. This perfectly befitted both the *form* and *substance* of Plekhanov's polemical method.

These articles of Plekhanov's, published in a single volume,[158] brought with them a mode of political-cultural polemic that was in many senses alien to the Italian socialist-Marxist environment. That is not to say that there had not been notable bitterness in the debate among tendencies (indeed, there still was), whether the discussion concerned immediately political questions, doctrinal ones or both. There had also been (and still were) attempts at political delegitimisation based on 'doctrine'. But never had the clear proclamation of an 'orthodoxy' shown how cold, sharp, irredeemable and full of consequences the separations operated by a consciously applied scalpel could be.

156 Labriola 1911, p. 186.

157 Labriola 1911, pp. 189–90.

158 Plekhanoff 1908. [Not available in English.]

Right from the introduction, the author declared that this text was an official declaration of 'Marxist orthodoxy', and that, in consequence, it wanted to clear the socialist terrain of all the wide range of elaborations that could not be considered congruous with this doctrinal dimension: 'Those of our comrades who consider syndicalism one of the aspects of socialism are deeply mistaken. *In realitiy the true syndicalism, that is, coherent syndicalism, stands in irreconcilable antithesis with coherent socialism*'.[159]

Many of Plekhanov's arguments were, indeed, well-founded. Together with his re-proposition of the usual themes of the anti-syndicalist polemic (its kinship with anarchism and with the bourgeois economists' free-tradeism; accusations of corporatism and a lack of sensitivity to the question of everyday improvements in the proletariat's living conditions), he also struck at the soft underbelly of arguments that had hardly been developed. We could say that he made rather light work of Labriola's set of arguments on the role of determinism and voluntarism in the process of social evolution. The rediscovery of the idealism of consciousness and of the will to which Labriola referred had no relation – or only purely nominal relations – with the pregnancy and complexity of a Hegelian idealism that he had caught wind of but was almost wholly ignorant about; Plekhanov's knowledge of it, meanwhile, was of a quite different order. As such, Plekhanov was easily able to demonstrate that the so-called 'orthodox' Marxists *à la Kautsky* were far from rigid determinists.

However, what ultimately stuck out from the set of articles offered in the volume was the conscious expulsion from the terrain of Marxism – and thus of socialism – of everything that exceeded confines established by personalities deputised to such a role on account of their recognised greater doctrinal knowledge. In this outlook, which would become paradigmatic of one of the traditions of Marxism, Arturo Labriola thus became *'Eduard Bernstein's Siamese twin'*,[160] and reformism and syndicalism 'identical' in their manner of considering the general process of modern capitalist development. 'Taken together', Plekhanov argued, 'these two currents represent something resembling a pair of gloves; the left hand is, in a certain sense, opposed to the right. But that does not take away the fact that the one is *perfectly similar to the other*'.[161] This was a logical model that would enjoy considerable fortune across a rather long period.

159 Plekhanoff 1908, p. 9; italics in the original.
160 Plekhanoff 1908, p. 48; italics in the original.
161 Plekhanoff 1908, p. 49; italics in the original.

Labriola's response was shot through with both excessive virulence and an excessive focus on detail,[162] but it does allow us better to clarify the meaning of the discussion then underway regarding the problem of 'orthodoxy' and revolutionary-syndicalist Marxism. First of all, he proudly declared his specificity as a theoretical economist, a different figure from that as a 'theorist of socialism'. This was to assert the possibility of accepting analytical elements from the baggage of pure economics, of being influenced even by the likes of Pareto and Pantaleoni, without this necessarily implying a general agreement with the marginalists regarding either the status of the discipline or the relations between the economic and social sphere. It was an economist's duty to draw new tools from the progress being made in his own scientific field; to conceive of Marxist economics as self-sufficient would ultimately mean condemning it to theoretical sterility. And self-sufficiency is one of the fundamental aspects of an 'orthodoxy'.

There was no doubt, for Labriola, that 'syndicalism is wholly to be found within Marxism'.[163] It was based precisely on the deep, philosophical core of Marx's anthropology, according to which the recomposition of the human totality consists of real, individual man's process of reappropriating his divided self, the abstract citizen. This was an operation of 'social synthesis', which was possible only within the sphere of workers' organisation. 'Only in the union', Labriola declared 'does there exist that fusion of concrete individual forces with abstract social forces that makes human emancipation possible ... The syndicalist conception is the legitimate continuation of the Marxist premise'.[164]

This was, however, a 'legitimacy' that did not aspire to the status of an 'orthodoxy', in that it was the product of a deep current of Marx's theory that had gone unexplored by the 'orthodox'. This was still a current of vital importance, and which should be concentrated on, without wasting time trying to exploit other currents from the same source that had now been exhausted or dried out. 'Orthodoxy', indeed, was a mental attitude from which there derived a merely comfortable political practice. Rather than attempting correctly to interpret a theory to which one should remain loyal on account of its operative capacities, 'orthodoxy' consisted of turning to stone a body of doctrine that programmatically excluded any element that the experts – guardians of the ideological construct – considered extraneous.

---

162 Labriola, 'L'onestà polemica contro G. Plekhanoff e per il sindacalismo', *Pagine Libere*, 1908.

163 Labriola, 'L'onestà polemica contro G. Plekhanoff e per il sindacalismo', *Pagine Libere*, 1908, p. 519.

164 Labriola, 'L'onestà polemica contro G. Plekhanoff e per il sindacalismo', *Pagine Libere*, 1908, p. 192.

This assertion of a non-'orthodox' Marxist 'legitimacy' also entailed a further delimitation of the spaces reserved to 'pure economics', in terms of its possibility of understanding the social dynamic. Labriola had argued that a revolutionary socialist scholar who stood on the terrain of a correct epistemological attitude, deeply marked by a privileged relation with Marx's theory, had the right/duty also to use marginalist categories for analysing social phenomena. However, these categories were almost wholly unknown to the economic analysis that allowed an 'intelligent understanding' of capitalism, even where – as we shall see – other revolutionary syndicalists had tried to use them.

For Labriola, the mechanism that encouraged the single worker's activity in the context of trade-union activity was not identifiable or quantifiable using any 'hedonometric' system, and nor did it correspond to any supposed 'hedonism'. Here one ought not to see 'a calculation of what is useful'[165] but rather 'a manifestation of his restored humanity', a moment of the reappropriation of the self that remained the essential core of the long march of working-class emancipation. This was a march that necessarily also had to make a long trek deep into the economic sphere.

As such, Labriola invited (with a certain rhetorical guile?) the now (1913) almost wholly marginalist 'official economic science' to learn the lesson of 'workers' unionism', and to reorganise 'its doctrinal complex', given that the union's ever greater social weight was one of the 'facts that have changed the economic world'.[166] He invited it to get to grips with the problems posed by a movement that was starting to become an imposing one, and which refused the 'economic' concept of human labour as a commodity and wages as a price. He invited it to pick up the thread of a discourse in terms of political economy; in a word, to repudiate its own methodological presuppositions.

'Modernity' was the bearer of phenomena like 'revolutionary syndicalism and capitalist imperialism, which are irreducible to the concept of individual egoism',[167] and whose genesis and development could only be understood within a 'theory of capitalism'. For this reason, a familiarity with the less immediately political parts of Marx's theory was indispensable.

Here, we have another type of 'return to Marx', posed in very different terms from that of the very beginning of the century.

---

165 Labriola, 'L'onestà polemica contro G. Plekhanoff e per il sindacalismo', *Pagine Libere*, 1908, p. 527.

166 Labriola 1913, p. 255.

167 Labriola 1912, p. 343.

There are two books that are key to understanding the fully analytical characteristics of *this* return to Marx. These two books are often rather overinflated – as was far from rare, with this prolific writer – encompassing a multiplicity of 'original' themes in accordance with a never fully subdued tradition of Loria's. The two books are on different subjects, but they are united by a common inspiration: the conviction that the models proposed by pure economics could not, in substance, be used to give account of the mechanisms of economic development or of their social determinations – fundamentally, the problems that had to be at the centre of the economist's attentions, in his function as a social scientist.

The first, which was modestly framed as a re-elaboration of a university course that he had given over 1907–8, in reality had a rather ambitious objective: to justify itself as a new model of economic history. This would be an economic history that, precisely because it was enlivened by the method of *Capital* and historical materialism in general, could leave behind the age-old quarrel between the 'empirical' and 'anecdotal' and the 'pure theorists' – between the descriptive method and that of the logical mechanism. Economic history, and in particular the history of capitalism, or rather, 'the determination of its historical essence', was an exemplary case offering itself up to be studied through the application of logical-historical methods. The knowledge-results obtained from this, moreover, would also prove able to facilitate a useful reflection regarding the use of determinate economic categories. 'The economics of men', Labriola declared, 'does not exist independent of certain socio-historical forms. Therefore, we always have to begin from these forms, in order then to get back to the logical categories used by economics'.[168]

In the second book he returned – this time explicitly – to posing as the central problem the question of the nature of the economic sciences, the questions to which they had to provide responses, the ideological meanings inevitably bound up with this, and the origins of 'the need to represent the social relation – to which the economic category necessarily refers – in an abstract manner'.[169]

He made clear that he was aware of the fact that economic science had, indeed, made enormous technical-sectorial progress in the last quarter century, but also that, at the same time, the new orientations had not proven able to give a response to the more profound questions of socioeconomics. If political economy was to work in this direction, it would have to take on board essential

168 Labriola 1910, p. 367.

169 Labriola 1912, p. 20.

aspects of Marx, who was 'the only author whose methods we consider justified, for the purpose of our research', as Labriola again insisted;[170] the Marx who was 'truly a man of our time'[171] because he had placed the rich body of *interests* that determine history and economics at the centre of his analysis.

Indeed, it does not seem that Labriola's journey through 'unknown lands' beginning at the end of the nineteenth century had brought him too far from his original homeland. While the – repeatedly mentioned – demands of disciplinary professionalisation (but so, too, his own intellectual restlessness, his curiosity for the seemingly novel, and the wish to get to grips with the scientific status of political economy) had brought him to seek a more direct relation with the Paretian version of political economy, his plans for such a closer encounter can essentially be considered a failure. Even his Marxist justification for revolutionary syndicalism fundamentally seems rather episodic, as compared to his long-term interpretation of Marx, which ultimately ought to be considered rather more coherent than it is usually presented as being.

When in 1926 he spoke of *Capital* as 'a monumental work, for which the ordinary, orthodox economics has no match', a work 'that still today constitutes an insuperable model of successful economic analysis, in which the observation of material economic forces is fully interwoven with a vital emphasis on the articulations of classes descending from this',[172] he was, at root, saying nothing that we cannot already pick out in the twists and turns of his journey 'through strange lands'.

Enrico Leone's involvement in the problematic tangle of the relations between Marxism and syndicalism, Marxism and pure economics, and finally syndicalism and pure economics, was, however, rather different in nature. He attempted to hold all the terms of this knot together in close relation, and give them an organic systematisation. In this sense, Leone can be considered the only Italian intellectual who posed himself the problem of constructing a complete syndicalist theory on the basis of Marxist revisionism. He was the most coherent proponent of the 'revolutionary *concorrenzialismo* [competition and/or combination]'[173] on which basis – by way of the 'economic moment' – it was possible for him to establish the most disparate theoretical compatibilities that the early twentieth-century climate had to offer. He remained loyal to the

170 Labriola 1912, p. 83.

171 Labriola 1912, p. 332.

172 Labriola 1943, p. 19. The third chapter of this book is undoubtedly one of the most penetrating texts that had been published in Italy at that point with regard to its titular subject, 'the method of exposition in Marxism'.

173 Macchioro 1993–4.

programme of his review, *Il Divenire Sociale*, with which he truly identified himself. This was a review that had even in its first issue declared its intention of delving into 'the relations between socialism and Political Economy', seeking to prove 'scientifically' that 'socialism [was] in accordance with economic laws; that it [was] also the natural product of these [laws], over the unfolding of time', and to demonstrate the terms within which 'Marx's *objective theory of value* [was] fallacious, integrating it with the hedonistic law of the "new school"'.[174] This was a programme that Leone pursued with particular intensity across many years, seeking elements of continuity with the cultural climate of end-of-the-century 'revisionism'.

Not by chance, in a long essay right at the start of the *Il Divenire Sociale* experience,[175] he organically addressed each of the themes that he would later seek to develop in more weighty studies:

- Firstly, the need for revisionism in order to conserve the scientific dimension of the Marxist approach, 'casting out all those elements that are not proven through a rigorous study of social reality'.[176]
- Secondly, an emphasis on a non-'collectivist' interpretation of Marxism. This was a reading that absolutely could not be deduced from the central aspects of the doctrine: namely, the theory of value and the process of capital valorisation.
- The non-contradictory – but rather, complementary – character[177] of the (objective) analytic dimension in Marx and the hedonistic (subjective) one. Marx's theory was a theory of capitalism, not a general economic theory. In the capitalist system the laws of history are of an objective nature, and thus Marx's method 'serves the examination of the historical form of the good, that is, of the commodity; the latter serves the general examination of the good in its logical form'.[178]
- The difficulty of giving any disciplinary definition of Marx's analysis, if economics is wholly identified with hedonism: hence the appearance of expressions like economic 'philosophy' or economic 'sociology'.[179]

---

174 See the inside back cover of *Il Divenire Sociale*, I, 1905.

175 A. Freedom (Leone), 'Lineamenti di socialismo scientifico', *Il Divenire Sociale*, 1905, pp. 203–5, 224–5, 259–60, 275–6, 281–2; 1906, pp. 44–5, 157–8, 174–5, 189–91, 204–6, 214–6.

176 A. Freedom (Leone), 'Lineamenti di socialismo scientifico', *Il Divenire Sociale*, 1905, p. 203.

177 'The two theories ... are not *parallel*, but *successive*': A. Freedom (Leone), 'Lineamenti di socialismo scientifico', *Il Divenire Sociale*, 1905, p. 225.

178 A. Freedom (Leone), 'Lineamenti di socialismo scientifico', *Il Divenire Sociale*, 1905, p. 204.

179 A. Freedom (Leone), 'Lineamenti di socialismo scientifico', *Il Divenire Sociale*, 1905, pp. 215, 282.

- And finally, insistence on the 'qualitative' character of Marx's analytical dimension, starting from the centrally important labour theory of value. Again in this case, his interpretation did not have the particular novelty that some historiographical interpretations have sought to attribute to it; rather, as we have seen, this was a rather common motif in Italian Marxist literature and literature on Marxism.

What were the passages through which a reading of Marx based on such fundamentals could become part of the explanation of revolutionary syndicalism? Through what processes did Leone intend to link a 'theory of capitalism' like Marx's – whose fundamental postulates he claimed to share – with the 'theory of socialism' now being built (a theory that he considered necessary, and whose explanation of syndicalism he considered its first constitutive element)? In his *La revisione del marxismo*[180] he attempted to build an interpretative framework capable of holding this problematic complex together.

Beyond the frequent moments of repetition and the many aporias of this work, owing also to Leone's assemblage of materials elaborated in different times, it was ultimately a rather linear design.

The crisis of Marxism had been 'determined by objective elements that [had] generated this *necessity*'.[181] Indeed, socialism had always followed the progress and the twists and turns of political economy. Marx was no exception, and leaving aside the particular theoretical function *sui generis* that the theory of value played in his system, this theory was itself a consequence of political economy, inheriting its high points. If economic science had become 'hedonistic', with 'almost all the university chairs now held by this school', 'Marxism thus remained the product of a scientific phase that had been surpassed'.[182] The task of modern socialism was, then, to fill the gap between the old Marxist economic framework and pure economics. This process of 'organic readaptation'

180 Leone 1910. This book was largely made up of materials that had already been published in *Il Divenire Sociale*, especially from 1908 onward. Leone noted this in the Introduction, but only with regard to the articles that had been published under his own name, and not those that had in fact appeared under the pseudonyms Adriano Freedom and Augusto Franco. This material had first been written at the beginning of the century, but was heavily revised, very probably starting with his 'return to Marx' period. See the observations in this regard in Gianinazzi 1989, p. 83. Moreover, there are notes in which Leone refers to literature later than that of the 'old' manuscripts of 1900–1.

181 Leone 1910, p. 47, my italics.

182 Leone 1910, pp. 48, 51.

could give rise to results that would mark 'an even more universalised triumph of socialist theories'.[183]

For Leone, the fundamental counterposition of Marx's method and the method of pure economics did not only lie in the evident antithesis between 'historic' and 'natural' laws. Precisely because Marx's economics was a theory of capitalism, it stood apart from the study of those economic behaviours that derived directly from *human nature* and not from a transient – however long and complex – historic period. On this terrain there could be no integration of Marxist and pure economics. 'There is only one possible comparison between the two: that of seeing if the effective and suggestive economic principles that spring from Marx's doctrine are reconfirmed and corroborated by other means in economic science, properly understood'.[184] This was the priority task that socialist theory had to pose itself.

Marx's theory of value is itself an evident product of the fully historical method on which basis he brought out his own analytical categories. This theory in fact proved a fundamental element in the explanation of the theory of *fetishism*,[185] and only in this context is this latter itself fully understandable. The logical form of Marx's conception of value thus descends 'from the perversion of the product of labour as a commodity, deriving from a merely historical phenomenon'.[186]

Certainly, this was a *true* theory within the terms of the speculative construction of which it was part, but it was a *false* one in the field of economics – as, indeed, was the theory of surplus-value, based upon it. More precisely, as a weighty volume specifically dedicated to hedonist economics would later explain, this theory – a keystone of Marx's theory – 'represents a chronologically surpassed phase, but can be re-elaborated scientifically and used in further advances of knowledge'.[187]

183 Leone 1910, p. 52.

184 Leone 1910, p. 80.

185 On this point, we might reflect on the longer continuities of intuitions that from time to time present themselves as 'new' ones.

186 Leone 1910, p. 101.

187 Leone 1910b, p. 222. He also posed this question with greater clarity: 'Is Marxism true because it is hedonism, or vice versa? Accepting such a principle, there are only two [possible] conclusions: a) Marxism is a special critique of capitalism and the mystery of surplus-value that keeps it alive, while hedonism is all 'economics'. This is the conclusion that Croce is approaching. Or else b) Hedonism can give account by other means of the main conclusions that Marxism reaches, confirming them'. Obviously this latter was Leone's own position.

But did the theories of value and surplus value also represent the analytical key to the theory of exploitation, and could socialism do without a theory of exploitation?

According to Leone, it is possible to start out from Marxian concerns and arrive at marginalist definitions: it is possible, in short, to arrive at a marginalist theory of exploitation that is also more 'concrete' than Marx's, given that it starts out from the worker's individual conditions. Building a system of labour utility and disutility curves, we can easily see that the wage-labourer

> is compelled to produce super-marginal amounts of utility, producing commodities that are goods for the capitalists and non-values for himself ... This super-marginality or surplus-marginality – of cost and utility – marks ... the exact measure of the degree of surplus product that the capitalist takes in, forming the basis of the surplus-value that regulates and feeds capitalist profits.[188]

For Leone, the concreteness of this way of considering and calculating the degree of exploitation on the basis of empirical-individual data on labour utility-disutility, as against a Marxian approach referring to the exploitation of the working class as a whole, explained the motive 'of interest' that 'pushes the proletarians to organise as a class, and for all of them to recognise themselves in [this class] as a single, indivisible whole'.[189] It also explained the *necessity* of working-class organisation, as the workers – subjects lacking any 'options' faced with capital – work to achieve the maximum individual utility through associative forms that *necessarily* lead to the achievement of the maximum collective utility. And this is one of socialism's end goals, and the premise of pure economics, when totally realised.[190]

From the formal point of view, the various moments of Enrico Leone's argument are organically composed, but certainly his attempt to reformulate

188 Leone 1910, pp. 121–2.

189 Leone, 'Il plusvalore nell'edonismo e nel marxismo', *Il Divenire Sociale*, p. 186. Moreover, he argued, the criterion of subjective utility, elaborated and explained as a natural law in the manner of mathematical economics, would allow an escape from Marx's over-general objectivism as well as the ethical subjectivism 'of Sorel, Bernstein [and] Merlino': Leone 1910, p. 153.

190 'Economic subjects whose *maximum hedonistic* has deteriorated – the proletarians, as Marx calls them, with a name popular even in his own time for those belonging to this class in the capitalist economy – are pushed by the natural force of hedonism to achieve this maximum': Leone 1910, p. 259.

Marx's problematic in marginalist terms, substituting the category of 'surplus-marginality' for that of 'surplus-value', is, as has rightly been noted, at best nothing more than a 'practice exercise'.[191] In short, the whole was notably lesser than the themes of some of its individual component parts, from which we can get a far from banal impression of the problems that a 'critical Marxism' had to address, even if it was one rather more commonplace in the Italian culture of the time than is widely believed. Leone was obsessed with constructing a systematic theory from which an *economic* theory of revolutionary syndicalism would also spring forth; and this was, moreover, a process parallel to the *economic theory* of reformism that Graziadei had built. But unlike this latter – whose theories were a real reference point for important sections of the CGL and the reformist cultural and trade-union milieux advancing the hypothesis of the 'party of labour' – Leone never succeeded in getting his system considered as a privileged explanation of revolutionary syndicalism. In certain regards, he did establish himself as the 'economist *par excellence*' of this movement,[192] but the fact remains that this movement's variegated culture little identified itself with an explanation centred on an *economic theory*.

His book explicitly dedicated to syndicalism doubtless had greater influence.[193] That is not to say that it contradicted the line of argument that Leone was continually proposing. Rather, this book, too, brought into relief the fact that the fundament of socialism consisted not in 'political-moral' aspirations, as reformist revisionism argued (according to Leone), but in the 'material conditions of the productive forces'.[194] This meant that conflict – the motor of social transformation – was a conflict among 'economic agents', subject to laws of utility that worked as the 'principal [economic] regulator'. Through this mechanism, *economics* gave way to *history*.[195] All this, however, was rather an implicit reference point, while the themes that most immediately stood out from the volume as a whole were the same ones as were widespread in the revolutionary syndicalist ideological milieu.

He made recourse to the authority of some of Marx's statements from 1868–9 concerning the importance of worker unionism and the need for the IWMA's adherents to dedicate themselves to organisation by trades, in order to deduce from this a priority of the union over the party.

191 Zagari 1975, p. 274.
192 Orano 1931, p. vi.
193 Leone 1907.
194 Leone 1907, p. 56.
195 Leone 1907, p. 58.

He mounted a 'rigorous' reading of historical materialism, deducing from this the argument that the state – the political factor – had no power to transform society's economic relations. As a corollary, 'parties [did] not make or change history', and thus the workers' union and not the socialist party was the primary subject of social transformation.[196]

He attempted a logical systemisation of the contradiction between the constantly-upheld argument as to the movement's 'practical' character – this being a movement of which 'action [was] the principle and essence'[197] and a movement that was by nature declaredly anti-intellectual – and the organic theoretical lineaments that had to guide action.

This last theme brings us back to the question – one continually present in the Marxist tradition – of the relation between determinism and voluntarism, between the necessary itinerary that the organised working class will progressively adopt fully autonomously, and the indication of this same path as the fruit of an elaboration external to working-class consciousness. For Leone, syndicalism was not the product of an intellectual construction external to the real movement, but was instead born 'as the spontaneous reflection of the aggregates of workers, in their trade associations ... responding to a psychological *instinct* of theirs'.[198] In this sense, the revolutionary decision became the fruit of a free choice that was continually proposing itself anew. At the same time, however, the class consciousness that was at the basis of this syndicalist choice was, in turn, the result of a formation process that could be 'fulfilled only through the natural unfolding of needs and *interests*'.[199] Once again, the economy created history, and the different components of the problem were thus interconnected in what were formally coherent propositions. Such formal coherence would not find particular good fortune in the overall ideological construction of revolutionary syndicalism.

4 Marxism and Elitism in the Universe of 'Minor' Syndicalist Intellectuals

In substance, the socialist experience – of which the syndicalist experience was one phase, albeit with a periodistion and an intensity of its own – near-coincided with the full sequence of Enrico Leone's and Arturo Labriola's exis-

196 Leone 1907, p. 73.
197 Leone 1907, p. 17.
198 Leone 1907, p. 53.
199 Leone 1907, p. 98.

tence. However, for the greater part of the revolutionary syndicalist intellectuals, it coincided with only part of their lives, representing a formative, transient moment of their own personal self-affirmation. For the old, revolutionary syndicalism represented the end point of this experience, while for the young it was the way in which they entered into relation with a dimension of socialism. For both the old and the young, a relationship with Marxism – in a period in which Marxism and socialism seemed to coincide – was, in any case, an obligatory one, a passage which they would go through, raising the banner of a claim to 'loyalty' to the 'truest' core of Marx's thinking and, simultaneously, a 'heretical' vein characterising the syndicalist mode of intellectual being.

One of the more 'elderly', Paolo Orano, would later reaffirm a connection of kinds between these two poles, writing in a different context and with different meanings now that he was established as an authoritative figure in the Fascist hierarchy: 'Marx was perfectly right in his diagnosis of capitalism', he declared, even if it was not possible to deduce any elements of socialist politics from this – any socialist 'realisation' – since the reality Marx analysed, the capitalist mode of production, could not be structurally transformed.[200] At the same time, a 'rib' of working-class organisation of Marxist inspiration had given rise to a syndicalism that inaugurated 'what is most new and constructive in the twentieth century ... the latent ideal of the formation of the believing, responsible worker, the moral man, discipline, obedience and, therefore, command'.[201] Had the 'heretical' re-elaboration of Marxism effected by the syndicalists, then, contributed to the formation of the 'new man', protagonist of the Fascist revolution and regime, both the elite in power and the responsible worker in the union? Certainly, Orano's was an *a posteriori* reading in which there are no lack of signs of retouching a personal history that was very closely linked to a certain group's experience; but even an attentive observer like Sorel attributed a symptomatic value to the processes through which figures like Orano evolved.[202]

200 Orano 1926, p. 27.

201 Orano 1931, p. vii.

202 'I have just read an article by P. Orano in the 10 November *Giornale d'Italia*, which seems to me to show that the Italians no longer have any interest in socialism; the author has always sought to follow the tendencies of the present day, so his evolution is probably symptomatic': Sorel 1993–4, p. 214. The article to which Sorel refers is 'La chimera socialista e la guerra', in which Orano declares the death of socialism and Marx's theory of class struggle.

Particularly in the case of those who had some socialist experience before becoming socialists, these processes of evolution expressed a long journey that took place amidst Italian culture's change sensibility, more open to the 'new' and alert to the changes in the existing equilibria.

In the period in which syndicalism remained an internal component of the socialist party, this milieu of 'minor' intellectuals shared and contributed to the wholly political use of Marx that we have already seen. However, there is one aspect that we ought to underline: the coexistence in the same discourse of a voluntaristic exaggeration of the political side and the reaffirmation of a rigidly deterministic vision of socio-economic development.

The 'Presentazione' of *Pagine Libere* – certainly the revolutionary syndicalist review giving us the most emblematic representation of this group of intellectuals' 'long journey' – expressed itself in a particularly telling manner, on this point:

> Each era is penetrated by an original note – its *leitmotiv* – that determines the orientation of a century, and which brands the physiognomy of an age on the sphinx of history. Our time is dominated by the workers' movement, which is the political expression of the obscure necessities of historical causality, technical and economic evolution, the serial development of thinking and of history. Here is the only expression of force amidst the general decadence, here the apparition of will, the appetite for joy and life that urges men to greater manifestations of energy.[203]

And it was not possible to 'jump' the stages of development at a whim. Even the revolutionary syndicalists only thought socialist revolution possible in countries with a mature capitalism. Commenting on an article giving account of the clashes between Bolsheviks and Mensheviks after the Duma was shut down, the review's editors presented Lenin's position as that of a *voluntaristic* figure arguing that there was a continuing tension in Russia toward fresh revolutionary outcomes, in the short term. They posed serious questions over both the inevitability and the possible results of revolution in Russia: 'Even were this effort victorious, through some hoped-for caprice of fortune, we might ask what use the mass of the people would be able to make of democratic institutions'. There needed to be a long period of growth in the productive forces, with the contemporary formation of a new, worker-ruling class ready to take over from the old one. In the meantime

203 'Presentazione', *Pagine Libere*, 1906, p. 3.

> The Italian syndicalists [considered] the need obeyed by the *Menshevik* fraction of Russian Social Democracy a very natural one … The Italian socialists ha[d] no interest supposing that socialism [was] about to triumph in a country as economically backward as Russia.[204]

This remained the point of view from which all backward countries were seen, from the Balkan chaos to the convulsions in Serbia.[205]

It was a dual reading in which Marx was at one moment the scientific guarantor of a very rigid social mechanism, and on the other the prophet of a 'revolutionary idealism … the logical expression of a strongly felt sentiment, a complex of emotions, instincts and wills'.[206]

In a short volume published in 1906 (but offered anew in almost the same form in 1913),[207] Olivetti, who also had, as has aptly been observed, 'an approach to the political-union struggle that gives … aesthetic pleasure … in an almost literary, lyrical search for a sort of epic of struggle',[208] he constructed a model explaining the Marxist bases of syndicalism – of what he explicitly called '*Marxist syndicalism*'[209] – wholly in line with his own end-of-the-century 'historical materialism', which we saw earlier.

For Olivetti, there was an immediate and direct correspondence between the political sphere, of whatever type (a party, the state …) and its economic basis. He fully accepted – picking up on Loria's term – 'the economic doctrine of political constitution', which allowed 'the dual study that in the science of chemistry takes place through the two operations of analysis and synthesis, and which can be translated into the political-economic field by posing these two problems: 1st, given a political party, research its economic bases; 2nd, given an economic party, establish its political significance and tendency'.[210] This was 'a law not subject to any exceptions',[211] and as such progressive economic growth,

204 'Postilla a R. Streltzoff, *Le due correnti della democrazia sociale russa*', *Pagine Libere*, 1907, I, p. 103.

205 See A. Semita (Olivetti), 'La rivoluzione in Serbia', *Pagine Libere*, 1907, I, pp. 141–2.

206 S. Panunzio, 'Il momento critico del socialismo', *Pagine Libere*, 1908, p. 207.

207 Olivetti 1913. This work was entitled *Questioni contemporanee*, but the 1906 edition had been called *Problemi del socialismo contemporaneo*. For the 1913 edition Olivetti expunged parts regarding the factional struggle of the time and also added a final chapter on the 'philosophy of syndicalism'.

208 From Perfetti's introduction to Olivetti 1984, p. 25.

209 Olivetti 1913, p. 187. Italics in the original.

210 Olivetti 1913, p. 105.

211 Olivetti 1913, p. 106.

the modernisation of social relations, must necessarily lead the antagonism between bourgeoisie and proletariat to extreme consequences. This was a radical antagonism, indeed one that was earth-shattering in tendency, whose *necessary* character the syndicalists had understood in full by following the original lesson from the Marx of the *Communist Manifesto* – a lesson that they accepted 'in its entirety'.[212]

Sergio Panunzio used this same expression of Loria's – 'the economic bases of social constitution'[213] – as well as his methodological determinations, as he mounted a severe polemic against 'juridical socialism' and in particular Anton Menger and the Italians Salvioli and Gabba. According to Panunzio, 'juridical socialism' was in fact nothing other than the extension of the idea of solidarity to the sphere of law. Its starting point was, then, not an *economic* but an *ethical* one – and as such, it turned on its head the Marxist assumption proper to 'revolutionary socialism', which instead sought to start from the *economic* to arrive at the *ethical*, 'conceiving law not as an entity that stands up by itself, but as a "hyperstructure", an "epiphenomenon" whose roots are found in the *underlying economic structure*'.[214] Juridical socialism thus appeared as a wholly abstract and ideological phenomenon, in that it did not 'respond to a necessity', not being 'the completion of an economic change' but, instead, 'an effect without a cause', 'a metaphysics, an *a priori* construction, empty and utopian'.[215]

Di Pietri Tonelli re-asserted a conception of the state 'wholly within the tracks of Marxism',[216] considering it purely descended from socio-economic equilibria, without the political sphere having any degree of autonomy. He considered this the fundamental dividing line between revolutionary syndicalism and reformism, with this latter not being so much the heir of Marx as of *Kathedersozialismus*.

212 Olivetti 1913, p. 187.

213 Sergio Panunzio, 'Il socialismo giuridico', *Il Divenire Sociale*, 1905, p. 304.

214 Sergio Panunzio, 'Il socialismo giuridico', *Il Divenire Sociale*, 1905, p. 288.

215 Sergio Panunzio, 'Il socialismo giuridico', *Il Divenire Sociale*, 1905, p. 304. In 1906 Panunzio published a volume with the same title, with Genoa's 'Libreria moderna'.

216 See A. Di Pietri Tonelli, 'Lo stato nella concezione marxista', *Il Divenire Sociale*, 1905, p. 274. He attempted a synthesis of Engels's *Origin of Family, Private Property and the State*, complaining that 'there really ought to be an Italian translation' of this work. In truth there was the 1885 edition translated by Pasquale Martignetti; and while this was probably difficult to find, there was also a new edition of the same translation, published in the 'Biblioteca di Critica Sociale' in 1901.

And even Paolo Orano, the figure whom Sorel rightly considered endowed with a very acute sensitivity to change, in this moment interpreted historical materialism as economic determinism – and in a wholly positive sense.[217]

This generalised dimension of argument took shape as the result of a long-term drift, inscribed within a context favourable to its contingent use. We cannot exaggerate the importance of Achille Loria's socio-economic construct to the formation of the young socialist intellectuals, still at the end of the 1890s or even in the very early 1900s. The assumption of this horizon would transform into a true and proper *forma mentis*, resistant even to the new scientific and philosophical demands, which were not lacking, and which, indeed, were of extraordinary significance. These demands were in some sense also 'registered' in cultural experiences' later stratifications, and sometimes explicit reference to them was made, but they were only integrated at the surface level. As syndicalism claimed Marx's 'revolutionary' inheritance by referring back to the *political* radicalism of the *Manifesto*, it became almost a conditioned reflex to justify the choices of 'absolute opposition' deriving from this by re-asserting the most immediate 'scientific' guarantees of their validity. And what was more immediate than the 'economic theory of political constitution' and the whole mechanism of a naturalistic sociology?

Sometimes it so happened that the long-term *forma mentis* met with the latest acquisitions of the cultural debate, within the very same lines of reasoning. The result was arguments distinguished by hybrid concatenations of concepts – even if they were not perceived as such, but rather as contributions capable of touching on a wide range of tonalities.

Typical of this was the case of Panunzio, who announced – with the end of the 'old organicist sociology'[218] – socialism's final divorce from sociology. Panunzio made use of Antonio Labriola, Werner Sombart, Benedetto Croce (indeed, among other things, he showed little capacity to distinguish among these writers) in order to recuperate the philosophical autonomy of historical materialism, denounce the determinism of the 'official science' that had given substance to socialist orthodoxy, and free Karl Marx of Marxist encrustations. The socialism that emerged from this attempt to liberate Marx was based both on the 'fundamental principles of Marxism' and the 'workers' union', considered the instrument most adequate to making the use of force subjective and conscious and not blind and mechanical. At the same time, the workers' union 'with all its different historical-political-ethical-juridical characteristics

217 P. Orano, 'Il materialismo storico e i suoi avversari', *Il Divenire Sociale*, 1905, pp. 30–2.

218 S. Panunzio, 'Socialismo, Sindacalismo e Sociologia', *Pagine Libere*, 1, p. 170.

[did] not escape the dominion of the laws that govern[ed] the marvellous concatenation of cosmic phenomena, but rather [was] the ultimate, conscious, deliberate, teleological, voluntary expression of these [laws]'.[219] Across the whole history of Marxism, the combination of 'determinism' and 'voluntarism' has represented a continually problematic question, but almost never has the 'concatenation' of logical processes arrived at these forms of expression.

In its 'foundational' moment, syndicalist culture had asserted its claim to a privileged inheritance, indeed one rigidly determining its characteristics; and this argument was an essential one in the context of a tendency struggle wholly internal to the Socialist Party. As it gradually emerged from this moment, its reading of Marx did conserve some of these basic characteristics. But it also became more polyvalent and 'tailored' to the peculiarities that the movement was now taking on, paying greater attention to external cultures that displayed appreciation of, and interest in, these peculiarities.

In 1905 De Pietri Tonelli had delineated a framework of Marxism's theoretical kernel on the basis of a set of very close and *necessary* interdependencies. In 1908 he dedicated a monograph to the Trier 'philosopher' that set itself precisely the objective of reacting to the tendencies – present in the epigones of the greats, from Kant to Marx – 'to push to extremes ... what seem to be the characteristics of a doctrine', and to make them a 'unilateral and immobile' system.[220]

De Pietri Tonelli also proved that he understood the often directly political motivations of certain catechistic systems. He reflected on the consequences of the fact that Marx was not only a great thinker of the nineteenth century, but had, more particularly, become established as a 'symbol of a great social movement', with all the difficulties that resulted from that for a freely critical approach to his thinking. These difficulties led him to conclude that 'the study of this author ... serious study ... dispassionate study ... is perhaps still to begin'.[221]

For his part, he tried to separate 'Marx as a student of capitalist society', who placed himself 'outside of and above all parties'[222] and the political Marx.

219 S. Panunzio, 'Socialismo, Sindacalismo e Sociologia', *Pagine Libere*, I, p. 236.

220 De Pietri Tonelli 1908, p. 6.

221 De Pietri Tonelli 1908, p. 72.

222 De Pietri Tonelli 1908, p. 64. He meant 'outside of all parties' also in the sense that all those who necessarily had to operate using capitalism's categories could legitimately draw on Marx: 'This is the true reason why neither reformists nor revolutionaries can or want to renounce Marxism: [that is,] neither the state socialists ... or the new theorists of the revolutionary workers' movement. These latters' claim to a monopoly in invoking Marx

Marx the theorist of capitalism, unsurpassed in this specific dimension, was, however, the last of the classical economists, and thus his fundamental categories could not be laid at the basis of the new economic science. The political Marx, conversely, 'was wholly the workers' own'. If studies on historical materialism by Antonio Labriola, Ettore Ciccotti, but also Arturo Labriola and Enrico Leone – and then by Benedetto Croce – had demonstrated its impracticability as a theory of pure social mechanics, what did nonetheless remain intact was 'the better interpretation of the realistic concept of history'.[223] It was precisely from Marx, 'the proletariat's Machiavelli', that the syndicalists had deduced a true and proper 'philosophy of the workers' movement'.[224]

So according to De Pietri Tonelli there were three points of reference for a syndicalist intellectual's culture: Marx the scholar (the theorist of capitalism), (neoclassical) economic science, and 'the philosophy of the proletariat' (inspired by the revolutionary, political Marx). It would not prove easy to develop a conceptual grid capable of maintaining a fruitfully functioning link between these levels, never mind cohering them together. It was easier to blur Marx the scholar into an ever more distant (classical) background, enter more directly into the horizon of present-day science (pure economics), and develop the 'philosophy of the proletariat' by following the paths of the difficult relationship between a real workers' movement and the logics of a group of intellectuals' self-affirmation. A large proportion of the syndicalist intellectuals would find themselves taking an itinerary profoundly shaped by these latter coordinates, even if in different ways corresponding to their personalities and/or professional specificities.

De Pietri Tonelli wanted to be an academic economist, and this choice inevitably brought him to Pareto. He continued to study Marx the scholar, and this allowed him to mature a conception of the state-civil society relation that

is no proof of their complete knowledge of Marx's system. Political injunctions do not coincide with the reality of things. In vain do they demand that the reformists renounce the Marxist label, when this is not only a question of labels. In short, all those who study or try to change capitalist society have the right to make recourse to one of its best investigators, who in so doing discovered that truth stands above political parties'. Those operating within the context of advanced capitalism could draw on Marx, but it was also sometimes true that 'in backward countries or backward parts of countries that have made progress, industrial interests themselves invoke Marxism in order to ground the single question of industrial development itself'. See 'Rammemorando', *Il Divenire Sociale*, 1908, p. 238.

223 De Pietri Tonelli 1908, p. 80.

224 De Pietri Tonelli 1908, p. 94.

was no longer boxed within the formula of the 'committee for managing the common affairs of the whole bourgeoisie';[225] but as for economic science, he would need different points of reference. From the end of the first decade of the new century, he who would later be defined as the 'St. Paul of the Paretians'[226] began to climb up the academic *curriculum* as he prepared his exam for a lecturing post, and at the same time began his correspondence with Vilfredo Pareto.[227]

In 1911, on the occasion of the severe, hard-fought political-cultural clash on the question of the state monopoly of insurance, *Pagine Libere* published an essay of De Pietri Tonelli's that earned Pareto's enthusiastic praise.[228] The hermit of Céligny, from his perspective, was right to be pleased. Even at the level of language – this being no secondary element – the young economist was now light years away from the last intervention he had made on the theme of state intervention in the economy.[229] He had begun to 'take the trimmings off his language, de-prettifying it, harking back to Galileo's style'. Since his only declared intent was to frame knowledge in a rational way, he had substituted 'commonplace terms with symbols, introducing and initiating a neutral, technical form of expression'.[230]

Here we can see impressive analogies – and certainly not only stylistic ones – with the first great specific preview of Pareto's own sociology, published just the previous year; the methodological schema used was exactly the same as in parts II and III of Pareto's text.[231]

---

225 De Pietri Tonelli, 'Il Socialismo come problema della libertà operaia', *Pagine Libere*, 1909, pp. 437–54.

226 See Giacalone-Monaco, 'Pareto e A. De Pietri Tonelli', *Giornale degli economisti e annali di economia*, 1963, pp. 687–94.

227 De Pietri Tonelli (ed.) 1961, with 47 letters from Pareto to Di Pietri Tonelli.

228 See De Pietri Tonelli, 'Lo Stato e gli affari', *Pagine Libere*, 1911, pp. 401–8, 507–13. Pareto wrote to his young interlocutor: 'It was with pleasure that I read your study on *Lo Stato e gli affari*, and what I most liked was your view of the method of the experimental sciences, which can only progress the social sciences and bring them to the level that the natural sciences have reached thanks to this method. I agree to the greater part of your observations … if you continue down the path that you have taken you can be of no little benefit to the social sciences': De Pietri Tonelli (ed.) 1961, p. 113.

229 De Pietri Tonelli, 'Lo svolgimento e la portata sociale della espropriazione forzata dei beni per causa di pubblica utilità', *Il Divenire Sociale*, 1907, pp. 211–18.

230 Giacalone-Monaco, 'Pareto e A. De Pietri Tonelli', *Giornale degli economisti e annali di economia*, 1963, p. 693.

231 Pareto, 'Le azioni non logiche', *Rivista italiana di Sociologia*, 1910, pp. 305–64.

De Pietri Tonelli put together a mechanism based on a system of social forces that clashed and combined over different hypotheses of state intervention in the economic sphere, with results that directly drew on the laws of physics. After having argued, on the basis of a historical *excursus*, that the assumptions that the forces favourable and opposed to state intervention started out from were erroneous – because they derived 'from an attempt to theorise particular and immediate interests' – the author concluded the first part of this essay by identifying this clash with the process through which new political and economic elites took form.

The democratic state, which could not fail to base itself on a relative consent given by the masses – the consent of the 'unions, workers' cooperation and coalitions' – was tendentially compelled to use extra-economic instruments like protectionism, social legislation and public monopolies. Faced with such a tendency, proper to all modern democratic states, the economic rationality of science had no possibility of bearing influence. In this context, two roads were left open to the socialists, divided into elites and the working-class element that constituted the passive mass. Part of the elites, leaning on part of the passive mass as its electoral base, could integrate itself into the 'state-ising' mechanism in order to obtain positions of power. This would also entail the renovation of the old ruling class's institutional sphere. Another part, would, however, make a different choice: it would assume 'a position, in its organisations, of struggle against the other classes – even a violent struggle – refusing as far as possible to cooperate with political and economic institutions'.

We should bear in mind that even this second type of action – with which De Pietri Tonelli identified himself as well as revolutionary syndicalism – excluded motivations of a rational or socially utilitarian kind. 'This group's action', the author specified, 'can evidently have a certain effectiveness in all kinds of history. It is an action that does not very much take immediate interests into account, and is therefore an ideal one'.[232] This was the action preferred by 'those who judge social movements not from the position of interested parties, but as aesthetes, and aesthetes who love even violent upheavals and even new social creations'. The revolutionary intellectual participated 'aesthetically' in the initiatives emerging from the social struggle. Doubling as a scholar, this same revolutionary intellectual would also establish the terms of rational social and economic logic, observing – from above the fray – the illogical preoccupations of men moved by myths and ideology, searching for satis-

232 De Pietri Tonelli, 'Lo Stato e gli affari', *Pagine Libere*, 1911, p. 513.

faction of their own particular interests, in an eternal alternation of elites in power.[233]

De Pietri Tonelli was here on the path to the theory of elites profoundly marked by Pareto's influence. This was a path also followed by other greater and lesser syndicalist intellectuals,[234] in a difficult and, for many, impossible balance between a conception of revolutionary minorities' vanguard role, and a conception of them as having *separate* ends.

Starting from a structurally conflictual view of society, the likes of Leone and Labriola recuperated – as against reformism and parliamentary, egalitarian democracy – aspects of the liberal tradition founded on competition, contractualism, individualism and anti-statism. They came to think of syndicalism also as a theory adequate to dominating and orienting the masses, using collective psychology and imagining new and sophisticated schemas of action appropriate to ever more complex and conflictual processes of social transformation.[235] They tried to settle accounts with the inevitably elitist structure of power, and undoubtedly breathed in the Paretian winds that were powerfully buffeting the Italian culture of the time, in this regard; but they did not make the jump separating a theory of vanguards from a theory of elites.

Rather, the atmosphere that would encourage such a jump was a numerous group of intellectuals' transformation of the 'syndicalist doctrine' into what one authoritative representative of this group called 'a state of mind'.[236]

This gradual slippage would be sharply accelerated by events in the real movement, within the party, the union, and the true and proper bastions of the proletariat that were the *Camere del lavoro*. There is no doubt that the three years from 1906 to 1908, in which revolutionary syndicalism went down to major defeats on several fronts, marked a point of no return for that tendency of syndicalist culture which, lacking any direct relation with the movement's organisational dimension, came to accentuate the logics inherent to

233 Many years later, recalling his own syndicalist past, De Pietri Tonelli would theorise it precisely as a moment of preparation of his elite function. See De Pietri Tonelli (ed.) 1961, p. 47.

234 Franz Weiss assimilated *tout court* Pareto's theory of elites to Marx's theory of class struggle: 'Pareto's theory of elites is nothing other than the theory of class struggle, rebaptised for the occasion with the high-sounding name of the "circulation of aristocracies"': 'Il proletariato e la scienza economica', *Il Divenire Sociale*, 1910, p. 238.

235 In this regard, see Cavallari 1983 and Gianinazzi's discussion of it in *Cahiers George Sorel*, 1984, 2.

236 Olivetti 1913, p. 2. Arturo Labriola had already used the same expression to define revolutionary syndicalism: Labriola 1911, p. 116.

this external position. In particular, the Parma strike ought to be considered a watershed in the history of Italian revolutionary syndicalism, in that it led to separation between worker-organisation and syndicalist intellectuals. While workers' organisation 'was maturing its definitive shape, overcoming the gap separating it from the European movement', in short aligning itself 'on the positions of the [French] CGT',[237] a large proportion of the syndicalist intellectuals projected themselves *outside* of the dense web of problems of workers' resistance. There was no lack of suggestive influences in the Italian culture of the time such as to confirm these intellectuals' extraneous position and to make it definitive.

All this was, however, facilitated by a way of experiencing (or exalting) militancy distinguished by a 'feverish ethical tension', 'disdain for bourgeois egoism and materialism' (as well as that of the reformist socialists) and an 'exaltation of the proletariat's heroism',[238] which in the right historical contexts could easily transform into disdain for the proletariat itself.

Still in 1906, Sergio Panunzio used Pareto in order to find analogies between the theory of elites such as it was espoused in *Les systèmes socialistes* and the explanation of the class struggle as the impulse for the 'effort with which an elite of workers seeks to replace the ruling ... elites, with the triumph of the proletariat'.[239] This was a proletariat that Marxism attributed consciousness only in a psychological and claim-making sense; in short, it gave it an elite function, already pre-existing in the 'workers' *mental horizon*'.[240]

In 1908 Panunzio continued to consider Marxism 'the logical, direct, rapid, cutting, cruel expression ... of the workers' psychological and mental horizon'.[241] He again went back to Pareto to give scientific dignity to the 'vital part of Marxism'. By this he meant a theory of class struggle; but one in which the class struggle was ever more understood as a site where a sort of social Darwinism played out, and where it was not so much the proletariat as a whole that transformed itself into an elite, as an elite within the proletariat that secured the dominant role for itself. And at the same time, he began openly to profess his affinity with Nietzsche's idea of the superman:

> ... this is what all of us syndicalists are made of, psychologically. We have trained our minds with Friedrich Nietzsche and his brilliant philosophy

237 Antonioli 1990, pp. 121, 123.
238 De Clementi 1983, p. 19.
239 Panunzio, 'Dove sta il socialismo?', *Il Divenire Sociale*, 1906, p. 301.
240 Panunzio, 'Dove sta il socialismo?', *Il Divenire Sociale*, 1906, p. 300.
241 Panunzio, 'Il momento critico del socialismo', *Pagine Libere*, 1908, p. 207.

> of force and will ... I am enthused by the Epic of the Revolution and the violent impulse of a class of the strong, tending to take over all the world's powers.[242]

Orano also began to ask if it was really possible that the workers could become a new elite, given the difficulties that revolutionary syndicalism faced in generalising itself among the proletariat. These difficulties could be imputed not to any missing capacity for 'vulgarisation' on the part of the 'syndicalists of the intellectual elites', but rather the fact that 'syndicalism demands a lot of the worker'.[243] Two years later, in 1909, Orano had definitively resolved the dilemma: 'there is no way to get ethical, aesthetic, critical, energetic syndicalism ... into the heads of the workers in the factories and fields'.[244]

Also in 1909, right on the brink of two years of defeats and disappointments, Olivetti decided to make explicit the transition from a theory of *vanguards* to a theory of *elites*. The opportunity came as a result of the conclusions of the Bologna syndicalist congress, which, with the affiliation of the workers' organisations still controlled by the syndicalists to the CGdL, marked an important moment of the recomposition of 'proletarian unity'. The results of the congress appeared to Olivetti as the Canossa of a movement defeated in the field on account of the congenital 'immaturity' of the greater part of its troops. This fact was, in substance, destined to remain impervious to change,[245] for which reason it was entirely pointless to tell tales about 'proletarian unity'. The syndicalists' task was not, then, to 'regiment large numbers of helots', but to select 'a healthy handful of the conscious and willing, who [would] open themselves a way through the capitalist forest using violence and guile'.[246]

With even greater clarity, after Tommaso Sorrichio objected that his vision of vanguards' role in the revolutionary process was not Marx's, but 'a true and proper parody of social revolution, leading the workers not to self-emancipation but to a change of boss',[247] Olivetti responded that 'Syndicalism must be

---

242 Panunzio, 'Il momento critico del socialismo', *Pagine Libere*, 1908, pp. 202, 204.

243 Orano, 'Perché il sindacalismo non è popolare in Italia', *Il Divenire Sociale*, 1907, p. 226.

244 Orano, 'La teoria sindacalista', *Pagine Libere*, 1909, p. 427.

245 'Out of a thousand men taken from the herd, nine hundred will adapt to any misery ... Of the hundred remaining ones, most will seek individual salvation ... What remains is but a handful'. Olivetti, '*Postilla* a T. Sorricchio, *Note all'articolo dell'Olivetti "Il congresso della dedizione"*', *Pagine Libere*, 1909, II, p. 11.

246 A.O. Olivetti, 'Il Congresso della dedizione', *Pagine Libere*, 1909, I, p. 626.

247 T. Sorricchio, 'Note all'articolo dell'Olivetti "Il congresso della dedizione"', *Pagine Libere*, 1909, II, p. 9.

… an experimental revolutionism. The object of this experiment is the working class. The hope that it could today, or ever, also be its subject, is a pious wish'.[248]

This was a point of arrival that Olivetti would never break from; indeed, after the First World War he would lay claim to it as an element of continuity with postwar neosyndicalism, as he now came to move between corporatist and revolutionary-fascist positions.[249] If Marxism had now become emblematic of the *forma mentis* that Germany had imposed on the socialist parties, as against syndicalism – 'that fine and free Latin flower, quivering in imposing winds' – in filigree it remained the old reading of history developing through stages that had to reach full maturity. Here, this was translated into a productivist ideology that ruled out 'in the most absolute sense the Bolsheviks' possibility [of making] an immature and incapable proletariat take over running society',[250] with their pretence 'of innovating society by changing … its political superstructure, on this point contradicting even the Marxist thesis itself'.[251] On this point, elitism and a never-fully relenting deterministic inheritance converged.

From 1908–9, the now-matured positions of the likes of Olivetti, Orano and Panunzio easily entered into the general context of 'agitated' intelligence of which *La Voce* represented the most significant moment. The shared 'heroic idealistic fervour'[252] would facilitate elements of osmosis, indeed ones that were perceived as such also within syndicalist circles. For example, Giulio Barni saw Prezzolini's considerations, and also those of the non-'*Voce*-an' Corradini, as offering elements of syndicalist consciousness, now made clear to the syndicalists themselves from the outside:

> The energetic syndicalism that emerges from Prezzolini's study and the imperialistic conception that nationalists *à la* Corradini have of it – in many senses relating back to the 'barbaric' conception of Marx's socialism – is virtually … an aspect of the workers movement, brought into relief by bourgeois minds.[253]

The 'barbaric' conception to which Barni here refers was nothing other than the reduction of Marxism to a 'philosophy of action', a 'philosophy of force', a

248 Olivetti, '*Postilla* a T. Sorricchio, *Note all'articolo dell'Olivetti "Il congresso della dedizione"*', *Pagine Libere*, 1909, II, p. 13.

249 Olivetti 1919.

250 Olivetti 1919, p. 10.

251 'Manifesto dei sindacalisti', written by Olivetti and De Ambris, *Pagine Libere*, 1921.

252 The expression is from Emilio Gentile: see Gentile 1972, p. 69.

253 G. Barni, 'Per la sincerità! Sindacati, sindacalismo e sindacalisti', *Pagine Libere*, 1909, p. 70.

'philosophy of violence', with a series of gradations that were not only chronological but also represented different contexts of culture and sensibility.

Certainly, these were not new themes in the revolutionary syndicalists' understanding of Marxism. They had taken on a certain weight and meaning in the movement's founding moment, when they appeared at the side of a theoretical complex of a quite different articulation, and with a conception of the working class as the primary (and more often, only) protagonist of the struggle for its own emancipation. Without this frame of reference, however, their weight and meaning was a rather different one.

Can we say that reading the Sorel of this period was the privileged site of this osmosis? Is it only from this moment that we can speak of an 'Italian Sorelianism'?

We can easily see that the period from 1908 onward marked a new phase in Sorel's fortunes in Italy. The publication of his *Reflections on Violence*, but in particular Croce's work editing them, expanded the horizons of the French thinker's influence on Italian culture. Croce's work was not, in fact, limited to presenting this text to an Italian audience, but also introduced an interpretation of Sorel that made itself felt even within the Crocean *moment* of democracy.[254] Not by chance, the expression '*Sorel notre maître*' would now be used indifferently by syndicalists, *Voce*-ans, nationalists, and in general by exponents of anti-democratic and anti-reformist currents of all kinds.

I think that we can say that the expression *Italian Sorelianism* is not fully able to define the phenomenon of revolutionary syndicalism on the Italian peninsula, a phenomenon of particular complexity that was articulated across what were often considerably different levels. It is inadequate not only with regard to Italian revolutionary syndicalism's structural-organisational dimension, rooted in a proletarian reality shaped by specific, endogenous factors, but also in terms of its general ideological and cultural construction.

While the most important intellectuals like Leone and Labriola did, in determinate contexts, use language and concepts taken from Sorel's work, they also preserved a theoretical autonomy of their own. Indeed, their autonomous theory was on many far from secondary points wholly irreducible to some of the central categories of Sorel's thought. The 'lesser' intellectuals, who were doubtless more sensitive to the influence of the '*maître*' beyond the Alps,

254 Sorel, moreover, declared himself perfectly in accordance with Croce's interpretation, after the text that would later be used as the introduction to the Italian edition appeared as a review in *La Critica*. See Sorel to Croce, 6 May 1907, in Sorel 1980, and B. Croce, 'Cristianesimo, socialismo e metodo storico', *La Critica*, V, July 1907, pp. 317–30.

nonetheless often mediated it through themes and concerns that had matured within their own context, in particular conjunctures. Here, too, then, this is a rather blurred line that lends itself poorly to serving as an interpretative paradigm.

However, an Italian Sorelianism really did emerge, and it was not without influence among significant cultural and political sectors. If it did not make itself felt as a movement, it certainly did so as a *climate*. This was a climate with different seasons and different effects according to latitude, longitude and the make-up of the territory. Revolutionary syndicalism was particularly influenced by it, but even in this case spaces and times played a fundamental role; it had no uniformity or characteristic 'essence'. Other settings – some of them contiguous to regions of syndicalism, and sometimes connected to it by difficult channels – were also affected by this climate; and these were settings that could open up to unexpected horizons. When the winds changed direction, it could lead – and did lead – even to currents with separate and distant sources and origins flowing together in unpredictable ways.

As such, while *Reflections on Violence*'s anticipations, coming out in Italian in 1906, initially with a preface by Leone (critical, among other things, of its aspects of apologia for violence) had had largely 'internal' echoes, after Croce's intervention in 1907, and in particular after his 1909 edition of this text, it was able to pluck very many different strings.[255] This led to what were sometimes dissonant notes, but which were part of one same melody.

There were some among the syndicalists, like Panunzio (or Orano, or Olivetti) who particularly grasped the radicalism of Sorel's counterpositions, the tension of a 'wholly epic state of mind',[256] and the cathartic effects of violence, which confirmed tendencies that had for some time already characterised their direction of travel. There were those like Longobardi who were little-inclined to move in this direction, continuing to consider Marx's school 'even truer and more profound in its realism' than Sorel's attempt to apply 'Bergson's philosophy of knowledge to the syndicalist movement', and yet also recognised the French 'master's' 'enormous' merit in 'making the socialist ideal more heroic'.[257] And there were those, *extra moenia*, like Corradini, who enthusiastically welcomed Sorel's call on the bourgeoisie to return to its origins, conform-

255 Leone contributed a preface to Sorel's *Lo sciopero generale e la violenza*, published by *Il Divenire Sociale* in 1906. This was made up of eight articles that had appeared in this publication between October 1905 and April 1906.

256 Sorel 1973, p. 365.

257 E.C. Longobardi, 'Il teorico della violenza (Giorgio Sorel)', *Il Viandante*, 1909, p. 27.

ing to the 'barbarism of its forebears' for the sake of a stronger, more consequential capitalism.[258]

Sorel's *Reflections on Violence* cannot only be read in the reductive, one-dimensional outlook of the 'apologia for violence'. The questions relating to the 'political myth', as a particular form of collective consciousness, have, indeed, given rise to a rich cultural inheritance. But in the specific context of the late 1900s, it was the echoes of his 'barbaric' conception of Marxism, as evoked by Barni, that seem to have reverberated most strongly among a non-negligible part of Italian culture and politics. It has been argued – wholly unconvincingly, indeed – that no-one could have interpreted 'the essence of Marxism' better than Sorel.[259] The 'essence' referred to, here, was a completely ideological one, cut off from any concrete analysis of capitalism's production processes and the working class, and which thus lent itself to reductive uses. This essence was then filtered also through other approaches bringing further elements of reductionism.

The man who took it upon himself to be Sorel's most faithful disciple, the man who wanted to be the Italian Berth, namely Agostino Lanzillo, identified the solution to the 'crisis of Marxism' in the 'theory of violence'.[260] And at the same time, reaffirming the elitist character of a syndicalist doctrine that was ill-adapted to 'drawing the crowds', he further reduced the 'theory of violence' to a pure 'philosophy of action', likewise arguing that 'the philosophy of Marxism [was] all to be found therein'.[261] Was it not, then, wholly in coherence with these assumptions that the nationalist Corradini argued in the syndicalist Orano's *La Lupa* that syndicalism was nothing but 'a form of *will to struggle*' and nationalism 'a form of will to war', with these thus being 'the same thing'?[262]

Nationalism and syndicalism were not 'the same thing', and nor was nationalism the same as *Voce*-anism, but the elements of intersection between them were hardly a matter of chance. 'Barbaric' Marxism, elitism, and catastrophism, represented mutually reinforcing moments of a vicious circle; and if in this composition it had a syndicalist epicentre, it also acted in a much wider political-cultural area, encountering elements that fed it still further.

The phenomenon of Mussolinianism ought to be considered wholly internal to this triad and this circle. It has rightly been noted that 'the influence of revo-

258 E. Corradini, 'La riforma borghese: Sorel – Considerazioni sulla violenza', *Il Marzocco*, 2 May 1909.

259 Giacalone-Monaco 1960, p. 13.

260 Lanzillo, 1910, p. 36.

261 Lanzillo 1910, p. 67.

262 E. Corradini, 'Nazionalismo e sindacalismo', *La Lupa*, I, 16 October 1910.

lutionary syndicalism represents a more or less evident, but always discernable red thread [running] throughout … [Mussolini's] long political evolution'.[263] However, it ought to be specified that Mussolini's involvement with revolutionary syndicalist milieux followed very particular and coherent paths. He had collaborated with *Avanguardia Socialista* in 1903–4, when Arturo Labriola consciously used Marxism as a purely ideological and political tool. Then came his more intense, important relations with Olivetti and Panunzio (indeed, his correspondence with this latter is particularly indicative of the direction of his ideological influences).[264] Conversely, he had no relation to revolutionary syndicalist culture's engagement with the analytical dimension of Marx's work. He was substantially ignorant of the elaborations in this regard by the likes of Sorel, Labriola and Leone. He moved from prophetic-deterministic Marxism to the 'sarcastic and tremendous' Marxism 'of social revolutions' to Marxism as a revolutionary 'state of mind', in substantial continuity and without the acquisition of one phase meaning the loss of the previous one. What was absent, as we have said, was analytical Marxism: and that was true both of Mussolini himself and to that revolutionary syndicalist milieu with which he was most attuned.

It was precisely the omission of this fundamental link – the one in which theory becomes an element of knowing reality, and in which interrogating the logics of theory becomes the precondition of knowledge – that allowed the co-presence, in the Marxism of Mussolini and many like him, of otherwise contradictory themes of rigid determinism and intense voluntarism. Of themes lacking in depth, assumptions and enunciations corresponding to old residues and impulses both old and new. This was a Marxism widespread among revolutionaries whether syndicalist or otherwise, amplified by an intelligentsia in large part made up of generic intellectuals, journalists, autodidacts, and sometimes all three at once.

In 1913 Mussolini founded a review, *Utopia*, with the declared goal of making this publication revolutionaries' 'theoretical consciousness'. In reality, the theoretical dimension – in the sense that we have discussed – was wholly absent from this initiative. Disregarding a very abundant and often high-level literature on this subject, he reasserted the 'present-day value' of the 'theory of growing immiseration, [the theory] of the concentration of capital and [the theory] apocalyptically predicting catastrophe'.[265] He moreover made a deterministic response to Prezzolini – who considered the effort to restore a theoretical

263 De Felice 1965, p. 40.

264 Perfetti 1986.

265 B. Mussolini, 'Al largo', *Utopia*, 22 November 1913, p. 2.

consciousness to Italian socialism 'hopeless' – arguing that theory is nothing other that the expression of the phase of development that capitalism is passing through. The important question, in his view, consisted of 'seeing whether reality ... allow[ed] for the prediction of socialism'. And this prediction ought to be not so much an object of science, as of faith: 'The Social Revolution', his conclusion exclaimed, 'is not a mental schema or a calculation, but, first of all, an act of faith. I, dear Prezzolini, believe in the Social Revolution'.[266]

This reduction of theory to absolute voluntarism perfectly coincided with what Sergio Panunzio was also arguing in *Utopia*, namely that revolutionary culture's priority task was that of 'reducing thought and action to an absolute unity', on the terrain of the '*must-be*'.[267] And Marxism was assigned the role of a revolutionary philosophy in that it was idealistic, and wholly extraneous to 'vulgar materialism'.[268] The 'reduction' was a triple one: of Marxism, of philosophy, and of idealism, a term that notwithstanding its nominal reference to Hegel was simply used as an opposite to the 'philosophy of the stomach' (materialism), and the 'viscous' character of consolidated socio-economic relations (realism).

On this terrain, Panunzio also considered Mussolini's 'spirit' – his 'intransigent geometrical style' – genuinely 'promising for ... the syndicalists'. Moreover, without *this* revolutionary syndicalism, Mussolini's 'revolutionary socialism' would have been 'living on the moon'.[269]

Not a small part of *this* Marxism would, within a few months, flow into the manifesto-appeal issued by the *Fascio rivoluzionario d'azione internazionalista*. And nor would it take long for Mussolini formally to sign up to these theses.

Perhaps it was not by chance that it was Sorel himself – a scholar who was truly familiar with Marx's texts – who expressed serious doubts 'that Marx would have signed the *Fascio Rivoluzionario*'s manifesto'.[270]

---

266 B. Mussolini, 'L'impresa disperata – a Prezzolini', *Utopia*, 15 January 1914, pp. 4–5.

267 S. Panunzio, 'Il lato teorico e il lato pratico del socialismo', *Utopia*, 15–31 May 1914, pp. 200–1. The italics are in the original.

268 S. Panunzio, 'Il lato teorico e il lato pratico del socialismo', *Utopia*, 15–31 May 1914, p. 201.

269 S. Panunzio, 'Il lato teorico e il lato pratico del socialismo', *Utopia*, 15–31 May 1914, pp. 203, 205.

270 Letter to Lanzillo, 27 November 1914, in Sorel 1993–4. In another letter to Lanzillo of 7 December 1914, he commended the wisdom of the Italian socialists who knew that keeping the country out of the war would save Marxism – a Marxism that the revolutionary interventionists were ready to destroy. He concluded 'I sometimes come to ask myself if Marxism will not, indeed, ultimately find its second homeland in Italy; and that would not be without importance to Italy, which would find itself alone in having a serious socialist

5 *De hominis dignitate*. A Workers' Syndicalist Marxism? *La Scintilla* in Ferrara and *Il Martello* in Piombino

According to Franziska Kugelmann's testimony, when Karl Marx was told that the workers enthusiastically followed his doctrine, he replied; 'They have a single desire, a rather understandable one, to escape from their poverty; but very few understand how they could do so'. Kugelmann also recalls that 'one time a delegation of workers went to Marx's place to ask him to handle the social question, because they were no longer managing to keep going'.[271]

Kugelmann's testimony refers to the 1860s, when 'Marxism' did not yet exist, or at least there were not major workers' organisations, be they trade-union or political, defining themselves as 'Marxist'. Nonetheless, they are indicative of the very great, indeed almost insurmountable obstacles to a 'working-class' reception of Marx that was even minimally capable of reaching a threshold of basic understanding of the mechanisms of theory. At the same time, they are also indicative of the fact that the workers' living and working conditions, including the forms that social clashes were gradually coming to assume, were essential elements of this reception, which absolutely cannot be overlooked. At not a few moments, the workers 'invented' for themselves the Marxism that they thought they needed.

Many years later, when Marxism had now become a macroscopic reality, at least in some regions of Europe, 'the mass of the socialist working class' within the SPD – the 'scientific party' *par excellence* – 'was absolutely distant from the theory of socialism and did not nurture any interest in the party's scientific literature'.[272] This, the author of an important study on the SPD added, 'was not an argument against the "maturity" of the German workers, who proved able to win the esteem even of their political opponents ... where they could be practically active'.[273]

While the literature on Italian socialist popular culture across the turn of the century is not very weighty, it does, nonetheless, allow us to say that the judgement here passed on the German workers can also be extended to their Italian counterparts. Nor is this an argument against the 'maturity' of the Italian workers, who in very difficult conditions often demonstrated capacities for

---

ideology'. Analogous concepts ('What if Italy became the leading country for Marxism?') appeared in his 9 December 1914 letter to Missiroli; Sorel 1963, p. 143.

271 Enzensberger (ed.) 1977, p. 270.

272 Steinberg 1979, p. 194.

273 Steinberg 1979, p. 196.

organisation, solidarity, and identification of connections lying beyond the immediate, concrete problems of their living and working conditions.

Notwithstanding the weak – almost non-existent – knowledge of the fundamental aspects of Marx's theory among the working class organised in the party and/or union, we should not imagine that there was any clear separation between the workers' 'practical activity' and an external, nebulous Marxism. This latter was anything but uninfluential; rather, it constituted, in often diverse and sometimes contradictory ways, the constant frame of reference for the former.

The revolutionary syndicalist experience developed among the Italian working class at a time when the Marxist frame of reference had already long been established. From the 1880s onward, 'high' Marxist literature had had time to grow, to become articulated and even to change its perspectives. We get the impression – as we shall see better in a moment – that the revolutionary workers' Marxism (if we accept that any such level can be clearly identified) held onto long-term, constant elements, without particular evolutions. In certain aspects, the somehow pre-Marxist Marxism of the old *Il Fascio Operaio* remained a model, yet to be surpassed.[274]

La Scintilla and *Il Martello* were the publications (the first was a weekly and very briefly a daily, the latter a weekly that was across some short periods a fortnightly) giving expression to two among the most important revolutionary syndicalist strongholds: Ferrara and Piombino. Among the very few publications that had a long continuity, covering the whole Giolittian era, they thus had an early 'socialist' phase and then came directly to represent the lineaments of the transition. That said, given that they were expressions of different contexts they were different in their characteristics, including with regard to the realities of the proletariat to which they spoke.

In Ferrara, the fundamental proletarian referent to which the socialists and syndicalists spoke was that of the peasant world. This particularly meant farm labourers, as classically understood, but also a wider range of workers belonging to the variegated and complex space of co-participation. At the same time, the city at the centre of the province retained its traditional urban fabric, a socially articulated one expressing political cultures that were largely autonomous with respect to the countryside. The editors of *La Scintilla* in their great majority belonged to this urban world, and the strong political-ideological link with a rural social base was not sufficient to changing the one-directional character of their cultural influences. Moreover, the paper would

274 Favilli 1988, pp. 21–5.

ultimately represent more the mediation-vulgarisation of Marxism than a mirror of its proletarian use.

In Piombino, conversely, across the whole period in consideration workers in the town's major steel industry represented slightly more than a third of the total urban population. Social stratification was thus particularly simplified, with the absolute predominance of the urban proletariat and the 'services' necessary for everyday life. *Il Martello* was a rather faithful expression of this reality. Almost all of its editors (and for long periods, all of them) were workers in factories connected to the steel industry, and it was they who set the general 'tone' of the publication, even if there were also 'outside' contributions (in particular during Umberto Pasella's leadership of the *Camera del lavoro*) and from figures belonging to the lower ranks of the intelligentsia.

In these papers, the syndicalists' Marxism encountered (overlapped with, was integrated with) some long-term coordinates that had already for some time defined the characteristics of existing Marxism. A socialist text celebrating Christmas 1902 allows a clear delineation of some of the basic themes of these coordinates. The editors of *Il Martello* tried to clarify the characteristics of their 'faith',

> a faith founded on science, which tells the workers of their redemption, which must be their own work, a faith that offers the remedy to the present life ...: this faith does not threaten, it asks nothing of the rich, because it knows that nothing, or at least too little can be expected of their kindheartedness, because their interests are inevitably in direct opposition with the workers' [interests]. As such, it says to [the workers]: You are the majority, you are labour, you have the right to the entire fruit of your toils: you have the right to life. And you will have this right *in reality*, when collective property is substituted for private property, and you will obtain this through the class struggle, organising yourselves economically and politically against the rich.[275]

Its style and contents were those traditional of popular divulgation; all the distinctive elements of the doctrinal nexuses that had become sedimented as Marxism were condensed in a brief, particularly effective text. And it was Marxism that was deemed necessary, even in formulations (like the right to the full product of workers' labour) that Karl Marx had expressly rejected. This all appeared in a context of references to the experience of Christianity, an

275 'Natale', *Il Martello*, 21 December 1902.

aspect of religiously experiencing one's own political belonging. This was an aspect of 'the intellectual and moral (that is, religious) "reform"'[276] of which the popularisation of Marxism and the characteristics of its reception represented the central moment.

The set of themes making up the passage cited above would not, in substance, be changed up till the First World War. Rather, the syndicalist experience privileged certain propositions, which it then often made yet more rigid. This ultimately made itself felt across the organic coordination of all its components. Workers' papers' experience of syndicalism – or, in any case, the experience of papers closely linked to advanced dynamics of class struggle – did not, then, produce a wide range of ideological 'innovations', but accentuated the dimension of 'the pure and simple return to "first principles"'.[277]

'Catastrophism' and 'fatalism' remained the North Stars of the long-term perspectives indicated to the Po Valley peasant whose 'more or less distant future wellbeing ... will inevitably be produced by the antagonism between the rich and the poor ever more reduced to shocking poverty'. 'And this', it was said, 'is the so-called catastrophist theory of Marxism'.[278] And the Piombino steelworker certainly would not operate according to different horizons:

> There is no doubt that socialism will conquer the future ... the so-greatly discussed and never disproven centralisation of wealth is ... a factual element that goes to show that not a small part of the bourgeoisie will find itself in front of the dilemma: either destroy wealth or collectivise it.[279]

This fundamental Marxism was certainly not, at least in *this phase*, an element of distinction among reformists and syndicalists, but at this very point the Marxism that did serve as the point of discrimination did now begin to appear also in the workers' press. The dominant theme of the operation now underway still remained the assertion of a privileged claim to Marxism's inheritance. *La Scintilla* exemplified this in the following terms;

> ... What did Marx say? *The emancipation of the workers must be the effort of the workers themselves*. What do the syndicalists say? *Workers, claim*

276 Gramsci 1975, Vol. III, p. 1985.

277 *Il Martello*, 26 August 1906.

278 Mugik, 'Le macchine sono utili o dannose? Continuazione del dialogo fra contadini', *La Scintilla*, 2 April 1905.

279 Curtius, 'Verso il socialismo', *Il Martello*, 18 August 1906.

> *your own interests for yourselves, without the intervention of lawyers.* What did Marx say? *The state is the executive committee of the bourgeoisie.* What do the syndicalists say? *Have no faith in the democratisation of the state, because it is and will remain capitalism's most effective defence.* What did Marx call parliamentary jousting among the politicians? *Parliamentary cretinism.* What do the syndicalists say to the worker-electors? ...[280]

Simultaneously, *Il Martello* claimed that the syndicalists had the merit of having risen up 'against those who tried to cut the Italian proletariat's nerves – against deviation from the socialist method of class struggle'. This was a syndicalism that was naturally none other than the 'appeal to the old, genuine form of fighting to conquer, which Marx and Engels exalted in their writings'. Marxism was presented as the keystone of the syndicalists' continuity with socialism:

> Marx wrote to indicate the guiding path: the efforts of the workers themselves. How so? With union: Proletarians of all countries, unite. United in trade unions to fight against the state, the political organ of the ruling class, which cannot serve, even once it is conquered, as an instrument of *workers'* emancipation ... Karl Marx and Friedrich Engels state in the preface to the *Communist Manifesto* that historical experience has proven that *it is not enough* [for the workers] *to take over the state machine such as it is* and wield it for their own ends. Certainly, the greats of Italian socialism maintain that Marx's theory is not applicable to our times, since Marx expressed his philosophical thinking many years ago, when, in their view, things could be seen rather differently than [they are] today. For my part, I think that the bankruptcy lies with our [Italian] reformists and not with Marx, when we consider the attitude that they take toward the bourgeoisie's governments, in antagonistic constrast with the socialist conception.[281]

This was syndicalism as revolutionism, then, and Marxism as a first guarantee of revolutionary purity. A single worker's intervention sought to interrupt this linear schema, and it is interesting to note that this took place not so much on the level of the movement's operative needs, as in terms of merely doctrinal projections. 'All us workers are in agreement on revolutionism', he declared,

---

280 Un operaio che vuol discutere, 'Spigolature di propaganda. Che cosa è il sindacalismo?', *La Scintilla*, 28 April 1906.

281 Etrusco, 'Il sindacalismo', *Il Martello*, 16 June and 1 July 1906.

then going on to define its coordinates – 'not whoring ourselves out to the bourgeois class, intransigence on the electoral question, no indulgence for parliamentary cretinism, the recourse to general strikes, and also violence, where it is needed'. However, the syndicalists also argued that 'their conception [was] a return to the very sources of Marxism and … in agreement with regard to practical action', but not with regard to the perspectives for socialism, in that Marx wanted to 'socialise, communise the means of production and exchange'[282] whereas the syndicalists wanted to assign property over it to trade organisations, which would have perpetuated the old system under new owners.

La Scintilla was now giving rise to a specific doctrinal complex, and the arguments for the syndicalist Marxism concerned were generally drawn from the national movement's intellectuals, whether through their direct intervention or from the republication of passages from writings of theirs that had appeared in books and journals. Thus Leone and Labriola were fairly constant presences in this paper's columns. But there was also no lack of articles signed by a far from negligible part of the 'minor' syndicalist intellectuals; indeed, even organisers like Guido Pasella and Michele Bianchi intervened on questions of Marxism.[283]

The themes proposed through this recourse to the various levels of the national Parnassus (with certain local aspects, too) were the ones that tended to consolidate elements of what was already a common sense circulating among syndicalist militants. They pointed to the state as a direct expression of the ruling class; the state's incapacity to change the economy and society; parliamentary cretinism; and Marxism as the philosophy of force.[284] The textual references generally almost exclusively concerned the *Communist Manifesto*. Starting from 1908, there was a repeated reproduction of passages from an interview on unions that Marx had given to *Volkstaat* – an interview considered 'the full and complete justification of syndicalism [as] the legitimate heir of Marx's thought'.[285] These were passages in which Marx explicitly recognised both the need for the union's independence from any 'political association' and the very considerable importance of union organisation and practice as

282 P. Dardini, 'Domando la parola', *Il Martello*, 29 September and 6 October 1906.

283 G. Pasella, 'Contro Giorgio Plekhanoff e per il Sindacalismo', *La Scintilla*, 17 January 1909; M. Bianchi, 'Marx in soffitta?', *La Scintilla*, 16 April 1911.

284 See, for example, E. Leone, 'Che cosa è il sindacalismo', *La Scintilla*, 18 November 1906; P. Mazzoldi, 'Cretinismo parlamentare', *La Scintilla*, 19 October 1917, A. Labriola, 'I sindacalisti di fronte allo Stato', *La Scintilla*, 1 May 1908, A. Labriola, 'Violenza proletaria', *La Scintilla*, 11 July 1908.

285 'Marx e il sindacalismo', *L'Internazionale*, 4 October 1908.

a moment of improving the working class's material living conditions as well as its political-cultural growth. They were organisations that functioned as true and proper schools of class consciousness; this was, indeed, the perspective of unions as 'schools of socialism'.[286] The paper that in some aspects served as a national hub of syndicalism drew the following (rather exaggerated) conclusions from these passages: '1st, Marx saw the unions as the moral instrument of socialism; 2nd, for Marx the only true workers' Party is the trade union; 3rd, the union must not depend on any party and, therefore ... not on the socialist party either'.[287]

La Scintilla also proved rather attentive to the literature on Marxism produced by syndicalist intellectuals, a literature presented in a section devoted to this purpose, 'Fra Libri e Riviste'. It often dedicated a considerable amount of space to this, as in the case of Di Pietri Tonelli's *Marx ed il Marxismo*[288] and in particular Labriola's *Marx nell'economia e come teorico del socialism* and Leone's *La revisione del marxismo*.

It was Guido Marangoni who devoted himself to covering these last two books. He was an atypical syndicalist who was both an organiser and a member of parliament; he did not belong to the coterie of syndicalist 'writers', but he represented well those figures who strongly linked organising to the radicalism of very harsh social clashes, without seeking useless and declamatory splits. What reading would such a figure, drawing on the deeper sentiments of the socialist movement, give of such undoubtedly high points of Labriola and Leone's theoretical elaboration? What images of Marxism would this 'link' figure, in turn, carry into the syndicalist sphere?

If, as we have seen, Labriola's book contained a constant tension between a more directly stated element that seemed to tend toward separation between Marx the economist (belonging to the past) and a revolutionary Marx (belonging to the present and future), and an analytical level that recovered Marx's 'intelligent understanding' of capitalism and, therefore, also his scientific dimension, Marangoni captured only the first of these elements. As such, he declared himself supportive of a 'current of ideas that while it affirms itself the most courageous in denouncing the faults and archaisms of Marx's system, of both an economic and philosophical order, [also] proves the most decisive

286 This was an account of Marx's conversation-interview with Hamann, head treasurer of the German metalworkers' union, in September 1869: see 'Marx über die Gewerksgenossenschaften', *Volkstaat*, 17, 27 November 1869.

287 'Marx e il sindacalismo', *L'Internazionale*, 4 October 1908.

288 A passage from this volume appeared in its 3 October 1908 edition, and a review-presentation in the 10 October 1908 issue.

and sincere in pursuing the revolutionary goals of the most formidable theorist of modern socialism'. Supportive, indeed, of a syndicalism that presented itself as 'the only legitimate heir of the surviving, triumphant part of the vast Marxist system'.[289] And reading Enrico Leone's *La revisione marxismo* had also confirmed, in his mind, that the 'surviving part' could not be that concerning Marxism the economist.[290]

Among the syndicalist organisers – in particular those of working-class backgrounds like Romualdo Rossi, and/or those closely linked to the everyday practice of fighting over demands, like the builders' union secretary Fabio Petrucci – there continued to dominate a rigidly mechanical-determinist vision of the social processes allowing them to maintain the unmediated priority of 'economic action', even in a climate of pervasive 'idealism'. 'The socialistic movement', Petrucci peremptorily declared, 'has its basis not in a political-moral sentiment that can unite men of different social conditions as one, but exclusively in the economic factor, which, through the never-disproven law of Marxist historical materialism forms the fundamental basis of any other "moral superstructure"'.[291] And seeing as once 'the economic conditions change, all the existing juridical relations above them must change',[292] it was not necessary to pose the problem of conquering power in the bourgeois state from a political point of view, but rather to 'transform economic relations, in the field of the economy itself, with organs that have a specific economic function, like the trade union, which is nothing other than the revolutionary organisation of the productive forces'.[293] To remove any doubt as to the 'idealistic' propensities of this type of organiser, the old manual labourer Romualdo Rossi, who would soon become the paper's lead editor (on 5 August 1912) dismissed in near contemptuous terms a 'state of mind' that was, conversely, widespread among other syndicalist milieux:

> The idealists are and will always be negative and Marxist theory is eminently positive … Faith is born of sentiment and expressed in thought – and Karl Marx, if I recall correctly, established incontestably that the development of both [sentiment and thought] is inherent to, dependent on and a consequence of the economic substructure …[294]

289 G. Marangoni, 'In tema di marxismo', *La Scintilla*, 24 October 1908.

290 G. Marangoni, 'La "revisione del marxismo" di Enrico Leone', *La Scintilla*, 18 December 1909.

291 F. Petrucci, 'Democrazia e socialismo', *La Scintilla*, 15 June 1912.

292 F. Petrucci, 'L'avvenire della donna', *La Scintilla*, 20 June 1912.

293 F. Petrucci, 'La "conquista del potere"', *La Scintilla*, 17 June 1912.

294 R. Rossi, 'L'illusione della fede e la fede dell'illusione', *La Scintilla*, 19 July 1912.

If *La Scintilla* could sound a Marxist note, as part of a relatively broad scale, the same cannot be said of *Il Martello*. Indeed, almost alone in the two years of Paselli's leadership of the *Camera del lavoro* (1909–11), the paper served the syndicalist divulgation of texts by national figures of reference – whether intellectuals or organisers – such as Barni, Orano and Mantica. Moreover, Giuseppe Vanni, the chief-editor who was subsequently replaced by Pasella, was still also a worker (a bricklayer), as were his predecessors. And this had evident repercussions on his way of considering and using Marxism.

We know that the proposition that opens the first paragraph of the IWMA's *Provisional Rules*, 'That the emancipation of the working classes must be conquered by the working classes themselves', had an essential role in the formation of Marxism in the 1880s, when it began to become renowned among the organised proletariat as 'Karl Marx's well-known phrase'. More than twenty years later, the syndicalists appropriated it as a further confirmation of their 'loyalty to first principles'. Independently of different circles' original spirit and positioning, this formulation was used in countless – often very different – contexts and areas of the syndicalist press (some of which we have already seen). Evidently neither *La Scintilla* or *Il Martello* was any exception to this, and at some points they also used it as an epigraph.

Providing a powerful impulse to working-class pride and identity, 'Marx's well-known phrase' had yet greater effects in situations in which the class struggle played out in particularly bitter forms, with little possibility of mediation. This was true in the countryside surrounding Ferrara just as in the steel plants of Piombino. The children of the agricultural labourers on strike in Massafiscaglia – with whom the very soldiers sent to protect the strikebreakers shared their provisions, moved by compassion – and the children of those locked out at the Piombino Altiforni – forced to look for shelter in other cities now that their parents were no longer able to feed them – sang the same fierce verses, the former against the landowners, the latter against the steel bosses.[295] This was but one sign of social clashes that were waged – and experienced – like a war; and the revolutionary syndicalist theorisations of these clashes certainly ought not be considered primary elements of this war. The motives driving the 'class war' among the agricultural and industrial proletariat, across many different contexts, instead drew on structural factors, and tended to persist even in the presence of 'a sort of interchangeability between reformism and syndicalism'.[296]

295 Roveri 1972, p. 274; Favilli.

296 See Procacci 1975, p. 110.

The strike was a declaration of war. The conflict between Magona and striking workers in 1906 was presented in the following terms:

> For two and a half months, an episode characteristic of the antagonisms among the classes in struggle has been playing out in Piombino. On the one hand, the capital employed in an industry that is almost unique in Italy, and thus highly profitable, and on the other the workers of this industry, requesting improved rates. Capital says no, and labour keeps on asking. Capital refuses, labour turns off the machines and crosses its arms. Battle is engaged, and two irreconcilable interests stand opposed ... It is a question of life and death.[297]

The concluding words of this paragraph must have had a lot of meaning for the workers hearing them, and not only a metaphorical one; there were constant examples of defeats leading to far-reaching decimations, using the weapon of mass sackings. In the practice of the strike, the components of the experience associated with working-class identity – in the deep sense of worker dignity, the difficult acquisition of an ennobling 'class' consciousness – were wholly put on the line. Defending this *dignitas* and this *nobilitas* could mean having to deal with even more devastating personal conflicts, as this letter demonstrates:

> Dear *Martello*, in order to protect my dignity as an honest worker I publicly declare my condemnation of my two brothers as well as my father, who during the strike went to the Stabilmento Alti Forni to carry out 'scab' labour [*krumiraggio*]. The blood ties that link me to them do not at all stop me breaking off all relations with those who stained themselves with cowardice, even when they knew that their son and brother was locked out and was thus being sacrificed. I have had to make this statement so that my mates [*compagni*] will not associate me with those who, unfortunately, also bear my name.[298]

The Marxism elaborated on the basis of Marx's 'well-known phrase' proved an essential confirmation of this *dignitas* and this *nobilitas*.

297 'Martello e incudine', *Il Martello*, 27 October 1906.
298 *Il Martello*, 1 October 1910.

References

AAVV, *La Critica in economia. Su Claudio Napoleoni*, Rome: Editori Riuniti.

Adorno, Theodor 1976, *The Positivist Dispute in German Sociology*, London: Harper and Row.

Agazzi, Emilio 1962, *Il giovane Croce e il marxismo*, Turin: Einaudi.

——— 1987, 'Il marxismo di Antonio Labriola: "socialismo scientifico" o "comunismo critico"?' in AAVV, *Marx e i suoi critici*, Urbino: QuattroVenti.

——— 1987b, 'Jürgen Habermas: "critico" o "ricostruttore" del marxismo?', in AAVV, *Marx e i suoi critici*, Urbino: QuattroVenti.

Albonetti, Pietro 1982, 'Andrea Costa tra gli Internazionalisti (1871–1874)', in *Andrea Costa nella storia del socialismo italiano*, edited by Aldo Berselli, Bologna: Il Mulino.

Allevi, Giovanni 1901, *L'utopia riformista*, Ascoli Piceno: Tip. Economica.

Allocati, Antonio 1990, 'Introduzione', *Carteggio Loria-Graziani (1888–1943)*, Rome: Pubblicazioni degli Archivi di Stato.

Anderson, Perry 2014, *L'Italia dopo l'Italia. Verso la Terza Repubblica*, Rome: Castelvecchi.

Andréas, Bert 1963, *Le Manifeste Communiste de Marx et Engels. Histoire et Bibliographie 1848–1918*, Milan: Feltrinelli.

Angelini, Giovanna 1994, *La cometa rossa. Internazionalismo e Quarto Stato. Enrico Bignami e 'La Plebe' 1868–1875*, Milan: Angeli.

Andreucci, Franco and Tommaso Detti 1977, *Il Movimento operaio Italiano. Dizionario Biografico*, Vol. III, Rome: Riuniti.

Ansart, Pierre 1977, *Idéologies, conflits et pouvoir*, Paris: PUF.

Antonioli, Maurizio 1983, *Sindacato e progresso. La FIOM tra immagine e realtà (1901–1914)*, Milan: Angeli.

——— 1990, *Azione diretta e organizzazione operaia*, Bari: Lacaita.

Anzi, Felice 1917, *Battaglie d'altri tempi (1882–1892)*, Milan: Avanti!

——— 1946, *Il Movimento operaio socialista italiano (1882–1894)*, Milan: Avanti!

Are, G. 1974, *Economia e politica nell'Italia liberale*, Bologna: Il Mulino.

Arena, Adele 1962, 'Formazione ideale e prima attività politica di Giuseppe Emanuele Modigliani', *Movimento Operaio e Socialista*: 3–33.

Artifoni, Enrico 1981, 'Un carteggio Salvemini-Loria a proposito di "Magnati e Popolani" (1895)', *Bollettino Storio-bibliografico subalpino*: 234–55.

Asor Rosa, Alberto 1975, *La cultura* in *Storia d'Italia*, Vol. IV/2, Turin: Einaudi.

——— 1996 *La sinistra alla prova. Considerazioni sul ventennio 1976–1996*, Turin: Einaudi.

Atkinson, Edward 1885, *Distribution of Products or the Mechanism and the Metaphysics of Exchange*, London: Putnam's and Sons.

Audenino, Patrizia 1995, 'La prefigurazione della società future nella propaganda del socialismo', in *Educazione e propaganda nel primo socialismo*, Rome: Riuniti.

Babel, Isaac 2014, *Red Cavalry*, ebook, London: Pushkin Press.

Badaloni, Nicola 1951, 'Le prime società operaie a Livorno', in *Bollettino Storico Livornese*, 1: 41–53.

Baczko, Bronislaw 1979, *L'utopia*, Turin: Einaudi.

——— 1979b, 'L'immaginazione sociale', *Enciclopedia*, Turin: Einaudi.

Bainton, Roland 1952, *The Reformation of the Sixteenth Century*, Boston: Beacon.

Bakounine, Michel 1974, *Oeuvres Complètes de Bakounine*, II, *Michel Bakounine et l'Italie*, Paris: Champ Libre.

Balibar, Étienne 1974, *Cinq études de materialisme historique*, Paris: Maspero.

Barbadoro, Idomeneo 1979, *Il sindacato in Italia. Dalle origini al congresso di Modena della Confederazione del Lavoro (1908)*, Milan: TETI.

Barbagallo, Francesco 1984, *Nitti*, Turin: Utet.

Barucci, Piero 1980, 'La diffusione del marginalismo', in *Il pensiero economico italiano 1850–1950*, edited by M. Finoia, Bologna: Cappelli.

Basso, Lelio 1962, 'La prima traduzione italiana di un brano del "Capitale" (1867)', *Rivista storica del socialismo*, 17.

Bellofiore, Riccardo 1993a, 'Quale Napoleoni', *Il Pensiero economico italiano*, I, 2: 99–135.

——— 1993b, 'Per una teoria monetaria del valore lavoro. La teoria marxiana tra radici ricardiane e nuove vie di ricerca', in *Valori e prezzi*, edited by G. Lunghini, Turin: Utet.

Benvenuti, Nicola 1981, *Partito e sindacati in Germania (1890–1914)*, Milan: La Pietra.

Bergami, Giancarlo 1985, 'La scoperta della questione sociale: Graf e De Amicis', in *Il positivismo e la cultura italiana*, edited by E.R. Papa, Milan: Angeli.

Berlin, Isaiah 1978, *Karl Marx*, Oxford: Oxford University Press.

Bernstein, Eduard 1900, 'Geschichtliches zur Gewerkschaftsfrage', *Sozialistische Monatshefte*, 4; 376–88.

——— 1901, *Wie is Wissenschsftlicher Sozialismus Möglich?*, Berlin: Verlag der Sozialistischen Monatshefte.

——— 1968, *I presupposti del socialismo e i compiti della socialdemocrazia*, Bari: Laterza.

Berselli, Aldo (ed.) 1982, *Andrea Costa nella storia del socialismo italiano*, Bologna: Il Mulino.

Berta, Giuseppe 1979, 'La formazione del movimento operaio regionale: il caso dei tessili (1860–1900)', in *Storia del movimento operaio, del socialismo e delle lotte sociali in Piemonte*, edited by Aldo Agosti and Gian Mario Bravo, Vol. I, *Dall'età preindustriale alla fine dell'ottocento*, Bari: De Donato.

Berti, Giampietro 1993, *Francesco Saverio Merlino. Dall'anarchismo socialista al socialismo liberale (1856–1930)*, Milan: Angeli.

Bidet, Jacques 1990, *Théorie de la modernité*, Paris: PUF.
Bloch, Ernst 1971, 'Karl Marx and Humanity: The Material of Hope', in *On Marx*, New York: Herder and Herder.
Bloch, Marc 2014, *Feudal Society*, London: Routledge.
Bobbio, Norberto 1987, 'Profilo ideologico del Novecento', in *Storia della Letteratura Italiana, Il Novecento*, Milan: Garzanti.
——— 1994, 'Umanesimo di Rodolfo Mondolfo', in *Maestri e compagni*, Florence: Passigli Editori.
Boccardo, Girolamo 1878, 'Del metodo e dei limiti dell'economia politica', preface to John Elliott Cairnes, *Alcuni principi fondamentali dell'economia politica* and John Stuart Mill, *Saggi su alcune questioni non ancora risolute di economia politica*, Turin: Utet.
Bodei, Remo 1995, *Libro della memoria e della speranza*, Bologna: Il Mulino.
Bonacchi, Gabriella and Alessandra Pescarolo 1980, 'Cultura della comunità e cultura del mestiere alle origini della "resistenza" proletaria italiana', *Movimento Operaio e Socialista*, I: 37–48.
Bonomi, Ivanoe 1907, *Le vie nuove del socialismo*, Milan: Sandron.
——— 1992, *Le vie nuove del socialismo*, Bari: Lacaita.
Bosio, Gianni 1951, 'Gli scritti di Marx ed Engels in Italia dal 1871 al 1892', *Società*, VII: 268–84, 444–7.
——— 1955, 'Introduzione', in Karl Marx and Friedrich Engels, *Scritti italiani*, Milan/Rome: Avanti.
Bortkiewicz, Ladislaus von 1952, *Value and Price in the Marxist System*, IEP, London: Macmillan.
——— 1984, 'On the Correction of Marx's Fundamental Theoretical Construction in the Third Volume of *Capital*', in Eugen von Böhm-Bawerk, *Karl Marx and the Close of his System*, Philadelphia: Orion Editions.
Bravo, Gian Mario 1962, *Marx ed Engels in lingua italiana*, Milan: Edizioni Avanti!
——— (ed.) 1970, 'Engels e Loria: relazioni e polemiche', *Studi Storici*.
——— 1978, *La prima internazionale documentaria*, Rome: Editori Riuniti.
——— 1979, *Marx e la prima internazionale*, Bari: Laterza.
——— 1992, *Marx ed Engels in Italia. La fortuna degli scritti le relazione le polemiche*, Rome: Editori Riuniti.
Briguglio, Letterio 1971, *Congressi nazionali socialisti e tradizione operaista 1892–1902*, Padua: Tipografia Antoniana.
——— 1978, 'Benoit Malon e le origini del socialismo in Italia', *Rassegna storica del Risorgimento*: 425–41.
——— 1979, *Benoît Malon e il socialismo in Italia*, Padua: Antoniana.
Brocchi, Renato 1907, *L'organizzazione della resistenza in Italia*, Macerata: Libreria editrice marchigiana.

Bulferetti, Luigi 1951, *Le ideologie socialistiche in Italia nell'età del positivismo evoluzionistico (1870–1892)*, Florence: Le Monnier.

——— 1975, *Cesare Lombroso*, Turin: Utet.

Bulgakov, Mikhail 1971, *The White Guard*, London: McGraw-Hill.

Burgelin, Henri, Knut Langfeldt and Miklós Molnár 1962, *La Première Internationale, Recueil des documents*, Vol. II, Geneva: Droz.

Busino, Giovanni 1974, *Gli studi di Vilfredo Pareto oggi. Dall'agiografia alla critica (1923–73)*, Rome: Bulzoni.

Calvino, Italo 1980 [1964], 'L'antitesi operaia', in *Una pietra sopra. Discorsi di letteratura e società*, Turin: Einaudi.

Cartiglia, Carlo 1967, *Rinaldo Rigola e il sindacalismo riformista in Italia*, Milan: Feltrinelli.

Castoriadis, Cornelius 1975, *L'institution imaginaire de la société*, Paris: Seuil.

Cavallari, Giuseppe 1983, *Classe dirigente e minoranze rivoluzionarie. Il protomarxismo italiano: Arturo Labriola, Enrico Leone, Ernesto Cesare Longobardi*, Camerino: Jovene.

Chekhov, Anton 2003, 'A Doctor's Visit', in *Chekhov's Doctors: a Collection of Chekhov's Medical Tales*, edited by Jack Coulehan, London: Kent State University Press.

Cherubini, Donatella 1990, *Giuseppe Emanuele Modigliani. Un riformista nell'Italia liberale*, Milan: Angeli.

Ciccotti, Emilio 1903, *Psciologia del movimento socialista*, Bari: Laterza.

Civolani, Eva 1977, 'Scioperi e agitazioni operaie dell'estate 1872 nei comparti manufatturieri di Milano e Torino', in *Movimento Operaio e socialista*, 1977: 427–55.

——— 1981, *L'anarchismo dopo la Comune*, Milan: Angeli.

Colajanni, Napoleone 1884, *Socialismo e sociologia criminale. Il socialismo*, Catania: Tropea.

——— 1887, 'Di alcuni studi recenti sulla proprietà collettiva', *Giornale degli economisti*, II/V.

——— 1889, *La Sociologia criminale*, Catania: Tropea.

——— 1899, *Il Socialismo*, Palermo: Sandron.

Coletti, Francesco 1925, 'Luigi Cossa e la sua scuola in Pavia', *Universitatis Ticinensis Saecularia Undecima*, Die XXI Maii Anno MCMXXV: 39–40.

Colletti, Lucio 1977, 'Marxismo e dialettica', in *Intervista politico-filosofica*, Bari: Laterza.

——— 1979, *Tra Marxismo e no*, Bari: Laterza.

Conigliani, Carlo 1890, *Teoria generale degli effetti economici delle imposte. Saggio di economia pura*, Milan: Hoepli.

Corradi, Cristina 2005, *Storia dei marxismi in Italia*, Rome: manifestolibri

Corradini, D. 1983, 'Politica e dialettica in Croce', in *Benedetto Croce trent'anni dopo*, Bari: Laterza.

Cortellazzo, Michele 1981, 'La diffusione del Manifesto in Italia alla fine dell'Ottocento e la traduzione di Labriola', in *Cultura neolatina*, XLI, 1–2: 89–104.

Cortesi, Luigi 1961, *La costituzione del Partito socialista italiano*, Milan: Edizioni Avanti!
——— 1971–2, 'Socialismo ed evoluzione tecnologica in Italia', *Le Machine*, Bollettino del Centro di studio sulla storia della tecnica, III.
Cossa, Emilio 1895, *Il metodo degli economisti classici nelle sue relazioni col progresso della scienza economica*, Bologna: Treves.
Cossa, Luigi 1892, *Introduzione allo studio dell'economia politica*, Milan: Hoepli.
——— 1895, *Primi elementi di Economia politica, I, Economia sociale*, Milan: Hoepli.
——— 1963, *Saggi bibliografici ed economia politica*, Bologna: Forni.
——— 1976, *Guida allo studio dell'economia politica*, Milan: Hoepli.
Costa, Andrea 1900, *Bagliori di Socialismo. Cenni storici*, Florence: Nerbini.
——— 1952 [1898], 'Memorie della mia vita', *Movimento Operaio*: 314–56.
Covelli, Emilio 1874, *L'Economia politica e la scienza*, Naples: Stabilimento tipografico Strada Medina 25.
Croce, Benedetto 1921, *Storia della storiografia italiana*, Bari: Laterza.
——— 1961, *Materialismo storico ed economia marxista*, Bari: Laterza.
——— 1961b, *Marxismo ed economia pura*, Bari: Laterza.
——— 1967, *Storia d'Italia dal 1871 al 1915*, Bari: Laterza.
——— 1981, *Lettere a Giovanni Gentile*, Milan: Mondadori.
——— 1989, *Contributo alla critica di me stesso*, Milan: Adelphi.
Croce, L.H. (ed.) 1987–8, *Sei lettere di Benedetto Croce ad Antonio Labriola (1898–1899)*, Annali dell'Istituto italiano per gli studi storici, X.
Cusumano, Vito 1873–4, 'Sulla condizione attuale degli studi economici in Germania', *Archivio Giuridico*, 1873, 2, 3 and 4, pp. 113–37, 240–65 and 395–420; 1874, 2–3, pp. 284–317.
——— 1875, *Le scuole economiche della Germania in rapporto alla questione sociale. La scuola del libero scambio, i socialisti cattedratici, i conservatori sociali, il socialismo*, Naples: Marghieri.
Dal Pane, Luigi 1975, *Antonio Labriola nella politica e nella cultura italiana*, Turin: Einaudi.
Dal Pra, Mario 1965, *La dialettica in Marx*, Bari: Laterza.
De Amicis, Edmondo 1980, *Primo maggio*, Milan: Garzanti.
De Clementi, Andreina 1983, *Politica e società nel sindicalismo rivoluzionario*, Roma: Bulzoni.
De Felice, Renzo 1965, *Mussolini il rivoluzionario (1883–1920)*, Turin: Einaudi.
De Giovanni, B. 1983, 'Sulle vie di Marx filosofo in Italia. Spunti provvisori', *Il Centauro*, 9: 3–25.
——— 1983b, 'Spinoza e Hegel: l'oggettivismo di Antonio Labriola', *Il Centauro*, 9: 26–47.
Degl'Innocenti, Maurizio 1995, *Filippo Turati e la nobiltà della politica*, Bari: Lacaita.
Del Bo, Giuseppe (ed.) 1964, *La corrispondenza di Marx e Engels con italiani (1848–1895)*, Milan: Feltrinelli.

Della Peruta, Franco 1952, 'L'Internazionale a Roma dal 1872 al 1877', *Movimento Operaio*: 5–34.

——— 1965, *Democrazia e socialismo nel Risorgimento*, Rome: Editori Riuniti.

De Marchi, Edoardo, Gianfranco La Grassa and Maria Turchetto 1994, *Per una teoria della società capitalistica*, Florence: La Nuova Italia.

De Pietri Tonelli, Alfonso 1908, *Marx e il marxismo*, Pistoia: Tip Ciattini.

De Pietri Tonelli, Pietro (ed.) 1961, *Scritti paretiani*, Padua: Cedam.

De Rosa, Gabriele (ed.) 1960, *Lettere a Maffeo Pantaleoni*, Rome.

De Tocqueville, Alexis 1964, *Œuvres Complètes*, Vol. XII, *Souvenirs*, Paris: Gallimard.

De Viti de Marco, Antonio 1888, *Il carattere teorico dell'economia finanziaria*, Rome: Pasqualucci.

Di Giovanni, Piero 1996, *Kant ed Hegel in Italia. Alle origini del neoidealismo*, Bari: Laterza.

Di Leo, Rita 2012, *L'esperimento profano. Dal capitalismo al socialismo e viceversa*, Rome: Ediesse.

Di Menza, Giuseppe 1874a, 'Le condizioni sociali dei nostri tempi', *Atti della Accademia di Scienze, Lettere e Arti di Palermo*, n.s., IV:1–25.

——— 1874b, 'Evoluzione del socialismo. Carlo Marx e le sue dottrine', *Atti della Accademia di Scienze, Lettere e Arti di Palermo*, n.s., IV:1–18.

Dmitriev, Vladimir Karpovich 1974, 'David Ricardo's Theory of Value. An Attempt at a Rigorous Analysis', in *Economic Essays on Value, Competition and Utility*, Cambridge: Cambridge University Press.

Dommanget, Maurice 1969, *L'introduction du Marxisme en France*, Lausanne: Rencontre.

Dostoyevsky, Fyodor 1917, *Crime and Punishment*, London: Collier.

Dowe, Dieter and Klaus Tenfelde 1983, 'La recezione di Eugen Dühring nel Movimento operaio tedesco intorno al 1870', in *L'Antidühring: affermazione o deformazione del marxismo?*, Annali della Fondazione Basso-Issoco, V, Milan: Angeli.

Droz, Jacques, 1981, 'Dalle organizzazioni operaie del 1848 al partito di Lassalle', in *Il Congresso di Gotha: Partito Operaio e socialismo*, Annali della Fondazione Basso-Issoco, III.

Durkheim, Émile 1986, *Durkheim on Politics and the State*, Stanford, CA: Stanford University Press.

Ellero, Pietro 1874, *La questione sociale*, Bologna: Fava e Garegnani.

——— 1879, *La tirannide borghese*, Bologna: Fava e Garegnani.

Engels, Friedrich 1880, 'Le socialisme utopique et le socialisme scientifique', *La Revue socialiste*, 3: 164–71; 4: 234–40; 5: 275–86.

——— 1883, *Il socialismo utopico e il socialismo scientifico*, Benevento: Stabilimento tipografico F. De Gennaro.

Enzensberger, Hans Magnus (ed.) 1977, *Colloqui con Marx ed Engels*, Turin: Einaudi.

Esposito, Edoardo 2013, 'Alla ricerca della verità (storica)', in Paolo Favilli (ed.), *Il letterato e lo storico. La letteratura creativa come storia*, Milan: FrancoAngeli.

Farina, Paolo 1996, *Pensare il mondo che cambia. Uno studio su economia e politica in John Locke*, Milan: Guerini.

Faucci, Riccardo and Enzo Pesciarelli (eds.) 1976, *L'economia classica. Origini e sviluppo*, Milan: Feltrinelli.

Faucci, Riccardo 1978, 'Revisione del marxismo e teoria economica della proprietà in Italia (1880–1900): Achille Loria e gli altri', *Quaderni fiorentini per la storia del pensiero giuridico moderno*, Milan: Giuffrè.

——— 1981, *La scienza economica in Italia (1850–1943)*, Naples: Guida.

——— 1995, 'Economia, storia, positivismo. Cognetti de Martiis e le origini del laboratorio di economia politica', *Società e Storia*: 599–618.

Favilli, Paolo 1974, *Capitalismo e classe operaia a Piombino (1861–1918)*, Rome: Editori Riuniti.

——— 1980, *Il socialismo italiano e la teoria economica di Marx (1892–1902)*, Naples: Bibliopolis.

——— 1983, 'Il sindacato riformista nelle lettere di Fausto Pagliari a Rinaldo Rigola (1907–1911)', *Ricerche Storiche*: 437–92.

——— 1986, 'Democrazia sociale e "grande riforma" in Carlo Conigliani', *Società e Storia*: 819–66.

——— 1988, *Herausgabe und Verbreitung der Werke von Karl Marx und Friedrich Engels in Italien*, Trier: Schriften aus dem Karl-Marx-Haus.

——— 1989, *Karl Marx, Friedrich Engels und Italien*, Teil I, *Katalog und Auswahlbibliographie*, Trier: Schriften aus dem Karl-Marx-Haus.

——— 1990, *Il labirinto della grande riforma. Socialismo e 'questione tributaria' nell'Italia liberale*, Milan: Angeli.

——— 2006, *Marxismo e storia. Saggio sull'innovazione storiografica in Italia (1945–1970)*, Milan: FrancoAngeli.

Fergnani, F. 1969, 'Marxismo e utopia', *Rivista di filosofia*, 4: 463–503.

Ferrara, Francesco 1975, 'L'italianità della scienza economica. Lettere al sen. Fedele Lampertico', in *Opere complete di Francesco Ferrara*, Vol. VIII, Rome: Associazione bancaria Italiana.

Filippi, Ignazio 1984, 'I socialisti della cattedra e Marx nella critica di Vito Cusumano', in AAVV, *Il marxismo e la cultura meridionale*, Palermo: Palumbo.

Fineschi, Roberto 2008, *Un nuovo Marx. Filologia e interpretazione dopo la nuova edizione storico-critica (MEGA2)*, Rome: Carocci.

Fiorot, Dino 1976, 'Lettere di Maffeo Pantaleoni ad Achille Loria: fasi e momenti del processo di maturazione intellettuale di due studiosi', *Storia e Politica*: 439–95, 553–604.

Foa, Vittorio 1973, 'Sindacati e lotte sociali', in *Storia d'Italia, I Documenti*, Vol. 5/II, Turin: Einaudi.

Franzina, Emilio 1974, 'La "buona stampa" liberista e le premesse ideologiche del liberismo di sinistra agli inizi del periodo crispino', *Critica Storica*: 38–93.

——— 1976, 'I "liberisti", Pareto e la Democrazia italiana', *Critica Storica*: 81–128.

Gallegati, Mauro 1984, 'Analisi parziale e teoria pura: l'economia politica marshalliana in Italia (1885–1925)', *Annali della Fondazione Luigi Einaudi*: 355–409.

Gallino, Luciano 1985, 'Achille Loria e la teoria dell'evoluzione delle società', in *Il positivismo e la cultura italiana*, edited by E.R. Papa, Milan: Angeli.

Galassi, Nazario 1989, *Vita di Andrea Costa*, Milan: Feltrinelli.

Ganci, Massimo (ed.) 1959, *Democrazia e socialismo in Italia. Carteggi di Napoleone Colananni: 1878–1898*, Milan: Feltrinelli.

——— 1968 [1959], 'Profilo di Napoleone Colajanni dagli esordi al Movimento dei fasci dei lavoratori', in *L'Italia antimoderata. Radicali, repubblicani, socialisti, autonomisti dall'Unità ad oggi*, Parma: Guanda.

Garegnani, Pierangelo 1981, *Marx e gli economisti classici. Valore e distribuzione nelle teorie del sovrappiù*, Turin: Einaudi.

Garin, Eugenio 1966, *Cronache di filosofia italiana*, Bari: Laterza.

——— 1983, *Tra due secoli. Socialismo e filosofia in Italia dopo l'Unità*, Bari: De Donato.

——— 1972, *Lettere a Benedetto Croce*, Florence: Sansoni.

Gentile, Giovanni 1955, *La filosofia di Marx. Studi critici*, Florence: Sansoni.

Gentile, Emilio 1972, *'La Voce' e l'età giolittiana*, Milan: Pan Editrice.

Gerratana, Valentino 1972, *Richerche di storia del marxismo*, Rome: Riuniti.

Giacalone-Monaco, Tommaso 1960, *Pareto e Sorel*, Padua: Cedam.

Gianinazzi, Willy 1989, *L'itinerario di Enrico Leone. Liberismo e sindacalismo nel movimento operaio italiano*, Milan: Angeli.

Gianola, G. Antonella 1988, *Alle origini del Movimento Operaio. L'associazionismo operaio in Asti. Dalle società di mutuo soccorso alla nascita delle camera del lavoro*, Cuneo: L'Arciere.

Giovannini, Claudio 1984, *La Cultura della "Plebe"*, Milan: Angeli.

Giuffrida, Vincenzo 1899, *Il III volume del "Capitale" di Karl Marx* (*esposizione critica*), Catania: Giannotti.

Giva, Denis 1985, 'Liberismo e positivismo nel gruppo della "Riforma Sociale"', in *Il positivismo e la cultura italiana*, edited by E.R. Papa, Milan: Angeli.

Gnocchi-Viani, Osvaldo 1875, *Le tre internazionali*, Lodi.

——— 1879, *Il collettivismo nel socialismo*, Milan: La Plebe.

——— 1879b, *Il Capitale Borghese*, Milian: Biblioteca di propaganda socialista.

——— 1880, 'La letteratura socialistica in Italia', *Rivista Internazionale del Socialismo*: 10–18.

——— 1886, *Il Socialismo moderno*, Milan: Pugni.

——— 1909, *Ricordi di un internazionalista*, Milan.

——— 1974 [1908], *Ricordi di un Internazionalista*, Padua: Tipografia Antoniana.

——— 1989, *Oltre la politica*, edited by G. Angelini, Milan: Angeli.

Gozzi, Gustavo 1986, 'Ideologia liberale e politica sociale: il socialismo della cattedra in Italia', in *Gustav Schmoller e il suo tempo*, edited by P. Schiera and F. Tenbruk, Bologna: Il Mulino.

Gramsci, Antonio 1975, *Quaderni del Carcere*, edited by Valentino Gerratana, Turin: Einaudi.

——— 1995, *Further Selections from the Prison Notebooks*, London: Lawrence and Wishart.

Grass, Günther 1993, *The Call of the Toad*, London: Minerva.

Graziadei, Antonio 1901, *Intorno alla legge del godimento descrescente ed al principio del grado finale di utilità*, Valparaiso: Hefman.

——— 1909, *Saggio di un'indagine sui prezzi in regime di concorrenza e di sindacato tra gli imprenditori*, Imola.

——— 1909b, *Socialismo e sindacalismo*, Rome.

——— 1913, *La questione agraria in Romagna. Mezzadria e bracciantato*, Milan: Uffici della Critica Sociale

——— 1921, *Gradualismo economico e gradualismo politico*, Rome: Libreria editrice del Partito Comunista.

——— 1927, *Capitale e colonie*, Milan: Casa editrice Sociale.

——— 1928, *Capitale e salari*, Milan: Casa editrice Monanni.

——— 1929, *Sindacati e salari*, Milan: Trevisini editore.

——— 1943, *Le teorie dell'utilità marginale e la lotta contro il marxismo*, Milan: Bocca.

——— 1948, *Il capitale e il valore. Critica dell'economia marxista*, Rome: Leonardo.

Graziani, Augusto 1887, *Intorno all'aumento progressivo delle spese pubbliche*, Modena: Soliani.

——— 1891, 'La ragione progressiva del sistema tributario in rapporto al principio del grado finale di utilità', *Giornale degli economisti*, I: 157–69.

——— 1897, *Istituzioni di scienza delle finanze*, Turin: Bocca.

——— 1908, 'Sulle relazioni fra gli economici in Italia e in Germania nel secolo XIX', in *Die Entwicklung der deutschen Volkswirtschaftslehre im 19 Jahrhundert*, Leipzig; Verlag von Dunder & Humblot.

Griziotti, Benvenuto 1909, 'I principi distributivi delle imposte moderne sul reddito e sugli acquisiti ed incrementi di capitali', *Giornale degli Economisti*, II: 455–505.

——— 1938, 'Intorno alla scuola di Luigi Cossa in Pavia. Glosse e controglosse di Maffeo Pantaleoni e Giovanni Montemartini a "una questione di metodo nella storia delle dottrine economiche"', *Studi nelle scienze giuridiche e sociali*: 222–60.

Grossi, Paolo 1977, *Un altro modo di possedere. L'emersione di forme alternative di proprietà alla coscienza giuridica postunitaria*, Milan: Giuffré.

Grossmann, Henryk 1977, 'Marx, Classical Political Economy and the Problem of Dynamics', *Capital and Class*, 2: 32–55 and 3: 67–99.

Grossmann, Vasily 2011, *Life and Fate*, London: Vintage.

Guastini, Riccardo 1977, 'Stato, produzione e classe dominante', in *Il ruolo dello Stato nel pensiero degli economisti*, edited by R. Finzi, Bologna: Il Mulino.

Guillaume, James 1905–7, *L'Internationale, Documents et Souvenirs*, Vol. I, *1864–1872*, Paris: Georges Bellais.

——— 1980, *L'Internationale, Documents et Souvenirs*, Vol. I, *1864–1872*, Geneva: Grounauer.

Gustafsson, Bo 1972, *Marxismus und Revisionismus. Eduard Bernstein Kritik des Marxismus und ihrere ideengeschichtlichen Voraussetzungen*, Frankfurt: Europäische Verlagsanstalt.

Haupt, Georges 1978, 'Marx e il marxismo', *Storia del Marxismo*, edited by Eric Hobsbawm, Vol. I, *Il marxismo ai tempi di Marx*, Turin: Einaudi.

——— 1981, 'Partito e sindacato: socialismo e democrazia nella II Internazionale', in *Il Congresso di Gotha: Partito Operaio e socialismo*, Annali della Fondazione Basso-Issoco, III.

——— 2011, *Aspects of International Socialism, 1871–1914*, Cambridge: Cambridge University Press.

Havemann, Robert 1965, *Dialettica senza dogma. Marxismo e scienze naturali*, Turin: Einaudi.

Hobsbawm, Eric J. 1974, 'La diffusione del marxismo (1890–1905)', *Studi Storici*: 241–69.

——— 1978, 'Gli aspetti politici della transizione dal Capitalismo al socialismo', in *Storia del marxismo*, Vol. I, Turin: Einaudi.

——— 1978a, 'Prefazione', in *Storia del marxismo*, Vol. I, Turin: Einaudi.

——— 1979 'La cultura europea e il marxismo tra Otto e Novecento', in *Storia del marxismo*, Vol. II, Turin: Einaudi.

——— 1982, 'Il marxismo oggi: un bilancio aperto', in *Storia del marxismo*, Vol. IV, Turin: Einaudi.

——— 1983, 'Quando siamo "marxisti"', in *Marx un secolo*, Rome: Riuniti.

——— 1984, *Workers: Worlds of Labor*, New York: Pantheon.

——— 1986, *Lavoro, cultura e mentalità nella società industriale*, Bari: Laterza.

——— 2011, 'The fortune of Marx's and Engels' writings', in *How to Change the World*, New Haven: Yale University Press.

Hunecke, Volker 1971, 'La diffusione dell'Indirizzo Inaugurale e degli Statuti Provvisori dell'Associazione Internazionale dei Lavoratori in Italia prima del 1871', in *Movimento Operaio e Socialista*, 1971: 115–37.

——— 1982, *Classe operaia e rivoluzione industrial a Milano (1859–1892)*, Bologna: Il Mulino.

Jaffé, William (ed.) 1965, *Correspondence of Léon Walras*, Amsterdam.

Jossa, Bruno 'Intervento', in *Marx e i marxismi cent'anni dopo*, edited by G. Cacciatore and F. Lomonaco, Naples: Guida.

Julliard, Jacques 1983, 'I rapporti sindacati-partiti. La pluralità dei modelli storici e il caso francese', in *Sindacato e classe operaia nell'età della seconda internazionale*, Florence: Sansoni.

Kautsky, Karl 1960, *Erinnerungen und Erörterungen*, The Hague: Mouton.

Kocka, Jürgen 1981, 'Il cambiamento strutturale della Germania nell'epoca di Bismarck', in *Il Congresso di Gotha: Partito Operaio e socialismo*, Annali della Fondazione Basso-Issoco, III.

Koestler, Arthur 1968, *Darkness at Noon*, Harmondsworth: Penguin.

Kolakowski, Leszek 1969, *Marxism and beyond: on historical understanding and individual responsibility*, London: Pall Mall.

——— 1974, *Marxismus: Utopie und Anti-Utopie*, Stuttgart: Kohehammer.

——— 1978, *Main Currents of Marxism*, Vol. I, *The Founders*, Oxford: Clarendon Press.

——— 1978b, *Main Currents of Marxism*, Vol. II, *The Golden Age*, Oxford: Clarendon.

Kuczynski, Jürgen 1967, *Nascita della classe operaia*, Milan: Il Saggiatore.

Labriola, Antonio 1946, 'Per uno studio sul III volume del Capitale', in *Fatti e teorie*, edited by L. Dal Pane, Milan.

——— 1965, *La concezione materialistica della storia*, Bari: Laterza.

——— 1973, *Scritti filosofici e politici*, Turin: Einaudi

——— 1977, *Saggi sul materialismo storico*, Roma: Editori Riuniti.

——— 1983, *Epistolario*, Rome: Editori Riuniti.

Labriola, Arturo 1899, *La teoria del valore di Carlo Marx. Studio sul III libro del Capitale*, Milan: Sandron.

——— 1901, *Ministero e socialismo. Risposta a Filippo Turati*, Florence.

——— 1904, *Riforme e rivoluzione sociale*, Milan: Società editrice milanese.

——— 1908, *Marx nell'economia e come teorico del socialismo*, Lugano: Edizioni di 'Pagine Libere'.

——— 1910, *Il capitalismo. Lineamenti storici*, Turin: Bocca.

——— 1911, *Economia, Socialismo, Sindacalismo*, Naples: Società Editrice Partenopea.

——— 1912, *Il valore nella scienza economica. Introduzione a una critica dell'Economia politica*, Naples: Società Editrice Partenopea.

——— 1913, *Economia, Socialismo, Sindacalismo*, second edition, Naples: Società Editrice Partenopea.

——— 1943, *L'attualità di Marx*, Naples: Morano.

——— 1945, *Spiegazioni a me stesso*, Naples.

Lagardelle, Hubert (ed.) 1905, *La grève générale et le socialisme. Enquête international*, Paris: Rivière.

Lanaro, Silvio 1979, *Nazione e lavoro. Saggio sulla cultura borghese in Italia (1870–1925)*, Padua: Marsilio.

Lange, Oskar 1935, 'Marxian Economics and Modern Economics', *Review of Economic Studies*, June.

——— 1963, *Political Economy*, Vol. 1, Oxford: Pergamon.

Lanzillo, Agostino 1910, *Giorgio Sorel*, Rome: Libreria Editrice Romana.

Larizza Lolli, Mirella 1985, 'Comte e l'Italia (1849–57)', in *Il positivismo e la cultura italiana*, edited by E.R. Papa, Milan: Angeli.

Laslett, Peter (ed.) 1970, *Two Treatises of Governement*, Cambridge: Cambridge University Press.

Lay, Adriana and Maria Luisa Pesante 1981, *Produttori senza democrazia. Lotte operaie, ideologia corporativa e sviluppo economico da Giolitti al fascismo*, Bologna: Il Mulino.

Lazzari, Costatino 1952, 'Memorie', edited by A. Schiavi, *Movimento Operaio*: 598–633, 789–837.

Leone, Enrico 1901, *Giubileo del manifesto Comunista (lineamenti di marxismo)*, preface by Giuseppe Caivano, Naples: Croce.

——— 1907, 'Il sindacalismo', Milan: Sandron.

——— 1910, *La revisione del marxismo*, Rome: Biblioteca del Divenire Sociale.

——— 1923, *Il neo marxismo – Sorel e Marx*, Bologna: Sindacato Ferrovieri.

Lequin, Yves 1968, 'Classe ouvrière et idéologie dans la région Lyonnaise à la fin du XIX siècle', *Le Mouvement Social*, 69: 4–18.

Levi, Giovanni 1990, 'Il piccolo, il grande e il piccolo', interview in *Meridiana*, 10: 211–34.

Limentani, Ludovico 1924, 'Il positivismo italiano', *Logos*, 7.

London, Jack 1982, 'Martin Eden', in *Novels and Social Writings*, New York: Viking Press.

Longinotti, Liana 1974, 'Friedrich Engels e la "Rivoluzione di maggioranza"', *Studi Storici*: 769–827.

Longobardi, Ernesto Cesare 1903, *L'Influenza degli alti salari sui profitti secondo le leggi dell'economia marxista*, Naples: Ettore Croce.

Loria, Achille 1880, *La rendita fondiaria e la sua elisione naturale*, Milan: Hoepli.

——— 1886, *Teoria economica della costituzione politica*, Turin: Bocca.

——— 1889, *Analisi della proprietà capitalista*, Turin: Bocca.

——— 1901, 'Movimento operaio e legislazione sociale', *Nuova Antologia*, September.

——— 1901b, *Il capitalismo e la scienza*, Turin: Bocca.

——— 1902, *Marx e la sua dottrina*, Milan: Sandron.

——— 1902b, *Il Movimento operaio*, Milan: Sandron.

——— 1927, *Ricordi di uno student settuagenario*, Bologna: Zanichelli.

Losurdo, Domenico 1986, 'Il paradise terrestre e il peccato originale: Marx profeta?', in *Attualità di Marx, Atti del convegno Urbino, 22–25 novembre 1983*, Milan: Unicopli.

Löwith, Karl 1957, *Meaning in History: The Theological Implications of the Philosophy of History*, Chicago: University of Chicago Press.

Lunghini, Giorgio 1994, 'Gramsci critico dell'economia politica', introduction to Antonio Gramsci, *Scritti di economia politica*, Milan: Bollati Boringhieri.

Luporini, Cesare 1973, 'Il marxismo e la cultura italiana del Novecento', in *Storia d'Italia, I documenti*, Vol. 5/II, Turin: Einaudi.

Macchioro, Aurelio 1970, 'Marxismo ed economia politica fra XIX e XX secolo', in *Studi di storia del pensiero economico*, Milan: Feltrinelli.

——— 1982, 'Marx, marxismo e politica economica', *Ricerche Storiche*: 463–90.

——— 1985, 'Evoluzione sociale e cooperativismo in Ugo Rabbeno', *Quaderni di Storia dell'Economia Politica*: 151–72.

——— 1985b, 'Crisi dello Stato e pensiero economico tra 1900 e 1925 in Italia', typescript of his intervention at a conference on *Ideologie, professioni e tecniche nel periodo fascista*, Milan, 14–16 November 1985.

——— 1989, 'Der Marxismus in der italienisch Nationalökonomie der 1890er Jahre', in *Karl Marx, Friedrich Engels und Italien*, Vol. II, Trier: Schriften aus dem Karl-Marx-Haus.

——— 1991, *Il momento attuale. Saggi etico-politici*, Padua: Il Poligrafo.

——— 1993, 'Sulla fortuna di J. Stuart Mill politico in Italia: A proposito di un libro di Nadia Urbinati', *Il pensiero economico italiano*, 1, 2: 239–51.

——— 1993–4, 'Liberoscambismo, sindacalismo rivoluzionario, Agostino Lanzillo', introduction to *"Cher Camarade" ... Georges Sorel ad Agostino Lanzillo 1900–1921*, edited by F. Germinario, Brescia: Annali della Fondazione Luigi Micheletti.

——— 1995, 'Gerolamo Boccardo e l'economia politica', in *Le origini del socialismo in Liguria*, Alessandria: Edizione dell'Orso.

——— 1996, 'Per una storia dell'economia politica Italiana nell'età del positivismo. Abbozzi', *Il pensiero economico italiano*, 1.

——— 1999, 'Sindacalismo rivoluzionario, pantaleonismo, mussolinismo', *Società e storia*: 109–138.

Maffi, Bruno 1969 (ed.), *Il Capitale*: Libro I, capitolo VI inedito (Karl Marx), Florence: La Nuova Italia.

Malon, Benoît 1879, *Histoire du socialisme*, Lugano: Veladini.

——— 1892, *Il Socialismo. Compendio teorico pratico*, Milan: Editori della Biblioteca Socialista.

Manacorda, Gastone 1963, *Il Movimento operaio italiano attraverso i suoi congressi (1853–1892)*, Rome: Editori Riuniti.

——— 1981, 'Associazione operaia, autonomia politica del proletariato e partito organizzato in Marx ed Engels', in *Il Congresso di Gotha: Partito Operaio e socialismo*, Annali della Fondazione Basso-Issoco, III.

——— 1992, *Il movimento reale e la coscienza inquieta*, Milan: Angeli.

Mannheim, Karl 1954, *Ideology and Utopia*, New York: Harcourt, Brace & Co.

Marmiroli, Renato (ed.) 1966, *Socialisti e non, controluce*, Parma: La Nazionale.

Marramao, Giacomo 1971, *Marxismo e revisionismo in Italia*, Bari: De Donato.
Martello, Tullio 1873, *Storia dell'Internazionale (dalla sua origine al congresso dell'Aja)*, Padua: Fratelli Salmin 1873.
Marucco, Dora 1981, *Mutualismo e sistema politico. Il caso italiano (1862–1904)*, Milan: Angeli.
Marx, Karl 1893, *Le Capital. Extraits par P. Lafargue*, Paris: Guillaumin.
Marx, Karl and Friedrich Engels 1902, *Pagine socialiste*, Genoa: Libreria Moderna.
——— 1955, *Scritti italiani*, Rome: Avanti.
Mascilli Migliorini, Luigi 1979, 'Camillo Prampolini e la cultura positiva', in *Prampolini e il socialismo riformista*, Vol. 1, Rome: Edizioni Avanti!
Masini, Pier Carlo 1951, 'La Prima notizia del "Capitale" in Italia in uno scritto di E. Covelli', Movimento Operaio, 431–6.
Masini, Pier Carlo (ed.) 1961, *La scapigliatura democratica*, Milan: Feltrinelli.
——— 1964, *La Federazione Italiana della Associazione Internazionale dei Lavoratori, Atti Ufficiali (1871–1880)*, Milan: Edizioni Avanti!
——— 1973, 'La preparazione della conferenze di Rimini (1871–1872)', in *Anarchismo e Socialismo in Italia (1871–1892)*, edited by L. Faenza, Rome: Riuniti.
Mazzola, Ugo 1885, *L'imposta progressiva in economia pura e sociale*, Pavia.
Meek, Ronald 1956, *Studies in the Labour Theory of Value*, London: Lawrence & Wishart.
Merli, Stefano 1972, *Proletariato di fabbrica e capitalismo italiano*, Florence: La Nuova Italia.
Merlino, Francesco Saverio 1897, *Pro e contro il socialismo. Esposizione critica dei principi e dei sistemi socialisti*, Milan: Treves.
Michels, Robert 1909, *Storia del marxismo in Italia*, Rome: Mongrini.
——— 1922, *La teoria di Carlo Marx sulla miseria crescente e le sue origini*, Turin: Bocca.
——— 1926, *Storia critica del movimento socialista italiano*, Florence: La Voce.
——— 1979, *Storia critica del movimento socialista italiano fino al 1911*, Rome: Il Poligono.
Mill, John Stuart 1880, *Sul socialismo*, Milan: Bignami e C.
Miller, Susanne 1985, 'August Bebel e le masse', in *Filippo Turati e il socialismo europeo*, edited by Mario degli Innocenti, Naples: Guida.
Mondolfo, Rodolfo 1908, *Il pensiero di Roberto Ardigò*, Mantua: Mondovì.
——— 1920, *Sulle orme di Marx*, Bologna: Capelli.
——— 1952, *Il materialismo storico in Federico Engels*, Florence: La Nuova Italia.
——— 1968, *Umanesimo di Marx. Studi filosofici 1908–1966*, Turin: Einaudi.
——— 1991, *Tra teoria sociale e filosofia politica. Rodolfo Mondolfo interprete della coscienza moderna*, Bologna: Clueb.
Montalbán, Manuel Vázquez 1993, *Autobiografía del general Franco*, Barcelona: La Planeta.

Montale, Bianca 1960, *La Confederazione Operaia Genovese e il Movimento mazziniano in Genova dal 1864 al 1892*, Pisa: Domus Mazziniana.

Monteleone, Renato 1987, *F. Turati*, Turin: Utet.

Montemartini, Giovanni 1896, *Il risparmio nella economia pura*, Milan: Hoepli.

——— 1899, *La teorica delle produttività marginali*, Pavia: Tip. Fratelli Fusi.

——— 1899b, 'Una questione di metodo nella storia delle dottrine economiche', *Rivista Filosofica*: 112–21.

Moretti, Mauro 1980, 'Preliminari ad uno studio su Pasquale Villari', *Giornale critico della filosofia italiana*: 190–232.

——— 1981, 'La storiografia italiana e la cultura del secondo Ottocento. Preliminari ad uno studio su Pasquale Villari', *Giornale critico della filosofia italiana*: 307–72.

Morgari, Oddino 1896, *L'arte della propaganda socialista*, Milan: Uffici della Lotta di Classe.

Muller, Jean 1911, *L'idée de lutte de classes et son evolution depuis le Manifeste communiste*, Paris: Jouve et c.

Musil, Robert 1997, *The Man Without Qualities*, London: Picador.

Napoleoni, Claudio 1972, *Lezioni sul capitol sesto inedito di Marx*, Turin: Boringhieri.

——— 1975, *Lezioni sul capitolo IV inedito di Marx*, Turin: Boringhieri

——— 1985, *Discorso sull'economia politica*, Turin: Boringhieri.

——— 1992, *Dalla scienza all'utopia*, Turin: Boringhieri.

Negro, Luigi 1900, *La centralizzazione capitalistica*, Turin: Piccarolo.

Negt, Oskar 1964, *Strukturbeziehungen zwischen den Gesellschaftslehren Comtes und Hegels*, Frankfurt: Europäische Verlagsanstalt.

——— 1979, 'Il marxismo e la teoria della rivoluzione nell'ultimo Engels', in *Storia del marxismo*, Vol. II, *Il marxismo nell'età della Seconda Internazionale*, edited by Eric Hobsbawm, Turin: Einaudi.

Nitti, Francesco Saverio 1973, *Discorsi parlamentari di Francesco Saverio Nitti*, Rome: Camera dei Deputati.

Nolte, Ernst 1983, *Marxismus und industrielle Revolution*, Stuttgart: Klett-Cotta.

——— 1987, *Der europäische Bürgerkrieg 1917–1945*, Frankfurt: Ullstein.

Nowak, Leszek 1980, *The structure of idealization: towards a systematic interpretation of the Marxian idea of science*, Boston: Reidel.

——— 1983, *Property and Power. Toward a Non-Marxian Historical Materialism*, Boston: Reidel.

Oldrini, Guido 1986, *L'Ottocento filosofico napolitano nella letteratura dell'ultimo decennio*, Naples: Bibliopolis.

——— 1994, 'La "Rinascita dell'Idealismo" e il suo retroterra napoletano', *Giornale Critico della Filosofia Italiana*, II–III: 205–25.

Olivetti, Angelo Oliviero 1898, *Per la interpretazione economica della storia. Alcune note sull'assegnazione coloniale nel diritto e nella vita romana*, Bologna: Libreria Fratelli Treves.

——— 1899, *Il pensiero del secolo che muore*, Bologna: Libreria Fratelli Treves.

——— 1913, *Questioni contemporanee*, Naples: Società Editrice.

——— 1913b, *Cinque anni di sindacalismo e di lotta proletaria in Italia*, Naples: Società Editrice Partenopea.

——— 1919, *Bolscevismo, comunismo e sindacalismo rivoluzionario*, Milan: Casa editrice Risorgimento.

——— 1984, *Dal sindacalismo rivoluzionario al corporativismo*, Rome: Bonacci.

Orano, Paolo 1895, *Il problema del cristianesimo*, Rome.

——— 1896, *La psicologia della Sardegna*, Rome.

——— 1926, *Lode al mio tempo (1895–1925)*, Bologna: Casa editrice Apollo.

——— 1931, 'Prefazione', in E. Leone, *Teoria della politica*, Turin: Bocca.

Ottaviano, Chiara 1985, 'Achille Loria: il successo di un intellettuale tipo', in *Il positivismo e la cultura italiana*, edited by E.R. Papa, Milan: Angeli.

Panaccione, Andrea 1988, 'Per una lettura di Labriola socialista internazionale', in AAVV, *Antonio Labriola nella cultura europea dell'Ottocento*, Bari: Lacaita.

——— 1995, 'L'ossessione del socialismo. L'ideologia socialistica in Italia attraverso la pubblicistica di propaganda di fine Ottocento', in *Educazione e propaganda nel primo socialismo*, Rome: Riuniti.

Pantaleoni, Maffeo 1882, *Teoria della traslazione dei tributi. Definizione dinamica e ubiquità della traslazione*, Rome: Tip. Adolfo Paolini.

——— 1883, 'Contributo alla teoria del riparto delle spese pubbliche', *La Rassegna Italiana*, October: 25–60.

——— 1889, *Principi di economia pura*, Florence: Berbera.

——— 1897, 'Del carattere e delle divergenze d'opinioni esistenti tra economisti', *Giornale degli Economisti*: 501–30.

——— 1898, 'Dei caratteri che debbono informare la storia delle dottrine economiche', *Giornale degli Economisti*: 407–31.

Papa, Emilio R. 1985, 'Criminologia e scienze sociali nel dibattito europeo sulla "scuola italiana" di antropologia criminale (1876–1900)', in *Il positivismo e la cultura italiana*, Milan: Angeli.

Pareto, Vilfredo 1966, 'La théorie de la valeur de Marx', in *Marxisme et économie pure*, Geneva: Droz.

——— 1974, *I sistemi socialisti*, Turin: Utet.

Pasternak, Boris 1958, *Safe Conduct*, New York: New Directions.

——— 1958b, *Dr. Zhivago*, New York: Pantheon

Pelger, Hans 1983, 'I concetti di "socialismo scientifico", "comunismo scientifico" e "scienza rivoluzionaria" in Marx ed Engels fino al 1848', in *L'Antidühring: affermazione o deformazione del marxismo?*, Annali della Fondazione Basso-Issoco, V, Milan: Angeli.

Pepe, Adolfo 1972, *Storia della CGdL*, Vol. 1, Bari: Laterza.

Perfetti, Francesco 1984, 'Introduzione' in A.O. Olivetti *Dal sindacalismo rivoluzionario al corporativismo*, Rome: Bonacci.

——— 1986, 'La "conversazione" all'interventismo di Mussolini nel suo carteggio con Sergio Panunzio', *Storia contemporanea*, 1: 139–70.

Perli, Diana 1972, *I congressi del Partito operaio italiano*, Padua: Tipografia Antoniana.

Perrot, Michelle 1974, *Les ouvriers en grève, France 1871–1890*, Paris: Mouton.

——— 1984, *Jeunesse de la grève, France 1871–1890*, Paris: Seuil.

Petretto, Alessandro 1984, 'Le funzioni, la struttura e gli effetti del sistema tributario secondo la tradizione italiana di scienza delle finanze', typescript of his intervention at the seminar on *La tradizione finanziaria italiana*, Pavia, Collegio Ghislieri, 18–20 September 1984.

Petry, Franz 1916, *Der soziale Gehalt der Marxschen Werttheorie*, Jena.

Pinzani, Carlo 1970, *Jean Jaurès, l'Internazionale e la guerra*, Bari: Laterza.

Pisano, Rossano 1986, *Il paradiso socialista. La propaganda socialista in Italia alla fine dell'ottocento attraverso gli opuscoli di "Critica Sociale"*, Milan: Angeli.

Plekhanoff, Georgij 1908, *Intorno al sindacalismo e ai sindacalisti*, Rome: Mongini.

Poggi, Alfredo 1925, *Socialismo e cultura*, Turin: Piero Gobetti Editore.

Poggi, Stefano 1978, *Antonio Labriola. Herbartismo e scienze dello spirito alle origini del marxismo italiano*, Milan: Longanesi.

Pogliano, Claudio 1976, 'Cognetti de Martiis. Le origini del laboratorio di economia politica', *Studi Storici*: 139–68.

Popper, Karl 2014, *Conjectures and Refutations: The Growth of Scientific Knowledge*, London: Routledge.

Portigliatti-Barbos, Michele 1985, 'Medicina ed antropologia culturale nella cultura positivista', in E.R. Papa (ed.), *Il positivismo e la cultura italiana*, Milan: Angeli.

Potier, Jean-Pierre 1986, *Lectures italiennes de Marx (1883–1983)*, Lyon: Presses Universitaires.

Prat, Michel 1983, 'Une lettre d'Eduard Bernstein à Sorel', *Cahiers Georges Sorel*, 1: 124–33.

Procacci, Giuliano 1975, 'Intervento al convegno di studi su *Il sindacalismo rivoluzionario in Italia* (1974)', *Ricerche Storiche*: 109–14.

Ragionieri, Ernesto 1961, *Socialdemocrazia tedesca e socialisti italiani (1875–1895)*, Milan: Feltrinelli.

——— 1968, *Il Marxismo e l'Internazionale*, Rome: Editori Riuniti.

Raffaelli, Guido 1955, 'Il Movimento operaio nel Trentino da mutualismo alle prime Camere del Lavoro (1844–1900)', *Movimento Operaio*: 230–51.

Ricca-Salerno, Giuseppe 1887, 'Nuove dottrine sistematiche nella scienza delle finanze', *Giornale degli Economisti*, 375–402.

——— 1894, 'La nuova fase delle riforme tributarie. Principio della progressività dell'imposta', *Nuova Antologia*, 35: 35–50, 260–80.

Ricci, Umberto 1939, *Tre economisti italiani: Pantaleoni, Pareto, Loria*, Bari: Laterza.

Rigola, Rinaldo 1946, *Storia del movimento operaio italiano*, Milan: Editoriale Domus.

Riosa, Alceo 1983, *L'esperienza italiana*, in *Sindacato e classe operaia nell'età della II Internazionale*, Florence: Sansoni.

Ritter, Gerhard A. 1959, *Die Arbeiterbewegung im Wilhelminischen Deutschland*, Berlin: Colloquium-Verlag.

Robbins, Lionel 1972, *An Essay on the Nature and Signification of Economic Science*, London: Macmillan.

Robin, Régine 1973, 'Langage et idéologies', *Le Mouvement Social*, 85: 3–11.

Robinson, Joan 1962, 'Marxism: Religion and Science', *Monthly Review Press*, 14, 8: 423–35.

——— 1966, *An Essay on Marxian Economics*, London: Macmillan.

——— 1978, *Contributions to Modern Economics*, New York: Harcourt Brace.

Romano, Aldo 1966, *Storia del movimento socialista in Italia*, Vol. I, *L'Unità italiana e la Prima Internazionale*, Bari: Laterza.

Rosenberg, Arthur 1939, *Democracy and Socialism*, New York: Alfred A Knopf.

Rosselli, Nello 1967, *Mazzini e Bakunin. Dodici anni di Movimento operaio in Italia (1860–1872)*, Turin: Einaudi.

Rossi, Pietro 1982, 'La sociologia positivistica e il modello di società organica', in Antonio Santucci (ed.) *Scienza e filosofia nella cultura positivista*, Milan: Feltrinelli.

Rota Ghibaudi, Silvia 1987, 'L'utopia e l'utopismo', in *Il pensiero politico contemporaneo*, edited by Gian Mario Bravo and Silvia Rota Ghibaudi, Vol. III, Milan: Angeli.

Roth, Guenther 1963, *The Social Democrats in Imperial Germany*, Totowa, NJ: Bedminster Press.

Roveri, Alessandro 1972, *Dal sindacalismo rivoluzionario al fascismo*, Florence: La Nuova Italia.

Roversi, A. 1986, 'Il "Verein für Sozialpolitik" e la questione sociale', in *Cultura politica e società borghese in Germania tra Otto e Novecento*, edited by G. Corni and P. Schiera, Bologna: Il Mulino.

Rubel, Maximilien 1974, *Marx critique du marxisme*, Paris: Payot.

——— 1983, 'Georges Sorel et l'achèvement de l'oeuvre de Karl Marx', *Cahiers Georges Sorel*, 1: 9–36.

Salvati, Michele 1994, 'Realismo e utopia', in *Carlo Marx: è tempo di un bilancio*, edited by P. Sylos Labini, Bari: Laterza.

Salvo, Roberto 1979, *Vito Cusumano dal liberismo al socialismo della cattedra*, Palermo: Quaderno della Facoltà di Magistero.

Sandirocco, Maria (ed.) 1969, *Carteggio Gentile-Jaia*, Vol. I, Florence: Sansoni.

Santarelli, Enzo 1977, *La revisione del marxismo in Italia*, Milan: Feltrinelli.

Sax, Emilio 1924, 'La teoria della valutazione dell'imposta', *Giornale degli Economisti*: 275–312.

Sbarberi, Franco 1986, *Ordinamento politico e società nel marxismo di Antonio Labriola*, Milan: Angeli.

Scaldaferri, Romilda 1992, 'I modelli straniero nel socialismo della cattedra italiano', in *La scienza moderata. Fedele Lamperico e l'Italia liberale*, edited by R. Camurri, Milan: Angeli.

Schröder, Wolfgang 1975, *Partei und Gewerkschaft, 1868–9 bis 1893*, Berlin: Tribüne.

Schiavi, Alessandro (ed.) 1947, *Filippo Turati attraverso le lettere di corrispondenti (1880–1925)*, Bari: Laterza.

Schiavone, Aldo 1999, *I conti del comunismo*, Turin: Einaudi.

Schieder, Wolfgang 1981, '"Socialismo" e "socialdemocrazia". Sull'uso dei concetti politici nel period dei primi programme dei partiti socialdemocratici', *Annali della Fondazione Basso-Issoco*, III, Milan: Angeli.

——— 1983, 'Sulla storia del concetto di "socialismo scientifico"', in *L'Antidühring: affermazione o deformazione del marxismo?*, Annali della Fondazione Basso-Issoco, V, Milan: Angeli.

Schiera, Pierangelo 1987, *Il laboratorio borghese. Scienza e politica nella Germania dell'ottocento*, Bologna: Il Mulino.

Schmidt, Conrad 1889, *Die Durchschnittsprofitrate auf Grundlage des Marx'schen Werthgesetzes*, Stuttgart: Dietz.

Schulze-Gävernitz, Gerhart von 1900, *La grande industria e il progresso economico e sociale*, Turin: Utet.

Schumpeter, Joseph 1986, *History of Economic Analysis*, London: Routledge.

——— 2003, *Capitalism, Socialism and Democracy*, London: Routledge.

Seen, P. 1966, 'What is "Behavioural Science"?', *Journey of the History of the Behavioural Sciences*, II: 107–22.

Sola, G. 1983, 'La sociologia di Napoleone Colajanni', in *Napoleone Colajanni e la società italiana fra otto e novecento*, Enna: Epos.

Sombart, Werner 1893–5, 'Studien sur Entwicklungsgeschichte des italienischen Proletariats', *Archiv für soziale Gesetzgebung und Statistik*, Vols. VI and VII, Berlin.

——— 1894, 'Zur kritik des oekonomischen System von Karl Marx', *Archiv für soziale Gesetzgebung und Statistik*, VII: 555–94.

Sorel, Georges 1894, 'L'ancienne et la nouvelle métaphysique', *Ère nouvelle*, II: 329–51, 461–82, 51–87, 180–205.

——— 1897, 'Sur la théorie marxiste de la valeur', *Journal des Economistes*: 222–31.

——— 1898, 'Préface' in Saverio Merlino, *Formes et essence du socialisme*, Paris: Girard et Brière.

——— 1903, *Saggi di Critica del marxismo*, Palermo: Sandron.

——— 1963, *Lettere a un amico d'Italia*, Bologna: Cappelli.

——— 1973, *Scritti politici*, Turin: Utet.

——— 1980, *Lettere a Benedetto Croce*, Bari: De Donato.

——— 1993–4, *Cher Camarade ... Georges Sorel ad Agostino Lanzillo 1900–1921*, edited by F. Germinario, Brescia: Annali della Fondazione Luigi Micheletti

Spirito, Ugo 1965, 'Gentile e Marx', in *Il comunismo*, Florence: Sansoni.

Spoto, Luciano 1984, 'Il socialismo e gli economisti siciliani', in AAVV, *Il marxismo e la cultura meridionale*, Palermo: Palumbo.

——— 1985, *Vito Cusumano e la fondazione della "Scienza delle Finanze" in Italia*, Palermo: Società Grafica Artifone.

Stedman Jones, Gareth 1977, 'Engels and the Genesis of Marxism', *New Left Review*, I/106: 79–104.

Steinberg, H.J. 1979, *Il socialismo tedesco da Bebel a Kautsky*, Rome: Editori Riuniti.

——— 1983, 'La formazione dell'ortodossia Marxista in Germania e il problema della recezione del marxismo da parte delle masse', in *L'Antidühring: affermazione o deformazione del marxismo?*, Annali della Fondazione Basso-Issoco, V, Milan: Angeli.

Stephan, Cora 1977, *'Genossen, wir dürfen uns nicht von der Geduld hinreißen lassen!' Aus der Urgeschichte der Sozialdemokratie 1862–1878*, Frankfurt: Syndikat.

Stuart Hughes, Henry 1977, *Consciousness and Society*, Londen: Transaction.

Sweezy, Paul 1964, *The Theory of Capitalist Development*, New York: Monthly Review Press.

Tarde, Gabriele 1887, 'Positivisme et criminalité', *Archives de l'anthropologie criminelle*: 32–51.

Timpanaro, Sebastiano 1970, *Sul materialismo*, Pisa: Nistri-Lischi.

Tolstoy, Leo 1899, *The Complete Works*, New York: Kelmscott Society.

Tomassini, Luigi 1984, *Associazionismo operaio a Firenze fra ottanta e novanta. La Società di Mutuo Soccorso di Rifredi (1883–1922)*, Florence: Olschki.

Topitsch, Ernst 1975, *A che serve l'ideologia*, Bari: Laterza.

Turati, Filippo 1898, *Il dovere della resistenza*, Milan: Uffici della Critica Sociale.

——— 1902, *Il partito socialista italiano e le sue pretese tendenze*, Milano: Uffici della Critica Sociale.

——— 1950, *Discorsi parlamentari*, Roma.

Turati, Filippo and Anna Kuliscioff 1959, 'Lettere di Anna Kuliscioff e Filippo Turati a Ivanoe Bonomi', *Rivista Storica del Socialismo*: 95–120.

——— 1977, *Carteggio*, Vol. I, Turin: Einaudi.

Turgenev, Ivan 1907, *Memoirs of a Sportsman*, New York: Charles Scribner's Sons.

——— 1950, *Fathers and Sons*, New York: Modern Library.

Turi, Gabriele 1996, *Giovanni Gentile*, Florence: Giunti.

Valiani, Leo 1950, 'Le prime grandi agitazioni operaie a Milano e Torino', *Movimento Operaio*, October–November 1950.

——— 1973, 'Considerazioni su anarchismo e marxismo in Italia e in Europa dopo la conferenza di Rimini', in *Anarchismo e Socialismo in Italia (1871–1892)*, edited by L. Faenza, Rome: Riuniti.

Veca, Salvatore 1973, *Marx e la critica dell'economia politica*, Milan: Il Saggiatore.

——— 1975, 'Sul Capitale', *in Marxismo e critica delle teorie economiche*, Milan: Feltrinelli.

Verzi, Ernesto 1907, *I metallurgici d'Italia nel loro sindacato*, Rome: Snt.

Vianello, Fernando 1978, 'L'anello spezzato', *Rinascita*, 15.

——— 1984, 'La critica dell'economia politica: ieri ed oggi', in *Marx e il mondo contemporaneo*, edited by C. Mancina, Rome: Editori Riuniti.

Vigna, Carmelo 1977, *Le origini del marxismo teorico in Italia*, Roma: Città Nuova Editrice.

Vilar, Pierre 1973, 'Marxist History, a History in the Making: Towards a Dialogue with Althusser', *New Left Review*, I/80: 64–106.

Villari, Pasquale 1984, 'La storia è una scienza?', *Scritti Varii*, Bologna: Zanchelli.

Volpe, G. 1966, 'Il movimento socialista a Napoli ed i moti del maggio 1898', *Clio*, 4.

Waldenberg, Marek 1972, *Il papa rosso Karl Kautsky*, Rome: Riuniti.

——— 1985, 'Karl Kautsky e Eduard Bernstein: due concezioni della strategia', in *Filippo Turati e il socialismo europeo*, Naples: Guida.

Willard, Claude 1965, *Les Guesdistes*, Paris: Editions Sociales.

Yourcenar, Marguerite 1987, *Two Lives and a Dream*, Chicago: Chicago University Press.

Zagari, E. 1975, *Enrico Leone e la teoria economica del sindacalismo*, Naples: Guida.

Zamagni, Stefano 1994, 'Sulla relazione fra economia e filosofia: argomenti per un ampliamento del discorso economico', *Economia politica*, XI, 2: 281–314.

Zanardo, Aldo 1974, 'Per una storia del marxismo contemporaneo' in *Storia del marxismo contemporaneo. I maggiori interpreti del pensiero marxista dopo Marx*, Milan: Feltrinelli.

——— 1979, 'Motivi e caratteri del marxismo di Rodolfo Mondolfo', in *Marxismo e filosofia nell'opera di Rodolfo Mondolfo*, Florence: La Nuova Italia.

Zangheri, Renato 1993, *Storia del socialismo italiano*, Vol. I, Turin: Einaudi.

Zavaroni, Adolfo 1979, 'Le origini del giornalismo socialista reggiano 1882–1890', in *Prampolini e il socialismo riformista*, Vol. I, Rome: Edizioni Avanti!

Index

www.ingramcontent.com/pod-product-compliance
Lightning Source LLC
Chambersburg PA
CBHW070858030426
42336CB00014BA/2245
* 9 7 8 1 6 0 8 4 6 8 0 3 4 *